ALSO BY HANNAH PAKULA

The Last Romantic: A Biography of Queen Marie of Roumania

An Uncommon Woman

The Empress Frederick
Daughter of
Queen Victoria,
Wife of the
Crown Prince of Prussia,
Mother of
Kaiser Wilhelm

Hannah Pakula

A TOUCHSTONE BOOK
Published by Simon & Schuster

⊼⊼⊼ TOUCHSTONE
Rockefeller Center
1230 Avenue of the Americas
New York, NY 10020

First Touchstone Edition 1997

TOUCHSTONE and colophon are registered trademarks
of Simon & Schuster Inc.

Designed by Edith Fowler. Contributing picture research by Natalie Goldstein.

Manufactured in the United States of America

10 9 8 7 6 5 4 3 2 1

The Library of Congress has cataloged the Simon & Schuster edition as follows:

Pakula, Hannah.
    An uncommon woman: The Empress Frederick, daughter of Queen Victoria, wife of the
Crown Prince of Prussia, mother of Kaiser Wilhelm / Hannah Pakula.
        p.   cm.
    Includes bibliographical references and index.
    1. Victoria Empress, consort of Frederick III, German Emperor, 1840–1901.   2. Victoria, Queen of
Great Britain, 1819–1901.   3. Germany—Relations—Great Britain.   4. Great Britain—
Relations—Germany.   5. Germany—Politics and government—1789–1900.   6. Great Britain—
History—Victoria, 1837–1901.   I. Title.
DD224.9.P35   1995
943.08′4′092—dc20   95-36848   CIP
ISBN 0-684-80818-8
ISBN 0-684-84216-5 (Pbk)

The author and publisher gratefully acknowledge permission to reprint extracts from the following
works:

Arthur Christopher Benson and Viscount Esher, Letters of Queen Victoria (1837–1861) (London: John
Murray, 1907). Reprinted with the permission of John Murray (Publishers), Ltd.

Hector Bolitho, Letters of Queen Victoria from the Archives of the House of Brandenburg-Prussia,
translated by Mrs. J. Pudney and Lord Sudley (New Haven: Yale University Press, 1938). Reprinted with
the permission of Methuen, c/o Reed Consumer Books, Ltd.

G. R. Buckle, Letters of Queen Victoria (2nd and 3rd series) (London: John Murray, 1926–1931).
Reprinted with the permission of John Murray (Publishers), Ltd.

Prince Bernhard von Bülow, Memoirs, Volume II: 1897–1903 (New York: Putnam, 1930–1932). Reprinted with the permission of The Putnam Publishing Group.

Egon Caesar Conte Corti, Alexander von Battenberg (London: Cassell, 1954). Reprinted with the permission of Simon & Schuster, Inc.

Egon Caesar Conte Corti, The English Empress (London: Cassell, 1957). Reprinted with the permission
of Simon & Schuster, Inc.

Andreas Dorpalen, "Frederick II and the German Liberal Movement," The American Historical Review
54, no. 1 (October 1948). Reprinted with the permission of the American Historical Association.

Erich Eyck, Bismarck and the German Empire (New York: W. W. Norton & Company, 1964). Reprinted
with the permission of HarperCollins Publishers, Ltd.

Friederich III, War Diary (London: Stanley Paul, 1927). Reprinted with the permission of Routledge.

Frederick Holstein, The Holstein Papers, edited by Norman Rich and M. H. Fischer. Reprinted with the
permission of Norman Rich and Cambridge University Press.

Credits continued on page 701.

To Anna, Robert, and Louis

Contents

A Note to the Reader

WHEN I STARTED THIS BOOK about the Empress Frederick, I was partially aware of the scope of her mind and the tragedy of her life. Her significance in terms of our world today became clear only as I made my way through the thousands of letters she exchanged with her mother, Queen Victoria. This correspondence, which opens a window on the personal and political life of nineteenth-century royalties, also provides a picture of the gestation of modern Germany different from those we usually find in history books. Like the birth of the Empress's son, Kaiser Wilhelm II, the emergence of the nation was fraught with irreversible problems. What is perhaps most remarkable about the Empress Frederick is her understanding of these defects and their consequences decades before the rest of the world.

A WORD ABOUT NAMES: The Empress Frederick's son, the leader of Germany in World War I, is commonly known as Kaiser Wilhelm II, or simply the Kaiser. I have used this name in the book, in spite of the fact that his mother and grandmother refer to him in their letters as William or Willy. By the same token, I use the Empress Frederick, her English name, and have taken the liberty of calling Frederick the Great by the name known to English-speaking readers. In making these and similar choices—Charles for Carl or Karl, Henry for Heinrich, Ernest for Ernst, Louis for Ludwig, and so forth—I have been guided by reader recognition rather than consistency.

The Empress Frederick and Queen Victoria were prone to underlining words for emphasis in their letters to each other, and I have preserved those underlinings, single and double, indicating the occasional triple in the footnotes. Both mother and daughter also used a whole vocabulary of abbreviations: gt = great; wh = which; wd, cd, and shd = would, could, and should; vy = very, etc. Except for the use of the symbol "&," I have taken the liberty of replacing most of their abbreviations with the entire word. And except in cases where a specific point was being made, I have used the lower case for the first letter of nouns, although both ladies often followed the German custom of capitalizing them.

Readers may want present-day equivalents for monetary amounts mentioned in the text. I have been warned not to try to provide these, because it is almost impossible to translate the currency of one country or century to another. Nevertheless, to the best of my ability, I have been able to determine the following (these figures do not account for inflation or the time value of money):

In the nineteenth century, one thaler was worth about 3 marks or 75 cents; guilders were worth about 2 marks; 133.33 thalers or 400 marks was the approximate equivalent of $100. Thus, in 1866, Bismarck was able to purchase the Pomeranian estate of Varzin, which included 14,200 acres of land and seven villages, for approximately $300,000, his gift from a grateful Wilhelm I after the Austro-Prussian War. The following year, Napoleon III and the King of the Netherlands settled on a price of about $1.4 million for the duchy of Luxembourg. And by the time he died in 1888, Wilhelm I of Germany had managed to accumulate $5.5 million in returns from the crown estates.

H. P.
New York, 1995

Principal Characters
and Their Relationship to the Empress Frederick

ALBERT, Prince Consort of England (1819–1861). Father. Born Prince of Saxe-Coburg-Gotha. Married Victoria, Queen of England.

ALBERT EDWARD, Prince of Wales; later King Edward VII of England (1841–1910). "Bertie." Brother. Married Alexandra, Princess of Denmark.

ALEXANDER II, Czar of Russia (1818–1881). Married (1) Marie, Princess of Hesse; (2) Princess Catherine Dolgoruky.

ALEXANDER III, Czar of Russia (1845–1894). Married Dagmar, Princess of Denmark (later known as Czarina Marie).

ALEXANDER I, Prince of Bulgaria (1857–1893). "Sandro." Born Prince of Battenberg. Married Joanna Loisinger.

ALEXANDRA, Princess of Wales; later Queen of England (1844–1925). "Alix." Sister-in-law. Born Princess of Denmark. Married Prince of Wales (later Edward VII).

ALEXANDRA, Czarina of Russia (1872–1918). "Alicky." Niece. Born Alix, Princess of Hesse-Darmstadt. Married Nicholas II, Czar of Russia.

ALEXANDRINE, Grand Duchess of Mecklenburg-Schwerin (1803–1892). Aunt by marriage (sister of Wilhelm I). Born Princess of Prussia. Married Grand Duke of Mecklenburg-Schwerin.

ALFRED, Duke of Edinburgh; later Duke of Coburg (1844–1900). "Affie." Brother. Married Grand Duchess Marie Alexandrovna of Russia.

ALICE, Grand Duchess of Hesse-Darmstadt (1843–1878). Sister. Born Princess of England. Married Louis IV, Prince of Hesse (later Grand Duke).

AUGUSTA, Princess of Prussia; later Queen of Prussia and Kaiserin of Germany (1858–1921). Mother-in-law. Born Princess of Saxe-Weimar. Married Wilhelm, Prince of Prussia (later King of Prussia and Kaiser of Germany).

AUGUSTA VICTORIA, Crown Princess of Germany; later Kaiserin (1858–1921). "Dona." Daughter-in-law. Born Princess of Schleswig-Holstein. Married Wilhelm II, Crown Prince (later Kaiser) of Germany.

BATTENBERG, Henry, Prince of (1858–1896). "Liko." Brother-in-law. Married Beatrice, Princess of England.

BEATRICE, Princess of Great Britain (1857–1944). Sister. Married Henry, Prince of Battenberg.

BERGMANN, Ernest von (1836–1907). German surgeon.

BISMARCK, Count (later Prince) Otto von (1815–1898). Prime Minister of Prussia, later Chancellor of Germany. Married Johanna von Puttkamer.

BISMARCK, Count (later Prince) Herbert von (1849–1904). German diplomat and Secretary of State; son of Otto von Bismarck.

BISMARCK, Countess (later Princess) Johanna von (1824–1895). Born Johanna von Puttkamer. Married Otto von Bismarck.

BÜLOW, Prince Bernhard von (1849–1929). German diplomat and statesman. Chancellor 1900–1909.

BULTEEL, Mary (1832–1916). Friend. Married Sir Henry Ponsonby, Queen Victoria's private secretary.

BUSCH, Moritz (1821–1899). German writer. Bismarck's press agent.

CAPRIVI, Count Leo von (1831–1899). German soldier and statesman. Chancellor 1890–1894.

CHARLES, Prince of Prussia (1801–1883). "Prince Charles." Uncle (younger brother of Friedrich IV and Wilhelm I of Prussia). Married Marie, Princess of Saxe-Weimar.

CHARLES, Princess of Prussia (1808–1877). "Princess Charles." Born Marie, Princess of Saxe-Weimar (sister of Augusta). Married Charles, Prince of Prussia.

CHARLES ANTON, Prince of Hohenzollern (1811–1885). "Prince Hohenzollern." Prime Minister of Prussia under Wilhelm I.

CHARLOTTE, Princess of Prussia; later of Saxe-Meiningen (1860–1919). Daughter. Married Bernhard, Prince of Saxe-Meiningen.

CHARLOTTE, Princess of Belgium; later Empress Carlotta of Mexico (1840–1927). Cousin. Married Archduke Maximilian of Austria, who became Emperor of Mexico.

CHARLOTTE, Czarina of Russia (1798–1870). Born Princess of Prussia (sister of Friedrich IV and Wilhelm I of Prussia). Married Grand Duke (later Czar) Nicholas I of Russia.

CHRISTIAN, Prince of Schleswig-Holstein (1831–1917). Brother-in-law. Married Helena, Princess of England.

ELISABETH, Queen of Prussia (1801–1873). Born Princess of Bavaria. Married Friedrich Wilhelm IV of Prussia.

ELISABETH, Empress of the Austro-Hungarian Empire (1837–1898). Born Princess of Bavaria. Married Franz Joseph, Emperor of the Austro-Hungarian Empire.

ERNEST II, Duke of Saxe-Coburg-Gotha (1818–1893). "Uncle Ernest." Uncle (Prince Albert's older brother). Married Alexandrine, Princess of Baden.

EUGÉNIE, Empress of France (1826–1920). Born Eugénie de Montijo de Guzman, Countess de Teba. Married Napoleon III, Emperor of France.

FEODORA, Princess of Hohenlohe-Langenburg (1807–1872). Aunt (half-sister of Queen Victoria). Born Princess of Leiningen. Married Prince Ernest of Hohenlohe-Langenburg.

FRANZ JOSEPH, Emperor of the Austro-Hungarian Empire (1830–1916). Married Elisabeth, Princess of Bavaria.

FRIEDRICH III, Kaiser of Germany (1831–1888). "Fritz." Husband. Born Prince of Prussia.

FRIEDRICH WILHELM IV, King of Prussia (1795–1861). Uncle (older brother of Wilhelm I of Prussia). Married Elisabeth, Princess of Bavaria.

FRIEDRICH, Grand Duke of Baden (1826–1907). "Fritz of Baden." Brother-in-law. Married Louise, Princess of Prussia.

FRIEDRICH, Duke of Schleswig-Holstein-Sonderburg-Augustenburg (1829–1880). "Fritz Holstein." Married Ada, Princess of Hohenlohe-Langenburg.

FRIEDRICH CHARLES, Prince of Prussia (1828–1885). "Fritz Carl." Cousin (son of Prince Charles.) Married Marianne, Princess of Anhalt.

FRIEDRICH CHARLES, Prince of Hesse-Kassel (1868–1940). "Fischy." Son-in-law. Married Margaret, Princess of Germany.

GEORGE V, King of Hanover (1819–1878). First cousin of Queen Victoria. Forced to abdicate his throne after Austro-German War (1866).

HELENA, Princess of Great Britain (1846–1923). "Lenchen." Sister. Married Christian, Prince of Schleswig-Holstein.

HENRY, Prince of Prussia (1862–1929). Son. Married Irene, Princess of Hesse and the Rhine.

HINTZPETER, George Ernest (1827–1907). "Dr. Hintzpeter" or "the Doctor." Tutor to Wilhelm II.

HOHENTHAL, Walpurga von (1839–1929). "Wally." Maid of Honor. Married Sir Augustus Paget, British diplomat.

HOHENLOHE-SCHILLINGFÜRST, Prince Chlodwig von (1819–1901). German diplomat and statesman. Chancellor 1894–1900.

HOLSTEIN, Friedrich von (1837–1909). German diplomat. *Éminence grise* of the German Foreign Ministry.

LASKER, Eduard (1828–1884). German statesman, liberal member of the Chamber of Deputies.

LEOPOLD I, King of Belgium (1790–1865). "Uncle Leopold." Great-uncle (both Victoria's and Albert's uncle). Born Prince of Saxe-Coburg-Saalfeld. Married (1) Charlotte, Princess of England; (2?) Karoline Bauer (morganatic); (3) Louise, Princess of Orléans.

LEOPOLD, Duke of Albany, Prince of Great Britain (1853–1884). Brother. Married Helena, Princess of Waldeck-Pyrmont.

LOUIS, Prince (later Grand Duke) of Hesse-Darmstadt (Hesse and the Rhine; 1838–1892). Brother-in-law. Married Alice, Princess of Great Britain.

LOUISE, Princess of Great Britain (1848–1939). Sister. Married John Campbell, Marquis of Lorne (later Duke of Argyll).

LOUISE, Grand Duchess of Baden (1838–1923). Sister-in-law. Born Princess of Prussia. Married Friedrich, Grand Duke of Baden.

MARGARET, Princess of Germany (1872–1954). "Mossy." Daughter. Married Friedrich, Prince of Hesse-Kassel.

MARTIN, Dr. Eduard (1809–1875). Gynecologist. Chief of Obstetrics at University of Berlin.

MOLTKE, Count Helmuth von (1800–1891). Prussian general (later field marshal).

MORIER, Sir Robert (1826–1893). British diplomat.

NAPOLEON III (Louis Napoleon), Emperor of France (1808–1873). Married Eugénie de Montijo de Guzman, Countess de Teba.

NICHOLAS II, Czar of Russia (1868–1918). "Nicky." Nephew. Married Alix, Princess of Hesse-Darmstadt.

PONSONBY, Sir Henry (1825–1895). Private Secretary to Queen Victoria. Married Mary Bulteel, a maid of honor to the Queen.

PONSONBY, Sir Frederick (1867–1935). "Fritz Ponsonby." Godson of Friedrich III. Secretary to Edward VII; son of Sir Henry Ponsonby.

RADOLIN-RADOLINSKI, Count (later Prince) Hugo Leszczyc von (1847–1917). German diplomat, Chamberlain of the Court of Friedrich III, Ambassador to Turkey, Russia, France.

SAXE-MEININGEN, Prince Bernhard of (1851–1928). Son-in-law. Married Charlotte, Princess of Prussia.

SCHAUMBURG-LIPPE, Prince Adolf von (1859–1916). Son-in-law. Married Victoria ("Moretta"), Princess of Prussia.

SECKENDORFF, Count Götz von (?–1910). Court Chamberlain to the Empress Frederick.

SIGISMUND, Prince of Prussia (1864–1866). "Sigi." Son.

SOPHIE, Princess of Germany (later Crown Princess and Queen of Greece; 1870–1932). Daughter. Married Constantine, Crown Prince (later King) of Greece.

STOCKMAR, Baron Christian Friedrich von (1787–1863). Physician and adviser to Queen Victoria and Prince Albert.

STOCKMAR, Baron Ernest von (1823–1886). Private secretary.

STOSCH, General Albrecht von (1818–1896). Chief of the Admiralty.

VICTORIA, Princess of Prussia (1866–1929). "Moretta." Daughter. Married (1) Adolf, Prince of Schaumburg-Lippe; (2) Alexander Zoubkov.

VICTORIA, Queen of England (1819–1901). Mother. Born Princess of England. Married Albert, Prince of Saxe-Coburg-Gotha.

WALDEMAR, Prince of Prussia (1868–1879). Son.

WALDERSEE, Count Alfred von (1832–1904). German general, Chief of Staff.

WILHELM I, Prince of Prussia; later King of Prussia and Kaiser of Germany (1797–1888). Father-in-law. Married Augusta, Princess of Saxe-Weimar.

WILHELM II, Prince of Prussia; later Kaiser of Germany (1859–1941). Son. Married Augusta Victoria, Princess of Schleswig-Holstein.

The Nine Children of
Queen Victoria and Prince Albert

VICTORIA
"Vicky"
(1840–1901)
m.
Friedrich Wilhelm
"Fritz," Crown
Prince of Prussia,
later Friedrich III,
Kaiser of Germany
(1831–1888)

Edward VII
"Bertie"
King of England
(1841–1910)
m.
Alexandra,
Princess of Denmark
(1844–1925)

Alice
(1843–1878)
m.
Louis,
Grand Duke of Hesse

One of their
daughters
(Victoria)
married Louis,
Prince of Battenberg;
Another (Alix) married
Czar Nicholas II
of Russia

Alfred
"Affie"
(1844–1900)
m.
Marie, Grand
Duchess of Russia
(1853–1920)

The Coburgs

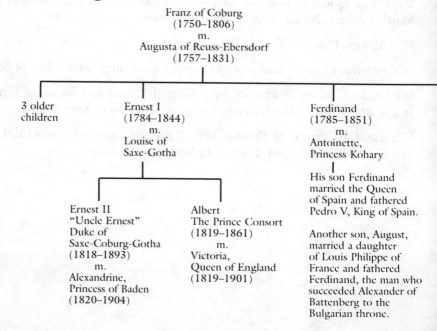

Franz of Coburg
(1750–1806)
m.
Augusta of Reuss-Ebersdorf
(1757–1831)

3 older
children

Ernest I
(1784–1844)
m.
Louise of
Saxe-Gotha

Ferdinand
(1785–1851)
m.
Antoinette,
Princess Kohary

His son Ferdinand
married the Queen
of Spain and fathered
Pedro V, King of Spain.

Another son, August,
married a daughter
of Louis Philippe of
France and fathered
Ferdinand, the man who
succeeded Alexander of
Battenberg to the
Bulgarian throne.

Ernest II
"Uncle Ernest"
Duke of
Saxe-Coburg-Gotha
(1818–1893)
m.
Alexandrine,
Princess of Baden
(1820–1904)

Albert
The Prince Consort
(1819–1861)
m.
Victoria,
Queen of England
(1819–1901)

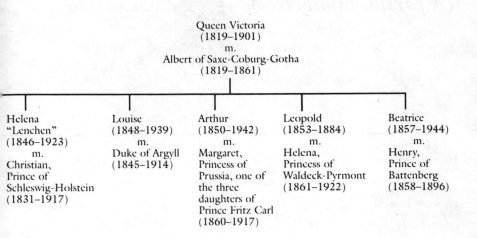

Queen Victoria
(1819–1901)
m.
Albert of Saxe-Coburg-Gotha
(1819–1861)

Helena "Lenchen" (1846–1923) m. Christian, Prince of Schleswig-Holstein (1831–1917)	Louise (1848–1939) m. Duke of Argyll (1845–1914)	Arthur (1850–1942) m. Margaret, Princess of Prussia, one of the three daughters of Prince Fritz Carl (1860–1917)	Leopold (1853–1884) m. Helena, Princess of Waldeck-Pyrmont (1861–1922)	Beatrice (1857–1944) m. Henry, Prince of Battenberg (1858–1896)

Victoria
(1786–1861)
m.
(1) Emich, Prince
of Leiningen
(1763–1814)

Charles
(1786–1861)

Feodora
(1807–1872)
m.
Ernest, Prince of Hohenlohe
(1794–1860)

(2) Edward, Duke of Kent

Victoria, Queen of England
(1819–1901)
m.
Albert (see Ernest I)

Their daughter Adelaide married the Duke of Schleswig-Holstein, whose daughter Augusta Victoria "Dona" married Wilhelm II of Germany

Leopold
(1795–1865)
King of the Belgians
m.
(1) Charlotte, Princess of England
(1796–1817)

(2?) Karoline Bauer (morganatic)

(3) Louise, Princess of Orléans
(1812–1850)

Their daughter Charlotte
(1840–1927) married
Maximilian, Archduke
of Austria, who became
Emperor of Mexico. She
went mad after he was
executed.

The Hohenzollerns
(A partial family tree)

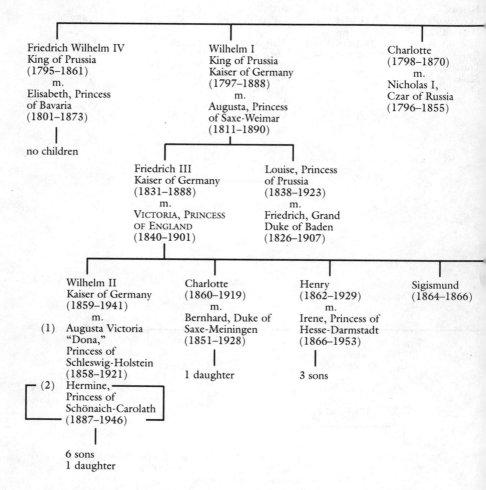

Friedrich Wilhelm IV
King of Prussia
(1795–1861)
m.
Elisabeth, Princess
of Bavaria
(1801–1873)

no children

Wilhelm I
King of Prussia
Kaiser of Germany
(1797–1888)
m.
Augusta, Princess
of Saxe-Weimar
(1811–1890)

Charlotte
(1798–1870)
m.
Nicholas I,
Czar of Russia
(1796–1855)

Friedrich III
Kaiser of Germany
(1831–1888)
m.
VICTORIA, PRINCESS
OF ENGLAND
(1840–1901)

Louise, Princess
of Prussia
(1838–1923)
m.
Friedrich, Grand
Duke of Baden
(1826–1907)

Wilhelm II
Kaiser of Germany
(1859–1941)
m.
(1) Augusta Victoria
"Dona,"
Princess of
Schleswig-Holstein
(1858–1921)
(2) Hermine,
Princess of
Schönaich-Carolath
(1887–1946)

6 sons
1 daughter

Charlotte
(1860–1919)
m.
Bernhard, Duke of
Saxe-Meiningen
(1851–1928)

1 daughter

Henry
(1862–1929)
m.
Irene, Princess of
Hesse-Darmstadt
(1866–1953)

3 sons

Sigismund
(1864–1866)

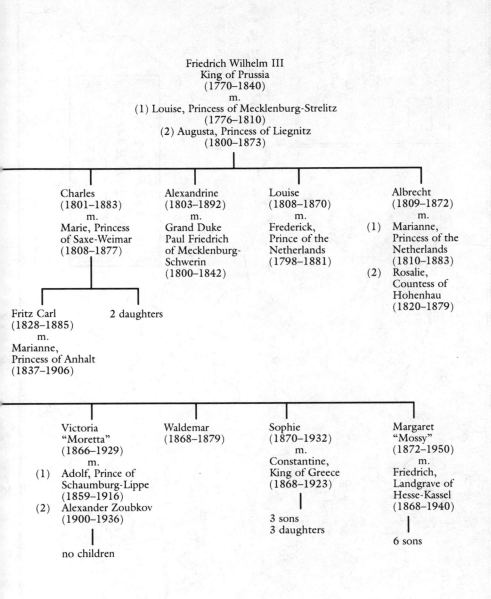

Friedrich Wilhelm III
King of Prussia
(1770–1840)
m.
(1) Louise, Princess of Mecklenburg-Strelitz
(1776–1810)
(2) Augusta, Princess of Liegnitz
(1800–1873)

Charles
(1801–1883)
m.
Marie, Princess
of Saxe-Weimar
(1808–1877)

Alexandrine
(1803–1892)
m.
Grand Duke
Paul Friedrich
of Mecklenburg-
Schwerin
(1800–1842)

Louise
(1808–1870)
m.
Frederick,
Prince of the
Netherlands
(1798–1881)

Albrecht
(1809–1872)
m.
(1) Marianne,
Princess of the
Netherlands
(1810–1883)
(2) Rosalie,
Countess of
Hohenhau
(1820–1879)

Fritz Carl
(1828–1885)
m.
Marianne,
Princess of Anhalt
(1837–1906)

2 daughters

Victoria
"Moretta"
(1866–1929)
m.
(1) Adolf, Prince of
Schaumburg-Lippe
(1859–1916)
(2) Alexander Zoubkov
(1900–1936)

no children

Waldemar
(1868–1879)

Sophie
(1870–1932)
m.
Constantine,
King of Greece
(1868–1923)

3 sons
3 daughters

Margaret
"Mossy"
(1872–1950)
m.
Friedrich,
Landgrave of
Hesse-Kassel
(1868–1940)

6 sons

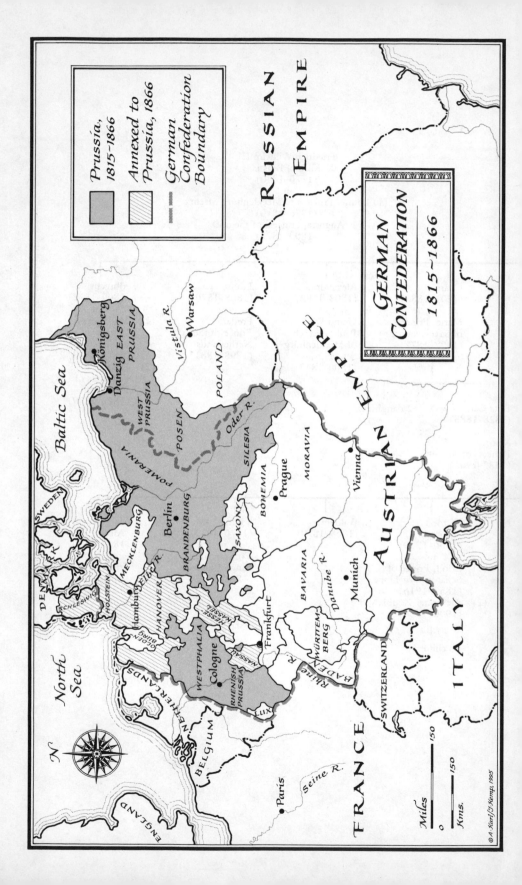

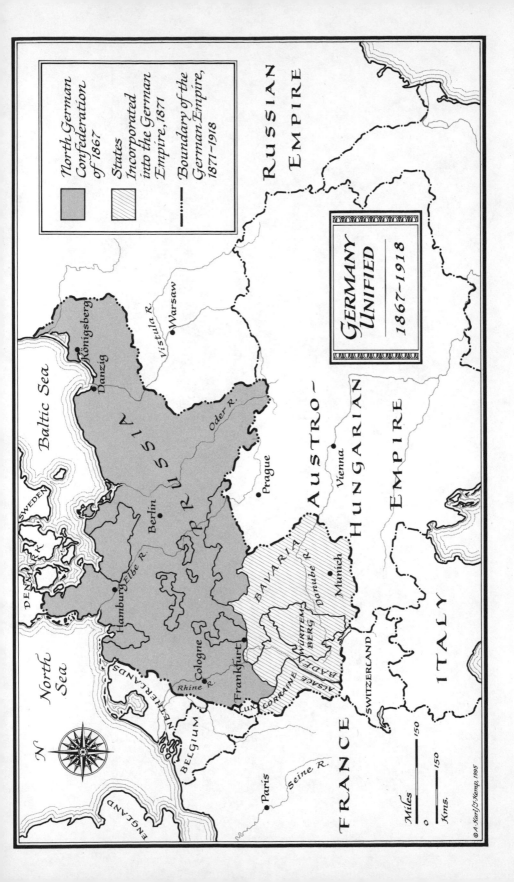

PART ONE

Princess Royal

CHAPTER
ONE

"[A]n ugly baby is a very nasty object—& the prettiest is fright-ful when undressed."

QUEEN VICTORIA, *1859*

*T*HE HOUSEHOLD into which Her Royal Highness Princess Victoria Adelaide Mary Louisa was born was surprisingly cozy. Her parents, Queen Victoria and Prince Albert, were only twenty-one and passionately in love. In the nine months between their wedding and Vicky's birth, they had established a domestic routine dedicated to fulfilling royal obligations, but lightened by the pleasures of reading aloud and playing four-hand Mozart. Compromises made for love had brought the young Queen and her consort closer together: while Victoria struggled to control her imperious temper, Albert battled his own shortcomings—a natural despondency and an aversion to the late hours and uninspiring social life of the court. Vicky provided a new and special focus for her parents' love and commitment to duty. They would mold an ideal royal offspring.

The young Queen described the birth of this, the first of her nine children, in her journal: "Just before the early hours of the morning of the 21st I felt very uncomfortable & with difficulty aroused Albert. . . . Tried to get to sleep again, but by 4, I got very bad & both the Doctors* arrived. My beloved Albert was so dear & kind. Locock said the Baby was on the way & everything was all right. We both expressed joy that the event was at hand & I did not feel at all nervous."

Before her marriage Victoria had admitted to her diary that having children was "the only thing I dread," and she had requested that the witnesses required to be present at the birth of an heir to the throne remain outside her green silk bedroom during the accouchement. Only those who could offer help or support —the obstetrician, the nurse-midwife, and her beloved Albert, who held her hand—were with her. The Queen's personal physician and two assisting doctors remained in an anteroom, while the Prime Minister, Foreign Minister, Archbishop of Canterbury, and other worthies were relegated to a room beyond— all eyeing the open doors and listening for signs of progress.

* *Sir James Clark, the Queen's physician, and Charles Locock, her chief obstetrician.*

It was, in Victoria's words, a "dark, dull, windy, rainy day with smoking chimneys." Tension both inside and outside the bedroom ran high, even for the first child of a queen. No one could forget that twenty-three years earlier the previous female heir to the throne, Princess Charlotte, had died giving birth to a stillborn son.

Medical sciences had progressed since 1817, and at one-fifty on the afternoon of November 21, 1840, the official witnesses, waiting in the outer room since before dawn, heard the doctor announce to the Queen, "Oh, Madam, it is a Princess."

"Never mind," Victoria replied in her clipped crystalline tones, "the next will be a Prince."

As soon as the umbilical cord was cut, the plump, healthy infant was carried out by a nurse and laid "stark naked" on a table for the witnesses to see. "[A]las! a girl and not a boy, as we had so hoped & wished for," Victoria wrote later. "We were, I am afraid, sadly disappointed, but yet our hearts were full of gratitude, for God having brought me safely through my ordeal, & having such a strong healthy child. Dearest Albert hardly left me at all, & was the greatest support & comfort."

The Prince Consort* was as disappointed as his wife. "Albert, father of a daughter, you will laugh at me," he wrote his brother Ernest in Germany. Two days later he felt less sheepish. "I should have preferred a boy," he told Ernest, "yet as it is, I thank Heaven." As did the English, grateful to have any offspring of the Queen placed in the succession before the Duke of Cumberland, Victoria's father's younger brother, who was next in line for the throne. Popularly seen as a one-eyed "ogre who devoured women and killed men in fits of rage," the Duke of Cumberland was the eldest living son of George III at the time of Vicky's birth.

While the national relief helped both parents overcome their disappointment over the child's sex, her arrival two to three weeks early threw the royal household into disarray. "Nothing was ready," the Queen complained, sending a page to ferry the wet nurse, wife of a sailmaker, over to Southampton from her home on the Isle of Wight, and ordering the old servants' rooms in the attic of Buckingham Palace, currently under alteration as a nursery, to be hurriedly completed.

Meanwhile, for the first eight days of her life, Vicky, or Pussy, as her parents called her, lived in her mother's dressing room. She slept in the royal crib—a nautilus seashell of gilded mahogany, lined with quilted green silk, embroidered in arabesques and the White Rose of England. Under a draped canopy of gold and silver silk surmounted by a royal crown, Pussy was rocked on gilded brackets attached to mahogany pillars. This fairy-tale caprice, solidly realized in the style of the nineteenth century, had been delivered just a week before by the Queen's favorite upholsterers, the Messrs. Seddon in Gray's Inn

---

* *Officially Prince Albert did not receive the title of Prince Consort until 1857, but it is used throughout this book.*

Road, along with two baths for the royal infant, one lined in silver, the other in marble.

The child was christened on February 10, 1841, the first anniversary of her parents' "dear marriage day," in a silver gilt lily font,* designed for the ceremony by the Prince Consort. He also composed a chorale for the celebratory banquet, which featured a christening cake topped with a sugar Britannia, bearing a tiny pink sugar Vicky in her arms. Albert was exceedingly proud of his firstborn, who did not cry but remained awake during the ceremony and "seemed to crow with immense satisfaction at the lights and brilliant uniforms." From this behavior, the baby's father concluded that his daughter was "very intelligent and observing." The Prime Minister, Lord Melbourne, also ventured to say that Vicky looked as if she was "quite conscious that the stir was all about herself!" adding portentously, "This is the time the character is formed!"

The only blot on the festivities was the absence of Albert's father, the Duke of Coburg. The Duke had kept Victoria and Albert guessing as to whether he could come or not, citing painful rheumatism and bad weather as reasons for not traveling. Although Queen Victoria complained that the fifty-six-year-old Duke expected her to pay his bills when he was in England and constantly called upon her for loans, Albert continued to hope he would arrive. It was not until the last minute that the Duke of Wellington was asked to stand substitute. There were too many godparents anyway, according to the Archbishop of Canterbury, who had advised the Prime Minister that the Church prescribed one godfather, two godmothers, and "no more" for a girl. Vicky was given three of each.

THE BIRTH of the Princess Royal made little immediate difference in Queen Victoria's life or routine. Once the baby was moved upstairs to the nursery, she was brought down to visit only twice a day, early in the morning when Victoria was still in her dressing room, and again in the afternoon. She was five weeks old when her mother saw her bathed for the second time. "She is amazingly improved since I last saw her undressed & is much grown & filled out," said Victoria. The Queen, who referred to childbearing as "the shadow side of marriage," and thought that babies were "froglike" in appearance, was clearly surprised by her rapidly growing attachment to her child. It was not long before she was paying flying visits upstairs to the nursery and having the baby brought down at odd times to be shown off to her ladies-in-waiting, visitors to the court, and even ministers, all of whom could be counted on to admire her. If the Princess Royal was not awake and performing in the manner of infants, Victoria had her produced a second or third time.

In spite of this, Vicky did not at any time assume first position in her mother's heart. For the young Victoria—a short, gentle-bodied girl in her early twenties—the greatest event of the highly eventful year of 1840 had been her marriage to Albert, and the wonder of it had not diminished. Even beyond the ·

---

* *It is still used by the British royal family, along with Vicky's christening robe of Honiton lace.*

enormous physical pleasure, there was the delight of companionship. It was part of a queen's duty to insure the succession, and Vicky was a prideful addition to her life, but with all the love and adoration Victoria expended on her beloved Albert, there was not much left over for anyone else.

This obsession with her husband is hardly surprising in light of the Queen's own rather grim childhood. Born in the spring of 1819 in the race among four of the middle-aged sons of King George III* to provide an heir to the throne, she had lost her father, the Duke of Kent, when she was only eight months old. Left in England with a German mother and her mother's two children from a previous marriage to a German prince, Victoria inherited all the hatred and resentment previously aimed at her spendthrift father and foreign mother by a jealous royal family. Her father's eldest brother, the Prince Regent, succeeded to the throne as George IV six days after her father's death. Determined to force Vicky's widowed mother to return to Germany, George refused to help settle his brother's enormous debts or help raise his brother's child. Although the King could not turn the penniless Duchess of Kent and her family out of Kensington Palace, he said "he would be d———d" if he'd support the child, since the widow's brother, Prince Leopold of Coburg, "was rich enough to take care of her."

George IV had never liked his former son-in-law, Prince Leopold of Coburg. The King begrudged Leopold the £50,000 annual allowance granted him by parliament when he married Princess Charlotte—£3000 of which Leopold now used to support his sister, the Duchess of Kent, and her daughter Victoria.

"I know not what would have become of you and your Mama, if I had not existed," Uncle Leopold wrote his niece when she was Queen some years later. "[W]e were very unkindly treated by George IV, whose great wish was to get you and your Mamma out of the country, and I must say without my assistance you could not have remained."

Despite a propensity for self-promotion, Uncle Leopold was by far the most intelligent influence on the young Victoria, and she called her visits to his home "the brightest epoch of my otherwise rather melancholy childhood." Her mother, an affectionate but weak-willed woman, preferred the charm and easy advice of Captain John Conroy to the practical admonitions of her politically minded brother. Conroy was a handsome and unprincipled Irishman, a former equerry to her husband, the Duke of Kent. Dubbed "Mephistopheles" by Prince Leopold, Conroy determined after the Duke's death that his road to power lay

---

* *Of the thirteen children of George III, none had any offspring qualified to inherit the throne after the death of Princess Charlotte. Three of the daughters were married, but none had children. (At least one of the unmarried princesses bore an illegitimate child.) Of the sons, the eldest, King George IV, was the father of the ill-fated Charlotte; the second was dead; the third, the Duke of Clarence, who became King William IV, had fathered ten children, all illegitimate; the fourth was the Duke of Kent, Victoria's father, who was followed in the succession by the Dukes of Cumberland, aged forty-six; Sussex, forty-four; and Cambridge, forty-three. Cumberland was already married, but Kent, Sussex, and Cambridge all hurried to find appropriate wives with whom to produce an heir.*

with his former employer's widow and infant, who would one day inherit the English throne, and he beguiled the Duchess into giving him complete control over her life and the education of her daughter.

To keep matters in his own hands Conroy developed what came to be known as the "Kensington System," a plan that isolated the young Victoria from every outside influence, especially members of her father's family, and forced her into total dependence on her mother and Conroy. She was allowed no companions besides Conroy's daughters, whom she loathed. Feodora, Victoria's adored half-sister,* who was eleven years her senior, was married off and sent back to Germany when Victoria was only eight. Three years later, her beloved uncle Leopold left England to become King Leopold I of Belgium.

Victoria's life should have improved in 1830 when she was eleven and her uncle, William IV, succeeded the now childless George IV to the throne. William, unlike his brother George, welcomed Victoria as his heir. He and his wife, Queen Adelaide, had always been fond of their young niece and wanted her to take her rightful place at functions of the court. But Conroy, looking forward to a regency that he could control through the Duchess of Kent, managed to keep the Duchess embroiled in endless quarrels with the King. Because of one such contretemps, the young Victoria, heir apparent to the throne, was prevented from attending her uncle William's coronation. She spent the day weeping bitterly.

An unwilling pawn in the intrigues of Conroy, whom she thoroughly detested, Victoria trusted no one besides her governess, Baroness Lehzen. Lehzen, devoted but possessive, had been appointed by Conroy when Victoria was five because she was German, not particularly well educated, and unlikely to harbor ideas of her own. With only "Dear good Lehzen" as the companion of her teenage years, it is not surprising that Victoria longed for diversions and friends her own age. Her diaries record the arrivals of even her most unprepossessing relatives with great enthusiasm and their departures with headaches and tears.

Not until she became Queen in 1837 at the age of eighteen was Victoria able to declare her independence from her mother and Conroy. Even then her infatuations with visitors to the court speak of the loneliness of her youth. Given a handsome, adoring husband like Albert when she was twenty, it is small wonder that the Queen, just discovering the joys of sexual love, found more pleasure in Vicky's father than in Vicky.

THE SITUATION was entirely different with Prince Albert, for whom Vicky's birth was the turning point in his relationship with his wife and his standing in his adopted country.

For the first nine months of his marriage to Victoria, Albert had functioned purely as the Queen's husband, a lover and companion, but nothing more.

* *One of the two children from the Duchess of Kent's previous marriage to the Prince of Leiningen.*

Although Victoria placed their writing tables side by side shortly after their wedding, she refused to delegate any work to him beyond running their palaces. One of Albert's biggest problems was Baroness Lehzen, who did whatever she could to undermine his position. "In my home life I am very happy and contented," he wrote a friend four months after his wedding, "but . . . I am only the husband, and not the master in the house." Tall and well built, handsome in a direct, masculine way, Albert was regarded by his wife as a beautiful but private treasure and by the English as a suspicious foreigner.

On the afternoon of Vicky's birth, however, Albert attended his first meeting of the Privy Council, invited by the Prime Minister to represent the Queen. Returning from the council chamber, he learned that his name was being introduced for the first time into the liturgy, so that the English would in the future pray for his wife, his daughter, *and* himself. Two days later Victoria gave him a key to her secret boxes. Within several months, Albert had taken advantage of his opportunities to advance himself to the position of the Queen's chief adviser. Soon he was sitting beside her when she received her ministers, writing many of her important letters, and making most of her decisions. "He is as much King as she can make him," Charles Greville, the famous chronicler, noted two years after Vicky was born.

Highly intelligent, Albert was a more devoted student of politics than his wife. Where she was inclined to act on impulse, he studied questions from every possible angle; where she was subject to temperamental outbursts, he was self-controlled. His natural intelligence, carefully nurtured throughout a rather bizarre childhood of his own, had prepared him to take an important place among the crowned heads of Europe.

Albert was the second son of Duke Ernest of Coburg, who was already a famous womanizer when he married Albert's mother, sixteen-year-old Louise of Saxe-Gotha-Altenburg, in 1817. Louise must have been an enchanting young woman—bright, lively, and gifted in music, a talent that Albert inherited. Duke Ernest and Louise had two sons, Ernest and Albert, born in the first two years of the marriage, after which the Duke returned to his mistresses. Rejected at eighteen, Louise fell in love with an army officer, an indiscretion seized on by her husband to force her to leave Coburg. Albert never saw his vivacious young mother again—she died at thirty-one—but he "never forgot her," and one of his first gifts to Victoria was a small pin his mother had given him before her departure. Totally insensitive to the emotional upheaval in the life of his sons, aged five and six, Duke Ernest went off on a hunting trip the day their mother left home.

It was his grandmother, the Duchess of Coburg, who picked the beautiful blue-eyed Albert to marry another of her grandchildren, Victoria. To that end, Albert's education was supervised (and sometimes paid for) by Prince Leopold, the same man who was subsidizing Victoria and her mother in England. Victoria's mother and Albert's father were Leopold's older siblings; he was their mutual uncle, adored by them both.

Albert was an exceptionally bright and capable boy, although serious, shy, and rather delicate. When he was eleven, he wrote in his journal that he intended to "train myself to be a good and useful man." Three years later he devised his own work schedule, which started at 6:00 A.M. with French translations and finished at 8:00 P.M. with compositions in Latin. He always rose and went to bed very early. "An irresistible feeling of sleepiness would come over him in the evening," his tutor said, "which he found difficult to resist even in after life."

This tendency to fall asleep too early—a trait inherited by his eldest daughter—created problems when Albert was taken to England at the age of seventeen to meet his cousin Victoria for the first time. Although the two cousins liked each other, the late hours and parties planned for his amusement made him ill. Uncle Leopold and Baron Stockmar, Leopold's doctor, friend, and secretary, who oversaw Albert's education, decided that the young Coburg Prince needed seasoning, and Albert was sent back to the continent for an intensive course of study, travel, and society.

When he returned to England three years later, he was more worldly and less self-conscious. He had grown taller and thinner, and his light brown hair fell in curls around his ears. "Albert is, in fact, so fascinating and looks so handsome," Victoria wrote the day after her twenty-year-old cousin's arrival at Windsor Castle, "he has such beautiful blue eyes. . . . His figure is fine, broad at the shoulders and slender at the waist, I have to keep a tight hold on my heart." Three days later they were engaged. Their marriage fulfilled not only the dreams of the Coburg family, but their own as well.

SHORTLY AFTER his engagement to Queen Victoria, Albert asked Baron Stockmar of Coburg to come to England as his personal adviser. Certainly there was nothing Christian Friedrich Stockmar preferred to the pleasure of giving advice. A diminutive, shivering, hypochondriacal sage, doctor by training, pundit by nature, Stockmar had accompanied Albert and Victoria's uncle Leopold to England when Leopold married Charlotte. He had remained in the service of the Coburgs ever since, helping Victoria prevent her mother and Conroy from establishing a regency over her head when she came of age to inherit the throne. Now, three years later, Albert asked Stockmar to return once again to England. The fifty-three-year-old doctor arrived a month before Victoria and Albert's wedding. Thereafter, he shuttled between Coburg and England, where he spent several months each year.

Baron Stockmar was an avid student of political affairs. His greatest gift to England—passed on through Albert to Victoria—was his conviction that the monarch must rise above party politics. Up until Victoria's time, British rulers had taken sides in the struggles of the political parties for control of Parliament. With Victoria, the crown gradually entered into an age of political neutrality— a position that would help keep the English royal family on its throne long after most other European monarchs had been chased off theirs.

In his position as adviser to Victoria and Albert, Stockmar dealt with family affairs as well, arbitrating marital squabbles and issuing long, sober tracts on the proper care of their children. With their determination to raise perfect princes and princesses, Victoria and Albert also wrote endless memoranda of their own.

The first appeared in November of 1840, the month of Vicky's birth. A collection of penciled notes in Albert's unsure English, it was an attempt by the young father to set up a proper nursery for his daughter, leaving no room for human error or even judgment. This rigidity can be only partly attributed to the external threats that dogged the lives of royal parents and children. Menaces such as these were dealt with, according to one member of the nursery staff, by means of "intricate turns and locks and guardrooms, and . . . intense precautions, suggesting the most hideous dangers . . . not altogether imaginary."

Beyond the necessities of safety, however, one senses the Prince Consort's possessiveness and desire for control as he outlined the duties and living arrangements of an enormous battery of attendants for his infant daughter—a superintendent of the nursery, a so-called monthly nurse, a nursery maid, an assistant nursery maid, a housemaid, and a wet nurse, as well as a "footman-in-waiting down stairs to take the various messages." Albert's first memo was followed by a second and even a third draft, each further refined. The end result, ennobled by the crests and signatures of both Queen and Prince, included the names of those who had been hired to fill these delicate positions.

Responsibility for Vicky's welfare rested with the superintendent of the nursery, who was admonished never to leave Vicky alone, not to show her to anyone or take her out without Victoria's or Albert's permission, not to act on physician's orders before consulting the parents, and to be sure that the wet nurse stood when she fed the child.*

The first superintendent of the nursery, Mrs. Kempthorne, left because of illness before Vicky was two months old. She was succeeded by Mrs. Southey, who lasted only a year. The pious widow of a naval captain, brother of Southey the poet, Mrs. Southey had run a school for boys before being employed by the royal family. The Queen said she was ineffectual. A more compelling reason for her early dismissal may be found in Southey's letter of resignation, which featured her credo of education:

> To teach the young idea how to shoot;
> To breathe th' enlivening spirit and to fix
> The gen'rous purpose in the glowing breast.

It was Southey's inefficiency more than her aggressive banality, however, that hastened her departure. Albert Edward, the future King Edward VII, known as Bertie, was born in November of 1841, just a year after his sister Vicky, dramatizing the need for a stronger, surer hand in the royal nursery. Pressed by her husband and Baron Stockmar, the Queen wrote the Prime Minister, Lord Melbourne, to ask his advice:

---

* *There seems to have been no medical reason for this directive beyond the fact that the wet nurse would have had to be young and healthy to stand that long.*

The present system will <u>not</u> do . . . Old Mrs. Southey is totally unfit to overlook the things & the Consequence is that the Children are left quite in the hands of low people—the Nurse & Nursery Maids . . . are vulgar, & . . . <u>constantly</u> quarrelling! Stockmar says . . . that our occupations prevent us from managing these Affairs as much ourselves as other Parents can & therefore that we must have someone in whom to place <u>implicit</u> <u>Confidence</u>. He says a Lady of Rank & Title . . . would be the <u>best</u>;—but <u>where</u> to find a person . . . <u>fit</u> for the place, & if <u>fit</u>,—one who will consent to shut herself up in the Nursery & entirely from Society.

They found her in their own court. Sarah Spencer, Lady Lyttelton, had served as a Lady of the Bedchamber to Queen Victoria for three years. A widow with five children, Lady Lyttelton was recruited by Baron Stockmar, who had to convince the Queen that the new governess would not "encroach upon" Victoria's own "maternal rights" and that she also had obligations vis-à-vis her own daughters. On this point Victoria refused to commit herself: "Her Majesty will permit <u>to</u> <u>have</u> <u>it</u> <u>laid</u> <u>down</u> <u>as</u> <u>a</u> <u>Principle</u> . . . that <u>Lady</u> <u>Lyttelton</u> <u>may</u> <u>devote</u> <u>as</u> <u>much</u> <u>time</u> <u>to</u> <u>her</u> <u>Children</u>, <u>as</u> <u>she</u> <u>herself</u> <u>finds</u> <u>conscientiously</u> <u>and</u> <u>practically</u> <u>consistent</u> <u>with</u> <u>the</u> <u>Duties</u> <u>she</u> <u>has</u> <u>undertaken</u>, bearing always in mind . . . that, whether absent from, or present with her charge, <u>her</u> <u>responsibility</u> <u>can</u> <u>never</u> <u>vary</u>."

It was weighty duty, made more so by the exacting Queen, ponderous Baron, and nervous Prince. Only a woman of Lady Lyttelton's tact could have succeeded. One of six children of a haughty and demanding mother, the new governess had grown up filling in the gaps of affection missed by her brothers and sisters, and it was natural for her to continue her sympathetic ways with Vicky, Bertie, and the seven younger brothers and sisters* who followed them into the nursery. Unaffected and imperturbable, Lady Lyttelton also dealt generously with the large staff under her command, treating their foibles and quarrels with gentle humor.

The birth of a male heir to the throne also galvanized Victoria, Albert, and especially Stockmar into presenting a plan for the education of the royal children. When Bertie was less than four months old and Vicky not yet a year and a half, Stockmar issued a memorandum of forty-six pages on the enormity of the task facing the royal parents:

"Good Education is very rare . . . and the higher the Rank of the Parents the more difficult it is," he proclaimed, but "to be deterred from attempting it . . . would be a dereliction of the most sacred Duties." In Stockmar's opinion, Victoria and Albert were too young to have sufficient "knowledge, maturity of judgment and experience" to guide their own children. What then were the royal parents to do? It was, Stockmar said, "their sacred Duty to consult . . . honest, intelligent and experienced Persons and not only to consult them but to follow their advice."

---

* *Alice, born in 1843; Alfred, 1844; Helena, 1846; Louise, 1848; Arthur, 1850; Leopold, 1853; Beatrice, 1857.*

The "honest, intelligent and experienced Persons" were, of course, Stockmar himself. "Having maturely meditated the subject in all its bearings and well considered all its difficulties . . ." he wrote, "there is no difficulty in the World, which would deter me from grappling with it, in order to triumph over it and to accomplish so necessary, so great and so sacred an object as a good Education of the Royal Children."

This is how Vicky's education came to be laid out by a middle-aged German pedant with little tolerance for human foibles. "The object of Education is, to develop and strengthen the good, and subdue or diminish the evil dispositions of our Nature," Stockmar told Vicky's parents, asserting that above all, education must regulate "the Child's natural Instincts" and "keep its Mind pure."

The fact that young Vicky survived and surmounted this burdensome directive is a testament to the buoyancy of her own God-given intellect.

CHAPTER TWO

*I*N ACCORDANCE WITH Stockmar's assurance that serious education begins on the day of birth, Vicky's French tutor arrived when she was eighteen months old and her German tutor when she was three and a half. All her governesses, including Lady Lyttelton, whom she dubbed "Laddle," were impressed with the child's intelligence. She was clever and quick, and she knew it. With a vocabulary in three languages far beyond her years, Vicky kept her parents and nursery attendants supplied with a constant fund of anecdotes to pass around the court.

"We drove with the Queen and the little Princess yesterday," wrote Lady Bloomfield when Vicky was two. "The latter chattered the whole time and was very amusing. . . . The Queen was not taking any notice of the Princess, who suddenly exclaimed, 'There's a cat under the trees'—fertile imagination on her part, as there was nothing of the kind; but having attracted attention, she quietly said, 'Cat come out to look at the Queen, I suppose.' "

Six months later, the Queen proudly wrote Uncle Leopold (King Leopold I of Belgium):

> Our fat Vic or Pussette learns a verse of Lamartine by heart, which ends with *"le tableau se déroule à mes pieds"* [the picture unfolds beneath my feet]; to show how well she had understood this difficult line . . . I must tell you the following bon mot. When she was riding on her pony, and looking at the cows and sheep, she turned to Mdlle [her French governess] . . . and said: *"Voilà le tableau qui se déroule à mes pieds"* [Behold the picture unfolding beneath my feet]. Is not this extraordinary for a little child of three years old? It is more like what a person of twenty would say. You have no notion what a knowing, and I am sorry to say sly, little rogue she is, and so obstinate.

Vicky was so bright that she spoiled things for her younger siblings, none of whom ever approached her in intellect. This was particularly painful in the

* *Vicky's aunt (Queen Victoria's half-sister).*

case of Bertie, one year younger and heir to the throne. Bertie, whom his mother referred to in his infancy only as "the boy," learned slowly and had difficulty concentrating. Subjected to intense pressure due to his future position, he suffered from the unreasonable demands of his parents and the inevitable comparisons to his older sister. His continued and deep fondness for Vicky throughout their lives is evidence of his basic goodwill.

But Vicky had all the problems of a firstborn. "The Princess," Lady Lyttel-ton reported when she was not yet a year old, "hid her head under the nurse's arm yesterday, and on the Queen peeping round to see why she did it, H.R.H. was detected in that safe corner sucking her necklace, which is forbidden. Then the Queen said, 'Oh fie! naughty! naughty!' . . . The Queen is, like all very young mothers, exigeante [demanding], and never thinks the baby makes prog-ress enough or is good enough."

There were other pressures on baby Vicky. "Oh, dear!" Lady Lyttelton wrote when the child was two,

I wish . . . that all her fattest and biggest and most forbidding looking relations, some with bald heads, some with great moustaches, some with black bushy eyebrows, some with staring, distorted, short-sighted eyes, did not always come to see her at once and make her naughty and her governess cross. Poor little body! She is always expected to be good, civil, and sensi-ble, and the Duke of Cambridge* . . . tells the Queen . . . that it is very odd the Princess should ever cry! "So very odd! my daughters never did cry!" . . . and Her Majesty believed her uncle.

Expected to behave like a miniature adult, Vicky was also dressed like one —stuffed into tiny gowns with wide sashes that had nothing to do with a child's body. On her second birthday she was decked out in diamonds and pearls over a velvet and lace dress, looking "too comical," according to her governess. On New Year's Day, 1844, the three-year-old toddler was done up in a floor-length blue-and-white silk gown with a low neck, tight sleeves, and bustle, copied from a portrait of Princess Charlotte. Victoria was an esthetic snob who never hesi-tated to comment adversely on her children's looks. Only Vicky's position as firstborn saved her in the early years from her mother's overly critical eye—that, or the Queen's recognition that the child looked strikingly like her.

Vicky's big failings, according to her parents and governesses, were her willfulness and her temper, also remarkably like that of her mother and a special problem for a child constantly in the public eye. "The evening of a festival is almost always disastrous," Lady Lyttelton reported, "people grow naughty after much excitement, and accordingly the Princess Royal fell into a transport of rage on perceiving that the day was nearly over; & shrieked and roared in the open carriage . . . luckily in a lonely part of the road."

Vicky also told what Lady Lyttelton termed "slight falsehoods." On one occasion, the governess noted that "the Princess Royal told an untruth, asserting

* *Victoria's uncle, the youngest surviving son of George III.*

that I had desired she should walk out after supper in her pink bonnet, which I had not done, nor even mentioned the subject. She was imprisoned with tied hands, & very seriously admonished; and I trust was aware of her fault in the right way."

Imprisonment was Vicky's usual punishment, and she was matter-of-fact about the stubbornness that got her into trouble. Lady Lyttelton, who approached her after one particular bout of misbehavior, was told, "I am very sorry, Laddle, but I mean to be just as naughty next time." When their father engaged a new physician, the children were admonished not to call him Brown, as their father did, but Dr. Brown. All complied except Vicky, who was told she would be sent to bed if she repeated the impertinence. The next day she greeted the doctor loudly, "Good morning, Brown," and then, catching her mother's eye, got up, curtsied, and continued, "Good night, Brown, for I am going to bed."

The Queen sought consolation for Vicky's faults from her half-sister, Feodora, who said she was "too severe" with Vicky. She also consulted with Uncle Leopold, whose daughter Charlotte was Vicky's age. "We find Pussy amazingly advanced in intellect but, alas! also in naughtiness," Victoria wrote her uncle. "I hold up Charlotte as an example of every virtue which has its effect, for whenever she is going to be naughty she says, 'Dear Ma, what does Cousin Charlotte do?' "

Naughtiness in any form was judged with great severity in the palace, and punishments were ordered accordingly by the royal parents. One suspects that Baron Stockmar's pronouncements on the solemnity of their task plus his continual, pointed references to the immorality of Victoria's uncles* blurred the lines in the nursery between major and minor sins. "Pussette, I am sorry to say, gets more & more naughty, & very strong measures will have to be resorted to, as nothing else has any effect," Queen Victoria told Uncle Leopold when Vicky was three and a half. And when Vicky's younger sister Alice misbehaved on a drive at the age of four, Lady Lyttelton reported, "I thought the case very grave, and that I should obey His Royal Highness's instructions best, by administering a real punishment, by whipping."

Fortunately, Lady Lyttelton usually exercised common sense in classifying childish behavior, writing the Queen when Bertie was two that "His Royal Highness's worst crime, being a tendency to throw his cows and his soldiers out of Windows," was unlikely to "furnish a dangerous precedent" for life.

In matters of the children's health, Lady Lyttelton also tried to inject moderation into the royal nursery. Vicky developed digestive problems toward the end of her first year, and her continuing loss of weight, which was treated with purgatives and a reduction in food, did not abate. Her father blamed her poor health on the incompetence of the family physician, Dr. Clark, and the perni-

---

* The seven surviving sons of George III, referred to by Queen Victoria as "my disreputable uncles," were known for their scandalous private lives (Cecil Woodham-Smith, Queen Victoria, p. 17).

cious influence of Baroness Lehzen. Claiming that Clark had "poisoned her with calomel and you have starved her," Albert threatened to "have nothing more to do with" Vicky's care: "[T]ake the child away and do as you like and if she dies you will have it on your conscience," he warned the Queen. Baron Stockmar had to intercede between husband and wife, and not long after this, Baroness Lehzen was pensioned off to Germany.

Like other English children of their day, Victoria and Albert's brood was subjected to frequent "doses," "powders," and "lavements" (enemas), and the state of their digestion was a subject of constant concern. Lady Lyttelton did have some effect on Victoria and Albert's anxiety over their health. When Bertie's nurse expressed fear that her charge showed signs of a cold, the governess wrote his absent parents, "I cannot detect them yet myself, but she is likely to be most in the right. Prince has however had a most delightful night's sleep; his appetite & spirits are excellent, & if he did not look unaccountably pale this morning, I should not attend to the 3 sneezes which constitute the ground of alarm."

Along with physical health, there was great concern over spiritual training. Both Victoria and Albert, although genuinely religious, were unaffected in the outward manifestations of their faith, and Victoria was particularly anxious to avoid an excess of religious fervor. "I dread the extreme & I must say, besotted notion of religion now so prevalent . . . as I dread it being attempted to instill these Doctrines into our daughter's mind," she wrote in one of her many memoranda. The Queen's only objection to Lady Lyttelton was that she was too High Church.

The great question was that of kneeling for prayers. Vicky, who sat up in bed to say her nightly prayers for her parents, knelt when she did so in the presence of Lady Lyttelton. Running through the halls at Windsor one day the six-year-old stepped on a large nail that almost tore through the thin sole of her satin slipper. Removing the nail, Lady Lyttelton pointed out that God had mercifully spared little Vicky "great pain." Vicky's response indicates that she understood more than the lesson intended. "Shall we not kneel down?" she inquired.

IN JANUARY OF 1844, the Prince Consort's father died. Although the old reprobate had driven Albert's mother away, demanded money for his dissipations from Albert's wife, and excused himself from attending Albert's daughter's christening, the Prince Consort was sincerely grieved at his passing. Anxious to please her beloved, Queen Victoria threw herself wholeheartedly into mourning. "You must now be the father of us two poor bereaved heart broken children . . . ," she wrote Uncle Leopold a week after her father-in-law's death; "we feel crushed, overwhelmed, bowed down by the loss of one who was so deservedly loved, I may say adored, by his children and family; I loved him and looked on him as my own father; his like we shall not see again."

The Queen, Vicky's governess observed, "is very affecting in her grief for the poor old Duke whom she scarcely knew. But it is, in truth, all on the

Prince's account." Vicky, of course, could not know this and burst out crying when she saw her mother's tears. "Poor, dear Grandpapa is very ill . . . ," she told her governess; "Poor, dear Papa and dear Mama cry so! But he will be quite well in two weeks." When told that her grandfather had died, she said nothing.

But within the year Vicky had started asking questions about God. Victoria conferred with Albert and solicited Baron Stockmar's advice on the subject of religious training. "I am quite positive," the Queen wrote Stockmar, "that she should be taught to have great respect & reverence for God, & for religion, but that she should have the feeling of devotion & love . . . not of fear & trembling; & that the thoughts of death & an afterlife should not be represented in an alarming & forbidding view, & that she should be made to know as yet no difference of creeds, & not think that she can only pray on her knees, or that those who do not kneel are less fervent & devout in their prayers."

In matters of the children's training, Victoria always deferred to Albert or a combination of Albert and Baron Stockmar. Stockmar never made things easy for the royal parents. A near parody of the German mania for obfuscation, he protected his position of resident oracle by burying his advice in an intricate maze of warnings, stipulations, and qualifications. Having determined that it was his personal duty to strengthen the dynasty, he set unrealistic goals of perfection for the royal offspring, taking little or no account of individual needs or even the talents of those involved.

In his early years of fatherhood, the Prince Consort was not yet completely warped by Stockmar's advice. Although he was prone to turn everyday events into cautionary tales like most Victorian parents, Albert was a deeply caring and devoted father. He was also physically agile, dancing baby Vicky in his arms and leading the children in their outdoor activities—chasing butterflies with Vicky and Bertie, teaching his sons to fly kites, and showing Bertie how to turn somersaults on a haystack. "He is so kind to them and romps with them so delightfully, and manages them so beautifully and firmly," the Queen commented in her journal when Vicky was eight. A less prejudiced reporter, Lady Lyttelton was also struck watching the Prince Consort help one of his toddlers struggle into a piece of clothing. "It is not every papa who would have the patience and kindness," she remarked.

Patience was not their mother's cardinal virtue. Nor did the Queen particularly enjoy children, although she tried hard to be a good mother by throwing herself into the task of teaching them. "The root of the trouble lies in the mistaken notion that, the function of a mother is to be always correcting, scolding, ordering them about and organizing their activities," Albert warned her. "It is not possible to be on happy friendly terms with people you have just been scolding."

Still, there was one lesson Victoria taught their children to which the Prince Consort could find no objection. Sympathizing with Albert's anomalous position as husband of the Queen, Victoria made sure that within their home he and he alone was respected as head of the family. This she accomplished by example, soliciting dearest Papa's opinion on everything, promulgating his words as law, and placing his pronouncements somewhere just below the commandments of the Almighty. Vicky grew up believing in her father's infallibility. She also knew she was his favorite child and, unlike her siblings, was never afraid of him.

IN JANUARY OF 1847, shortly after Vicky's sixth birthday, her parents issued a memorandum dividing their brood, now five in number, into classes according to age. Leaving Alice, Alfred, and Helena in the nursery, Vicky and Bertie entered a new class, dedicated to elementary education and "the submission to the supervision & authority of one person for the Development of Character." That person was Sarah Anne Hildyard.

Nicknamed Tilla, the new governess was chosen by Baron Stockmar, and, as with Lady Lyttelton, Vicky was fortunate in the Baron's choice. Miss Hildyard, the daughter of a clergyman, was intelligent, well-read, and a stimulating teacher. She was also lucky with her eldest pupil, who was blessed with a remarkable mind and an infinite sense of curiosity.

Vicky's day started at eight-twenty in the morning with "Arithmetic, Dictation, Poetry or Questions in History" and ended at 6:00 P.M. with "Geography, History or Work Chronology as far as Edward 6th." This last class was replaced twice a week by dancing lessons. There was Scripture study three times a week, usually with her mother, and reading, writing, German, and French every day.

The Princess Royal was also given music lessons, although she showed more appreciation than talent in that area. Her artistic gifts lay in drawing and painting, and she started sketching with her tiny easel next to the Queen's when she was still a toddler. As she grew older, she began to take her drawing seriously, exhibiting the pride of an anxious perfectionist. "Don't look at it, Papa!" she would beg, hiding her work in her portfolio. "It is so bad, you must not see it."

Vicky's closest companion as she grew up was her sister Alice, two and a half years younger, with whom she soon shared Miss Hildyard and, when they were old enough, rooms away from the nursery. Alice was, as Vicky later wrote her husband, "always the diplomatically lovable one . . . easy to praise and hardly ever in trouble. Quite to the contrary was your fatty, who was always quite capable of stepping in it, wherever possible getting punished, yelled at, hit and disgraced."

But Vicky was never in as much trouble as brother Bertie. Called by his father "the nation's child," the heir to the throne was given his own tutor and an even more rigorous schedule than Vicky from the age of seven onward.

Unable to force Bertie into any enthusiasm over his studies, Prince Albert and Baron Stockmar rejoiced over Vicky's interest in history, which they made great efforts to develop. "From her youth onwards," Stockmar wrote, "I have been fond of her, have always expected great things of her, and taken all pains to be of service to her. I think her to be exceptionally gifted in some things, even to the point of genius."

■

VICTORIA, ALBERT, and their children lived in two residences, Buckingham Palace in London and Windsor Castle in the countryside. During Vicky's toddler years the family tried vacationing at Brighton, but George IV's Chinese Pavilion there, with its gorgeous dragons and serpents, was ill suited to the young family. Wedged as it was between resorts and lodging houses, it afforded no way for the children to walk on the beach without being mobbed. Victoria and Albert gave up using the Pavilion in 1845 and bought Osborne House on the Isle of Wight. A year later, after tearing down the old house and building a Neapolitan villa, they moved in. Vicky was six at the time.

Osborne House belonged to the family, not to the nation, and life there was informal. "In our island home," Prince Albert wrote his stepmother, "we are wholly given up to the enjoyment of the warm summer weather. The children catch butterflies, Victoria sits under the trees, I drink the Kissingen water." They also sketched and rode and picked strawberries in season. When the children were old enough they were taught to swim in a floating bath in the bay, designed by their father. They were understandably fascinated by their mother's bathing machine—a contraption with high, frosted glass windows, which slid down the sloping pier to the beach. Inside, her modesty protected, the Queen walked out onto a curtained porch and down five steps into the sea. Only after she was safely hidden by the water was the bathing machine removed.

About a half mile from the main residence was the children's playhouse, a miniature Swiss chalet of carved black wood with balconies. It was given to the royal brood so they could learn carpentry, cooking, and housekeeping. They had a room for natural history collections, and they grew vegetables in the garden, each child keeping a set of tools marked with his or her name in the summerhouse. For moral instruction, there were sayings from the Psalms and Proverbs inscribed around the walls and outside staircase. All the furniture was scaled down in size, including two small charcoal stoves with appropriately sized pots and pans. It was here in the blue-and-white-tiled kitchen that Vicky baked her first cake.

Whether in the state residences in London and Windsor or the private family retreats of Osborne and (later) Balmoral Castle in Scotland, family occasions were celebrated with amateur plays, concerts, and fancy dress. For their parents' twelfth anniversary, the children acted a portion of Racine's play *Athalie,* in which Vicky naturally took a leading role. Another Victorian favorite, *tableaux vivants,* were put on by the children for their parents. On Victoria and Albert's fourteenth anniversary, they appeared as the Four Seasons. Ten-year-old Alice was Spring, distributing flowers and poetry; Vicky, now thirteen, appeared as Summer with three-year-old baby Arthur; Alfred, age nine, was dressed as Autumn in the skin of a leopard; and Bertie, twelve years old and covered with icicles, was Winter, holding five-year-old Louise by the hand. For the last tableau, all the Seasons gathered together on stage with Helena, age seven, dressed in white and holding a large cross. The children then intoned a blessing on their parents.

Except for important state occasions, Victoria and Albert went to some pains to keep their children away from the corruptions of court life. Once outside the royal circle, however, there was little anyone could do to counteract the attention they received. At eight, the Princess Royal accompanied her mother to Ascot and made her first official appearance at the opening of the Coal Exchange in London. All done up in a green-and-white silk frock, black velvet cape, and pink satin bonnet trimmed with a pink feather, Vicky told her dresser how proud she was to be the "only great lady present."

The Queen was down with chicken pox, and Vicky attended the event with her father and brother. A half hour after leaving Buckingham Palace in a state carriage, she was seated in a gilded barge, rowed by twenty-seven oarsmen from Westminster to the City. The Lord Mayor and his functionaries, "dazzling" in crimson velvet, traveled in a boat just ahead of the royal party, while live swans were transported in their own barge attended by their keeper. "Every inch of ground, every bridge, roof, window, and as many vessels of all sorts as could lie on the river . . . were . . . close packed, with people," reported Lady Lyttelton, who added that the public looked "so affectionately, quite like parents" on her two young charges, "stretching over one another to see and smile at them."

Only Vicky and Bertie had been considered old enough to attend this celebration, and even they were not allowed to go to the public banquet, but were given lunch by themselves in a private room. The gentleman who brought the wine was so overcome at the honor of serving the children of his Queen that he broke down in tears and had to leave the room. "What a striking curious thing is that loyalty!" commented Vicky's governess. "And how deep and strong in England!"

As the world was about to discover, this was not the case in the rest of Europe.

CHAPTER THREE

*D*URING THE FIRST HALF of the nineteenth century, England stood in sharp and enviable contrast to her European neighbors. She had been separated by the Channel from the terrors of the French Revolution at the end of the eighteenth century and the humiliations of Napoleon's conquests that followed. By 1812, the French Empire, along with her satellites and allies, encompassed Spain, the kingdoms of Italy, Naples, and Sardinia, the Netherlands, Belgium, Switzerland, Prussia and the other German states, the Austrian Empire, the Grand Duchy of Warsaw (Poland), Denmark, and Norway.

It was England's Foreign Secretary, Viscount Castlereagh, who took advantage of Napoleon's retreat from Moscow to join the Fourth Coalition, an alliance of Russia and Prussia* that marched on Paris in March of 1814 and secured Napoleon's abdication a month later. And it was the British army under the Duke of Wellington that, after Napoleon's return from Elba, defeated him at Waterloo. Britain then joined Austria, Russia, and Prussia at the Congress of Vienna, which met in 1814–15 to put France back where it had been before the great conqueror and redraw the map of Europe.

Britain could rarely be convinced—except in a special case like Napoleon —to join the wars of her neighbors across the Channel. She remained aloof from the politically stultifying repression required to prop up the outmoded status quo reimposed on Europe by the Congress after the Napoleonic Wars, and in 1832 she passed the Great Reform Act, widening the voting franchise and opening up politics to the commercial class. While Prussia, France, Austria, and Russia bent their energies to reinventing prerevolutionary Europe, England marched forward under the twin banners of commercial and moral progress— leaders in the industrial revolution and colonial expansion, believers in the perfectibility of man. By the middle of the nineteenth century, England's cows were fat, her factories humming, her ships unbeatable, and her monarchy firmly in place.

* *Later joined by other German states, Sweden and Austria.*

This was not true of the countries on the other side of the Channel, where neither industrialization nor advancement by merit had caught up to England and where monarchs enforced their "divine rights" with armed soldiers and secret police. Throughout the period from 1814 until the middle of the century, popular discontent surfaced throughout Europe with some regularity—finally culminating in the widespread eruption known as the Revolution of 1848.

Arguably the beginning of the modern age and the major monarchical upheaval of the century, the Revolution of 1848 was not a single event but a confluence of individual uprisings that deposed, juggled, or at the very least called to account rulers all over Europe. The seminal revolt—the one that encouraged rebels in other countries—occurred in February in Paris, where Louis Philippe, the Citizen King who had fought in the revolutionary army and been elected to the throne by a liberal Chamber of Deputies, was forced to abdicate, leaving France a republic for the second time* in her history. Shortly thereafter, the Austrian Chancellor Prince Metternich, the major force behind the Congress of Vienna, was forced to flee that city, some say in the humbling guise of a woman.

In March, fighting also broke out on the streets of Berlin, and Prince Wilhelm of Prussia, the fifty-one-year-old heir to his brother Friedrich Wilhelm IV's throne, was compelled to trim his conspicuous whiskers in order to get out of Prussia alive. Nicknamed "the Grapeshot Prince" because he advised the King to use cannons against the rioters, Wilhelm left the Fatherland for both his own safety and the good of other members of the Prussian royal family, who were trying to make an accommodation with the revolutionaries. In spite of warnings from several of their ministers, Victoria and Albert offered their friend Wilhelm asylum. Treated as an honored guest, the Prince of Prussia remained in London for three months and returned home with his soldierly dignity intact.

This was not true for Louis Philippe, who escaped to England disguised as a Mr. Smith wearing goggles and a cap. His plight and that of his family—"wretched refugees," some of whom arrived at Buckingham Palace with nothing more than rags on their backs—must have made a deep impression on seven-year-old Vicky, who watched her father collect clothes and other necessities for the exiled Orléans family.

Even for the most secure of Europe's crowned heads, 1848 was a frightening phenomenon. Revolutionary fever finally jumped the Channel to the British Isles, where the Irish, suffering since 1801 from a desire for independence and now from potato famine, engaged in an abortive revolution, while the Chartists, a working-class movement aimed at electoral and parliamentary reforms, planned an enormous demonstration to take place on April 10 on Kennington Common. Albert was anxious about the safety of his wife, who was about to give birth to their sixth child. "We have Chartist riots every night . . . ," he wrote Baron Stockmar. "The organization of these people is incredible. They

---

* *The first came after the French Revolution and lasted from 1792 to 1804.*

have secret signals and correspond from town to town by means of carrier pigeons."

Fortunately for the royal family, Princess Louise made a timely appearance in the world, and two days before the dreaded demonstration, the Queen was pronounced well enough to leave London. The public was barred from the platform at Waterloo Station, which had been filled with hundreds of special constables, detailed to speed Victoria, Albert, and the royal children out of danger to their home of Osborne on the Isle of Wight.

IF THE REVOLUTION OF 1848 gave Albert reason to worry about his family, it also provided him with an opportunity to expound on his favorite subject—the future of Germany. When he left his home in Coburg in 1840 to marry the Queen of England, Albert had vowed to remain "a loyal German." Eight years later, with nearly a decade of experience in constitutional government behind him, the Prince Consort was in a unique position to express his views on German politics. In letters to King Friedrich Wilhelm IV of Prussia, Albert advocated the unification of all the small German states (there were nearly forty of them) under the leadership of Prussia. To accomplish this, Albert said, Prussia must discard the outdated autocratic ways of its partners in the Holy Alliance,* Russia and Austria, and turn itself into a modern constitutional state. Then and only then could it take its rightful place in the forefront of European politics and enter into an alliance with England.

Albert took advantage of Prince Wilhelm's asylum in London to press his solutions to the German problem. Wilhelm was a tall, impressive-looking soldier with a small closed mind—a reactionary who had once proclaimed himself a "sworn enemy" of the "impudent claims" of parliamentarians. But by the end of his exile in England, Albert believed he had succeeded in modifying his friend's attitude by convincing Wilhelm to cooperate with the new Prussian constitutional government established during his absence.

Albert's influence on Wilhelm, twenty-two years his senior, was helped by the relationship of their wives, who were only eight years apart in age. Victoria had entertained Wilhelm's wife, Princess Augusta of Prussia, in England in 1846. "I find her so clever, so amiable, so well informed, and so good," the Queen wrote Uncle Leopold after the visit; "she seems to have some enemies, for there are whispers of her being false; but from all that I have seen of her . . . I cannot and will not believe it. Her position is a very difficult one; she is too enlightened and liberal for the Prussian Court not to have enemies; but I believe that she is a friend to us and our family, and I do believe that I have a friend in her, who may be most useful to us."

If Augusta was not as trustworthy as Victoria would have liked her to be,

---

* The Holy Alliance was a declaration of Christian principles conceived by the Czar of Russia and signed by the monarchs of Prussia and Austria, obliging the signators to act together to maintain the status quo in Europe. Other European sovereigns signed on later.

she was politically liberal, and the Queen, who had had very limited intercourse with women her own age, felt she had found a soulmate. For Christmas that year Princess Augusta, known to Victoria and Albert's children as "Aunt Prussia," sent Vicky four miniature fruit and vegetable shops just like those in Berlin, and to brother Bertie, five cartons of Prussian toy soldiers in wood and lead. In return, Queen Victoria sent Augusta's son Fritz, age fifteen, a Scottish kilt, which his mother forced him to wear for a state dinner at the Prussian court. Soon Augusta and Victoria were exchanging letters on an intimate basis—a correspondence that continued in varying degrees of warmth and frequency for over forty years.

THERE IS SOME QUESTION as to who originated the idea of a marriage between Vicky and Fritz. It was probably Victoria and Albert's uncle Leopold. Leopold, named the first King of an independent Belgium in 1831 after its successful revolution against the Netherlands, was always looking for a way to extend the Coburg influence and guarantee his country's independence.* Or it might have been Baron Stockmar, the family adviser who believed in anything that would bring together "the two great Protestant dynasties in Europe" and who had begun raising the issue when Vicky was only six. Finally, there was Albert himself. If not the originator, he was certainly the catalyst in the match between his daughter and the future heir to the Prussian throne.

Albert's vision—a progressive Germany, unified by the Hohenzollerns of Prussia, living under constitutional law, and allied to England—seemed a realizable dream from the other side of the Channel. King Friedrich Wilhelm IV of Prussia, who was suffering from what was then called softening of the brain, but was probably a series of strokes, would not last long on the throne. The King was childless, and the next in line to the throne was his brother and Albert's friend Wilhelm, who now seemed less autocratic after his edifying three-month exile in England. In any case, Wilhelm would not be likely to rule for long, since he was already in his fifties. That left Wilhelm's son Friedrich Wilhelm, known as Fritz, a young man in his late teens, trained in the liberal tradition by his mother, Augusta, and open to good English influences. What better way to introduce reform to Albert's beloved Germany than to bring Fritz into the English royal family by marrying him to Vicky?

There is another school of thought that says the idea of a match between the two royal houses originated with Fritz's mother, who brought it to a head

---

* *Shortly after ascending the Belgian throne, King Leopold married the daughter of the French King, Louis Philippe d'Orléans, thus ensuring his country's safety from its southern neighbor. But Louis Philippe was deposed in the Revolution of 1848; Leopold's French wife died in 1850; Napoleon III confiscated all the Orléans property in 1852; and by 1855, the year of Vicky's engagement, Belgium once again lay open to French aggression. Because of his relationship with Victoria and Albert, Leopold counted on England as the primary guarantor of Belgian independence. A marriage between Vicky and the heir to the Prussian throne would bring Prussia, France's natural enemy, into alliance with England and guarantee Belgium's territorial integrity vis-à-vis France. Or so he hoped.*

when her husband suggested that Fritz marry a member of the royal house of Russia. The Romanovs and Hohenzollerns had close political and familial ties. Both had belonged to the Holy Alliance since 1815, and the King of Prussia's sister Charlotte was married to Czar Nicholas I. To forestall the possibility of yet another autocratic Russian in the bosom of the family (so this version goes), Augusta eagerly pursued her friendship with Victoria with an eye to marrying her only son to Victoria's eldest daughter.

Whoever instigated the plan—and it was probably a concurrence of desire on both sides—Victoria and Albert invited Wilhelm and Augusta and their two children to come to England for the opening of the Great Exhibition in London in 1851 so that they could meet Wilhelm and Augusta's son, Fritz, and introduce him to Vicky. Since Fritz was nineteen and Vicky not yet eleven, no one dared speak of marriage, but it was certainly at the back of everyone's mind. To disguise their intentions, Victoria and Albert invited several European monarchs as well. No one else accepted. Memories of 1848 were still too vivid in 1851 for crowned heads to risk leaving home for any but the most urgent reasons.

Moreover, London, the site of the Great Exhibition, was deemed by other European monarchs both intellectually and physically unsafe. Not only did the Czar of Russia refuse to issue passports to Russian courtiers for fear of their "contamination" by constitutionalism, but the Crystal Palace, built for the exhibition and a triumph of nineteenth-century engineering, was regarded by many as a catastrophe waiting to happen. Doomsayers predicted that the enormous glass structure would collapse from the weight of bird droppings or that it would shatter from the salvo of the guns on opening day.

It looked for a while as if even the Prussians would not be able to attend. Scarcely two weeks before their expected arrival, the reactionary King of Hanover, another German kingdom, wrote the King of Prussia to warn him that London was a hotbed of potential republican assassins, far too dangerous a city for his brother. "I would not like anyone belonging to me exposed to the imminent perils . . . ," he said. "Letters from London tell me that the Ministers will not allow the Queen and the great originator of this folly, Prince Albert, to be in London while the Exhibition is on, and I wonder at Wilhelm's wishing to go there with his son." Friedrich Wilhelm's subsequent letter of concern to Albert, in which he asserted that "countless hordes of desperate proletarians" were "on their way to London" to assassinate his brother, provoked some sarcasm on the part of the Prince Consort:

"Mathematicians have calculated that the Crystal Palace will blow down in the first strong gale," Albert answered the King of Prussia,

engineers—that the galleries would crash in and destroy the visitors . . . doctors that owing to so many races coming in contact with each other, the Black Death of the Middle Ages would make its appearance . . . theologians—that this second Tower of Babel would draw upon it the vengeance of an offended God. I can give no guarantee against all these perils, nor am I in a position to assume responsibility for the possibly menaced lives of your Royal relatives. But I can promise that the protection from which Victoria and I benefit will be extended to their persons—for I presume we also are on the list of victims.

The King withdrew his objections, and Wilhelm and Augusta, accompanied by their children, Fritz and Louise, arrived in London on April 29, 1851. Vicky met Fritz, a strikingly handsome blond soldier, for the first time in the Chinese drawing room at Buckingham Palace. History does not record what the plump little princess, undeveloped and unaware of the implications of the

meeting, wore, but she usually dressed for occasions in white lace over white satin, her gowns trimmed with pastel sashes and bows, her soft brown hair twisted into a large curl tucked neatly into a silk net at the nape of her neck. Nine years younger than Fritz but intellectually precocious, she answered his faltering English in fluent German.

Next day, the families visited the Great Exhibition—in reality the first international trade fair.* Vicky took Fritz on a guided tour, astonishing him with her knowledge, her curiosity, and her unabashed opinions. She was certainly

The headdresses worn by the Queen and Vicky, Opening Day of the Great Exhibition, 1851, as sketched by Victoria.

a contrast to his sister, Louise; Louise was two years older than Vicky, but as docile and uninquiring as German princesses were expected to be.

"You cannot form an idea," Fritz said later, "what a sweet little thing the Crown Princess was at the time; such childlike simplicity combined with a woman's intellect, . . . and . . . dignity. . . . She seemed almost too perfect; so perfect, indeed, that often I caught myself wondering whether she was really a human being."

It was not only Vicky who enchanted the German visitor, but the entire picture that now composed itself around her. Raised in the rigidity of the Prussian court, Fritz was amazed to find so much less pretension in a far more powerful family. Invited to accompany them to Osborne, he was thoroughly engaged by their relaxed style of life. It was obvious that Victoria and Albert, unlike his own parents, genuinely loved each other. More at ease than he had ever been, Fritz engaged in long, earnest political discussions with the Prince Consort, which nourished his liberal leanings. He returned home an enthusiastic Anglophile and entered into correspondence with Vicky, answering her childish enthusiasms with a gentleness surprising in an officer of the Prussian army.

---

* Along with American cotton machines and French works of art, the exhibition featured an alarm bed that flung its occupant out at the prescribed hour and a doctor's walking stick containing the equipment for an enema in its handle. This, of course, Vicky would not have been permitted to see.

More to the point was the correspondence between their mothers. Victoria, who had dropped the formal *"Sie"* in favor of the intimate *"Du,"* wrote to Augusta a week after her departure. "With all my heart I reciprocate the feelings of love, friendship and attachment which you so touchingly express. . . . A true and lasting friendship demands not only similarity of character, but also a sympathetic agreement upon the serious aspects of life, particularly in regard to politics and religion; and I have found this in you."

The Queen had already reported on the meeting to Uncle Leopold. "Never did a visit go off better," she wrote the King of Belgium; "we lived all so comfortably & happily together, quite *en famille* & quite at home. Vicky has formed an amazing friendship for that charming Child Vivi [Fritz's sister Louise], & also for the young Prince; Might this, one day, lead to a union! God knows it would make us very happy, for I never saw a more amiable, unspoilt, & good young man than he is. This is all in God's hands. We can only hope it & wish it."

SHORTLY AFTER THIS auspicious family gathering, however, some realignments among the nations of Europe began to threaten the hoped-for marriage. A reshuffling of loyalties that culminated in the Crimean War, this series of international couplings and uncouplings had a significant effect on Vicky's future life.

At the close of the fateful year of 1848, the French had elected Prince Louis Napoleon Bonaparte, nephew of Napoleon I, President of the Second Republic. As soon as he gained the presidency, Louis Napoleon began scheming to establish a hereditary dynasty of Bonapartes. Called by Victor Hugo "Napoléon le Petit," this Napoleon had none of his uncle's military genius. His power was based on personal charm and the skill with which he balanced state-sponsored repression against material prosperity and concessions to the Catholic Church. Louis Napoleon's need for constant and spectacular successes to impress his own people made other crowned heads nervous, particularly after the end of 1851, when he succeeded in establishing the Second Empire and declaring himself Emperor Napoleon III.

"With such an extraordinary man as Louis Napoleon," Queen Victoria wrote in February of 1852, "one can never be for one instant safe." But with the Czar of Russia, ruler of the largest empire in the world, showing alarming signs of aggression, England needed allies, and Queen Victoria agreed to assume an attitude of watchful cordiality toward the new French Emperor.

In the middle of the nineteenth century, Russia controlled vast expanses of land in Asia and over half the territory of Europe. One of the last strongholds of serfdom, it was ruled by Czar Nicholas I, whose wife, Charlotte, was a sister of King Friedrich Wilhelm IV and Prince Wilhelm of Prussia. An adamant foe of progress and a narrow legitimist who refused to recognize Napoleon III's new title, the Czar bore Napoleon a grudge for outwitting him in an ancient conflict over the so-called Holy Places of Christianity: No sooner had Napoleon become Emperor than he secured the rights for Latin monks under French protection to oversee the most sacred Christian shrines in Palestine, thus taking the privilege away from Orthodox monks under the protection of the Czar.*

Far more important than Nicholas I's petty resentments of Napoleon III were his imperialistic ambitions. These were aimed at Turkey, which he dubbed the "sick man" of Europe and whose vast holdings he proposed to acquire during the course of the patient's extended demise. Assuming that the Western powers could be kept, if not quiet, at least at bay, the Czar sent his soldiers in June 1853 to occupy the Turkish principalities of Wallachia and Moldavia (later Romania). His excuse—that he was protecting the twelve million Christians who lived there under Moslem rule—fooled no one. Nine months after the initial occupation, in March of 1854, England and France joined Turkey in the fight against Russian expansion—the Crimean War.

Neither the English government nor the royal family wanted war, but were carried into it by one of those outbreaks of anti-Russian ferocity that swept periodically through England. The Czar's position as the leading reactionary in Europe had long earned him the dislike of English liberals, and his acquisitive nature had raised the antennae of British imperialists. When Nicholas I sent the Russian Black Sea fleet to patrol the Turkish coast, he raised the hackles of Home Secretary Palmerston and the press. The seas, Britons felt, belonged to them. And when the Russians destroyed a Turkish fleet lying at anchor, England exploded. Although other members of the British government tried to maintain peace with negotiations, threats, and naval maneuvers, war fever raged throughout the country. Like many people in the throes of impotent fury, the British looked around for a scapegoat. They found it in the person of the most conspicuous foreigner in their midst—Prince Albert, the German husband of their Queen.

Albert had never been popular with members of the English aristocracy, who derided the stiffness of his manners and the cut of his clothes. But the English upper class was an insular body that usually kept its opinions to itself, away from the masses. Now both press and public raised accusations against Albert of "improper interference" in the government by plotting with his German relatives to keep England out of the war. Accused of being an agent of "the Austrian-Belgian-Coburg-Orléans clique, the avowed enemies of England, and the subservient tools of Russian ambition," the Prince Consort was rumored to have been impeached for treason. Ordinary Englishmen gathered before Traitors Gate at the Tower of London to see if it was true. The charges against the Prince were laid to rest in parliament, but public reaction indicated the depth of feeling in England against Prussia.

The Crimean War would, in any case, have been an unlikely place for Prussia to take a stand against an ally in order to join the developing consort of Western Europe. Besides, the King of Prussia, Friedrich Wilhelm IV, was a

* *The most important of these were the Church of the Holy Sepulchre in Jerusalem, said to have been built over the tomb of Christ, and the church in Bethlehem, believed to incorporate Christ's manger.*

weak and confused romantic. He had been wavering for some time between two factions in Berlin—the reactionaries who supported his brother-in-law, Czar Nicholas I of Russia, and the party surrounding his brother Wilhelm, who supported an alliance with England. Eventually convinced by the Russophiles that Prussia owed the Russians, who had saved them from Napoleon I in 1813, he decided to stay out of the war altogether, much to the disgust of the English and French. "It is impossible to make these people understand the duties and responsibilities of a great power," the British Ambassador to Berlin complained to the Foreign Secretary. "It is sad that Prussia has renounced her position as a Great Power by this behavior," Queen Victoria wrote the Prussian King.

Personal and national anger toward Friedrich Wilhelm did not, however, prevent Victoria and Albert from continuing to pursue their close relationship with his brother Wilhelm and wife, Augusta, and their goal of marriage between their children. In a letter inviting Augusta to England as godmother to one of her sons, Victoria added a description of Vicky. "Vicky is counting on seeing her dear friend Vivy once more. . . . Vicky will look small beside Vivy, although she has grown a great deal. . . . She has made much progress with her music, and has a great deal of talent for drawing; she has a genuine love of art and expresses opinions about it like a grown-up person, with rare good sense."

In trying to impress Augusta, Victoria could not have chosen a less fortunate example of Vicky's virtues, for Augusta, highly opinionated herself, strongly disapproved of young princesses with ideas of their own. But Queen Victoria continued writing to her friend throughout the war, conveying expressions of political solidarity and news of her eldest daughter, who, she informed the girl's prospective mother-in-law, was "growing fast and her figure . . . developing."

The Crimean War was a tragic and humiliating chapter in English history. The British army made the long and exhausting journey to the Crimea, "alighting like a flock of birds," as one historian* put it, "with no means of flying away." Raging cholera, lack of medical equipment or even soap, gross mismanagement of transport, and the coldest weather in memory reduced their numbers by forty to seventy percent, exclusive of battle casualties. In September 1854, the allies laid siege to Sebastopol. The following spring, they were still there. To boost his sagging prestige with his people, who had never approved of the war, Napoleon III announced that he would go to the Crimea himself, personally assume command of the Western armies, and bring the siege of Sebastopol and the ghastly war to an end.

But French soldiers did not want to be commanded by a civilian, and England, her troops pitifully reduced, did not want the honor of victory to fall to the French. In March 1855, Victoria's Foreign Secretary, Lord Clarendon, was hastily dispatched to Paris to extend to Napoleon an invitation from Queen Victoria to come to England as her official guest.

For Napoleon III, a parvenu among nineteenth-century monarchs, it was a bribe he could not refuse.

---

* *Cecil Woodham-Smith.*

CHAPTER
FOUR

> "[O]nly four things matter at the [court of the] Tuileries: youth, beauty, diamonds—and a dress."
>
> S. L. BURCHELL

NAPOLEON III AND HIS EMPRESS journeyed to England in April of 1855. Five months later, Victoria, Albert, and their two eldest children returned the compliment with a state visit to Paris. These elaborately choreographed monarchical gatherings were Vicky's first ventures into royal society. She was fourteen years old—an appropriate time in the life of a nineteenth-century princess to be exposed to a world of pleasure and pomp.

Having previously excluded their eldest daughter from the more ceremonial aspects of court life, the extent to which Victoria and Albert now included her was remarkable. This was probably a conscious decision on their part to expose the young teenager to what might be expected of her in the future. Among the European royalties of the day, certainly none were better suited to introduce the Princess Royal to the sophistication ordinarily shunned by her parents than the French Emperor and his Spanish-born Empress. Not too surprisingly, Vicky developed an instant crush on the beautiful and glamorous Eugénie.

Tall and unusually graceful, with an "exquisitely proportioned" body and undeniable chic, Empress Eugénie was blessed with the kind of face most admired in the nineteenth century—aquiline nose and widely spaced eyes, set off by an abundance of heavy auburn hair. Even that wizardly painter Winterhalter, justly famous for transforming plain or ugly royalties into acceptable icons, could represent Eugénie with honesty. The daughter of a Spanish count,* fascinating and anxious to please, this unusually handsome woman was quite a contrast to her imperial spouse.

Small, unattractive, with a pointed beard† jutting out from the top of his

---

* Eugénie was falsely rumored to be the illegitimate daughter of Queen Victoria's Foreign Secretary Lord Clarendon, with whom her mother had had a well-known affair. "But Sire," the lady protested to her son-in-law, Napoleon III, when the subject came up, "the dates do not correspond" (Sir Herbert E. Maxwell, Life and Letters of the Earl of Clarendon, Vol. II, p. 91).

† This type of beard, called an "imperial" after Napoleon III, consisted of a thick tuft of hair grown under the lower lip.

chin and a mustache resembling the whiskers of a cat, Napoleon III had none-theless earned a reputation as the ultimate Gallic charmer. Observers said that it was his quiet manner and his ability to listen that drew people to him. Known as a famous ladies' man, eager to place himself on an equal footing with the sovereign of the most powerful nation of Europe, Napoleon set out in the spring of 1855 to woo Queen Victoria. He succeeded in seducing the entire family.

Even before the arrival of the imperial pair, there was enormous excitement at Windsor. "All the children on the tiptop of expectation," the Queen reported on the morning of April 16, 1855, as she, her husband, and seven offspring trooped down to the royal stables to inspect the Emperor's fourteen horses, sent ahead of their master to England, and back to the palace to admire the apartments refurbished for the Emperor and Empress. Napoleon and Eugénie's taste for luxury had preceded them, setting in motion a frenzy of redecoration. Old heirloom furniture had reappeared from storage. Jewel-toned satins—crim-sons, greens, and purples—had been hung in Eugénie's bedroom and dressing room, where the Queen's personal gold toilet set was laid out for the Empress's use. The Vandyke Room, the Rubens Room, and the Tapestry Room were "beautifully done up" in fresh new silks, while the ninety-foot-long Waterloo Room, built in 1830 and decorated with portraits of generals, admirals, states-men, and kings, had been thoughtfully rechristened the Music Room—in defer-ence to the sensitivities of the honored visitor.

Bulletins of the Emperor's progress reached Windsor all day long—his landing at Dover, his arrival in London, and his departure from London, which sent the family scurrying to dress. By 6:00 P.M. the court had gathered "in a state of anxious anticipation" for the formal welcome—Victoria in light blue with pearls and thirteen-year-old Bertie in full Highland dress. As soon as the first outriders appeared among the crowds lining the road to the castle, the doors were thrown open and the Queen stepped out. Trumpets blew, the band played, and the carriage carrying Napoleon III, Eugénie, and Prince Albert, who had gone to Dover to meet the visitors, drew up. "These great meetings of sovereigns . . . are always very agitating," the Queen commented in her journal. She embraced both the Emperor and Empress, noticing that the latter was "very nervous." As was Vicky, who made her deep, respectful curtsies with "very alarmed eyes."

The teenager's fluster was still evident the next day, when she joined the adults for breakfast, a long walk to the royal kennels, and a visit to her grand-mother, the Duchess of Kent. As they walked, she listened to intense discussions of the siege of Sebastopol, the climactic struggle of the Crimean War still under way. She was included at luncheon and afterwards given a place of honor in the first carriage with the Queen and the Empress for a grand review of the troops. Invited to rejoin the company for dancing after dinner in the newly renamed Music Room, she wore a light blue dress and pulled her hair back like the other ladies of the court. Vicky was a "daring and lively" dancer, but when the Emperor asked her for the second waltz, she was noticeably frightened. "Vicky behaved extremely well," the Queen noted in her journal, "making beautiful curtsies, and was very much praised by the Emperor and Empress, whom Vicky raves about."

Eugénie was the first lady of fashion with whom Vicky had ever had close contact, a woman totally different from Vicky's mother in both attitude and style. One can easily imagine the young Princess following the Empress around, as one can imagine the Empress, a woman of basic goodwill but unsure of herself in Queen Victoria's court, flattered by the adoration of the Queen's eldest daughter. Before she left, Eugénie gave Vicky her own ruby and diamond watch with its chain, seal, and watch key, a gift that sent the teenage girl into "ecstasies." When she and the Emperor said good-bye, the children cried.

FOUR MONTHS LATER, in August of 1855, Vicky and Bertie accompanied their parents on a return state visit to Paris. It was an historic journey, the first time a British sovereign had visited Paris in over four hundred years, and it came at a time when the war in the Crimea had begun to turn in favor of the West. While English and French soldiers stormed the fortifications of Sebastopol, Napoleon III made elaborate preparations to welcome the Queen of England. He counted on the visit to prove to his people that the Bonaparte dynasty was worth the terrible sacrifices they had been called upon to make in the war.

Paris of the Second Empire was a city devoted to outward show, where the frothier aspects of civilization—decor, clothing, jewels, even makeup—were often more important than substance. Offenbach played at the Opéra. The theaters featured comedies of manners. At Napoleon III's newly reconstructed palace of the Tuileries (it had been damaged in the Revolution of 1848), there was more attention paid to the crinoline than the war. The Goncourt brothers, chroniclers of their day, heard of one woman who ordered her dressmaker: "Make sure I always have something black on hand. You know I've got three sons at the Crimean front."

The English entourage docked at Boulogne, where the quay had been carefully massed with troops and large cheering crowds. Whisked off by Napoleon to Paris, Victoria and her family were treated to a second, even more elaborate welcome featuring some sixty thousand men in uniform: "[R]eally it is impossible for the imagination to conceive anything so gorgeously magnificent as the entry into Paris . . . ," one of the Queen's ladies-in-waiting wrote home. "Strasbourg Railway Station . . . was fitted up and brilliantly lighted like a theatre, with thousands of magnificently dressed people."

In spite of a "broiling" sun and intense heat, the Queen and her party were escorted through gold-fringed, crimson velvet canopies, which had been draped over the arches of the railway station, to their carriages for a triumphal ride down the Boulevard Strasbourg. A crowd of 100,000 people had been waiting to see the Queen of England. "[N]o description can give an idea of the splendour of the whole scene . . . ," Victoria wrote in her journal. "Vicky and I sitting together (it seemed to me a dream that she should appear *comme une grande personne*), the Emperor and Albert opposite . . . banners, flags, arches, flowers, inscriptions, and illuminations; the windows full of people . . . the streets lined with troops . . . everybody most enthusiastic."

If the French loved the Queen, they did not like her outfit. General François Canrobert, a Crimean War hero, complained of her "shocking toilette"—a white flounced gown topped with a "crude green" mantle. "In spite of the great heat," he wrote, "she had on a massive bonnet of white silk . . . with streamers behind and a tuft of marabout [*sic*] feathers on top." Worse than the bonnet was the purse on her arm—a "voluminous object . . . made of white satin or silk on which was embroidered a poodle in gold."

Remarking on Victoria's lack of chic during their spring visit to Windsor, Eugénie, who wanted Vicky to enjoy the full approval of the sartorially snobbish Parisians, had found a way to make sure that at least the Princess Royal's wardrobe was up to French standards. Armed with the measurements of a life-size doll belonging to Vicky, she and her husband had a number of gowns made and sent to London before the visit, addressed somewhat artfully to Her Royal Highness's doll. Vicky, if not her mother, arrived in Paris dressed in style.

The family stayed at the palace at St. Cloud, a magnificent old château situated on the left bank of the Seine a few miles outside the city. Vicky, who still shared a room with sister Alice, was given her own bedroom for the first time in her life. Refurbished for her in fairy-tale splendor, it overlooked the city of Paris and opened onto an exquisite flower garden, filled with the scent of orange blossoms and the sound of splashing fountains.

It was a "never-to-be-forgotten week," according to the Queen, who admitted to Baron Stockmar that afterwards she could "<u>think</u> and talk of nothing else." If Victoria was that impressed, one can only guess at the effect on her daughter. From St. Cloud the royal party made excursions into the city in the Emperor's small barouche; Vicky, who, her mother admitted, "looked nice in her different smart dresses," always traveled in the first carriage with her parents and Napoleon III. (Eugénie, who was pregnant, joined the party only in the evenings.)

Paris in 1855 was in the throes of reconstruction, the result of Napoleon III's program to transform the overgrown, semimedieval capital into the city of architectural splendor we know today. Widened boulevards, public parks, running water, covered sewers—these were all part of the Emperor's plan, along with the elaborate rebuilding of national monuments. Partly to distract the Parisians from his repressive regime, but mostly because the modernization of Paris had been his lifelong dream, Napoleon III was in the process of rebuilding when his royal guests arrived, and he could scarcely wait to show them what he was doing.

They visited the recently restored Tuileries, the newly completed Louvre, Nôtre Dame, the Hôtel des Invalides, and in the evenings the Opéra and the theaters. They drove through the Bois de Boulogne—one of the Emperor's most inspired additions to the city—and attended a hunt in the forest of St. Germain. Napoleon III, who grew "very communicative when in the carriage," was proud of his achievements and highly solicitous of the ladies' well-being.

Victoria even felt comfortable enough to bring up the subject of the dethroned Orléans family, with whom she was on intimate terms. The Emperor, who had used funds from their confiscated properties to improve slum conditions, replied that he "quite understood" her loyalty to friends and relatives.

This ten-day tour of Paris and its environs—"the domain of a debonair tyrant with waxed moustaches"—was Vicky's introduction to adulthood, and it culminated, rather appropriately, in a grand ball at Versailles. Although Victoria did not want her daughter to attend, Eugénie interceded on Vicky's behalf. Dressed in a French gown of white net over silk trimmed in pale peach roses, Vicky was driven in torchlight with Napoleon, her parents, and brother Bertie to the palace, where they were met by the willowy Empress, gowned in white and looking, according to the Queen, "like a fairy queen or nymph." *

Balls of four or five thousand guests were not unusual in the French court, but this one—decorated in the style of Louis XV—was more spectacular than most. Upon entering, the royal party was escorted through the great Hall of Mirrors—a shimmering gallery of reflected light, lined with gentlemen in uniform and ladies in ball gowns, Nubian servants, and lackeys in knee britches, plumes, and powdered wigs. For entertainment there was a spectacular display of fireworks, "the like of which," Victoria said, she had "never before seen." One of the reasons for the Queen's enthusiasm may have been the last twinkling outburst—an homage to herself in the form of a representation of Windsor Castle. After the fireworks came the dancing.

While Vicky, "blushing deeply," waltzed with the Emperor, her parents met the famous Prussian politician Count Otto von Bismarck, the man considered responsible for convincing King Friedrich Wilhelm IV to keep Prussia out of the war against Russia. To Queen Victoria, Bismarck seemed "very Russian and Junker." † Although Prince Albert seems to have made a special effort to be courteous, Bismarck later claimed that he felt a "malevolent curiosity" in the Prince Consort's manner.

Before Vicky left France, the Empress gave her another gift of rubies and diamonds—a bracelet containing strands of Eugénie's own hair, a popular Victorian expression of affection. The Princess Royal "melted in tears" at the moment of departure; "she is much devoted and attached to the Empress," her mother commented.

It was thirteen-year-old Bertie, however, who asked Eugénie if she could not "get leave for them to stay there a little longer," explaining that he and Vicky had enjoyed themselves so much and were unhappy at the thought of going home. The Empress said that this would unfortunately not be possible,

---

* *Eugénie may have already started wearing a crinoline—a fashion, it was said, that she devised to cover her bulging stomach. Since political commentary was strictly censored under Napoleon III, the French press, desperate for news, pounced on the new fashion. "The number of words written about the crinoline," observed one historian, "passes human understanding" (S. C. Burchell,* Imperial Masquerade, *p. 13).*

† *The Junkers were Prussian landed gentry known for their militarism and conservative politics.*

"as the Queen and the Prince would not be able to do without them." Bertie disagreed. "Not do without us!" he replied. "[D]on't fancy that, for there are six more* of us at home and they don't want us."

If during the visit Victoria ever felt a twinge of jealousy over the Empress's beauty, she did not show it, going out of her way to praise Eugénie's gorgeous toilettes and drawing pictures of her in the royal sketchbook. The Queen herself, according to one of her maids of honor, Mary Bulteel,† was always "badly dressed." Nevertheless, the maid of honor hastened to explain that this "did not in the least signify," since Victoria's "wonderful dignity, her manner of bowing to the crowd, and her want of all preoccupation were far more impressive than dear Empress Eugénie's manner, who, though she was very beautiful, could not help always worrying over trifles."

It was not only Mary Bulteel who noticed the difference between the Queen and the Empress. After the national anthems were played at the Opéra, the audience was amused to see Eugénie look around to see if her chair was in place before sitting down. Victoria, observers noted, stared straight ahead and sat. Born to her position, she knew the chair would be there.

If Victoria and Albert had formerly regarded the imperial French couple with well-bred suspicion, by the end of these two state visits the Queen was referring to Napoleon III as her "nearest and dearest ally!" She had, she said in a letter to Baron Stockmar, "personally . . . conceived a real affection" for the French Emperor. "He is . . . so full of tact, good taste, high breeding. . . . To the children (who behaved beautifully) . . . his judicious kindness, was great. . . . In short, without attempting to do anything particular to make one like him or ANY personal attraction in outward appearance, he has the power of attaching those to him who come near him and know him, which is quite incredible." Or, as the Queen's Foreign Minister, Lord Clarendon, sagely observed on the subject of Victoria's new infatuation: Napoleon III's "love-making was of a character to flatter her vanity without alarming her virtue."

As to Victoria's eldest daughter, Vicky, her adolescent passion, while it centered primarily on the Empress and had no immediate political repercussions, was as strong as that of the Queen. For the rest of her life, regardless of shifting political loyalties and demands, Vicky carried an untarnishable image in her heart of the two people who opened her eyes to the splendid if superficial delights of a world she had not known existed. For the present, the fairy-tale trip to the court of Napoleon III had put her into an appropriate mood for the romance about to descend upon her.

---

* *Princess Beatrice, Victoria and Albert's ninth child, had not been born yet.*

† *Later Lady Ponsonby. (She married Henry Ponsonby, Queen Victoria's private secretary, in 1861.)*

CHAPTER
FIVE

"Impressions one receives in childhood cannot be erased from the soul."

FREDERICK THE GREAT

WITHIN THREE WEEKS of the family's return from Paris, Crown Prince Friedrich Wilhelm of Prussia arrived at Balmoral Castle to look Vicky over as a prospective wife. The invitation, which was considerably less enthusiastic than it would have been before the Crimean War, had been issued by Vicky's mother. Pressured by Prince Albert, Baron Stockmar, and King Leopold, the Queen wrote Fritz that the "present political position of Prussia is certainly difficult, but I believe that better times will come." Albert had also been in correspondence with Fritz's mother, Augusta, whom he referred to as the "matchmaker," and whose "most friendly and confidential" letter he destroyed after reading it.

There had been so much resistance to Fritz's trip by the pro-Russian, anti-English entourage of Friedrich Wilhelm IV of Prussia that the King kept his reluctant consent a secret even from his wife. Against the wishes of the court but armed with the encouragement of his parents, Fritz arrived at Balmoral to see what had happened to that charming child he had not met since 1851, when she was ten. He was welcomed by Victoria and Albert, who were nearly as jumpy as the prospective suitor—Victoria, because she did not think her daughter was pretty enough to attract the handsome Prussian prince; Albert, because his dreams for his native land were about to be realized or destroyed.

The young man himself had improved since his first visit. He had settled more comfortably into his six-foot, two-inch frame and had added a becoming tawny-colored mustache to his face. He had broad shoulders that he carried in an erect "soldierly" way, but there was nothing else about Fritz to suggest the arrogant Prussian officer, typical of the caste.

As a matter of fact, Victoria had always been concerned about the lack of self-confidence in Wilhelm and Augusta's son—and with good reason. She quite rightly blamed his parents and had even written to Augusta urging her to treat Fritz with more love and respect. Caught between his liberal mother and ultraconservative father, Fritz had been forced into the role of reluctant peacemaker from a very young age. Insecure, eager to do the right thing, he was a sincere, blond Teutonic knight in search of a mission worthy of his ancestors and a wife who could help him realize it.

BORN IN 1831, nine years before Vicky, Fritz, like the Princess Royal, had been dedicated from the cradle to his parents' dreams and ambitions. Unlike Vicky's father and mother, however, Wilhelm and Augusta harbored opposite ideas of Prussia's future, and Fritz's upbringing reflected this political schizophrenia. With only one sibling, a girl seven years his junior and his father's favorite, Fritz was the battleground on which his parents played out their animosities, personal and political, toward each other.

He grew up in the Neues Palais of Potsdam, a magnificent but uncomfortable rococo edifice built in 1763–69 by his ancestor Frederick the Great. But Frederick never lived there, and by the time Fritz came along sixty years later, it had fallen into serious disrepair: the fabulous silver furniture had tarnished; the great tapestries were moth-eaten; lice and dead vermin were commonplace. Since the Hohenzollerns considered modern conveniences unnecessary and extravagant, there were no bathtubs or water closets in the palace, and a courtyard pump supplied all the water. Eggs were served in liquor glasses, since there was no appropriate china in which to present them.

Like all Hohenzollern boys, Fritz was dressed as a miniature soldier and sent out to march with the adult males in the family. At seven he was given a military governor who introduced him to drilling, artillery, and the care of cavalry horses. On his tenth birthday, he received his commission as a Second Lieutenant in the First Regiment of Foot Guards. Along with his all-important military education, there was a young theologian to instruct him in the creed and masters from the public schools of Berlin brought to the palace to teach history, languages, mathematics, and science.

While his father made sure he became a good soldier, his mother supervised the rest of his education, purposefully inculcating in Fritz a liberal outlook antithetical to Prussian militarism. Augusta felt that her son had fine character, but deprecated his intelligence—a judgment that made him diffident and shy. His lack of self-assurance was not improved by his father's obvious disapproval. "[I]t has come to the point that Fritz starts up at hearing his father come," Augusta commented when her son was young.

The fact that Fritz also suffered from depression would not have been recognized or taken into account in the middle of the nineteenth century. Because of this, it is difficult to determine precisely when these bouts started— whether in childhood or when he was a young man. One thing is certain: his parents' attitude toward him did not help.

Fritz's military governor, General von Unruh, described the young red-headed Prince as a very serious child. Each year for Fritz's birthday his grandfather Friedrich Wilhelm III gave him fifty gold coins (Friedrichsdor) to spend as he liked, and Unruh recalled finding the boy very late on the evening of his eighth or ninth birthday at his writing table, deep in mathematical calculations.

"The task which had absorbed the Prince up to such a late hour . . . had been to find out to whom he would give pleasure [with his gift money] and . . . how much he might be able to spend upon each." According to Unruh, these computations were carefully detailed as to the circumstances and the merits of each individual. "I was filled with astonishment by the earnestness of the work; the insight into human nature, the loving forethought . . . and the charitable spirit. . . . I added the . . . entries together and found that Fritz . . . had allotted the whole of the fifty Friedrichs-d'or."

Wilhelm was not a sympathetic father, but Fritz was an absolutely obedient and respectful son. He must have repressed tremendous hostility, which manifested itself in concern about his father's life. At one point Fritz complained to Unruh about a teacher who had said that one day, when his father was dead, Fritz would be king. "I know nothing about this," Fritz interrupted furiously; "I have never thought of it, and I do not wish my father's death to be referred to."*

When Fritz was thirteen, he was put in the hands of Professor Ernest Curtius, a famous archaeologist and authority on ancient Greek culture, charged with giving the future heir to the throne instruction in history and the classics and developing his taste in literature and the arts. It was fortunate that the young teenager loved to read, for there was not as much in the way of theater or concerts in Berlin as in the capitals of other, more cultured capitals around Germany. It is said that Fritz's father, Wilhelm, loathed music and once rather conspicuously left the performance of a Wagnerian opera to go on military maneuvers.

The major trauma of Fritz's young life, the Revolution of 1848, occurred when he was seventeen. During the revolution, he and his younger sister, Louise, stood helpless while the citizens of Berlin fired on his father's palace and eventually took it over, turning the wine cellars into public drinking houses. It was Fritz who was sent to get the scissors to lop off his father's beard and prominent mustaches, so Wilhelm would not be recognized as he escaped Germany. While Wilhelm sat out the terror in England, Fritz was confined with his mother and sister at Babelsberg, his parents' summer palace in Potsdam.

In 1849, the year after the revolution, the young Prince was invested with the Order of the Black Eagle, the highest Prussian order. General von Gerlach, the King's adjutant general, reported how shocked he was by Fritz's conversation that evening at dinner. Seated next to the Prince, Gerlach said that he "envied" him his youth, "for he would no doubt survive the end of the absurd Constitutionalism" forced on King Friedrich Wilhelm IV by the revolution. Much to the courtier's surprise, Fritz answered that "representation of the people would become a necessity" in Prussia.

According to Professor Delbrück, a historian of the day, Fritz believed that

---

* *Many years later, when Fritz was discussing an appropriate title for himself as the son of the Kaiser of Germany, he told Bismarck he hated titles like "Heir to the Reigning Prince" and "Hereditary Grand-Duke" because they "undisguisedly speculate on the death of the father" (Margaretha von Poschinger, Life of the Emperor Frederick, p. 19).*

he must be given free intercourse "with every class and with every honest man of other views." This attitude, said Delbrück, brought Fritz "early into conflict with the old Prussian reactionary party. The members of this party . . . held that the King of Prussia should surround himself exclusively with personages of their own station and opinions. The Prince, however, even before he became Crown Prince . . . rebelled against these narrow views."

Shortly after his eighteenth birthday, Fritz left for the University of Bonn. He was the first heir to the Prussian throne to attend a public university—a break with military tradition brought about by his mother, Augusta. The experience affected him deeply:

"No one can deny that no true picture of the life and doings of men can be gained at Court, and that it can only be acquired from the frequent intercourse with persons of all classes," he wrote in a somewhat ponderous essay during his third year. "At Court one is surrounded by people who invariably meet royalty with politeness . . . and only too frequently with deceitful flatteries. . . . At Court the growing Prince is mostly surrounded by older people, but here he enters the circle of his contemporaries. . . . He gains an insight into . . . the prevailing aims and the hopes which they hold out."

This was not enough for Augusta. "Fritz's knowledge of human nature has certainly improved," she wrote at the time, "but his intellectual development does not equal that of his peers."

At Bonn the heir to the throne studied law—German, international, civil, criminal, and ecclesiastical—political science, history, French and English literature, and the science of fortifications. His professor of political science was F. C. Dahlmann, a leading liberal thinker, who believed in hereditary monarchy, but also in constitutional and representative government. When Fritz was still a young child, Dahlmann and the brothers Grimm (collectors of the fairy tales) had been thrown out of Göttingen University by the reactionary King of Hanover for refusing to rescind their oaths of allegiance to a liberal constitution, abrogated by the King in 1837.

If not a particularly gifted student, Fritz was a hardworking, persevering one. He enjoyed companions of his own age, although like most royalties, he bridled if they forgot who he was. According to his English professor, he "manifested the keenest interest for all that I was able to tell him of England's political and social life, and when our more serious studies were over, we amused ourselves by writing imaginary letters to Ministers and leading members of English society."

He was still at Bonn when he visited England with his parents and sister in 1851, the journey that, according to a German biographer,* "undoubtedly had the greatest influence upon his whole life." The following spring he finished his formal studies and was given command of a company of infantry. A natural leader, blessed with a good memory for faces, Fritz knew nearly every one of his soldiers by sight and concerned himself with their off-duty comforts and

* *Margaretha von Poschinger.*

accommodations, often bivouacking with them in the field during maneuvers. (On one such occasion, he found that mice had eaten the lining of his helmet during the night.) When he was not soldiering or attending royal functions, he indulged his passion for travel—mostly in Italy where, as the representative of a Protestant power, he refused to kiss the hand of the Pope.

As the heir to the throne moved up the military ladder, he was given the famous Colonel (later Field Marshal) Helmuth von Moltke as his personal aide-de-camp. Thirty years older than Fritz, a dedicated soldier and cultivated intellectual, Moltke developed a warm friendship with the Prince, based on a similar fondness for reading, writing, and foreign travel. It was Moltke, a cosmopolite married to an Englishwoman, who accompanied Fritz to England in 1855 to see Vicky and determine whether she was really the girl for him.

As is almost never the case, the parents' choice turned out to be the choice of the young people as well.

CHAPTER SIX

*T*HE GIRL WHOM *FRITZ* had come to see was an unusual combination of intellectual maturity and emotional naïveté. Assigned a program of study that would have daunted any would-be sovereign or consort, she had been kept in social and sexual ignorance. Still, she would not have deserved her reputation for perceptiveness had she not guessed that there was more to the arrival of this tall blond German officer than she had been told.

At nearly fifteen the Princess Royal was not unlike her mother at the same age, but taller (five feet, two inches) and better-looking. Her nose was smaller and straighter, her mouth less set. But it was her remarkable blue eyes with their level gaze, curiosity, and humor that were her best feature. That and a ready smile, which lit up her soft, young face and "bewitched those who approached her." She struggled against weight, ached to be "thin & interesting," and knew that her body type was against her.

Stubborn but eager, opinionated and informed, she spoke in a gentle, "almost timid" manner, although she was very definite in her likes and dislikes. Her critics complained about her penchant for making instant judgments based on minor physical traits, a tendency that often led her into misguided enthusiasms. Candid to a fault, she was a thoroughly successful product of Stockmar's educational theories and Albert's prideful love.

"That he should love me was my most ardent wish, my greatest ambition . . . ," Vicky once wrote her mother about her father. "I cared more for a kind look or word from him than for anything else in the world. . . . But I never thought he could really care for me. I felt so much too imperfect for that. I never dared to expect it."

If Albert never let on to Vicky how much he adored her, Victoria was doubtless aware of the intensity of the father-daughter bond, based on an intellectual companionship that she did not share. While Albert had seen to their daughter's mind, Victoria had also paid attention to Vicky's appearance, manners, and deportment. The Queen, according to Lord Clarendon, was "always finding fault with her daughter's looks, and complaining of her being ugly and coarse very unjustly." What Clarendon did not understand was that the Queen's attitude toward Vicky was an extension of Victoria's dissatisfaction with her own face and body. Neither mother nor daughter ever considered herself remotely good-looking, and it was with close to a sense of wonder that they collected and shared photographs of other women whose faces and figures they admired.

Moreover, Victoria did not seem to realize that the reason Vicky's willfulness drove her mad was that it came straight from her. As did Vicky's budding sexuality. At thirteen, the Queen had found it appropriate to squash the first signs of the coquette in her eldest daughter when she caught Vicky flirting with the soldiers at a military review. Ignoring her mother's disapproving looks, the young girl dropped her handkerchief over the side of their carriage. As two or three young soldiers started to scramble for it, the Queen ordered them back. "Stop, gentlemen. Leave it just where it lies. Now, my daughter, get down from the carriage and pick up your handkerchief." Blushing deeply, Vicky obeyed.

Tradition decreed that prospective royal brides were kept innocent of the marital schemes of their parents, and the Queen worried that her daughter, who looked on Fritz as an old friend, would not make enough effort to attract him when he came to visit in the fall of 1855. What if the fourteen-year-old stood on one leg, laughed too loudly, gobbled her food, or waddled when she walked? But Vicky surprised her mother. Dressed in Highland tartan, she met Fritz with her family at the castle door, gracefully holding out her hand to be kissed. To the young Prince, she seemed much more elegant and stately than the diminutive Queen, who wavered nervously between wanting Vicky to make a good impression and not wanting to lose her.

Vicky committed the unpardonable sin of coming in a few minutes late for dinner the first evening of Fritz's visit. When she appeared, however, dressed in white with bright red ribbons, she was apologetic, enthusiastic, and completely charming. During the meal she chatted happily to Fritz in German and French, laughing and smiling and looking at him admiringly, coloring only when she was caught doing this by her father. Vicky was, in fact, the only one of the four at the dinner table who was even remotely comfortable. Having agreed that they would never force their daughter into an unwanted marriage, Victoria and Albert watched anxiously as the young people exchanged glances. "We looked at each other a great deal," the prospective suitor wrote his parents.

Fritz spent his first full day in Scotland stalking deer with Prince Albert. The Prince Consort, who developed painful rheumatism in the shoulder from standing in the rain, insisted on more of the same three days later. Fritz complained that he would have far preferred to be with "someone" who "really attracted him," but said that his ordeal was made easier by Vicky, who pressed his hand "very hard" at breakfast. Albert was very pleased with the young man. "Great rectitude, openness and honesty are his most outstanding qualities," he wrote Baron Stockmar. "He seems to be unprejudiced and well-meaning to a high degree."

For his part, the Prussian Prince found the English Princess "sweet, natural, friendly and unaffected." She had, as he wrote his parents, "a pleasant mixture of childlike simplicity and virginal charm, as I like it. . . . She possesses great feeling and intelligence and has a lively interest in art and literature, particularly that of Germany. Without exaggeration I think I may say that we will be well suited to each other."

After a sleepless night, a very nervous Prince spoke to Victoria and Albert. "It has long been my wish to beg the Princess to be my wife. I have the concurrence and the approval not only of my parents, but also of the King, and as I find Vicky so sweet I cannot wait any longer and must pour out my heart." The delighted parents wept with happiness. Victoria squeezed Fritz's hand and told him frankly that she and Stockmar had worried that Vicky might not be good-looking enough for him.

One condition was placed on their acceptance. Victoria did not want her daughter to marry until she was seventeen, and Fritz must wait to propose to Vicky herself until she was confirmed the following spring at the age of sixteen. Meanwhile, the Queen and Prince Consort sent excited letters to Fritz's father, their Foreign Secretary, Baron Stockmar, and King Leopold—letting them all in on the secret before the prospective bride.

But when Fritz asked Victoria and Albert's permission to give Vicky a bracelet, they realized that "something had to be told her and he had better tell her himself!" A few days later, during an excursion up the heather-covered slopes of Craig-na-Ban, Fritz and Vicky managed to fall behind. He picked a sprig of white heather for good luck, which he offered her with his first kiss, saying that he hoped she would come to Prussia. She answered that she would be happy to go there for a year. He added that he hoped it would be "always," at which she blushed bright red. Had he said anything to annoy her? "Oh! No." "Might he tell her parents?" No, she would tell them herself. They shook hands, and Fritz told her that "this was one of the happiest days of his life."

When Vicky got home, she appeared in her mother's room, "very much agitated." Her father asked if she had anything to say. "Oh! yes, a great deal . . . it is that I am very fond of the Prince."

Both parents kissed her and her father explained how Fritz had asked permission "to offer her his hand . . . & to see more & more of her." Did she want the same thing?"

"Oh! Yes, every day," she answered, kneeling by her mother.

Had she always loved him?

"Oh always!"

Her mother took her in to see Fritz, who was waiting in an outer room. Vicky, the Queen said, was "nervous but did not hesitate or falter in giving her very decided answer." When Fritz kissed Vicky's hand, "she threw herself into his arms, & kissed him with a warmth which was responded to by Fritz again and again. I would not for the world have missed so touching and beautiful a sight," said the Queen, pleased that her daughter "behaved as a girl of 18 would, so naturally, so quietly & modestly & yet showing how very strong her feelings are."

Later, after Fritz left, Victoria and Albert spoke to Vicky alone. She promised her parents that she "would improve" and "would conquer herself," and said that she "hoped to be like" the Queen.

"My joy, my gratitude to God knows no bounds!" said Victoria.

Fritz was similarly ecstatic. "It is not politics, it is not ambition," he said; "it was my heart." He wrote his parents that the visit had been "like a beautiful dream" and that "the love and trust that the parents shower upon me makes me happier with each passing day." Back in Prussia, Wilhelm and Augusta were "in raptures," while King Friedrich Wilhelm IV, far less enthusiastic, strained to hail the engagement "with cordial satisfaction."

The next day Fritz left Balmoral. Vicky, who controlled herself until he was gone, fled to her mother's rooms, where they both surrendered to the prevailing fashion for extravagant tears. Vicky admitted to her mother with great embarrassment that she had never been so happy as when Fritz kissed her. That evening, confirming her new status as a woman, she was invited to dine alone with her parents.

"The young lady improves daily & an attachment of that kind will have the most beneficial effect on her," Victoria wrote King Leopold a few days later. "I cannot say how I love him [Fritz], his devotion & affection towards & confidence in me, not to speak of his decided passion for V. have touched and delighted me." Fritz had been instructed to stop in Brussels to pay his respects to the Belgian King, who was gratified to see his great-niece as the future Queen of Prussia, having promoted the marriage partly to protect his own country from France.

A month later Victoria wrote "dear darling Augusta" about her daughter:

I have hardly ever discussed Vicky with you, partly because it seemed somewhat immodest to mention her gradual development or to praise her unduly, and also because she was so largely the object of our secret hopes and desires. However, now that God has graciously granted our wishes I will keep silent no longer. . . .

She has developed amazingly of late and her visit to France proved beneficial in every way. . . . I find her very good company and this important event in her life has now brought us even closer together. . . . Her health is excellent. Early this year she went through a critical time * and did not suffer even the slightest indisposition. But she is still half a child and has to develop herself both physically and morally before their marriage takes place in two years' time.

THERE WERE FEW PEOPLE who greeted the alliance between the royal houses of England and Prussia with the same satisfaction as the parents. In a scathing article about the rumored engagement, the London *Times* dismissed the Hohenzollerns as just one of many "paltry German dynasties" dependent for their survival on Russia, and it attacked Prussia for fifty years of a "vacillating and

---

* *Obviously the onset of menstruation.*

discreditable" foreign policy. The Prussian royal family, the *Times* said, was destined for extinction because it had not lived up to the promises given its subjects during the Revolution of 1848: "What sympathy can exist between a Court supported like ours on the solid basis of popular freedom . . . and a camarilla . . . engaged . . . in trampling out the last embers of popular government? For our part, we wish for the daughter of our Royal House some better fate than union with a dynasty which knows neither what is due . . . to the rights of the people over which it presides, nor to the place it occupies in the great European confederacy."

Unfortunately for Vicky, the *Times* succeeded primarily in creating Prussian ill will toward the "daughter of England," whose interests it purported to defend. By pointing out Prussia's dependence on Russia, as exemplified by its neutrality in the Crimean War, its consequent loss of clout in the councils of Europe, and King Friedrich Wilhelm's obvious failings as a sovereign, the paper wounded Prussian pride and prejudiced Vicky's future subjects against her.

Nor was the engagement popular with the English people. There would certainly have been more of an uproar had Victoria and Albert not already earned the respect and loyalty of their people by their exemplary family life and had Vicky herself been less well regarded. The American Ambassador, who dined with the royal family about this time, was said to be "in raptures" about the Princess Royal, whom he described as "the most charming girl he had ever met: 'all life and spirit, full of frolic and fun, with an excellent head, and a heart as big as a mountain.' "

In Prussia, the reaction to the engagement was predictably mixed—liberals delighted, reactionaries infuriated. The ultraconservatives were appalled by the proposed union, as were most members of the royal family and their courtiers, who launched veiled barbs in Fritz's direction when he returned from England. Albert's older brother, Duke Ernest of Coburg, who was far less principled but often more pragmatic than the Prince Consort, predicted that this pro-Russian clique would go underground with its hostility, since no one dared criticize what the King had sanctioned.

When asked his reaction, Bismarck, then Prussian delegate to the German Diet in Frankfurt,* voiced his fear of English influence on the Prussian people. Bismarck's agenda revolved around the competition in the diet between the two most powerful German states, Prussia and Austria, for supremacy in Germany. To win this game, Bismarck believed that Prussia must not look to England and the West, but retain the goodwill of the Russian Czar to the East. In response to a letter from General Leopold von Gerlach, he had this to say:

> You ask me . . . what I think of the English marriage. I must separate the two words to give you my opinion. The "English" in it does not please me,

---

* *The German Diet was the organ of the Germanic Confederation, a loose consortium of thirty-nine German states and four free cities established by the Congress of Vienna in 1814 and dominated by Austria. It was not a parliament but more like a diplomatic congress whose members represented the monarchs of the various German states.*

the "marriage" may be quite good, for the Princess has the reputation of a lady of brain and heart. If the Princess can leave the Englishwoman at home and become a Prussian, then she may be a blessing to the country. Royal marriages generally give the House from which the bride comes an influence over the other, not vice versa. This is still more the case when the wife's country is more powerful and has developed a greater feeling of nationality than that of the husband. If our future Queen therefore remains even only partly English, I can see our Court in danger of being surrounded by English influence.

Bismarck resented what he called the "servile admiration" in Germany for English ways and the current "Anglomania of the Chambers [parliament], newspapers, sportsmen, landowners and judges." His real fear was that Vicky might bring with her dangerous democratic influences.

Bismarck's concern was not surprising in a country searching for a national identity. Nor did he misgauge the popularity of English institutions among Germans of the educated classes. Bismarck's goal—to wrest the leadership of the German Confederation away from Austria—required building Prussia's self-confidence. For the Prussians, currently suffering under the leadership of an incapacitated King and the onus of having sacrificed their position as a major factor in the European equation, it was not yet clear how this was to be accomplished.

But new opportunities arising from the end of the Crimean War were about to open for Prussia, as tension increased between the English, who wanted to continue the fight, and the French, who wanted to get out of the Crimea as quickly as possible. In the middle of January 1856, King Friedrich Wilhelm IV of Prussia sent Queen Victoria a secret cable announcing that his nephew* Czar Alexander II of Russia was ready to make peace on reasonable terms. For its role in bringing about this peace, Prussia expected to be included as a major participant in the peace conference, and to this end, the Prince Consort was bombarded by letters from the King and Prince of Prussia, as well as King Leopold of Belgium.

But Albert was a man of principle. "As for the special claims of Prussia . . . to take part in the negotiations . . . it would be a most perilous precedent . . . that a Power may take part in the great game of politics, without having laid down their stake," he wrote Uncle Leopold. Prussia was not invited to the peace conference until after the terms had been settled, although it was allowed to sign the General Treaty of Paris, which formally ended the Crimean War in March of 1856.

Ironically, it was Prussia who benefited more from the Crimean War than any of the participants. These gains were made at the expense of Austria, currently the dominant member of the German Confederation. During the Revolu-

---

* *The King's sister Charlotte was the widow of Czar Nicholas I and mother of Alexander II.*

tion of 1848 the Czar had helped the Austrian Emperor put down the rebellion, but the Austrians had turned around six years later and allied themselves with France and Britain against Russia in the Crimean War. The rift that now opened between Russia and Austria helped Prussia in her struggle against Austria for dominion over the German-speaking peoples of central Europe.

TEN DAYS BEFORE the official end of the Crimean War, Vicky was confirmed in the chapel at Windsor Castle. Dressed in what the *Times* described as a "rich silk glacé gown, with five flounces pinked, the body richly trimmed with white riband and Mechlin lace," she was led into the chapel by her father, followed by her mother and her great-uncle, King Leopold. Lord Granville, the leader of the Liberals in the House of Lords, commented acidly on the proceedings: "The Princess Royal went through her part well. The Princess Alice cried violently. The Archbishop read what seemed a dull address; luckily it was inaudible. The Bishop of Oxford rolled out a short prayer with conscious superiority."

As they had promised, Vicky's parents agreed to a private announcement of her engagement to Fritz after her confirmation. The Queen's great worry was that people might say that she and Albert had pushed Vicky into a decision at too young an age—which in fact they had. Although confident in public about their decision, Victoria was anxious and growing more so with each passing month. "Poor dear child, I often <u>tremble</u> when I think <u>how</u> much is expected of her!" she wrote her half-sister Feodora in Germany shortly after the engagement. Two months later, she confided similar worries to her journal. "I resent bitterly the conduct of the Prussian Court and Government and do not like the idea now, of our Child going to Berlin, more or less the enemy's den!"

The Queen's fears were confirmed some months later by Lady Bloomfield, wife of the English Minister in Berlin. "I fear Her Royal Highness's position here will be *more* difficult than perhaps Your Majesty is fully aware of . . . .the real fact is without living here & seeing the curious anomalous state of this country, & the violence and bitterness of [political] party spirits, it is almost *impossible* to value the true state of affairs at this Court . . . the unhappy divisions and jealousies which exist in the Royal family itself."

The Princess Royal, now confirmed, entered her first season, appearing at a drawing room in white with feathers, train, and cornflowers in her hair.* Fritz came from Prussia, and her parents gave her a coming-out party in the new ballroom at Buckingham Palace, designed under the supervision of her father. Because of Vicky's engagement and the end of the Crimean War, the 1856 social season was a particularly spectacular one. "Never were there so many balls and banquets," Disraeli wrote in early July. "No roof so hospitable this year as the Palace itself."

* *In flight from the Napoleonic Wars, Queen Louise (wife of Friedrich Wilhelm III) stopped to rest in a meadow with her children, who gathered cornflowers and made her a chain to wear to replace her lost jewels. The cornflower had become a Hohenzollern family tradition.*

The engagement, which lasted for nearly two years, gave everyone at court an opportunity to pass judgment on Vicky's fiancé. One of the Queen's maids of honor, Mary Bulteel, dismissed him as "a good-humoured . . . lieutenant, with large hands and feet, but not in the least clever." Disraeli thought somewhat better of him. "The Prince of Prussia . . . is well informed, and appears able—but more like a German student than a Prince."

When they were not being feted, Fritz and Vicky presented Queen Victoria with something of a problem. The Queen told Uncle Leopold that her daughter's fiancé was "so much in love, that, even if he is out driving and walking with her, he is not satisfied and says he has not seen her, unless he can have her for an hour to himself." Victoria, who believed it her duty never to leave the couple alone, complained peevishly of the boredom attached to chaperoning young lovers—all the more so because, as Prince Albert wrote his brother, "she cannot imagine that the child [Vicky] can arouse such [sexual] feelings." Vicky herself, "horribly shy and embarrassed to be with Fritz before others," was miserable seeing her mother's routine upset. Things went better when the Queen delegated the chaperoning to Vicky's fourteen-year-old brother, Bertie, who managed to occupy himself with their younger siblings in an adjoining room, leaving the door ajar just in case their mother returned unexpectedly.

During the winter of 1856, Fritz stopped in Paris on his way home from England to try to allay Napoleon III's concerns over the coming Anglo-Prussian marriage. Received by the Emperor on the palace steps as if he were a fellow sovereign, the heir to the Prussian throne was nonetheless an unwelcome addition to Napoleon's political calculations. "The Prince of Prussia pleased us very much," he wrote Queen Victoria with as much restraint as he dared, "and I have no doubt that he will bring happiness to the Princess Royal, for he seems to have all the qualities characteristic of his age and rank."

Empress Eugénie was more enthusiastic about the future groom. "The Prince is a tall, handsome man, almost a head taller than the Emperor [Napoleon]," she wrote a friend; "he is slim and fair, with a light yellow moustache—chivalrously polite, and not without a resemblance to Hamlet. . . . The Germans are an imposing race. Louis [Napoleon] says it is the race of the future. Bah, we are not there yet."

Another quasi-diplomatic foray, far less pleasing to his future in-laws, had been undertaken by Fritz a few months earlier, when he was sent by the King of Prussia to represent his country at the coronation of Czar Alexander II in Russia. "It is impossible to imagine a greater contrast than the way in which you and we are living," Albert wrote Fritz from Balmoral,

> you in the Oriental splendour of the Moscow festivities and we in the quiet isolation of the Scottish Highlands . . . I understand that your future alliance is looked on askance in Russia. . . . The German stands in the centre between England and Russia; his high culture and his philosophic love of truth drive him towards the English conception, his military disci-

pline, his admiration of the asiatic greatness . . . which is achieved by the merging of the individual into the whole, drives him in the other direction.

It is hardly surprising that the German-born Albert understood this basic dichotomy in his people. What is amazing is that he expected the weight of a fragile girl to tip the scales in favor of individual liberty and constitutional government.

CHAPTER SEVEN

"[O]ur marriage [ceremony] is no amusement but a solemn act and generally a sad one."

QUEEN VICTORIA

*A*s soon as Vicky became engaged to Fritz, the Prince Consort sent Baron Stockmar to see Prince William and Princess Augusta in Berlin. Shocked by Augusta's "pitiable" state of nerves, which he ascribed to the difficult political climate in which she lived, Stockmar warned Albert that they must begin immediately to prepare Vicky for her "special mission" and impress upon her "the seriousness and difficulty" of her future position. "She has the qualities of mind and feeling required," Stockmar said, "but that will not be enough. . . . For I foresee that she would have to suffer her whole life from mistakes and faults which are to be feared at the very beginning."

Spurred by Stockmar, the Prince Consort started Vicky on an intensive course in political science, particularly the history of Prussia and the Hohenzollerns. He gave her letters from his various correspondents around Europe to read; he discussed the international situation with her; and he laid out her future role in what he fervently believed would be the coming of age of Germany under the leadership of Prussia.

Albert taught Vicky that the future of the German states lay in a "national union" to be created under Prussian military might in conjunction with "progress in constitutional institutions." Like Bismarck, the Prince Consort believed that Austria cared "nothing for Germany but much for her influence over it." His solution for Prussia, however, was not to placate Russia in order to have a protector, but to "encourage Prussia to have confidence in herself," lead the other German states into voluntary union, discard the conservatism of Russia and Austria, and join the progressive Western powers.

"Vicky is . . . very busy: she has learned . . . many and diverse things, but they are all somewhat haphazard in her mind," Albert wrote Fritz early in the engagement. "She now comes to me every evening from six to seven, when I put her through a kind of general catechizing; and, in order to give precision to her ideas, I make her work out certain subjects by herself, and bring me the results to be revised. Thus she is now engaged in writing a short Compendium of Roman History."

"From dear Papa I can learn more than from anyone else in the world," Vicky wrote her fiancé a year later; "he explains everything so well and discusses things like no one else."

However well Vicky understood the political lessons her father taught her, she had problems with precision of language. This lack of specificity continued to dog her throughout her life. Reading her political analyses, one marvels at the gist, but frequently longs for the grace and wit of the teacher.

Along with intellectual training, Albert instilled in his favorite child a belief in the perfectibility of character. Eight years later, at the age of twenty-two, Vicky would write her mother from Prussia that it was "a serious and disheartening thing to look back . . . and think how far short of ones mark one has always remained. . . . How often one has thought of oneself instead of others, of ones own pleasure and convenience before duty. . . . if I were to die today how little how very little I should have done of what I ought to have done. . . . I am sure Heaven and Hell are in ones own conscience."

As presented by Prince Albert, precise standards of rectitude applied not only to people but to nations. Sitting at his feet, Vicky imbibed a rigidity in political outlook that would prove less than helpful to a girl embarking on life in a foreign culture.

WHILE ALBERT WORKED on their daughter's mind, Victoria prepared her trousseau—an enormous array of personal and household items. Along with twelve evening gowns, six ball dresses, three court dresses, and fifteen miscellaneous gowns, there was enough velvet, silk, and summer lawn folded into her trunks to make at least forty more elaborate ensembles. Underwear was ordered by the gross—twelve dozen shifts, twelve dozen pairs of drawers, twelve dozen handkerchiefs (embroidered and plain), and twelve dozen nightdresses, plus eight dozen petticoats, four dozen dressing gowns, quantities of mourning dresses, shoes, stockings, shawls, bonnets, caps, mantillas, mackintoshes, and so forth. It took a year and a half to assemble all this, and by the time it was ready, there were three huge shipments—one hundred packing cases, crammed with everything from furniture, carpets, and wallpapers to paintings, linens, and saddles. There were delicacies from Fortnum and Mason and a carton of the popular *Illustrated London News*.

For Fritz, Vicky ordered an engagement ring set with an emerald exactly like the one her mother had given her father. Vicky asked her fiancé to wear it in the same way, on his little finger. Fritz sent Vicky his diaries for 1848, the year of the revolution, so that she could learn what this period of terror had been like for him. "You have had sad experiences; the scenes of horror which you went through appalled me. God grant that such things may never happen again in your country," she wrote in response.

Separated from each other, Vicky and Fritz corresponded in the way of lovers. "That you now are everything in the world to me you already know," Fritz wrote. "I no longer undertake anything without thinking constantly of you and look upon you as my good angel." To which she replied, "If you only knew how your love moves me, how happy it makes me and how much I return it, I do not deserve so much. Dear, dear Fritz, I think of you day and night." The envelope containing this sentiment was inscribed, "For my precious madly-loved Fritz from his own Vicky." Not too surprisingly, the people around the young couple found these letters less fascinating than did the correspondents themselves. Fritz's aide-de-camp, Count Moltke, reported that the Prince received a forty-page letter from the Princess Royal written one day after he left her. "How the news must have accumulated!" Moltke remarked.

Vicky's new status as an engaged girl entitled her to spend her evenings with Victoria and Albert away from her siblings, and she wrote her fiancé that "the hours I spend with my parents are the happiest in the day." Her mother felt differently. "We dined with Vicky, who generally leaves us at 10," the Queen noted in her journal shortly before her daughter's seventeenth birthday, "and then I have the rare happiness of being alone with my beloved Albert."

In the spring of 1857, the Queen asked parliament for a dowry for the Princess Royal "suitable to the dignity of the crown and the honour of the country." She hoped for £80,000 with an annual income of £10,000, but settled for £40,000 with an income of £8,000. "Her allowance is not large," Prince Albert wrote Vicky's future mother-in-law, "but it makes her independent, which is most important for her."

The truth was that Fritz had very little money, and the interest from Vicky's dowry would have to be added to the groom's income to defray their household expenses. After the announcement of the engagement, the King of Prussia granted Fritz an annual income of nine thousand thalers in lieu of the usual "morning gift" bestowed on a Hohenzollern bride after the consummation of the marriage; in the case of Fritz's mother, Augusta (the King's sister-in-law), the morning gift had been far more generous and had included clothes and jewels. The Prince Consort was never happy with Vicky's financial arrangements, feeling quite rightly that the Prussians took advantage of Queen Victoria's wealth.

The wedding was set for January 25, 1858, and as the time drew closer, other problems arose. First was the issue of where the ceremony should take place. The Prussians let Queen Victoria know that they expected their future King to be married at home in Berlin. Victoria was not pleased. "Whatever may be the usual practice of Prussian Princes, it is not every day that one marries the eldest daughter of the Queen of England. The question therefore must be considered as settled and closed."

The next disagreements arose over the members of Vicky and Fritz's future household—always a touchy point when the bride was foreign. Vicky had to have *Palastdamen* (palace ladies) to serve at important court functions, *Hofdamen* (ladies-in-waiting) who took turns in attending her, and maids of honor. As chosen by the Queen of Prussia and Fritz's mother, Fritz and Vicky's household was composed mainly of dreary middle-aged courtiers, the best of whom had already been assigned to Fritz's sister, Louise, recently married to the Grand Duke of Baden. Prince Albert's request for a few English girls of Vicky's age was answered with the inclusion of two young German ladies-in-waiting, Countess Walpurga Hohenthal and Countess Marie Lynar.

Fritz disagreed with Prince Albert over the addition to Vicky's staff of Ernest von Stockmar, old Baron Stockmar's son, whom the Prince Consort had with difficulty convinced to act as his daughter's private secretary. "The Princess Royal of England is expatriating herself . . . ," Albert wrote his future son-in-law. "She will have an English dowry, which will be administered separately. . . . For this she has need of a man of business who knows the country and its ways." Regarding Fritz's objection that people would call Stockmar, whose father was well known for liberal views, a "secret political agent," Albert had little patience. "[I]t is not in either of your interests . . . to placate enemies who desire both the political and social failure of the marriage. It is rather your duty to fight for its success in spite of them."

Vicky's last big family festivity before her marriage was her father's thirty-eighth birthday—the culmination of a long series of tearful good-byes to places, people, and events that started a full year before her wedding. "You can guess what anyone must feel at the idea of parting from such a father," she wrote Fritz. "You know and love him too, but you do not quite know how eminent is his mind, how great his soul. There is certainly no one like him on earth, there cannot be another."

TWO WEEKS BEFORE the wedding, the members of Fritz and Vicky's Prussian court arrived at Windsor Castle. They were ushered into Victoria's small blue and gray sitting room to be presented to the Queen, the Prince Consort, and the Princess Royal. Vicky, who looked "almost a child" at seventeen, was noticeably shy when her mother motioned her to step forward, but managed to greet her future attendants "with great composure and gentleness," while her father looked on with obvious pride.

The most promising of Vicky's future ladies was Walpurga Hohenthal, the orphaned daughter of a German diplomat, only a year older than the bride herself. A handsome young woman, she had been chosen by Vicky's future father-in-law, who had an eye for good looks. When Queen Victoria first saw Wally Hohenthal, she laughed. "The Princess is 17, the Maid of Honor, 18. What a respectable court that will make."

The German ladies had been instructed to leave their crinolines at home, since that particular fashion had not yet reached England, and Victoria was always put off by clothes she considered too smart (her word) or too avant-garde for royalty. Young Wally found this "rather a trial," although she admired the colored woolen petticoats worn by the English ladies under their skirts to keep out the winter chill. Like everyone who ever visited Queen Victoria, the German visitors complained about the cold inside her palaces.

A few days after their arrival, the court moved to London for the wedding festivities. Before she left Windsor, Victoria inspected the suite refurnished for Fritz and Vicky's brief honeymoon. A new brown carpet strewn with orange flowers had been placed in the redecorated flowered bedroom, along with the marriage bed painted with the young couple's initials. "[I]t gave me quite a pang looking at the rooms . . . ," Victoria said. "I do so feel for my poor child."

Twenty-five years later, on the occasion of the marriage of her youngest daughter, the Queen had not changed her opinion about sex, which she loved, and pregnancy, which she resented. What worried her was the wedding night, although she never seems to have enlightened her daughters about the sexual act. Even the nicest, most thoughtful bridegroom was almost sure to shock his bride with demands for which she was unprepared. Victoria was also anxious about the dangers of childbirth.

"That thought—that agonizing thought . . . of giving up your own child, from whom all has been so carefully kept & guarded, to a stranger to do unto her as he likes, is to me the most torturing thought in the world," she wrote Vicky many years later. "While I feel no girl could go to the altar (and would probably refuse) if she knew all, there is something very dreadful in the thought of the sort of trap she is being led into."

Within a few days the rest of the guests had arrived at Buckingham Palace —Fritz's parents, "radiant at the realization of their long-cherished project," his huge German cousins, and a whole galaxy of the royal and near-royal. King Leopold of Belgium was one of the first to appear. Nearly as pleased as those immediately involved, he "glided about distributing advice in soft low tones." Between seventy and eighty people sat down to dinner every evening. There were hunting parties for the gentlemen, a great ball with over one thousand guests, and three galas at the theater. The Queen, who dismissed the command performance of *Macbeth* as "perfectly atrocious," preferred the scene offstage. "Here we all sat," she commented, "in a wonderful row of royalties."

Two days before the ceremony, the groom, looking "pale and agitated" but describing himself as "the happiest of the happy," arrived. Next day—"Poor dear Vicky's last unmarried day!" according to her mother—the Queen led the young couple into a large drawing room to survey their wedding presents. Fritz had brought his bride a necklace of diamonds and turquoise, and his parents had presented her with a string of thirty-six "enormous" pearls, valued by the newspapers at £5,000. Victoria said that Vicky was "almost startled by the magnificent display," as she and Albert presented the groom with three huge silver candelabra.

For Vicky there was also a diamond diadem from the King and Queen of Prussia; a dressing case in gold and corals from her grandmother the Duchess of Kent; Brussels lace from Uncle Leopold; a diamond "corsage" to be worn as a necklace or head ornament, along with three extra diamond clusters from the Queen; a bracelet and pendant in large emeralds and diamonds from her father; a parure* of opals and diamonds from both her parents; and from each of her four sisters a brooch of the same pattern worked in different stones—diamonds, rubies, sapphires, and emeralds.

---

* *A matching set of jewelry, usually a necklace, earrings, a pair of bracelets, and a tiara. Necklaces often had a pendant which could be detached and worn as a brooch.*

At the end of this momentous day Victoria and Albert took Vicky to her room, where they kissed her and gave her their blessing. Vicky cried. Afterwards in her own rooms Victoria herself broke down. "[I]t is like taking a poor Lamb to be sacrificed," she told Albert.

THE MORNING OF THE WEDDING, the Queen was far more agitated than the bride herself. "I felt almost as if it were I that was being married over again, only much more nervous . . . ," she wrote in her journal. "Vicky came in to see me, looking composed. . . . This relieved me greatly." Vicky's calm would last all day. "Not a bit of bridal missiness [sic] and flutter," Lady Lyttelton remarked on observing her former charge's serenity during the ceremonies.

After breakfast, Victoria invited Vicky into her rooms to dress, and they had their hair done. For her wedding, Vicky wore a gown of white silk moiré over a petticoat flounced in lace and wreathed in sprays of orange blossom and myrtle. Her train was trimmed with white satin ribbons and lace. Her lace veil was held in place by a matching wreath, and she wore a diamond necklace, earrings, and brooch. The Queen, who had chosen lilac silk moiré with a velvet train, wore the crown diamonds and a royal diadem of diamonds and pearls. Before they left for the chapel, Vicky gave her mother a "very pretty" brooch with a lock of her hair, saying, "I hope to be worthy to be your child!" She was also daguerreotyped with her parents. This early photographic process required the subject to remain utterly still for between thirty seconds and one minute. Although Vicky came out quite well, Victoria trembled so much that her likeness was a blur.

It was a brilliant winter day, and the streets were filled with thousands of people waiting since dawn to watch the procession that led from Buckingham Palace to St. James's Chapel. They were not disappointed. There were some eighteen carriages with outriders, over three hundred soldiers and 220 horses, along with carriage drivers and musicians. One carriage bore three of Vicky's sisters,* dressed in white lace over pink satin. Her four brothers followed in Highland dress. Then, with drum rolls, trumpet flourishes, and cheers from the crowds, the last carriage appeared with Vicky and the Queen. At St. James's they joined the Prince Consort, Uncle Leopold, and Vicky's eight young bridesmaids for the traditional entrance down the aisle. In her journal, the Queen described it:

"A procession was formed. . . . Mama came last, just before me, then Lord Palmerston, with the Sword of State, Bertie and Alfred, I, with the 2 little Boys (on either side of me), which they say had a most touching effect, & the 3 girls following."

Vicky's future mother-in-law, Princess Augusta of Prussia, had already entered the chapel wearing a dress of the same white silk as the bride, but with a blue velvet train. She was accompanied by two ladies-in-waiting, one of whom, Countess Louise Oriolla, was considered too "conspicuous" in bright orange.

* Alice, Helena, and Louise. Baby Beatrice was less than a year old.

The Countess, a difficult and demanding woman, was said to be one of the mistresses of Prince Wilhelm.

With the spectators in place, the participants entered, preceded by trumpets and drums. "[T]he effect was thrilling & striking as one heard the music coming nearer & nearer," said Victoria. "Fritz behaved with the greatest self-possession . . . bowing to us, & then kneeling down before the altar in a most devotional manner." According to the *Morning Post,* the groom "bore himself manfully on an occasion where few men appear to much advantage." He wore the dark blue tunic and white trousers of the Prussian Guards and carried his shining silver helmet in his hand.

"Last came the bride's procession," Victoria continued,

> our darling "Flower" looking very touching & lovely, with such an inno-
> cent, confident, & serious expression on her dear face. She walked between
> her beloved Father & dear Uncle Leopold, who had been present at both
> her christening and confirmation.
>
> My last fear of being overcome vanished, when I saw Vicky's calm &
> composed manner. It looked beautiful seeing her kneeling beside Fritz,
> their hands joined, her long train born [*sic*] by the 8 young ladies . . .
> hovering round her, as they knelt near her. How it reminded me of my
> having similarly, proudly, tenderly, confidently knelt beside my beloved
> Albert, in the very same spot. . . . The Archbishop was very nervous,

the Queen added, commenting that "Vicky and Fritz spoke very <u>plainly</u>."

The bride and groom walked out of the chapel to the Mendelssohn "Wedding March," composed sixteen years earlier and played for the first time at a royal wedding.* They took their places in a carriage for the ride through the crowds back to Buckingham Palace. For the rest of their lives, whenever they were driving in London, Fritz always took Vicky's hand and squeezed it when they passed the Chapel Royal.

Before the wedding breakfast, the newly married couple stepped out on the balcony at Buckingham Palace to be cheered by the public below. Seated opposite their parents afterwards, they were hidden by an enormous wedding cake, placed in the middle of the table. A triumph of confectionery folly, it stood over six feet tall and had been baked in three tiers, separated by rows of pearls and festooned with garlands of orange blossom, jasmine, and silver leaves. The top tier, formed like a dome, rested on columns and contained an altar with two cupids holding medallions of Vicky and Fritz. Around this were busts of Victoria, Albert, Wilhelm, and Augusta. The second tier was cut by niches containing allegorical statues (Wisdom, Innocence, etc.); the third was decorated with the arms of Great Britain and Prussia.

---

* *Felix Mendelssohn had been a guest at Victoria and Albert's court in 1842, the year he composed the incidental music to* A Midsummer Night's Dream, *from which the "Wedding March" is taken. Victoria and Albert, both in their twenties, had surprised Mendelssohn with their musicianship, while he had astonished them by improvising the Austrian National Anthem with one hand and "Rule Britannia" with the other.*

While Vicky and Fritz were changing into their traveling clothes, Prince Albert added a last paragraph to a letter he had started to Baron Stockmar earlier that day. He thanked Stockmar, who had been too ill to come to England, for the "work in which you have had a large share," reminding him that it was "just eighteen years since you . . . were present in the same Chapel Royal at my union with Victoria" and forty-two years since Stockmar had first accompanied Uncle Leopold to London for his marriage to Charlotte.

That evening Victoria and Albert gave a state banquet for which Tennyson had written two less than inspiring verses to "God Save the Queen."* Outside the palace, London sparkled with illuminations in the public buildings and fireworks in the parks. In honor of the occasion, gifts were bestowed on "the deserving poor." In Nottingham, the mayor distributed two thousand quarts of soup and bread, while in Birmingham, between twelve hundred and thirteen hundred needy sat down to a free dinner of "beef, plumpudding, ale and tobacco," served them by the local gentry.

Meanwhile, Fritz and Vicky had arrived at Windsor, where they were met by fireworks, cannons, a guard of honor, and more cheering crowds. The white ponies had been unhitched from their carriage, and one hundred schoolboys from Eton next door had yoked themselves in their places to pull the carriage from the railway station up the long hill to the castle. Before settling in for their two-day honeymoon, Vicky sent a messenger back to London with a note for her mother: "I cannot let this day close, which has brought me so much happiness without one more word to you, one more word of the deepest tenderest love. Can I ever forget your kindness to me today, or shall I ever be able to express all my gratitude to you and dear Papa, as I feel it!"

The morning after their wedding night, the bride and groom took their first walk alone together and then went ice-skating. Just as they were sitting down to breakfast, a letter arrived for Vicky from the Queen, describing marriage as

> a very solemn act, the most important & solemn in every one's life, but much more so in a woman's than in a man's. I have ever looked on the blessed day which united me to your beloved & perfect Papa as the cause . . . of my own happiness (a happiness few if any enjoy). . . . You have also the blessing of a dear, kind, excellent husband. . . . Let it be your study & your object . . . to be of use to him. . . . you can never give your parents more happiness & comfort than when they know & see that you are a truly devoted, loving and useful wife.

Vicky, who declared herself "really quite at a loss how to thank" the Queen sufficiently for this advice, answered at once, saying that the letter would be "a

---

* *"God save our prince and bride*
God keep our lands allied
God save the Queen . . . etc."
("The Marriage of Her Royal Highness, the Princess Royal, 1858," Morning Post, *January 26, 1858.)*

treasure to me all my life." She assured the Queen that she was "not the least tired or nervous or excited and had no headache either yesterday evening or this morning." Nor, she said, had she ever "felt a joy so serene & pure as I do now."

Unlike most royal brides of her day, Vicky was in fact blissful. Like her mother, she had been given to a man who offered not only sexual pleasure, but concern and tenderness rare in princes of the day. She grew to adore her Fritz with his gentle manliness, as he obviously loved and desired her. But as was the way with royal honeymoons, the rest of the wedding party migrated back to Windsor two days after the wedding. "Everything seems to be as one would wish," the Queen wrote in her journal, "& the great happiness of the 2 dear young people, their simple, pure love & affection for one another is truly delightful." Still, the Queen found it "quite strange" to see Vicky "walking off with Fritz" at bedtime.

On January 29, everyone returned to London once again for a series of festivities preceding the inevitable departure for Prussia. On her last day at home, February 1, 1858, Vicky stayed quietly with her mother and spent the early evening lying on a bed, playing with her nine-month-old sister, Beatrice. "I think it will kill me to take leave of dear Papa!" she told the Queen.

The next day's weather—overcast sky and freezing temperatures—fit the ladies' bleak mood. Before Vicky left, it had begun to snow. Victoria described her eldest daughter's emotional departure:

> We went into the Audience Room where Mama & all the Children were assembled & here poor Vicky & Alice's, as well as the other's tears began to flow fast. . . . Still I struggled but as I came to the staircase my breaking heart gave way. . . . The Hall was filled with all our people & theirs [the Prussians] . . . amongst the many servants there, I don't think there was a dry eye. Poor dear Child. . . . I clasped her in my arms, not knowing what to say & kissed good Fritz, pressing his hand again & again. . . . Again at the door of the carriage I embraced them both. . . . What a dreadful moment, what a real heartache to think of our dearest child being gone & not knowing how long it may be before we see her again!

Accompanied by her father, brothers Bertie and Affie (Alfred), and her mother's uncle, the Duke of Cambridge, Vicky and Fritz drove through London and on to Gravesend, where they were to board the royal yacht for their crossing to the Continent. Passing under huge arches emblazoned "Fairwell, Fair Rose of England" and "We give her to your care," they found that the streets leading to the dock had been decorated with flags and garlands. Young girls with wreaths in their hair were scattering flowers over the snow, and a thousand people waited at dockside for the Lord Mayor of London to deliver a congratulatory address. Both sixteen-year-old Bertie and thirteen-year-old Affie cried. Father and daughter said good-bye alone in the privacy of Vicky's cabin, and Vicky sobbed.

Albert, the only member of the family who kept a semblance of composure during Vicky's departure, wrote her the next day. Unlike his usual letters to the women in his family, which were light and often witty, this note revealed the depth of his love for his eldest daughter. "My heart was very full when yesterday you leaned your forehead on my breast to give free vent to your tears. I am not of a demonstrative nature and therefore you can hardly know how dear you have always been to me, and what a void you have left behind in my heart."

SOME YEARS LATER Albert's older brother, Duke Ernest, wrote about the Prince Consort's role in Vicky's marriage:

> My brother . . . loved his eldest daughter much too tenderly, to be influenced entirely by political considerations in respect of her marriage. For many years . . . his heart's desire had been to see his favourite child . . . in a great position. He took a paternal delight in fancying his promising, talented, and precocious daughter on a powerful throne, but, above all, I knew how much he also desired to render her inwardly happy. . . . the son of the Prince of Prussia, above all other scions of reigning Houses, afforded the greatest hopes for the future.

As Vicky left for Prussia, the Prince Consort was sure that he had trained her adequately for that future. "Vicky is very reasonable," he had written his brother at the time of the engagement; "she will go well prepared into the labyrinth of Berlin."

PART TWO

Crown Princess

CHAPTER
EIGHT

*T*HE SNOW CONTINUED TO FALL as the *Victoria and Albert* moved out into the Thames. Vicky and Fritz settled themselves down in an alcove on deck, where she tried to read aloud to him. They were soon cut off from the rest of their party by the falling snow, which filled up the footsteps of the sailors frantically sweeping to keep the decks clear. The scene reminded Vicky of a book Miss Hildyard had read to her and Alice when they were little girls about someone's voyage to the North Pole.

Feeling "so unwell, and so shaky" from her leavetakings, Vicky begged Fritz to allow her to remain in her cabin during dinner while he entertained the enormous entourage of ladies and gentlemen, English and German, who accompanied them on their journey. She wrote her mother "to cheer up, and to console yourself with the thought . . . that this cruel separation is but for a while. . . . My comfort," she assured the Queen, "is in my beloved Husband, heaven reward him for his kindness to me, for indeed it is greater than I can say, and makes me feel that I care not where I go to now as it is with him."

Sometime during the night the *Victoria and Albert* headed into the open sea toward the continent. The water had been extremely calm, but the German ladies' maids, noting the accumulated snow, bewailed "the dreadful storm . . . in the night." Prone to seasickness herself, Vicky wrote her mother that they "made us laugh very much as it was so particularly quiet and really no motion at all."

It was dull and gray in Antwerp, where they dropped anchor the next morning. Crowds of Belgians, eager to catch a glimpse of the royal honeymooners, stood waiting, thoroughly drenched by early-morning rains. Before facing them, Vicky wrote home: "May God bless and protect my Parents for whom I would lay down my life. May he give me strength to prove myself worthy of being their child, worthy of their love which I can never requite as I ought."

Although she wrote words of comfort to her mother, it was to her father that Vicky confessed her own sadness. "The pain of parting from you yesterday was greater than I can describe. I thought my heart was going to break when you shut the cabin door and were gone. . . . I miss you s̲o̲ dreadfully dear Papa, more than I can say; your dear picture stood near me all night. . . . To you, dear Papa, I owe most in this world. . . . you possess the deep confidence, reverence and affection of your child . . . and I may say of my husband too; and we feel secure and happy in the thought that you will never refuse us your precious advice."

Vicky and Fritz were met on the quay by Uncle Leopold, who escorted them to Brussels. That evening there was a ball in their honor; most of their attendants did not arrive in the ballroom until well after midnight, since the ballgowns and dress uniforms packed in their luggage had been left in Antwerp. In spite of the lateness of the ball and of her bedtime, Vicky was up writing her mother at six-forty the next morning before her scheduled eight A.M. departure for her new country.

Once inside the German states, Vicky found herself the centerpiece of a long procession stretching from Hanover, where she crossed the border, all the way to Berlin. She and Fritz traveled by train, stopping frequently to greet the local townsmen and admire their villages, decked out with flags, triumphal arches, and illuminations. Pompous mayors, town elders, and nervous school-girls in starched white dresses waited expectantly at every station. According to Wally Hohenthal, Vicky was "gentle, charming, and affable, not for one mo-ment relaxing her endeavour to make the best impression. There was in her appearance a childlike dignity and goodness which was most captivating."

Ease of manner was not Vicky's strong suit, and what young Wally noted was obvious to their entire suite: the new Prussian Princess was determined to do everything in her power to fulfill the role her parents had set out for her. No matter what she felt—shyness, homesickness, even disapproval—she would present a cheerful, gracious exterior to the world.

This became evident during their first evening at the Hanoverian court. From the early eighteenth century until 1837, the King of England was also sovereign of the German state of Hanover. This peculiar overlap of dynasties had ended in 1837 when Victoria became Queen of England, since under Salic Law* a woman could not sit on the Hanoverian throne. As soon as Victoria's uncle Ernest Augustus, the eldest surviving and most unpopular son of George III,† became King of Hanover, he instituted a lawsuit against his niece over some of the best of her jewels—the ones she wore for state occasions—and a fabulous gold dinner service. This dispute was not settled until 1857, the year before Vicky's marriage, when a royal commission ruled in favor of Hanover; by this time, however, the dreadful Ernest Augustus was dead, and his son George V had succeeded him. Probably through oversight rather than malice,

---

* *A code from the Salian Franks and other Germanic tribes specifying the exclusion of females in the inheritance of land. It was extended by the French and others to include the succession to the throne.*

† *A London newspaper of the day said that Ernest Augustus had "committed every crime in his life except suicide" (Hajo Holborn,* History of Modern Germany, 1840–1945, *p. 27).*

it was this contested gold dinner service that Vicky found on the table at the banquet in her honor. Although "much hurt," the seventeen-year-old behaved with aplomb. Only her intimates guessed that she was even upset. Nor did she mention anything about it in her letters home, remarking only on the kindness of King George and his wife.

From Hanover the party proceeded to Magdeburg, where Fritz and Vicky visited the cathedral, one of the earliest examples of Gothic architecture in Germany. The crowds at the cathedral, anxious to get close to the young couple, tore shreds of Vicky's velvet gown off her back. In her letter to her mother, the bride spoke only about "the magnificent, enthusiastic receptions we have met with everywhere."

One incident lightened the otherwise formal royal progression. Just before they reached Potsdam, old Field Marshal Wrangel, once "the most daredevil and original of Prussian generals," boarded the train to welcome the young couple on behalf of the Prussian army. They had just passed through the town of Wittenberg, where the citizens, known for their pastry, had presented the Princess with an enormous apple tart covered with meringue. A sudden jolt of the train threw the portly Wrangel onto the seat opposite Vicky and into the tart. The seventeen-year-old laughed helplessly while her ladies struggled to clean the backside of his uniform to make him presentable in Berlin.

Heralded by cannons, soldiers in helmets and armored breastplates, and "a veritable forest of flags," Vicky entered Berlin for the first time through the famous Brandenburg Gate, enclosed in a golden state coach with painted panels and huge glass windows, drawn by eight horses. Nicknamed "the gilded monkey-cage" by Fritz, it swayed and bobbed "like a ship at sea."

For a young woman brought up in London, Berlin of the late 1850s—minus the display arranged in her honor—would not have been an impressive sight. According to the British attaché who arrived the same year as Vicky, "Berlin is the most insupportable place I ever was in." With a population of 400,000, one-fifth of whom were uniformed soldiers, it most resembled a military encampment.

Situated on what a contemporary guidebook called "a dreary plain of sand, destitute of either beauty or fertility," the town had presented quite a challenge to Frederick the Great when he set out toward the end of the eighteenth century to create a capital to impress his neighbors. Fritz's most illustrious ancestor had laid out wide streets, enclosed the area with walls, and ordered his citizens (there were only forty thousand in his day) to fill it with houses. "As the population was scanty," the handbook explained, "the only mode of complying with the wishes of the sovereign was by stretching the houses over as wide a space as possible."

Vicky arrived in Berlin in February of 1858, nearly three-quarters of a century later. On the day of her entry, the marching soldiers and cheering crowds would have filled the emptiness, camouflaged the miserable paving, and hidden the inadequacy of the Spree—called by one visitor a "sluggish, dirty little stream on which the name of a river has been undeservedly conferred." The icy weather would also have masked the smell of raw sewage, a major problem in a city where the land was flat and water stagnated in the open drains, giving off "noxious odors . . . very unwholesome as well as unpleasant."

From her seat in the swaying coach, Vicky would not have seen much of this, nor would she have had time to contemplate the cultural aspects of a city devoted to soldiering. "The mere passing traveller in search of amusements will exhaust *the sights* of Berlin perhaps in a fortnight and afterwards find it tedious without the society of friends," the guidebook concluded. For the young newcomer, there were, at the moment, more than enough people and events to make up for the inadequacies of her future home.

"We were received in the *most* kind & enthusiastic manner," she wrote her mother; "the crowds in the streets were not to be described—and the noise—! —the shouts & Bells & guns. The whole town had turned out, I think, the multitudes of flags, banners, ribbons, streamers etc. fluttering in the brightest of suns & the bitterest coldest of east winds!"

Although it was freezing, Vicky and her ladies were required to wear court gowns, cut very low. Shivering in her corner of the carriage, Vicky's lady-in-waiting Wally Hohenthal was amazed that the new Prussian Princess insisted on keeping the windows of the state coach down so people could see her. By ancient right, the parade through the city was led by the master butchers of Berlin, looking somewhat incongruous in their top hats and frockcoats, mounted on less-than-glamorous steeds. The procession, which took nearly two hours, ended at the Old Schloss, where Fritz and Vicky were to live and where King Friedrich Wilhelm IV and Queen Elisabeth waited to formally receive them. Queen Elisabeth, a noted Anglophobe, had openly opposed the British marriage, but was quite impressed with the sight of the young girl running up the palace steps in her low-cut gown, apparently oblivious to the cold.

"Are you not frozen to death?" the Queen asked as she greeted Vicky.

"Yes, I am," Vicky answered quickly with a smile; "I have only one warm place and that is my heart!"

"Every one says how well you behave . . . ," her mother wrote. "How thankful & happy do we feel! How right your sometimes not very patiently and kindly listened to Mama was, when she told you, you could do every thing, if you would but take pains, control yourself & conquer all little difficulties—as you had such great qualities, such a heart of gold!"

A telegram from Fritz dated three days after their arrival confirmed Vicky's success: "The whole Royal Family," he claimed, "is enchanted with my wife."

The fact that Vicky was winning "golden opinions" encouraged her father to drive home a moral message. "This kindly and confident welcome of a whole nation to a total stranger must have aroused and strengthened your efforts to prove yourself worthy of such feelings . . . ," he wrote his daughter, warning her a few days later of the inevitable "little reaction" that was bound to follow such unqualified success. "Just because they were delighted and enthusiastic, the public will now turn to sharp criticism and pull you to pieces. The family, who were courteous to the stranger . . . may now be inclined to put you back to what they consider your proper place and to reassume theirs. But even this must not surprise you. Your place is your husband's wife, your mother's daughter; you must not expect anything else, but you must not give up anything which you owe to your husband or your mother."

It is rather remarkable that the Prince Consort, an intelligent and perceptive man, never seems to have realized that he was asking the impossible of his child, since there was no way on earth that Vicky could fulfill the task of becoming her husband's Prussian wife and remain her mother's English child. Closing his eyes to this anomaly, Albert chose to regard Vicky's reception as a happy prelude to the fulfillment of his deepest desires for his old homeland.

Albert knew that the mantle of countryhood worn by the German Federation since its creation at the Congress of Vienna in 1814 was perilously thin—a skin stretched over a patchwork of petty, quarreling kingdoms guarding their ancient traditions and privileges at the expense of the whole. Of these dynasties, the Hohenzollerns of Prussia were certainly not the oldest, the most enlightened, or the most cultured, but they were the best soldiers and therefore the most likely agents of change. The only other powerful dynasty, the Austrian Habsburgs, whose territories had once blanketed Europe from Spain to the Balkans, were on the decline as a European power.

But Albert, who had taught his child that "history is the best guide for Royalties," seems not to have taken into account the fact that the Hohenzollern family, which Vicky had now joined, was essentially a tribe of warriors with beliefs utterly at odds with his own. This was because he was out of touch with the land of his birth.

The Prince Consort had left Germany nearly twenty years earlier—before the Crimean War, before the Revolution of 1848, and before the reactionary backlash that had surged through continental Europe, reviving princely legitimacy as the cornerstone of political order and returning to their thrones frightened kings determined to hold parliamentary government at bay. In sending Vicky to Prussia, Albert was not only consigning her to a political entity in flux, but asking her to help mold it into a viable nation under principles of constitutionalism that were anathema to the family to which she now belonged.

CHAPTER NINE

"I am tired of ruling a nation of slaves."

FREDERICK THE GREAT

*I*F HISTORY IS A CHRONICLE of the most successful conquerors and defenders, then the Germans, who lived in the middle of Europe without protective barriers, had to have been the best soldiers of all. Descended from Scandinavian tribes who migrated south before the birth of Christ, the earliest Germans were described by Julius Caesar and Tacitus as tall, blond men noted for courage in battle, drinking, and the open-air worship of deities who they believed inhabited the imposing forests that covered their land. Nine hundred years later, when Charlemagne joined the Catholic Church to the remnants of the Roman Empire, creating the Holy Roman Empire, it was the descendants of these tribes who repelled the barbarian hordes and brought relative peace to the middle of Europe.

The medieval German Empire surpassed both France and England in the sophistication of its political institutions. In size, it encompassed Burgundy, Italy, and the kingdom of Sicily—a fact that eventually led to its deterioration, as German emperors, neglecting the core of their empire in the north, fell prey to the sybaritic pleasures of life in the south. They also incurred the enmity of the papacy, which schemed with individual princes to throw them off the throne. To keep these minor German princes in line, the emperors were forced to grant concessions, including the right to bear arms, raise taxes, maintain their own courts, mint coins, and rule the towns lying within their territories.

This withering away of imperial prerogatives was underscored by the method in which German emperors came to power. After the middle of the fourteenth century, the crown no longer passed from father to son, but to the man elected by seven other princes called "electors." Those elected—usually from the House of Habsburg—valued the vast Habsburg holdings in Austria, Burgundy, the Netherlands, and (later) Spain over their German territories. While monarchs in England and France struggled against their feudal aristocracies to consolidate their power, the Habsburgs allowed the Holy Roman Empire to deteriorate into a loose confederation of autonomous principalities whose rulers defied central authority and cultivated differences that would keep their part of Europe fragmented for five hundred years. Unprotected by nature or a strong government, these tiny duchies became the unwitting battleground for the wars that followed the Reformation.

The Reformation—the sixteenth-century revolt against the corruption and worldliness of the Catholic Church—gave Germans of diverse political loyalties their first national hero. Martin Luther, the son of a miner who became an Augustinian priest, nailed his Ninety-five Theses against the misuse of absolution and indulgences to the door of the court church in Wittenberg in 1517. Basing religion on faith alone, introducing the liturgy in German, and eliminating the offices of the priests as intermediaries between man and God, Luther founded a new religion. By the same token, he divided Germany between Protestants (Lutherans) in the north and Catholics in the south, thus reaping additional benefits for the feudal princes, who were given power over the religion of their subjects.

The Reformation was followed by the Thirty Years' War (1618–48), the political reaction to this religious split, which decimated these small, defenseless German principalities. It is estimated that one-third the population of Germany died or starved to death during this war, as Bohemians, Danes, Swedes, Frenchmen, and Austrians fought back and forth, up and down across Germany, ravaging its cities and villages, farms and feudal strongholds, reducing it to what has been called a mere "geographical expression."

Dubbed by a French diplomat "one of the finest jewels in the French crown," the Treaty of Westphalia, which ended the Thirty Years' War, divided Germany into some three hundred principalities, duchies, free cities, and bishoprics—a rich mosaic of tiny domains, each with its own ruler, constantly squabbling and vulnerable to French encroachment. Too many of these sovereigns were petty tyrants who spent vast sums of money aping the French court at Versailles and indulging in ridiculous, often brutish behavior. To show his mistress what a man would look like falling from a great height, the Margrave of Ansbach-Bayreuth shot his chimney sweep down from the roof of his castle, while Wilhelm I, the Elector of Hesse, engaged in the highly profitable business of kidnapping soldiers for the army of his cousin, George III of England.

To compete with the rulers of other fiefdoms, German princes built up large, provincial bureaucracies that hampered the overall economy. Commerce ceased to thrive in a land where goods had to pass through countless frontiers and innumerable customs; a traveler on his way from Hamburg to Vienna, a little over 450 miles, had to negotiate ten different borders, each with its own passport control, customs check, and currency exchange.

This loss of economic vitality accounts in large part for the deterioration of the German middle class. Deprived of the commercial opportunities that gave their peers in other countries independence from the aristocracy, members of the German bourgeoisie were reduced to entering the lower echelons of princely administrations, where they degenerated into frightened little props of provincial establishments. Serving at the whim of autocrats, they grew servile, narrow, and unproductive. The caricature of the officious bureaucrat, toadying to his superiors and disdainful of his inferiors, stems from this period in German history. In undermining the independence of the middle class, this system of princely autonomy put a curse on Germany from which it did not recover until after World War II. As one German publisher wrote in 1758: "Every nation has its principal motive. . . . in England [it is] freedom; in Holland, trade; in France, the Honor of the King." The motive ascribed by this gentleman to his native Germany was "obedience."

Of the three hundred or so petty rulers whose fiefdoms made up the Holy Roman Empire, only the Habsburgs had any real power, but, as noted before, this was based on their holdings in Hungary, the Netherlands, Italy, and Spain. Three other German electors also held kingdoms and titles outside Germany. The Elector of Hanover was King of England; the Elector of Saxony was King of Poland; and the Elector of Brandenburg was King in Prussia.

It is with the last of these dynasties that we are concerned—the Protestant* House of Hohenzollern in Brandenburg-Prussia, which began its rise in the seventeenth century, successfully challenged the supremacy of the Catholic Habsburgs, and by the time Vicky entered the family, had become the preeminent dynasty in Germany. The Hohenzollerns based their success on militarism, authoritarianism, and political conservatism—beliefs and values clearly at odds with the teachings of Prince Albert.

THE HISTORY OF the House of Hohenzollern, like many family chronicles, is a tale of action and reaction, as sons rebelled against their fathers and ended by repeating, updating, and frequently magnifying the errors of their grandfathers.

The story starts in 1417 when the German Emperor, grateful for the services of Friedrich of Hohenzollern, created him Elector of Brandenburg, a district in northeast Germany around Berlin. Two hundred years later, Friedrich's descendants inherited the province of East Prussia, separated from Brandenburg by a hefty slice of Poland. With their lands scattered inconveniently around northeast Germany, the Hohenzollerns of Brandenburg-Prussia remained a second-rate power until the middle of the seventeenth century, when Friedrich Wilhelm of Hohenzollern (1620–1688), the father of what came to be known as Prussia, set out to expand his territory.

A formidable-looking man with a large nose and dreadful temper, Friedrich Wilhelm was called the Great Elector for his ambitious pursuit of the interests of his state. Only twenty years old when he became Elector of Brandenburg, he inherited a domain in ruins, devastated by the Thirty Years' War, the end of which was still eight years away. By playing one power off against another, however, he managed to strengthen his army, rebuild his cities and towns, and reorganize his treasury. At the end of the war he added the eastern half of Pomerania and several well-placed bishoprics to the family holdings.

* The House of Hohenzollern was not entirely Protestant; there was and remains today an ancient Catholic branch of the family from Sigmaringen in Swabia, near the Swiss border.

More important than these substantial additions of territory was Friedrich Wilhelm's concept of service to the state. In a day when other German princes taxed their subjects in order to indulge themselves in luxuries, the Great Elector followed a program of personal austerity, which earned him the loyalty of his people. By the same token, he demanded that the landed aristocracy, the so-called Junkers, pay for the maintenance of a standing army that he needed to defend his widely scattered territories.

In 1701 the Great Elector's son Friedrich bought the title of King of Prussia for himself and his heirs from the Emperor of Austria. The price was eight thousand soldiers and a promise to support the House of Habsburg in perpetuity. Crowned at Königsberg, East Prussia, on the Baltic Sea, Friedrich I of Prussia (1657–1713) was a dwarfish, humpbacked second son, whose father never forgave him for outliving his tall, handsome older brother.

A hands-off ruler, Friedrich I left decisions to his ministers and concentrated on spending money he did not have imitating the court of Louis XIV, including its sexual conventions. Although he was still in love with his black-haired wife, Sophia Charlotte, sister of George I of England, Friedrich I took a mistress *en titre,* a lady whose sole duty seems to have been promenading daily and showily with the King for one hour through the Palace of Charlottenburg, which he built for his wife.

After Sophia Charlotte's death, Friedrich remarried. The new Queen, who suffered from a kind of religious lunacy, materialized in his room one night in her underwear. Having heard all the superstitions about the "White Lady"—an apparition that was supposed to appear to Hohenzollern kings immediately before their deaths—Friedrich collapsed in fear. Turning quaint legend into self-fulfilling prophecy, he died a few days later.

Starting the seesaw pattern that was to plague the Hohenzollern dynasty and all of Europe into the twentieth century, Friedrich I's son, Friedrich Wilhelm I (1688–1740) rejected his father's way of life and reverted to the militarism of his grandfather. To reform the army, Friedrich Wilhelm I recruited soldiers from his own people, replacing the mercenaries employed by most princes of his day. Called the "Soldier King," Friedrich Wilhelm I declared military uniform the proper dress garb for gentlemen of the Prussian court—a tradition that did not die out until the last ruling Hohenzollern, Kaiser Wilhelm II, was toppled from his throne.

Of Friedrich Wilhelm's many eccentricities, perhaps the most bizarre was his collection of gigantic men. His agents roamed Europe, bribing and kidnapping men of over six and often nearly seven feet to serve in the ranks of the Potsdam grenadiers. His fellow rulers knew that no gift pleased Friedrich Wilhelm as much as one of these physical giants, and eventually, through fair means and foul, he acquired two thousand of them.

Because his father had loved France, Friedrich Wilhelm I hated it. Turning up his nose at French sexual mores, he chose to live quietly with his wife and twelve children, in whom he tried to instill solid Protestant virtues. Given this aggressively sober German upbringing, it is hardly surprising that Friedrich Wilhelm I's son, Friedrich II (Frederick the Great), pushed the pendulum back again and fashioned his life and his court directly after the French.

It was under Frederick the Great, who ruled during the last half of the eighteenth century, that Prussia grew to be a major power. Utilizing the army and treasury built up by his father, he increased Prussia's status and territory dramatically and fought the Austrian Habsburgs for dominance over the German-speaking peoples of central Europe. Frederick the Great became King of Prussia in 1740, the year that the Habsburg Emperor Charles VI died, leaving his crown to his daughter, Maria Theresa. Frederick immediately laid claim to the Austrian duchy of Silesia, a rich crescent of land that he wrested from the Empress in the War of the Austrian Succession.

Ten years later, Maria Theresa formed alliances with France, Russia, Sweden, and Saxony to win Silesia back. Allied only with England, Frederick fought half of Europe in the course of the Seven Years' War (1756–1763). It was a bitter struggle, but his military genius, dogged perseverance, and some well-timed luck* brought eventual victory. Under Frederick the Great, the Prussian army grew from 90,000 to 150,000 men and consumed three-quarters of the annual budget, prompting Mirabeau to say that Prussia was not a country that had an army but an army that had a country.

Frederick the Great spent the first half of his forty-six-year reign at war and the last half consolidating Prussia's gains. In 1772, he acquired what was known as West Prussia, the part of Poland that separated Brandenburg from East Prussia. With his lands joined and strengthened, Frederick devoted himself to proving that Prussia was the dominant of the two great German powers and belonged in the first rank of European powers along with England, France, Austria, and Russia.

A Prussian icon in his military and political pursuits, Frederick the Great was an arrogant Francophile in his artistic life, "a virtual foreigner" in the intellectual and cultural Germany of his day. He abhorred German literature, refusing even to recognize Goethe, while he corresponded avidly with Voltaire, whom he brought to live in his palace of Sanssouci. Frederick's literary output fills thirty volumes, and his highly competent musical compositions, like his writing, survive today.

Twenty years after Frederick the Great's death, Napoleon I, fresh from an easy victory over the Prussian army, visited Frederick's tomb in Berlin. "Hats off, gentlemen," he commanded his companions; "if he were still alive we should not be here." Queen Louise, wife of one of Frederick's successors, agreed. "We went to sleep on the laurels of Frederick the Great," she said.

THE PRUSSIAN KINGS who followed Frederick the Great—the Friedrich Wilhelms II, III, and IV—were pale imitators of the man his people fondly called

---

* *Notably the death of Empress Elizabeth of Russia, whose successor, Peter III (husband of Catherine the Great), idolized Frederick and ordered his soldiers to change sides.*

"Old Fritz." Friedrich Wilhelm II (1744–1797), a fat nephew of Frederick the Great, was a weak, sensual man who saw nothing more in the cultural romanticism of his day than a license for self-gratification.

The Hohenzollerns were not in any case (except Frederick the Great) interested in literature, philosophy, or the arts, and the Romantic movement, which swept through Germany in the late eighteenth century with an impact like that of Napoleon's army, seems to have passed them by unnoticed. German Romanticism was actually several parallel movements in intellectual and artistic fields, all sharing the belief that truth is better apprehended through intuition than by reason. Vastly appealing to a people with an ingrained sense of the mystical, the Romantic movement changed not only philosophy and the arts but eventually spilled over into political thought as well.

Up through the time of Frederick the Great, the Germans were cultural slaves of the French. In their romantic rebellion against French domination in the arts lay the first seeds of German middle-class pride, which eventually sprouted into German nationalism. That this process took as much time to germinate as it did was largely the fault of Friedrich Wilhelm II's painfully inept son, Friedrich Wilhelm III.

Like all Hohenzollern kings, Friedrich Wilhelm III (1770–1840) started his reign by repudiating the ways of his father, which in his case meant assuming a bogus militarism. Called the "simple" King by those who mistook dullness for virtue, Friedrich Wilhelm spoke in brief commands—"Proceed regardless!"; "Take into consideration!"; and "Put it right!" In spite of this, he was an insecure, wavering monarch who refused to join two of the European alliances (1799 and 1805) formed to fight Napoleon I, thus helping the French Emperor defeat Austria and gain control of central Europe.

In July of 1806, the victorious Napoleon created a new German political entity, the Confederation of the Rhine. Tied into a permanent military alliance with France, the Confederation was forced to support Napoleon's Grand Army of 170,000 men billeted in its territory and provide the French Emperor with more soldiers in case of war. Eventually, all the German states but four joined the Confederation, the most notable exceptions being Prussia and Austria. Within a month of its creation, the Confederation of the Rhine seceded from the German Empire, and on August 6, 1806, Napoleon forced Franz I of Austria to renounce the ancient title of Holy Roman Emperor,* thus erasing the last vestige of ancient German glories.

Friedrich Wilhelm III was now driven by an outraged populace to take on Napoleon virtually alone, and in a disastrous encounter, he and his army were quickly defeated. When the French took possession of Berlin, the King and his dynamic wife, Queen Louise, who had ridden beside him into battle, were forced to flee to the town of Memel, near the Russian border. They were so poor that the Queen wrote a friend to send her some underwear. "I possess but one set," she explained, "and have to stay in bed while it is being washed."

---

* He retained his Habsburg title, Emperor of Austria.

Meanwhile, the two victorious Emperors, Napoleon I of France and Alexander I of Russia, having failed to destroy each other, met on a raft in the Niemen River to negotiate the peace and trade outrageous flatteries. "If he [the Czar] were a woman," Napoleon said, "I think I would make him my mistress." Napoleon I admired Alexander I but had nothing but contempt for Friedrich Wilhelm III of Prussia, whom he left pacing the shoreline in the rain during the negotiations.

The heroine of the peace talks was Queen Louise, Friedrich Wilhelm III's blond, blue-eyed wife, sent to charm Napoleon into better terms for Prussia. Known as a great beauty and flirt, Louise was only mildly successful with Napoleon, who caddishly intimated that she had gone so far as to offer him her favors for the town of Magdeburg. "The queen of Prussia is really charming and full of coquettishness toward me," he wrote Josephine. "But don't be jealous. . . . It would cost me too dearly to play the gallant." Desperate by the end of their tête-à-tête, Louise seems to have thrown herself at the conqueror's feet to beg him to spare her country from annihilation. He asked her to rise and take a seat. "Nothing is better suited for cutting a tragic scene short," he explained. "Once a person has sat down, it turns into comedy."

Napoleon's comedy lasted for seven years—from 1807 to 1814. During that time the Prussians, humiliated by peace terms that deprived them of nearly half their territory, began to look at themselves for the first time as an embattled nation. As one historian* wisely noted, Napoleon made a great mistake in dealing with Prussia. Had he wiped it off the map, he would have been rid of it. Had he been more generous, he would have earned the loyalty of the Prussians. As it was, he was the unwitting catalyst that turned a submissive and apathetic people into a self-aware and vengeful war machine.

THE COMPLIANCE with which the average Prussian accepted Napoleon's victory appalled a small group of reformers,† and during the reign of Fritz's grandfather Friedrich Wilhelm III, they seized on Prussia's defeat to press on the King some much needed political changes. These included the abolition of serfdom, the institution of a council of ministers to advise the king, and the reorganization of town governments to include ordinary male citizens. The reformers also changed the Prussian army. They abolished corporal punishment and introduced universal military service, making it possible for anyone who qualified to become an officer.

Forced into a revolt against the French by his generals and this newly awakened populace, Friedrich Wilhelm III sent his army to pursue Napoleon as he limped away from Moscow in the famous retreat of the winter of 1812. The Prussian army was joined by Austria six months later. Aided by subsidies from England, an enlarged but largely untrained Prussian force and the more seasoned army of the Czar formed the kernel of the vast European uprising known

---

* *J. Christopher Herold in* The Age of Napoleon.

† *Men like Baron von und zu Stein and Prince von Hardenburg.*

as the Wars of Liberation, which eventually drove Napoleon back to France and off the throne.

During the Congress of Vienna, the nine-month orgy of peace talks and social functions that followed the victory over France, representatives of Austria, France, England, Russia, and Prussia redrew national borders designed to restore monarchical Europe and maintain future peace by a careful balance of power. Prussia was doubled in size by the addition of north Saxony and territory on both sides of the Rhine. After Napoleon's return from Elba and defeat at Waterloo, the Prussians gained three more towns in the Rhineland. Thus constituted, the new Prussia splashed diagonally across the center of Europe—a bulwark against France, strong enough to withstand Russia, but not so strong as to threaten Austria.

The least hint of nationalistic yearnings, however, terrified the Congress of Vienna, especially Prince Metternich of Austria, who associated nationalism with revolution.* Instead of a united Germany, the Prussians, Austrians, Hessians, Bavarians, and other principalities were once again scooped up into a loose confederation of thirty-nine states and four free cities. This new German Confederation was primarily a defensive alliance conceived, as one Prussian delegate put it, "to ensure tranquility" in Europe.

The Congress of Vienna ushered in a long period of conservatism, which effectively stifled German participation in the basic political trends of the nineteenth century toward nationalism and self-government. Called the "Metternich System," the new order depended on so-called legitimate monarchs, censorship, and police surveillance to preserve the outdated status quo. This suited Friedrich Wilhelm III of Prussia nicely. He supported Metternich's Central Investigative Commission for the Detection of Popular Revolutionary Activities, a task force that managed to unearth political heresies in any number of reasonable citizens, who were then forced to flee Prussia.

Having aroused its citizens to their political responsibilities during the Napoleonic Era, the Prussian government cut them down to pygmy size during the first half of the nineteenth century. Farmers, tradesmen, and bureaucrats brought up in servile obedience to authority fell back all too easily into their pigeonholes in a society topped by an unsympathetic monarch, a greedy aristocracy, and an arrogant military class. Even the 1830 July Revolution in Paris, which spilled over into Germany and toppled the Kings of Saxony, Brunswick, and Hesse-Kassel, did not affect the kingdom of Prussia, where renewed persecution of dissidents sent hundreds of people to prison and death.

But if the Prussian government willingly followed Metternich in the suppression of civil rights, it broke from Austria in economics and trade, establishing a new system of tariffs that excluded the Austrians and became a major threat to their power. Known as the Zollverein, the new customs union did

---

* In the case of Metternich, this was hardly surprising, as the greater part of the Austrian Empire was composed of non-Germans—Hungarians, Italians, Czechoslovakians, and so forth—ethnic groups who would prove themselves anxious to throw off the Habsburg yoke.

away with the internal customs duties that had crippled commerce for hundreds of years in Germany. As one after another of the German states joined the Zollverein, Prussia became the leading economic force in Germany—and gained a framework for future political dominance.

In 1840, the year of Vicky's birth, Friedrich Wilhelm III of Prussia died. The last monarch of the Napoleonic era, he left the Prussian people economically well-off but politically discontent. As Karl Marx observed, "There was universal agreement that the old system had had its day and would have to be abandoned, and what people had silently endured under the old King was now openly pronounced to be unbearable."

Because of this, the accession of forty-five-year-old Friedrich Wilhelm IV of Prussia (1795–1861) was met with great enthusiasm, particularly when he announced an amnesty for political prisoners, reduced press censorship, and offered concessions to the Catholic Church. When he also moved his court to Sanssouci, the home of Frederick the Great, the public took it as the sign of a fresh start. Those who knew the new King, however, realized that this was only the first expression of his passion for restoration—both architectural and political. For Friedrich Wilhelm IV, progress meant resuscitating a chivalrous paternalism that he mistakenly attributed to his ancestors and believed he could retrieve by renovating their castles, reviving the splendid liveries of their courts, and resurrecting rituals from the Middle Ages.

Mired in past glories and oblivious to the political currents of his day, Friedrich Wilhelm IV neither anticipated the Revolution of 1848 nor understood the reasons for it. Not until the overthrow of Louis Philippe in Paris and the threatened dissolution of the Habsburgs' Austrian Empire did he take action, and then it was the wrong one. While rulers in the south and west of Germany hastened to try to fulfill their subjects' demands for constitutional law, freedom of the press, and a unified nation, the King of Prussia did what generations of Hohenzollerns had done before him: he called out the Prussian army.

But the sight of his "beloved Berliners" getting themselves beaten and killed by his soldiers brought Friedrich Wilhelm IV to a quick accommodation with the revolutionaries. Riding through Berlin under the red, black, and gold flag of the new Germany, the King of Prussia promised "German freedom and German unity," but reneged as soon as the tide began to turn against the revolutionaries. All the Prussians got out of the Revolution of 1848 was a constitution that created two houses of parliament, chosen under a system that favored the rich, left the primary power in the hands of a king whose "divine right" was reaffirmed, and exempted members of the army from taking an oath to uphold it.

Meanwhile, a national assembly had convened in Frankfurt to write a constitution to unify all Germans. Nicknamed the "Parliament of Professors" because of the large number of academics in attendance, the high quality of their debates and their inability to get things done, the Frankfurt parliament got sidetracked into the issue of whether or not to include Austria in its plans. By the autumn of 1848, when it finally got around to the central issue of a German constitution, the revolution had collapsed. When the parliament promoted the King of Prussia to Emperor of Germany, Friedrich Wilhelm IV, king "by divine right," refused to accept a throne freely offered by a popularly elected assembly of ordinary men,* and in so doing postponed the chance to unify Germany. With the suppression of a few more uprisings, the Revolution of 1848 came to a dismal end.

The revolution did nothing to help Friedrich Wilhelm IV of Prussia solve the problem of Austria. When the tyrannical Elector of Hesse asked his fellow monarchs to support him against his own parliament, both the Austrians and the Prussians sent in troops. War between the two armies, vying for military jurisdiction in Hesse, seemed inevitable until Friedrich Wilhelm capitulated to the Habsburgs. Over the next few years, Prussia revenged herself for this diplomatic defeat by refusing to allow the Austrians into the Zollverein and reducing customs duties so much that Austria could not compete in the marketplace. More states, seeing Prussia's economic success, joined the Zollverein, and by 1853 it encompassed all of German-speaking Europe except Austria.

In 1857, the year before Vicky's marriage, Friedrich Wilhelm IV suffered a stroke, and by the time Vicky arrived in Berlin in February 1858, he was no longer functioning. The revolution had been over for ten years, but the basic problems that had caused the upheaval still remained.

Prussia in 1858 was a kingdom in transition—a state waiting to be a nation, a society waiting for a rationale, a court waiting for a king. It was this passage that Albert hoped to influence through Vicky. To start, the seventeen-year-old Princess had to learn to negotiate the court of Berlin, a world vastly different from anything she had ever known. Her aunt Feodora, Queen Victoria's German half-sister, worried about her. "The Princess is so young and inexperienced in the world," she warned, "and Berlin is a hotbed of envy, jealousy, intrigue and malicious knavery."

---

* Henry Kissinger blames the King's refusal of the German crown on Friedrich Wilhelm's belief that "only Austria had a historical claim to it," but this author believes it was more likely the King's belief in his "divine right" (Kissinger, The White Revolutionary: Reflections on Bismarck, p. 902).

CHAPTER
TEN

"Unmarried people do not know what happiness is."

PRINCESS VICTORIA OF PRUSSIA, *1859*

F OR A TEENAGE PRINCESS like Vicky, used to the harmonious, moralistic world of her parents, life in the confines of the Hohenzollern family was a shock for which neither Stockmar's warnings nor her father's lessons had prepared her. Added to the political tensions were rivalries and jealousies that invariably turned family occasions into verbal prizefights. Worse was the lack of affection between Fritz's parents.

"I shall be very curious to hear . . . from you of the different relationships in the family of which we have often talked," Queen Victoria wrote her daughter the week after her arrival in Berlin. "<u>How</u> do you find the relationship between the Prince and Princess . . . ?" she asked coyly a week later. "What a <u>sad</u> family it must be! How melancholy!"

The Queen's eagerness for descriptions of Vicky's squabbling in-laws fell somewhere between sympathy for her daughter and sanctimonious dismay. Everyone knew about the acrimony that existed between Wilhelm and Augusta. Their marriage, an enforced relationship of state, had been doomed from the start.

FRITZ'S FATHER, WILHELM, the second son of King Friedrich Wilhelm III and Queen Louise, had been a delicate child, subject to constant colds—a tendency that made him forever impatient with illness in himself and others. Easier to raise than his mercurial older brother, Friedrich Wilhelm IV, he was given no training beyond his military education, which began at age ten. Dutiful, sober, and religious, Wilhelm acquitted himself well in the Wars of Liberation from Napoleon, which were the high point of his life. His greatest sadness—an aborted love affair with Elisa Radziwill—underscored the virtues, limitations, and narrow sense of duty created by his peculiar upbringing.

Elisa was the big-eyed, rosebud-lipped daughter of a Princess of Prussia who had married a charming prince of the Polish Radziwill clan—thus downgrading her offspring in the eyes of the Hohenzollerns, who believed that members of their family should marry only royalty. The drama of Wilhelm and

Elisa's doomed courtship was played out over a period of nine years, during which his father, Friedrich Wilhelm III, dithered between his son and the pro-Russian (i.e., anti-Pole) faction at court, much as he vacillated between France and Russia during the Napoleonic Wars. In the end, Wilhelm was forced to give up Elisa, although one of her ancestors had been the wife of the Great Elector himself. When she died of tuberculosis at the age of thirty, Wilhelm had been married to Augusta for four years. "I always think of her; she was, and is still, the guiding star of my life," he maintained half a century later, at the age of eighty. Under these circumstances, it is not surprising that his wife could never please him.

Fourteen years younger than Wilhelm, Augusta was the daughter of the Grand Duke of Saxe-Weimar, whose court, for all its proximity to Prussia, seemed to belong to another world. The Duchy of Weimar was not only the first German state to give its citizens a constitution, but a center of the Romantic movement. Goethe had served as Augusta's grandfather's tutor, and her mother was the subject of some of his more rhapsodic poems.

Augusta's education, which was predominantly French, left her with a passion for France. The murder of her mother's father, Czar Paul of Russia, was the basis of her intense hatred of the Russians. Coming of age in an atmosphere of humanism, Augusta had acquired what was unusual for princesses of her day, a "very firm and independent character."

At the age of seventeen, tall and full of life and opinions, Augusta had entered into marriage with Wilhelm with few illusions. She knew about Elisa, but she was a determined and imperious young woman, Wilhelm was a charming challenge, and as a bride she tried to seduce him into love. But with nothing intellectual in common and her outsized pride to keep them apart, the marriage turned quickly into a state convenience. After the very difficult births of her two children—Fritz two years after the wedding and Louise seven years later—Augusta announced that their conjugal life was over. From then on, she concentrated on changing Wilhelm's political attitudes, a crusade at which she was no more successful than she had been at romance. A constant goad to her husband, she was extremely unpopular in the ultraconservative Prussian court. As time went on, she drew close to the Catholic Church, taking up the papal cause with the same zeal she applied to liberal politics. It was an odd dichotomy, one she never tried to reconcile.

Because she was so disliked at court, Augusta rarely stayed in Berlin past the social season. She spent summers in Baden, weeks in Weimar, and long stretches at her huge country palace in Coblenz. From there, she kept track of the comings and goings of other royalties and took umbrage when any of them passed by without paying her a visit. Reprimanded for doing just that, King Leopold of Belgium dubbed her "the Dragon of the Rhine."

As was usual with kings and heirs apparent, there were plenty of ladies eager to fill in for Augusta, and Wilhelm was blessed with the grace and manners that attracted them. "He could kiss one's hand as charmingly as any man," said the Empress Eugénie. But the ballroom charmer became a different person in the barracks and on the battlefield, exacting precise discipline from his soldiers and meting out excessive punishment to his enemies. It says something about Wilhelm that his was the only royal palace attacked during the Revolution of 1848 by the Berliners, who threw stones at his windows, painted graffiti on his walls, and set up a rallying cry, "Away with the Prince of Prussia." While he was in exile in England, his name was struck from the church prayers, and when word got out that he was coming home, twelve thousand citizens gathered in the Tiergarten to demonstrate against him.

Convinced by Prince Albert to join the Prussian assembly on his return, Wilhelm was hissed by his fellow delegates. Appointed commander of the anti-revolutionary forces of Prussia and Hesse, he put down the last remnants of the revolution with undue brutality and ordered summary executions of the revolutionaries—thus earning the order of Pour le Mérite from his brother, Friedrich Wilhelm IV, and leaving "the very name of 'Prussia' a horror" in southern Germany. When he and his family subsequently withdrew to Coblenz, he was advised by the mayor of the city not to go out into the streets unguarded.

By the time Vicky married Fritz ten years later, much of the animus against Wilhelm had dissipated. Tall and striking, with huge whiskers and the manners of a great chevalier, he was admired by the Prussians for his excellence as a soldier and pitied within the court for the misery of his marriage. Disillusioned with the wavering Friedrich Wilhelm IV, the public had begun to look forward to a change of kings.

WHEN VICKY ARRIVED in Berlin in the winter of 1858, there were two generations of Hohenzollerns at court. The older generation, ranging in age from sixty-two to forty-eight, included King Friedrich Wilhelm IV; Vicky's father-in-law, Wilhelm; and their two younger brothers, Charles and Albrecht. "If we four had been born the sons of a petty official," the King had once said, "I should have become an architect, Wilhelm a sergeant-major, Charles would have gone to prison, and Albrecht would have been a ne'er-do-well." There were also three sisters—Charlotte, Alexandrine, and Louise—but only Alexandrine, the wife of the Grand Duke of Mecklenburg-Schwerin, a neighboring duchy, lived in Germany.* In spite of her reactionary politics, Alexandrine sent a complimentary letter about Vicky to a friend in England, who showed it to Queen Victoria. Gratified that her daughter was found pleasing, Victoria was nonetheless irritated by the Duchess's comment that Vicky was "very small." This, the Queen wrote Vicky, "considering that you are a good deal taller than me, & I am not a dwarf, is rather hard."

Victoria did not realize that stories of Vicky's short stature had preceded her to Berlin, along with the kind of rumors prevalent in royal reportage—tales that made the English Princess sound nearly deformed and worried the Prussian

---

* *Charlotte was married to Czar Nicholas I of Russia, and Louise was the wife of a Prince of the Netherlands.*

royal family about the future of the dynasty. Since the Prussian princesses were all very tall (some reaching five feet ten inches) and some very fat, Vicky, with her diminutive body, did look undersized to her new relations.

Of all the Prussian relatives, Vicky's nemesis was Prince Charles, Fritz's fifty-six-year-old uncle, third in line for the throne. During the Revolution of 1848, Charles, an ultraconservative, had tried to maneuver his two older brothers, Friedrich Wilhelm IV and Wilhelm, out of the succession in order to establish himself as Regent for sixteen-year-old Fritz. In doing this, he had used Bismarck as his intermediary. Fritz's mother, Augusta, who had refused to take part in these machinations, never got over her fury at Charles and regarded Bismarck as her "mortal enemy."

Charles liked Augusta no more than she liked him, and he included Vicky in that hostility, going out of his way at court dinners to tell stories he knew would make the seventeen-year-old bride blush in front of her new relations. Both Prince Charles and his wife, Marie, who was Augusta's elder sister, resented their inferior position at court. Charles took out his frustrations in womanizing and political schemes, while Marie vied with Augusta in clothes, wigs, and jewels. Unlike the sober Wilhelm and intellectual Augusta, Charles and Marie ran a fashionable household, surrounding themselves with the sort of café society from which Vicky had been carefully protected in England.

Prince and Princess Charles had one son and two daughters. Their younger daughter, Princess Anna, was Fritz's favorite cousin. Vicky, who said that Anna had "the most splendid figure you ever saw," thought her gowns were too full in the skirt (even larger than the Empress Eugénie's) and far too low-cut. Having never been allowed to dance with anyone but princes, Vicky was shocked to find Anna "dancing about with everybody."

Princess Anna's brother, Prince Friedrich Charles, was three years older than Fritz. Known within the family as Fritz Carl and outside as the "Red Prince" (for his favorite Hussar uniform, not his politics), he was a morose bully—"one of the most brutal men in existence." Vicky was immediately drawn to his twenty-one-year-old wife, Marianne, whom she liked best of all the people at court.

When Vicky met Fritz Carl, he was excessively polite to her, and she could not understand why Marianne seemed "so cowed by her husband." Marianne, Vicky reported to her mother, "is very amiable, the cleverest of them, and decidedly the most sensible, but she has received very little education and stands terribly in awe of her husband." Three months earlier, however, Marianne had given birth to a daughter, their third. Fritz Carl, who had boasted of "the brave soldiers all his sons would make," was so infuriated that he boxed his wife's ears, leaving her with impaired hearing for the rest of her life.

Victoria's primary concern was that Vicky not grow too close to anyone in the Prussian royal family. "No familiarity—no loud laughing . . . ," she warned. "Kindliness, friendliness & civility but no familiarity except with your parents (in-law)." Vicky was also told to keep her opinions of her new relatives to herself, as every Hohenzollern palace harbored a spy. Victoria was particularly upset when her daughter made the mistake of sending a letter about the royal family by ordinary mail, rather than the usual private messenger.

"It was indeed most imprudent of me to have written as I did by the post —and it gave me a great deal of uneasiness after my letter was gone, but I hope you will forgive that piece of folly . . . ," Vicky wrote her mother in what would be the first of many abject apologies for minor sins. "But please, Mama and Papa, never cease to remark to me anything that strikes you as not right or anything you hear. . . . We shall always be deeply grateful—we are young and inexperienced in a difficult position, you have made for yourselves a reputation, and a happiness—such as no other—you will not deny your children your help —we know that all you say to us is only in our interest, and we wish to imitate your example."

That was the problem.

Prussia was not England, and Vicky and Fritz were not Victoria and Albert. This did not, however, prevent the Queen from trying to control every detail of Vicky's personal life, and the Prince Consort her political one. Advice sped to Berlin two, three, even four times a week. Albert, who mistakenly believed that the Prussians regarded Vicky's English background "as an asset," insisted that she keep her English title, the Princess Royal, thus causing resentment in the pro-Russian, anti-English court. When the Duchess of Orléans, one of the unfortunate French exiles and a much-beloved relative of Augusta of Prussia, died, Victoria took Vicky to task for following the practices of the Prussian court, which dictated a week's rather than a full month's mourning as in England. An excessive mourner herself, the Queen told Vicky that she had a duty "as my daughter and Princess Royal" to follow English practices within her own palace for those related—in this case very distantly!—to her English family, no matter what the custom in Berlin.

Proud of her daughter, Victoria was prone to give approval with one hand and take credit away with the other, reminding Vicky every so often of how difficult she had been as a child. "[W]hen . . . we receive your dear, clever, sensible letters—so full of all that is excellent and good and right, then we thank God for such a blessing as such a dear, distinguished and loving child is—and feel . . . rewarded for all the anxiety and trouble we had about you," she wrote at the end of her daughter's second month of marriage.

No matter how often or how completely Vicky wrote, it was never enough for the Queen. Even when she told her daughter that "an affectionate little line" would suffice, it never did. Victoria demanded fully detailed accounts—of the gowns and jewels Vicky had worn for particular occasions, her daily schedule, her feelings about Fritz, her health, how much exercise she took, how much time she spent in the fresh air, her menstrual periods, what she ate and drank, whether she was pursuing her drawing, what she saw at the theater and opera, the layout of her palace, the furnishings, outlook, and temperature of her rooms, the members of the Prussian royal family—how they behaved, what they said, what they wore, where they went. She insisted that Vicky number her letters consecutively and was irritated when she forgot.

When words were insufficient, Victoria asked for a little "scribble"—a drawing of rooms, events, or gowns that Vicky dutifully sent along, usually accompanied by apologies for the inadequacy of her sketches. The Queen also demanded complete weekly reports on Vicky's activities from her ladies-in-waiting, Wally Hohenthal and Marie Lynar, letters that caused the young women some consternation, as Vicky, whom they loved, was not above saying, "Don't tell Mamma this." Added to the domestic information required by her mother were the observations on the political climate of Prussia and Europe that Vicky exchanged with her father.

Albert, who limited his correspondence with his daughter to once a week, tried to get his wife to temper her demands. "If you knew how Papa scolds me for (as he says) making you write! . . . he says that I write far too often to you, & that it would be much better if I wrote only once a week! . . . I think however Papa is wrong & you do like to hear from home often."

To which Vicky made a careful response:

"Letters from home as you can fancy must always be a great comfort & delight to me; and I feel deeply grateful to you for spending so much of your precious time & thought upon me; but I think as a principle it is better not to write too much. . . . That your letters cause me pleasure, that I think you need not doubt; but I must say that my extended correspondence takes up a good deal of my time, particularly as I cannot write as quickly as you can."

One of the reasons the Queen clung to the correspondence with her eldest daughter was her need for female companionship. Ruling is a lonely business, and marriage, she felt, had turned Vicky overnight into a grown-up woman with whom she could exchange confidences she had never before been able to share. The Queen also wanted reassurance that Vicky's old home compared favorably with her new one. "[I]t gives me a pang . . . to see & feel my own child so much happier than she ever was before, with another," she wrote three weeks after Vicky's wedding. Nor would the Queen entertain the possibility that anyone, even her daughter, could be as well mated as she herself. "You know, my dearest that I never admit any other wife can be as happy as I am— so I can admit no comparison for I maintain Papa is unlike any one who lives or ever lived or will live!"

Nevertheless, Vicky was ecstatic with her Fritz. "I feel happier from day to day," she wrote her mother shortly after her arrival in Berlin; "in fact I never knew before what it was to be so happy." A few months later, she tried to explain. "I feel proud when I go out walking alone with Fritz, and when I look at his dear face and think that I belong to him & that he is my husband, that I have a right to be more to him than any one else; did you ever feel that dear Mama; at least I hope you will think it pardonnable."

Fritz, whose duties to the Prussian army would keep him away from home much of the time, was allowed to be with his bride during the first few weeks of their married life in Berlin. He took Vicky on long drives or walks in the Tiergarten, where, Vicky reported, people "stared" at them in surprise, as it was "quite unheard of" for a prince to walk or drive with his wife. "Fritz says he never can remember having seen his father and mother or any of his uncles walking together with their wives; but that usually the Princess drove out with the Lady in Waiting and the Prince with his Aide de Camp, and that they sometimes met each other in this way!"

Vicky's happiest moments were those spent alone with Fritz, although they were rare. The court in Berlin was far more active and formal than the one in London, with obligatory dinners nearly every night, theater and after-theater parties at her mother-in-law's palace. Wilhelm and Augusta were sticklers for protocol, demanding Vicky's attendance at every court function. The only Princess who pursued any intellectual or physical activities, she struggled to find enough hours.

"I'm sure that you will succeed in bringing order to your life and your thoughts and also find quiet time to devote to your intellectual development and spiritual growth," Albert wrote his daughter shortly after her arrival. "Your report on the situation in France is very well thought out. . . . you should devote one hour of your free time every day to this. . . . Are you dutifully reading the English and the German newspapers?"

Vicky and Fritz got up at eight and read together before breakfast. While he attended to his military duties, she read the papers and composed the essays demanded by her father, wrote letters, worked at her painting, and met with the members of her household—the Lord Chamberlain, who received her instructions for the day's meals, guest lists, and audiences; young Baron Stockmar, who dealt with her political and financial affairs; and Dr. Wegner, who checked daily on her health.

When Fritz returned, they had lessons together in everything from electricity and chemistry to German medieval history. Fritz's old tutors were pressed into service, as well as leading historians of the day. Vicky went back to studying geometry, which, she told her father, helped her organize her "stupid confused mind . . . I have such a wish to learn all I possibly can. . . . I always get so frightened now I have not got you to remind me now, that time is going on, that I have this and that to learn and to do; I always fear I am going back instead of forward if I do not continually remind myself of the necessity for activity. Laziness was always my greatest fault."

As time went on, Vicky rose earlier and earlier to make time for the reading and studies recommended by her father and the fresh air required by her mother. "I quite agree to what you say about my going out & taking more exercise," she wrote dearest Mama after a few months, "but here in Berlin it is perfectly impossible. . . . I am always out 2 full hours . . . dinner is always at 5 you know then one is in evening dress—consequently has to dress at half after 4, after dinner one goes to the theatre. I do not always, because I am usually so tired that I nearly fall asleep. . . . after the play we have to go to the . . . Prince and Princess. . . . if I did not secure the morning to myself, I should pass my whole time in doing nothing at all. . . . no one who has not been here can understand the busy idleness . . . that goes on."

Vicky was not the only one who suffered from the rigorous social schedule. "Being young and strong I bore up gallantly against these ghastly hours . . . ," said her lady-in-waiting Wally Hohenthal; "the only thing I could never achieve satisfactorily was the early dinner by daylight in full evening dress. . . . The afternoons were passed by the victims of these barbarous customs in a state of coma . . . and it is only latish in the evening that they begin to arouse themselves, for the amusements which filled the evening."

Sunday dinners, which took place between two and five in the afternoon, were attended by the entire Prussian royal family in full evening dress, jewels, uniforms, and decorations. On one of these occasions shortly after she moved to Berlin, Vicky was publicly reprimanded by Queen Elisabeth for sneezing while standing behind the King's chair. The young Princess made the mistake of saying that this kind of natural accident was not regarded as a sin "at home" in England. The Prussian court, particularly the pro-Russian contingent that saw its power waning with the ailing King, deeply resented Vicky's English origins, and her conviction that everything was better at home did not add to her popularity.

ONE OF VICKY'S DIFFICULTIES was the inconvenience of her living quarters. Since their own palace was in the process of renovation, she and Fritz took up temporary residence in the Royal Palace of Berlin, an enormous seventeenth-century structure, parts of which dated back even further. Standing on the main street of Berlin, Unter den Linden, it was the gathering place for the formal dinners of the royal family.

No one had actually lived in the Old Schloss for nearly twenty years, and Wally Hohenthal described it as "badly heated and hardly lit. Endless dark corridors connected huge mysterious-looking rooms, hung with large pictures of long-forgotten Royal personages; the wind whistled down through the large chimneys, and the unspoken terror of the 'weisse Dame'* brooded over all." Wally wrote that she lived "in constant dread" of meeting the apparition during the time she lived there with Vicky.

The suite of rooms assigned to the honeymoon couple was on the second floor of the palace. Very grand and gloomy, it had belonged to Fritz's grandfather, Friedrich Wilhelm III. In a gesture of reverence, the room in which he died had been left untouched by his children. Musty and frightening, this room was next to Vicky's private sitting room; each time she wanted to go to her bedroom or dressing room she had to pass through it. Moreover, the door between her sitting room and the "death chamber" had a habit of opening by itself, lending credence to stories that the palace was haunted by other ghosts as well as the White Lady. Fritz insisted on taking a solitary walk every evening

---

* *The White Lady, i.e., the ghost who was supposed to haunt the Hohenzollern family, appearing to members of the male line before their deaths.*

for an hour—a habit from his bachelor days—leaving Vicky alone with her fears.

Aside from the more macabre aspects of the Old Schloss, life in Prussian royal palaces, according to Wally Hohenthal, was one of "utter discomfort." There were "large and stately sitting-rooms, but wretched bedrooms, and no accommodation for the servants. I do not believe anyone washed in former days, for if you were lucky you found a basin, the size of an entrée dish of some precious porcelain, Dresden or Carl Theodore, and a bottle of water of priceless ruby glass."

No bathtubs, no toilets, no cupboards for Vicky's beautiful new clothes, and no alterations allowed without the ailing King's personal permission. Used to life in comfortless splendor, Fritz had difficulty understanding Vicky's needs; nevertheless, he ordered a bathroom built for her with hot and cold running water.

But the carpets in the Old Schloss remained dirty and threadbare; Vicky was expected to dress and read by the light of a single flickering candle; the family portraits lining her walls were permanently black from smoke, which none of the palace servants bothered to clean; and the English maids never stopped complaining that they could not attend to their mistress, since their rooms and all the kitchens and laundries were at the opposite end of the palace. A little over two months after Vicky's arrival, a large section of the ceiling in her sitting room fell with an enormous crash. "[W]hat a blessing that I was not standing where I always do . . . ," she wrote her mother; "it would have occasioned a serious bruise or have killed one. . . . [T]hings are so dreadfully neglected here."

Vicky had arrived in Berlin in the middle of a particularly harsh winter. Although she instructed the servants to keep the fireplaces going in all the rooms, the warmth did not penetrate the corridors and narrow stairways, full of icy drafts from arctic Russian winds that blew across the northern plains through ill-fitting windows and doors. From England, Victoria hounded Vicky about being too warm. She had provided her daughter with one of her famous ivory thermometers—the kind she placed on the mantelpieces of all her rooms —so that she would be equipped to check the temperatures in her new palace and guard herself from excessive heat. Victoria did not understand why Vicky complained about trying to keep warm. "The cold I am sure, dear, helps to keep you so well & brisk."

Vicky soon caught cold with a hacking cough. Queen Victoria to Vicky, February 18, 1858:

"I was distressed to hear of your having a cold—& a little cough tho' I am not surprised with the cold weather & at night the fearfully hot, oppressive rooms which Lady Churchill* says are dreadful. You fortunately do not suffer from them, as I & most people do but still you know how very unwholesome

---

* *Lady Churchill, a Lady of the Bedchamber to Queen Victoria, accompanied Vicky to Berlin to report to the Queen on her early weeks there.*

they are. I hope you keep your's [*sic*] not over-poweringly hot & air them & use my little thermometer?"

Queen Victoria to Vicky, four days later:

"You ought to have a capuchon* made . . . to put on at night. People think you didn't dress warm enough, which considering this fearful heat of the rooms at night . . . may be the case. . . . I asked you several questions . . . about your health, cold sponging—temperature of your rooms etc. & you have <u>not</u> answered one! . . . My good dear child is a <u>little</u> <u>unmethodical</u> & unpunctual still."

"I beg your pardon dearest Mama for not answering your question, you bear my confusions with great kindness and patience and I am very grateful for it . . . ," Vicky wrote back. "My rooms are exactly the same temperature as in England. . . . I always use my cold water baths every morning & could not exist without them. I always have your thermometer lying on my table. I have several times read good Sir James's† admirable letter of advice, which I keep sacredly under lock & key with your memorandums. . . . Will you tell him that I am most grateful for his advice, and will endeavour in every possible way to carry it out."

As Vicky was discovering, it was not always easy—even in minor matters —to satisfy the requirements of one court in another.

---

* *Hooded cape.*

† *Sir James Clark, Queen Victoria's physician, who had convinced the Queen of the salutory effects of cold air and exercise.*

CHAPTER
ELEVEN

"[W]e poor creatures are born for <u>Man's pleasure</u> & <u>amusement</u>."

QUEEN VICTORIA, *1859*

*E*ACH YEAR TOWARD THE END OF SPRING, the Prussian court migrated to Potsdam, sixteen miles southwest of Berlin. Called by a contemporary guidebook "the Prussian Versailles," Potsdam was built on the Havel River, which at this point in its course forms a lake with gently sloping, wooded banks. Vicky and Fritz arrived in early May of 1858. Married just three months, they moved into his parents' summer palace of Babelsberg.

Set on a hill with lovely green lawns rolling down to the river, Babelsberg was (and is still) a charming, faux Gothic, *altdeutsch* construction of turrets, turnings, and crenellated galleries. Inside, it was crammed with enormous furniture and creeping plants trained to climb over mirrors and screens—a more pleasing home for Fritz's bride than the Old Schloss in Berlin, but lacking in creature comforts.

Vicky complained that she was not allowed to move chairs and tables where she wanted them, that her floors were uncarpeted and noisy, and that there was nothing in the windows to block the sun. She blamed these shortcomings on the fact that German palaces had no women housekeepers, only what were called *Hofmarschalls*. Men, Vicky wrote her father, "cannot know about all these little conveniences, and cannot see that rooms look tidy and comfortable. I think it wants a woman's eye."

Nonetheless, Babelsberg was closer to the military headquarters where Fritz reported daily, and life in the country was simpler than in Berlin. Vicky's husband was now sent out on maneuvers for days at a time. "What shall I feel like this evening," she wrote him, "when I have to go to bed without my angel. . . . I cannot live without you . . . you are my protector, my dearest and best friend, my lord, my guardian angel, my better self."

Two days after she arrived at Babelsberg, Vicky slipped on a staircase and sprained her ankle. "[Y]ou and Papa will say, 'Vicky is so awkward and clumsy and always tumbles,'" she wrote home, explaining that she had been trying to get out of the way of a lamplighter who was coming up the steps of the palace as she was going down. That night, as she "did not like to make a fuss," she attended the opera. To reduce the pain and swelling next day, Dr. Wegner applied leeches, which made her sick and faint—"horrid slimy cold things slipping about. . . . I do not think I ever saw any before."

Marooned on the sofa in her sitting room, Vicky assured her mother that she was becoming neither lazy nor fat, but that she could not do as dear Mama wished and be carried downstairs: "[T]he stairs are so dreadfully steep and the passages so narrow, Wegner thought it dangerous and forbid[s] it." News that her father was coming to Coburg for a visit in late May provided a reason to obey the doctor.

But Dr. Wegner forbade her going to Coburg—not because of the ankle, which was healing, but because it looked as if she might be pregnant. Told she could not travel, Vicky was devastated. "I who had rejoiced at the very idea of seeing dearest Papa . . . to tell him all the thoughts I have been collecting for months to ask his advice about, and now to know this to be impossible is quite dreadful."

"It is not only a question of a nascent human life," Albert wrote his daughter, "but of your health and of your mutual future domestic happiness, of the founding of your family and the future of your country and people, and thereby one might almost say, the welfare of Europe. In comparison with the importance of this, all other considerations, desires, predilections must be suppressed."

But Albert changed his itinerary to include two days in Potsdam in early June with his favorite child. He was pleased with what he found and wrote Victoria that the "relation between the young people is all that can be desired. . . . I have had long talks with them both, singly and together, which gave me the greatest satisfaction. . . . Vicky . . . is very sensible and good."

The possibility of a pregnancy upset Victoria. The Queen, who had given birth to two children within the first two years of her marriage, had resented giving up what she called the "enjoyments, etc." of an unrestricted life—dancing, late parties, sex*—for the "constant precautions" plus the "sufferings and miseries and plagues" of pregnancy. "If I had had a year of <u>happy</u> enjoyment with dear Papa, to myself—<u>how</u> thankful I should have been!" she wrote Vicky. "But I was 3 years & ½ older; & <u>therefore</u> I was <u>in for it</u> at <u>once</u>—& furious I was."

When Fritz wrote some weeks later to say that the pregnancy was a reality, the Queen was no more resigned. "I must admit, dear Fritz, that what fills you

---

* *Medical theories of the day recommended extreme caution or abstinence in sexual relations throughout pregnancy. "I can see no law or reason which justifies the husband in approaching the wife for the purpose of sexual gratification, at any time during pregnancy," one doctor asserted as late as 1901 (Emma F. A. Drake, M.D., What a Young Wife Ought to Know, p. 90). The Victorians generally believed that "sexual indulgence" or even "amative excitement on the part of the mother, without indulgence" would damage the health of the unborn child or lead it into future vice (Edward B. Foote, M.D., Plain Home Talk, p. 224). If this was the advice given ordinary women, one can only imagine the restrictions placed on a queen carrying a future monarch in her womb.*

with joy, brings me sorrow and anxiety, for it is bound up with so much suffering and danger for the poor and very young mother! You men are far too selfish! You only have the advantages in such a case, whereas we poor women have to bear all the pain and suffering (of which you can have no conception)."

Vicky was apparently not much bothered by her mother's reaction. "That you regret my being (perhaps) in this state I can understand," she wrote, "but I assure you dear Mama, I think it no great hardship . . . if it is really true. . . . you know I love little children so much. . . . I own one must feel rather proud to think that one has given life to an immortal soul."

"What you say of the pride of giving life to an immortal soul is very fine, dear," Queen Victoria answered, "but . . . I think much more of our being like a cow or a dog at such moments; when our poor nature becomes so very animal & unecstatic."

"I could not help laughing at what you said in answer to my remark," Vicky wrote back; "being like an animal is very hard. But . . . I cannot look upon what God has ordained as a degradation, although I should be thankful indeed if we could be spared many things which shock our feelings of propriety."

Vicky suffered most of the annoying symptoms of pregnancy—morning sickness, dizziness, vomiting, headaches, problems with her teeth, and swelling of her feet. She looked quite ill to those around her. Although she complained regularly in letters to the Queen, she tried valiantly to hide her discomfort—not always easy for a girl on constant display. In the middle of an important military celebration, she felt faint and had to sit down. "I hope no one observed it," she wrote her mother, "as Princess Charles being tired asked for a chair too."

Vicky's pregnancy gave Queen Victoria more opportunities to send advice to Berlin and to give vent to long-repressed comments on the unfairness of being a woman. "I hope Fritz is duly shocked at your sufferings, for those very selfish men would not bear for a minute what we poor slaves have to endure."

> I know you will not forget, dear, your promise not to indulge "in baby worship," or to neglect your other greater duties in becoming a nurse [i.e., nursing the child]. You know how manifold your duties are, & as my dear child is a little disorderly in regulating her time, I fear you might lose a great deal of it, if you overdid the passion for the nursery. No lady, and still less a Princess, is fit for her husband or for her position, if she does that. . . . with your great passion for little children (which are mere little plants for the first 6 months) it would be very natural for you to be carried away by your pleasure at having a child.

Along with advice, Victoria sent corsets for Vicky's figure, tincture for her toothaches, camphor lozenges for insomnia, patterns for infant clothes, a baby quilt she worked herself, and detailed notes about her own confinements. The Queen had insisted that the young couple's physician-in-residence, Dr. Wegner, come to England shortly before the birth of her last child, Beatrice, born just nine months before Vicky's marriage, in order to "see how these things are managed here."

"My 2 first confinements . . . were far from comfortable or convenient . . . ," she wrote her daughter, explaining that she was "particularly anxious" that Vicky "profit" from her experience.

The Queen also sent Mrs. Innocent, the midwife who had attended her during the births of her children, and Mrs. Hobbs, a nurse for the baby. In August, two months after Albert's solo trip, she herself arrived with the Prince Consort and the family physician, Sir James Clark. Although Victoria and Albert insisted that their trip to Germany was no more than a family visit, they were accompanied by their new Foreign Secretary, Lord Malmesbury. And as if his presence did not make enough of a statement, the Queen also convinced Baron Stockmar to come out of retirement at Coburg to join the family at Babelsberg. Despised by the court for advocating parliamentary democracy in Germany, Stockmar was the bane of the conservatives, who were growing more desperate as Friedrich Wilhelm IV grew more frail. The visit, which helped Vicky's emotional well-being, damaged her and Fritz politically.

Still, the Queen of England was cheered in Berlin, where she mistook Prussian reverence in the presence of royalty for agreement with the English form of government. She attended a large and "dreadfully hot" dinner and was delighted to hear seventy-six-year-old Field Marshal Wrangel call Vicky "an angel." There was also the inevitable military review.

Sir James Clark, the Queen's physician, whose political observations often seem more acute than his medical ones, was disturbed by the ubiquity of "the perpetual uniform," observing in his diary that "none of the Royal family or princely class ever appear out of the stiff military dress." That this was indicative of a way of life soon became abundantly clear to Sir James. "The whole court seems occupied in playing at soldiers & the officers are perpetually occupied in drilling the young conscripts. . . . The officer corps seems to think of nothing but military matters. This is very sad." Even the Crown Prince, whose "agreeable manners" impressed the Queen's physician, seemed "devoted to military matters."

Victoria and Albert spent two and a half weeks in Germany, most of it at Babelsberg. Guests invited to dine with them had to leave Berlin in full evening dress at midday, since Augusta and Wilhelm served dinner at four P.M. When they were not entertaining, there were family evenings, during which Vicky played duets with her father and Victoria talked to Stockmar. There were also excursions to country castles belonging to the royal family. On one of these, Fritz and Vicky decided to acquire a summer home of their own.

In spite of Queen Victoria's delight with Babelsberg, which she called a "Gothic jewel," it was neither comfortable nor healthy for Vicky, whose blue boiserie bedroom was directly over the palace kitchen. Because of this, Prince Albert recommended that the young couple try to refurbish part of the Neues Palais, where Fritz had been born, for themselves.

A three-story, two-hundred-room structure, the Neues Palais had been built by Frederick the Great to demonstrate that Prussia was still rich and dangerous, unexhausted by the series of wars that had raised it into the pantheon of great powers. Surmounted with a cupola held up by three scantily clad ladies—supposedly representing Frederick's enemies: Maria Theresa of Austria, Catherine the Great of Russia, and Mme. de Pompadour of France—and designed to accommodate princely visitors, it was then and remains today one of the most lavish palaces in Europe. Magnificent marble galleries and huge public salons lead to ornate boiserie bedrooms. Nearly all the ceilings are embellished with delicate gold-leaf tracery.

Albert's choice of a summer residence for his daughter was by far the largest building in Sanssouci Park—a square mile of buildings, outbuildings, and gardens, which included two other palaces,* a church, picture galleries, an obelisk, a grotto, a Chinese teahouse, and two small temples. The Neues Palais is actually two palaces in one; the second, an enormous structure called the Communs, was built to hide a swamp behind the palace proper. In Vicky's day, it was used to house kitchens, laundries, servants' rooms, and offices.

Neglected for many years, the Neues Palais had fallen into filth and disrepair, occupied only by a few old servants who had taken refuge there along with large numbers of insects and vermin. Years later, Vicky said that she had found "1000's of dead bats . . . in one big empty room, and bugs by the 100. The beds I begged all to have burnt, but they were not. W.C.s and water there were none. . . . How furious the royal Hofmarschalls were with me when I rowed and complained and begged for money and reforms."

In spite of these drawbacks, Vicky and Fritz would love their new summer home. It was full of curiosities to restore, like the *Tassenzimmer* (cup room), a room shaped like a cup with conforming furniture, and the *Muschelsaal* (shell hall), a huge fantasy grotto with walls covered in nineteen thousand different kinds of stones and shells—everything from mother-of-pearl to fossil fish—taken from the lands conquered by Frederick the Great and arranged in designs as simple as swirls and as complex as dragons.

Before she moved into the Neues Palais the following summer, Vicky received instructions from her mother to install toilets, or as Victoria called them, "very <u>necessary</u> <u>conveniences</u>, which are <u>totally</u> wanting in <u>Germany</u> & really make one's life very uncomfortable & very unwholesome." The Queen, who had put them in Claremont and Kensington Palace, said that she was sure her daughter "would be benefitting <u>all</u>, if they could be <u>generally</u> introduced."

Vicky agreed, but her one attempt at indoor plumbing—a modern bath for herself in the Old Schloss in Berlin, had not been a success. "[H]ow was it arranged at Claremont, Holyrod [sic], Kensington & in the French Palaces . . . ," she asked, "when there are no pipes whatever in the house and no water laid on any where. . . . I do not know whether we may make such changes in the New Palace [Neues Palais]. . . . As to Babelsberg, I will certainly mention it to the Princess, because you know it is so bad there, there are mephitic smells

* *Sanssouci, which still exists, and Belvedere, seriously damaged during World War II.*

all the summer. . . . altogether it is quite dreadful in Germany without these things."

Vicky's campaign to bring indoor plumbing to Germany was never very successful. Twenty-three years later, she was still complaining to Queen Victoria that drainage and ventilation were nearly "non extant" and that she could give her mother "details which would make your hair stand on end!"

AFTER VICTORIA AND ALBERT had settled on Vicky's future summer home, they left Germany. Their departure was a tearful one, but within a few weeks Vicky's brother Alfred (Affie) came to see his sister, and two months later so did Bertie. Vicky, who adored her brothers, was under explicit instructions from England to watch carefully to be sure they benefited from their visits. Victoria and Albert had always used Vicky as a sobering influence on her brothers, and it is a mark of true sibling generosity that their affection for her withstood this unfortunate practice.

Affie, who was fourteen that year, commented pointedly on his sister's enlarged stomach, and Vicky, who had received no instructions from her parents, did not know how to respond. Victoria had adamantly refused to tell him about his sister's condition, choosing to believe that, although he was about to enter the navy, he was unacquainted with the most rudimentary facts of life.

The code by which the Queen shut her eyes and tried to close those of her children to sexual curiosity was not only silly but, in the case of Vicky, dangerous. Raised in an atmosphere where pregnancy itself was considered a social indiscretion, Victoria's eldest daughter was too embarrassed to even discuss her symptoms with her doctor. "Dearest Fritz . . . always talks to Wegner for me, and then tells me afterwards," she wrote her mother. "But I do not mind asking Wegner what I am to eat, or what medicine he wishes me to take or how long I am to drive. Wegner is so extremely discreet & pleasant in that respect."

It was this combination of Wegner's discretion, Vicky's ignorance, and Victoria's insistence on the proprieties that contributed to a situation which no one could have foreseen early in the pregnancy, but which, at the penultimate moment, nearly cost Vicky her life and that of her unborn child.

CHAPTER
TWELVE

> *"[T]he political reformation of Germany lies entirely in the hands of Prussia."*
>
> PRINCE ALBERT, 1847

WHILE VICKY WAS PREPARING to give birth to the next generation of Hohenzollern rulers, the old King, Friedrich Wilhelm IV, was deteriorating fast. At the time of Vicky's arrival in Prussia, he was still partially coherent, but as the months went by, he became less intelligible, jumbling his words and losing interest even in his beloved architectural projects. In the fall of 1858, eight months after Vicky's marriage, the Prussians were told that he was going to the Italian Tyrol for a rest. Before he left, his family insisted he sign over his powers to his brother Wilhelm, who assumed the title Prince Regent of Prussia.

"What a pity that he [Wilhelm] has not yet had any serious conversation with Stockmar on the difficulties ahead of him!" Albert wrote Vicky. "I cannot understand how anyone dares to enter upon such a hard and dangerous struggle unequipped, unarmed, unprotected, and unaided."

But Wilhelm sailed into power on a hopeful crest of Prussian dreams. Many managed to forget his cruelties during the Revolution of 1848. Others, who had chafed at life under a king who walked dutifully behind the Emperor of Austria and took his political cues from the Russian Czar, now looked to his younger brother to change the national agenda. Their hopes for progress seemed justified when Wilhelm dismissed Friedrich Wilhelm IV's reactionary Prime Minister, Otto von Manteuffel, as well as his Chief of Police, who had harassed Wilhelm for his advocacy of England during the Crimean War and set his spies poring over Vicky's letters to her parents. Now, Vicky informed her mother, it was no longer necessary to send everything important by messenger.

On the surface, the new Regent seemed to be steering Prussia toward the kind of enlightened monarchy advocated by German liberals and the Prince Consort of England, who hailed the "new era" as the dawn of a new Prussia. But Wilhelm was at heart an unshakable conservative, and his actions had little to do with reform. His antipathy to Manteuffel was based not on Manteuffel's reactionary ideology but on his role in capitulating to Austria after the Revolution of 1848. Wilhelm's apparent antagonism to the Conservative Party had less to do with its place in the political spectrum than with the intrigues of the court camarilla that supported it. And when he replaced two conservative ministers with liberals, he was only trying to keep his royal authority independent of all political parties.

Albert and Victoria rejoiced along with Vicky when Wilhelm's appointed Prince Charles Anton of Hohenzollern, a member of the Catholic branch of the Hohenzollern family, as Prime Minister. "Prince Hohenzollern" was a great favorite of the English royal family and had been a guest at Fritz and Vicky's wedding. More progressive in his thinking than most men of his class, his appointment as Prime Minister helped elect a liberal majority in the Prussian Chamber of Deputies.

"You may indeed congratulate us on the change which has taken place," Vicky wrote her father in a state of naïve political euphoria. "This is indeed a most important step & one which will satisfy the nation, please all patriotic men, raise the Prince in the eyes of all, make his work easier for him, in course of time I hope restore this country to its place and position in Europe, & altogether do Germany good. This measure will put an end to the X . . . Party* & make the Queen† very angry & her friends too. Whether the poor King will understand what is happening I do not know, he ought to be thankful to his brother for trying to repair the evil his reign has done."

It was all very well for Vicky to write this sort of letter to her father, but in the excitement of the moment, she made the mistake of expressing her delight over the political changes to one of the gentlemen at court. Her words, repeated and exaggerated, created deep, undying resentment in members of the Conservative Party, especially their representatives at court, the pro-Russian camarilla.

Had someone with political savvy counseled her during this period, the new Prussian Princess might have been saved a lifetime of ill will. But Vicky was only following the lead of her father, who bombarded the Regent with advice on what to do and how to do it—presumptuous letters on liberalizing the Prussian government, which, it is said, Wilhelm did not always open. If Albert was that mistaken about the Regent, it is not surprising that Vicky was similarly naïve about his court.

Moreover, the tendency of courtiers to report only the good and suppress the uncomfortable prevented Vicky's parents from seeing what was really happening in Berlin and from advising their daughter more realistically. Reports like that of the Duchess of Manchester, Mistress of the Robes to Queen Victoria, who visited Prussia during the military maneuvers of 1858, were misleading:

> The English could not help feeling proud of the way the Princess Royal was spoken of, and the high esteem she is held in. For one so young it is a most flattering position, and certainly as the Princess's charm of manner and her kind unaffected words had in that short time won her the hearts of all the officers and strangers present, one was not astonished at the praise

---

* The ultraconservative party, sometimes called the Kreuzzeitung Party.

† Elisabeth, wife of Friedrich Wilhelm IV.

the Prussians themselves bestow on Her Royal Highness. The Royal Family is so large, and their opinions politically and socially sometimes so different, that it must have been very difficult indeed at first for the Princess Royal, and people therefore cannot praise enough the high principles, great discretion, sound judgement and cleverness Her Royal Highness has invariably displayed.

The Duchess was dead wrong. If there was anything the Prussian court did not admire, it was the new Princess's principles and her cleverness.

ON VICKY'S EIGHTEENTH BIRTHDAY, November 21, 1858, she and Fritz moved into their own palace* on the main street of Berlin, Unter den Linden. An updated seventeenth-century structure with a plethora of Corinthian columns, it struck Wally Hohenthal as an "ugly structure . . . with not a good room in it." Wally complained that Vicky furnished it too much like Osborne House on the Isle of Wight, but Vicky loved her alterations, particularly the red-and-green marble added to the staircase and the white and gold paint that lightened the doors of her private apartments.

Her new home was next to the Opera House, which opened onto Opera Square—an open space with the royal library in one corner and a cathedral in another. On the opposite side was the Prince Regent's palace, where Wilhelm lived on the ground floor and his wife one floor above.

The physical separation of husband and wife was an apt metaphor for the emotional and intellectual distance between them, a rift that already posed a major problem for Vicky. Like others, she found her father-in-law's old world gallantry appealing, but her assigned role as the missionary of progress made it hard for her to talk to him on any but a superficial level. Vicky also realized how little Wilhelm actually cared for his son and how much he mistrusted him politically. (He had invited Fritz to attend meetings of the crown council, but had forbidden him to speak.) Thanks to her careful upbringing and Wilhelm's considerable charm, she succeeded in preserving a veneer of dutiful and caring daughter. At the same time she managed to appease her ever-demanding mother-in-law.

If Wilhelm was a difficult father-in-law, Augusta was, in the words of a frequent visitor to court, "one of the most disagreeable persons imaginable." Intelligent but resentful, disappointed and insatiable, Augusta took out her own insecurities in fomenting intrigue among others. Because of this, she neither inspired nor received loyalty from relatives or courtiers. Her sister, Princess Charles, loathed her, and one of her favorite ladies-in-waiting had an affair with her husband.

"Mama is influenced by such fluctuating moods," Fritz had warned Vicky before their marriage, "that sometimes when opinions differ it is wiser to pretend to agree so as not to irritate her still further." While Augusta's son took the

---

* *Called the Kronprinzenpalais (the Crown Prince's palace).*

road of least resistance, Vicky tried to rationalize her mother-in-law's waspish temperament by attributing it to her "active restless mind," which needed "a larger field" like politics in which to graze. She felt sorry for Augusta at first, but soon wrote home, "I know what it is to suffer from the faults of her temper, and it is that that makes her so little beloved."

To make up for her lack of popularity, Augusta had created around herself a maelstrom of social activity into which her new daughter-in-law was expected to plunge. Vicky was remarkably patient, particularly for a young woman accustomed to parental bliss: "[I]t is really a pleasure when I can do something to please or to pacify her . . . ," she wrote home, "but how anyone can exist in that perpetual whirl of excitement, annoyance & fatigue . . . is a miracle to me."

As the eighteen-year-old Princess approached the end of her pregnancy, her own mother's demands, accentuated by distance and worry, also grew more unreasonable. Vicky had sent Victoria a description of the christening of the ill-fated* daughter of Fritz's cousin Fritz Carl and his wife, Marianne. As was the custom in the Prussian royal family, the new mother watched the service reclining on a sofa in a recessed room at the side of the altar.

In response, Vicky received a letter from the Queen, insisting that she "promise . . . never to do so improper & indecorous a thing as to be lying in a dressing gown on a sofa at a christening! It would shock people here very much, & as my daughter & an English Princess I expect you will not do it." This letter —which included admonitions never to forget what she owed both England and Prussia plus the Queen's assertion that there was "nothing in these two-fold affections and duties which need ever clash"—finally jarred Vicky out of her usual deference.

"I think I am not likely to forget . . . the duties I owe to my country . . . ," she replied. "But my first duties are here now, and in fulfilling them to the utmost I can only be doing what my own country would wish and expect. . . . as to the possibility of being . . . on a sofa at . . . a christening, I can give no promise against. . . . I fear I should make myself justly disliked if I showed a contempt for a custom which is after all an innocent one."

It was about this time that old Baron Stockmar, who kept up with Vicky through his son, her personal secretary, decided to do something about Victoria. He approached her former Foreign Secretary, Lord Clarendon, who was visiting Berlin at the time. "I want to talk to you on a very important matter and to invoke your aid," Stockmar said.

It relates to this poor child here. Her mother is behaving abominably to her; and unless a stop can be put to her conduct I know not what may be the consequences, for she is not in good health, and she is worried and frightened to death. The Queen wishes to exercise the same authority and control over her that She did before her marriage; and she writes her constant letters full of anger and reproaches, desiring all sorts of things to

---

* *The child died in infancy.*

be done that it is neither right nor desirable that she should do, and complaining . . . of her forgetting what is due to her own family and country, till the poor child . . . is made seriously ill.

Vowing that he was going to write Queen Victoria "such a letter as she probably had never had in her life," Stockmar asked Clarendon to discuss the matter with Prince Albert. The Prince Consort admitted to Clarendon that he, too, questioned "the 'aggressive' system" his wife had pursued regarding their children, but rationalized his acquiescence to Victoria on the madness of her uncle George III,* which, he was afraid, might be "excited by an opposition to her will." Nevertheless, judging from Victoria's subsequent letters, Albert must have convinced his wife to moderate her demands on Vicky.

What seems to have escaped the well-meaning participants in this somewhat comical exchange is the irony of Baron Stockmar's new-minted concern about Vicky. It was Stockmar who had originally pushed Vicky's marriage to Fritz. And it was he who had issued frantic warnings to Vicky's parents, aimed at making sure that the English Princess was properly trained to carry out her mission abroad. Now that Vicky was trapped between two irreconcilable cultures, Stockmar suddenly began to worry about the position in which he and her family had placed her.

His empathy had clearly come too late.

---

* *George III suffered from porphyria, an agonizing disease of which one symptom is intermittent psychosis.*

CHAPTER
THIRTEEN

> *"It may well be claimed that Queen Victoria's greatest gift to her people was a refusal to accept pain in childbirth as woman's divinely appointed destiny."*
>
> ELIZABETH LONGFORD

*T*HE FACTS SURROUNDING THE BIRTH of Vicky's first child, the future Wilhelm II of Germany, will never be fully known. But because of the unsettled nature of her eldest son—an instability blamed by many on the circumstances of his birth—several versions have sprung up over the years to fill the vacuum left by royal reticence. Dr. Eduard Martin, chief of obstetrics at the University of Berlin, presided over the event and issued a written report* which, along with letters and cables sent to Queen Victoria by Dr. James Clark, tells the most reliable story. But since professional ethics called for doctors to cover up for each other, none of the available information can be taken completely at face value.

"[W]hen I look at the baby things & feel I shall not be, where every other mother is—& I ought to be & can't—it makes me sick & almost frantic," Queen Victoria wrote Vicky two months before the baby was due. "Why in the world did you manage to choose a time when we could not be with you?"

Committed to being in London for the opening of parliament, Victoria sent her midwife, Mrs. Innocent; her doctor, James Clark; and a bottle of chloroform, the recently discovered painkiller that had helped her through her own last two confinements.† The Queen took every precaution for Vicky's welfare except one—instructing her daughter in the basics of the birth process.

Vicky's labor began shortly before midnight on January 26, 1859, the day after her first anniversary; she spent the rest of the night on the bed prepared for the birth or walking around the room, supported by Fritz, Countess Blücher, and Countess Perponcher, "clutching" a table when the pains came.

At the onset of labor, the court physician, Dr. Wegner, who lived in the palace with the young couple, wrote a note to Dr. Martin, the specialist whom

---

* *Released seventy years later, when his son felt he must defend his father's name and reputation from the now-dethroned Kaiser.*

† *Victoria's use of chloroform made it fashionable; it was known as anesthesia* à la reine.

Vicky's father-in-law had engaged for the confinement,* telling him to come to the palace. Wegner gave the note to a palace servant. Instead of delivering it, the man put it in a mailbox, which meant that it did not arrive at the doctor's residence until eight o'clock the next morning, after Martin had already left on his rounds. It was not until 10:00 A.M., when Martin was getting into his carriage to go to the lecture hall, that the note was handed to him along with the rest of his morning mail. At the same time, another footman appeared asking him to come immediately. It was almost too late.

When Martin arrived around 10:30 A.M. at the palace, he walked into a nearly completed tragedy. After eight or nine hours of agonizing and fruitless labor, during which Vicky had screamed and moaned and "begged everyone for forgiveness," she lay exhausted in a state of semiconsciousness. Fritz, who had been forced several times to "put a handkerchief in her mouth . . . to keep her from grinding her teeth and biting herself," was in despair, as were Countess Blücher and the midwife, Mrs. Innocent. The doctors had given up trying to help the young Princess, and one of them had actually said "in her presence" that he thought both she and her baby "would die." Obituary notices were on their way to the newspapers.

Presiding at royal births was always a dangerous business,† and the doctors obviously preferred to let Vicky die rather than expose themselves by interfering with the natural course of events. Fortunately for Vicky, Martin was able and willing to take charge. First, he insisted on an internal examination, from which he determined that the infant was in a breech position‡ and would have to be manually turned and/or extracted from the mother's womb.

Dr. Clark later assured Queen Victoria that Wegner had discovered the breech "long before Dr. Martin arrived." But Augusta wrote Victoria to the contrary, and it is doubtful that Wegner, a typical court physician, would have jeopardized the sensitivities of his royal patient by conducting the necessary examination. As it was, he tried to cover himself in a report to Queen Victoria, writing that a "difficulty, which could not have been determined earlier . . . delayed the course of the delivery and endangered in particular the life of the child."

What Martin found on his arrival was a patient in spasmodic labor, which, though "very painful," had been "of little consequence" in expelling the infant. He told Clark to give Vicky a few whiffs of chloroform, which seemed to help, although she still "complained of unbearably great pain, and begged in the most touching fashion for compassion and forgiveness." Martin gave her a uterine stimulant to increase the frequency and intensity of the pains. Ordering Clark to assist the now seriously debilitated girl with heavy doses of chloroform, he undertook to remove the child.

---

* *Apparently at the suggestion of old Baron Stockmar.*

† *Old Baron Stockmar, a trained German gynecologist, had declined to assist at the accouchement of Princess Charlotte, knowing that as a foreigner he would be blamed if she died.*

‡ *Today, in a case like this, a cesarean section would be performed.*

In his report Martin described how he extracted the infant, who was born "seemingly dead" but started to breathe "after the usual life saving attempts" had been made. "After careful consideration of all circumstances and in view of my many years of experience," he said, "I am . . . of the opinion that the Prince, if I had acted differently, would have lost his life."

This is probably accurate. It was Martin's skill and willingness to assume responsibility for the consequences that brought Vicky through the process and produced a living infant. What is questionable in the proceedings is not Martin's ability, but the role of Dr. Wegner. Not only did professional jealousy apparently interfere with Wegner's duty to his patient, but once the specialist arrived, the court physician tried to hinder the administration of chloroform, admonishing Clark over Martin's orders not to give the suffering girl "so much." From this, one might conclude that Wegner was more interested in protecting his own skin than in helping Vicky. Whatever the explanation, incompetence or malfeasance nearly cost the Hohenzollerns an heir to the throne.

Once the child was born, it took some time for Martin to start it breathing,* and there may well have been loss of oxygen to the brain during the hiatus. "[S]ince it was brought in immobile and still," Augusta wrote Victoria, "we all thought it had died." . . . "Then I heard people rubbing the child and doing all manner of things to it, and then a cry and immediately following another voice saying: 'it is alive and it is a boy.' " A 101-gun salute informed the Berliners that there was a new heir to the Prussian throne. "Soon after the salute," Augusta continued, "the crowd [outside the palace] grew to such an extent that the three of us [Wilhelm, Augusta, and Fritz] had to step onto the balcony, where we received cheers." That evening, Wilhelm hosted a celebratory dinner for the royal family.

Vicky's mainstays through her trial were her husband and Countess Madeleine Blücher, a round, ruddy-faced Englishwoman of indeterminate age—a friend of Augusta, an intimate of Queen Victoria, and one of the few women Vicky could trust in Berlin. Even Dr. Clark, who criticized the ladies attached to Vicky, said he had "rarely met a woman . . . of more good sense" than the Countess. "[T]he friendship of this lady . . . ," he wrote in his diary "is one of the most fortunate circumstances attending the Princess . . . in her adopted country." Always in the room as the representative of Queen Victoria when Vicky gave birth, Countess Blücher was a much-needed source of maternal kindness and wisdom.

"God be praised for all his mercies and for bringing you safely through this awful time . . . , Victoria wrote her daughter two days later. "My precious

* We know from Martin's report that it was half an hour before he handed the baby to Mrs. Innocent to put him in the waiting bath. From a recent article, we have the following information. "It is likely that the future Kaiser was hypoxic (hyposia is a reduction in oxygen) for eight to ten minutes, possibly even longer, sufficient to produce what we now call 'minimal brain damage.' " It was this damage that "set the background" for Wilhelm's "hyperactivity and emotional lability [instability]." (William B. Ober, "Obstetrical Events That Shaped Western European History," The Yale Journal of Biology and Medicine 65 [1992], pp. 208–9.)

darling, you suffered much more than I ever did." Indeed, according to Dr. Clark, even Dr. Martin "was observed to shed tears" over Vicky's agony, while Clark himself, who used up two-thirds of a bottle of chloroform during the proceedings, reported to Vicky's mother that he could never "go through such" an ordeal again.

IN THE EUPHORIA that followed the birth of an heir, no one seems to have noticed that the infant's left arm hung useless from its socket. Nerve damage was (and is still) not uncommon in breech births like Wilhelm's, where speed is of the essence in saving the life of the child; even today, half of all breech babies delivered vaginally suffer some damage. But it was three or four days after Wilhelm's birth before Mrs. Innocent discovered the lifelessness of the arm and showed it to the doctors, who informed the child's father.

According to Martin's son, the disability was caused by "disastrous" pressure on the nerves that control the arm at the neck, a result of the position of the baby in the womb, along with the problems of the birth—the loss of amniotic fluid and the spasmodic nature of Vicky's contractions. He denied that an injury could have taken place during the birth without his father's discovering it. Newborns are routinely examined by the obstetrician immediately after birth, and in the case of royal infants, were shown to official witnesses within minutes of their appearance in the world.

Once the deformity was discovered, the doctors minimized its seriousness, indicating that it would improve with exercise, and agreed to postpone telling Vicky, who "hovered for days between life and death." (Since Prussian infants were swaddled in layers of clothing, she would not have noticed it herself.) When they finally told her, she, like Fritz, accepted the doctors' diagnosis and wrote nothing about it to her parents. The public, of course, was not informed.

The fact that Vicky said little about Wilhelm's arm at the beginning of his life, however, does not mean that it did not haunt her day and night. Ignorant of her own anatomy and frightened of the doctor whose hands had invaded her womb, she must have suffered from severe guilt over her son's arm. Had she injured the child when she fell down the stairs at Babelsberg? Had she not borne down strongly enough during the birth process? If she had labored harder or withstood the pain with more fortitude, Martin might not have had to pull the baby out with such force. Vicky would always believe that Wilhelm's arm was wrenched during his birth. Brought up to account for her every thought and action to an excessive degree, the barest possibility of having contributed to the deformity would have led to terrible feelings of culpability, reinforced every time she looked at her son.

Unable to voice her worries, Vicky could and did share with her mother— in veiled terms suitable for letters—their now common experience of childbirth, a subject that Victoria had warned her to discuss with no one else. "You ask me in your letter how I liked Wegner through this whole disagreeable business," she wrote. "I can only say that he has showed a great deal of tact, discretion, feeling during the whole time & that he is personally very agreeable to me, but I do not know what I should have done without Sir James."

Poor Martin, when I first saw him I took a violent dislike to him. I thought him vulgar, rough and fancied he was indiscreet, but it was very wrong I am sure because he is an excellent man & I feel the greatest confidence in his skill, but now I feel so much ashamed that although I quite retract my former opinion of him I never can look him in the face. . . . Mrs. Innocent is perfection of a nurse and a good kind person with such nice manners, a real comfort to me. . . . There is not much love lost between her and Wegner.

What seems clear is that Vicky was never made aware of the extent of Dr. Martin's role in saving her life and that of her child. Certainly Wegner did not give his colleague the credit due. The court doctor went to some lengths in his report to point out "slight indications of bruises" on the inside of the child's upper arm and in the armpit, which, he claimed, "must have occurred when the arms were moved at birth."

With Wegner as her primary source of information, it is small wonder that sixteen years and eight births later, Vicky would continue to blame Martin for Willy's useless arm, writing her mother that she still had "a horror" of Martin and "the bungling way in which I was treated." Like most people in pain, she clung to familiar hands and faces—dear old Dr. Clark, in whom her mother had enormous faith; Mrs. Innocent, who had appeared at the birth of her sister Beatrice at home; and Dr. Wegner, who seems to have been more courtier than medical practitioner.

IT WAS SOME TIME before Vicky recovered from Wilhelm's birth. Christenings in the Prussian court usually took place three weeks after birth, but Wilhelm's was postponed owing to his mother's delicate health until he was almost six weeks old.

He was christened Friedrich Wilhelm Victor Albert. "We are thinking of calling him Wilhelm," Fritz wrote to an aunt, "in order to lessen the confusion which is liable with the legions of Fritzes." Young Wilhelm was given forty-two sponsors, a "somewhat alarming" number, according to Victoria. "May our dear child only possess one quarter of all your virtues . . . ," Vicky wrote her father; "this was my earnest prayer during the ceremony which has just taken place."

As a compromise between Prussian and English custom, Vicky was seated at the door of the chapel during the ceremony, which took place under a purple canopy embroidered in jewels and golden crowns. "Afterwards," she told Victoria, "I shall sit in an arm chair in the blue room, and the whole company will pass before me as they do at your balls and drawing rooms without speaking."

According to the wife of the British Ambassador, Lady Bloomfield, Vicky seemed "flushed and nervous," spoke in a weak voice, and looked as though she still needed "considerable care." Victoria and Albert's formal representatives at the christening also returned from Berlin with descriptions of the new mother that raised concern in the English court. "I gather from them that you look rather languid and exhausted . . . ," Albert wrote his daughter.

I am, however, delighted to hear you have begun to get into the air. Now pass on as soon as possible to cold washing, shower baths, etc., so as to brace the system again, and to restore elasticity to the nerves and muscles. . . . In reference to having children, the French proverb says: *Le premier pour la santé, le second pour la beauté, le troisieme gâte tout.** But England† proves that the last part of the saying is not true, and health and beauty . . . are only injured when the wife does not make zealous use of the intervals to repair the exhaustion, undoubtedly great, of the body, and to strengthen it both for what it has gone and what it has to go through.

Vicky's health, to say nothing of her child's, would have responded more quickly had she been allowed to follow her own instincts and nurse her baby. But neither her mother nor her mother-in-law approved of such practices, and a wet nurse was immediately engaged. Nursing was considered inconsistent with the more exalted obligations of a royal princess.

Both Vicky and Fritz adored their baby and lavished enormous affection on him. The first of nine siblings, Vicky had always loved infants, but it was Fritz who proudly carried young Wilhelm around the palace. "Papa . . . ," Victoria wrote Vicky, "cannot quite enter into Fritz's ecstasy about him [William]; he never has felt that himself. After a certain age if they are nice . . . he is very fond of playing with them."

Victoria herself, she said, had "no adoration for very little babies, (particularly not in their baths till they are past 3 or 4 months, when they really become very lovely) still I know what a fuss and piece of work was made with you; far too much I think. . . . All that was very foolish, & I warn you against it—but one is very foolish with one's first child."

"I think and hope we are sensible with our little boy . . . ," Vicky answered, explaining that she saw her baby early in the morning while she was dressing or, if he was not awake, just before breakfast, and twice more during the day. "I am completely guided by Mrs. Hobbs‡ who knows what is good for him, I never interfere in any thing as she must know best; and I never would think of showing him to any one without Fritz's being there or having given his especial permission. He is really a dear little child, he is so intelligent and lively & cries so little, but as he is so forward, great care must be taken not to excite him."

---

* *The first for health, the second for beauty, the third spoils everything.*

† *I.e., Queen Victoria herself.*

‡ *The baby nurse sent by the Queen from England.*

1. The Royal Family, 1846—a famous picture by the royal portrait painter, Franz Xaver Winterhalter. Vicky is seated on the right with Alice and baby Helena; Bertie, the heir to the throne, is next to his mother, and Alfred (in a skirt) is in front of her.

2. Baron Stockmar, the *eminence grise* of the English court, taken from a lithograph based on a portrait by Winterhalter.

3. "Uncle Leopold." King Leopold I of the Belgians, at the age of 67.

4. The first photograph ever taken of Queen Victoria, 1844–45. The child is Vicky.

5. The first photograph of Prince Albert, a daguerreotype made at Brighton in 1842, two years after his marriage to the Queen.

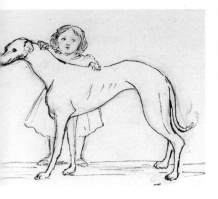

6. Queen Victoria's sketch of Vicky and the greyhound Eos, her father's favorite dog, 1843.

7. Pen drawing of Vicky and Bertie by Prince Albert, 1842.

8. Drawing of Vicky in eighteenth-century dress by the Queen, 1843.

9. Sketch of Vicky by Prince Albert, 1841.

10. Three studies of Vicky and her nurse by the Queen, 1843.

11. Vicky, Bertie, Alice, and Affie, 1853.

12. Vicky and Alice, Osborne, 1855.

13. Vicky and Queen Victoria in 1857, the year before Vicky's marriage.

14. Portrait of Fritz in 1856, the year after he and Vicky became engaged.

15. Photograph of Vicky taken at Osborne in 1855, the year of her engagement.

16. Group photo, Balmoral, September 29, 1855, the day that Vicky and Fritz became engaged. Left to right: Affie, Fritz, Alice, Bertie, the Queen, Prince Albert, Vicky.

17. *The Marriage of the Princess Royal, with Prince Frederick William of Prussia, 25 January, 1858,* a painting by John Phillip.

18. Vicky with her parents, daguerreotyped the day of her wedding, January 25, 1858. Queen Victoria was so nervous that she moved and nearly spoiled the picture.

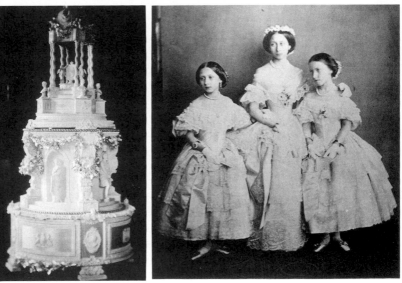

19. Vicky and Fritz's three-tiered wedding cake. Six feet tall, it hid the bride and groom from their parents during the wedding breakfast.

20. Vicky's sisters in the dresses (white lace over pink satin) they wore for her wedding. Left to right: Louise, Alice, and Helena.

21. Queen Victoria's sketch of Vicky and one of her bridesmaids.

22. Portrait of Fritz, taken from a painting by Lauchart.

23. Portrait of Vicky by Winterhalter, 1858, the year of her marriage.

24. Fritz and Vicky's marriage bed painted with their initials.

25. Vicky and Fritz photographed at Windsor, four days after their wedding.

26. Vicky with Willy, March 1859.

27. Queen Victoria and Willy, age five, in 1864.

28. Fritz and Willy, four years old, in Scottish dress at Balmoral, 1863.

29. Queen Victoria's sketch of Willy at twenty-one months, made during her visit to Coburg, October 1860.

30. Fritz and Vicky with Willy, Charlotte, Henry, and baby Sigismund, November 1865.

31. Fritz with his two younger daughters, Sophie (right) and Mossy, August 1874.

32. Waldemar with his sisters (left to right), Sophie, Moretta, and Mossy, 1878.

33. Wilhelm I of Germany, c. 1880s.

34. Queen Augusta.

35. Vicky with her two maids of honor the year after she arrived in Berlin. Left to right: Marie Lynar, Wally Hohenthal, Vicky.

36. King Frederick Wilhelm IV, known as "Fat Head." He was suffering from strokes and aphasia by the time Vicky moved to Berlin.

37. Queen Elisabeth, wife of King Frederick Wilhelm IV. She hated Vicky at first, but eventually left her the crown jewels.

38. Dr. Wegner, the court doctor —more courtier than medical man.

39. Fritz Carl, Fritz's cousin, who boxed his wife's ears for giving birth to a third girl.

40. Vicky at twenty-two and Willy, four, on horseback, June 1863.

41. Wilhelm I and Wilhelm II, six years old, saluting from the window of Wilhelm I's palace on Unter den Linden, 1865.

42. George Hintzpeter in 1869. He became Willy's tutor in 1866.

43. Vicky and her sisters in mourning around the bust of their father, 1862. Left to right: Alice, Helena, Beatrice, Vicky, and Louise.

44. Queen Victoria and Queen Augusta of Prussia, probably at Frogmore, 1867.

Willy was four months old before Vicky told her parents about his useless arm, but once the issue was raised, she shared her worries with them. Certainly, there was little sympathy to be found in the older generation in Berlin. Her father-in-law, who was extremely kind to her after the birth and gave her a string of twenty pearls, was hardly the sort of man to whom one could confide one's concerns. Thrilled as she had been at the birth, Augusta does not seem to have liked the infant very much and was constantly remarking to others on his small size, a subject about which Vicky was understandably sensitive.

Even with her own parents, Vicky was apologetic—about the intensity of her love for Wilhelm (she had been warned repeatedly against "baby worship") and her worries over his infirmity. Still, her letters home detailed every microscopic improvement in the arm, the various treatments tried, doctors consulted, advice sought, and tales of other children with the same condition who had grown out of it. It was a sad litany: "Your grandson is in perfect health and my whole delight, clever little thing," she wrote her father when the baby was nearly six months old.

> His arm is better certainly, but his hand not much, he can move all his fingers, clench his hand and open it and extend his fingers but very feebly, but the hand itself is about half the size of the other and that is what frightens me. . . . he has a crease up to his shoulder . . . but Wegner says that comes from the muscles under the arm being stronger than the rest. . . .
> I wish so very much to consult a surgeon, no one has ever had anything to do with it except Wegner, and I should be afraid of offending him. . . . the principal surgeon . . . is Langenbeck, who is a fussy important talkative disagreeable man, and . . . we don't wish the arm talked about. . . . Oh how I wish you could see it, that I could hear what you think. . . . It is certainly much improved . . . but he cannot bend it himself or raise it higher than an inch or 2, although it does not hang behind his back as it used, and is not so thin and limp. Do tell Sir James this, but . . . not to mention what I say to Wegner or it might offend him. Forgive me for this long uninteresting explanation which I fear will bore you.

Langenbeck was called in two weeks later, but was of little help. "[H]e said nothing at all except a few casual remarks such as it was a great deal better than he expected . . . and he hoped it would soon come right etc," Vicky reported, "but this sort of thing does not satisfy me. I want to hear exactly what he thinks & what ought to be done."

One of the things Wegner recommended (seconded by the English doctors) was tying Wilhelm's good arm to his side for an hour a day so that he would be forced to use the weak one. "He does not mind it in the least," Vicky reported, "but lies on his back on the floor or the sofa kicking his legs about, and laughing and crowing to the ceiling as happy and contented as possible. . . . I do not think he knows as yet that he has another arm as he has not much feeling in it. Wegner pricks his hand with a pin and pinches his arm to see whether he feels it. . . . He of course cannot crawl and never will . . . but Mrs. Hobbs thinks he will walk all the sooner."

Along with cold compresses and sprays of seawater, Wegner prescribed "animalic baths"—bizarre treatments that consisted of placing the child's useless arm twice weekly into the body of a freshly killed hare and leaving it there for half an hour to give it strength. The baby did not mind at all. "He is as fond of warmth as I am," Vicky reported; "he crows and talks in his own way all the time and enjoys the proceeding immensely."

By the time Wilhelm was a year old, there was some improvement in the arm, particularly its appearance. Whereas his head and left shoulder had formerly drooped to one side, young Willy was now more normal looking. "[T]he shoulders are exactly alike now and he holds his head as free and erect as possible," the happy mother wrote her father; "his back is as flat as every other child's." At sixteen months, the child took his first step, and Fritz wrote Victoria and Albert that their grandson could now walk "completely alone and independently with an adorable self-assurance."

But at four, Willy's head tilted to the right, inhibiting his ability to turn it. The doctors recommended putting him into a steel device that forced him to hold his head straight; this, they hoped, would eventually lengthen the muscles on the right side. After some infighting between physician and surgeon over whether the child's muscles should be cut first, they tried the contraption without the surgery.

"I cannot tell you what I suffered when I saw him in that machine . . . ," Vicky wrote Victoria;

> it was all I could do to prevent myself from crying. . . . The machine consists of a belt round the waist to which is affixed an iron bar or rod which passes up the back to which a thing looking very like the bridle of a horse is attached. The head is strapped into this and then turned as required with a screw which moves the iron. . . . When the head is firm in the leather straps it is made to turn towards

The apparatus used on Willy, as sketched by Vicky in a letter.

the left, so as to stretch the muscles of the right side of the neck; the object is to prevent his head from being drawn down to the right side. . . .

William is very good about it as it does not hurt him but I fear in a few times more it will and then we shall have a great piece of work to make him wear it—as he flies into such violent passions when he does not wish to do a thing. It seems so cruel to torment the poor child, still it would be no kindness to save him inconvenience now at the expense of causing him much greater hereafter.

BECAUSE OF HIS INFIRMITY, the future Wilhelm II started life as the center of even more concern than most royal babies. A bright child, he quickly learned to manipulate his elders, particularly his mother. In trying to compensate for his medical problems and the dreadful solutions imposed by nineteenth-century medicine, Vicky paid more attention to her first son than was good for him. Mother and son soon developed an overly intense relationship—a symbiosis that would serve them both badly in the end.

CHAPTER
FOURTEEN

"At the Court of Napoleon they play, they make love, enjoy themselves, dream and between sleeping and waking make decisions on matters of the greatest importance."

PRINCE ALBERT

NOT LONG AFTER Wilhelm's birth, Vicky was confronted with a clash between personal feelings and national loyalties. It was a dilemma that often plagued nineteenth-century royalties, who belonged to an exclusive monarchical club in which members addressed each other as brother and sister, but frequently found themselves on opposing sides of international issues. In this case, the problem was Italy and the efforts of Napoleon III to use Italian unification to further his territorial ambitions.

By the middle of the nineteenth century, the only other major ethnic group in western Europe besides the Germans still seeking unification were the Italians. As a result of Metternich's enormous influence at the Congress of Vienna, Austria had been left the dominant power in the several states of Italy, controlling Lombardy and Venetia directly and the others through alliances and influence. Only the kingdom of Sardinia (which included the state of Piedmont), had emerged from the Revolution of 1848 with a liberal constitution. Led by Count Cavour, a square-faced, bespectacled aristocrat who admired English parliamentarianism, the Piedmontese had taken part in the Crimean War on the side of France and Great Britain.

Napoleon III agreed to help Piedmont in its war of independence against Austria in exchange for the Piedmontese states of Savoy and Nice. Rationalizing his support on his often-trumpeted interest in freeing subjugated nationalities, he sent the French army to join the Italians when the Austrians invaded Piedmont at the end of April 1859.

Vicky's father-in-law was in a quandary. It was feared that victory for the Italians and French might lead to further French aggression on the Rhine. Various of the smaller German states had begun agitating for military support for their fellow Germans in Austria, and the appearance of Napoleon's soldiers in Piedmont and next-door Lombardy accelerated everyone's concern. "It is difficult to imagine . . . the fear and distrust the name of Louis Napoleon [Napoleon III] inspired in Germany then," said one member of Vicky's court.

Bismarck, now Prussia's Ambassador to Russia, recommended that Wilhelm take advantage of Austria's military involvement elsewhere by sending the entire Prussian army south *against* the Austrians "with the boundary-posts in the soldiers' knapsacks,"—a violation of the Germanic Confederation, which prohibited the German states from aggression against one another. But in mid-May, Wilhelm ordered partial mobilization of the Prussian army in support of Austria. This was the moment for which Fritz had been waiting. Trained as a soldier, he was eager to prove himself on the battlefield. His enthusiasm for war was lost on Vicky.

"Your anxiety [about the possibility of war] must be dreadful," she wrote her mother,

> but think of what I feel when I hear Fritz talking of the arrangements to be made for a campaign, of what people and horses he will take, etc. It breaks my heart, and he cannot or rather will not understand my distress. It is all very fine of the men talking of defending their country, of a soldier's life being the only one that becomes a man, that death on the field of battle is the thing they wish for; they don't think of their poor unhappy wives whom they have taken from their homes and whom they leave at home alone! . . . Nothing else is talked of but war, I hear nothing else all day.

In the middle of Fritz's preparations, Vicky left for a long-planned visit to her parents. She traveled alone, as Dr. Wegner refused to allow her to take her son, nearly four months old, with her. "Wegner will not hear of the child's travelling in the heat of the summer," she explained, although it was only May.

At home, Vicky impressed her parents with a newfound womanliness, and she was complimented by their unexpected candor. "Mama has been treating me with a friendliness and warmth that I have hitherto not experienced . . . ," she wrote Fritz. "We are together most of the day, more like sisters than mother and daughter. We have gotten along as never before. Everything I do meets with her approval, and even my wardrobe is applauded!!!!!!!!!" Her mother shared her pleasure, referring to the "delightful intercourse" that she found "so soothing & satisfactory to . . . my heart which requires sympathy & the possibility of pouring out its feelings quite openly to one who will feel for & understand me!" This, she assured Vicky, she now "found in you, my dearest child!"

Albert, too, was delighted with his married daughter, who, he wrote Fritz, "has grown, become prettier and has a feminine poise which makes her totally unlike the girl who left England." He was pleased that his favorite pupil had retained her liveliness and intellectual curiosity, along with her new maturity, and he enjoyed discussing the oncoming war with her. Furious at Napoleon III for joining the Italians, Albert also blamed Alexander II of Russia, who had assured Napoleon that Russia would remain neutral. This was the Czar's way of punishing Austria for supporting the French and English against Russia during the Crimean War.

Although she was gone only twelve days, Vicky missed Fritz enormously. "I am settled here in the rooms I had before my marriage," she wrote him. "In this room I experienced the happiest moment of my life when you took me into your arms as your wife and pressed me to your heart; when I even think of that moment my heart beats madly and I have a terrible longing for you, and I think I would hug you to death if I had you here now. I find the parting unbearable. . . . I feel quite crazy with longing for you." Away from her husband and child, Vicky realized that England was "no longer my homeland and . . . I do not belong here any more."

She returned home in time to see Fritz take command of the First Infantry Division of Guards. Her father-in-law's willingness to take up arms for Austria against Italy and France had largely depended on two things: Austria's acknowledging Prussia's importance in the Germanic Confederation and his own appointment as Commander-in-Chief of all the German forces on the Rhine. Hesitant at first, the Austrians acquiesced after they had been defeated by the Italians and French at Magenta in early June. Only then did Wilhelm order full mobilization of the Prussian army. Overnight, Vicky turned jingoist.

"All is preparing for war . . . ," she wrote home. "I am getting up all my courage, and hope that we shall soon be engaged—and pass the Rhine—the sooner the better—and by a successful war obtain for us a lasting and honorable peace, secure our position as the first in Germany and help the Austrians by helping ourselves and make for ourselves a great political position. . . . I wish for once I was a man, and baby too to fight the French."

But war did not come to the eager Prussians. Wilhelm did not have a chance to lead the combined German army into the field, nor did Fritz have an opportunity to win his military spurs. On the evening before Prussia's official declaration of war, in the middle of a celebratory dinner hosted by Fritz and Vicky for the Prussian generals, Wilhelm was handed an unexpected and unwelcome telegram. He interrupted the excited company with the news that a peace treaty had been signed at Villafranca between the Emperor of Austria and the Emperor of the French.

His announcement was greeted with "dead silence."

Franz Joseph of Austria, whose army had suffered a second major defeat at Solferino toward the end of June while Prussia was still mobilizing, had agreed to an armistice proposed by Napoleon in which France and Austria would redivide Italy along the old lines, giving everything back to Austria except Lombardy.* Count Cavour resigned in fury as Premier of Piedmont. Frustrated at his aborted military career, Fritz blamed the Austrians for coming to an agreement without consulting the Prussians. The Austrians rationalized their capitulation, blaming it on Prussia's hesitation in coming to their aid.

The sudden peace humiliated Wilhelm, who had managed to antagonize both his Austrian allies and his French enemies in his first foray into foreign

---

* *Lombardy was first ceded to Napoleon, who agreed to give it to Piedmont. Over the next two months, four other Italian states (Parma, Modena, Tuscany, and Romagna) refused to take back Austria's puppet princes and voted for union with Piedmont. Piedmont could not annex them without Napoleon's approval, which was negotiated by the reinstated Cavour in January of 1860, thus beginning the unification of the Italian states into the country we know today.*

relations. Frightened by the time and money it had taken to bring Prussia to full mobilization, Wilhelm embarked on a campaign of army reform. His military expertise would be his compensation for an obvious and acute incompetence in European affairs. Fritz attended the meetings of a military commission appointed to overhaul the army; in the field, he drilled the soldiers under his command until both he and they were exhausted.

"We are as surprised as you are at this Peace," Vicky wrote her mother, adding that her personal joy did not blind her to the "sad and dangerous position" of Prussia or "to the mistakes that have been made." She blamed Austria for accepting the peace and questioned if it was really "because they cannot go on or because they want to revenge themselves upon us for not having helped them; that is most likely the cause," she told her father, claiming that the Austrians wanted to put Prussia "in the worst light possible." From England, Victoria urged a different view of Austro-Prussian relations, stressing "the immense importance to Europe & Germany of Austria & Prussia keeping well together. And the more you love Prussia as you truly ought," she warned Vicky, "the more you should strive not to fan the flame of irritation & annoyance but to urge & encourage 'Unity.' "

The midsummer return of Vicky's mother-in-law, who had been in Weimar throughout the war crisis, heightened the tension at court, as Augusta's fondness for the French came into conflict with Prussian foreign policy. Forced to witness a number of "rather disagreeable scenes" between her parents-in-law, Vicky sympathized with Wilhelm and blamed Augusta's position on the influence of the pro-French Count Pourtales, a member of the Prussian Foreign Office and an intimate friend (some say lover) of the Princess.

Vicky handled her own ambivalence somewhat better than her mother-in-law did. When Victoria cautioned her daughter against "too great violence of feelings" against Napoleon III, Vicky responded by citing her duty to Prussia. "That I should feel strongly with this country . . . I am sure you will think natural as you know that I am with heart and soul attached to it, and should be unworthy to belong to it if I was not. Against the E.N. [Emperor Napoleon] personally I have not a feeling. . . . I cannot forget the visits in 55 and 57—and our visit to Paris and never shall and love the dear Empress as much as I ever did . . . but I must dislike the enemies of my country when they become such."

Albert, who had never trusted Napoleon III, was convinced that the French Emperor was "not the slightest bit interested in the independence of Italy . . . but only in . . . absolute supremacy in Europe." Frustrated by England's neutrality, convinced that the Russians were largely responsible for the situation, Albert wrote his son-in-law Fritz that he was "itching to strike a blow" at Napoleon. "May God destroy the wicked French!" he said.

At this point, Vicky seems to have been more objective than either her parents or her in-laws. Writing her mother at the end of July, she was forced to defend her position. "I am sorry you . . . say I have so much bitterness against Austria—as I am the only one here that has not any. . . . I have no violent feelings either against the E.N. or the Austrians, but I think the former does [not] much care for veracity and that the latter does not love us—that we ought to be armed against the French and be civil to the Austrians."

THE UPRISINGS IN ITALY and the successful Italian drive toward nationhood, most of which was completed by early 1861, created a surge of liberal and nationalistic sentiment in Prussia and the other German states. In opposition to the liberals, who spearheaded the movement toward a united Germany, were the conservatives, who wanted to preserve Prussia as a military autocracy and the other states as semifeudal fiefdoms. One of the most important factors weighing in on the side of conservatism was Prussia's friendship with Russia. Ever since Wilhelm's sister Charlotte had married Czar Nicholas I in 1817, there had been close ties between Berlin and St. Petersburg, familial bonds that were usually stretched to include politics.

Early every summer, the Hohenzollerns' Russian relatives made an annual pilgrimage to Prussia, inundating Berlin and Potsdam with "a flood" of Russian grand duchesses and their servants. In addition to the political implications of these visits, Vicky was kept busy going back and forth between Berlin and Potsdam for parades, luncheons, dinners, balls, and receptions, often having to change clothes six times a day. Even Fritz complained that his aunts kept himself, his wife, and the entire Prussian court running around as if they were "waiters." Vicky, whose days often started with 7:00 A.M. trips to the railway station and ended long after midnight when she was finally released from the nightly court soirées, suffered from headaches, swollen feet, and resentment.

In the summer of 1859, Vicky was left alone to do the social honors since Augusta was in Weimar, visiting her dying mother. During their visit, the Russian ladies tried to convince her father-in-law not to go to war against Napoleon III. Although neither Wilhelm's sister Charlotte nor his pro-Russian sister-in-law Queen Elisabeth (wife of the ailing Friedrich Wilhelm IV) succeeded in changing his position, Vicky did not trust any of Fritz's Russian relations after that.

When Augusta's mother died, Vicky informed Victoria that the court would stay in mourning for three months, the ladies in high black woolen dresses (in spite of the heat) and veils to the ground. Palace servants were required to wear mourning except those in the nursery.

"I think it quite wrong that the nursery are not in mourning, at any rate I should make them wear grey or white or drab—& baby wear white and lilac, but not colours. That I think shocking. . . ." Victoria replied, "[Y]ou must promise me that if I should die your child or children & those around you should mourn; this really must be, for I have such a strong feeling on this subject." To prove it, the Queen put on mourning for her eldest daughter's husband's grandmother. Vicky assured dearest Mama that it would "please the family."

If Victoria was strict about the rituals of death, the Prussians were even more demanding. It was the custom in the Prussian royal family for descendants to gather on the anniversary of the death of an important relative for a religious ceremony in a room that had belonged to the deceased. In 1860, the annual trip of the Dowager Empress Charlotte of Russia to mark the death day of her father, King Friedrich Wilhelm III of Prussia, coincided with the last weeks of Vicky's second pregnancy.

This pregnancy had been far easier than her first, although Dr. Martin had insisted upon an internal examination. "I was poked at in every direction," she wrote her mother, "but he wished it so much & seemed to think it of such importance as all went wrong the last time, that Fritz thought it better and so of course then I said nothing more."

After her first experience with Dr. Wegner, Vicky had asked her mother to have Sir James Clark send a bottle of chloroform directly to her and to instruct the court doctor that this time she was to be given enough of it. "I am sure they will not give me sufficient if he does not write . . . as the last time what little I got I owe to good Sir James who held it to my nose in spite of Wegner. . . . here you know they have such different ideas on that subject. . . . If Sir James does write about it will you tell him *not* to mention . . . *my* having wished him to do so—or it will offend."

With everything arranged for the birth of her baby, Vicky still had to contend with the Russians, who appeared in Potsdam the month before her confinement. Offered rooms in two other palaces, one of which had been recently rebuilt and redecorated specifically for her use, the Dowager Empress Charlotte (widow of Czar Nicholas I) insisted on staying in the Neues Palais in rooms directly below Vicky's.

Of the annual Russian visitors, the Dowager Empress was the most venerable. Tall, thin, and erect, the sixty-one-year-old former Czarina always wore black with a black lace scarf over her hair for day and white with cascades of pearls for evening. The previous summer, she had treated Vicky to a showing of her other jewels, for which members of the Russian royal family were justly famous. "Yours are finer," Vicky had assured Victoria. "Hers are huge things and really in such profusion that it seems almost magic—sapphires, emeralds, pearls, rubies, etc., but the quality is not very fine—her diamonds excepted which are magnificent."

The Dowager Empress always traveled with an "enormous suite" including four maids of honor (gowned in black cashmere), each with several maids of her own. Their arrival upset Vicky's preparations for her confinement. Russian servants always slept on the floor, and it was considered necessary to gut their quarters and redecorate after each imperial visit.

"[T]he noise just underneath won't be over & above pleasant," Vicky complained to her mother;

the slamming of doors and steps on the uncarpeted floors & in those high rooms are heard very loud—then the low talking & smoking of the Russian servants and suite. . . . She knows <u>when</u> I expect to be laid up—and <u>where</u> my rooms are as she was here last year. . . . I cannot help feeling that it is not <u>the</u> most considerate thing in the world to live with that immense train of people in the house. . . . 'Enfin' I don't care about the inconvenience to myself so much as the inconvenience our servants are put to when those dirty Russians are in the house.

Worse, the room in which the Russians planned to gather to mourn the death of Friedrich Wilhelm III was Vicky's personal sitting room, which had been stripped of all her furniture and pictures, hung with black crepe, and left in that depressing state throughout the entire visit.

The final irritant came in the form of an invitation from Queen Elisabeth, requesting Vicky's presence at the Neues Palais on the seventh of June, the day of Friedrich Wilhelm III's death. "I think to be invited to . . . one's own room is rather too much," Vicky wrote her mother. To express her anger, Vicky sent her own invitations to all the people invited to the ceremony "so that at least they know in whose house they are!"—and then declined to attend herself. This was just as well, for Fritz's ultraconservative aunt Alexandrine (one of Wilhelm's sisters) had announced that "she would never put her foot" in the Neues Palais while the liberal Crown Princess was there. As the irate girl wrote her mother, "[S]he can have the extreme satisfaction of going there on the 7th . . . as I shall not trouble her with my presence!"

On July 24, 1860, Vicky gave birth to a girl. This delivery, according to Fritz, who rubbed her feet during labor, was "much easier" than her first. They named the child Victoria Elizabeth Augusta Charlotte and called her Charlotte. No one was satisfied with the name. Queen Victoria confined herself to a mild rebuke: "<u>I</u> <u>do</u> hope <u>one</u> of <u>your</u> <u>daughters</u>, if you have any more, will be <u>called</u> <u>Victoria</u>, so that there may be the <u>4</u> <u>generations</u> <u>of</u> <u>Victorias</u>," she chided.

Queen Elisabeth vented her anger in full force:

"The Queen was so much displeased at the name that it made her <u>still</u> <u>more</u> cross and ungracious the two times she has been to see me . . . ," Vicky wrote her mother. "I just wish you could have heard the exclamations of all my relations when they have come to see me. I wish you could have stood behind a screen—and heard all the senseless remarks and seen the upturned eyes and shrugging of shoulders at everything I did and had on—they were not satisfied with anything. . . . when we meet I will make you laugh with all the things that have been said to me." The attitude of the pro-Russian court did not improve at Charlotte's christening. This time, Vicky said she was "ready to cry at all the cutting remarks and sour faces."

Beneath the silly cuts and slights lay something far more significant— the competition for Prussia's future between Russian autocracy and English constitutionalism. It was this drama that would be played out in the events of the 1860s and 1870s. And it was in this arena that Vicky, who had been sent to Prussia as the ambassador of parliamentary government, would finally win or lose the game.

CHAPTER
FIFTEEN

"The past is a foreign country; they do things differently there."
L. P. HARTLEY, The Go-Between

*I*N THE FALL OF 1860, two months after the birth of Vicky's first daughter, her parents came to Germany to see her. It was their second visit in two years. In spite of these early trips and their constant correspondence, it is unlikely that Albert or Victoria understood what life was really like for their eldest daughter. When they traveled around Germany, they were surrounded by cheering crowds, eager to welcome anyone royal, particularly the most powerful monarch in Europe. Vicky, too, received the adulation of the public, but inside the court, she was an object of both fear and hatred—fear of her potential power and hatred of what she represented.

In consigning Vicky to the Prussian court, Albert and Victoria had hoped to counteract the influence on the Hohenzollerns of the absolutist Romanovs. Bismarck had been right when he said at the time of Fritz and Vicky's engagement that there was real admiration in Prussia for English ways. But unfortunately for Vicky, most of it came from the professional and intellectual class, a group that had never—except for the few months of the Revolution of 1848—gained enough power to override the military establishment or the Junkers (landed aristocracy), the two pillars on which the Prussian monarch rested his power.

It was this ruling triumvirate—the king, the army, and the Junkers—to which the petty Prussian bureaucrat owed his livelihood and his ethic. Loyalty to their conservatism gave him the conviction of borrowed superiority, an arrogance that sat poorly with non-Germans, particularly the English. Only a week before Victoria and Albert's second visit to Germany, in September of 1860, a minor incident involving an Englishman traveling in Prussia exposed this resentment.

On September 12, 1860, a Scotsman, one Captain Macdonald, had a dispute with a railroad official over a seat in a train at Bonn. Apparently rather high-handed in his behavior, Macdonald was put off the train and clapped into prison by the Prussian police. He was kept there for nearly a week before being brought to trial, where he claimed he had been the object of violence by the police and mistreatment by his jailers. Nevertheless, he was fined by the judge and forced to pay minor court costs. The matter would have ended there, had not the public prosecutor seized the occasion to denounce the behavior of Englishmen abroad, claiming they were "notorious for the rudeness, impudence, and boorish arrogance of their conduct."

Macdonald's ordeal, coupled with this statement from a member of the Prussian judiciary, provoked angry outbursts in England, speeches on the floor of parliament, and indignant answers in the Prussian Diet. Notes flew back and forth between London and Berlin. The Prime Minister, Lord Palmerston, demanded that the judge in the case be dismissed and reparations made to Macdonald. The press on both sides, led by the London *Times,* profited from the furor, scratching and inflaming irritations that were festering beneath the veneer of diplomatic niceties.

One of the problems in cases like this was the difference between English and continental newspapers and the misconceptions of the public on both sides of the channel. In Germany, newspapers were usually the organs of political parties, funded by them for the purpose of disseminating a particular position; in England, where the press was purely commercial, the opinions published in a given paper represented nothing more sinister than the bias of its owner. This was something that the Prussians, whose conservative party took its very name, Kreuzzeitung, from its newspaper, did not understand. When the London *Times* attacked their king or his politics, they naturally assumed that the attack had been launched by the English government.

Even without the Macdonald affair, Victoria and Albert's trip in the fall of 1860 was plagued with troubles. Albert's stepmother, the Dowager Duchess of Coburg, died while they were en route, and the scene that met them in Coburg was a gloomy one—Albert's brother Duke Ernest and Vicky's Fritz, dressed in black, standing at the train station surrounded by a joyless crowd. When they reached the palace, Vicky was waiting with Ernest's downtrodden wife, Alexandrine, both ladies in deep mourning with long black veils.

Only a few days after the funeral, while Albert was driving in a coach-and-four, the horses took fright and ran into a railway barrier. The coachman was seriously hurt, one of the horses was killed, and Albert had to jump from the carriage in order to escape severe injury. Although he suffered only minor cuts and contusions, he was clearly shaken by the accident and fell into a deep depression. The last day of his visit, he asked his brother Ernest to go for a walk with him. While they were out, Albert dissolved into tears and told Ernest that he was sure he would never see his ancestral home again.

Her parents' visit to Germany was Vicky's first opportunity to show them their grandson, Willy, now nearly two, and their infant granddaughter, Charlotte. Knowing her mother's insistence on superbly mannered children, she was nervous. "I only hope William will behave himself," she had written her father; "he is . . . so noisy & naughty, we have a great deal of trouble to keep him in order—he is so jealous of the baby. . . . He is growing immensely and looks very well—only his poor arm makes very little progress."

Willy was brought in the first day, holding his nurse Mrs. Hobbs's hand, and in spite of Vicky's fears, the twenty-month-old behaved very well. Dressed in a white dress trimmed in black bows, he impressed his grandmother as "a fine fat child, with a beautiful soft white skin." Although Queen Victoria saw him every day during the visit, she apparently did not refer directly* to his useless arm, writing only to her own mother, the Duchess of Kent, that it was "much better."

It was common knowledge in Berlin that the children of the heir to the throne had an English nursemaid and were being raised in accordance with their mother's foreign ideas and customs, which called for well-aired nurseries, cold baths, and babies who were not immobilized in swaddling clothes. Such peculiarities fanned the ordinary Prussians' distrust of *die Engländerin* (the Englishwoman), as she was called, laying the groundwork for more serious suspicions. There were rumors that it was Vicky herself—the opponent of good German *Hausfrau* practices—who had instigated the attacks on Prussia in the English newspapers, and Lord Clarendon claimed that the anti-Prussian stance of the English press "materially" affected her position in her new country.

Faced with this animosity, Vicky undertook to monitor newsprint on both sides of the channel, as well as the diplomats sent by the Foreign Office to represent her native land in Berlin. Her special friend at the British Embassy was the attaché, Robert Morier, an articulate young diplomat with liberal leanings, sponsored in his career by her father and old Baron Stockmar. Posted to Berlin at the time of Vicky's marriage to Fritz, Morier immediately came under attack from the ultraconservatives. But the British Foreign Secretary, who considered Morier an authority on Germany, which he was, continued to consult him on "most important, confidential, and delicate" matters.

The British Ambassador was another matter. Up until the fall of 1860, the post had been filled by John Bloomfield, a kindly and tactful man who had shown sensitivity to the anti-English feeling in Prussia by distancing himself from Vicky during her early days in Berlin. Now the Foreign Office proposed replacing him with the current Ambassador to Austria, Augustus Loftus.

Vicky complained to her father that in the continuing struggle between Prussia and Austria for control of Germany, Loftus had, in his Viennese posting, exhibited "a great leaning towards Austria." Moreover, he was "personally disagreeable, pompous, conceited, indiscreet & very <u>forward</u>." Apologizing for her presumption, she begged her father to speak to the Foreign Secretary about the choice of Loftus† as well as "the necessity of fostering . . . good feeling of

---

* *This is true insofar as we know. In one of the great misfortunes in modern recorded history, Queen Victoria's journals were edited after her death by her youngest daughter, Princess Beatrice, who excised everything she felt should not be seen by the world and recopied what was left in her own hand.*

† *Vicky's animosity to Loftus was short-lived. When his replacement, Lord Napier, turned out to be a great admirer of Bismarck, she was, in fact, delighted to get Loftus back in Berlin on his second tour of duty there.*

the 2 countries which is . . . very bad since the *Times* uses language so grossly insulting."

Although Vicky was not successful in changing ambassadors, her attempt to do so is indicative of the depth of her concern over the ongoing deterioration of Anglo-Prussian relations. When she lost the battle, she retreated with dignity. "You can rely on our being as civil to Lord A.L. as to Lord Bloomfield," she wrote Prince Albert, "and that every mark of consideration due to him as Mama's representative he will receive from us."

IF THERE WAS LITTLE that Vicky could do to slow the breakdown in Anglo-Prussian relations, she was still expected to serve her family in a variety of ways. One of these was to search out dynastically appropriate spouses for her siblings. Her own marriage was an example of the naïve faith of nineteenth-century monarchs in the efficacy of political matches, but even when there was no specific alliance in mind, there was the need to keep the blood blue, and power in the hands of the powerful.

Queen Victoria had waited less than two months after Vicky's wedding before charging her with the task of finding a husband for her sister Alice, now fifteen, and a wife for sixteen-year-old brother Bertie, the future Edward VII. Half German herself, married to a German, the Queen of England generally preferred German princes and princesses as potential spouses for her children, and her eldest daughter was now in a position to ferret them out. Vicky's job was facilitated by the fact that most of Germany's petty kings, grand dukes, and their families came to Berlin at one time or another to call at the Prussian court, and Vicky made it her business to go and see the ones who stayed at home.

Visiting in the castles of minor German royalty in the middle of the nineteenth century was not an altogether pleasurable experience. If the rich and powerful Hohenzollerns of Berlin did not subscribe to English standards of hygiene and convenience, their counterparts in the duchies and kingdoms cared less about making their guests comfortable than impressing them with useless grandeur. Vicky was frequently given rooms that had not been inhabited for years, where no one had thought to open the windows in summer or light a fire in winter before her arrival. On a trip to the grand duchy of Weimar, which took place less than three months after her marriage, the bride was assigned a suite of rooms on a different floor of the castle from those of her husband, who would not allow her to visit him because of the freezing drafts on the stairways and the fact that she had to pass through a scullery to get to him. "How can married people live in that sort of way!" Vicky complained to her parents.

Nevertheless, she continued to travel about dutifully, sending reports back to England on the looks and manners of various young princes and princesses of Germany. One of the first families to come under scrutiny were the Hesses of Darmstadt, an ancient dynasty whose lands lay in the area of Frankfurt. The head of the house, Grand Duke Louis of Hesse, had no children, but his brother and heir, Prince Charles, married to a member of the Prussian royal family, had fathered three sons and a daughter. It was the daughter, Princess Anna, who interested Queen Victoria as a possible wife for the Prince of Wales, and she sent Vicky to Darmstadt to look her over.

Although Anna was said to be attractive and charming, Vicky's reaction to her was decidedly tepid. "I do not think her pretty—she has not a fine figure . . . and her teeth are nearly all spoilt," she reported to her mother. Vicky was particularly distressed by Anna's unfortunate habit of twitching, which, she assured Victoria, "her father and second brother Heinrich do continually."

Anna's eldest brother, Louis, however, had escaped the family twitch, and he impressed Vicky as a possible husband for sister Alice. Louis and Heinrich were therefore invited to Windsor during Ascot week. "I think them the nicest young men I have seen for very long . . . ," Victoria wrote Vicky during the visit, adding that "Louis gets on extremely well with Alice." When Louis left Windsor, he asked for Alice's photograph, and Alice made no secret of the fact that she was attracted to him.

Proud of her matchmaking, Vicky was also delighted at the possibility of having her closest sister settle near her in Germany. For her part, Queen Victoria thought that by marrying Alice to a minor German prince, she might have her at home as much as she liked. The Queen was more ambivalent about this match than she had been about Vicky and Fritz, primarily because she realized she had married off her eldest daughter too young. Although Alice and Louis became engaged later that year, Alice did not marry until she was nineteen.

More important than finding a husband for Alice, however, was finding a wife for Bertie, the future King of England. Neither Stockmar's theories nor Albert's exhortations and punishments had succeeded in turning Vicky's charming younger brother into the moral and intellectual paragon his parents had envisioned. Discouraged by what they considered his laziness, Albert and Victoria had convinced themselves that the lighthearted Bertie must be protected from sexual experimentation, and the only way to do this was to provide him with a delicious wife.

Vicky's first efforts in this direction were discouraging. Anna of Hesse had that disturbing twitch; the young Princess of Weimar's teeth were "almost black," and the Princess of Sweden was still undeveloped. Vicky had gone as far as Düsseldorf, where her family's friend and father-in-law's Prime Minister, Prince Hohenzollern, had arranged a dinner party attended by the eligible princesses in that part of Germany, but none of them was interesting enough to become a future Queen of England.

The search for Bertie's wife had come to a standstill when Victoria and Albert arrived in Coburg in the fall of 1860. It would have been surprising had Vicky and her mother not spent some hours during their time together studying the bible of royal and aristocratic Europe, the *Almanach de Gotha,* listing all the princesses lurking in the petty courts of Germany. Help in this matter soon came from an unexpected quarter, however, involving Vicky's lady-in-waiting, Wally Hohenthal.

One of the blessings of Vicky's first three years in Prussia was the companionship of her two young German ladies-in-waiting, the charming, high-spirited Wally (Walpurga) Hohenthal and pretty Marie Lynar. "We three suited so well," Vicky later wrote Wally, "and were so happy together, like three friends only can be who love each other truly." But it was inevitable that the two eligible young German countesses would not stay single long, and during 1860, both married and left the court.

The first to go was Marie Lynar, who married one of Wilhelm's aides-de-camp in the spring. Then Wally Hohenthal married Augustus Paget, a British diplomat, in October, just after Victoria and Albert's visit. Their wedding took place in the British Legation, where they stood in front of a portrait of the Queen for the service.

At the time, Wally's husband was posted to the British Embassy in Copenhagen, where he had met young Princess Alexandra of Denmark, whom he called "the most charming, pretty and delightful young Princess" in Europe. On their way from Berlin to Copenhagen, Wally and Augustus stopped at Windsor, where he told Victoria and Albert about the girl. Wally was instructed to meet Alix and send back photographs.

Meanwhile, Vicky continued to explore other eligible princesses. Queen Victoria, who fretted about her eldest son, was growing impatient. She would have settled quite happily for Anna of Hesse and tried to ignore Vicky's hints that this girl simply would not do. "I am much <u>pleased</u> with the account of Princess Anna, (minus <u>the</u> <u>twitching</u>)," Victoria declared.

The Queen also urged Vicky to look at another German princess, Elisabeth of Wied, who had always appealed to Victoria as a prospective daughter-in-law, for reasons best known to herself. Elisabeth was an overwrought sixteen-year-old with artistic leanings whose childhood had featured séances and visits to the local lunatic asylum. She was spending the social season at the court in Berlin, where, it was hoped, she might be tamed into a docile, marriageable princess.* "I do not think her at all distinguée looking—certainly the opposite to Bertie's usual taste" was Vicky's reaction. In contrast, the pictures of Princess Alexandra of Denmark showed a girl of uncommon beauty—tall, slender, elegant, and, as Vicky put it, "just the style Bertie admires."

It took some effort for Vicky to say this, because she knew that as a Prussian, she should not wish Bertie to marry the daughter of the man next in line to be King of Denmark. For years, Prussia had been at loggerheads with Denmark over the duchies of Schleswig and Holstein, coveted by German nationalists as a link between the Baltic and North seas. By sponsoring this marriage, Vicky ran the risk of being harshly criticized in Berlin. Whatever the cost, however, she wished her brother the loveliest princess in Europe. "I never

---

* *Elisabeth was a hard case. She was twenty-five, a veritable old maid by the standards of the day, before Prince (later King) Carol of Romania decided that she would make a good wife, and she became Queen Elisabeth I of Romania.*

saw anything so sweet," she wrote Victoria, enclosing a photograph of Alix, saying that if Bertie saw the picture, "he must fall in love with it."

Albert agreed. "[F]rom that photograph I would marry her at once," he told his wife. But Queen Victoria, who called Alix "outrageously beautiful," still objected to her on the grounds that her "mother's family are bad"* and her "father's foolish." "You know, dearest . . . ," she wrote Vicky, "the beauty of Denmark is much against our wishes. . . . If Bertie could see and like one of the others first, then I am sure we should be safe."

Vicky did not give up trying to find a candidate who would answer both her mother's and her brother's needs. "I am so anxious to be of use to you . . . ," she wrote Victoria in the spring of 1861. "At present, although I do not like to own it even to my own self, the balance is inclining on the side of the Danish beauty, but I have never seen her and how can one judge without having seen a person!"

Three months later, pressed by the knowledge that the Russians were now considering Alix for the heir to *their* throne, a meeting was arranged between Vicky and Princess Alix at a point midway between Prussia and Denmark. Like the young Pagets, both Vicky and Fritz were enchanted by Alix, whom she described to her mother in precise detail:

> I never set eyes on a sweeter creature. . . . She is lovely! . . . a good deal taller than I am, has a lovely figure . . . a complexion as beautiful as possible, very fine white regular teeth and very fine large eyes. . . . Her voice, her walk, carriage and manner are perfect, she is one of the most ladylike and aristocratic looking people I ever saw! She is as simple and natural and unaffected as possible. . . . You may go far before you find another princess like Princess Alix. . . . Oh if she only was not a Dane . . . I should say yes —she is the one a thousand times over.

It remained only for Bertie to see Alix, an encounter that took place at the cathedral in Speyer, near Heidelberg, during the annual Prussian military maneuvers. The meeting was a disappointment to Vicky and her mother. Although Bertie told his sister that "he had never seen a young lady who pleased him so much," he was clearly not as bowled over as she wished. When he got back to England, his mother reported that although "certainly much pleased," he had not fallen in love at first sight. "[A]s for being in love I don't think he can be," Victoria wrote Vicky, "or that he is capable of enthusiasm about anything in the world."

Frustrated after all her efforts, Vicky was more than a little surprised that the kind of beauty she herself had always longed for had not brought her brother to his knees. "Bertie may look far before he finds another like her," she answered; "if she fails to kindle a flame—none ever will succeed in doing so."

---

* *Alix's mother's cousin, the current King of Denmark, had divorced two previous wives and was living with a third (morganatic) one.*

But neither Vicky's words nor pressure from his parents could budge the young Prince of Wales. He wanted to see the sixteen-year-old Danish Princess again before committing himself to spend the rest of his life with her, and he asked her parents to bring her to England before he made up his mind. There matters lay until the end of 1861, when minor scandal and major tragedy intervened to change all their lives.

CHAPTER
SIXTEEN

*"There are many who make it their business to make princes fear
their own people."*

PRINCE ALBERT, *1861*

ON NEW YEAR'S EVE of 1860, Vicky and Fritz were awakened at 1:30
A.M. by a telegram saying that King Friedrich Wilhelm IV was dying at the
palace of Sanssouci in Potsdam. They dressed and ran through the cold, dark
square separating Wilhelm and Augusta's palace from their own, reaching it just
in time to board his parents' carriage for the railway station. When they arrived
at Sanssouci, they found Queen Elisabeth sitting in a chair by her husband's
bed, her arm supporting his head, her head on his pillow beside his. With her
free arm, she was wiping the perspiration from his face.

"We approached the bed and stood there at the foot of it," Vicky wrote
Victoria,

> not daring to look at one another, or to say a word. . . . no sound was
> heard, but the crackling of the fire and the death rattle. . . . every now
> and then the King breathed very fast and loud, but never unclosed his
> eyes—he was very red in the face, and the cold perspiration pouring from
> his forehead. . . . 3,4,5,6,7 struck and we were still standing there—one
> member of the family came in after the other and remained motionless
> in the room, sobs only breaking the sadness. Oh it is dreadful to see a
> person die!

Morning dawned, the lamps were removed from the room, and the King
still struggled. Everyone moved into an adjoining room. Around noon, Vicky
and her friend Marianne returned to the King's bedroom where they kissed
Queen Elisabeth's hand, knelt by the bed to kiss Friedrich Wilhelm's, and remained until 5:00 P.M., when supper was served. By then Vicky was "so sick
and faint and unwell" that Fritz put her to bed. At one o'clock in the morning,
hearing that the King had only a few more minutes to live, she got up and
dressed quickly, but by the time she got back to his bedside, Friedrich Wilhelm
IV of Prussia was dead.

"I went into the room where the King lay, and I could hardly bring myself
to go away again," Vicky wrote her mother.

There was so much of comfort in looking . . . at that quiet peaceful form at rest at last after all he had suffered . . . his mouth and eyes closed and such a happy expression. . . . Fritz and I stood looking at him for some time. I could hardly bring myself to believe that this was really death, that which I had so often shuddered at and felt afraid of; there was nothing there dreadful or appalling—only a heavenly calm and peace. . . . I am not afraid of death now, and when I feel inclined to be so, I shall think of that solemn and comforting sight, and that death is only a change for the better!

The next morning Vicky returned to sit alone with the widowed, childless Queen, who complained that she was "no longer of any use in this world." Elisabeth obviously appreciated Vicky's attentions. She was, as Vicky wrote her mother, "so kind to me, kinder than she ever has been yet, and said I was like her own child and a comfort to her!"

Friedrich Wilhelm IV's death marked the end of Queen Elisabeth's hostility toward Vicky. The old woman made it clear that of all her relations, the new Crown Princess had been the only one who worried about the widow. Berlin society, which had reveled in the antagonism shown by the pro-Russian Queen toward her nephew's English wife, was robbed of one of its favorite topics of gossip.

Twelve years later, when Elisabeth herself died, she left her "magnificent" jewels to Vicky instead of to the Prussian crown, as was traditional with queens of Prussia. Vicky's mother-in-law, Augusta, never forgave Vicky.

THE DEATH OF FRIEDRICH WILHELM IV, which raised Wilhelm and Augusta to the position of King and Queen of Prussia and Fritz and Vicky to Crown Prince and Princess, stirred up a hornets' nest of new jealousies in the court. As the youngest matron and wife of the heir to the throne, Vicky found herself in a coven of quarreling middle-aged women, sisters and sisters-in-law of Friedrich Wilhelm IV and Wilhelm I. "My day is spent at Sans Souci between the 2 Queens [Elisabeth and Augusta] the Grand Duchess of Mecklenburg-Schwerin & Princess Charles—and it is neither an easy nor a pleasant life . . . ," Vicky reported home. "Of course I cannot write all that passes, that must always remain to be told when we meet."

The chief troublemaker was Wilhelm's sister, the reactionary Grand Duchess Alexandrine of Mecklenburg-Schwerin. Minutes after her elder brother's death, Alexandrine threw herself sobbing into the new King's arms, begging him not to trust his wife. Augusta, she claimed, "was an intriguer who would try to meddle with the affairs of state and place her own friends in important positions." A large woman, filled with piety and her own importance, Alexandrine was nearly sixty at the time and a formidable foe. Next, she turned on Vicky.

Members of the royal family were required to pay homage several times each day to the King's corpse as he lay on his deathbed, a task that the twenty-year-old Crown Princess found hard to perform, explaining to her mother that the deteriorating body of the old man "did not make a pleasant impression upon me." Fritz's aunt must have sensed Vicky's revulsion because, during one of Vicky's first visits, she pushed the twenty-year-old girl's face down almost to Friedrich Wilhelm's pillow and stood behind her so she could not rise—a piece of mischief that gave Vicky, as she wrote Victoria, "a great shudder."

In keeping with Hohenzollern tradition, Friedrich Wilhelm IV's body was taken after two days to be embalmed, dressed in uniform, and placed in an open coffin for his lying-in-state. The coffin was set in an alcove in the room in which Frederick the Great had died, draped in purple velvet and massed with lighted candelabra. A purple marquee, the same marquee that had been used for Wilhelm's and Charlotte's christenings, was hung over the coffin.

Masked by all this splendor, Friedrich Wilhelm's body was less intimidating, but Alexandrine's trick had done its work. "[T]oday when I went up to the coffin," the new Crown Princess wrote her mother, "I kept my eyes cast down —I had not courage to look at the King's face. I only looked at it when I was a little further off . . . and I own it costs me a great struggle to overcome my feelings now whenever we are obliged to go in."

The King was not buried until six days after his death, but Queen Victoria raised an eyebrow at this "very quick funeral," writing her daughter how astonished she was at the "fearfully dangerous* habit" of the Prussian royal family "of burying people so early." The day of the funeral was bitterly cold, so cold that the King's oldest friend caught a chill and died, and some of the soldiers ordered to march from Berlin to Potsdam at 2:00 A.M. to serve in the cortege had to have toes and fingers amputated due to frostbite.

By then the new King and Queen had already had an enormous fight along the lines predicted by Alexandrine. Only a few days after Wilhelm's succession, Augusta suggested to the Foreign Minister, Baron Schleinitz, that he get her husband to contact Napoleon III personally before the French Emperor received the formal announcement of Wilhelm's accession, so as to establish more friendly relations between Prussia and France. To make sure it was done right, she drafted the letter to Napoleon III herself. Schleinitz was agreeable. He wrote his concurrence to the Queen; at the same time he addressed a letter to the King as she had suggested.

Unfortunately, the groom of the chambers, to whom the letters were entrusted for delivery, mixed them up. When Wilhelm received the letter intended for his wife, he was furious at her for meddling in state business. Matters grew so bad between them that for the first time in over thirty years of bickering, they considered an official separation. It was Fritz who finally intervened, convincing his parents that they must remain together in the interests of Prussia.

"Every day I have a new opportunity of admiring all dear Fritz's sober qualities," Vicky wrote home; "if you knew how good he is and how well he behaves, he is the only one of us who does not get discouraged & who does not lose his head . . . really I wish more people knew. He is such a good son, such a

* I.e., *dangerous to the position of monarchs.*

good husband & such a good brother! & always thinks of his duty before his pleasure."

Both Vicky and Victoria were distressed by the fact that Fritz, who did not call attention to himself, was so consistently undervalued in the Prussian court. "From his own mother he seldom or rather never hears . . . words of affection," Vicky complained.

Queen Victoria, who looked for opportunities to make up for this, found one a few months later after a brief visit from her son-in-law. "Allow me to tell you, my dear Fritz," she wrote him after his return, "how fond I am of you . . . and how we have learned to appreciate, love and respect you more and more every day!"

"You can imagine how happy I am to possess such proof of your parents' approval and trust! . . . ," Fritz wrote his wife, to whom he gave credit for his ability to function in a difficult situation, "you know exactly what it takes to make me happy through good times and bad, and you know exactly what is best for me. . . . you accept me the way that I am; you have taught me how to gain confidence and see the world in a better way than I did before."

"If 'marriages are made in heaven,' " he added three days later, "then God has obviously done so in our case."

BEFORE HE DIED, Friedrich Wilhelm IV had added a caveat to his will, urging his successors to the throne to refuse to take an oath to uphold the Prussian constitution. Prince Albert was shocked by this "breach of faith" with the people and even more by the efforts of Friedrich Wilhelm's old camarilla to pressure Wilhelm to comply "out of respect" for his dead brother. But Wilhelm had his own ideas about constitutions.

"Having found a constitution," the new King had explained while he was still Regent, "I consider it my duty to conform myself to it. . . . it was not my intention to discuss whether Constitutions as such were conducive to the well-being of a nation, but only to express the conviction that, where they did exist . . . it would be the height of danger to put oneself in contradiction. . . . Upon this same ground of distrust, it was my opinion, that it was a false policy to seek the security of the throne in the limitations of the Constitution."

In other words, the new King did not like constitutions, did not trust constitutions, and refused to take his mandate to govern from them. Nonetheless, he would not openly oppose the Prussian constitution, lest he find himself in the middle of a revolution.

Sensing Wilhelm's attitude from the "bitter, aggressive tone against the people" he detected in the new King's first manifesto from the throne, Prince Albert wrote his old friend a long letter urging him to actively support the Prussian constitution, thus "serving as a model" for the rest of Germany and attracting the other German states into a union. In that union, Albert said, lay the future security of Europe.

This was not what Wilhelm wanted to hear. Unsolicited advice from the Prince Consort only set him against Fritz and Vicky, who he knew shared

Albert's vision. At sixty-four, the new King of Prussia was already set in his ways. Unlike his quasi-artistic predecessor, he was a typical Hohenzollern, perhaps even the archetypal one in terms of his fanatic militarism, his lack of interest in culture, and his almost religious belief in duty. But it was duty as he saw it, not as Queen Victoria's husband, a former prince of a minor German duchy, pointed it out to him.

Victoria was also anxious about Wilhelm. Dangling a carrot instead of a stick, she offered the new King of Prussia the Order of the Garter. Unaware that the Queen was instructing the bearer of the order, Lord Breadalbane, to bestow political advice along with the much-coveted honor, Wilhelm was delighted. "The King makes such a fuss about receiving the Garter," Vicky wrote her mother, "it gives him so much pleasure it would quite make you laugh if you saw how much he thinks about it."

This was the first time since his accession to the throne that Vicky had seen her father-in-law "smile & look pleased." Since the day of his accession, she said, Wilhelm's mood had "really been something dreadful." Deploring the "advanced age" at which he had come to power, which left him "little time to accomplish anything," Wilhelm was tormented by the idea that the constitution he had inherited had raised a barrier between the Prussian people and himself. He became obsessed with the danger of revolution and charged his secret police with the job of taking the public temperature.

One of his agents, a man named Jacobi, scanned the newspapers, clipping all references to revolution or democracy, which he then pasted out of context on bits of paper, added some inflammatory comments of his own, and turned over daily to the new King. Vicky wrote to complain about this practice to her father: "[I]f there is a sharp or strong expression in an article of which the whole tenor is moderate & loyal he [Jacobi] cuts that expression out, even though it be in the middle of [a] sentence—and often in the <u>middle</u> of a line!"

To earn his keep, Jacobi apparently also frequented the beer houses and taverns of Berlin, where he provoked his drinking companions into adverse political comments so that he would have something to report back to his employer. Fooled into believing he possessed "the best police in the world" and was "better informed than his ministers," Wilhelm was "delighted" with the results of these spurious investigations. "[I]f only he could be removed from the pernicious reactionary atmosphere he breathes and from the poison daily poured into his ears," Vicky wrote her father, "I know he would be another man." But the insecurity and suspicion that characterized Wilhelm's first few months on the throne were as much a part of him as his elegant manners. The ultimate responsibility thrust upon him had only narrowed and hardened his political arteries.

The new King had also become extremely suspicious of his own family. Within the court, his relatives now learned to ask his permission for almost any plans they made, and it was particularly difficult to gain his consent to travel abroad. Court gossips contended that this was his way of preventing Vicky from going home too often and being contaminated by English liberalism.

When Vicky's grandmother, the Duchess of Kent, died two months after his accession, however, he could scarcely refuse to allow her to attend the funeral.

Vicky found her mother inconsolable. In spite of the Queen's youthful problems with the Duchess of Kent, she had played the role of dutiful daughter to the best of her ability. Now, her ambivalence toward the Duchess came out in excessive mourning. Victoria wept for days, surrendering to the paroxysms of tears as "a welcome friend," taking all her meals alone for three weeks, and leaving the running of the family and official duties entirely to her husband, who had not been particularly well himself. It is generally accepted that the Queen suffered a minor breakdown over her mother's death. Certainly, the court grew anxious as it observed what one biographer called her "hysterical indulgence in sorrow." But Vicky empathized, as she always did, with her mother's mood.

When she returned to Berlin in early April, however, the Prussian Crown Princess discovered that stories about her mother's nervous state had been escalated by the anti-English element at court; even Victoria's old friend Augusta believed that the Queen of England had gone mad and that doctors from all over Europe had been called in for consultation. "[I]ll natured people circulate this report with the greatest certainty," Vicky warned her father.

She also found that her father-in-law's mood had not improved in her absence. "I cannot tell you how difficult it is to get on with the King—," Vicky wrote after her return. "I do not mean personally, he is kind and amiable as usual—but it is perfectly impossible to come to a conclusion on any business matter with him, he gets very angry and always keep talking of Fritz's immense riches, etc . . . refusing to grant necessary things, and then putting off final decisions *à l'infini*."

Both Vicky and her father must have been hoping that when Fritz became Crown Prince, the financial burdens on her dowry would be lessened. But the new King refused to increase his son's allowance. A frugal man himself, particularly in his personal habits, Wilhelm was said to sleep in torn sheets with a threadbare blanket. As king, he personally controlled the pursestrings of all the members of the family, since their expenses—their living allowances and the upkeep of their palaces—were paid directly by him out of the income from the crown estates. Although these estates were huge, Vicky, who needed a new *grande maîtresse* for her palace, could not come to satisfactory living arrangements with the woman she wanted because of her father-in-law's control over her finances.

"It is obvious to me that a certain party is opposed to the practical financial independence of the Princess," Albert wrote Vicky's secretary, Ernest von Stockmar. "That was noticeable in the negotiations for the marriage settlement. . . . She does not get one penny from Prussia, which is shabby enough, and gives away the whole of her dowry, which she is not obliged to do. If the poor Crown Prince is refused things because he has a 'rich wife,' then this is a plan to impoverish her."

The Prince Consort does not seem to have been too far off the mark. As plans for Wilhelm's coronation in the fall began to take shape, Vicky complained regularly to both parents about the cost of her gowns and all the paraphernalia necessary for the celebration. Clearly, she was still spending her own money on what might rightly be called Prussian court expenses.

She was also concerned about her father, and as word of his sickly appearance reached Berlin, she urged Fritz to go to England with her and the children during the summer. There she found her mother on the mend but, as she had suspected, her father overworked. Her own concerns did not add to his peace of mind, and they passed long days at Osborne mulling over the political situation in Prussia and Wilhelm's obsession with revolution. Suddenly, on July 24, word came that the King, who was summering in Baden-Baden, had been the object of an assassination attempt by a student from Leipzig, who was upset because Wilhelm was not doing enough to bring about the unification of Germany. The King had been shot in his neck just below his ear. The wound was not serious, but Fritz rushed home, leaving Vicky in England with her parents.

She returned a few weeks later, in time to prepare for her father-in-law's coronation. In trying to bring England and Prussia closer together, she had arranged for Lord Clarendon, her mother's representative at the coronation, to arrive in Berlin early in order to find a residence where he could entertain as well or better than the representatives of other countries. At the age of not quite twenty-one, the Crown Princess was clearly more adept at symbolic gestures than the new British Ambassador, Lord Augustus Loftus.

"To our despair," she wrote her mother two weeks before the big event,

all the pains we have taken . . . were of no use. The Italian, Spanish and French Ambassadors arrived before him [Clarendon]. . . . he is in a hotel in rooms quite unfit for him, so that he cannot even give a dinner. . . . Now I fear the English Embassy will be the *only* one that will not shine, which is a great pity as here where the feeling is alas not good towards England, every body will say the English don't think it worth their while. . . . I should have thought it such a good opportunity to set the relation between England and Prussia on a better footing. . . . Lord A. Loftus did not take enough trouble. . . . he only took a wretched set of apartments in the Hotel Royal, fit for travelers but not for a Special Mission.

In spite of Fritz, who begged his father to hold the ceremony in Berlin, the current capital of Prussia and of what many hoped would soon be a united Germany, Wilhelm insisted on Königsberg, on the Baltic Sea, the site of the coronation of the first Hohenzollern King 150 years earlier. When he arrived in Königsberg, there were black-red-and-gold flags everywhere, symbolizing the people's desire for unification.* "It is strange," Vicky wrote her parents, "up in the furthest corner of Prussia to find more liberal & German feeling than at

* *These were also the colors of the democratic movement in Germany.*

Berlin." What pleased Vicky angered Wilhelm, who repeatedly told his daughter-in-law that he "regretted that Prussians were ashamed of their own colours and preferred those of the revolution!"

The fact that Wilhelm I saw revolution rather than a desire for unity in the German flag was typical of a man who was determined to make his coronation into an expression of personal sovereignty. His proclamation of the divine right of kings—"I receive this crown from the hand of God"—distressed his old friends Victoria and Albert. (The English had given up the concept of divine right two centuries earlier.) When, contrary to the advice of his ministers, he insisted upon crowning himself and demanded an act of homage from the estates of his realm,* it was clear that Prussia's new King was determined to hold off both the symbols and substance of constitutional government as long as he could.

As Lord Clarendon wrote the Queen from Berlin,

> Her Royal Highness is much alarmed at the state of things here and Lord Clarendon thinks with great reason, for the King has quite made up his mind as to the course he will pursue. He sees democracy and revolution in every symptom of opposition to his will. . . . The King will always religiously keep his word, and will never overturn the institutions he has sworn to maintain, but they are so distasteful to him, and so much at variance with his habit of thought and settled opinions as to the rights of the Crown, that His Majesty will never, if he can avoid it, accept the consequences of representative Government, or allow it to be a reality.

If the spirit was medieval, the coronation itself was splendid. The ceremony took place on Fritz's thirtieth birthday. Wearing the crimson velvet mantle of the Knights of the Black Eagle sweeping down from his broad shoulders to the floor, the Crown Prince looked as if he had stepped out of an ancient German legend just in time to place the coronation mantle around his father's equally imposing frame. Vicky, too, according to Lord Clarendon, was a creature of "exquisite grace" as she paid obeisance to her father-in-law and her adopted country, dressed in a gown of shimmering white satin. As always, Clarendon was impressed with her intelligence.

"Lord Clarendon has had the honour to hold a very long conversation with her Royal Highness, and has been more than ever astonished at the states-manlike and comprehensive views which she takes of the policy of Prussia, both internal and foreign, and of the duties of a constitutional king," he wrote London.

But what impressed a former English Foreign Secretary did not help the new Crown Princess in Prussia. If anything, her views and the fact that she dared express them made her more suspect than ever in her father-in-law's court.

---

* *The estates of the realm: a prerevolutionary concept in which the country was divided into three estates—the nobility, the middle class, and the peasants. Each of the Prussian provinces had a diet composed on these lines.*

CHAPTER
SEVENTEEN

*"[S]he [Vicky] not only always remained the favourite, but, in
many things, the image of her father."*

ERNEST, DUKE OF COBURG

*T*HE FATIGUES OF THE PRECORONATION activities left Vicky with a bad
cold, which turned into an abscess in her ear, accompanied by high fever. On
the day of the ceremony, she excused herself from several activities, and by the
time everyone returned to Berlin, she was confined to bed, temporarily deaf
from the infection. Weeks later she was still tying a cloth around her head and
pouring warm oil in her ear to relieve the pain.

The newly crowned Queen resented the fact that the Crown Princess was
not well enough to accompany her on her social rounds. "I ask you," Vicky
wrote her mother, "how I could go to [a] Party with a tied up head?!" Writing
to her old friend Victoria, however, Augusta put on a different face. Vicky, she
told Victoria in what remained an intimate, sisterly correspondence, was the
only Princess at court allowed to do as she liked.

"But how <u>can</u> the Queen say that I am more at liberty to do what I please
in that respect than the other Princesses," Vicky wrote home.

Morning, noon and night she expects me to be at her beck & call. . . . it
ends in my being a sort of slave. Two winters ago I resisted . . . and the
consequence was that I was not in favour. So Fritz always says, 'Never
mind how tired you are, if it keeps Mama quiet, it is in everybody's interest.'. . . The Queen <u>lives</u> upon society . . . & does not know what fatigue is
when she is amused. . . .

Then you know that the etiquette here is very stiff & that Fritz likes
its being adhered to. Consequently, the respect due to the King & Queen
demands that wherever they appear, I should appear too. . . . The Queen
has no pity, nothing makes her so angry or impatient as when anyone is
unwell, either the King or one of us, or her ladies, or her maids. They are
sure to fall into disgrace.

Furious at her mother-in-law, Vicky enjoyed a certain grim satisfaction
when Dr. Wegner told Augusta that there could be no parties to celebrate the
Crown Princess's twenty-first birthday on November 21. Vicky was in a low

mood anyway. The weather was miserable, and she had broken out in an ugly rash from the quinine prescribed by the doctor. She was also in mourning for King Pedro V of Portugal, a twenty-five-year-old first cousin once removed of her mother and father, whom the Prince Consort had regarded as a surrogate son.

A cult of adoration had been built up in the English court for Pedro—a mystique forged by Albert's wife and his eldest daughter, vying with each other to adore most what Albert loved. Historians disagree with the Prince Consort's esteem for this distinctly ordinary young man. One goes so far as to call Pedro V "the poorest administrator" ever to sit on the Portuguese throne and blames him for neglecting urban sanitation, which ironically brought on the cholera that killed him. Nevertheless, Pedro's death in early November of 1861 produced a flurry of extravagant eulogies flying between London and Berlin, glorifying the young paragon in whom Albert had placed such hopes: "Here I find no one who can understand this, only the greatest astonishment that the death of a cousin whom I have only seen once and that several years ago, should be a grief to me!" Vicky wrote her mother, adding that she would "not take off my mourning but put on black & white or grey."

"It has been a terrible blow to us—& to dearest beloved Papa—who found in him one entirely worthy of himself—which he alas! does not find in those where it was most expected & wanted," Victoria answered. "We have been much crushed by it & have since Tuesday (the day the fatal news arrived) not dined in society. . . . I have been much shaken again—but try to bear up as dear Papa (who has many worries) is so dejected & wants cheering."

Victoria's not-so-subtle comparison of the worthy Pedro to the unworthy Bertie was typical of the Queen, who often contrasted her eldest son with other young men and nearly always found him wanting. This time, however, there was a hidden meaning in her words not lost on Vicky, who was privy to the newest gossip whirling through royal family circles.

At the age of nineteen, the Prince of Wales had spent the summer of 1861 in a training program at the camp of the Curragh of Kildare near Dublin. Sent to live with the general in command of the camp, he had been kept under constant supervision, totally isolated from other men his age, and expected to master the duties of every rank from ensign on up. Visiting Ireland at the end of the summer, Victoria and Albert could not understand why the reports on their son were not good.

But Bertie's dreary summer vacation had ended with a party given the night before his departure, during which his fellow officers, appalled by the Prince of Wales's chaste and restricted life, smuggled a young actress named Nellie Clifden into his bed.

Whether it was Nellie bragging about her conquest or the young officers boasting about their part in it, someone was indiscreet, and the story was soon all over the London clubs. It was not long before old Baron Stockmar in Coburg heard that the Prince of Wales had taken his first mistress and that she had followed him to Windsor. Lord Torrington, "one of the great gossips of

London," passed the news along to Bertie's father just about the time Albert was mourning the death of Pedro.

The Prince Consort was in no state of mind to deal with information of this sort. Ever since his trip to Coburg the previous year, he had been in a serious depression—obsessively overworking and suffering from sleeplessness. Now he directed all his anxieties onto his eldest son, turning what was normal behavior for a man his age into a situation "which," he told Bertie, "has caused me the greatest pain I have yet felt in this life."

Although the Prince Consort's overreaction can be partially blamed on his worries over Bertie's profligate ancestors—Victoria's uncles and his own syphilitic brother, Ernest—it is still true that, as one of Queen Victoria's biographers* says, "on the subject of sex, the Prince Consort was unbalanced." As was the Queen. When Albert told her about their son's escapade—minus, of course, "the disgusting details"—her reaction was as unreasonable as his: "Oh! that boy—much as I pity him I never can or shall look at him without a shudder."

Tormented by insomnia, the Prince Consort's nights were haunted by worries that Nellie would interfere with a visit Alix was supposed to pay to England so that Bertie could see her again. What if Alix's parents heard about it? What if the actress became pregnant? In his irrational state, Albert wrote Bertie a letter, detailing a nightmarish scenario in which the Prince of Wales would be dragged into court and forced to own up to his paternity while the girl regaled "the greedy Multitude" with "disgusting details" of his "profligacy."

The death of the "good son" Pedro had exaggerated Albert's concerns about the next generation, and on November 21, 1861, Vicky's twenty-first birthday, the Prince Consort wrote her a low-spirited letter describing his "sad heart" and begging her to take care of her own health. "The frightful event in Portugal stands in strong outline before our eyes. Therefore see that you spare yourself now, so that at some future time you may be able to do more."

But the advice Vicky's father gave to her he was unable to follow himself. The day after his daughter's birthday, the Prince Consort insisted on going out in the pouring rain to inspect new buildings at Sandhurst, returning to Windsor shivering and suffering from rheumatism. He came down with a cold and fever that kept him awake at night, while he thrashed over his anxieties about Bertie. Finally, on November 25, a day of bitter weather, he traveled to Cambridge, where Bertie was at the university (although he was not allowed to live on campus), to see his son and discuss his transgression with him. The meeting was successful. Bertie apologized to his father and impressed him by refusing to name the officers responsible for Nellie. "It would have been cowardly to sacrifice those who have risked themselves for you," he wrote approvingly to his son, "even in an evil deed. . . ." The Prince Consort then voiced, rather touchingly, his greatest fear. "You must not, you dare not, be lost. The consequences for this country, and for the world, would be too dreadful!"

* Cecil Woodham-Smith.

Albert returned from Cambridge still suffering from cold and fever. The first Vicky heard of this was a letter from him written four days later. "I am at a very low ebb," he told his daughter. "Much worry and great sorrow (about which I beg you not to ask questions) have robbed me of sleep during the past fortnight. In this shattered state I had a very heavy catarrh and for the last four days am suffering from headache and pains in my limbs which may develop into rheumatism."

Her father's unhappy state was confirmed by her mother, who wrote that the Prince Consort was suffering from "a cold with neuralgia—a great depression which has been worse these last 3 days. . . . The sad part is—that this loss of rest at night (worse than he has ever had before) was caused by a great sorrow & worry, which upset us both greatly—but him, especially—& it broke him quite down; I never saw him so low."

Low, but not critical, and this report was soon followed by others that were quite encouraging. On the last day of November the Queen wrote that "dear Papa is in reality much better—only so much reduced and as usual desponding as men really only are—when unwell. He was never confined to his room—and able to come to dinner and other meals—every day—and yesterday he went out with us to see the Eton Volunteers. . . . Dr. Jenner said yesterday evening Papa was so much better, he would be quite well in two or three days —but he is not inclined himself ever to admit he is better!"

It was letters like these that kept Vicky from realizing the seriousness of her father's illness. Either the Queen did not want to worry her eldest daughter, who could do nothing in Berlin and had been refused permission to go to Windsor, or she could not commit to paper what she was afraid even to admit to herself. The result was that Vicky, who saw her father's condition only through her mother's eyes, was not prepared for what happened.

The first inkling the Prussian Crown Princess had of anything out of the ordinary came in a letter from Victoria written on December 6, admitting that she had had "3 days of dreadful anxiety" over Vicky's father, who was suffering from an "abominable feverish attack," symptomatic of typhoid fever. The Queen told Vicky that she had given Albert their bedroom and moved into the dressing room next door to sleep, "so as to be near him at night."

It was a difficult time for Vicky, who was just recovering from the flu. Fritz, who seldom pleasured himself, was off hunting. There had been an accident at sea in which the children's governess lost her brother, a naval officer who had been one of Fritz's playmates; Vicky had been caring for the governess's family, as they waited for word about their son, which never came. "Really the door never opens now except for someone to come in with bad news," Vicky wrote her mother at the end of the first week in December. Still shut in, she worked on some drawings to give her father for Christmas. He was proud of her artistic talent and had asked her to try illustrating Tennyson's "Idylls of the King," which they had read together during the summer. She decided to skip her weekly letter to him because, as she put it, "I fear I should bore him, and all I have to say is of a serious nature and not calculated either to cheer or amuse."

There were also political troubles brewing in Berlin. Wilhelm was furious because new elections had brought "almost all radicals" to power. "The state of things here appears to me most threatening," Vicky wrote Victoria. "I cannot tell why but I have a sort of presentiment that something is going to be amiss and go wrong."

"Don't be alarmed about adored Papa. . . ." was the next word from Windsor, dated December 7. "[I]t is a sort of feverish attack which will be tedious—and you must not expect his being better for some days." On the tenth: "Thank God! beloved Papa had another excellent night and is going on quite satisfactorily." And on the eleventh: "The doctors are satisfied; he holds his ground and contrary to what is generally the case with such fevers—he is not weaker, though he gets sadly thin."

Two days later, however, there was a telegram for Fritz from Prince Albert's secretary, telling him to prepare Vicky for the worst—a warning temporarily contradicted by a wire that arrived the next morning.

"Thank God that the news are so much better this morning!" Vicky wrote her mother on December 14.

Of course I was much frightened at the telegram last night, as it seemed to us . . . completely inexplicable, the news I had been receiving every day were so reassuring and cheerful that I thought all was now going on perfectly well. . . . Oh how I wish I were with you and could try to comfort you and be of use. . . . If you had allowed, I would have come to you immediately. I wanted to do so last night, but Wegner and Fritz & the King and Queen would not allow it on any account, which I think is very cruel.

But I have hopes of which I did not tell you because I was afraid it would annoy you . . . & Wegner will not allow me to think of moving. I myself think that at this early stage it would not matter at all. . . . I am at the end of the 2nd month. I did not tell you because I thought you were worried about dearest beloved Papa & it was no use saying anything which might vex you. Forgive my speaking of it now.

This letter was written on the morning of December 14, about the time that the Prince Consort, who had been delirious on and off for several days, lapsed into final unconsciousness. He emerged only a few times more—to kiss his wife or smile wanly at his children. During an early delirium, he had spoken of his eldest daughter, whose health was one of his obsessions during his own illness. "If only nothing happens to Vicky," Albert said; "now since Pedro's death I no longer trust any one."

A little before 11:00 P.M. on the evening of December 14, 1861, Vicky's father died at the age of forty-two. In his depression, he had, it seemed to observers, simply resigned himself, fading into oblivion without even a struggle. The next morning the telegram arrived in Berlin. "Why has the Earth not swallowed me up?" Vicky asked. "He was too great, too perfect for Earth that adored Father whom I ever worshipped with more than a daughter's affection."

■

THE DEATH OF HER FATHER robbed Vicky of the most stable element in her life, the person who understood and admired her, the mentor to whom she applied for approval. Much as the Prussian Crown Princess loved her mother, and she did enormously, the Queen had dealt primarily with the female side of Vicky's life—manners and clothes when Vicky was young; childbirth, social custom, and court gossip after she was married. Even in the realm of religion, where Victoria was responsible for Vicky's early and deep faith, it was Albert who had explained the creed to his adolescent daughter's more questioning mind and laid to rest her doubts. It was clear to everyone that Victoria and Albert's first child was the only one whose intellectual capacities equaled those of the father, and it was she, next to his widow, who would miss him the most.

The Prince Consort's death not only deprived Vicky of her "oracle," it left her with unrealistic burdens. First, there was the need to live up to her image of her sainted father. "[L]et us take up his glorious task of being good and doing good," she wrote her mother three days after Albert's death. "I will try to follow his example to fulfill his every wish, to be to you all I possibly can, to banish and overcome every wrong feeling & to live but for others as he did. He wished it, he expected it. May his blessing now from above rest on my endeavours!" she added the next day.

There was also the additional obligation to her mother. The one person who had kept the Queen on a semi-even emotional keel was gone, and as their eldest child, Vicky could not help but feel the need to offer emotional ballast to his grieving widow. How could she consider her own loss when her mother's was so much more painful? Waking up every morning next to Fritz, Vicki wondered what it must be like for her mother to wake up alone.

This empathy comes through in the Crown Princess's letters to the Queen in the weeks and months that followed the Prince Consort's death. Muddled by the supreme effort to make sense out of tragedy, devastated by her own grief and bewilderment at being abandoned, Vicky tried to convince her mother (and herself) that her father's death was God's will and that dearest Papa, the most perfect of human beings, had been too good for this earth and was better off in Heaven. A true believer, she did find comfort in her faith, but her attempts to communicate it failed. The Queen's lamentations continued:

"Yes, dearest child, you may well preach to me alive & well! I may drag on an utterly extinguished life, but it will be death in life." Victoria blamed the Prince Consort's demise on his anguish over Bertie's escapade. "I never can see B. without a shudder!" she wrote Vicky, who came to her brother's defense. "I know you will be kind, pitying, forgiving and loving to the poor boy. . . . he is not like Papa and you, but he cannot help it . . . and I assure you he knows it and he feels it. . . . He has really the best intentions."

Unlike her mother, who was surrounded by sympathy, Vicky knew that she herself was in hostile territory. Who among those hard-line Prussians was not secretly thrilled to have such a dangerous voice of constitutionalism silenced and removed from the European stage? Only her loving Fritz and, to a minor degree, her in-laws shared her grief. Whatever the other members of the Prussian royal family said, Vicky knew that there was little genuine sympathy in their appropriate phrases, carefully mouthed.

She felt particularly isolated when Fritz left for her father's funeral. She herself had been denied permission to attend because of the early stage of her pregnancy. She would, she wrote her mother, come just as soon as the doctor and her parents-in-law allowed her to travel. Meanwhile, she dreamed about dear Papa every night. "[L]ast night I dreamt that I took his dear hand and kissed it so long and so often, and cried over it and did not like to let it go! Waking was such unutterable misery!" She continued to dream about her father for months, dreams in which he appeared "alive and well," while the rest of his family was in mourning.

At her mother's request, Vicky sent Albert's letters to her back to England. They were returned some months later by the Queen. "[H]ow admirably, how perfect, all are! . . . read them again & again & drink in from them wisdom & virtue to give you strength in the battle of life," she exhorted her daughter.

The day of Prince Albert's funeral was the most difficult of all for the Prussian Crown Princess, who got through the hours with photographs of "dear darling blessed" Papa propped up on her knees, "devouring them with my eyes" and kissing them. "Dear Mama . . . how cut off I feel so far away out here!" she said.

It was not until March of 1862, three months after the Prince Consort's death, that she was given permission to visit her mother. The journey was a frustrating one, as Vicky took upon herself the task of comforting someone who would not be comforted. "Mama is dreadfully sad . . . ," she wrote Fritz; "she cries a lot; then there is always the empty room, the empty bed, she always sleeps with Papa's coat over her and his dear red dressing-gown beside her and some of his clothes in the bed! . . . Poor Mama has to go to bed, has to get up alone—for ever. She was as much in love with Papa as though she had married him yesterday. . . . she feels the same as your little Frauchen . . . and is always consumed with longing for her husband."

But if Vicky still had her Fritz, she had other problems. "I feel so discouraged . . . ," she admitted to her mother two weeks after her father's death;

all the efforts that I made for doing my duty here, in this position which is no easy one, were made in hopes of pleasing Papa—a word of satisfaction from him was more to me than the praise of any one else—and for that I could have done anything. I felt so full of determination and courage. . . . I did not care what I went through, I knew Papa would be satisfied, and now I feel I don't care about anything anymore. It is not right I know, he would not approve it . . . but at present I confess it to you, hoping you will not think the worse of me for it, and that you who are setting a better example will pity me! I am but beginning life and the unerring judgment on which I built with so much security and so much confidence for now and for the future is <u>gone</u>! <u>Where</u> shall I look to for advice? I am only 21 and things here wear a threatening aspect!

Vicky was right. The world around her was menacing her most profound beliefs. But it is doubtful, even if Albert had lived, that his presence in the wings of German history would have made any significant difference. What he could have offered was sympathy and understanding. As it was, Vicky and Fritz now had to face the first political crisis of their lives without the intellectual and emotional succor on which both of them had come to depend.

CHAPTER
EIGHTEEN

"[I]f an alternative to liberalism could have worked anywhere, it should have worked in Germany. Where else was the authoritarian tradition still so strong, the bureaucracy so efficient . . . the military so respected . . . the populace so law-abiding and so unconsciously docile?"

FRITZ STERN

*T*HE YEAR AFTER her father's death, 1862, was one of turmoil and frustration for the Prussian Crown Princess. There were rumors in February that her marriage was in trouble—stories she and Fritz believed were spread by the Kreuzzeitung. Pregnant for the third time in four years, she gave birth to a son (Henry) in August, attended by Dr. Locock and Mrs. Innocent. "I have lost all confidence in the German treatment," she wrote her mother, "and I really thought if I did not have Sir Charles or an English doctor I should not get through the business at all."

It was particularly unfortunate for Vicky that Albert had died at this point in German history. Caught between duties to her English and Prussian families, she muddled through these familial crises while at the same time trying to cope with devastating changes in the Prussian political climate—developments that were totally antithetical to the precepts inculcated in her by her father.

WHEN WILHELM I SUCCEEDED to the throne in early 1860, there were four political parties in Prussia: two factions of conservatives, the Kreuzzeitung and the Wochenblatt; the Liberals; and the Center (Catholic).

The Kreuzzeitung party, which centered around its newspaper of the same name, was furthest to the right; it was the political home of the feudal Junkers, who wanted to rescind the great reforms of the Napoleonic period and return Prussia to "a sort of modern Gothic edifice, in which the castes and hierarchic gradations of medieval societies should be revived." This revisionism appealed to both the "Squirearchy of the provinces" and the higher echelons of society in the cities and around the court. The Kreuzzeitung was the faction of Bismarck and the pro-Russian court clique that had supported Friedrich Wilhelm IV before his death and had opposed Vicky as the wife of their future King.

The Wochenblatt faction supported Wilhelm. Its members had kept faith with him when he was ostracized for his pro-English, anti-Russian stand during the Crimean War. The Wochenblatt took its inspiration from the glorious days of Frederick the Great and believed in the Prussian army as the protector of all the German states. Like Wilhelm himself, his party was an enemy of representational government, regarding the Prussian Parliament not as a legislative body but as a political adjunct, "entrusted with the high privilege of giving its advice to the Crown."

Slightly to the left in the political spectrum were the Old Liberals. A half century earlier, at the end of the eighteenth century, they had supported the great reformers who rid Prussia of much of its fossilized feudalism and helped defeat Napoleon I. A "much-maligned minority" under the reactionary Friedrich Wilhelm IV, they had reemerged during the Revolution of 1848, only to be silenced during the conservative reaction that followed. They surfaced again at the beginning of Wilhelm's reign and had been gaining steadily in power.

The fourth party called itself the Center and was the party of the Roman Catholic minority in a Protestant country. It sought temporal as well as spiritual power for the Church, but it was not yet a political force.

These parties operated in the two houses of the Prussian Parliament, established by the constitution following the Revolution of 1848. The lower house, or Chamber of Deputies, was elected by a three-class system that favored the wealthy and held veto power over the budget. The House of Lords (Herrenhaus) was dominated by the Junkers. It was empowered to veto legislation, a prerogative it never failed to exercise to the advantage of the nobility. But it was the king who held the final power. He could call parliament into session, adjourn or dissolve it, and issue emergency edicts when it was not sitting.

A PROFESSIONAL SOLDIER, Wilhelm had few interests outside the army. His one-sided military education had made him deeply suspicious of parliamentary procedures, antagonistic to the will of the people to share in government, and intellectually incapable of separating the desire for German unification from the revolution that had brought it to his attention. Nor had his enforced exile in England left any permanent liberalizing effect. It was only the aborted Italian War, highlighting as it did the length of time needed to mobilize the Prussian army, that had given Wilhelm a mission. An old-fashioned soldier-king, Wilhelm made army reform the personal and central issue of the early years of his reign, and it was these reforms that led him into conflict with the Prussian Parliament—a situation that later came to be known as the Constitutional Crisis of 1862.

Certainly there was need to reform the Prussian army, which was still operating on regulations established at the end of the Napoleonic Wars, when every able-bodied boy and man had been needed to wrest Prussia back from the French. To do this, the Prussian military reformers of 1814 had established a national guard, the *Landwehr*, that served as a bridge between the regular army and the Prussian people. Over the ensuing fifty years, however, the *Landwehr* had deteriorated. Its officers were poorly trained and its soldiers mostly raw recruits; "dirty militiamen" is how they struck Wilhelm when they straggled before him, ragged and imprecise, in military reviews.

In striking contrast was the regular Prussian army, the "state within a state" —a rigidly disciplined but shrinking force led by aristocratic officers, who were quite literally a class apart. In 1859, when Wilhelm started his army reforms, two-thirds of the lieutenants, three-fourths of the senior officers, and nine-tenths of the generals in the Prussian army were of noble birth. The number of ordinary soldiers had dwindled in fifty years, while the population of Prussia itself had nearly doubled. There were no more recruits in Wilhelm's day than there had been in the days of his grandfather, Friedrich Wilhelm III.

At the end of 1859, Wilhelm appointed General Albrecht von Roon to the post of Minister of War with the specific job of implementing military reform. Roon, a so-called "intelligent conservative," had more wide-ranging intellectual interests than Wilhelm but still believed in the mystique of his caste. According to Roon, the world was divided into two groups, soldiers and civilians. Professional soldiers were trustworthy on the battlefield; citizen-soldiers, who had to believe in a cause before they would risk their lives, were not.

Roon was sincerely devoted to Wilhelm, but there is some question as to whether this was true of General Edwin von Manteuffel, a man of insatiable ambition who served as Wilhelm's other military adviser. A former member of Friedrich Wilhelm IV's camarilla, Manteuffel had remained at court by ingratiating himself with the new King. It was Manteuffel who advised Wilhelm to guarantee his personal authority over the army by creating a "royal military cabinet," independent of the War Ministry and hence not answerable to parliament. Not too surprisingly, Manteuffel himself became the first chief of this cabinet, which lasted until 1918, as long as there were Hohenzollerns on the throne.

Both Roon and Manteuffel contributed to Wilhelm's army reforms, which underscored the King's determination to keep a barrier between his soldiers and his people. The object was to increase the regular army while reducing the national guard, the *Landwehr*. To do this, they proposed universal conscription, increasing active service to three years, followed by service in the reserves for four or five years more, thus robbing the national guard of all the young men and excluding it from wartime service. An expensive proposal, it was made more costly by Wilhelm's unshakable belief, not shared by his advisers, that it took three years to train a good soldier. "Discipline, blind obedience, are things which can be inculcated and given permanence only by long familiarity," Wilhelm claimed. The proposal was rejected by the Prussian Parliament, which was asked to vote an increase of twenty-five percent in taxes to fund it.

Parliamentary opposition was based as much on political as economic concerns. The national guard, a bridge between the elite army and the citizenry, was extremely important to liberals everywhere and the upper middle class in particular, which provided most of its officers, as opposed to the exclusively aristocratic officer corps of the regular army. Moreover, the liberals quite rightly discerned that Wilhelm and his advisers were trying to turn the army into the "school of the nation"—a training camp whose well-indoctrinated pupils would automatically support the conservative King with "cadaver obedience" for the rest of their political lives.

Rejected by parliament and convinced by his military advisers that he and his army should function independently of the legislative branch of government, Wilhelm withdrew his proposals for military reorganization and the taxes to implement them. In their place, he substituted a request for blanket appropriations to cover military expenses for one year. Parliament approved these blind appropriations—not only in 1860 but in 1861 as well. In return, Wilhelm's ministers had promised to drop the reorganizational provisions to which parliament objected. Manteuffel now urged the King to disregard this pledge, which he did, forming thirty-six new regular army regiments to replace an equal number from the national guard and appointing aristocratic officers to lead them. In allowing Wilhelm and his military cabinet free rein in the development of the army, the Prussian Parliament had acquiesced, however unwittingly, in the dominance of the military over Prussia. It was one of the great miscalculations of history.

Not everyone agreed with the "spineless tactics" of the moderate liberals in parliament, and a group that called itself the Progressive Party split off from the Liberal Party. Demanding unification of Germany and true constitutional government, the Progressives affirmed their loyalty to the King, but insisted on preserving the national guard and cutting military training to two years. At the end of 1861, they gained an enormous victory at the polls.

VICKY WAS VISITING the recently bereaved Queen in England in March of 1862 when the newly liberalized Chamber of Deputies passed a bill requiring Wilhelm to account for his military budget for the first time in two years. In answer to what he considered an affront to his royal prerogatives, Wilhelm dissolved the Chamber and fired his few remaining liberal ministers, whom he blamed for the liberal landslide in the previous election. As the wheels of government ground to a frightening halt, Otto von Bismarck, a pro-Russian member of the Kreuzzeitung Party currently serving as Ambassador to St. Petersburg, began to be mentioned as the only man strong enough to bring order out of governmental chaos.

"Rumour has it that the candidate for a new Conservative Ministry is von Bismarck-Schönhausen," Fritz wrote Vicky in early March. "I cannot get used to this idea, although in actual fact there are no men of great ability, look where you will." Vicky also heard from her mother-in-law, one of Bismarck's earliest and most determined opponents, that Roon, coauthor of the King's military reforms, had helped bring about the downfall of the liberal ministers in order to open the way for a Bismarck ministry.

"For heaven's sake <u>not that</u> man as Premier. . . . he has no principles!" she wrote Fritz. "I keep on repeating the same thing and cannot express myself strongly enough, as I am so convinced that our only duty is to make this dear country so perfect, strong and mighty by means of a liberal practical constitution and by orderly and legal methods. . . . then . . . we shall have the confidence of the whole of Germany and Europe, which we have not now."

But back in Berlin, Vicky's husband was forced to deal with his father, and Wilhelm was very much on the defensive. He accused Fritz of disloyalty to the crown and excoriated him for what the liberal papers characterized as the Crown Prince's "opposition to the King." These recriminations stung Fritz, for whom reverence for his father and king were the basic tenets of life as a Hohenzollern Prince. "I hardly know of anything which can hurt one more than reproach from his father," Vicky wrote him from England. "I loved my father so much that one mere hint of disapproval from him made me unhappy for weeks, but he never unjustly accused me of anything! . . . I wish to protect you and guard you from anything which could trouble your great and golden heart."

In May of 1862, six weeks after Vicky's return, new elections for the Prussian Parliament took place. Following the trend of the previous winter, voters sent even more Progressives to the Chamber of Deputies, thus putting the forces in opposition to the crown in control of parliament.

Ironically, this gave the conservatives the ammunition they had been seeking. "The reactionary Party get stronger every day, and have the King now completely on their side and in their power," Vicky wrote her mother in early July. The Crown Princess's assessment was correct. During these critical months, the strongest influences on the King were Roon, who was doing everything he could to bring his friend Bismarck home as Prime Minister, and fanatics like Manteuffel, eager to find an excuse to do away with the constitution. Having predicted revolution for the past year, Manteuffel drew up a precise campaign for the subjugation of the citizens of Berlin, "street by street." To advance his own ambitions, he played skillfully on Wilhelm's deepest fears—a repetition of the Revolution of 1848 and his undignified flight to England.

Sent on a ceremonial tour in the middle of the summer, Fritz was warned by his father to say nothing "oppositional" and to allow no "criticism of the Government in his presence." But as Vicky complained to her mother, it was "perfectly impossible" to know what the King called opposition, as he took offense "at the most harmless expressions."

For Fritz, the position of Crown Prince, difficult at best, was becoming impossible. "[Y]ou can and must not oppose him [the King], and you cannot sacrifice your liberal opinions," Vicky advised her husband; "there is only one way of reconciling the two—silence!" But while Fritz struggled between filial piety and the beliefs of his conscience, he was badgered by the liberals, who wanted him to break with the King, and denounced by the military establishment, rumored to be planning a coup in favor of his reactionary cousin, Prince Fritz Carl.

Unlike the fanatics, the liberal factions in parliament wanted compromise, not conflict, and they were even willing to abandon their support of the national guard in the fight over army reform. Joined by the Progressives, all they asked the King to do was agree to reduce the training period for soldiers from three years to two, an amount of time most army generals and his cabinet deemed absolutely sufficient. Wilhelm would not listen.

In early September of 1862, Vicky wrote Victoria that there was "a storm blowing up. The Chambers have refused to vote the money necessary for the new organization of the army if the 3 year service is adhered to. They will only hear of the 2 years, and this the King said 'he never would agree to, even were it to cost him his head.' Fritz is in despair, he has seen several deputies yesterday & is gone to Berlin today to a Counsel held on purpose for him."

On September 17, the Chamber voted down the King's army reorganization bill by 308 to 11. In a towering rage, Wilhelm declared to his ministers that he would sooner abdicate than compromise. He wired Fritz, who had gone with Vicky to see Queen Victoria, who was visiting in Gotha, demanding that he return immediately to Berlin.

"I have sent for you to prepare you for my abdication if the Ministers insist on their demands," Wilhelm told Fritz, when he arrived at Babelsberg at eight the next morning. "God and my conscience do not allow me to do anything else. . . . For thirty-three years I have been opposed to military service of less than three years, and I cannot show such inconsistency to the world at large. Everything is ready for my abdication. Here is the document, it only needs my signature."

Fritz was appalled. He believed in the army as the instrument of the monarchy, not the parliament, and for the next forty-eight hours tried to mediate between the King and his ministers, explaining to his father that compromise on one year of military training would be far preferable to abdication, which would "constitute a threat to the dynasty, country and Crown." He even argued that Wilhelm was establishing a dangerous precedent by abdicating over a parliamentary decision, a precedent that might endanger his son's future reign. The one thing the Crown Prince never considered was accepting his father's abdication and taking over the throne himself.

Not so Vicky, who saw the matter in an entirely different light. She was still in her father's old duchy of Gotha with her mother and her mother's Foreign Secretary when she sent Fritz the advice which, had he followed it, might well have changed history: "If the King sees that he cannot take the necessary steps to restore order and confidence in the country without going against his conscience, I consider it wise and honest to leave it to others who can take over these duties without burdening their conscience," she wrote him. "I see no way out and consider you should make this sacrifice for the country. If you do not accept, I believe that you will regret it one day."

But Fritz's father had tears in his eyes when he spoke of abdicating, and he looked like a "poor broken old man" to his son. How calculated this was will never be known. Wilhelm was unquestionably sincere in his concept of duty and his stand on military reform. At the same time, he was being directed by men with minds far more devious and clever than his own. He had to have known how Fritz would react to his abdication threat and was certainly aware that he could count on his son's acute sense of filial honor to save him from carrying it out. Had he really wanted to abdicate, he would have signed the paper first, then called in Fritz.

Two days later, Fritz heard that Bismarck had arrived in Berlin. Unbeknown to the Crown Prince, Bismarck had been in constant touch with General Roon, who had been trying to secure his appointment as Prime Minister. Fritz asked to see him. It was a cool encounter, with Bismarck clearly "resentful" of the Crown Prince, refusing to commit himself until he had spoken to the King. That evening Fritz returned to his wife and family in Gotha.

On September 22, 1862, after having assured his son that he was "opposed to engaging this man," Wilhelm summoned Bismarck to his summer palace of Babelsberg: "I have done my utmost and can see no way out," the King said. "I cannot reign against my convictions. My Ministers are against me; my son has ranged himself on their side. . . . I should be acting against my conscience if I were to sacrifice the reorganization of the army."

Bismarck begged Wilhelm to give up the idea of abdication.

"Will you try to govern without a majority?" Wilhelm asked him.

"Yes," Bismarck answered.

"Without a budget?"

"Yes."

The two men took a walk in the palace park, during which the would-be Prime Minister assured Wilhelm that he would carry through his army reorganization and that it was "not a question of Liberal or Conservative . . . but rather of monarchical rule or parliamentary government, and that the latter must be avoided at all costs." A master of psychology, Bismarck said what he knew Wilhelm wanted to hear. "I will rather perish with the King than forsake your Majesty in the contest with parliamentary government."

Thus, over the objections of the Queen, the Crown Prince, and the Crown Princess, Bismarck secured for himself the major role in the political future of Prussia and Europe.

He had been waiting for this chance for a very long time.

CHAPTER
NINETEEN

> *"The German nation is sick of principles and doctrines, of literary greatness and of theoretical existence. What it wants is power, power, power! And whoever gives it power, to him it will give honor, more honor than he can imagine."*
>
> JULIUS FROBEL, *1859*

*I*N PROMISING WILHELM to defy parliament in the interests of royal inflexibility, Bismarck was doing more than just flattering his King to achieve the post he had long coveted. Count Otto Eduard Leopold von Bismarck-Schönhausen believed in everything the Hohenzollerns had always stood for—an autocratic monarch, a strong army, a feudal aristocracy, a quiescent bourgeoisie, and a suppressed peasantry. Unlike Wilhelm, however, Bismarck was brilliant. He was also self-confident, psychologically astute, and articulate.

Bismarck was a big man physically, oxlike in strength, thin but starting a paunch. Already half bald, he had a pale complexion, bushy brows and mustache, and piercing eyes with heavy bags. His high-pitched voice seemed inappropriate to a man of his size and demeanor. Forty-seven years old when he became Prime Minister of Prussia, he had had plenty of time to hone his skills and solidify his political philosophy.

BISMARCK WAS BORN in 1815 into the Junker class, a group exclusive to Prussia. The Junkers were country squires, landed noblemen, neither as rich nor as politically influential as their aristocratic counterparts in England, but even more conscious of their separation from their inferiors. All Junkers, not just firstborns, were entitled to use *von* before their names, thus distinguishing them from the middle class. The army officer corps in this militaristic nation was drawn from their ranks. Other Junkers joined the labyrinthian bureaucracy of the civil service, where they were guaranteed similarly favored treatment.

Although the great reforms of the early nineteenth century had freed city dwellers from the constraints of outdated feudalism, life in the countryside had not changed a great deal. The local aristocracy continued to administrate the rural areas for the peasants, in whom the habit of obedience to authority remained very strong. It is easy to understand why the Junkers (with few free-spirited exceptions) belonged to the Kreuzzeitung Party. Like any endangered species, they fought to retain their prerogatives. These, they felt, had been slipping away with the emancipation of the serfs and laws that permitted members of the middle class to buy estates. They resented the intrusion of nonaristo-cratic neighbors, complaining that the reformers had tried to turn "good old Prussia into a new-fangled Jewish state."

Bismarck, who was proud of his noble origins, was an aristocrat only through his father, whose family had owned land in Brandenburg for five hun-dred years. His mother, by far the more intelligent of his parents, was from the middle class. Her ancestors were academicians and civil servants; her father, a diplomat, had risen to the position of secretary of the cabinet of Frederick the Great and his two successors. She herself was more attracted to the political and social scene at court than to life in the country.

Bismarck did not like his mother. He felt she had been too busy for him when he was young (she sent him away to school at six) and too demanding as he grew up. An ambitious woman, she objected to his favorite pastimes of drinking, dueling, and womanizing—activities that he pursued with notoriety during his student years and for some time after. A portrait of the future politician at eighteen shows a good-looking and determined young man with a surprisingly soft and full mouth, whose sensuality was covered by his famous bristling mustaches by the time he came to middle age and power.

The story is told that during his university days Bismarck was invited to a ball, for which he ordered a new pair of boots. The day before the event, having heard that the boots would not be ready, young Otto went to the cobbler with two "enormous and ferocious dogs," threatening the man that the dogs would "tear him in pieces if the boots were not ready by the following morning." To drive his point home, he hired another man to parade the dogs back and forth in front of the cobbler's shop throughout the day with the admonition, "Unfortunate shoemaker, thou art doomed to death by the dogs unless Herr Bismarck's boots be finished." Needless to say, the cobbler worked all night, and Bismarck went to the ball in new boots. The anecdote, repeated "with great gusto" by Bismarck's fellow students, may be apocryphal. If true, it presages Bismarck's later successes in intimidating those who might be inclined to op-pose him; if not, it says something about the standards of behavior for aristo-cratic students of the day.

Arrogant and pugnacious, Bismarck tried life as a provincial bureaucrat after university, but gave it up after two years as "petty and tedious" work. "The Prussian official is like a member of an orchestra," he explained in a famous quote many years later, "but I want to play only the music which I myself like, or no music at all."

Young Bismarck then tried farming the family lands in Pomerania, the part of eastern Germany lying to the south of the Baltic Sea. That, too, failed to satisfy him. Bored, discontented, the "wild" or "crazy" Bismarck, as he was called by the local gentry, was nearing thirty and seemingly a failure when a charming young woman, Marie von Thadden, changed his life.

When Bismarck met Marie, she was engaged to one of his friends. Young Otto, who declared himself a cynic and agnostic, had given up religion at sixteen, but Marie, a devout Pietist, wanted to bring him back into the fold.

The Pietist tries to find personal union with God. Pietism dates back to the end of the seventeenth century; it flourished in the nineteenth century under the leadership of men like Marie's father, a close friend of General Leopold von Gerlach, the King's personal aide-de-camp, and Ludwig von Gerlach, founder of the Kreuzzeitung. The Gerlach brothers were intimates of the mystical King Friedrich Wilhelm IV.

Bismarck fell in love with Marie, but she married his friend and died in an epidemic during the first year of her marriage. Word of her illness, Bismarck said, "tore the first ardent prayer from my heart, without pondering as to its reasonableness." That prayer, Bismarck claimed, was his conversion back to the faith. According to Henry Kissinger, Bismarck's covenant was "more in the nature of a diplomatic pact with God than the mastering of a spiritual dilemma."

Marie had introduced Otto to another young Pietist, Johanna von Putt-kamer, whom she wished him to marry. With her long face, longer nose, and short upper lip, Johanna was not pretty like Marie, nor was she particularly appealing. Essentially mean-spirited, Johanna was already accomplished at spot-ting other people's foibles and attacking them with sardonic humor. This judg-mental aspect of her personality is obvious in a portrait done at the time of her marriage. Johanna's mouth, already turned down at the corners, exhibits a humorlessness strange in a young woman of twenty-three.

But Johanna fell in love with Bismarck, and he learned to love her, too. To marry her, he had to convince her father of the validity of his conversion. "I think I am entitled to count myself among the adherents of the Christian reli-gion," he wrote his prospective father-in-law in December of 1846, adding, "I like piety in women and have a horror of feminine cleverness."

This was not entirely true. Bismarck liked piety in his wife and intellectual stimulation in other women, and he soon discovered the disadvantages of the one without the other. "No one believes how difficult it was for me to make out of Fräulein von Puttkamer a Frau von Bismarck," he once complained. Still, Johanna was an excellent foil for a man who had felt used and unloved by his mother. She adored him unreservedly, gave him three children within five years, and made no demands whatsoever. Frau von Bismarck was, according to the eldest of those children, one of those unfortunate souls "composed only of a sense of duty and self-denial." Permitting herself no pleasures and no opinions, she seized eagerly on her beloved Otto's enemies as her own.

If Bismarck's Christianity stabilized his life and gave him an adoring wife and a secure home, it did not soften his attitude toward those outside his private domain. Untempered by love, it was a harsh faith, cruel to his enemies but well within the Lutheran tradition of service to the state and the monarch. In this regard, Bismarck rationalized his behavior in one simple sentence: "I believe that I am obeying God when I serve the King."

Pietism did something even more important for the young Bismarck. It established him in the court of King Friedrich Wilhelm IV through the Gerlach brothers. Invited to attend the United Diet in Berlin in 1847, Bismarck arrived for his first political stint with powerful friends already at court. His attendance at the diet, however, was pure historical serendipity. Unpopular at home, he was appointed to represent his fellow Pomeranian Junkers only after the original delegate took ill. "No one would ever have heard of me in my rural retreat," Bismarck later wrote, "if I had not become a member of the united diet by chance."

At that meeting, called by King Friedrich Wilhelm IV for the purpose of getting money for a new railway, Bismarck made a name for himself by attacking the liberal delegates, who refused to authorize the railway funds, put forward proposals for citizenship for all Jews, and tried to reform the hunting laws. Later, on his honeymoon with Johanna in Venice, Bismarck was presented to the King himself, who spoke to him at length, signifying approval of the young man's behavior at the diet.

Bismarck was back in Pomerania when the Revolution of 1848 broke out. Hearing of the uprisings in Berlin, he armed the peasants of Schönhausen, then left for Berlin to start a counterrevolution. But Friedrich Wilhelm IV seemed impotent; his generals refused to help without an order from above; and the King's brother Wilhelm, with whom Bismarck had hoped to speak, had already fled to England. Desperate, Bismarck approached Augusta, who had retreated to the country, to recommend Prince Charles's scheme to push both the King and Wilhelm aside in favor of sixteen-year-old Fritz. Augusta, who hated her brother-in-law Charles, resented Bismarck's suggestion that she might be persuaded to betray her husband and her king and use her son to do it. She refused him indignantly and never forgave him for his part in the intrigue.*

After the Revolution of 1848, there was no place for a hard-line Junker like Bismarck in the Prussian National Assembly, which was engaged in the business of writing a constitution for Prussia. To fill his time, Bismarck began working behind the scenes with the Gerlachs, who, along with some generals of the army, were trying to shore up the weak King and undermine the official government. Toward this end, Ludwig von Gerlach founded the Kreuzzeitung, based on a theory that German "constitutionalism," unlike that in other countries, drew its power from the divine right of the king, whose ministers were responsible only to him, not to parliament or the people. To bolster their doctrine and their party, the Gerlachs also started a daily newspaper, the *Kreuzzeitung*, to which Bismarck was a frequent contributor, fighting for the prerogatives of the Junkers and attacking liberal innovations such as the real estate tax, which he claimed, was "not a tax, but a confiscation of capital."

Bismarck's parliamentary career got under way again with the first Prussian Parliament, established under the constitution that was forced on Friedrich Wilhelm IV. As the most outspoken representative of the ultraconservatives, Bismarck defended the King's indignant refusal to wear the crown offered by the Frankfurt Parliament. He was rewarded for his loyalty with an appointment

---

* *In his* Recollections and Reminiscences, *published after Augusta's death, Bismarck reversed the story and said that it was he, not Augusta, who refused to take part in the scheme, which he labeled "high treason" (p. 63).*

in 1851 as Prussian minister to the German Diet in Frankfurt, the parliament at which all the German states were represented. It was the most important post in the Prussian diplomatic service.

Austria was then the dominant member of the German Diet, and Bismarck made a reputation by attacking her. He believed that the only valid basis for foreign policy is self-interest, and that historically and geographically, Prussia and Austria were headed for a clash. "If we do not prepare for ourselves the role of the hammer," he said, "there will be nothing left but that of the anvil."

His hostility to Austria manifested itself during the Crimean War, in which Friedrich Wilhelm IV vacillated between Russia on the one side and England and France on the other. For Bismarck, the war was simply an opportunity to cement relations with the Czar, since Prussia would one day need Russia's help in its struggle with Austria over the domination of the German peoples. Determined to keep Prussia out of England's orbit, he was a major factor in convincing the King not to join the English and French, thus incurring the dislike of Albert and Victoria, whom he met for the first time at Eugénie's ball in Paris in 1855.

"The Prince [Albert], handsome and cool in his black uniform, conversed with me courteously," Bismarck wrote of the meeting, "but in his manner there was a kind of malevolent curiosity from which I concluded that my anti-occidental influence upon the King was not unknown to him. . . . In the eyes of the Prince . . . I was a reactionary party man who took up sides for Russia in order to further an Absolutist and 'Junker' policy. It was not to be wondered at that this view . . . had descended to the Prince's daughter, who shortly afterwards became our Crown Princess."

Soon after Fritz and Vicky's wedding, when Wilhelm became Prince Regent, he dismissed Bismarck from his post at the diet. Wilhelm did not like or trust Bismarck, but he could not help but realize his remarkable capabilities and sent him off as Ambassador to Russia. In spite of his Russian sympathies, Bismarck was angry and probably blamed his demotion on Wilhelm's wife, Augusta, and her new English daughter-in-law.

Bismarck stayed in St. Petersburg from 1859 to 1862. During the Italian campaign of 1859, he urged Wilhelm to defy the laws of the German Confederation and go to war—not on behalf of Austria, as Wilhelm planned to do, but against her.* The German Confederation, he told the Prussian Foreign Minister, was a "disease . . . of which we have to be cured, sooner or later."

In March of 1862, Wilhelm called Bismarck back from Russia. But instead of offering him a position in the cabinet, which Bismarck had hoped and expected, the King sent him as Ambassador to Paris.

Thinking this would be a good time to meet the statesmen who ran England, Bismarck used the excuse of an industrial exhibition to visit London. The experience was a blow to his ego. "He thought the English ministers . . .

---

* He wanted the King to send Prussian soldiers south to occupy Austrian territory while the Austrians were busy fighting the Italians elsewhere (see Chapter 14).

would attach more importance into entering into direct relations with him," recalled the Russian Ambassador to the Court of St. James's. "Disappointed in this expectation, he felt a touch of annoyance." It was at a diplomatic dinner party given by this same ambassador that Bismarck reportedly stated that if he became Prime Minister, he would reorganize the army and, as soon as it was strong enough, settle accounts with Austria and dissolve the German Confederation. "Take care of that man," was Disraeli's reaction; "he means what he says."

Warned by Roon to be ready to come to Berlin at the right moment, Bismarck did not take his appointment as French Ambassador as a permanent situation. "My things are still in Petersburg and will be frozen in there," he complained; "my carriages are in Stettin, my horses in the country near Berlin, my family in Pomerania, and I am on the highway." Since no diplomat ever stayed in Paris in the heat of August, he moved on to Biarritz, where he met a twenty-two-year-old Russian Princess, Katherine Orlov, the wife of the Russian Ambassador to Belgium, and fell in love.

Not since Marie von Thadden had Bismarck been so taken with a woman. They bathed in the sea together, picnicked, and went climbing in the mountains. Katherine was a pianist, and in the long summer evenings she played Mendelssohn, Beethoven, and Schubert for him. She was also, according to her stepsister, Catherine Radziwill, "a woman of alert intelligence who lived in close intimacy with the Imperial family . . . [and] knew more about the secrets of politics than perhaps any other woman in Russia." It is said that the affair was never consummated. Prince Orlov seems not to have resented it, nor seemingly did Johanna von Bismarck, off in Pomerania and by now the mother of three adolescents. To his wife and his sister, Bismarck wrote rapturous letters about his seaside idyll.

"Since the Orlovs arrived I have been living with them as though we were alone in the world. . . . I am a little in love with the enchanting Principessa," he wrote his sister. "Invisible to all the world, hidden in a steep ravine cut back from the cliffs, I gaze out between two rocks on which the heather blooms at the sea, green and white in the sunshine and the spray," he wrote Johanna. "At my side is the most charming woman, whom you will love very much when you get to know her, a little like Marie Thadden . . . but with a personality all her own—amusing, intelligent, and kind, pretty and young."

Few women would have swallowed this without a murmur, but the all-accepting Johanna did. "Were I at all inclined to jealousy and envy I should be tyrannized to the depths now by these passions," she wrote a friend. "But my soul has no room for them and I rejoice quite enormously that my beloved husband has found this charming woman. But for her he would never have found peace for so long in one place or become so well as he boasts of being in every letter."

Her husband's peace was short-lived. Two weeks later, back in Paris, Bismarck received the coded telegram from General Roon for which he had been waiting. The wording had been decided on beforehand, as had the name of a bogus sender. *"Periculum in mora. Dépêchez-vous"* * read the message. As the recipient himself put it, he "did not hesitate to set out."

Four days later, Wilhelm offered Bismarck the position of Prime Minister.

BISMARCK'S APPOINTMENT was not received kindly—either in Berlin or around Europe. The English scarcely knew him, the Austrians feared him, and most people thought he was a temporary, if belligerent, nuisance. As one Swiss newspaper commented acidly, "These Junkers would like to have a try, but whether they have any ability remains to be seen. There is no need to fear that fattened geese will soar like eagles."

Within Prussia itself, the appointment damaged Wilhelm's already lowered prestige. The members of Bismarck's own party, the Kreuzzeitung, distrusted him because he had supported an upstart Napoleon III over the Habsburgs. The liberals liked him less. One leader of the Progressive Party claimed that he would lead Prussia into "government without budget, rule by the sword in home affairs, and war in foreign affairs." The man was right on every count.

But the person who probably felt the worst about the appointment was Fritz, now forced to question whether he had done the right thing in ignoring Vicky's advice and not taking over for his father. At the time, Wilhelm had reassured him that he would not resort to Bismarck. Now, informed that his father had named Bismarck his Prime Minister, Fritz sent letters from Gotha warning both Wilhelm and Bismarck that he, the Crown Prince, would regard any breach of the Prussian constitution as "disastrous." At the same time, Fritz worried about his father. "People will immediately smell reaction . . . ," he wrote in his diary, "and poor Papa will cause himself many difficult hours through this dishonest character. Poor Mama, how bitterly grieved she will be at this appointment of her deadly enemy."

Bismarck's first appointments were certainly not inspiring. He formed his cabinet with men of reactionary stamp and little merit, and in later years referred to his Finance Minister as "a liar" and the Agricultural Minister as "an ass." Never enthusiastic about Wilhelm's insistence on a three-year training stint, he thought at first that he might be able to convince the King to compromise. In conversation with a liberal politician, Bismarck compared Wilhelm to a horse who "takes fright at an unaccustomed object, will grow obstinate if driven, but will gradually get used to it." When he discovered he could not prod or wheedle Wilhelm from his *idée fixe,* he realized he had to find another way.

Bismarck had once told Roon that the only way for the King to overcome a recalcitrant parliament was to divert its attention abroad. Since this was not yet practicable, he temporized. In his maiden speech to parliament as Prime Minister, he said nothing about the crisis that had brought him into power, but everything about his blueprint for the future. "Germany," he told the delegates, "does not look to Prussia's liberalism, but to her strength. . . . The great ques-

---

* *"The time is ripe. Hurry."*

tions of the day will not be settled by speeches and majority decisions—that was the great mistake from 1848 to 1849—but by iron and blood."*

The speech made a sensation. Although the words were no more than a new Bismarckian term for the old Prussian militarism, the speech offended both liberals and conservatives. Even a hard-line militarist like Roon took exception to such "racy excursions" from the man he had brought to power. The man who was most frightened of all, however, was King Wilhelm. Bismarck blamed the King's disapproval on the fact that he was still in Baden with his liberal wife, daughter, and son-in-law. To avert disaster, he set out to intercept Wilhelm on his way home from Baden to Berlin.

Bismarck met the King's train in an unfinished railway station in the junction of Jüterbog, fifty miles south of Berlin. The platform was piled with timber, and there were mounds of bricks waiting to be laid. Seated on an upturned wheelbarrow, the new Prime Minister waited for the train in a crowd of third-class passengers and construction workers. When it finally arrived, he had difficulty locating the King, who was sitting alone and unsmiling in the only first-class carriage.

"I can perfectly well see where all this will end," Wilhelm told Bismarck after giving him permission to join him for the remainder of the trip. "Over there, in front of the Opera House, under my windows, they will cut off your head, and mine a little while afterwards."

"*Et après, Sire?*"† Bismarck asked.

"*Après,* indeed; we shall be dead," Wilhelm answered.

"Yes," Bismarck answered, "then we shall be dead; but we must all die sooner or later, and can we perish more honourably? I, fighting for my King's cause, and your Majesty sealing with your own blood your rights as King by the grace of God; whether on the scaffold or the battlefield, makes no difference to the glory of sacrificing life and limb for the rights assigned to you by the grace of God."

Bismarck clearly knew his man, and he watched while the despondent King assumed once again the attitude of "an officer fighting for kingdom and Fatherland."

The new Prime Minister was triumphant:

[I]n a few minutes he [Wilhelm] was restored to the confidence which he had lost at Baden, and even recovered his cheerfulness. To give up his life for King and Fatherland was the duty of an officer; still more that of a King, as the first officer in the land. As soon as he regarded his position from the point of view of military honour, it had no more terror for him. . . . This raised him above the anxiety about the criticism which public opinion, history, and his wife might pass on his political tactics.

* *Later changed by history to "blood and iron."*

† *"And afterwards, Sire?"*

Bismarck was a brilliant psychologist. He had come to his new position armed with remarkable intuitive gifts and years of thoughtful observation. He did not have to play anyone else's music anymore, just his own, and he played Wilhelm I like a virtuoso—full of bravura, sure of his notes, confident in knowing exactly when, where, and with how much force he must attack for the effects he wished to produce. It was a fine performance, signifying a unique talent that Bismarck would use to the awe of his supporters and the despair of his enemies.

CHAPTER
TWENTY

"If the Lord means well by Germany, he'll never let the Crown Prince ascend the throne."

OTTO VON BISMARCK

ANXIOUS TO DISTANCE THEMSELVES from a Bismarck government, Vicky and Fritz left for a holiday journey to Italy in early October of 1862. It had taken them months to get his father's permission. In the first place, the King did not approve of their destination. A friend of Austria and an enemy of Napoleon III, he had thus far refused to recognize the new kingdom of Italy, promoted by Napoleon and proclaimed the previous year. Moreover, Wilhelm, who always resented their travels, was more adamant about their leaving Prussia during the constitutional crisis. "[H]e thinks Fritz wishes to avoid being drawn into affairs under the present circumstances," Vicky wrote her mother, "which the King considers disobedience and opposition."

But once he had named Bismarck as his new Prime Minister, the advantages of getting the Crown Prince and Princess away from the political scene became apparent. Fritz and Vicky traveled part of the way in her mother's yacht and took Bertie with them. Queen Victoria wanted to get the Prince of Wales out of the way so that she could spend time alone with Alexandra (Alix) of Denmark. The Queen had finally met the young Danish Princess in Brussels the previous month and had given her unqualified, if self-absorbed, approval:

"You did <u>not</u> say too much about dear Alix . . . ," she wrote Vicky.

No, she is a dear, lovely being—whose bright image seems to float—mingled with darling Papa's—before my poor eyes—dimmed with tears! Oh! <u>While</u> I write to you, they are streaming down my face! Oh! <u>who</u> can know <u>what</u> my . . . life is now! . . . <u>none</u> of the agonies of despair . . . [of] . . . my warm passionate loving nature so full of that passionate adoration for that Angel whom I dared call mine. And at <u>42</u>, <u>all</u>, <u>all</u> those earthly feelings must be crushed & smothered & the never quenched flame . . . <u>burns</u> within me & wears me out! Dearest child! this very prospect of opening happiness of married life for our poor Bertie—while I thank God for it, yet wrings my poor heart, which seems transfixed with agonies of longing! I am alas! not old—and my feelings are strong and warm; my love is ardent.

Much to everyone's relief, Bertie had followed his mother's sanction with the long-awaited proposal of marriage, which was accepted immediately by the Danes. But the announcement of the engagement of Vicky's brother to a Princess of Denmark, coming as it did in the middle of the Prussian constitutional crisis, fell "like a clap of thunder," seriously damaging Vicky's position at home, as she had known it would. Liberals and conservatives, Prussians and non-Prussians alike attacked the Crown Princess for promoting an alliance between Denmark and England. Men like Uncle Ernest in Coburg, a leader of the German unification movement, and Max Duncker, Fritz's political adviser chosen by old Baron Stockmar, warned that Vicky had done herself "much harm" with German nationalists, who coveted Schleswig and Holstein for the future Germany.

Leaving Prussia at the beginning of Bismarck's first ministry also hurt Fritz and Vicky's image as guardians of the flame. Liberals felt that their only supporters at court had deserted them, while conservatives used the trip to point out that the Prussian Crown Prince and Princess were traveling around the Mediterranean in an English yacht with an escort of English warships during a Prussian political crisis.

THEY SPENT MUCH OF THEIR TIME in Italy admiring the art, then went to Rome, where they had an audience with the Pope. Pius IX, known somewhat euphemistically as "the Pope of Progress," seemed to them a good-natured, cheerful man. For his part, the pontiff was most enthusiastic about Vicky, telling the English representative to the Vatican, Lord Odo Russell, that "he was an old man, but in the whole course of his long life he had never been more favourably impressed by anyone than by her Royal Highness the Crown Princess of Prussia."

It was fortunate that Pius was not able to read Vicky's letters to her mother, in which she gave an unflattering impression of High Mass at St. Peter's. "The fine music would have lifted one's soul up to Heaven had it not been for the dumb foolery going on down below—dressing and undressing of priests and bobbing up and down, and mumbling latin so fast that no one could understand it. I thought it very shocking, & had a hard struggle once or twice not to laugh." In Vicky's report to Victoria, the Jews of Rome, whose synagogue she also visited, fared better than the Catholics. Judaism, of course, was no threat to the Church of England, while popery was the traditional bugbear of the English royal family.

Fritz and Vicky's last stop was Vienna, where they were entertained by Emperor Franz Joseph, who at thirty-two was just a year older than Fritz. His twenty-five-year-old wife, Elisabeth, three years older than Vicky, was famous for her beauty and faddish diets. "I am quite charmed with the Empress," Vicky wrote Victoria; "her beauty though not regular is surpassing. I never saw anything so dazzling or piquant. . . . She is immensely tall & wears very high heels besides. . . . She seems to be laced dreadfully tight which surely is not necessary with such a magnificent figure." Elisabeth, however, was shy, and it was difficult for Vicky to engage her in conversation. "[S]he neither sings, draws or plays, speaks very little of her children. . . . The Emperor seems to dote on her, but I did not observe that she did on him. He is most insignificant, very plain . . . which you would not suppose from his pictures or photographs."

Vicky had explained to her mother that she was planning to spend December 14, the first anniversary of her father's death, on board the train from Trieste to Vienna "in strict incognito." She had, in fact, partly planned the trip so as not to be in Berlin, where she would be reminded of the previous year. "[O]h how I dread that day, the thought of your suffering makes me quite miserable," she wrote Victoria as she had written many times throughout her journey.

Whatever Vicky's plans, it became abundantly clear that she and Fritz would not be permitted to slip quietly into Vienna. They were met at the station with the usual royal fanfare by Emperor Franz Joseph. Queen Victoria was outraged:

"I have to thank you for 2 letters from Rome . . . & for the one from Florence . . . ," Victoria wrote her eldest daughter.

> But I have had none for the sacred & heartrending anniversary of the 14th, & only heard of your spending that day in the railroad & arriving that evening at Vienna—where the Emperor received you!!! Even now I can hardly believe it! I should have thought that you would have preferred remaining in the smallest wayside inn and going to pray to God to support your broken-hearted mother rather than do that! . . . I will therefore not speak of the solemn, touching and edifying way in which we spent that day or of the deep anguish of my broken heart! One dreary, lonely year has been passed, which I had hoped never to live to the end of, & now with a weakened, shattered frame I have to begin the weary work again.

Vicky explained to her mother that it was a day "of sorrow" for her, too, that she had been thwarted in her wish to spend it quietly and alone, and that she "never dreamt" Victoria would suppose she had arranged for her formal reception that evening. Moreover, she had written the Queen a letter from Florence that she had been assured would arrive on the "dreadful" fourteenth, but it had obviously been delayed.

This explanation, less anxiously apologetic than earlier responses, shows a change in Vicky's attitude. Not only was she learning to answer for her actions, but she was also dealing with the real world as it existed outside her mother's house of mourning—a world in which she, the twenty-two-year-old Crown Princess of Prussia, continued to face immediate and serious problems. Although she never stopped trying to console her mother, Vicky realized that she had to get on with her own life, with or without help from home. As she explained in her last letter from Vienna, she dreaded returning to Berlin. "We shall have a hard time of it, and I shall thank God if Fritz comes unscathed out of it all!" She longed for her father's advice.

"If I were a man," Vicky wrote,

I should not feel a bit frightened as I am in no doubt about the course I should take and care very little for the opposition I met, but with Fritz it is so different. You know how he loves his Father and <u>what</u> his sense of duty is both towards his King and his Father, besides he is not born a free Englishman, and all Prussians have <u>not</u> the feeling of independence & love of justice & constitutional liberty they ought to have, though Fritz is as you know . . . so free from the absurd and dangerous prejudices to which the poor King and the whole of the Prussian aristocracy are a prey.

Oh all this weighs upon me at times more than I can say—Fritz and my future existence, that of our children and in fact that of our country is at stake, and the government is playing a foolish and desperate game!

"I <u>tremble</u> at the state of Germany and especially <u>your</u> affairs!" Victoria wrote after the New Year. "What <u>on earth</u> will happen, God almighty knows. I only wish I could <u>help</u> you. But alas! he who could is above us & above earthly trouble & worry."

WHEN VICKY AND FRITZ returned to Berlin, the political situation was worse than she expected. A fight over the budget between the upper and lower houses of parliament had provided Bismarck with an excuse to adjourn the lawmakers until the beginning of the following year (1863). With no approved budget to fund the government, he argued that "since the life of the state cannot stand still," the King should collect taxes and spend the money to govern as he saw fit, regardless of parliament. Accused of violating the Prussian constitution, Bismarck rationalized his action on a so-called gap—a flaw in the constitution that compelled Wilhelm to carry on the government without a budget.

"The King thinks only of his duty . . . ," Vicky wrote her mother. "He never would with open eyes break the constitution—or do away with it—but his ministers have so tampered with it that it is broken already, which the King & M. de Bismarck . . . call . . . interpreting the constitution. . . . There is no knowing where 'interpreting' . . . may not lead."

Vicky was no happier with Bismarck's handling of foreign affairs, particularly his policy toward the Poles. Poland was partitioned among Russia, Austria, and Prussia, and the Poles were in the middle of a revolt against the Czar. As Alexander II began to crush the rebellion and England and Austria raised their voices in protest, Bismarck offered to cooperate with the Russians, thus enabling the Czar to ignore diplomatic pressure from the other powers.

Bismarck, for whom Russian goodwill was essential to Prussia's future, saw in the Polish uprising a chance to earn the Czar's gratitude, and he signed a treaty with Russia providing for mutual support in putting down the rebels. England and France objected, and the Prussian Chamber of Deputies demanded an inquiry into his negotiations. The Prime Minister refused, convincing the King that the liberal members of the chamber sided with Prussia's natural adversaries, the Poles, and that he, Bismarck, was engaged in the noble business of fending off revolution in Europe. Years later, he admitted that his tactics had been highly unethical, but at the time, he boasted about his inexpensive victory: "As things are shaping in Poland," he wrote Wilhelm, "it is unlikely that we shall be called upon for active participation, and through the treaty we shall in future have the advantage of securing Czar Alexander's gratitude and Russian sympathy cheaply."

Wilhelm, who saw Prussia condemned on all sides because of his Prime Minister, soon fell ill. In Vicky's judgment, it was "chiefly moral & not physical suffering" that had attacked her father-in-law, "striving to do his duty in every way, seeing that his mode of doing it does not produce any good results, yet determined not to give way to any other opinion and persuaded that all those of different opinion wish to limit his power, destroy his army and despoil the crown of its rights."

A FEW WEEKS AFTER the Prussians signed a treaty* with Russia providing for mutual military assistance in repressing the Poles, Vicky left Berlin for Bertie's wedding to Alix of Denmark, which took place on March 10, 1863, at Windsor. "Oh! if it only was all over!" Victoria wrote her eldest daughter before she left. "I dread the whole thing awfully & wonder even how you can rejoice so much at witnessing what must I should think be to you, who loved Papa so dearly, so terribly sad a wedding! Dear child! your ectasies at the whole thing is to me sometimes very incomprehensible!"

The Queen had requested that Vicky and Fritz arrive well ahead of time so that Vicky could represent her mother at the premarital celebrations and "do all to help me in checking noise & joyousness in my presence." Fritz was to serve as one of Bertie's two supporters.

Thrown into the spotlight, Vicky began for the first time in her life to talk about her looks. Never before had she been so candid about her embarrassment over her own face and figure. Perhaps it was the comparison between herself and the lovely, slim Alexandra or perhaps her recent meeting with Elisabeth of Austria—whatever brought it on, the young Crown Princess bewailed what "a perfect monster" she had been as a child and "how exceedingly ugly and uninteresting" she looked now. Although the winter of 1863 was one of the few times during the early years of her marriage when Vicky was not pregnant, she was already beginning to thicken out from childbirth and realized that she would never be an adornment to society.

She was, however, "awfully cheered" (in the words of an Eton boy) when she came down the aisle of the chapel after her siblings. And she was delighted at having been allowed to bring her elder son, now known as Willy, who had

---

* *Known as the Alvensleben Convention, after the Prussian envoy to St. Petersburg.*

talked of "nothing else" in the weeks preceding the trip and was "very much occupied with his scotch dress," wanting to know "whether Uncle Arthur and Uncle Leopold * will put on theirs."

Dressed in his miniature Highland kilt, Willy was led into St. George's Chapel by his mother and put under the charge of his eighteen-year-old uncle Alfred (Affie). "Such a dear, good little boy!" said Queen Victoria, who observed the service in mournful privacy from the closet of Catherine of Aragon † in the gallery above. But the "good little" four-year-old, irritated at being kept out of sight between his young uncles and bored by the long ceremony, could not keep still. He scratched Arthur and Leopold on their bare legs (they, too, were in kilts) to get their attention. When Affie told him to be quiet, he brandished the dirk (dagger) he had found in his stocking. Scolded for throwing his sporran (purse) into the choir, Willy bit Uncle Affie in the leg. It was the first version of a scene that would be repeated many times in the course of Willy's lifetime—the future Wilhelm II of Germany trying to take the spotlight away from his uncle Bertie, the future Edward VII of England.

The following evening the British Ambassador to Prussia gave a dinner in Berlin honoring the marriage of the Prince of Wales, to which he invited Wilhelm and Augusta. Because of the feeling against the Danes, Bismarck did not want the King to accept, warning him that "all kinds of unpleasantness might result." For once, Wilhelm ignored Bismarck. But when his son and daughter-in-law returned from the wedding, there was no one to greet them at the railway station. The King had apparently expended all his goodwill in lending his presence to the English dinner.

BY THE TIME VICKY AND FRITZ returned to Prussia, Bismarck's campaign to suppress opposition to his policies was well under way—in parliament, the civil service, the judiciary, and the army. In defiance of the Prussian constitution, which guaranteed deputies against reprisals for positions taken on the floor of the chamber, the new Prime Minister had instituted a series of punitive financial measures aimed at forcing liberal deputies to give up their seats in parliament. To justify his acquiescence in this travesty of the legislative process, Wilhelm asserted that he was only penalizing parliamentarians who opposed his wishes out of "personal considerations," not those who stood up for what they believed out of "conviction."

To control the civil service, Bismarck's new Minister of the Interior was instructed to inform members of his department that their first duty was to give "unconditional" support to the policies of the King. In the judiciary, a traditionally independent arm of the state, Bismarck tried but failed except in one category to make political conviction rather than seniority the basis for promotion. In the army, "spying and terrorizing" were sponsored by Manteuffel's military cabinet, while the King and Roon forbade members of the armed

---

* *Victoria's third and fourth sons.*

† *The first wife of Henry VIII.*

forces to vote in the elections of September 1863, explaining that the election process was bad for military discipline.

During this initial period of repression, perhaps a thousand deputies, civil servants, and judges were victimized, and a fund to help those in need was set up in Britain where it could not be touched by Bismarck or his police. Required to give a ball "in powder" (i.e., costumes and wigs) to celebrate the centennial of Frederick the Great's Neues Palais, Vicky told her mother that she wished she could "bring back" Frederick the Great himself, who "would be astonished to see the mess his country is in, and the blockheads which his great nephew has got for ministers. . . . All is going from bad to worse—that wretched B. will not stop his mad career until he has plunged his King into ruin & his country into the most dangerous difficulties!"

Just how dangerous, Vicky had not begun to guess.

CHAPTER
TWENTY-ONE

> *"Prussia is a place where you are free to move, but with a gagged mouth. . . ."*
>
> KARL KRAUS, *Austrian satirist and critic*

*T*HE BEGINNING of the Bismarck era was characterized by suppression in all branches of life and government, particularly in the realm of free speech. A "pitched battle" between the new Prime Minister and the Chamber of Deputies ended in late May of 1863, when Bismarck again dissolved parliament and, with the deputies out of the way, launched a full-scale attack on the liberal press.

In the fall of 1862, when Bismarck had become Prime Minister, liberal newspapers outnumbered conservative by more than six to one. The major political asset of a professional middle class clamoring to take its place in the power structure beside the aristocracy and the army, these papers advanced the liberal ideas of national unification and an increase in personal freedoms. Their best articles were often written by impecunious politicians who used journalism to supplement their incomes, since members of parliament were not paid for their services. Moreover, articles in the German press were published anonymously, and only the editor, who was frequently instructed to burn the originals, knew their source.

Faced with this "virtual monopoly" by the opposition, Bismarck began to secretly subsidize the existing conservative press. He also organized an elaborate network of rural papers through which he could funnel official news, often directing exactly what was to be printed. Although both these classes of papers were supposed to be independent, they spread the Bismarck gospel and were supported by public funds.

The Prussian constitution guaranteed only nominal freedom of the press, a right that had been subverted by legislation passed in 1851—laws Bismarck now used to confiscate liberal publications or fine and imprison editors for so-called distortion of the news or contempt. But the system was inefficient, as each case had to be proven in court. Just five days after parliament was dissolved, on June 1, 1863, Bismarck presented Wilhelm with a decree for his signature, banning all newspapers and magazines deemed by the government as "dangerous to the public welfare." There was no appeal to this ruling except to the king's cabinet. To justify such blatant censorship, the government claimed that the press had abused its freedom of speech to "undermine every foundation of orderly government and of religion and morality as well."

The edict was issued under an article of the constitution that gave the king the right to take the law into his own hands when parliament was not sitting "for the preservation of public safety or the settlement of an unusual emergency." This was clearly no emergency. Bismarck had, in fact, prepared the decree before dissolving parliament. Although Wilhelm's conscience bothered him, he allowed himself to be convinced by Bismarck and his other ministers that the liberal press had already turned the lower classes against the crown. The army, he was warned, would be the next target of their corrupting influence.

Fritz was conveniently away on a tour of the provinces when Wilhelm signed the press edict.

"[F]eeling in the country . . . is very bad indeed," the Crown Princess wrote Victoria when the news of the dissolution of parliament caught up with them, "and the belief that . . . nothing good can ever come out of this dynasty is pretty generally expressed in many intelligent circles. People are angry with Fritz for not coming forward," she added, saying that the Crown Prince had just received a letter from his father ordering him to go to Poland, a journey that, because of Bismarck's support for the Czar, would be difficult and possibly life-threatening. Vicky lamented the fact that her father-in-law "could think of exposing his son if not to absolute danger," then to "every sort of disagreeable" experience.

It was surely not Wilhelm but Bismarck who had sent Fritz away. Realizing what the Crown Prince's reaction would be to the press edict, he wanted him out of Berlin, to prevent him from both influencing his father and being a rallying point for other liberals. Before Fritz left for his tour, however, he had written his father a letter "warning him and begging and imploring him never to give his consent to any unconstitutional measures his ministers might propose." Otherwise, it would be his (Fritz's) "painful duty" to "protest." Fritz also sent a similar message to Bismarck.

Knowing how difficult it was for Fritz to cross his father, Vicky wrote to say how proud she was of him. Other German liberals like his brother-in-law, the Duke of Baden, had also been urging the Crown Prince to speak out "so the people could have hope." Queen Victoria supported his position, which had previously been one of passive resistance, as did Vicky, who told her husband that he "must satisfy the demands of your conscience before those of your father and king."

Wilhelm responded by ordering Fritz not only to abide by the government position but to speak out in favor of it. Vicky, who "travelled all night in a state of great anxiety" to join her husband, arrived in the town of Danzig with the King's letter on June 4. It was there, in the local newspaper, that she and Fritz read the announcement of the press edict.

A parade of the town garrison in honor of the Crown Prince had been planned for the next day, but the streets were nearly empty. "[P]eople are truly enraged about the press decree," Fritz wrote in his diary. "We are in a dreadful position," Vicky wrote Victoria, "the country loudly clamouring for Fritz to come forward and he receiving the most peremptory commands from the King as thanks for the tact and self-denial Fritz has been showing this last whole year —only reproaches for having opposed the King."

At a reception, the Mayor of Danzig, a prominent liberal and friend of the Crown Prince and Princess, apologized for the meager nature of the gathering and joined Vicky in urging her husband to speak out. "I did all I could," she wrote her mother, "to induce Fritz to do so, knowing how necessary it was that he should once express his sentiments openly and disclaim having any part in the last measure of the government."

Fritz finally broke his silence. But even then, he phrased his disavowal of the press edict in such a way as to make himself "publicly known as an opponent of Bismarck and his evil theories," while assuring the people of the "noble and fatherly intentions and magnanimous sentiments" of their King. "I did not know anything of this order beforehand," he said. "I was absent. I am not one of those who advised it."

It was Fritz's first public stand against Wilhelm's position and Bismarck's government. In light of his sense of filial responsibility, it was an extremely difficult thing for him to do, and it created what Bismarck angrily referred to as "a sensation both at home and abroad." The King sent Fritz a "furious letter," accusing him of "disobedience," insisting he issue a public retraction, and threatening him with expulsion from the Prussian army and the crown council.

That night Vicky and Fritz sat up until 1:00 A.M. composing an answer to Wilhelm's letter. The Crown Prince said that although he was "almost broken-hearted" at the pain he had caused his father, he must "stand by his opinions." "I realize the possible consequences of such an attitude," he wrote, "but please be convinced that I shall take risks and suffer for my convictions with the same courage with which you, dear Papa, once did for yours." Since he said he realized that this would make it "impossible" for him to serve the King, either in a civil or military capacity, he offered to resign from his various official positions and to retire to any place his father chose inside Prussia or abroad. "If I am not allowed to speak my mind," he said, "I must naturally wish to dissever myself entirely from the sphere of politics."

Fritz's position was not unlike that of his father a decade earlier during the Crimean War, when the pro-English Wilhelm withdrew to Coblentz rather than conform to his brother King Friedrich Wilhelm IV's support for Russia. But Wilhelm, trying to justify an uneasy conscience, refused to see his son's action as honorable. "Your behavior has offended the King, your country and your father," he wrote Fritz. For a time it looked as if he might actually court-martial the Crown Prince and confine him in a military fortress—a plan supported by Fritz's reactionary uncle Prince Charles and General Manteuffel. But Bismarck was too smart to allow Fritz to become a martyr, reminding Wilhelm that when Friedrich Wilhelm I of Prussia imprisoned his son, Frederick the Great, "the sympathy of contemporaries and posterity was with the latter."

As was the free press in England, Europe, and even Germany itself. Someone leaked the correspondence between Fritz and Wilhelm to the papers outside Bismarck's sphere of intimidation. Many, like the *Saturday Review* or *Europe* (a publication printed in the free city of Frankfurt), took Fritz's part. Proud of its native daughter, the London *Times* applauded Vicky for giving the Crown Prince "so much assistance in a momentous and critical juncture. It is not easy," the *Times* asserted, "to conceive a more difficult position than that of the princely pair placed, without a single adviser, between a self-willed sovereign and a mischievous cabinet on the one hand, and an incensed people on the other."

Bismarck tried to locate the source of the leak, scattering accusations around liberally and mobilizing the police to follow them up in what Vicky called "a regular inquisition." The first victim was young Baron Stockmar. "There is a devil of a row about the *Times* article . . . ," he wrote his friend Morier of the British Embassy, "of which . . . the Ministers . . . suppose me to be the author. I am as innocent as a newborn babe. Can you give me a clue?" Stockmar's cheerful insouciance was quickly shattered by Bismarck's witch hunt. He became so ill under pressure that he begged Vicky's permission to withdraw to a spa and shortly thereafter took a leave of absence that led to his early retirement. This was a major loss for the Crown Princess, who was left unprotected from the spies with whom Bismarck now began to infiltrate her court.

After young Stockmar, the Prime Minister turned on Heinrich Geffcken, a diplomat, jurist, and friend of Fritz's whom he would one day destroy. Finally, he settled on Max Duncker, Fritz's political adviser, against whom he instituted legal proceedings. These were unsuccessful, but Bismarck managed to use Duncker far more effectively—seducing him away from the Crown Prince but leaving him as an informant within Fritz and Vicky's court. A professor of history with close ties to other academic journalists, Duncker eventually became the head of Bismarck's domestic press bureau, charged with disseminating pro-Bismarck propaganda.

The source of the leak was never uncovered. Judging from the wording of the article in the *Times,* which was remarkably similar in feeling to Vicky's reports to her mother, it may well have taken place in London. Vicky, who had copied out the letters between her father-in-law and her husband for Victoria, was frightened enough to ask the Queen if anyone else had seen it.

"The correspondence was seen by no one but General Grey . . . ," Victoria answered, "it never left the house nor indeed [did] any of the ministers ever see it. Only one of your letters . . . was read to Lord Russell [Foreign Secretary], and Sir George Grey [Home Secretary]—but it never left our hands. You know that it was no secret what Fritz did & said & that his views were necessary to be known. But no one saw the correspondence. I think the King should look nearer home, for such things." Queen Victoria was clearly not disturbed that her son-in-law's views had been splashed across the European papers.

Inside Prussia, however, the press edict had done its work, and no one dared support the Crown Prince. A "graveyard stillness" permeated the liberal press, "over which," as one historian phrased it, "could still be heard the strident voices of the conservative newspapers and the bought journals of the government." It was into this hostile atmosphere of Berlin that Fritz and Vicky returned from their tour of Poland to pick up their children for a summer vacation on the island of Rügen in the Baltic Sea.

The beaches of Rügen, the largest island in Germany, offered an oasis of peace to the beleaguered couple. From her bedroom window in the home of her friends Prince and Princess Wilhelm of Putbus, Vicky looked out beyond flower gardens and woodlands to chalky cliffs and the sea. After a day spent hunting seals in a little boat with Fritz, she wrote her mother that the island seemed like "sort of a second Osborne . . . a perfect Eldorado."

In this idyllic atmosphere, away from the strain of the past months, the twenty-two-year-old Crown Princess had time to think over her situation, writing her mother a rambling letter detailing her thoughts and feelings about what had taken place. Everyone, she said, assumed that it was she along with Stockmar and Morier who had leaked the correspondence to the *Times*. Unlike other royalties, Vicky was remarkably philosophical about the hostility of the Prussian newspapers and journalists, explaining that "I have always held they had a right to say what they liked, and to pick up their information wherever they could." Still, she told her mother, "You cannot think how painful it is to be continually surrounded by people who consider your very existence a misfortune and your sentiments evidence of lunacy!"

It was even more complicated within the royal family, where Vicky felt particularly bad at causing such distress to her father-in-law, "whose kindness & whose endearing and amiable qualities make him creep into one's heart." As she explained to her mother,

> Fritz <u>adores</u> his father, and till now in his eyes obedience and subordination was *[sic]* the first duty. Now I see myself in duty bound as a good wife— and as a really devoted and enthusiastic <u>Prussian</u> (which I feel every day more that I am), of using all the influence I possess in making Fritz place his opinions & his political conscience above his filial feelings. . . .
>
> I <u>know</u> what a responsibility I take upon myself in taking advantage of my husband's reliance on my judgement. . . . Until I find the person whose judgement I can feel greater confidence than in my own, I <u>shall</u> go on with might and main trying to assist Fritz in pursuing the only road I consider right and safe. . . . It is <u>very</u> disagreeable to me to be thought meddling and intriguing. Mixing in politics is <u>not</u> a ladies' profession. . . . But I should not be a free-born Englishwoman and your child if I did not set all those things aside as minor considerations. I am <u>very</u> ambitious for the country, for Fritz and the children and so I am determined to brave all the rest!

This is one of the rare instances that Vicky dared speak openly about the anomaly of her position as her husband's mentor. In her letters to Fritz (and no doubt in person), she was careful to maintain the appearance of a submissive German wife, formulating her views in careful prose, making excuses for her opinions and suggestions. With Albert dead, Victoria was the only person left with whom Vicky could be totally frank.

It is also clear from this and other letters that Vicky felt she and Fritz had acted correctly vis-à-vis the press edict and that because of this, an all-knowing Providence would eventually reward them. But what historians later referred to as "the Danzig affair" had been an isolating experience. It was Fritz and Vicky's first major skirmish without Prince Albert, author of the plan for unifying Germany under a morally righteous Prussia—a concept that seemed to be slipping further and further out of their reach.

CHAPTER
TWENTY-TWO

"A government that encroaches on the constitution at one point, cannot stop there. It is forced by circumstances and by its own action from one illegality to another."

ERICH EYCK

*D*URING MOST OF THE UPROAR that resulted from Fritz's Danzig speech, Vicky's mother-in-law was in Baden-Baden with her daughter or in England visiting Queen Victoria. Since Augusta listened patiently to the Queen of England's lamentations over her widowhood, she found great favor with her hostess: "She is so clever, so good, so noble-minded, so free from all pettiness, so adores adored Papa, misses him so dreadfully; feels so deeply for me & pities me so truly," Victoria wrote Vicky. "She sees how crushed, & worked & fagged I am & has such forbearance. . . . We are both so unhappy, that we understand each other so well."

A few weeks after Augusta's departure, Victoria heard that old Baron Stockmar had died: "And now that loving father, as he ever was to us both (Papa & me) and God knows to you too, is gone & I am more & more desolate!!" the Queen wrote Vicky.

Raised to revere the sage of Coburg, Vicky wrote Augusta that her "only comfort" was "that Fritz's conduct in the past dark days were his last pleasure."

In that regard, the Crown Prince was ordered to meet his father and Bismarck in August in Bad Gastein, where the King was taking the waters. It was the first face-to-face encounter between father and son since Danzig, and Vicky knew that Wilhelm would play on Fritz's well-known sense of filial and dynastic responsibility. "[I]t does seem such a shame to torment one so good as Fritz," she wrote her mother; "scenes with his father are what he dreads of all things."

At their meeting, Wilhelm said that he planned to continue dissolving parliament until "obedience" was "re-established in the country." To which Bismarck added that Prussia could not exist under parliamentary government and that a "constitutional regime" was "untenable."

From Gastein, Fritz traveled to Coburg to join his wife and Queen Victoria, who was on a pilgrimage to one of Albert's ancestral homes. The Queen's visit coincided with a new crisis in Prussian affairs, arising over Bismarck's determination to keep Wilhelm from attending a congress of the reigning monarchs of the German states. The meeting had been called by the Austrians in order to settle the differences between themselves and the Prussians. Since the Austrian plan provided for strengthening the German Confederation largely at Prussia's expense, they sent Emperor Franz Joseph himself to invite the Prussian King to Frankfurt. The invitation, implying as it did the solidarity of kings against the encroachment of parliaments, was nearly impossible for Wilhelm to refuse.

But Bismarck had resolved to thwart any reform of the German Confederation, let alone one that would keep Prussia in a position inferior to Austria. When Franz Joseph arrived at Gastein, the Prime Minister was there, too. Bismarck managed to convince Wilhelm that the invitation, delivered on August 3 for a meeting on the sixteenth, was an insult and must be refused. Plans for the congress proceeded without the King of Prussia, who moved on to his favorite summer spa at Baden-Baden, tailed by Bismarck.

As soon as the congress gathered, it sent a second emissary to invite the King of Prussia in the name of all the German monarchs to come to Frankfurt. King Johann of Saxony, a highly respected man and personal friend of the Prussian King, was waiting in Baden-Baden when Wilhelm arrived.

"Thirty reigning princes and a king as messenger? How can I refuse?" Wilhelm asked his Prime Minister. Bismarck, who found the King lying on his sofa weeping after a visit from Johann, eventually succeeded in extracting a letter of refusal from Wilhelm, but was so undone by the effort that he "tore the handle off the outer door" as he left the King's chambers. Back in his own rooms, he smashed a huge porcelain bowl on the floor and burst into tears as well. But they were tears of triumph. Without the King of Prussia, the congress of German princes was a meaningless gathering.

In Coburg, Fritz discussed the worsening of Austro-Prussian relations with his wife and mother-in-law. Victoria and Vicky wanted to see the ties between the two great German powers strengthened, but Fritz agreed with Bismarck that Prussia must wrest the leadership of the German states from Austria. Albert had said that Prussia must show the way to unification with a viable constitutional government. Fritz believed that unification might well precede liberalization.

On the last day of August, Wilhelm himself arrived in Coburg with Bismarck and Roon, both clearly unwilling to let him out of their sight. "The conflict as to whether I should accept or refuse the invitation to Frankfort," he told Victoria, had made him "quite ill." To which she replied that she was "very much in favour of the closest rapprochement between Prussia and Austria." Victoria did not receive Bismarck, although she ran into him at one point, noting the "horrid expression" on his face. The visit left the Queen of England "so done up, so worn, so worried . . . so agitated" that she had trouble sleeping and woke up "very trembly" the next day.

Three days later, Franz Joseph arrived. Again, Victoria tried to mediate between the two German powers. When Franz Joseph complained that Wilhelm had "made a great mistake" in not attending the congress, Victoria explained that he was worried that the Austrian Emperor wished to subordinate Prussia to Austria. She herself, she said, hoped to see "equal rights for both" of the two great German powers. "Yes," Franz Joseph replied, "but how can we arrange it if the King withdraws from all discussion of the subject? I regret his non-appearance, but Bismarck is entirely to blame."

ALONG WITH HIS DETERMINATION to separate Prussia from Austria in foreign affairs, Bismarck continued his domestic campaign to subvert the constitution. While Victoria was still in Coburg, the Prussian Parliament was once again dissolved. Fritz, who was not allowed to speak at the crown council when the decision was taken, saw his father the next day. What, Fritz asked, did the King think would become of the Prussian Parliament?

"Repeated dissolutions, one after the other," Wilhelm replied. "[T]he King of Prussia was never intended to be a powerless figurehead with the power to rule vested in parliament." When Fritz asked him how many times he planned to dissolve parliament, he answered that he would "continue until it became obedient, or until barricades were raised in the streets" and he himself "ascended the scaffold." "[T]his abominable constitutional system can't continue" he added; "it will only bring about the destruction of royal authority and the introduction of a republic with a president as in England."

Fritz begged to be excused from future crown councils "in order to avoid opposition," but his father said that it was his "duty as Crown Prince" to attend. Screaming repeatedly at his son, the King threatened to "deal very severely" with whoever it was that was putting "these ideas" into Fritz's head. But Fritz said that he was expressing his "own convictions." He could not, he said, "be silent and watch my King and Father go to destruction."

The next day Fritz sent Bismarck a letter, outlining his position. "A momentous decision was yesterday taken in the council; in the presence of the ministers I would not in any way oppose His Majesty; today I have done so; I have expressed my views, I have set forth my grave apprehensions as to the future. The King now knows that I am the determined foe of the ministry."

It was always easier for Fritz to express his opinions in writing than in person. Faced with his father's belligerence (based on the unexamined theories of a limited mind) and Bismarck's withering wit, the Crown Prince was often at a loss for words. This led him into doubt and depression. "I consider myself a particular species of 'blockhead' . . . ," he wrote Vicky two weeks later. "My courage and persistence will no doubt prevail, but . . . I am increasingly aware of my startling lack of knowledge about domestic problems, foreign policy and government personnel. You must forgive me, my angel, for telling you all these confidential matters, but I cannot keep silent, least of all with you, when I am in such low spirits!"

"My poor dear treasure . . . ," Vicky wrote after Fritz's argument with his father. "Don't lose your courage and don't take things so hard. . . . Keep up your spirits darling, don't be downhearted and never mind other people's nonsense."

Ever since the end of June, Fritz had been requesting his father's permission to absent himself from the crown councils attended by Bismarck, the ministers of his cabinet, and the King. But Bismarck had told Wilhelm that Fritz's opposition to his policies was seen by the Prussians "as a revolt against . . . paternal authority"—an argument the Prime Minister knew Wilhelm could not resist. "When the authority of the father and the King is assailed by the son and the heir apparent," Bismarck asked, "to whom shall it still remain sacred?"

This was skillful manipulation by a Prime Minister bent on the political emasculation of the heir to the throne. As expected, the King decided that the Crown Prince must continue to attend the councils at which he was still prohibited from voting. Wilhelm sent Bismarck to tell Fritz of his decision.

The choice of messenger was even more devastating than the message. "I asked him why he held so aloof from the government," Bismarck wrote thirty-odd years later in his memoirs; "in a few years he would be its master; and if his principles were not ours, he should rather endeavour to effect a gradual transition than throw himself into opposition. That suggestion he decisively rejected. . . . The refusal was accompanied by a hostile expression of Olympian disdain, which after all these years I have not forgotten; today I still see before me the averted head, the flushed face, and the glance cast over the left shoulder."

Written at the end of his life, Bismarck's version of this encounter with Fritz illustrates the skill with which the Prime Minister twisted scenes around to his own advantage. It was a tactic he had learned to use with stunning effect in the slippery world of European diplomacy. The Crown Prince of Prussia, however, was neither a diplomat nor a trained negotiator. He was a straightforward thirty-two-year-old man, torn between filial and political duty. "When I see him," General Roon, the Minister of the Army, said, "he looms like a thundercloud."

Silenced but seething, Fritz continued to attend the crown councils, but on the proviso that after each one he be allowed to submit his opinions in writing to his father. "I have considered my negative and passive attitude a duty to my conscience from the moment when I heard . . . from the Prime Minister himself that he regarded the annulment of the constitution as the last and quite admissible outcome of the present conflict and confusion in Prussia . . . ," Fritz wrote the King. "I regard the constitution . . . as the immovable and focal point of our state and law."

"NOW BEGINS THE ELECTION SWINDLE," Bismarck said on September 4, 1863, two days after he had dissolved parliament for the third time in a year. Certainly, every tactic was tried to intimidate voters. In the countryside, where approximately two-thirds of the nineteen million Prussians lived, elections were controlled by royal appointees on the government payroll, who drew up the lists of eligible voters, outlined the precincts, supervised the voting, and traveled through rural areas campaigning in favor of conservative candidates. Owners of country taverns—the meeting places for most political groups—were told they would lose their licenses if they allowed liberals to use their premises for assembly or the distribution of political pamphlets. Village mayors were instructed to vote for conservative candidates under penalty of fines and loss of position; rural pastors made support of the king's government a religious duty; and Junkers pressured their tenants to vote for the conservative delegates. Bismarck himself had one group of railway employees suspended for failing to stop a demonstration against him at a station in Pomerania.

Pressure was also applied to liberal members of parliament not to run for reelection. If they insisted, those who made their living as civil servants were assessed for the cost of substitutes named by the government to take over their positions when parliament was in session. Were they reelected, they were told, they were bound by their oath to support the King.

But in spite of all this, the conservatives made only smallish gains in the Chamber of Deputies (the lower house of parliament), while the liberals retained a hefty majority. "The Prussian monarchy and our present constitution are irreconcilable things," Bismarck said when the elections were over. His plan, he said, was to maneuver the former into "complete and unconditional elimination" of the latter.

The political atmosphere was beginning to weigh on Vicky, who had been trying to take her three children to England since the beginning of 1863. But her in-laws kept changing their minds as to when she and Fritz might leave, with the result that when they were finally given permission, their place at Balmoral Castle in Scotland had been filled by her sister Alice and her family.

"I am grieved to think they [Alice and her husband, Louis of Hesse] should by their devotion to me cause you, dear child, a disappointment," Queen Victoria wrote Vicky, "but . . . you will, I know, at once see that I, in my forlorn position, have a prior claim. . . . I need not tell you how constantly & anxiously I think of you and your great troubles & difficulties. It adds much to my many sorrows & anxieties!"

In the end, the Queen managed to make room for Vicky and her family. While they were in England, they made arrangements to consult a specialist for Willy—a man known for his work on the spinal cord* who had been recommended by Victoria's physician. Before there was a chance to talk to him, Fritz was ordered by his father to return to Berlin for the opening of parliament. Fritz and Vicky hastened home, leaving the children and their nannies with the Queen.

"[A]s you are not here, it may be a satisfaction to you if I see him [the specialist] himself—which I shall do & take care a full report is written of what he says," Victoria wrote Vicky. The Crown Princess was deeply grateful for her mother's help, but upset by a disagreement between the English doctors, who ordered "galvanization" (the application of electricity to damaged muscles), and the German doctors, who refused to perform it. "What am I to do?" she asked

---

* *Édouard Brown-Séquard, whose other work was in the field of blood and the internal secretions of organs. He later developed a fluid prepared from sheep testicles that he prescribed to prolong life and sexual vigor in men—a fact that gives one pause over his medical expertise.*

Victoria. "I feel so convinced that electricity . . . does the child no harm—but I cannot have it done." This letter was written on Christmas Day of 1863, a day that brought the inevitable recollection of the terrible Christmas two years earlier following her father's death. "Thank God that dreadful time is passed!" Vicky wrote her mother, not realizing how her words would be taken.

"How you can be as merry & happy as formerly—& how you can say 'Thank God those dreadful days are past'—is to me incredible," Victoria wrote back. "How have these days passed? They have left your old home desolate & wretched & broken your mother's heart & health, & hastened her end! Is this 'thank God! that they are passed'? My good, dear child, you have wonderful spirits—& you like ever to shake off all that is sad!"

IT IS FORTUNATE that Vicky retained those "wonderful spirits" denigrated by her mother. At twenty-three she had already survived two major misfortunes— the death of her father and the advent to power of her enemy. Albert's death had forced her to begin to think for herself, and it was this nascent self-reliance, those "wonderful spirits," that kept her fighting in spite of the odds that now began piling up against her.

Ever since he had been named Prime Minister, Bismarck had been trying to neutralize the effectiveness of the heir to the throne and his English wife. Only once had Fritz dared speak out in public against his father, and Bismarck had managed not only to silence his outburst in the press, but use it as an opening wedge in his drive to separate father and son. The Prime Minister began by infiltrating Fritz and Vicky's palace with courtiers more sympathetic to his agenda, ensnaring men like Duncker and getting rid of those like Stock-mar whose loyalty he could not change. He then set out to portray Fritz and Vicky's intimacy with Queen Victoria as potential treason.

In a memo dated at the end of 1863, Bismarck told Wilhelm that Vicky's relationship with Queen Victoria would remain a problem until the Crown Prince and Princess "fully realized that in ruling houses the nearest of kin may . . . represent other interests than the Prussian. It is hard that a frontier line should also be the line of demarcation between the interests of mother and daughter . . . ," Bismarck said, "but to forget the fact is always perilous to the state."

If this last was calculated sanctimony, it was also common sense from Bismarck's point of view. Having once determined that the key to Prussia's future as leader of the German states lay in subduing Austria—a policy that necessitated the support of Russia—the Prime Minister was understandably eager to cut the link with Russia's rival, England. This determination was of course reinforced by the fact that the British stood for limited monarchy and constitutionalism, ideas inimical to Bismarck's political and emotional tempera-ment.

But before Fritz's speech at Danzig, Wilhelm would not have tolerated such innuendos about his daughter-in-law and his old friend, Victoria. It would have been an attack on family honor, both in the Prussian royal family itself and in the farther-flung family of nineteenth-century monarchs. Danzig was a watershed in the relationship between the King and his heir. With Bismarck guiding Wilhelm and insinuating filial disloyalty, the relationship between Wilhelm and Fritz now began a long, sad descent to distrust and alienation. The month after Bismarck's memo to the King, Wilhelm informed his son that he would no longer be allowed to see government dispatches.

PART THREE

Three Wars

CHAPTER TWENTY-THREE

> *"Only three men ever understood the question of Schleswig-Holstein. One was Prince Albert, who is dead. The second was a German professor who became mad. I am the third and I have forgotten all about it."*
>
> LORD PALMERSTON

*B*Y NEW YEAR'S OF 1864, Bismarck had been in office for a little over a year. He had successfully orchestrated what one historian called "a steady crescendo of dictatorial measures" culminating in the muzzling of the press, but his early efforts to change the direction of Prussia's foreign policy had been wobbly. Now, however, as conflict began to unroll in the semi-German duchies of Schleswig and Holstein, he saw his chance to pursue the aggrandizement of Prussia on his own terms—without the German Confederation, without the moral leadership vaunted by Prince Albert, and without the watered-down but still inconvenient constitutionalism to which Fritz and Vicky clung. Having warned parliament from the very beginning that "blood and iron" would be Prussia's new creed, Bismarck seized upon the Schleswig-Holstein controversy with hearty if well-concealed gusto.

The issue of the duchies of Schleswig and Holstein had first entered the Prussian political arena during the Revolution of 1848, when they became a litmus test for German nationalists. Located between the North and Baltic seas on the extension of land jutting out from Germany toward Scandinavia and separated from each other by the Eider River, Schleswig, the northernmost duchy, was about half German and half Danish, while Holstein, which lay in the mainland to the south, was almost entirely German. Both duchies belonged personally to the King of Denmark, and they were considered inseparable. Nonetheless, in one of those territorial inconsistencies inherited from generations of overlapping monarchies, Holstein was a member of the German Confederation, while Schleswig was not. Moreover, Germany and Denmark operated under different laws of succession; in Germany, which observed the Salic Law, the crown could pass only to male heirs, while in Denmark it could descend through the female line.

In 1848, King Frederick VII of Denmark announced that Denmark was taking over next-door Schleswig. It was the year of revolutions, and the Schleswigers, rebelling against the occupying Danes, established a provisional government with the Holsteiners at Kiel. The people of the duchies preferred as their master the Duke of Augustenburg, who rushed off to Berlin to ask for Prussian assistance. He arrived in the middle of the revolution, offering the Prussian government a heaven-sent opportunity to improve its badly damaged prestige by exhibiting its devotion to German nationalism.

The liberal Frankfurt Parliament, which was enjoying its brief moment of power, recognized the provisional government of the Duke, welcomed Schleswig into the German Confederation, and sent the Prussian army to occupy the duchies. But King Friedrich Wilhelm IV distrusted rebels, whatever their cause. Heeding threats from England and Russia, who were trying to keep Prussia geographically contained in the middle of Europe, he signed an armistice with the Danes. Left in the lurch, the Duke of Augustenburg was forced to flee.

The confusion was temporarily settled in 1852 by the Great Powers through the Treaty of London, a makeshift document that guaranteed the integrity of Denmark itself and designated Prince Christian of Glücksburg as heir to the current King. Along with Denmark, Christian was also to inherit Schleswig and Holstein, provided that Denmark never again try to incorporate either duchy into its territory.

For his part, the Duke of Augustenburg, impoverished by the confiscation of his lands, promised on his honor as a prince, for both himself and his heirs, to do nothing further to disturb or endanger this settlement of the duchies. To pay off his debts, he turned over his extensive properties in the duchies to the King of Denmark, in return for which he received 2.75 million thalers, about half of what they were worth. It is not insignificant that the person who negotiated this agreement was Otto von Bismarck, then Prussian minister to the Frankfurt Diet.

The Treaty of London lasted only a decade, until the Danish Parliament ratified a new constitution incorporating Schleswig into the kingdom of Denmark. Before he could sign the constitution, however, the old King died, leaving his heir Christian IX with a major problem.

Christian of Schleswig-Holstein-Sonderburg-Glücksburg,* an obscure German prince, none too bright, had been chosen by the Great Powers to succeed to the throne because his wife, Louise, was a first cousin of the previous King, who had left no direct heirs. With his throne, Christian IX of Denmark, as he was now known, inherited a seemingly insoluble dilemma. If he signed the new constitution, approved by the Danish Parliament, he was validating a document that negated the terms of the treaty that had made him King of Denmark; if he refused to sign, he denied the will of the people he had been designated to rule. Forced to choose between evils, he signed, just three days after becoming King.

Reaction followed at once. Duke Friedrich of Schleswig-Holstein-Sonderburg-Augustenburg, the son of the Duke of Augustenburg who had renounced his lands in the 1852 Treaty of London, immediately proclaimed himself Duke of Schleswig-Holstein and assembled a rival government. The

* *Father of Alexandra (Alix), Princess of Wales.*

Duke of Augustenburg, or Fritz Holstein as he was known in the family, was a former schoolmate of the Crown Prince. An intelligent, somewhat pedantic man, he had married a niece of Queen Victoria* and was a close friend of both Vicky and Fritz.

A confirmed constitutionalist and liberal, the Duke of Augustenburg quickly gained the support of most of the small German states. Wilhelm favored his claim, which was based on the Duke's contention that his father had had no right to renounce the succession in his name since he was of age in 1852 when the treaty was signed. The citizens of Schleswig-Holstein agreed, alleging that the Augustenburg claim to the duchies could not be resigned without their approval, which had never been given.

By now the question of Schleswig-Holstein had become a *cause célèbre* among statesmen, politicians, and greater and lesser royalties—one of those nineteenth-century Euro-muddles in which many had a stake and everyone offered opinions. Vicky and Fritz were at Windsor, on their way back from Balmoral, when the Schleswig-Holstein crisis broke, and the Queen and Fritz had a snappish political discussion at breakfast on the day King Christian signed the new constitution.

This was the first time that Queen Victoria, who was intimately related through marriage to both claimants, had been faced with such a situation. Her eldest son and new daughter-in-law, Alix, were naturally on the side of Alix's father, Christian of Denmark. On the other side were Fritz and Vicky, who supported their old friend and political ally, Fritz Holstein (the Duke of Augustenburg), as well as the Queen's beloved half-sister, Feodora, the Duke's mother-in-law. Family tension rose to fever pitch when Bertie and Alix arrived at Windsor, and the Queen banned political discussions altogether.

"Oh! God, why, oh! why . . . now this year everything that interested my Angel and that he understood takes place, and he is not here to help us, and to write those admirable memoranda which are gospel now," Victoria wrote Uncle Leopold. "Oh! my fate is too too dreadful!"

Prince Albert had never approved of the pro-Danish Treaty of London, believing that "Schleswig is entitled to insist on union with Holstein; Holstein belongs to Germany, and the Augustenburgs are the heirs." Victoria, taking her cue from Albert's "admirable memoranda"—already over ten years out of date —lent her support to Prussia.

The most passionately partisan member of the Queen's family was the normally quiet young Alix, by now six months pregnant, tearful, and claiming between sobs that "the Duchies belong to Papa." The British government agreed. Prime Minister Palmerston had gone so far as to warn Bismarck a few months earlier that if "any violent attempt" were directed at Denmark, "those who made the attempt would find . . . that it would not be Denmark alone with which they would have to contend."

But Bismarck knew that England, for all of Palmerston's threats, was un-

---

* *A daughter of Victoria's half-sister, Feodora.*

likely to go to war for little Denmark. The Prussian Prime Minister was, in fact, the only person with a clear-cut plan for Schleswig-Holstein. It was a secret plan, one he could confide to no one, because it contradicted everything in which his King, his countrymen, and his fellow Europeans believed. Bismarck was determined to wrest the duchies from Denmark, not in order to establish them as separate states in the German Confederation, not to honor the claim of the Duke of Augustenburg—but to annex them to Prussia.

VICKY AND FRITZ arrived back in Berlin two days before Christmas of 1863. Although the impeccably mannered King was polite to them, Vicky noted a definite coolness. This may have been due to the distrust engendered by Bismarck's memorandum on the dangers of their intimacy with Victoria or even to wounded pride, based on the fact that Bismarck's press edict, source of the family rift, had been soundly rejected by the Chamber of Deputies and annulled several weeks earlier. More probably, Wilhelm's irritation can be traced to a letter Fritz and Vicky brought from Victoria, in which the Queen of England expressed herself rather openly on matters that Wilhelm no doubt considered private.

"Allow me to say how greatly relieved my mother's heart is . . . ," Victoria wrote, "at your decision to exempt Fritz in future from the ministerial sessions. I am convinced that you yourself will realise how much better it is that your dear, excellent son should not be compelled to take part in what his conscience and feelings bid him avoid. And you surely could not wish that he should act against his own firm conviction, a conviction which rests on the belief that he is acting only in your and your country's interests."

The Crown Prince and Princess arrived home just in time to do their bit for the winter social season, already in full swing. Five days after their return, they hosted a state dinner to which they invited, as Vicky put it, "all our enemies." She was genuinely surprised by Bismarck's geniality, discovering that both he and General Manteuffel could be "very agreeable" when they wished.

But neither Fritz nor Vicky was lulled by Bismarck's charm. Fritz worried about what he called the "web of lies" surrounding his father, and he realized that state documents and important information were now being withheld from him. Like other liberals, Fritz and Vicky supported the Duke of Augustenburg, whom Bismarck disliked for his progressive outlook and his relationship to Queen Victoria. Like many successful politicians before and since, the German Prime Minister had managed to brand opposition to his policies as a lack of patriotism. "The more German one feels," Vicky wrote Victoria on New Year's Day of 1864, "the more jealous and ambitious for one's country's honour and welfare, the more one has to suffer here!"

Vicky was becoming more and more dedicated to Prussia and more determined that Schleswig and Holstein should become part of Germany. She not only urged Fritz to speak on the Duke of Augustenburg's behalf with his father, but herself outlined the terms of the negotiation. Embarrassed that she had promoted the Danes into the British royal family, she managed to blame the situation on the King of Denmark.

"King Christian has himself to thank for the fix he is in," she wrote her mother. "Why did he accept [the throne]—and allow himself to be put in a place not rightfully his own? He might now be living in peace and quiet!" This was specious reasoning, aimed at overcoming personal ambivalence as well as asserting royal prerogatives. By accepting the Danish throne, King Christian had made a mistake, according to Vicky. He had crossed an invisible line guarded by sovereigns of every political stripe from the Queen of England to the Czar of Russia. Monarchy, to those born to the throne, was an exclusive club into which one should never allow oneself to be drafted.

Basically rational, Vicky did not cling to convenient sophistries. "My thoughts and wishes are with Fritz Augustenburg . . . ," she wrote Victoria. "But I feel much for poor King Christian; with his kind feelings and good heart he must find the position he is in doubly disagreeable. I hope dearest Alix does not fret too much about it all."

But Alix did fret, and on January 8, 1864, Vicky was shocked to receive a telegram from Bertie saying that his wife had given birth prematurely to a seven-month, three-and-three-quarter-pound son.* Queen Victoria and Vicky were convinced that Alix's unabated social life and constant physical exercise had brought the baby on early, but those outside the family blamed it on the Princess of Wales's worry over Schleswig-Holstein, a conflict that Bismarck was purposefully escalating into war.

BISMARCK HAD DECIDED that the question of the duchies would be determined on the battlefield. The Schleswig-Holstein affair, which he later called his "proudest" success, was the first of three Bismarck-induced conflicts that turned Prussia into Germany and permanently changed the face of Europe. It was also the first real demonstration of Bismarck's foreign policy in action, and, as he himself boasted, the attendant "diplomatic intrigues" would have provided an elaborate plot for a play. A master at balancing the forces around him, Bismarck kept potential enemies at bay with half-promises that catered to their weaknesses and their greeds. The ultimate pragmatist, he guiltlessly embraced whatever position or relationship he thought would advance his goal—the aggrandizement of Prussia—and then dropped it when it had outlived its usefulness. For Bismarck there was neither good nor evil, only allegiance to the Fatherland.

He began his monumental coup by posing as a supporter of the status quo, calling on the Austrians to join him in demanding that Denmark conform to the Treaty of London. This stratagem—basing Prussian intervention on the terms of the treaty and gaining Austria as an ally—kept the other European powers from interfering with Prussian designs.

There were, in any case, only two potential brakes on Bismarck's plan—

---

* *Prince Albert Victor (Eddy), 1864–1892.*

England and Russia. The English, who had raised false hopes with the Danes, were not prepared to go to war for Denmark, at least not without an ally, and the only logical partner-in-arms, Napoleon III of France, was still smoldering over England's slight to his Polish policies the year before.* To keep France neutral, Bismarck let Napoleon think that he supported the Emperor's expansionistic policies, even when they involved the German Rhineland. Russia was less of a problem, since Czar Alexander II wanted to see Bismarck remain in power as a bulwark to conservatism. The Czar knew that the best way would be for Bismarck to have some tangible victory to wave before the Prussians.

On January 16, 1864, Prussia and Austria issued a joint ultimatum to Denmark, demanding the repeal of the November constitution in which they incorporated Schleswig. Much to the delight of Bismarck, who needed an excuse to occupy the duchies, the Danes refused. Three days later, an Austro-Prussian army marched into Holstein and two weeks later, into Schleswig. The reconstructed Prussian army, cause of Wilhelm's budget crisis and Bismarck's rise to power, was about to be exhibited in all its fighting splendor. Although the King himself was too old to lead the troops, three members of the younger generation of Hohenzollerns were there, among them the Crown Prince.

Vicky was philosophical about her husband's role in the fray, although she wrote him that she wished his "mission were of a different nature!" As she told her mother, "I do not say a word to prevent him, as first it would not be listened to & secondly it is best for him to do what would be justly expected of him!" To keep from brooding, she had helped Fritz prepare for his departure. As befitted his rank, he took two aides-de-camp, five servants, several grooms, and six of their best horses.

The Crown Prince headed for army headquarters where he was to serve on the staff of Field Marshal Wrangel. Wrangel was now eighty years old and no longer capable of running a war, but since he was the only German officer who outranked the Commander of the Austrian troops, he had been appointed in order to keep the combined Austro-Prussian army under Prussian command. Fritz's cousin Fritz Carl had been named Commander of the Prussian army—a blow to Fritz, whose father had still not forgiven him for his objections to Prussian domestic policy. As it happened, however, Fritz had been placed in the most influential position of all—a post from which he could countermand the indecisive Wrangel, who issued orders in the morning only to reverse them later in the day and then change them back again. "I can assure you that my presence here at Headquarters is of particular importance," Fritz wrote Vicky with uncharacteristic pride. "At times Wrangel is really half crazy, and his . . . energy and verve have turned to obstinacy and stubbornness."

Some Prussian officers—doubtless those who saw beyond politics—

---

* *During the Polish insurrection against Russia, Napoleon had proposed sending identical notes from Paris, London, and Vienna censuring Prussia for intervening on the side of Russia, but London had refused, preferring to censure the Russians.*

claimed that the Crown Prince was the only man who showed a clear under-standing of military strategy on a large scale, and the most chauvinistic historian of his day, Heinrich von Treitschke, credited him with introducing bolder tactics into the Prussian army. Fritz's concern for his soldiers had always won him affection from the rank and file, but now, with added respect from his fellow officers, he was promoted to what was essentially a joint command with Wrangel. This meant that he bore the ultimate responsibility for the success or failure of the Austro-Prussian forces.

"That you are in fact really leading the armies, although without the title, makes me proud and happy," Vicky wrote him. "May you succeed in doing good effectively as you have done up to the present. . . . I consider it a very good thing that poor old Wrangel has been spared and his outward reputation preserved."

Fritz, who was a modest man, agreed. When he suddenly heard that his father had given him the Order of the Red Eagle, with Swords, he was genu-inely distressed. "What Orders are still left for really brave deeds?" he wrote in his diary. "They will laugh at me in the Army because I, who am sitting comfort-ably at Headquarters, have been honoured. Dear Papa! . . . I am afraid it will be ascribed to fatherly weakness. I am quite beside myself . . . for I feel ashamed."

What the Crown Prince really wanted was the chance to see action. Ever since the invasion of Schleswig in early February, the Danes had been retreating before the vastly superior forces of the Prussians and Austrians, finally with-drawing to the fort of Düppel, their last position on the mainland. Fritz had requested his father's permission to join the troops in storming the fortifica-tions, but Augusta tried to talk William into refusing Fritz's request. "She thought she was doing me a favour thereby . . . ," Vicky wrote her husband, "but I declared that you knew best yourself what your life was worth. This seemed incomprehensible to Mama and she said she was your mother and I answered that I was your wife. This matter worried me and I went this morning to your Papa and begged him to give you a free hand; he said he had already wanted to do that yesterday, only Mama had made such a fuss; but he would do it."

On April 18, 1864, when the Prussians stormed Düppel, Fritz was in the thick of the fighting, and it was his plan of attack that was credited with the victory. He was not entirely jubilant. "I am sorry for my sister-in-law, the Princess of Wales," he wrote in his diary. "It is true we have a wonderful army, but what will be the result of her victories under a Bismarck? This question has a crushing effect."

Fritz had recently received two letters from the Prime Minister, soliciting his advice on the wisdom of occupying the whole of Jutland (the largest part of modern Denmark). Bismarck was having trouble convincing Wilhelm that it should be done and was trying to get Fritz to help him. "The sly fox," Fritz said. "He leaves no stone unturned to force me to make some statement from which he can later derive advantage for himself."

The Crown Prince's formal response to the Prime Minister, composed after consultation with his wife and Ernest Stockmar,* was aimed primarily at not getting caught in Bismarck's web. "The question . . . comes, I must confess, as somewhat of a surprise to me," he wrote back, "as up to the present I had no reason to suppose that you attached any value to my judgment. . . ." Assuring Bismarck that if he could respond "as a soldier pure and simple," he would do so, but to "fulfil your wish to support the occupation of the whole of Jutland would mean that I was supporting your policy, and this I am unable to do, principally because I am unaware of the object of that policy."

Bismarck did not give up. The letters continued. "He writes most confidentially as if he were devoted to you," Vicky wrote her husband. "But how obvious are his ulterior motives—to swallow up the Duchies later on."

The Crown Princess was right.

During the first crown council held after the accession of Christian IX to the throne of Denmark, Bismarck had raised the subject of annexing the duchies to Prussia, reminding Wilhelm that "every one of his immediate ancestors, not even excepting his artistic brother, had won an increment of territory for the state." Wilhelm, who supported the claim of the Duke of Augustenburg, was shocked, but Bismarck knew that if he could undermine the King's trust in the Duke's loyalty and appeal to Wilhelm's ingrained militarism, he could eventually turn him around.

At the same time, Bismarck tried to get Austria to agree to Prussia's annexation of Schleswig and Holstein, claiming that this was already being discussed in Berlin in spite of *his* personal objections. Should it become a real possibility, he promised that Austria would not only receive compensation in Italy, but would earn the appreciation and future services of the Prussian army. Austria, however, refused to be talked out of sharing the duchies. By agreeing to sever Schleswig and Holstein from Denmark and give them to the Duke of Augustenburg, however, she allowed Bismarck to proceed one step further toward annexation. By now, Austria feared Prussia far more than she feared the liberal-minded Duke.

In early May, England called another international† conference in London to try to stop the fighting and return the duchies to their original status before the war. For purposes of negotiation, a temporary armistice was signed. "When the conference opens," Vicky wrote Fritz, "Bismarck will hold forth our aims in a most confusing and unclear manner so that the back door can be left open . . . [and] . . . the Duchies can be swallowed up later."

Which is essentially what happened. Prussia and Austria astounded the diplomats in London by reversing their position and calling for the "complete separation" of Schleswig and Holstein from Denmark "and their union in a single state" under the Duke of Augustenburg, who had "the greatest right to

* *After his retirement, Stockmar continued to advise Vicky.*

† *Austria, Prussia, the German Confederation, England, Denmark, France, Russia, and Sweden.*

the succession." This left the conferees with nothing to do but agree on a line of demarcation between Schleswig and Denmark—a compromise that should have been fairly simple to find, but which, because of Bismarck, now became unattainable. The last thing in the world that Bismarck wanted was a cessation of hostilities or a return to a peaceful status quo. Only the revamped and superefficient Prussian army, the "blood and iron" of his prophesies, could help him achieve his ultimate goal—annexation of Schleswig and Holstein to Prussia.

CHAPTER
TWENTY-FOUR

> *"Bismarck espouses a doctrine . . . that any action in foreign affairs will ease domestic turmoil—this is an immoral principle."*
>
> VICTORIA, CROWN PRINCESS OF PRUSSIA, 1862

*A*S THE OBVIOUS TARGET for anti-Danish, anti-British sentiment during the Schleswig-Holstein War, Vicky bore the brunt of hostility inside and outside the court. As long as Fritz was with her, she was able to withstand the barbs and even laugh them off, but when he left for war, her pluck gave way. "I . . . wish I could join you at Headquarters where I could play cards, smoke and tell off-color stories. . . ." she wrote; "it would be much nicer than moping about around here!"

The Crown Princess asked Victoria to send Countess Blücher to Berlin, but the Queen was none too gracious. "You know she is my guest & . . . had settled to stay with me, a good way into Feb. I was . . . rather hurt at this want of consideration. When you . . . say how sad & alone you are, I am ready to give her up, painful as it is—but, dear child, this must not . . . happen again."

By the time Countess Blücher arrived in Berlin, Fritz had been gone three weeks and Vicky had brought five-year-old Willy down from the nursery to stay in her room—an honor that made him "very proud." Unlike the other princesses whose husbands were at the front, the Crown Princess did not attend the seasonal balls and fêtes, explaining to her mother that she could not dance when her beloved Fritz might at "that very moment be exposed to danger." Queen Victoria, who favored any diminution of social activity, approved. "You are not only quite right not to go to balls etc. but it would have been quite improper if you had done so while Fritz is with the Army. Altogether going out & about without one's husband I disapprove—and never did!"

But along with the praise, there were reproaches for the war: "I had hoped that this dreadful war might have been prevented but you all (God forgive you for it) would have it!" Victoria wrote her eldest daughter.

Vicky's mother-in-law also used Vicky to let out her frustrations. "Your Mama wants me to tell you that everything is in a very bad way," she wrote Fritz; "in the last two Councils Bismarck talked Papa round to all his ideas! . . . Your mother is in the worst possible mood, she made a terrible scene yesterday with most bitter and cutting remarks which, at such moments, she always has at her command. . . . Why must she come here and make such scenes."

Finally, there was the "grief for our country," which the Crown Princess outlined in a letter to her husband.

> It is not only the worry about your personal safety which depresses and torments me, but . . . [the] lives that are sacrificed, our changeable policy, the shameful role which we are forced to play against our wishes . . . because an adventurer like Bismarck wishes it, and because he is successful in lying to his King and dominates him. . . . Just fancy, rumours are being spread here that I had found out everything about a Council of State and had immediately telegraphed it to Lord Palmerston.

Vicky's agitation was augmented by the fact that she was physically unwell. For over a month she had been fighting one of those feverish colds that always seemed to plague her during the Berlin winters. Dr. Wegner prescribed leeches, but these only weakened her further. And she was once again—she finally admitted it to her mother—pregnant.

"I think I am quite sure now, as next Monday something will have staid *[sic]* away for the 3rd time. . . . ever since the beginning of January I have been so awfully sick regularly twice a day and often as many times as 3 & 4. . . . I did not say anything about all this before, as I know it is a subject distasteful to you, dear Mama, & I was afraid of making you angry by saying how happy and thankful I am that I have hopes again."

"I cannot tell you how grieved & how surprised I am at the news conveyed in your letter received today," wrote the Queen, who described herself as "quite shattered" over the Schleswig-Holstein conflict. "I thought you both knew how highly important the doctors . . . thought it that you should have 2 years complete rest before these—for you—particularly trying events—again began. . . . I will say no more except that I pray God fervently to protect you & the child! I little needed this additional anxiety in my present sorrow & worry! May God order all for the best!"

After the stunning victory of the Prussians over the Danes at Düppel, Vicky thought Fritz would be able to come home, but soon learned that, "as he has virtually the command of everything out there & Wrangel only the name," he had to stay until the final armistice. Her husband had already been away for over three months. She had been ill the entire time.

Her winter grippe had left her with a retching cough for which the doctors had prescribed the usual range of mustard poultices, warm baths, and liniments. "[I]t makes me afraid to sneeze or laugh, or blow my nose as it hurts so much," she told her mother. Confined to bed at the end of April, she was furious at Queen Augusta, who had insisted that she continue to appear at court functions in spite of her illness.

By the middle of May, however, she was well enough to travel to Hamburg to meet Fritz. It was a joyous reunion in spite of Queen Victoria's admonition that "in the midst of your joy" at being with her husband, Vicky should "think of your poor unhappy Mama to whom this for ever is denied in this world!"

"Indeed I did think of you when we met, we both did, and we always do whenever anything reminds us . . . of the joy of being with those we love!" Vicky wrote back.

The Crown Princess was very proud of her handsome husband and thrilled by the praise he received for his role in the war. "He is so modest about it himself—but every one knows that what successes we have had are to be attributed to him and not to Fritz Carl," she wrote Victoria in a slap at Fritz's bad-tempered cousin, whom the King had just appointed to succeed Wrangel as Commander-in-Chief of the Prussian army.

The King, who had promoted his son to the rank of general, was still cool to him and had given him only the command of the Second Army Corps. This involved Fritz's spending a great deal of time at the corps headquarters in Pomerania—possibly an attempt to keep him away from Vicky. Wilhelm also appointed as Fritz's new Chief of Staff a man whom the Crown Prince recognized immediately as an "arch-spy of the Kreuzzeitung."

Fritz's war record should have insulated him and his wife from the rancor of the anti-British faction in Berlin, but it did not. Other Hohenzollern princes referred to Fritz scathingly as "the democrat of the family," while the papers wrote openly about the dangers of the Anglo-Coburg connection—the ties between England and Germany forged by Prince Albert, promoted by his brother Ernest, and sealed by Fritz and Vicky's marriage. These speculations were encouraged unwittingly by the English press and knowingly by Bismarck. The London *Times,* astride what one diplomat referred to as its "Danish hobby-horse," published an ongoing spate of anti-Prussian invectives, which the Bismarck papers answered by charging the Crown Princess with disloyalty. Vicky was furious when one of her ladies-in-waiting told her that she was continually being asked whether the Crown Princess was happy about the Prussian victory at Düppel. When the lady-in-waiting replied that of course she was, she inevitably encountered disbelief and the comment: "[A]fter all she is an Englishwoman."

"The family here look upon me with a certain look of virtuous indignation and raise their eyes to the skies when they mention England . . . ," she wrote her mother.

The Grand Duchess of Mecklenburg-Schwerin [Alexandrine, the King's sister] said yesterday to Aunt Charles [the King's sister-in-law] she never ceased regretting that there was an Englishwoman in the family. . . . People spread at Berlin that I was unhappy at the success of our troops. . . . I cannot do the simplest thing without its being found to be in imitation of something English, and therefore anti-Prussian. . . . I never was popular here, but since the war you can well imagine that my position has not improved.

Vicky had hoped, as she wrote Fritz during the war, that "the people's admiration for you will be carried over to me and that I will not be referred to as your 'unfortunate' partner as is the case with your Mama." Matters had not worked out that way. "[T]hey reproach me here for being too English, at home I am too Prussian; it seems I cannot do anything right."

The peace conference to end the Schleswig-Holstein War was scheduled for April of 1864 in London. "If your Government obstinately refuses to accept the frontier line which they [the English and Danes] propose . . . it will not only probably make peace impossible but also confirm the prevailing opinion that Prussia started this war on a false pretext, with ambitious intentions of her own," Queen Victoria wrote Wilhelm I. The Queen, whose personal sympathies were with Prussia and against her own government, did not trust Bismarck.

Her fears proved to be correct. The Prussians proposed a line of demarcation; the English countered with a more advantageous frontier for Denmark; and the Danes, having allowed themselves to be convinced by Bismarck that England would still enter the war on their side, held to the English line. The London Conference broke up at the end of June with nothing settled. Three days after the temporary armistice expired, the Prussian army was steamrolling through Jutland, crushing the Danes and bringing them to their knees. By early July the Schleswig-Holstein War was over. The Danes sued for peace, and a conference to settle the terms opened in Vienna—without the English, the French, the Russians, or anyone else to challenge Bismarck's demands.

Queen Victoria was not the only one to question Wilhelm about Prussia's real intentions. At a meeting between the King of Prussia and the Emperor of Austria, which also took place in Vienna in the summer of 1864, Franz Joseph asked Wilhelm face to face if he was intending to annex the duchies. Bismarck, who had accompanied the King to Vienna, did a curious thing. Instead of stepping in to save Wilhelm from the embarrassing position for which he himself was responsible, the Prime Minister added that he, too, would like to know what was in the King's mind. Wilhelm's hesitant reply—that "he had no right to the duchies and hence could lay no claim to them"—testifies either to his ignorance of Bismarck's intentions or to his capacity to hide the truth from himself.

WHILE THE VICTORS and vanquished haggled over peace terms in Vienna and Fritz visited his new command in Pomerania, Vicky settled down at the Neues Palais in Potsdam for the summer. She had with great difficulty succeeded in getting her father-in-law's permission to send Willy to his grandmother at Osborne. Worried about the five-year-old's physical condition and determined that he should spend the summer by the sea—the English remedy for weakness and underdeveloped muscles—she had tried to send him to the German shore, but Wegner had said he "would not allow it." Sea bathing, he told the Crown Princess, was "dangerous for children," as it "excited their nerves."

Vicky knew that Willy's trip would damage her and Fritz with the public, "as the feeling is at this present moment so violent here against England. . . . But as I cannot help thinking that every sensible persons <u>must</u> see how natural and harmless a thing it is to send a little child to the place that is thought best for his health and to the House of his grandmama, I do not much mind." If Vicky's concern for her son's welfare was admirable, her sense of public relations was abysmal. It must have been only too easy for Bismarck to use this trip as proof of the Crown Princess's disloyalty to Prussia.

Seven months pregnant, heavy but stronger than during her other pregnancies, the twenty-three-year-old girl who was reviled for her Englishness spent much of her summer organizing medical attention for Prussia's soldiers and financial assistance for their families. For the King's birthday in March, Fritz and Vicky had presented Wilhelm with money to start a fund to help the families of dead or disabled soldiers. Fritz's experience on the front lines had alerted them both to the lack of proper medical attention for the soldiers in the field as well. Vicky, who remembered meeting Florence Nightingale at the time of the Crimean War, undertook the job of starting an army nursing corps. She enjoyed this sort of work and did it very well.

She was also determined to enlarge her own and her husband's intellectual horizons. "This summer we will have to be diligent and read many important books," she had written him in March. "If you are pressed for time, I will summarize any books you won't have time to read. I'm ashamed to think just how much I have yet to learn!" While pushing her husband to fill in the gaps in his education, Vicky was proud of the "enormous strides" Fritz had made since their marriage.

She also revamped her household to cut excess, particularly from her wardrobe—the last place other princesses economized. A born *Hausfrau*—a trait that should have endeared her to the Germans—Vicky was extremely generous with charities, but not in running her homes. As with her mother, who once wrote the name of the offending housemaid in the dust on a cupboard, dirt and waste drove Vicky wild. She was probably difficult to work for at this point in her life—intimate with servants one moment and distant the next, demanding full value from those who served her. Perhaps because her father had taught her to make a budget and stick to it, perhaps because her father-in-law gave his son and daughter-in-law very little allowance, or simply out of an exaggerated sense of thrift, Vicky made far too much of getting the most out of each pfennig and thaler.

During the summer of 1864, she also consulted with her mother on the drawings for the many memorials to her father, helped Queen Victoria and Queen Augusta abort a plan to marry her sister Helena off to a young cousin of Fritz's (both countries would be embarrassed by further ties), and painted a series of pictures of soldiers in uniform that were sold for the benefit of the families of the dead and disabled soldiers. Queen Victoria bought one anonymously.

■

VICKY'S FOURTH CHILD* in six years of marriage arrived on September 15, 1864. It was another son, whom the King named Sigismund. By the time this baby was born, Vicky had enough self-confidence to defy her mother and mother-in-law and nurse the child herself. "I am sorry to find that Vicky's determination to nurse her baby makes you so angry," Victoria's sister Feodora wrote Victoria from Baden; "the Queen of Prussia feels the same as you. I have no opinion . . . as I have always felt it a <u>duty</u> for a mother to nurse her child if she <u>can</u> and if the doctors approve."

"My little darling is grown so fat!" Vicky wrote one of her mother's ladies-in-waiting two months after the baby's birth. "He has not had a single ache or pain . . . and sleeps like a top. He lives next door to me, and I wash and dress him every night myself. I nurse him 5 times a day. . . . I cannot say how happy I am with him and what a delight nursing is. I really think I never was so happy, & I certainly never loved one of the others so much. . . . It is too strange that crowned heads have sworn such enmity to this very innocent occupation."

Queen Victoria not only disapproved of Vicky's nursing her baby, but was furious at her for influencing sister Alice to nurse her newborn as well. The Queen had thought that Alice, like their mother, "<u>disliked</u> the <u>disgusting</u> <u>de</u>-<u>tails</u> of the nursery . . . '<u>all</u> & <u>every</u> one of which <u>Vicky</u> <u>delights</u> <u>in</u>,' " and was pained to discover otherwise. "There is in everything the <u>animal</u> side of <u>our</u> nature . . . ," Victoria wrote Alice,

> but . . . this—when one is high born—one <u>can</u> avoid & . . . <u>ought</u> to avoid. . . . <u>I</u> maintain . . . that a <u>Child</u> <u>can</u> <u>never</u> be <u>as</u> <u>well</u> nursed by a <u>lady</u> of <u>rank</u> & <u>nervous</u> & <u>refined</u> <u>temperament</u>—for the <u>less</u> <u>feeling</u> & the <u>more</u> like an <u>animal</u> the <u>wet</u> <u>nurse</u> <u>is</u>, the <u>better</u> for the child. . . .
> It hurts me <u>deeply</u> that my <u>own</u> 2 daughters should <u>set</u> at <u>defiance</u> the <u>advice</u> of a <u>Mother</u> of 9 <u>Children</u>, 46 years old. . . . <u>You</u> said you did it only for your health . . . & <u>because</u> <u>you</u> had <u>no</u> <u>social</u> <u>duties</u>. Well Vicky . . . has <u>none</u> of these excuses, & <u>indeed</u> has <u>very</u> <u>important</u> <u>public</u> & <u>social</u> <u>duties</u> to perform which <u>she</u> <u>cannot</u> <u>with</u> the nursing . . . & <u>if</u> she gives up her <u>duties</u> as Crown Princess . . . she will <u>with</u> <u>right</u> <u>enrage</u> the King & Queen & the whole of Society. . . . <u>I</u> <u>think</u> <u>you</u> . . . could speak to her much more strongly than any one else. . . . I never say anything more to Vicky for she always disagrees with me.

The Queen was currently upset with Vicky for another reason. On her last visit home, the Crown Princess had mentioned her interest in Darwinian theory, which she had recently discussed with the English geologist Sir Charles Lyell. Writing to Charles Darwin, Lyell reported that the Crown Princess was "very much *au fait* with the 'Origin.' . . . She said . . . the old opinions had received a blow from which they would never recover."

Victoria felt that Darwin was turning Vicky into a disbeliever. "[I]t is my

---

* *William was born in 1859, Charlotte in 1860, Henry in 1862.*

fear that Vicky's <u>faith</u> & <u>belief</u> in the <u>future</u> <u>are</u> <u>gone</u> & I fear from reading philosophical sceptical books, which dear Papa always deprecated . . . ," Victoria wrote Alice. "I <u>fear</u> that she is <u>becoming</u> <u>very</u> <u>un</u>-christian in her views." The Queen worried that Vicky might influence Alice in this as well as in nursing. "[D]on't <u>you</u> <u>listen</u> to her, don't you let <u>your</u> firm faith which you so <u>often</u> speak to me about, <u>ever</u> be shaken," she warned, "don't <u>you</u> read <u>those</u> books, don't <u>follow</u> <u>her</u> advice in <u>many</u> things, <u>pray</u>, <u>pray</u> don't. . . . Did she speak to you about it?"

Like the seesaw that carried Bertie and Affie up and down in their mother's estimation, the Queen frequently raised one daughter only to drop the other. At the moment, it was Vicky who was "very self-willed & selfish," unfeeling toward their mother, and far too ambitious. Vicky and Alice did not reverse positions until the following autumn, when Alice's disapproval of her mother's choice of husband* for sister Helena sent her crashing down, bouncing Vicky back up.

THE NEGOTIATIONS ENDING the Schleswig-Holstein War were concluded at the end of October 1864, when King Christian of Denmark signed a peace treaty in which he agreed to cede all his rights to the duchies to the King of Prussia and the Emperor of Austria and pay a substantial war indemnity. Although Austria now urged that the Duke of Augustenburg should be placed at the head of the duchies, Bismarck refused, saying that this would preclude claims from other pretenders—a ruse to keep the Duke out. "I am thankful the peace is signed," Vicky wrote Victoria, "but I shall not be happy until Fritz Augustenburg's position is clear and settled. If he ever is Duke it will be in <u>spite</u> of that mischievous M. de B."

The December social season was enlivened by a marathon of peace celebrations—a military parade, nightly dinners, balls and soirées. "I did not drink to Bismarck at the Gala Dinner as all the rest did," Fritz wrote in his diary. "Also, I did not say anything to him."

Upset by the self-congratulatory air of the Berliners, preening and boasting about their victory over the small army of the Danes, Fritz and Vicky realized that Bismarck had tapped reservoirs of nationalistic pride that could overwhelm their hopes for Germany. Bismarck's plan for a nation unified through war had a more direct appeal for his fellow Prussians, raised in a military autocracy, than the benign constitutional monarchy envisioned by Fritz and Vicky. Moreover, they knew they had few weapons to fight the chauvinism that Bismarck was just beginning to exploit.

---

* *Prince Christian of Schleswig-Holstein.*

CHAPTER
TWENTY-FIVE

> *"For heaven's sake no sentimental alliances in which the consciousness of having performed a good deed furnishes the sole reward for our sacrifice."*
>
> OTTO VON BISMARCK, 1854

*B*Y SEPARATING SCHLESWIG AND HOLSTEIN from Denmark, Bismarck had overcome the first great obstacle in his plan to bring the duchies under the Prussian crown. The next step—severing their connection with Austria—would require a second war.

Austria was not interested in the duchies themselves. Nearly bankrupt from war and her continued exclusion from the Zollverein (German customs union), threatened internally by the demands of the Hungarians and other nationalities under her rule, Austria needed the Prussian alliance for protection against the forces of self-determination both inside and outside her empire. All she wanted was to settle the future of the duchies in a manner that would not increase Prussia's power in the German Confederation. This, Austria and everyone else had assumed, would be managed in the interests of the Duke of Augustenburg under the umbrella of the confederation.

But Bismarck had insisted that the peace negotiations be conducted without representatives from the other German states, the Duke's most ardent supporters. "I am sure B will try all he can to delay Fritz H's [Fritz Holstein, i.e., the Duke of Augustenburg] being recognized in the hopes of still being able to persuade the King to keep the Duchies!" Vicky wrote her mother. She was right. When Austria wanted to install the Duke temporarily after the peace, Bismarck introduced another claimant, the Grand Duke of Oldenburg. After the Oldenburg claim was declared invalid, he was forced to declare the terms by which he would accept the Duke of Augustenburg. He designed them to be unacceptable to both Austria and the Duke.

Long before the Prussian victory, the Duke of Augustenburg had assured the King of Prussia that if he were reinstated as Duke of Schleswig and Holstein, he would bring the duchies into the Zollverein, allow a Prussian naval base to be built at Kiel, and organize his army along Prussian lines. When the Duke met with Bismarck, however, the Prime Minister upped the ante, demanding territory that he knew could not be given and a conservative government that would run contrary to the constitutions of the duchies.

The Prime Minister now needed to blacken the Duke in King Wilhelm's eyes, create the appearance of an indigenous political movement in the duchies against him, and accustom the King of Prussia to the idea of annexation through war. First, he stressed the army's demand for Schleswig and Holstein—land for which its men had fought so bravely and died. Although Wilhelm was happy to add the duchies to the greater glory of the House of Hohenzollern, as a man of basic decency operating under an old-fashioned code of honor he was loath to take by force something that belonged to another prince. But Bismarck quickly planted doubts in his mind about the Duke of Augustenburg's loyalty to the Hohenzollerns, using the Duke's refusal to abide by his (Bismarck's) impossible terms to convince Wilhelm that the Duke would favor Austria over Prussia as the leader of the German states. So successful was Bismarck that even the British Ambassador spoke of the Duke's conduct as "ungrateful & mean."

At the same time, Bismarck prepared Schleswig for annexation by organizing the local government along Prussian lines and buying up the local newspapers for anti-Augustenburg propaganda. These measures increased the friction with Austria. For Bismarck, the heightened tension was all to the good. To further goad the Viennese, he instructed the Prussian Minister of War to announce that Prussia intended to establish a naval base at the port of Kiel in Austria-occupied Holstein.

When the members of the German Confederation finally passed a resolution demanding that the administration of Holstein be turned over to the Duke of Augustenburg, Bismarck used their support to point an accusatory finger at Augustenburg as the source of dispute within the states. The Duke, he alleged in a remarkable twist, had become a danger to the future union of Germany; henceforth Prussia would oppose his claims in favor of its own.

During a crown council held at the end of May 1865, Bismarck put forward the desirability of annexing the duchies, a policy, he said, that would "sooner or later" lead to war with Austria. "We cannot advise His Majesty to follow this course," he said disingenuously; "the decision can only proceed from his own royal conviction. Should he take such a determination, the entire Prussian nation would joyfully follow him." When Wilhelm asked General Moltke if the army was ready, Moltke assured him of probable success. "The gain is so great that it is well worth a war," he said. Three days later, the King sent the Duke of Augustenburg a letter advising him to quit Schleswig and Holstein, since by virtue of the peace treaty, only Prussia and Austria were allowed to be there.

Of all the members of the council, only the Crown Prince voiced any objection. Prussian hostilities against Austria and the southern German states (Austria's natural allies) would be tantamount, he said, to "German civil war." As he had made clear before, Fritz supported the Duke of Augustenburg as the best choice for a peaceful solution to the problem of the duchies, and he looked forward to the time when the union of Schleswig and Holstein with Prussia would serve as a model for the future unification of Germany under Prussian leadership.

Although he was unable to budge Fritz, Bismarck spread the word that the

Crown Prince had been converted to annexation. Then he sent Fritz's Privy Councillor, Max Duncker, to talk to him. Named by Baron Stockmar as the old man's successor and dispenser of political wisdom, Duncker's job was to interpret the news for the Crown Prince and advise him on what positions he should take. A former professor of history and liberal deputy in parliament, Duncker was liked and respected by both Fritz and Vicky. Unlike Stockmar's son Ernest, who had collapsed under pressure, Duncker was rapidly adjusting to the Bismarck era and had become one of the Prime Minister's mouthpieces. Like Bismarck, he believed in the efficacy of the sword. "The German question is a question of power," he had written a few years earlier, "and will never be solved without the deployment of Prussian power, without proofs of the national use of power and success of power."

Duncker told the Crown Prince that "an overwhelming majority" of Prussians wanted to annex the duchies. "The army is unanimous in this wish; they want to have fought for Prussia, not for Duke Friedrich [Augustenburg]." He reminded the Crown Prince that he had "stronger duties towards Prussia than towards Duke Friedrich," contending that it was "the fate of Princes to be forbidden to be magnanimous where the interests of their State are at stake." Finally he told Fritz that the duchies were at the very heart of Prussia's destiny, "the future of Prussia and Germany."

But Fritz would not be swayed. When Bismarck redoubled the diplomatic pressures on Austria during the early summer of 1865 with a series of menacing communiqués aimed at bringing the two countries to the brink of war, Fritz urged his father to come to a personal understanding with Emperor Franz Joseph and the Duke of Augustenburg. When it was suggested that he mediate with the Duke over the terms laid down by Bismarck, he attacked governmental hypocrisy:

"[H]ow shall I now prevail on him to consent to those conditions, after Bismarck's remark to me on June 18 that they were drawn up so as to be impossible for Duke Friedrich [the Duke of Augustenburg] to accept them? . . . ," the Crown Prince wrote Duncker. "And even if Duke Friedrich were to yield, and were he to accept even more onerous conditions, we should still manage matters so that new complications might arise in order to obtain war. . . . If it was desired to settle the affairs of the Duchies . . . an agreement might have been made with Duke Friedrich. . . . But the plan was to ruin him. . . . A conflict is desired, in order to adjust our present incurable internal dissensions."

Fritz had put his finger on the crux of the situation—Bismarck's belief in the use of foreign adventures to overcome domestic problems. Early in the Schleswig-Holstein crisis, the Chamber of Deputies had denied the government's request for funds to finance the war against Denmark and had declared the use of public money without parliamentary approval unconstitutional. But the subsequent victory over Denmark had had a chilling effect on the delegates' concerns over parliamentary procedures. Wilhelm's military reforms, carried out in spite of the Chamber's opposition, had won Prussia her first victory in fifty years. Moreover, the deputies were hard put to find supporters among their quiescent constituents, for as one historian put it, "Two centuries of absolutism had lamed the capacity for popular initiative."

Having outmaneuvered the liberals in foreign affairs, Bismarck continued his domestic war, striking out aggressively against the opposition. In East Prussia, seventeen deputies were prosecuted and fined for publishing an advertisement "mildly critical" of the Bismarck cabinet. When the citizens of Cologne wanted to honor their liberal deputies, they were prevented from meeting by the police, and newspapers reporting the incident were confiscated. In Königsberg, a liberal mayor, reelected by the citizens of his city, was not allowed to take his seat, but was replaced by a "commissar" sent by Bismarck. Military supplies were purchased only from firms displaying the proper political attitudes; liberal physicians were no longer hired for positions in public health.

Worse was the assault on the judiciary and the traditional concept of equality under the law. In May of 1865 Wilhelm approved salary raises for judges based not on time served but political attitude. When a deputy from the Progressive Party who was also a judge* attacked the government in parliament for using the courts as a political tool, Bismarck and his Minister of Justice called for an indictment against him. In what an historian calls "one of the darkest pages in the history of Prussian jurisdiction," the highest court of the Prussian monarchy decided for the government. As one leader of the Progressive Party put it, "For those in disfavor, there is no justice any more in Prussia."

WITH THE DOMESTIC PRESSURE to conform increasing, and the tension between Prussia and Austria rising according to plan, Bismarck needed to get the only rallying point left for the opposition, the Crown Prince and Princess, out of his way. In July of 1865, Fritz and Vicky were dispatched on a visit to Prussian-occupied Poland. Although the Crown Prince had been sent the year before to Russian-occupied Poland, it was the first time any member of the Prussian royal family had visited the German sector. The Poles, who made up 12 percent of the Prussian population, were its single largest minority, permanently disaffected from the Prussian regime. "I have every sympathy for their plight," Bismarck said in 1861, "but if we are to exist we can do nothing other than exterminate them." Well received by the peasants and the townspeople, the Crown Prince and Princess were boycotted by the nobility.

"The middle and lower classes are happy enough (which they are not in Russian Poland),"† Vicky wrote Victoria. "It is only the aristocracy (and chiefly the ladies and the priests by whom they are ruled) who are the elements of disturbance. . . . of course all difficulties are increased by our unfortunate, illiberal government at home, the ill effects of which are felt everywhere."

---

* *Karl Twesten. Twesten had had his right arm shattered four years earlier in a duel to which General Manteuffel had challenged him over a pamphlet Twesten had written critical of Manteuffel's military cabinet.*

† *Poland was at this time still divided among Russia, Austria, and Prussia.*

From Poland, the Crown Prince and Princess moved on to the Isle of Föhr off the coast of Schleswig with their four children, now aged one to six. On the way, they stopped in Hamburg to visit the beleaguered Duke of Augustenburg, whom they warned to "hope for the best & prepare for the worst." Two weeks later, the Crown Princess wrote her mother a gloomy letter from Föhr:

If you are furious at the way these unfortunate Elbe Duchies and Fritz Holstein [the Duke of Augustenburg] are treated what do you think we are! . . . I wish we and the nation were rid of him [Bismarck] and all that are like him. If my letter is opened by the Post Officials I shall be accused of high treason—but I am as loyal as anyone as I love the King and would do anything to serve him. . . . One resents the injury done to a noble nation by . . . one reckless adventurer. . . . But no more of politics, we breakfast, dine and sup on the same sad subject and are unable to change it in the least!

Shortly after this letter, in early August of 1865, Austria sent an ambassador to see Wilhelm, who was in Bad Gastein for his annual cure. The diplomat returned to Vienna carrying Bismarck's proposal to divide the duchies—Schleswig to go to Prussia, Holstein to Austria. Anxious to preserve the peace, Vienna accepted the so-called Gastein Convention, adding a proviso that the division applied only to the administration of the duchies, not their sovereignty.

But by agreeing to divide the "indivisible" duchies and sacrifice the Duke of Augustenburg, Austria had been forced by Bismarck into a serious loss of prestige with the other German states and the world. And by not settling the matter of sovereignty, Austria had given Prussia an excuse to intervene in Holstein's affairs. Austria's only gain from the Schleswig-Holstein War was a piece of land (Holstein) she did not need and had never wanted. And she had been manipulated into sharing international opprobrium for a war that had been started in the name of preserving the integrity of the duchies as a whole, but had ended with a cynical division of the spoils.

An enormous outcry greeted the Gastein Convention. Public opinion in the other Germany states rose up against this blatant defiance of the indivisibility of the duchies. From England, Lord Clarendon said that the Gastein Convention was "the most infamous act since the partition of Poland," adding that "King Bismarck I is the only man among forty million Germans who has a purpose and the will to give effect to it." To which the French Minister of Foreign Affairs, Drouyn de Lhuys, added, "Every principle of justice, right, and equity had been set aside. . . ." Even Prussia's own diplomats were appalled. The Prussian Ambassador to France, Count von der Goltz, wrote the Prussian Ambassador to the Court of St. James's, "The Gastein Convention puts us permanently on the path of trickery, force, and violation of law."

It was not world opinion but local opposition to his policies that concerned the Prime Minister. Since this centered on the Crown Prince, Bismarck had determined that the Gastein Convention should be signed without Fritz's knowledge. "If . . . a hint . . . should reach Queen Victoria, the Crown Prince and Princess, Weimar or Baden,"* Bismarck wrote Wilhelm, "the fact that we had not kept the secret . . . would . . . bring failure upon the negotiation."

The Crown Prince and Princess were already on their way back to Berlin when they again met Fritz Augustenburg, who told them about the Gastein Convention. Fritz, according to his friend, was "stupefied at the news of the partition."

IF DUKE FRIEDRICH OF AUGUSTENBURG had been cast by Bismarck in the role of public obstacle to King Wilhelm's plans for Prussia, his younger brother Prince Christian soon became a private irritation to the entire Hohenzollern clan. At the end of August, two weeks after the signing of the Gastein Convention, Queen Victoria arrived in Coburg to meet Christian, the man she had selected as a husband for Vicky's sister, nineteen-year-old Princess Helena, known in the family as Lenchen. With both Vicky and Alice living in Germany, Victoria had decided to marry the next daughter in line to someone who could be counted on to move to England. What better than a homeless Augustenburger, recently dispossessed of his share of the family properties?

Vicky had sent a photograph and description of Christian to her mother the previous spring, noting that Christian was a close friend and an intimate of their home who "comes and goes when he likes. . . . He is the best creature in the world, not as clever as Fritz [the Duke of Augustenburg] but certainly not wanting in any way. . . . we like him very much."

A penniless thirty-four-year-old prince, Christian had not only lost his stake in the family duchies but also his commission in the Prussian army, which had been taken away by Bismarck as punishment for being the Duke of Augustenburg's younger brother. With little else in his future, he readily accepted the idea of marrying Queen Victoria's third daughter, and she, too, acquiesced in her mother's plans. "You know that Lenchen could not & would not leave me," the Queen wrote Vicky, "as in my terrible position, I required one of my daughters to be always in England." As for Christian, he "entirely" accepted the Queen's conditions for the marriage and, as she put it, took "a noble & right view" of his future mother-in-law's "very forlorn & difficult & almost unbearable position."

Helena's engagement to Christian, coming as it did at that particular time, infuriated the Hohenzollerns. Before the war, Helena had been considered as a match for one of Fritz's cousins, but the idea had been abandoned because of tensions between their two countries. Now the Prussian royal family jeered at her comedown from a member of the reigning House of Hohenzollern to the pathetic, defeated House of Augustenburg. As for Bismarck, just raised to the rank of count, he took the match as a personal offense, since he had made it clear that he considered the Augustenburgs his enemies.

In October of 1865, Fritz and Vicky left for England—the first time the

---

* *Other liberal supporters of the Duke of Augustenburg related to the King. Augusta was a Princess of Weimar, and the King's son-in-law was Grand Duke of Baden.*

Crown Princess had been able to go home in two years. Although she asked her mother's permission to bring the children and stay for Christmas, the Queen refused, citing her "poor nerves," which made her "quite & totally incapable of bearing joyousness and merriment."

On the way to England, the Crown Prince and Princess stopped to see seventy-four-year-old Uncle Leopold (King Leopold I of Belgium), who had not been well. By the time they got to England, Prime Minister Palmerston had died, the country was in mourning, and Queen Victoria was at Windsor dealing with a new cabinet. Pregnant once again, Vicky was ill, and there was no one to meet them when they disembarked. They had not been invited to Buckingham Palace, so they stayed at the Prussian Ambassador's residence in London. From there they moved to Bertie and Alix's country home at Sandringham, where Bertie got Vicky a doctor. "Bertie and Alix are most amiable hosts," Vicky wrote Victoria as if to assure their mother that the tensions between them over Schleswig-Holstein were coming to an end. Later they joined the Queen at Windsor.

Victoria was grateful for Fritz and Vicky's support in the matter of Helena and Christian's marriage, over which she was having trouble with Helena's other siblings. Not only were Bertie and Alix against the match, but Alice had joined the fray, objecting that it was unfair to Lenchen, whose happiness was being bargained away to solve the problem of their mother's loneliness.

Vicky urged Victoria to forgive Bertie and Alix, explaining that her brother "has much too kind a heart and is too fond of you to keep up a long opposition to anything you have so much at heart." She was shocked, however, to learn that Alice and Affie were angry with her for taking their mother's part.

"Words cannot express how deeply I have felt your love & affection, your help & understanding . . . when others behaved so ill!" Victoria wrote her eldest daughter shortly after she left England. "May God bless & reward you both for it. . . . Fritz's conduct to Christian was beautiful, & he was so dear and affectionate to me. When one is in such a sad & desolate position as I am—love, affection & sympathy is doubly felt. . . . Your love & affection, our own beloved child, did my poor heart so much good. I must tell you how much improved I found you in every way and yet always the same, simple unspoilt child. God bless & protect you."

Back in Berlin in early December, Vicky felt anything but loved. "I miss the kind words and kind looks as much as I do the mild and genial air of dear England," she wrote her mother.

I plunged yesterday all at once into the freezing depth of the family circle here. It began with a pail of cold water being poured upon my head in the shape of a visit to Charlottenburg where I found the three aunts together, viz the Queen Dowager, the Grand Duchess of Mecklenburg and Princess Louise of the Netherlands.* The conversation was neither amusing nor

* _King Wilhelm's sister-in-law, the sixty-four-year-old widow of Friedich Wilhelm IV, and his sisters, aged sixty-two and fifty-seven._

cheering to one's spirits, consisting in cross little remarks about nothing. I was not asked after Lenchen by any of them; neither has the King mentioned the subject to me as yet. It wants a deal of heroism to take the life here kindly after having been at home (and so <u>much</u> spoilt) and I am afraid I have not got it.

Three days later, on December 10, 1865, Albert and Victoria's uncle and the family patriarch, King Leopold I of Belgium, died in Brussels. In four years Vicky had lost her three principal mentors—her father in 1861, Baron Stockmar in 1863, and now Uncle Leopold. They had been the architects of her life, the men who had matched her up with Fritz and sent her off to liberalize the Hohenzollern dynasty and bring it into concert with western Europe. Three devoted Germans, none had foreseen the meteoric rise of a Bismarck, but had pursued their vision of Germany at Vicky's unwitting expense. Now, at the beginning of 1866, all three were gone, leaving behind a twenty-five-year-old English girl to try to counteract a brilliant political manipulator and the militarism he espoused—a combination that had already taken over Prussia and was threatening to engulf the rest of Germany.

CHAPTER
TWENTY-SIX

> *"Prussia has become great not through liberalism and free-think-ing but through a succession of powerful, decisive and wise regents who carefully husbanded the military and financial resources of the state and kept them together in their own hands in order to throw them with ruthless courage into the scale of European politics as soon as a favorable opportunity presented itself."*
>
> OTTO VON BISMARCK

WHILE THE SEPARATION of Schleswig and Holstein appalled other Europeans with its flagrant disregard for princely legitimacy, it disturbed Napoleon III of France for entirely different reasons. Like Bismarck, Napoleon needed territorial gains to divert public attention from interior repressions. There were only two areas in which France could expand—French-speaking Belgium and Luxembourg to the north, or German territory on the Rhine to the east. To keep the French Emperor on Prussia's side, Bismarck had been dangling the German Rhineland before him.

But when Prussia took the province of Schleswig, signaling a shift in the balance of power in central Europe, Napoleon grew restive. To reassure him, Bismarck hastened to the Villa Eugénie, the summer home that Napoleon had built in Biarritz for his Spanish-born Empress. Before the meeting, Bismarck told a French diplomat that if France would support Prussia's expansion in Schleswig now and Holstein later, she would be similarly entitled to spread out "everywhere in the world where French is spoken" (i.e., Belgium and Luxembourg). No one knows exactly what Bismarck promised Napoleon during their private encounter, but when Bismarck left Biarritz, he reported that Napoleon would "dance the cotillion with us, without knowing in advance when it will begin or what figures it will include."

With France more or less in place, Bismarck resumed his taunts at Austria, installing General Manteuffel as Prussian governor in Schleswig with instructions to interfere as much as possible with the Austrian government in Holstein. The operation backfired, and the Holsteiners began demonstrating for the Duke of Augustenburg. Bismarck countered by insisting that Austria suppress all "democratic" and "revolutionary" actions in Holstein on penalty of Prussia's ending their alliance, or worse. He told the English Ambassador to Berlin, Lord Augustus Loftus, that he would force Austria "either into concessions or to war." According to Loftus, the political atmosphere in Berlin "smelled of powder."

Either Wilhelm did not understand or he did not want to know what his

Prime Minister was doing, but it was obvious that he accepted everything Bismarck told him without question. At a crown council held on the last day of February 1866, the King told his ministers that Austria had not kept her part of the Gastein Convention. At the same meeting, Bismarck said that a struggle for power between Prussia and Austria was inevitable, since Austria had always stood in the way of Prussia's "natural and very justified" desire to lead Germany. With military conditions currently favoring Prussia, the Prime Minister asked the King's permission to negotiate with France for "more definite guarantees" of neutrality and with Italy for an alliance, just in case the projected war should extend into the other German states.

This, of course, was the real issue. "We should never go to war for the Duchies," Bismarck told Loftus, adding that it would be "folly" to risk war for a territory with a population of only 500,000 "when half that number might possibly be sacrificed to obtain it." What Bismarck was aiming at was German supremacy.

Although he refused to admit it, the Prime Minister also counted on victory over Austria to regularize army reform and pay the government's debts, refused by the chamber since the constitutional crisis that had brought him into power three years earlier. Neither the Prussian people nor their representatives in parliament wanted to fight Austria, but out of the entire council, only the Crown Prince spoke for the rest of the country in voicing his objections to Bismarck's war.

Vicky, nearing the end of her fifth pregnancy and having difficulty sleeping, spent her "bad nights" that winter and spring lying in bed and thinking "of all the sad and dangerous eventualities" to which Bismarck's policies were leading them. It was all the harder because, as she put it in a letter to her mother in early March, "officially we know nothing. Fritz is kept quite out of it all, the King does not speak to him on the subject & the ministers never communicate anything to him. . . . The Queen is much alarmed, and fears the King will be provoked into it [war]." Like her mother-in-law, Vicky believed that Wilhelm did not want war, but "he may be forced into it by Bismarck & his colleagues & many of the generals."

Pressured by his wife and sister-in-law,* who believed that war with Austria would be fratricide, the King asked Fritz to send Queen Victoria a letter saying that he was "anxious to accept an offer of mediation" from England. Vicky guessed correctly that Bismarck knew nothing of this piece of private diplomacy. "Austria has done nothing to offend us. . . . ," the Crown Princess wrote her mother. "The feeling in the country here is strongly against war."

But, according to the English Ambassador, all efforts to keep the peace "vanished under the withering influence of Count Bismarck." When the British Foreign Secretary offered to take Prussia's complaints about Austria to Vienna, he was told that Bismarck wanted no explanations from the Austrians and that the alliance between Prussia and Austria was at an end. Moreover, Prussia

---

* *Friedrich Wilhelm IV's widow, Elisabeth, who was Franz Joseph's aunt.*

would on no account give up her intention of annexing both Schleswig and Holstein.

"[I]t is evident that all hope of the interference of England must be abandoned," Queen Victoria wrote Fritz in a formal letter to be shown to his father, cautioning the King against "the violent annexation of the duchies . . . against the known feelings and wishes of the People." Composed in consultation with her ministers, Victoria's letter included unmistakable hints that Bismarck had been repeating confidential conversations with his sovereign outside Prussia in order to sabotage Wilhelm's peace efforts.

This official attempt to show the Prussian King that his Prime Minister could not be trusted was followed by a personal letter from Victoria to Wilhelm. "Beloved Brother . . . ," she wrote, in the traditional salutation of fellow monarchs, "You are deceived, you are made to believe that you are to be attacked, and I, your true friend and sister, hear your honoured name attacked and abused for the faults and recklessness of others—or rather more, of one man! As you value the life of thousands . . . pause before you permit so fearful an act as the commencement of a war, the responsibility of which will rest on you alone."

But Wilhelm was no longer master of Prussia. His muddled explanation, written in answer to Victoria's letter, made Vicky "quite sad" when her mother sent her a copy. As she wrote Victoria, "[I]t touched me, because I know he felt what he said. . . . I know it all by heart, & you will see by it how useless it is to combat the errors it contains." Fritz was more disturbed. In a letter to the Duke of Baden,* he made it clear that he was opposed not only to the war but "to the lawless and illegal domestic conditions of the country on which the government bases its foreign policies." Fritz's letter, according to the Duke, betrayed "a great deal of depression and helplessness."

In contrast was the King's cheerfulness. "Unconcerned" and "very amiable" were the adjectives the Crown Princess used to describe her father-in-law during these weeks of crisis. "The King . . . did not wear an appearance of care . . . ," Lord Loftus confirmed after a large dinner. "His Majesty was gifted with the rare faculty of casting off momentarily all . . . anxiety of mind, and of evincing his usual gaiety and amiability."

In such circumstances, it was impossible to pin Wilhelm down to any sort of meaningful exchange. A letter from Vicky's aunt, the Duchess of Coburg, verified what everyone knew—that "NO ONE" wanted war, that Bismarck was concealing from Wilhelm the warnings sent by other countries, and that he had arranged matters so that Wilhelm believed it was Austria who wished to attack Prussia.

But all the efforts at peace and mediation were stymied by the combination of Bismarck's determination to fight Austria and Napoleon III's territorial ambitions, which Bismarck had carefully kept alive. As the British Foreign Secretary knew and Vicky had repeated several times to Queen Victoria, civil war in Germany was "by no means displeasing" to the Emperor of France.

* The liberal Duke was his brother-in-law, married to Louise.

On April 8, 1866, Wilhelm signed a secret treaty with the Italians. Concluded by Bismarck with Napoleon's help, it obligated Italy to join Prussia if war broke out between Prussia and Austria within three months. For this, Italy would receive as her share of the spoils the Austrian province of Venetia, located at the northern end of the Adriatic Sea.

It was this treaty, according to one historian,* that "destroyed the German Confederation." Certainly it broke both the spirit and the letter of the law. The Confederation had been created for the mutual protection of all its members, and as a signator, Prussia was prohibited from waging war on any other member. It must have taken a great deal of hard persuasion on Bismarck's part to convince the King to put his name on such a paper, and for the remainder of his life, Wilhelm kept the treaty a secret. One can only imagine the extent of the King's moral discomfiture when, some weeks later on the eve of war, he had to give Franz Joseph his word of honor that no such document existed.

At the same time that Bismarck was negotiating with the legitimate representatives of Italy and France, he was also establishing some more questionable alliances with Austrian minorities, reaching far into the empire itself to contact frustrated malcontents in Hungary, Italy, and Serbia—nationalist groups willing to foster insurrection against the Habsburgs. This process, which Bismarck instigated long before war broke out, produced something called the Hungarian Legion, ultimately a great disappointment and embarrassment to its sponsor. Nevertheless, the effort expended demonstrated the lengths and depths to which Bismarck was prepared to go to defeat Austria and gain hegemony over Germany.

Another ploy was Bismarck's proposal for a new all-German parliament based on universal suffrage. The possibilities of popular government had been suggested to Bismarck by the German socialist Ferdinand Lassalle, a disciple of Karl Marx and a man whose mind Bismarck had greatly admired. While Lassalle aimed at shooting down middle-class liberalism by enfranchising the urban proletariat, Bismarck counted on votes from the masses of rural poor (whom he knew from his days as a Junker squire) to support conservatism, royalism, and everything that carried with it the weight of traditional authority.

In proposing universal suffrage, Bismarck had three objectives: first, to take the fire out of the Prussian liberals; second, to destroy the German Confederation; third, and most important, to antagonize Austria, who could not afford to oppose it for fear of goading her restless minorities, eager for self-expression, into revolution. Although Bismarck claimed that he had the interests of all Germans at heart, his proposal was primarily a maneuver to precipitate Austria into war.

By early April of 1866, both Austria and Prussia had started to mobilize. "I have induced a king of Prussia to break off the intimate relations of his House with the House of Habsburg," Bismarck boasted to the French Ambassador,

---

* *Erich Eyck.*

"to conclude an alliance with revolutionary Italy, possibly to accept arrangements with Imperial France, and to propose in Frankfurt the reform of the Confederation and a popular parliament. That is a success of which I am proud."

ON APRIL 12, 1866, A FEW DAYS after the Italian treaty was signed, Vicky gave birth to her fifth child. The child was a girl, named Victoria after her grandmother, and later nicknamed Moretta. "I am much pleased & touched that the dear, new baby (& long may she remain the Baby!) is to be called after me," Victoria wrote Vicky, "as I cannot deny that it pained me very much that 4 children were born without one being called after either of your parents. However I know that you could not help that."

The Crown Princess lapsed almost immediately into postpartum depression. The excitement of mobilization and preparations for war in the palace made her weep. Although the christening was planned for Queen Victoria's birthday, it hardly promised to be a festive affair, as the baby's father was due to leave the next day to assume command of the Second Army in Silesia.

Even now, there were last-minute attempts to stop the inevitable. These were not too difficult for Bismarck to counter, because the Austrian war machine required three or four weeks more than the Prussian to get rolling, and Bismarck was adept at using the defensive actions of others to justify his own advances. Austria was also in the unpleasant position of having to choose whether to concentrate her forces on the German or the Italian front, since she had neither the money nor the military capability to mount a strong campaign in both places at once.

Bismarck's most difficult problem was sustaining the King's warlike frame of mind, and his ability to keep Wilhelm on track astonished everyone. In Berlin, the wits had it that Bismarck was Wilhelm's "last mistress," for, they reasoned, "only such a creature can wield so magic a power over an old man."

Early in May, the Prime Minister was the object of an assassination attempt in Berlin. Walking down Unter den Linden, he was assaulted by Ferdinand Cohen, the stepson of a famous exiled German revolutionary. Although the young assailant fired five shots, the Prime Minister was unhurt. "How bad revolvers in this country are!" complained one professor from the University of Berlin. Vicky was glad that Bismarck would live to see "the consequences of his reckless madness" and not die "a martyr pitied by all."

By early summer of 1866, the only obstacle between Bismarck and his war was Napoleon III. Having exacted as many concessions as possible from both sides,* the French emperor could still not decide if war or peace was more to

---

* After helping the Prussians conclude a treaty with Italy, Napoleon turned around and signed a treaty in June with the Austrians, whereby he guaranteed French neutrality in return for Venetia (which he would then cede to the Italians), Belgium (to be annexed outright by France), and the Rhineland (to become a buffer state).

his advantage. At the end of May, he proposed a European congress under the aegis of France, England, and Russia to settle the problems of Schleswig-Holstein, the German Confederation, and Italy. Bismarck was furious.

"I see a glimmer of hope if the congress assembles," Vicky wrote Victoria in early June. "If the Emperor N. is <u>determined</u> there <u>shall</u> be <u>peace</u>, of course there will be, and that will be an utter defeat of Bismarcks' *[sic]*, in which case, I suppose, we shall get rid of him in some way or another. He is more bent upon the war than ever and keeps pushing on the King who would rather avoid it, but who[se] military feelings are being continually worked upon."

In early June, this last hope was dashed—not by Bismarck but by the Austrians, who issued such impossible conditions that Napoleon's congress could not convene. When the telegram announcing the abortion of the congress arrived at Bismarck's office, the French Ambassador to Berlin, Count Benedetti, was with him. "Now it is war," Bismarck announced to Benedetti, as he rose from his chair. "Long live the King!"

CHAPTER
TWENTY-SEVEN

"Genius is knowing where to stop."

GOETHE

THREE MONTHS BEFORE STARTING the war against Austria, Bismarck had begun lining up allies among the other members of the German Confederation. In diplomatic dispatches demanding that they take sides in the oncoming struggle under threat of revenge, the Prussian Prime Minister offered territorial spoils in return for support. "We appeal to the noble sentiments: patriotism, honor, principles of law, energy, courage, decision, sense of independence, etc.," said one frustrated Austrian diplomat. "*He* reckons on the lower motivations of human nature: avarice, cowardice, confusion, indolence, want of decision, and narrow-mindedness." Nevertheless, when Prussian troops marched into Holstein in early June of 1866, most of the German states joined Austria in censuring Prussia in the Frankfurt Diet. In response, the Prussian Minister to the diet announced his country's withdrawal from the German Confederation. The diet then ordered mobilization against Prussia.

Back in Berlin, Bismarck asked the King to declare war on Austria. Before giving his response, Wilhelm excused himself and withdrew into an adjoining room, accidentally leaving the door ajar. Looking into a mirror, the Prime Minister could see his sovereign on his knees praying. Shortly thereafter, the King reappeared and gave his assent.

At midnight on June 15—well within the ninety-day limit set by Italy*— the Prussian army began its advance into other German states. Bismarck was walking in his garden with the British Ambassador when the clock struck 12. "At this moment our troops are marching into Hanover, Saxony, and Hesse-Cassel," Bismarck told Loftus. "The struggle will be severe. . . . If we are beaten, I shall not return here. I shall fall in the last charge. One can but die once; and if beaten, it is better to die."

But Bismarck knew that Prussia was unlikely to lose. The war, which was fought in three separate theaters—Italy, Germany, and Bohemia—was over in

---

* *It will be remembered that Italy had signed a treaty that obligated her to join Prussia if war broke out between Prussia and Austria within three months.*

less than two months, thus becoming known in history as the Seven Weeks' War. Austria's only substantial victories were against Prussia's ally, Italy. The kingdom of Hanover, which supported Austria in the north, was easily defeated within two weeks, and the rest of the war was decided in Bohemia a little over a month later.

General Moltke, Fritz's former aide-de-camp, was Commander-in-Chief of the Prussian forces. Chief of Staff during the Schleswig-Holstein campaign, he was an oddity among the homogeneously dull, arrogantly provincial officers of the Prussian army. Well traveled and literate, Moltke brought to his job ideas absorbed from the recent American Civil War on how to utilize the railways and telegraph to gather concentrations of men and supplies when and where he needed them. Because of the development of the railways, Prussia's position in central Europe was no longer a handicap. Troops could be brought to the battlefield in top condition, not exhausted by forced marches; ammunition and food came to the soldiers, who no longer had to forage off the land. "Every new development of railways," Moltke had written during the period of quick railway expansion, "is a military advantage."

Another advantage was the breech-loading gun, used extensively by Prussia for the first time in 1866. The Austrians as well as the British and French still used muzzle-loaders, which dated back to the fifteenth century and were slow and innacurate. The Prussian needle gun could fire six shots to every one fired by the enemy.

Taking into account these new developments in warfare, Moltke formed three separate armies in the south—the First Army, of 100,000 men under the command of Fritz's cousin Fritz Carl; the Army of the Elbe, 40,000 men under General Bittenfeld; and the Second (Silesian) Army, under the Crown Prince.

Fritz, who led 120,000 men, was a popular commander, calm and self-possessed, slow to make up his mind, but firm once he had decided on a particular course. General Julius von Verdy du Vernois, a former Minister of War, considered himself very fortunate to have been assigned to the Crown Prince's staff, as did Prince Kraft zu Hohenlohe-Ingelfingen, who wrote admiringly of the Crown Prince's equanimity under stress and his "eminence as a commander." Fritz's positive influence on those serving him was also noted by Colonel Charles Walker, military attaché to the British Embassy in Berlin, who served as British military commissioner at the Crown Prince's headquarters. "I like the Crown Prince better every hour . . . ," Walker wrote. "The Prince is charming, firm enough when required, but so frank and modest that any one can always find an opportunity of saying what is desirable. . . . The Prince also has no taste for small interferences, and no jealousy of those under him."

The Crown Prince, according to his Chief of Staff, Field Marshal Count von Blumenthal,

> possessed that rare gift of a commander, of not interfering unnecessarily with his subordinates in their own sphere of duty, and yet keeping the general course of the action well under his control. In the most advanced

lines and under the heaviest fire, he maintained his composure and gave the troops a fine example of coolness and devotion to duty. . . . He showed great sympathy with the wounded, and . . . visited them, looked after them, and comforted them in the field-hospitals after the battle, so that every soldier would have gladly given his life for his beloved leader.

Blumenthal admired Fritz's strategic sense, pointing out that whereas his more vaunted cousin Fritz Carl employed a system of combined commands (whereby the cavalry and the artillery advanced together), the Crown Prince favored the flexibility of separation, sending his forces on different roads if possible and uniting them only for specific battles. It was, in fact, this aspect of Fritz's strategy that saved his cousin's army and won the decisive battle of the Austro-Prussian War.

The week after the war started, Moltke sent the First Army under Fritz Carl and the Army of the Elbe under General Bittenfeld into Bohemia, while Fritz was ordered to take his Second Army southward through Silesia. When Moltke discovered that the Austrian army was within range of attack in Bohemia, he sent for the Crown Prince and his troops. Apparently jealous of his cousin, the heir to the throne, Fritz Carl wrote Fritz to say that the march through the mountains would be extremely difficult and that even their famous ancestor Frederick the Great had avoided it. "Well, then, *we* will do it," Fritz told his Chief of Staff, "and it will not be so difficult, considering the improvement in the state of the passes and the tactical mobility of our troops."

Meanwhile, the Crown Prince engaged the enemy at the Battle of Nachod, a victory for Fritz and his first opportunity to prove himself as a military leader. He sent Vicky a cornflower picked from the battlefield. Worried that her husband would relapse into the mold of the Hohenzollern warrior kings, Vicky's letters of love and support included political caveats. "We know too well how this war came about, and we know that our policy was unjust, brutal . . . ," she had written him the day before the battle. "What has been brought about with blood and iron could have been achieved by moral conquests. . . . a bloodbath was not necessary."

"You think that I am completely absorbed in my military career," he wrote back a few days later. "As far as my duty demands it, yes, certainly, but you must believe me when I say that even if the little campaign against Schleswig-Holstein gave me a dislike of the idea of war, then these last days have sufficed to arouse a veritable horror of the misery caused by such a decision. . . . It is certainly not easy to be a Commander-in-Chief. . . . the physical effort is child's play compared to the mental. May this be the last war we shall experience."

On July 2, Fritz received orders to take his army only to the Elbe River, instead of joining the other two Prussian armies as previously planned. He disagreed with the plan and sent Chief of Staff Blumenthal to see the King, who was with Bismarck and Moltke at army headquarters. Blumenthal relayed the Crown Prince's message that the time was ripe for the three armies to join and engage the Austrians. Late that night, Moltke ordered the First Army and the Army of the Elbe to attack at dawn the following day and sent word to Fritz to come quickly with the Second Army.

During the Battle of Königgrätz,* the last and decisive battle of the Austro-Prussian War, King Wilhelm himself rode through his regiments, delighting the Prussian officers, who rushed to kiss his hands, and terrifying their commanders by putting his own life in jeopardy. The generals' concern was warranted. The Austrians were well on their way to victory early in the day, and Fritz Carl's First Army was hard pressed to hold its position. Wilhelm asked Moltke what arrangements had been made in the event of defeat. "Your Majesty," Moltke replied, "the fate of Prussia decides itself today here, and the Crown Prince comes."

It was Fritz's swift arrival with the Second Army and his astute choice of approach that brought the Prussians victory at Königgrätz. "[T]he honour rests with the Crown Prince," said Colonel Walker, who claimed that Fritz "not only won the battle, but saved his cousin. . . . I was with him throughout, and I cannot say too much of his good sense, clear judgment, and firm decision."

The cousins embraced in front of their men as the Austrians began their retreat, and at eight o'clock that evening, the Crown Prince, surrounded by cheering soldiers, made his way to his father, who decorated him with the order Pour le Mérite. "Thanks to his own energy and clear decision the Prince saved Prussia . . . from a serious defeat," Walker said. "The King gave him the order . . . and well he has won it." Bismarck said nothing to the Crown Prince, but, according to Walker, sat "sulky as a bear" while Wilhelm "showered kind words and embraces" on his son.

The Battle of Königgrätz marked a popular high point for Fritz, both with his father and the Prussian people. For several months after the war, Wilhelm was particularly kind to his son. It was said that Napoleon III, dismayed at the quick succession of Prussian victories, was even more perturbed when he got word of Fritz's prowess on the battlefield. "The future King a good general, too!" he exclaimed, hitting his hand on the table. "That is the last straw!"

The victory had been expensive. Close to ten thousand Prussians were killed or wounded in the final battle, while Austria lost nearly forty thousand men, eighteen thousand of them taken prisoner. "War is a frightful thing, and the civilian who brings it about with a stroke of his pen at the Council table has no idea of what he is preparing," Fritz wrote in his diary the evening after Königgrätz.

Vicky was in the middle of a letter to Fritz when news of victory arrived. "Darling husband . . . ," she wrote,

> God grant that the work of devastation will soon be over. The brilliant and glorious victories of our 'nation under arms' can never change my opinion of Bismarck. For me war will ever be a crime brought on by the irresponsibility and temerity of this one man, not by force of circumstances. . . . The

* *Also known as Sadowa.*

work that is now (perhaps) being done by blood and iron should have been done by intellectual forces. Your Papa owes his people a great deal for the terrible sacrifices they have made. . . . Who knows whether we may not have to wage a third war in order to keep what we have now won.

This was one of Bismarck's concerns as well. Inflated with victory, Wilhelm demanded Austrian territory as the proper spoils of war. Bismarck counseled that Prussia could not afford to turn Austria into her permanent enemy. "If we do not exaggerate our demands and do not believe that we have conquered the world," Bismarck wrote his wife, "we shall get a peace worth the efforts we have made. But we—that means, of course, the King—are . . . easily intoxicated . . . and I have the thankless task of pouring water into his wine and bringing home the truth that we do not live alone in Europe but with three neighbours."*

Matters reached such an impasse between the King and his Prime Minister that on July 20, Bismarck sent for the Crown Prince. On his way up the hill to military headquarters in Nikolsburg, Fritz ran into Moltke. "Your Royal Highness will find everything in a terrible state up there," the Commander told him; "the King and Bismarck won't even see each other."

It was true. Bismarck met Fritz alone to ask for his help in convincing the King that he must not insist on the traditional territorial recompense. "I must say that Bismarck is acting very correctly in this matter, and I am giving him considerable support . . . ," Fritz wrote in his diary. "For the last three days Papa has said such things to him that he [Bismarck] actually cried last evening and was really afraid to go in again. I had to calm down both of them."

In his memoirs, Bismarck says that he was ready to offer his resignation. He retired to his own quarters, where, as he put it, he contemplated falling "out of the open window, which was four storeys high." While he was standing there, the Crown Prince quietly entered the room behind him. Although he did not turn around, Bismarck guessed that it was Fritz.

"I felt his hand on my shoulder," Bismarck recalled. "You know that I was against this war," Fritz said. "You considered it necessary, and the responsibility for it lies on you. If you are now persuaded that our end is attained, and peace must now be concluded, I am ready to support you and defend your opinion with my father." The Crown Prince then left to speak to the King. He was back within thirty minutes "in the same calm, friendly mood," according to Bismarck. "It has been a very difficult business," Fritz told him, "but my father has consented."

Wilhelm acknowledged his consent in a note scribbled in pencil on the margin of one of Bismarck's memoranda. "Inasmuch as my Minister-President has left me in the lurch in the face of the enemy . . . ," Wilhelm wrote, "I have discussed the question with my son, and as he has associated himself with the

---

* He probably meant Austria, France, and Russia, since Italy was not much of a potential threat.

Minister-President's opinion, I find myself reluctantly compelled, after such brilliant victories on the part of the army, to bite into this sour apple and accept a disgraceful peace."

The preliminary Peace of Nikolsburg and the definitive Treaty of Prague that would follow in August left Austria territorially intact, but put an end to the old German Confederation established by the Congress of Vienna a half century earlier. It combined east and west Prussia by the annexation of Hanover. Other annexations included the states of Hesse-Kassel and Nassau and the free city of Frankfurt, thus adding thirteen hundred square miles of territory and more than four million people to the Prussian state. The remainder of the German states north of the Main River were joined to Prussia in the new North German Confederation. The southern states of Baden, Württemberg, and Bavaria were given very generous terms, in return for which they agreed to conclude military alliances with Prussia in case of an eventual, and now probable, war with France.

Napoleon III, who could not sit back and allow Prussia to assume control of central Europe, was devastated by the sudden victory of Prussia over Austria. He had counted on a long war to debilitate both sides and create opportunities for French expansion. Hadn't Bismarck virtually assured him of Prussian acquiescence should France wish to extend its borders into Belgium and Luxembourg? Hadn't he hinted at similar possibilities for the French in the Rhineland? The French army still had the reputation, established in the days of the first Napoleon, of being the finest fighting force in Europe. But with his finances strained by an attempt to establish a Mexican empire and with the best of his troops in Mexico and Algeria, there was not much the French Emperor could produce in the way of immediate military intervention. The fact that he had not sent French troops to the Rhine during the Austro-Prussian conflict—in spite of urging by his Foreign Minister and his wife—is an indication that there may have been a deal struck between him and Bismarck, an understanding that enabled Prussia to withdraw its forces from its French border and concentrate them against Austria and the other German states.

Although Napoleon III offered himself as official peacemaker between Prussia and Austria, it was only a face-saving gesture. At the end of the Austro-Prussian War, the French Emperor was nearly paralyzed by illness.* "The Emperor can neither walk nor sleep and can hardly eat," Eugénie told the Austrian Ambassador to France. The Austrian Foreign Minister, who hastened to Paris in search of help after his country's defeat, was stunned by Napoleon's physical deterioration. According to him, the Emperor could do little more than stammer over and over, "I am not ready for war."

Nevertheless, at the close of the Austro-Prussian War, Napoleon put forward his claims for territorial compensation along the Rhine. It was easy for Bismarck to reject this demand out of hand. In the middle of August, the French Ambassador, Count Benedetti, came back with a request for Belgium

---

* *He was suffering from bladder stones.*

and Luxembourg—the French-speaking countries that Bismarck had suggested as appropriate places for French expansion. Bismarck induced Benedetti to put this proposal in writing, presumably so he could present it to King Wilhelm. But taking advantage of illness and vacation to delay giving the French an answer, Bismarck simply tucked the confidential draft away for future use against its authors.

It was clear that Bismarck had outfoxed Austria, France, the other German states, his own King, the Crown Prince, and the Prussian liberals. "I have beaten them all! All!" he claimed in triumph, pounding his fist on the table.

And so he had.

CHAPTER
TWENTY-EIGHT

> *"Prussia must do for the whole of Germany what it has done for itself . . . erase the distinction between victor and vanquished . . . replacing the consciousness of belonging to separate states . . . with a proud and happy loyalty to a German commonwealth headed by the King of Prussia."*
>
> OTTO VON BISMARCK,
> *letter to the Crown Prince,*
> *April 2, 1867*

*A*S SOON AS HE HAD enabled Bismarck to come to terms with the King, Fritz left headquarters to spend a few days with his wife. Vicky was in a very fragile state; she had retreated to the small town of Heringsdorf on the Baltic Sea to cope with "the hardest trial" of her life, the death of her youngest son, twenty-one-month-old Prince Sigismund.

"A little child is no loss to the rest of the world," she wrote her mother a few days before her husband's triumph at the Battle of Königgrätz; "none miss it, but to me it is a part of myself. . . . my little Sigie's loss has cast a gloom over this House and over my . . . whole existence which will never quite wear off." Although this was written when the Crown Princess was still in a state of shock, she never did recover completely from Sigismund's death, partly because of the circumstances—her utter aloneness and helplessness during the swift, terrifying illness that attacked her son.

On June 4, Vicky had said good-bye to Fritz, who was on his way to the front. The next day, Sigi, who had been fretful with what was thought to be teething, was unable to eat or sleep. Within twenty-four hours, he could no longer stand by himself. Wegner and the other doctors had all left with the army, and Vicky was forced to consult an incompetent practitioner from Potsdam. For five days, she watched her son in the "most frightful convulsions," and on June 18, two weeks after his father's departure, Sigismund died of meningitis. "Oh to see it suffer so cruelly, to see it die & hear its last piteous cry was an agony I cannot describe, it haunts me night and day!" Vicky told her mother when she was finally able to write about the death.

Queen Augusta set out immediately for the front to tell Fritz. Although Wilhelm gave his son leave to go home for the funeral, the Crown Prince refused. "I am in the service of the fatherland," he explained. "I would never forgive myself if we were attacked when I was absent from my post." Vicky did not understand. "In you, of course, the soldier is uppermost," she wrote. She prepared an anteroom of the Freedom Church in Potsdam with carpets and cushions, pictures and flowers to receive the tiny coffin and was the only person at the services who did not cry.

Two weeks after Sigi's death, the Crown Princess picked up her four remaining children and took them with her to the Baltic. "I feel I must be alone with such grief," she wrote her mother. "I have felt now and then as if my reason would give way. . . . I want all my powers of mind and endurance at this moment when our country is being convulsed by the most violent shocks. . . . one must have one's wits about one, which I feel I have not yet."

During the worst of her despair, Vicky turned to her mother, who, she felt, well understood the pain of death. Indeed, one would have thought that there was no one in the world more suited to sympathize than the English Queen, who was making a life work of mourning—rarely appearing for state ceremonies, clinging resolutely to her widow's weeds, and welcoming the spasms of self-pity that still erupted with some regularity.

But unlike Victoria, who never offered excuses for her lamentations, Vicky apologized continually for "wearying" her mother with her sorrow, explaining that she tried to write about other things but kept falling back on "that little face in its last agony." It haunted her lonely nights, and she could not drive it out of her tortured mind.

For over a month, the Queen was a model of support and sympathy, accepting everything that came pouring out of her often irrational daughter with love and understanding. But she lost patience when Vicky claimed that she would give up "house & home, future & all" if she could bring back her dear little boy.

"[I]t is not right in you, dear child," Victoria wrote, "to say you would give up everything . . . to get little Siggie back. That is really wrong, dearest child! It is tempting providence. Think what is a child in comparison with a husband."

But Vicky remained inconsolable. She sculpted a waxen image of her dead son and placed it in his crib. Next to the bed were his shoes, as well as his silver rattle and ball, "lying," according to one observer, "as though flung aside by the little hand." Ten years later, a friend reported being taken to a small room in the Neues Palais and shown this pathetic sight, still locked away in the inner recesses of the building.

In spite of or perhaps because of her tragedy, the Crown Princess threw herself into war work—collecting supplies and clothing for the soldiers, turning sections of her Berlin palace into a private hospital, and visiting the wounded and dying men. Wherever she was—and she moved around a good bit that summer—she made one or two daily forays to the hospitals, taking flowers, books, newspapers, cigars, and other comforts, and arranging for the suffering men to be given special culinary treats. Since she made no distinction between her own soldiers and those of the enemy, this meant having goulash cooked for the Hungarians, polenta and macaroni for the Italians, and whatever else might tempt wounded men from the various ethnic groups that made up the Austrian

Empire. The only cases she avoided were those with cholera, a disease that assumed epidemic proportions during the summer.

But the constant sight of death, the loss of one shattered young soldier after another, plus the knowledge that the war had not been necessary, only increased her personal despair. When she left Potsdam for Heringsdorf—which meant leaving her son's tiny crypt—she was so despondent that she apologized to her mother for even sending the letter.

It was in Heringsdorf on the Baltic that Vicky began to receive details of the Prussian victory at Königgrätz and Fritz's role in it. His name, she reported, was "on every one's lips," and "his praise sung by all his countrymen." The news brought her back to life.

"What do you say to all those <u>dreadful</u> battles?" she wrote Victoria.

Are you not a little pleased that it is <u>our</u> Fritz <u>alone</u> who has won all these victories? You know how hard I tried to help in preventing the calamity of war—& how Fritz did too, but now it is there I am thankful to think that our cause under Fritz's leadership has been victorious! You cannot think <u>how</u> modest he is about it—never seeking praise, always doing his duty. The soldiers adore him. I am told that when they get sight of him there is always a perfect burst of enthusiasm amongst them.

Vicky was irritated that the newspapers gave Fritz Carl more credit than her husband. This, she wrote Victoria, was "not fair as my Fritz has the largest share of all the difficulties & ought to have the most glory."

Nervous at the idea of meeting the returning hero in her present state of mind, she drove into a small wood near Heringsdorf, where the family was able to enjoy a private reunion before being mobbed. One of the members of Fritz's military staff described the Crown Prince as he must have appeared to his wife and children, swinging down off his horse to clasp them in his arms. With his new, fuller beard and great height, Fritz at thirty-four was "as fine a man as one could wish to see." Even the new lines on his face, witnesses to the "tremendous events he had passed through," made him more attractive. "He is looking well only thinner and perhaps a little older," Vicky wrote her mother; "at least his beard and his serious expression make him appear so, he has gone through a <u>great</u> deal, but is as humble and modest about all he has done as possible." She was also thinner than usual, although she referred to her picture in a photograph sent her mother as "my hideous self."

From Heringsdorf they moved on to the town of Erdmannsdorf, where Fritz devoted himself to improving conditions at the local war hospital. Vicky wanted to avoid Berlin, partly because cholera was still rampant in the city, but mostly because she was expected to continue her social rounds and was not allowed to wear mourning for her son, dead less than two months. Stopping off with Fritz at the capital en route to Erdmannsdorf, she had been required to appear at a dinner and evening tea at the King and Queen's "as if nothing had happened." She was furious. "You know . . . they think that a week is time enough to mourn and forget that grief cannot be so quickly shaken off!" she complained to Victoria. She was hurt that Queen Augusta had never worn mourning for Sigi at all.

But in late September, she took off her black gowns to join Fritz and the rest of the royal family for the triumphant entry of the victorious army into Berlin. Riding in front of the King, the Crown Prince, and Prince Fritz Carl were Commander-in-Chief Moltke, General Roon, and Count Bismarck. The King had just rewarded Bismarck with 400,000 thalers to purchase the Pomeranian estate of Varzin, which included 14,200 acres of land* and seven villages.

"[T]he universal enthusiasm was . . . so spontaneous and I shared it with all my heart," Vicky wrote her mother. Her mood had changed when the King, drawing his sword and taking a position at the head of the Rifle Battalion of the Guards, led them past the Crown Prince—a mark of honor to his son.

The Crown Princess was also pleased to see her father's brother Ernest, Duke of the duchies of Saxe-Coburg and Gotha who had supported Prussia in the war, riding at the head of his battalion in the victory parade. "I am not accustomed," she noted drily, "to hearing so much praise of Coburg here." Her uncle, she was happy to tell her mother, was "not among the crushed and beaten foe, it is sad enough as it is to see so many of one's friends suffering from the effects of their miscalculations."

CERTAINLY THERE HAD TO BE quite a few petty German kings, princes, and dukes who wished fervently that they had supported Prussia, not Austria, in the war. For if Bismarck had prevented King Wilhelm from rewarding himself with pieces of the Austrian Empire, he was not anxious to restrain the King when it came to the other German states. Under the terms of the peace, the King of Hanover, the Duke of Nassau, and the Elector of Hesse† were swiftly deposed. "Only under Napoleon I," said one historian, "had Europe experienced such a ruthless destruction of sovereignties." The Russians, upholders of monarchy at any price, were appalled. "The monarchical principle," Czar Alexander II complained to King Wilhelm, "has suffered a rude shock."

Considering Wilhelm's princely sentiments about his fellow monarchs, it is amazing that he joined so enthusiastically in this blatant takeover of their states. Perhaps this was Bismarck's way of compensating the King for his enforced restraint over Austria. Vicky, who had deplored the "continual opposition" and "petty conflicting jealousies" that had always prevented the German states from joining together to assume a more significant position in Europe, still did not agree with Bismarck and Wilhelm's route to unification. "I remain faithful to my principles which are: that annexation without the expressed wish of the population is an act of injustice . . . ," she wrote Victoria. "My ideal has always been a free and united Germany under the protection and leadership of Prussia

---

* Bismarck eventually increased it to twenty thousand acres.

† Hesse-Kassel, i.e., the northern part of Hesse. Hesse-Darmstadt, the southern part where Alice lived, was only required to surrender part of her territory to Prussia, and her sovereign Grand Duke was left in place.

. . . a liberal Prussia and the other states enjoying each the development of their local interests under their own sovereigns. . . . I would have nobody's rights upset. . . . this is not Bismarck's ideal and much less the King's with his spirit of military despotism."

More than the annexations themselves, the Crown Princess regretted the methods used. "The only way they [the other states] can become reconciled to their hard fate is to allow them to preserve their own particular customs . . . their laws, their town and community regulations and their jurisdiction," she told her mother-in-law, adding that it was a "very great pity" that the government planned to "impose" the Prussian constitution and "the whole machinery of our officialdom" on the defeated states. But, as she had come to realize, "Bismarck never even considered a liberal policy."

Of the three states annexed by Prussia, it was Hanover that caused the biggest concern in royal circles, particularly in England. George, the blind King of Hanover, was Queen Victoria's first cousin and head of one of the oldest dynasties in Germany. Enormously rich and reactionary, he had sent what he could of his private fortune plus nineteen million thalers in public monies to England for safekeeping during the war. Determined to honor his obligations to the German Confederation, he had hesitated a long time before declaring himself on the side of Austria and had been roundly defeated a few weeks later.

Victoria was ambivalent about King George. It was crucial that the dignity of her family be preserved, but she wanted to discourage her cousin from following his fortune to England. Vicky's brother Affie had fallen in love with George's daughter, whom the Queen and her advisers considered a dangerous match on the grounds of politics and health.* Still, the Queen wanted George treated well.

But there was nothing the Crown Princess could do to help her mother's cousin after the Austro-Prussian War. Prussians rejoiced at the annexation of Hanover, which provided a territorial link between the divided lands of East and West Prussia for the first time in two hundred years. Her father-in-law, Vicky explained to her mother, had tried to get King George of Hanover to join Prussia, but had failed. Hanover had been conquered during the war and "is by right of conquest no longer his; my father-in-law cannot reinstate him. . . . I am certain that whatever can be done to make him comfortable—that is to say secure his immense fortune to him—the King will do."

Bismarck, however, had other plans. The Prussian Parliament ratified an

---

* Ernest Augustus, the Duke of Cumberland and father of the current King George of Hanover, had been next in line after Victoria's father, Edward, the Duke of Kent, for the English throne. Since both Victoria's mother and her husband were Coburgs, it could be said that the Coburgs had dispossessed the Hanovers of the throne, and a marriage between their houses might be construed as a restoration.

The Queen's concern about the health of the Hanovers, based largely on what she called "three generations of blindness," was less warranted. Ernest Augustus had lost the sight of one eye in battle; George was blinded by an accident; and only his son, George III, had gone blind from natural causes (Fulford, Dearest Mama, p. 331, QV to V, 5/10/64).

agreement granting the exiled King of Hanover the income from the sixteen million thalers and property he had left behind in Germany in return for the nineteen million in public monies he had sent to England. But Bismarck reneged on this settlement, arranging for King George's entire income to come to the Prussian government for the alleged purpose of controlling Hanoverian espionage.* This money, known as the Guelph Fund, or "Reptile Fund," provided Bismarck with an annual income of more than one million marks outside parliamentary control to do with as he liked. Treating the Hanoverian funds as his personal bank account, Bismarck used the money to finance an extensive network of Prussian espionage (he claimed that he knew what King George had eaten for breakfast) and—far more important—to increase his control over the liberal press.

Ever since his advent to power four years earlier, Bismarck had used the conservative press to spread his message. Now he had the wherewithal to buy the liberal newspapers as well. In some instances, he paid to have his own articles published in domestic or foreign papers one day in order to quote them the next—as if the ideas and opinions they expressed came from an independent source. In other cases, he used the Foreign Ministry and the Literary Bureau of the Ministry of the Interior to distribute government handouts that encouraged journalists to disseminate the Bismarck line "as apparently private reporters, for the best papers in Germany." The money needed to subsidize these "official, semi-official and secret news sources" came largely from the Reptile Fund, which was not restored to the rightful heirs for some thirty-five years, after Bismarck was out of power.†

If it was hard to feel sorry for the King of Hanover, it was difficult not to pity others on whom the victorious Bismarck imposed his revenge. Except in circumstances when leniency could be measured in political profits, he extracted heavy indemnities and retribution from all the defeated states. His most cruel demands were made on the free city of Frankfurt. Frankfurt had not participated in the war and had put up no resistance whatsoever to the occupying Prussian troops, but because of its liberal traditions it was treated like an enemy.

The Prussian army, which marched into the city on July 16, levied huge requisitions from its citizens. After six million guilders was paid, General Manteuffel demanded an additional twenty-five million guilders to be delivered within twenty-four hours. Unable to comply within the time specified, the mayor of Frankfurt hanged himself. Bismarck ordered that the amount be raised one million guilders for every day that it remained unpaid, that the city gates be closed, and that all trains be stopped in and out of the city, thus starving the

---

* *From his residence near Vienna, the deposed King sent money to support the so-called Guelph Legion, a group of around one thousand ex-soldiers from the Hanoverian army who had fled to France.*

† *In a study made in 1977 of Bismarck and the press, the author concludes that the "influence of Bismarck's secret press apparatus cannot be underestimated"* (Robert H. Kayserlingh, Media Manipulation, the Press and Bismarck in Imperial Germany, *p. 144).*

inhabitants into submission. To Rudolph von Bennigsen, a leader of the moderate liberals in parliament, this was "unspeakably miserable" behavior, and Queen Augusta begged her husband not to mistreat a city that was about to fall under his sovereignty.*

The citizens of Trautenau, a small town in Bohemia, fared little better. They had come under fire in the early days of the war when Prussian troops invaded the town and were driven out by the Austrians. Angry at their defeat and claiming that the citizens of Trautenau had fired on them from their homes, the Prussian corps abducted the town mayor and nine other elderly citizens, whom they imprisoned in shackles. After holding them for seven weeks without charges, Bismarck found a use for them.

The Prussian Prime Minister's Hungarian Legion, the group he had raised from Austria's political malcontents, had proved both unpopular and incompetent. The legion had not invaded Austrian territory until after the armistice, crossing the line of demarcation in a failed attack from which it had to withdraw in some haste. This would have been the stuff of comic opera, had not the commander's aide-de-camp been taken prisoner by the Austrians and sentenced to death. When the aide appealed to Bismarck, it was the ten innocent burghers from Trautenau whom Bismarck threatened to shoot if the Hungarian was not released.

Along with true stories like these, vague tales of Prussian atrocities circulated through royal circles. When Queen Victoria repeated them to Vicky, the Crown Princess jumped to defend Prussia and its army.

> The Prussian army is a body of well-trained, well-educated and thoroughly disciplined men, the Austrians are the very reverse, all sorts of different, half-barbarous nationalities jumbled together. That many of our men and some of our officers may have forgotten themselves I do not doubt; they cannot all be angels and one cannot be answerable for all. But this is a fact that our army is, because composed of better elements, superior in behaviour & kindness & humanity to any other. . . . The Austrian wounded prayed & begged to be treated by our doctors as theirs were so rough & cruel. Many of the prisoners and wounded we have here are very sorry to go home.

WHATEVER THE TRUTHS of the battlefield—and there were surely as many as there were soldiers—Bismarck's two wars had seriously damaged Prussia's image among the other countries of Europe, and Fritz's role in them had left him and his wife in a difficult position with many of their peers in Europe. As

---

* *Three years later, when Frankfurt, still impoverished from her war indemnity, was having trouble getting money from the government, Wilhelm gave the city one million guilders from his own pocket. This was done in complete agreement with Fritz, to whom his father had originally promised the money as part of his inheritance. Bismarck, Vicky said, was "frantic" (RA: Z 23/21, V to QV, 2/24/69).*

life returned to postwar normality in the fall of 1866, Vicky began to face problems with members of her family.

Among the most outspoken critics of Prussian aggression was Vicky's brother Bertie, and she worried about what might happen when her husband and brother saw each other during the festivities celebrating the wedding of the Russian Czarevitch, the future Alexander III, to Alix's sister Dagmar. The wedding was due to take place in early November of 1866, two years after the bride's father, the King of Denmark, had lost the duchies of Schleswig and Holstein to the Germans and scarcely three months after Prussia had wrested them both from Austria.

Vicky, whose experience with her husband's Russian relatives had not changed the anti-Russian bias of her upbringing, did not want Fritz to go. Queen Victoria did not want Bertie to attend either, but was relieved that her son-in-law would be there to keep an eye on her pleasure-loving son.

"[Y]ou know my brothers have no feeling of companionship for Fritz," Vicky wrote her mother the day Fritz left for Russia; "they soon get bored in his company, his tastes, occupations & interests are quite different to theirs, he is much older*—& cannot enter into their amusements so well. Therefore, I fear Bertie will avoid him as much as he can. All I hope and trust & pray is that B. may be prudent in what he says about politics. I know quite well what the feelings of English people at this moment are against us . . . & I tremble for fear anything unpleasant might happen."

Any possible friction was averted by Fritz himself, who declared openly to the bride that it must be "very unpleasant" for her to see him at her wedding "after the events of these past years." Grateful for his candor and his hopes that her marriage would turn out as happy as his own, Dagmar thanked him.

A dutiful young Princess with a highly ambitious mother, Dagmar had agreed to take on the bearlike, lumbering Alexander in place of his attractive older brother, who had died at twenty-one before he could marry her. Loveless marriages like this were far more common among young royalties than love matches such as Vicky's, and she felt strongly about them. "A young life is thus being sold and sacrificed . . . ," she wrote. "They say that Dagmar was absolutely determined about it, but that he cared little about her and had no wish to marry at all."

In this rarefied stratum of European society, there were only a limited number of young royalties eligible to marry and extend the power of their family dynasties. Everyone in this tiny group knew one another personally or knew about one another, and it was hard for them not to compare their lives. If Vicky felt sympathy for Dagmar, she was profoundly shaken by news of her second cousin Charlotte, known as the Empress Carlotta of Mexico, which reached her just before Dagmar and Alexander's wedding.

Charlotte was Vicky's age and the only daughter of her uncle Leopold of

---

* Fritz was thirty-five, Bertie twenty-five at the time.

Belgium.* Their mothers were close; they had been constantly compared as children (to Vicky's detriment); and shortly before Vicky's marriage to Fritz, Charlotte had married Archduke Maximilian of Austria, a brother of Emperor Franz Joseph. Maximilian and Charlotte had gone to Mexico under the aegis of Napoleon III, who had been trying to build a Catholic empire in the new world while the Americans were busy fighting the Civil War. But in early 1866, Napoleon, threatened by the United States and needing soldiers to back up his demands vis-à-vis Prussia, had pulled out of Mexico. The deserted Maximilian sent his wife back to Europe to beg for aid against the Mexican republicans. Unable to find help for her husband, Charlotte's mind apparently gave way.

"Oh how much better to be . . . in one's grave than to live on deprived of one's reason . . . ," Vicky wrote Victoria in October of 1866. "She who was so quiet and self-possessed. . . . I should not have been astonished if my brain had turned during the war and after my little one's death . . . but you know what a sensitive, nervous, excitable, lively being I am with an imagination which is a burden to me . . . but dear Charlotte . . . whose reason and caution was always above her years . . . what she must have gone through to . . . come to that!"

Charlotte, whose husband was arrested and shot eight months later, spent the next sixty-one years locked up in a château outside Brussels. Her fate continued to haunt Vicky, who feared that she herself might one day lose her mind as well.

But Vicky was not Charlotte. Despite all her anxieties, complaints, chronic winter colds, and family problems, she did not break under stress, but continued to function and play a role in the ongoing unification of Germany. It was, to be sure, the role of an unwelcome conscience in a bellicose society. For as Bismarck's brilliance in foreign policy began to force the rest of the German states into Prussia's orbit, there were fewer and fewer people who dared question his methods. Of these, the twenty-six-year-old Crown Princess remained one of the most outspoken.

---

* *Charlotte's mother was Louise d'Orléans, Leopold's third wife. Louise was the daughter of Louis Philippe of France, who had escaped France with his family during the Revolution of 1848 and taken up residence in England. Leopold's first wife was the ill-fated heir to the English throne Princess Charlotte; his second (morganatic) wife was Karoline Bauer.*

CHAPTER
TWENTY-NINE

> *"[T]he trophies of war exercise a magic charm upon the child of peace. One's view is involuntarily chained and one's spirit goes along with the boundless rows of men who acclaim the god of the moment—success."*
>
> GUSTAV MEVISSEN, *liberal leader,*
> *on watching the entry of troops into Berlin*
> *after the Austro-Prussian War*

*T*HE CLOSE OF the Austro-Prussian War marked the end of Bismarck's fourth year in office. During this time, he had changed the course of Prussia's domestic policy and engineered two full-scale wars—all without the moral or financial backing of the Prussian Parliament. Among those who urged ending the constitutional crisis was the Crown Prince. With the King now past his seventieth birthday, it became important for Bismarck to pay more attention to Wilhelm's successor.

Elections conducted during the war had decreased the number of liberals in parliament, but they were still the largest faction in the country, soon to be increased by the majority of voters in the newly annexed states of Hesse, Hanover, and Nassau, and the city of Frankfurt. In the postwar confederation of states that Bismarck was in the process of establishing, he needed liberal cooperation to offset the natural hostility of the heads of the individual states—petty princes with feudal minds who resented giving up any of their traditional rights in the interests of the German whole. A reconciliation with the liberals would give Bismarck the weapon he needed to extract cooperation from the reactionary princes, while the latter gave him ammunition to defend the power of the monarchy in the face of liberal demands.

Shortly after the Battle of Königgrätz, Bismarck presented parliament with an indemnity bill granting the government retroactive indemnity for expenses incurred in running the country for four years without an approved budget. Faced with the overwhelming success of the Prussian army, it was difficult for deputies to question King Wilhelm's army reform—the issue that had led to a constitutional crisis. And with Bismarck well on his way to accomplishing a major goal of the liberals—unification of the German states—it would have seemed ungrateful to deny him financial absolution for his sins. As could be expected, the indemnity bill passed by more than three to one.

A milestone in Prussian political life, the indemnity bill of 1866 split the liberals into two parties—the Progressives on the far left and the dominant National Liberals in the center. It was the first significant liberal capitulation to

Bismarck, and it came about partly because of Bismarck's shrewdness in dealing with his old adversaries, but mostly because of the nature of German liberalism itself.

This liberalism did not spring from the masses, but from the educated bougeoisie—professors, judges, doctors, lawyers, and their ilk. Like the liberals of 1848, who had squandered their mandate while the revolution collapsed around them, the liberals of 1866 were elitist, parochial, and frightened of peasants and workers. Suffering from what historian Otto Pflanze called the "delayed growth" of the German middle class, as well as its paralyzing admiration for authority, they were easily pushed into consigning their principles to the Prime Minister, as long as he delivered their dream of a united Germany. "The liberals," says Pflanze, "were the victims of their own limited ends, their lack of genuine popular support, and their lust for national power."

These same weaknesses made it possible for Bismarck to seduce the liberals into accepting his constitution for the North German Confederation—the new German entity created after the Austro-Prussian War. Dominated by Prussia, the North German Confederation included the twenty or so German states north of the Main River left intact after Prussian annexations. Bismarck himself drafted this constitution, which he designed specifically to preserve the power of the king, free the king's first minister—Bismarck himself, now called Chancellor—from responsibility to anyone but the monarch, and liberate the government from parliamentary controls. The constitution placed the armies of the allied states under the King of Prussia, investing in him absolute authority for all military matters, including the army's budget. Believing that the laboring classes were basically conservative, Bismarck wrote one of the first European constitutions that mandated universal male suffrage. It was also the first constitution in history not to include a bill of rights.

Though Fritz approved of the North German Confederation, Vicky did not. She still believed that unity could be based on leadership rather than force, and objected strongly to what she called the mere "expansion of Prussia." "I have been in the Reichstag today," Vicky wrote her mother at the end of March 1867, "and heard some very good speeches. . . . Of course no true patriot considers present arrangements anything else than quite provisory but hope [sic] . . . for better laws in the future—in which I earnestly believe they will not be disappointed."

Better laws, however, were figments of liberal dreams. As all but radical leftists fell before the lure of expediency, they justified their willing surrender by redefining the seducer, reshaping the image of the man they had once called the devil into that of a seer. "To be sure, liberalism has lost out . . . ," one prominent liberal leader wrote. "But this is not important now. First of all a great state, everything else can wait."

Bismarck assumed his new role of national hero with relish, offering sops to the liberal conscience and pocketbook. There was something for everyone. Parliamentarians liked his indemnity bill, militarists reveled in his annexations, and nationalists applauded his new North German Confederation.

There was an outside factor, however, that made swift passage of Bismarck's regressive constitution easier to achieve—a sudden threat of war with France over the duchy of Luxembourg. It was Napoleon III who inadvertently provided the goad used by Bismarck to prod the members of the confederation into accepting his personal blueprint for the future of Germany. Waving the threat of French expansion before the delegates to the constituent assembly, Bismarck was able to unite them behind a document that, in essence, robbed them of their power in the future state.

LIKE SCHLESWIG AND HOLSTEIN before 1864, Luxembourg—an odd little duchy nestled in central Europe, surrounded by Belgium, France, and the German Rhineland—was governed by potentially conflicting elements. Before the Austro-Prussian War, Luxembourg had been a member of the German Confederation, which had maintained a fortress there manned by the Prussians. But the Grand Duke of Luxembourg was also King of the Netherlands. This dual role created problems immediately after the Austro-Prussian War, because the peace settlements stated that neither the Netherlands nor its possessions were to be included in the new North German Confederation.

Prussia's victory in the war had left Napoleon III and the French in a vulnerable position. With the threat of a larger, stronger Germany looming in the middle of Europe, France felt she must restore the balance of power by expanding her territory and improving her military frontiers. Having failed to find compensation in the Rhineland, Napoleon fell back on Bismarck's previous offers of help in securing French-speaking Luxembourg.

During the summer of 1866, Bismarck had told the French Ambassador to Prussia, Count Benedetti, that the only thing standing in the way of France's acquiring Luxembourg was sufficient compensation for the King of the Netherlands. But once he had elicited a written draft of the proposal in which France agreed to union between the German states if Prussia acquiesced to French expansion in Belgium and Luxembourg,* Bismarck left Berlin for the country, where he remained incommunicado for nearly three months. Claiming illness and fatigue, he had spent this time drafting the constitution for the North German Confederation.

Returning to Berlin at the end of 1866, Bismarck told Benedetti that although he personally was in favor of their agreement, he had yet to win over King Wilhelm. Then he withdrew once again from Benedetti's sight, declaring himself too weak and too ill to receive the French Ambassador. "The French," Bismarck wrote at the time, "must retain hope and especially faith in our good will without our giving them definite commitments." He gave instructions to this effect to the Prussian Ambassador in Paris, "for," as he put it, "we shall win time thereby for the consolidation of our relationships in northern Germany and with southern Germany."

It was the large and powerful states of southern Germany—Bavaria, Baden,

---

* See Chapter 27, pages 236–237.

and Württemberg—that Bismarck still needed to bring into line with the new North German Confederation. Possessing large Catholic populations, fearful of Prussian hegemony, and distrustful of her authoritarian government, they had counted on Napoleon III for support during the peace negotiations with Bismarck, who threatened them with annexations and exorbitant reparations if they did not agree to sign military treaties with Prussia. Impotent to press even his own demands, however, Napoleon was no help to the south Germans, and Bismarck pushed through treaties that placed their armies in the service of Prussia. When Bismarck published these treaties in the spring of 1867, Napoleon, who had been counting on using his friendship with the southern states as leverage for Belgium and Luxembourg, was devastated.

Nevertheless, the French Emperor continued to negotiate with the King of the Netherlands for Luxembourg, and they agreed on a price of five million guilders. But the Dutch King said he must have the approval of the King of Prussia, thus bringing Bismarck back into the negotiations. Although Bismarck had suggested time and again that France might improve her security by expanding into her French-speaking neighbors, the moment it looked as if she might do so he began raising obstacles. Feigning innocence and moral injury, Bismarck complained that Prussia's "sense of honor" was at stake and that the undue precipitiousness of the French in making the offer made it nearly impossible for him to secure the requisite approval either from the Prussian people or their King.

To some extent, he was telling the truth. "People are in a wonderful state of excitement about Luxemburg," Vicky wrote her mother, "and I must say I think anything preferable than giving France a bit of Germany—as a sort of compensation for our unity. France has no right to interfere in our internal affairs. . . . Should there be a war against France—which would be a dreadful calamity on the one side—the unity of Germany would be effected at once."

Bismarck himself cared little for Luxembourg. "The population of the country is hardly homogeneous with ours," he said, noting that the people were, in fact, "anti-Prussian." Nor was the Prussian fortress in Luxembourg of such value that it could not easily be replaced by one in a more strategic location. What Bismarck was doing was what he did best—adopting the exigencies of foreign relations (exigencies that he himself often created) to impose constrictions on parliamentary procedures at home. In this case, Napoleon III's move to expand came at the opportune moment to rally the forces of German nationalism behind the new constitution of the North German Confederation. This was achieved on April 16, 1867, when the new parliament (to be known in the future as the Reichstag) voted to accept Bismarck's version of parliamentary government in order, as Vicky put it, "not to put fresh difficulties in the way of the government in case of a war with France."

At the same time that he was lobbying for his constitution, Bismarck managed to continue to thwart Napoleon's bid for Luxembourg. He refused to withdraw the Prussian garrison from its fortress there, advising the Dutch King not to go through with the sale to Napoleon, since public opinion would then force Prussia into war with France. For about two weeks in the spring of 1867, war did seem imminent—a war that would have been easy for Bismarck to blame on Napoleon, since only Bismarck, Napoleon, and their ambassadors knew how far Bismarck had gone in encouraging the French Emperor to expand into Luxembourg in exchange for French neutrality during the Austro-Prussian War.

Vicky for one was certainly fooled. "I do not think he [Bismarck] is in the wrong for once in his life," she wrote Victoria. "The aggression comes from France—and it is there they wish for the war and not here. . . . if our honour is at stake . . . we must not hang back. That is my feeling and Fritz's and most people here. . . . I think the great united empire of Germany will never consolidate itself in peace—before France is reduced to a second power on the Continent. . . . But please do not betray me to anyone—this is my own individual opinion and may be worth nothing."

Victoria was "surprised" at her daughter's letter. "In the present instance it is not France or the Emperor who wish for war," she wrote back, "quite the contrary; & I repeat it again—it is Bismarck who has for the last 8 months encouraged the Emperor to believe he could get Luxemburg [sic] without difficulty."

In that regard, the Queen of England wrote the King of Prussia, appealing to him to meet Napoleon III halfway, or "the world will appear only too well justified in accusing Prussia of desiring the war." When Vicky explained to her father-in-law that the English believed Bismarck had "encouraged" Napoleon in his desires to expand into Luxemburg, Wilhelm denied any such possibility.

The Crown Princess also found an opportunity to speak with Bismarck, reporting to her mother that she had told the Chancellor her "admiration for him would be greatly increased if he found a means of honourably preserving peace." Bismarck refused to commit himself. "[O]ne never can know what he really means . . . ," Vicky wrote Victoria. "The King wishes for peace, so does Fritz, so does the Minister for War. . . . If I am to sum up all our impressions, I should say that peace seems more likely."

In the end, since no one wanted war, the matter was submitted to another of those international conferences, this one held in London in May of 1867. It left King William III of the Netherlands sovereign over Luxembourg, affirmed the neutrality and independence of Luxembourg under the guarantee of the Great Powers, and ordered the destruction of Prussia's fortress.

Queen Victoria claimed that Napoleon III was "quite delighted" at not having to go to war. "[H]e from the first was against it," she told Vicky. "I repeat this again as a positive fact. You always seemed to doubt it—& that is what makes me always believe that Bismarck exaggerated all the reports from France in order to bring on the war."

If the Queen of England did not fully understand the motivation behind Bismarck's war propaganda, she understood very well his role in the war scare and saw through his actions far more clearly than her daughter or son-in-law.

∎

OUTMANEUVERED BY BISMARCK and anxious to improve his image with scenes of thriving industry at home, Napoleon III had planned an international exposition to take place in Paris during the spring and summer of 1867. Although their trip was nearly canceled because of the Luxembourg crisis, Fritz, Vicky, and Wilhelm proceeded with their journey late in May. Paris was *en fête*, as sightseers streamed in from all over Europe. Thomas Cook brought in tours from London, and visitors like Mark Twain came from America. Napoleon, now fifty-nine, was showing the ravages of his political misfortunes, and his "half closed" eyes disturbed Twain with their "deep crafty scheming expression."

Among the other guests of the French Emperor were Czar Alexander II of Russia, Sultan Abdul Aziz of Turkey, King Leopold II of Belgium (Uncle Leopold's son), and Emperor Franz Joseph of Austria. The Prince of Wales also attended the exposition, but not at the same time as his sister. This was just as well, for it was said that when Bertie was not participating in official functions, he was at the Théâtre de Variétés in the rosy dressing room of Hortense Schneider, watching the most popular actress and courtesan of the day apply her makeup. For less privileged spectators there was the famous aerealist Blondin, who tied Roman candles and Catherine wheels to his body and lit them before swaggering across a tightrope. Theaters and restaurants were filled to "suffocation," according to one contemporary report, which noted that the sidewalks of Paris were not wide enough "for the overflowing torrent of prostitutes."

Fritz and Vicky arrived on May 24 and were met at the station by Napoleon III. The next day they drove in state to the Tuileries, and that evening Napoleon and Eugénie gave a banquet in their honor. Along with visits to the exposition, they attended the races in the Bois de Boulogne, the Comédie Française, and a ball held by Prince Metternich* at the Austrian Embassy. They also made the acquaintance of Ernest Renan, the celebrated author of *La Vie de Jésus*, whom Vicky invited to the Prussian Embassy to discuss philosophy, metaphysics, and literature.

"I cannot tell you how I think of you here and of darling Papa and 12 years ago, and of all that has happened since!" Vicky wrote Victoria from Paris. "I delight in the Exhibition, the English things are the best to my taste." Vicky's preference for English china and works of art is not surprising, since the objects of greatest popularity in the German exhibit were the huge cannons made by Krupp, the armaments manufacturer.

Vicky's brother Affie was also in Paris, but having too good a time to see much of his sister. Alice was there, too—"looking so pretty," Vicky reported to their mother. Napoleon accompanied Fritz and Vicky to Fontainebleau shortly after their arrival, and on their last day, Eugénie took them to St. Cloud, where Vicky had stayed when she was fourteen.

Both Vicky and Bertie had fallen in love with Paris in their teens, and both had succumbed to the charms of Napoleon III and Eugénie, who provided

---

* *Son of the Austrian Chancellor Klemens Metternich.*

quite a contrast to their virtue-oriented parents. But the experience had affected them differently. Bertie always retained a passion for France itself that colored his political opinions, while Vicky was forced, by virtue of her marriage, to separate personal friendship from political loyalties. Moreover, Vicky never lost the prudishness instilled by their parents. She was far too embarrassed to enjoy the titillations of a less rigid sexual code and wrote her mother that a play about Julius Caesar at the Tuileries had made her "very hot and uncomfortable." As she admitted to Victoria, "There is much that shocks and disgusts me here, and I would not live here for the world. . . . What I care about is sightseeing, looking at the works of art and the lovely things in the shops."

Nevertheless, she remained enchanted with her hosts—"the charming way in which they do the honours and the trouble they give themselves to please their guests." She was particularly pleased that the Emperor and Empress continued to talk to her about her parents. "They spoke so often and with such real attachment of you and dear Papa," she wrote Victoria, "and asked so much after you. The Emperor said of dear Papa, 'He was surely the most distinguished and the most remarkable man I ever knew.' "

Her father-in-law was also treated to Napoleon III's calculated charm. "The King's reception at Paris was very fine and gratified him," Vicky wrote her mother. Wilhelm, who was always in the best of humor when separated from his wife, enjoyed himself immensely in Paris, behaving, as his daughter-in-law noted, much "like a schoolboy on a holiday."

But Vicky herself was depressed. She used the anniversary of Sigi's death as an excuse to leave Paris a full week ahead of schedule, offending her hosts, who had orchestrated the succession and appearances of their royal guests with great care. Pregnant again and never one for constant social life (she had stopped dancing when Sigi died), she was clearly in no mood for any more of the balls and galas that other royalties found so amusing.

"Dear Vicky was so low the last days," Alice wrote their mother, "and dislikes going to parties so much just now that she was longing to get home. . . . She was in such good looks . . . everybody is charmed with her." Despite King Wilhelm, who asked her to stay, and Napoleon and Eugénie, who were miffed that she would miss the grand ball at the Hôtel de Ville, Vicky hurried back to Potsdam to spend the few days preceding the anniversary of the death day quietly.

Before leaving for Paris, she had sent her mother a picture of baby Moretta, now a year old, in a little jacket and bonnet worn by her dead brother when he was taken ill. Understandably "distressed" by the photo, Queen Victoria cautioned her daughter against dwelling "so much on all that you cannot get back . . . surrounded as you are too by so many blooming children, and above all and worth 20 children, by your dear, good husband."

It was a loving reprimand. "Your Darling—God took to himself," the Queen told her daughter, "and he is safe & happy! You will see him again there, where there is no sorrow or pain or parting & if you would but dwell on that (as I <u>do</u>) . . . & have that faith & trust you would not have that sad and agonising repining. . . . I say all this in <u>love</u> & <u>affection</u> & in <u>perfect</u> <u>sympathy</u> with your loss."

Fritz and his father returned to Berlin the day before the anniversary of Sigi's death. That same morning, Alexander II of Russia also arrived in Berlin, and Vicky, immersed in her own sadness, resented the obligatory parade, endless dinners, and gala entertainments that necessarily accompanied such a visit.

A few days after Wilhelm and Fritz's departure, Napoleon III used an awards ceremony at the international exhibition to deliver a major speech in which he promised an era of peace. During the event, news reached the Tuileries of Emperor Maximilian's execution in Mexico. A sad postscript to the Austro-Prussian War, Maximilian's death and his wife Charlotte's madness were the direct results of the withdrawal of French troops by Napoleon III, who brought his soldiers home in order to deal with the threat of the newly expanded Prussia.

But this royal tragedy was only a minor prelude to the enormous loss of life that would be involved in the ongoing rivalry between the leaders of France and Prussia. In spite of his pledges of peace, Napoleon III was ripe fruit for Bismarck, who soon found a better provocation than Luxembourg to draw the French into war and establish Prussia as the major power in central Europe.

CHAPTER
THIRTY

"I love Germany. I glory in national feeling, and I am ambitious for her greatness, unity & happiness."

CROWN PRINCESS VICTORIA, 1867

*A*LTHOUGH THE CROWN PRINCE had played a major role in the first two wars leading to German unification, Bismarck continued to denigrate him and his wife to the German people. At the same time, the Chancellor used Fritz as a goodwill ambassador abroad, sending him on two major trips to prove to potential allies that the future monarch of the North German Confederation was more than just a successful warrior.

In 1868, Fritz went to Italy for the wedding of Crown Prince Humbert of Italy to Margaret of Savoy. Greeted with cheers of "Long live the hero and victor of Sadowa [Königgrätz]!" the man who was seldom allowed acclamation in his own country was delighted. "I do not suppose that any German . . . ever before received such an ovation as the Italians gave me this year," he wrote a friend.

The Italians were indeed grateful to Fritz for his role in defeating the Austrians in the Austro-Prussian War, thus winning for them the province of Venetia and furthering Italian unity. Led by Garibaldi, they were still trying to incorporate Rome into the nearly completed kingdom of Italy, but so far had been defeated by papal soldiers supported by Napoleon III. Bismarck, who insisted that Fritz's jubilant welcome "surprised nobody except the Crown Prince himself," was well satisfied. Italy was one of the two nations (Austria being the other) that France would look to for support in a conflict with Prussia. "Our aim has been achieved," Bismarck said on hearing the news of Fritz's enthusiastic welcome. "A Ministry hostile to us is no longer possible."

Fritz's popularity was partly due to his personal efforts and imposing appearance. "The Prince is a fine-looking man, tall and well made with a martial air," said one newspaper. "He smiles almost constantly, and . . . is much liked by our soldiers, who speak with pleasure of the interest displayed by His Royal Highness in all that concerns the minutest details of the military service."

Commended by the Italian press for his "extreme politeness" and "amiable courtesy" to his fellow soldiers, the Crown Prince of Prussia was also a success in society. When a clumsy partner stepped on the edge of Margaret's ball gown, leaving a piece of lace trailing on the floor, Fritz pulled a small pair of scissors from a case in his pocket, knelt down, and cut off the torn trim. When the Crown Princess of Italy held out her hand to take it from him, Fritz stood up, put the lace to his heart, folded it, and tucked it away in his coat pocket, earning oohs and ahs from the crowd. "These Prussians are sharp fellows, always armed, and ready for everything," commented one newspaper in the south of Germany.

The political implications of Fritz's trip pleased Vicky, a great admirer of Garibaldi and supporter of Italian unity, but infuriated Augusta, who had tried to stop her son's journey. "You know she has a great leaning towards the Roman Catholic religion," Vicky wrote Victoria, "and [is] much interested in the Pope's temporal power."

When Queen Victoria asked her daughter about the "coquetterie between Prussia and Rome," Vicky explained that in this area Bismarck "gives way completely" to the Queen. Although the Chancellor did not remotely agree with the pro-Catholic Augusta, he believed that a Prussian queen with papal sympathies might prove an asset in attracting the Catholics of the south German states to the North German Confederation. Taking into account Bismarck's determination to find some means of unifying Germany, we must assume the Prussian Chancellor calculated that it cost him little or nothing to keep the Catholic ball in the air along with the Italian one.

While Fritz was in Italy, Vicky was recuperating from the birth, on February 10, 1868, of her sixth child, a boy whom they named Waldemar. Shortly before her own confinement, her close friend Princess Putbus had died of puerperal fever. Wanda Putbus was Vicky's age; she had married around the same time and left five little girls. Nevertheless, Vicky wrote Victoria that Wanda's death "has not made me apprehensive for myself. . . . indeed I have hardly thought about myself with regard to that sad event."

This was hardly true, but the Crown Princess, who complained endlessly about minor illnesses, was remarkably gallant when it came to situations that were potentially life-threatening. One milestone had helped her through a nervous waiting period—the "great and undeserved" happiness of her tenth wedding anniversary at the end of January 1868. "These years have not been without trials and sorrows . . . ," she said, "but as long as it pleases Heaven to let us share them together no burden will be heavier than we can bear."

Vicky knew Queen Victoria disapproved of her having babies so close together, and Moretta was barely a year old when she realized she was pregnant again. "People are very anxious for us to have another son," the Crown Princess explained to her mother, "as we had the misfortune of losing the 3rd." She had in fact not told Victoria or Fritz's family she was expecting until she was five months along. "We should at any rate not have told the Queen [Augusta] . . . ," Vicky said, "as the last times it made her so cross and was so unpleasant for us."

No one got along with Augusta, but no one dared cross her. The Queen did not, as Vicky wrote Victoria, "get softer or easier to live with." Nothing, she realized, would change her mother-in-law's bad temper or hyperactivity.

"The Queen . . . has parties <u>every</u> <u>night</u>," Vicky wrote Victoria. "She is <u>never alone</u>. . . . When she leaves Berlin there is hardly a person . . . who has not a feeling of intense relief."

Augusta entertained every Thursday at what one guest called "small" receptions, explaining that "never more than two hundred and fifty people were invited." The entertainment—overweight, elderly singers performing two hours of music—was repeated each week. Upon entering the Queen's white drawing room, guests were assigned tables from which they were not permitted to stray either during the recital or the supper that followed. "These Thursday evenings were considered very smart, but this did not prevent those privileged to attend them from complaining of their extraordinary dullness," said one of the chosen.

Augusta's daily teas, on the other hand, were highly selective gatherings with only ten or twelve in attendance. The Queen sat at a small round table covered in red velvet with gold fringe and chose the guests she wanted to sit with her. She poured the tea, while footmen passed sandwiches, ices, and roasted chestnuts with claret. "The plates . . . were ugly and common looking . . . ," according to one guest. "The conversation was entirely small-talk. . . . The events of the day were discussed, together with the gossip going round the town, of which the Empress [Queen] was extremely fond."

One of the things that kept Augusta engaged was meddling in the affairs of others. A disappointed, spiteful woman, she clearly enjoyed making trouble where she could. As Countess Blücher, who was a friend of both Queen Augusta and Queen Victoria, wrote the latter, "[T]here is a system of <u>constantly</u> interfering in the little domestic arrangements of the Princess [Vicky] which is certainly very provoking." This showed itself when Vicky, who had not been in England for three years, obtained the King's permission to go home in November of 1868. She hoped to be allowed to stay for Christmas, but as soon as she got to England, she heard that Augusta had started lobbying to get her back. "I think it is <u>unkind</u> & <u>selfish</u> of the Queen to wish to spoil me of the pleasure of being with <u>you</u> . . . my <u>own</u> dear Mama whom I have not seen for 3 <u>years</u>!" Vicky fumed. "You know that the Queen cares very <u>little</u> for my presence, therefore it is not out of <u>love</u> she wishes for me back—if that were the case it would <u>touch</u> me. I hope now dear Mama you will . . . write to the King saying you knew the Queen was against my staying but that in this case you appealed to <u>him</u> . . . that you allowed <u>your</u> daughter-in-law [the Danish Princess of Wales] to go home to her parents & you thought for once <u>he</u> might let me stay."

Victoria wrote Wilhelm, and Vicky, Fritz, and three of their children were allowed to remain in England for Christmas of 1868. But this extended visit, pleasurable as it was, turned out to be both personally and politically damaging to Vicky. Before the travelers returned home, Queen Victoria received a strongly worded letter from King Wilhelm complaining about his son and daughter-in-law's long absence, Vicky's lack of interest in the social life of Berlin, and the fact that the Crown Princess insisted upon driving out in her carriage with fewer than four horses.

The Queen of England was not easily cowed: "As regards this prolonged absence of our dear children . . . ," she wrote back,

> I have merely to observe that . . . they have not been here for the last 3 years. . . . I have no doubt that you will allow me to see our dear daughter more often . . . for you, dear brother, see your own daughter . . . several times every year. . . . Your loving paternal heart will surely understand that I should not like to be parted from Vicky again for three whole years.
>
> She will, of course, do her best to comply with your wishes as regards social life, only you and dear Augusta will certainly show consideration for her, for she does not really stand very hot rooms and late hours well. As for her drives, I am really not in a position to say anything, for I leave it to our daughter-in-law to follow her own wishes entirely in this respect, and in any case, in our day, driving with four horses has quite gone out of fashion almost everywhere.

Although Victoria was able to whisk away complaints lodged by the King, she could do nothing to help Vicky counter a campaign launched against her during her absence from Berlin. It was started by Gustav and Elisabeth von Putlitz, a well-known German writer and his wife, whom Vicky had appointed Chamberlain and *Grande Maîtresse,* respectively, of her household.

Putlitz had met Vicky four years earlier when he came to write a history of the Neues Palais. At that time, he could not find enough words to express his admiration for her. Vicky was "marvellously well-read"; her painting was "conceived with real genius"; she discussed history "like a historian" and was, in sum, the "most wonderful woman, rich in mind, culture, energy, kindness and benevolence."

The Putlitzes were only one of many examples of Vicky's inability to judge character. Raised by the Crown Princess to positions of eminence in her court, they left in a huff after a row with the children's governess, Fanny Reventlow, turning on their benefactor and spreading nasty rumors about her. Vicky complained about these stories to her mother, although she never specified what they were. Clearly as absurd as Putlitz's excessive flatteries, they were magnified and repeated by the members of the Anglophobic court, anxious to blacken the character of *die Engländerin.*

Far more dangerous was Bismarck, who jumped into the fray with some inventions of his own. "The stories about me and Fanny Reventlow are the main talk of all the salons," Vicky wrote Victoria two weeks after her return; "there is <u>nothing</u> people do not say particularly <u>Bismarck</u>. I am very weary and discouraged." The Chancellor went so far as to tell the children's tutor that Vicky "detested Germans so much" that she invited only the old men and generals to ride horseback with her so that she could exhaust them "and injure their health!"

Vicky's enemies were also miffed because her brother the Prince of Wales and his Danish wife were due to arrive for a visit at the end of January 1869.

King Wilhelm, on the other hand, was delighted. It was clearly Alix's beauty and not her friendliness that captivated the old man, for during the previous fall she had made a point of refusing to see him when he tried to call on her at Wiesbaden. Since she had given ill health as an excuse and was then observed enjoying a band concert in the public gardens, there had been a royal brouhaha over her behavior. But the rift—a result of the Schleswig-Holstein War—had been papered over, and the King was feeling very friendly when the Prince and Princess of Wales arrived in Berlin three months later.

"Dearest Bertie and Alix's visit is going off as well as possible," Vicky reported to her mother; "nothing can be more kind, amiable and good natured than they both are. . . . The King quite touches me by the unfeigned pleasure he has in being as kind and cordial as possible. . . . The King gave Alix a nosegay last night for the ball. I don't think he has ever done such a thing for any one before, not for the Empress of Russia even."

During the visit, King Wilhelm invested the Prince of Wales with the Order of the Black Eagle, and there were endless entertainments planned around them. During an ice-skating party, the British Military Attaché told Queen Augusta "how the Berliners raved about the little Danish Rose." Not surprisingly, Augusta, who resented the young and beautiful Princess of Wales, looked for an excuse to pick a quarrel with her. She found it during Alix and Bertie's last evening in Berlin at a ball in the palace.

"I thank Your Majesty for all your kindness and friendship," Alix said as she left the Queen's presence.

Augusta complained that Alix was "very impolite" to call her "Your Majesty" instead of "Aunt Augusta" and made a scene: "[Y]ou may call me as you wish, it does not make any difference to me," she barked at the Princess of Wales, turning her back on the twenty-four-year-old in front of the rest of the guests and stalking away. The Queen must have regretted her actions later, because she wrote Vicky a note asking her to give Alix a "very handsome" collection of green-and-gold display porcelains.

The Queen's behavior toward her guest indicates what she must have been like as a mother-in-law. Much to Vicky's distress, she was left alone with this difficult woman a good deal during the years following the Austro-Prussian War, as Fritz's duties—inspecting troops within the country and representing Prussia abroad—took him away for weeks and months at a time. In September of 1869, the Crown Prince was sent to attend the opening of the Suez Canal.

Vicky was concerned about her husband going so far away with her father-in-law at such an advanced age. Did she worry that something might happen to Wilhelm and Bismarck might find a way to take over the government completely? No matter. The Chancellor decreed that someone had to go, and he himself was too busy; the King was too old; and the King's brothers, known to be "very anxious" to represent Prussia, were too bellicose.

When word got out that Fritz was to attend the Suez opening, Emperor Franz Joseph of Austria decided to go too. He did not want to make the journey, but knew that any lesser representative of the Austro-Hungarian Empire would have to give precedence at the official ceremonies to the Crown Prince of Prussia. Having been recently defeated by the Prussians in war, he could not afford to lose diplomatic face as well.

Bismarck's choice of Fritz had, in fact, everything to do with Austria and little to do with Egypt. The German Chancellor had been looking for an opportunity to improve relations with the Austrians, with whom he wanted to renew old German ties in light of the war that might one day break out between Prussia and France. Who better than the Prussian Crown Prince, well-known in royal and political circles for his sincere pacifism? Fritz and Vicky realized that he was being used by the Chancellor, but there was little they could do about it. Fritz traveled to Suez via Vienna.

The Prussian Crown Prince was warmly welcomed by Franz Joseph, who put on the uniform of a Prussian officer to greet him. They exchanged "words of old friendship," avoiding recent politics with the sort of pleasantries and compliments at which men of their time and training excelled. After spending several days together, they journeyed separately to Constantinople, where the Sultan established Fritz in a palace on the shore, gave up his own apartments to the Austrian Emperor, and moved into his harem.

From Constantinople, Fritz proceeded to Jerusalem and from there to Port Said, the point of departure for the formal passage through the Suez Canal. He was joined by his host the Khedive of Egypt, Emperor Franz Joseph, Prince Henry of the Netherlands, and Empress Eugénie, who disembarked from her ship dressed in an officer's cap and a skirt fetchingly looped up, revealing bright yellow leather leggings. After the formal opening of the canal, each of the royalties boarded his own separate ship for the two-day voyage from Port Said to Suez. These royal barges were followed by a large flotilla of smaller boats. The highlight of the festivities was the premier of the opera *Aïda,* written by the Italian patriot and champion of Garibaldi, Giuseppe Verdi, for the occasion.

From Egypt the Crown Prince returned to Europe, stopping in the south of France to pick up Vicky. Partly because of the expense, but mostly because she did not want to leave her children alone for over two months, Vicky had not accompanied her husband but had taken Willy and Henry to Cannes for their health.

IT HAD BEEN A PLEASANT two months for the Crown Princess. She was joined by Alice, whose husband, Prince Louis of Hesse, traveled with Fritz. Due to the exigencies of war, the sisters had not been together for four years, and Alice's last visit, coming in the middle of the Berlin social season, had not given them much time alone. They stayed at the Grand Hotel with rooms overlooking the sea, while Vicky's sons occupied a separate villa with their attendants.

Both young women needed a vacation—Vicky from the rigors of life as handmaiden to Queen Augusta, Alice from chronic rheumatism, neuralgia, and a sense of being economically deprived. The contrast in the sisters' lives had increased with the years. Vicky now traveled with twenty-five in her suite; Alice had four, including her lady-in-waiting and a baby nurse. Yet they enjoyed each other's company enormously and discovered certain interests in common— subjects that caused their mother intense embarrassment and displeasure.

One of these was religion. Alice was going through a crisis of faith, based on the teachings of a man who challenged the Bible as history, and Vicky was enough of a Darwinist not to damn Alice for asking difficult questions. Another forbidden topic was human anatomy. Alice, who had nursed her father during his fatal illness and cared for soldiers in the hospitals during the wars, was fascinated by the human body. Vicky never ventured onto the subject of anatomy with "dearest Mama," but both girls had wasted countless words defending their "awful and disgusting" preference for nursing their own children. "[I]t does make my hair stand on end to think that <u>my</u> 2 daughters should turn into *des vaches* [cows]," the Queen said.

Vicky was both an intellectual stimulus and a practical help to Alice. As the wife of a minor German prince, Alice had very little money and very little hesitancy in asking their mother for help—a habit that annoyed the Queen. So it was Vicky who begged Victoria to give her sister the things she needed, such as a good doctor the following year for Alice's fifth confinement. Alice had incurred Victoria's wrath when she opposed Helena's marriage to Christian, and ever since, the Queen seemed to find more fault with her than with any of her other children.

The Crown Princess was proud of her younger sister, especially her good looks, and though occasionally jealous, she rarely allowed it to color their relationship. Vicky was convinced that Alice was a beauty and had sent her mother a picture of the two of them taken with their babies in the fall of 1864 with the comment, "the ugly sister & the pretty one (the 1st of course myself)." Her father-in-law's clear preference for Alice only underscored Vicky's embarrassment about her plainness. He was, she said, never "so amiably disposed" toward her as when her prettier sister was around. "[H]e thinks me ugly and a bore and therefore I have not the same influence with him as she has," she told their mother.

FRITZ AND LOUIS ARRIVED back in Cannes in time for Christmas, and the next day, Fritz and Vicky left together for Paris. There, they were welcomed affectionately by Napoleon III and Eugénie. Vicky thought they both looked "very well." More objective observers said that the Emperor seemed old, ill, and depressed.

By 1870 there had been a marked shift to the left in French political life. Republicanism, radicalism, and trade unionism were ascendant, and Napoleon III had been forced into sweeping domestic constitutional reforms. He was no better off in the area of foreign affairs, where the new North German Confederation had left France—considered predominant in Europe for over three-quarters of a century—a declining power. In trying to get territorial compensations in Belgium, Luxembourg, and on the left bank of the Rhine, Napoleon had been continually outwitted by Bismarck, who had made a fool of their Emperor before the French people.

During the three years following the Austro-Prussian War, there was a general feeling throughout Europe that war between France and Prussia was inevitable. Because of this, Napoleon had attempted to secure written alliances with Italy and Austria, but his efforts had foundered—in the first case over Italy's insistence that France withdraw her troops from Rome, and in the second over Austria's hesitancy to commit itself to nearly certain war, particularly when neutrality might elicit more profit. Nevertheless, Napoleon and his ministers believed that in the event of a war against Prussia, both Italy and Austria would fight on the side of France. It was a dangerous miscalculation.

Napoleon III had another problem when he contemplated a fight against Prussia. France prided herself on a small army of professional soldiers, an elite and complacent corps, jealous of its prerogatives. Having never considered Prussia a worrisome military power before, the French military ascribed the Prussians' victory over the Austrians to the use of breech-loading guns. If they were to purchase the same weapons, they would regain the military superiority they had enjoyed since the days of the first Napoleon.

Napoleon III did not subscribe to that theory. The Prussian army was much larger (1.2 million men to 288,000 French in 1866), more easily mobilized, and more efficiently supplied. But when the Emperor tried to strengthen French forces, he ran headlong into his own past sins: French liberals were afraid to enlarge the regular army, which had supported the coup that had brought him into power and forcibly kept him there; French conservatives balked at creating an army reserve of discontented citizens who might at any moment turn revolutionary. Although by 1870 Napoleon managed to increase the regular army to 500,000 and the reserves to 400,000, he had been able to do little to change basic military organization, which had yet to take into account the changes in warfare brought about by the industrial revolution.

The situation in Prussia was quite the reverse.

The results of Wilhelm's army reform had already delivered easy victories over both the Danes and the Austrians. Much of this success was due to the Prussian general staff, created by Fritz's old friend and aide-de-camp General Moltke. Dedicated to the continual improvement of the craft of warfare, Moltke's general staff analyzed the advantages of the new railway system and the telegraph, synchronizing shipments of men and arms so that large concentrations of soldiers could be swiftly gathered for major battles and efficiently dispersed for minor skirmishes. A special line-of-communications department was charged with the task of making sure that supply trains did not languish unloaded or clog the railway lines—a problem that plagued all armies of the day and caused as many defeats as mistakes on the battlefield.

The father of the modern staff system and nerve center of this newly reformed Prussian army, Helmuth von Moltke, was now its Commander-in-Chief. Tall, lean, and bald, the Field Marshal wore a wig not for vanity but to keep from catching cold. Known in military histories as a "commander of genius," he combined strategic vision with attention to detail. Convinced of the inevitability of war with France, Moltke had twice urged Bismarck to attack France—at the end of the Austro-Prussian War and during the Luxembourg crisis—both times when he knew Prussia had the military advantage. Frustrated with Bismarck's delays, he spent the years between 1866 and 1870 perfecting plans of attack, and by 1870, every unit of both the regular Prussian army and the reserves was prepared to spring into action.

Moltke was no more anxious for a showdown with France than Bismarck, who was only waiting for the most propitious moment to bring it about. Although the Austro-Prussian War had reduced France's weight on the European scales, it had not increased Prussia's sufficiently for the nationalists, the militarists, or the Prussian Chancellor. Ever since the Austrian peace, Bismarck had tried to attract the states of southern Germany to the North German Confederation, but nothing broke down south German suspicions and antipathies toward Prussia. "We don't want to be Prussian," Bavarian conscripts shouted at their officers, indicating that their enforced military alliance with Prussia was neither popular nor likely to forge a spontaneous union between north and south. As 1870 approached, it had become increasingly clear to Bismarck that nothing short of a common enemy on the battlefield would unite the states of Germany.

THIS WAS THE SITUATION when the Prussian Crown Prince and Princess arrived in Paris from Cannes in December of 1869. Their "very kind and civil" welcome by Napoleon III was an ironic prelude to the future. Within six months, Prussia and France would be at war—the struggle for military and political supremacy in western Europe on which Bismarck had been counting for some time. If the still disunited German states were the most backward politically of all the great nations, they were militarily the most precocious. It was this dichotomy that their Chancellor, the nimble master of pragmatic politics, finally chose to exploit as the last available means to German unification. In this struggle, neither Napoleon III nor his country were adequate rivals for Bismarck's cunning and Prussia's new army, called by historians "a military wonder of the world."

CHAPTER
THIRTY-ONE

"Hatred of the foreigner is the best possible cement for a divided nation."

OTTO PFLANZE

*I*F THE UNDERLYING CAUSE of the Franco-Prussian War was the rivalry between France and Prussia for preeminence in western Europe, the immediate excuse was a candidate from the House of Hohenzollern for the throne of Spain. Ignited by Bismarck and fanned by the French, this issue erupted into a conflagration that united the German states against a common enemy and transferred the dominant military power and political prestige in Europe from France to Germany. It is a story that verges on tragic farce—the tragedy being the sacrifice of innocent lives, and the farce the outrageous charade put on by the men who wanted the war.

IN 1868, SPANISH LIBERALS revolted against Queen Isabella II, deposed her, and set about looking for someone to take her place. Isabella's personal life had been as fraught with discord as her political one.* Married to a man who, she claimed, wore more lace than she did on their wedding night, the Queen of Spain had sought solace in food and lovers, growing monstrously fat and wildly indiscreet. When she elevated her newest paramour, the son of a cook and an actor by profession, to the post of Minister of State, she was forcefully relieved of her throne.

Vicky was "shocked" by Isabella's "depravation and vice," but attributed her poor governance to a lack of education. Royalties of the period were apt to rationalize the bad behavior of their peers, and neither Vicky nor Queen Victoria was an exception. "The poor Queen of Spain is a most unfortunate woman," the Queen wrote her eldest daughter. "Every excuse must be made for her private conduct—on account of her <u>cruel</u> marriage. But her misgovernment is to me incredible."

---

* *The elder child of Ferdinand VII of Bourbon, Isabella had inherited the throne at the age of three. Serving under a series of regents, she had survived a bid by her uncle for the throne, numerous insurrections, and a series of dictatorial premiers before fleeing to France at the age of thirty-eight.*

In 1869, the year after Isabella fled Spain, an emissary from the Spanish provisional government arrived in Germany to sound out Prince Leopold of Hohenzollern-Sigmaringen, a distant cousin of King Wilhelm of Prussia, on the possibility of accepting the Spanish throne.

Leopold was the eldest son of Wilhelm's first Prime Minister, Charles Anton Hohenzollern. A remarkably good-looking man, the thirty-four-year-old seemed admirably suited to the job. He was Catholic; his wife was a Princess of the Portuguese royal family; he had already fathered three sons; and he was related not only to the Prussian royal house but also to Napoleon III. There was one minor obstacle: Leopold did not want the job.

Leopold's life as the eldest son and future head of the House of Hohenzollern-Sigmaringen, the southern branch of the Hohenzollern dynasty, was an extremely pleasant one, full of predictable feudal pleasures. Although his father had relinquished his line's sovereignty to the ruling branch of the Hohenzollern family during the Revolution of 1848, the Hohenzollern-Sigmaringens still lived as petty monarchs at home and members of the royal family when they were in Berlin. The tranquillity of their turreted old castle of Sigmaringen by the still waters at the mouth of the Danube must have seemed very appealing to Leopold when contrasted with the turbulence of a Latin country in monarchical uproar. Leopold was not alone in his reluctance to move to Spain. Four other princes—Portuguese, Italian, French, and Spanish—had also declined what was considered to be one of the most unstable thrones in Europe.

If Prince Leopold was not anxious for greater glory, his father was. Charles Anton, who had recently dispatched Leopold's younger brother Charles to rule over the precarious kingdom of Romania, was seriously tempted by the Spanish offer. But like most Hohenzollerns, Charles Anton prided himself on living by old-fashioned rules; he had sworn allegiance to the King of Prussia, and Wilhelm's word, right or wrong, was his law. In February of 1870, when the Spanish formally offered the throne to his son, his only stipulation was that Leopold must obtain the approval of the King. When queried, Wilhelm declared himself "utterly against the affair."

Bismarck, who had conferred with Charles Anton, was not. Although he denied his role in this drama, the Prussian Chancellor had already started negotiating behind the scenes to promote Leopold's candidacy. Delighted by anything that would discomfit Napoleon III, he had sent two of his agents to Madrid to advance the Hohenzollern candidature with Marshall Prim, President of the Spanish Council of Ministers.

Bismarck also tackled Wilhelm. It was in "Germany's political interest," he insisted, "that the House of Hohenzollern should gain an esteem and an exalted position in the world such as does not find its analogy in the past record of the Habsburgs since Charles V."* Except for the obvious advantage to be gained if

* *Charles V, the sixteenth-century Holy Roman Emperor and King of Spain, whose colossal empire encompassed Germany, Austria, Hungary, Bohemia, Spain, Sicily, Naples, the Netherlands, and much of the New World.*

Napoleon III had to maintain troops to guard the Spanish-French frontier, Bismarck's arguments were a blatant appeal to Hohenzollern pride.

But Wilhelm dismissed Bismarck's reasons out of hand, contending that only a fool would believe that a Spanish monarch could count on Spanish soldiers for protection, as Bismarck claimed. "Reliable support from an army which has made all the revolutions for the last forty years is hardly to be expected!" Wilhelm insisted. The combined forces of his Chancellor, Minister of War, Chief of Staff, and Minister of the Interior were not enough to change the King's mind, and Wilhelm refused to sanction the operation unless Leopold himself felt bound to accept the throne. For once in his life, Fritz agreed with his father.

Shortly after this conversation, Bismarck fell ill with jaundice and retired to his home at Varzin. He was there for over a month. When he returned to Berlin in late April of 1870, his emissaries had been recalled by the King, and a telegram of refusal had been sent to Madrid. "Bismarck is unwell again but nothing serious," Vicky wrote Victoria on April 26, 1870. She had written her mother six weeks earlier on behalf of Fritz and his father, asking Victoria's views on this "most profoundly secret" subject—an opinion the Queen's Foreign Secretary told her she had no business expressing. Nevertheless, Vicky knew how her mother felt. "You will be glad to hear that all thoughts about Spain are entirely given up," she said.

But Vicky was mistaken. On the advice of Bismarck's agents, the Spanish Prime Minister had ignored the telegram of refusal and was waiting for the Chancellor's return to Berlin. Meanwhile, Bismarck wrote Charles Anton saying he had "no doubt" that Germany had a "vital interest" in Spain and that during times of crisis "the pointer on the scales might well register differently," depending on who was sitting on the Spanish throne. "I have once more begged H.M. the King to reconsider the question in this light," he added, "and received the answer that as soon as any prince of the House of Hohenzollern showed any inclination to accept the crown he would raise no opposition whatsoever to this inclination."

This was, of course, a lie, but Charles Anton, eager to be convinced, ordered Leopold to accept the throne. Having set the project back into motion, Bismarck again took sick and removed himself in early June to Varzin, where he claimed he had no code book and no access to the Foreign Ministry—i.e., where no one could trace his hand in what he later referred to as a private "family" matter of the Hohenzollerns. "It is possible that we may see a passing fermentation in France . . . ," he explained to an underling; "undoubtedly they will cry 'intrigue,' they will be furious against me, but without finding any point of attack."

With Bismarck hiding in Varzin, his office continued to dispatch the telegrams and couriers necessary to bring the Spanish candidacy to an affirmative conclusion. On June 19, King Wilhelm, in Bad Ems for his summer cure, was handed a letter stating that Leopold of Hohenzollern was accepting the throne of Spain. He was not pleased, but, having said that the decision rested with the candidate, was forced to accede.

"I fear it is a sad mistake on the part of the Hohenzollerns . . . ," Vicky wrote Victoria in early July. "I cannot but regret their decision, not for Spain but for themselves and us." Vicky explained that her in-laws were having as little to do with the affair as possible, "dreading as we do that complications may arise for Prussia, as it is easy more or less to identify the Hohenzollerns with us—and with our government."

It is clear from Vicky's letter that neither she, Fritz, nor Wilhelm had any inkling of Bismarck's role in reviving Leopold's candidacy, and if the process had progressed according to Bismarck's plan, Leopold would have been settled on the Spanish throne before the French knew what had happened. But because of a mistake in Madrid, matters did not work out that way.

To become King of Spain, the candidate had to be approved by the Spanish Parliament. To this end, Prime Minister Prim had kept the delegates in session through the first three weeks of June while his representative, Don Salazar, negotiated with the Hohenzollerns. On June 21, Salazar wired that Leopold had accepted and that he himself would return to Madrid around June 26 with the confirming letter. But an error made by a clerk in decoding the wire put the date of Salazar's return at some two weeks later. Pressured to relieve the delegates working in the heat of the Madrid summer, Prim suspended parliament until November. He hoped to keep the identity of the new Spanish monarch from the French until then, but the news was all over Paris within a week.

The French were outraged, particularly when Bismarck's office disclaimed all responsibility, announcing that "so far as the Prussian Government is concerned the affair does not exist." Backed by Napoleon and Eugénie, the French Foreign Office protested that the right of the Spanish people to put whomever they wished on their throne did not include upsetting the balance of power in Europe to the detriment of France. In such a case, the French warned, "we would know how to fulfill our duty without hesitation and without weakness." Bismarck answered by calling on the Prussian press to stoke the fires of outrage at home. "The newspapers . . . ," he said, "must be very rough and as many of them as possible."

While Bismarck agitated for war, the Prussian royal family tried to maintain peace. "I think every thing ought to be avoided which might wound the susceptibility of the French nation . . . ," Vicky wrote Victoria in early July. "When General Prim originated the idea of Leopold Hohenzollern, nobody was more taken aback than the Hohenzollerns themselves who had never dreamt of such a thing. . . . Leopold Hohenzollern is an independent Prince, though he is a member of our family, but the Government has nothing to do with his decision. I fear the French will not understand this."

They certainly did not. The French Ambassador to Berlin, Count Benedetti, was assigned the unpleasant task of asking the King of Prussia to order Leopold to withdraw his candidacy—a demand Wilhelm refused, explaining that he could not do any more than acquiesce in his kinsman's decision. The King did, however, send an emissary to Sigmaringen to speak with Leopold's father. Besieged by his King, as well as Napoleon III of France, Queen Victoria of England, and King Leopold II of Belgium, Charles Anton finally withdrew his son's candidacy for the Spanish throne.

"[T]hank goodness there seems more chance of a good turn in affairs since we learn that Leopold Hohenzollern has resigned of his own accord—of course the best thing he could do under the circumstances," the Crown Princess wrote her mother on July 13. And for a brief moment, it did look as if war had been averted. It would have been, had Bismarck not stepped in.

On the same day that Charles Anton withdrew his son's candidacy, the Prussian Chancellor set out from Varzin for Berlin in order to stop the King's efforts at mediation. When he arrived and found out that Charles Anton had, in fact, already capitulated, he was furious. Only slightly less satisfied were the French, who labeled the withdrawal of Leopold's candidacy an "insufficient and almost derisory concession." On the grounds that they were entitled to a full-fledged apology, the French told Ambassador Benedetti to ask King Wilhelm for his personal guarantee that Leopold's candidacy would never be renewed.

The next day, July 13, 1870, while respectful onlookers stood watching, Benedetti waited on the promenade in the public gardens at Bad Ems for Wilhelm, who was out taking his daily stroll. With typical courtesy, the King raised his hat and congratulated the French Ambassador on the happy outcome of their mutual crisis. Benedetti, hoping to embarrass Prussia, pressed forward with the request from the French government for guarantees. Wilhelm refused. Some say they argued, some that they parted amicably, but in any case Wilhelm told one of his aides to wire Bismarck the gist of their conversation.

Back in Berlin, Bismarck had been busy contacting representatives of the other European countries, sounding them out as to their leanings in case of war between Prussia and France. The dispatch arrived from Ems while Bismarck was dining with Chief of Staff Moltke and Minister of War Roon. Bismarck asked Moltke if the army was prepared for war. Moltke replied that Prussia would be better off engaging France now before she had a chance to make any further military reforms.

With this assurance, Bismarck doctored the King's telegram, removing words to make it appear as if the French had issued a presumptuous and insulting demand. What started out as an informative dispatch from the King's aide to his Chancellor evolved under Bismarck's pen into an acrimonious rupture of diplomatic relations. When he had finished, Bismarck showed his handiwork to Moltke and Roon. "Yes," the generals agreed, "that will do."

A few hours later, a special edition of "the most faithful" of Bismarck's outlets, the *Norddeutsche Zeitung,* appeared on the streets of Berlin featuring the doctored dispatch. The effect was exactly what the Prussian Chancellor hoped. France erupted in indignation, and mobs poured into the streets of Paris shouting "Down with Prussia" and "To Berlin!" Labeling the "Ems Dispatch" a "slap in the face," the French Foreign Minister demanded war credits from the French Parliament.

Convinced by his Chancellor that the French were entirely responsible for the oncoming conflict, the King of Prussia returned to Berlin, where he delivered a stirring speech to the members of the North German Reichstag. Written by Bismarck, it was meant to solidify Germany by building up grievances against France. Until the nineteenth century, Wilhelm said, Germans had been forced to put up with foreign incursions on their soil and on their honor. The defeat of Napoleon I in 1813 had bound them more closely together. Now, over a half century later, they must again defend themselves in a struggle for "our freedom and our right against the brutality of foreign conquerors."

But the *causi belli* clearly lay elsewhere. In an astute and dispassionate letter, the British Foreign Secretary, Lord Granville, outlined the situation for Queen Victoria. Describing the week's diplomatic thrusts and parries as something out of a "feverish dream," Granville condemned both the French, whose language he termed "undiplomatic and unstatesmanlike," and Bismarck, who "must have known how distasteful" Leopold's candidacy would be. But even granted the secrecy of the negotiations and the discourtesy of the announcement, Granville contended, it was "inconceivable" that in a civilized world, "hundreds of thousands of Frenchmen should be hurled against like numbers of Germans, on a point limited to a matter of etiquette."

As was the case with all but the most intimate associates of Bismarck, the Crown Princess was kept in the dark about the Chancellor's machinations. Nearly a decade later, she would write Victoria that "Bismarck (who in my eyes is the most mischievous & dangerous person alive) did . . . not fan the flame— until of course there was no option left—& then of course he tried to animate his nation against the enemy." Members of the royal family were nevertheless prey to constant anxiety, since they would be blamed if things went badly for Prussia. The day that Bismarck received the dispatch from Ems, Vicky wrote her mother complaining of "violent headache" and an "hysterical feeling" in her throat. The "agitation, suspense and fear of these last few days have upset me terribly," she admitted.

Vicky's fragility can be explained partly by the fact that she had just given birth to her seventh child, a girl named Sophie. The confinement had taken place in Potsdam on June 14, a week or so before Leopold accepted the throne of Spain. Although Fritz tried to keep the developing crisis from his nursing wife, by the second week in July he felt he must tell her that events were taking "a serious turn."

The Crown Princess was thrown into panic. Much of her fear was based on the conviction, seemingly held everywhere except the innermost circles of the Prussian army, that the French army was indomitable. The enemy, Vicky wrote Victoria, "are well prepared and we not at all." They could not, she believed, "choose a better moment for themselves nor a worse one for us."

But on July 15, her husband learned differently. The Crown Prince joined Chancellor Bismarck, Minister of War General Roon, and Chief of Staff General Moltke on a journey to Brandenburg to see his father and request full mobilization. In conversations with Moltke, Fritz learned something of the overall strength of the Prussian army, "making our prospects," as he put it, "more favourable than has been supposed."

Returning to Berlin with his father, Fritz announced the mobilization of the troops to an excited public waiting on the station platform. The King and Crown Prince embraced for the onlookers, then drove off together along streets lined "shoulder to shoulder" with 100,000 cheering citizens. Back at the palace, Wilhelm had to come out to show himself "again and again" to the crowds. The next day, July 16, 1870, Fritz traveled to Potsdam to tell Vicky that the war was on.

"All hope is now at an end," Vicky wrote her mother,

and we have the horrible prospect of the most terrible war Europe has yet known before us, bringing desolation and ruin, perhaps annihilation! . . . We have been shamefully forced into this war. . . . Bernstorff [Prussian Ambassador in London] writes that Bertie had expressed his delight . . . that the Austrians were going to join the French and his hope that we should fare ill. This he is said to have loudly expressed at a dinner of the French Ambassador's. Perhaps it is exaggerated, but of course it is a story related everywhere.

Although the Prince of Wales issued a formal denial, the story was immediately seized on by the anti-English faction to prove that the Crown Princess's brother was allied with the enemy and that she, too, had French sympathies.

As a matter of fact, while France and Prussia were rushing to take up arms, the other countries of Europe were quietly withdrawing to protect their own interests. Assured by Bismarck that Prussia had no designs on Austria, Franz Joseph declared neutrality, and the members of the Italian cabinet refused to honor their King's commitment to France. It is said that Russia was lulled into passivity by Bismarck's assurance of acquiescence, should the Czar care to slide out of certain punitive clauses of the Crimean War treaty that neutralized the waters of the Black Sea.*

For her part, England wanted guarantees from France of nonaggression toward Belgium, which Napoleon III hastened to give. It was at this crucial juncture that Bismarck made public the secret treaty draft Benedetti had foolishly left with him four years before, offering Prussia a free hand in unifying Germany in exchange for Belgium.† Not only did Bismarck release this document, but he tried to give the impression that the draft was a recent one and

---

* This promise came back to haunt Bismarck in the middle of the Franco-Prussian War when Russia repudiated these clauses. England and Austria threatened to get involved in the war, and Bismarck had to call a conference in London to revoke them, thereby preserving the inviolability of treaties, Russian pride, and his own free hand in arranging the peace.

† See Chapter 27.

that only Prussia's refusal had saved Belgium from being taken over by the French. Queen Victoria asked Vicky if what Napoleon said were true, i.e., that the suggestion to take Belgium had originated not with him, but with Bismarck. "I don't trust him [Bismarck] _ever_," the Queen told her daughter. Nevertheless, the English declared their neutrality.

This did not satisfy Bismarck, who now told the Prussians that England could have and should have prevented war. He complained to the British Ambassador that Great Britain ought to have "forbidden France" to declare war. "She was in a position to do so," he said, "and her interests and those of Europe demanded it of her." In this way, the Prussian Chancellor set in motion one of his favorite games—shifting the responsibility for his actions onto someone else. The success of this scenario can be measured by the fact that the Europeans blamed the French for declaring war, and the Prussians blamed the English for not stopping her.

"The feeling is very general here that England would have had it in her power to prevent this awful war," she wrote her mother, "had she in concert with Russia, Austria, and Italy declared she would take arms against the agressor [sic], and that her neutrality afforded France advantages and no disadvantages." Her father-in-law, Vicky told Victoria, was "frantic" over reports that the English continued to sell France horses for their cavalry, coal for their ships, and cartridges for their guns. "People . . . say that England sides with the French against us, and has interpreted her neutrality to the exclusive benefit of France. . . . One hears nothing but the bitterest complaints of England's partiality." Because of this, Vicky wrote a few days later, she was being "looked on with suspicious eyes."

Bismarck was in his element. Looking "clear and healthy," better than at any time since the Austro-Prussian War, the Chancellor told Colonel Walker, the British Military Attaché, who complimented him on his recently improved health, "Now the uncertainty is off my mind I have no care, and am perfectly well again." To which Walker added, "I don't believe he ever was really ill."

With two German sons-in-law (Crown Prince Friedrich Wilhelm of Prussia and Prince Louis of Hesse) and a German brother-in-law (Duke Ernest of Coburg) in the war, the Queen of England now came down firmly on the side of Prussia. Unable to influence her government to follow her lead, she took consolation in writing Vicky. "Words are far too weak to say _all_ I _feel_ for you or what I _think_ of my neighbours!! We must be neutral _as_ _long as_ we can, but _no one_ here conceals their opinion as to the _extreme iniquity_ of the _war_, and the _unjustifiable_ conduct of the French! Still _more publicly we cannot_ say; but the feeling of the people & country here _is all with you_, which it was not _before_. And need I say what _I_* _feel_?"

WHILE VICKY RECUPERATED from Sophie's birth in Potsdam, Fritz spent most of the time in Berlin, refining war plans with his father, Roon, Moltke, and

---

* _Underlined three times in original._

Bismarck. During their first council of war, the subject of his cousin Fritz Carl was raised. "[N]o one would speak right out when the question came up as to . . . his appointment to a high command," Fritz noted in his diary, "until His Majesty in some excitement insisted on an expression of opinion, and then all were unanimous that the Prince should lead the Army (the IInd Army as it is entitled) which the King would accompany and so be on the spot to exercise special control."

While Fritz Carl was offered the glory, the Crown Prince received the most difficult assignment. In the Austro-Prussian War, he had been given hostile Poles to command. Now his Third Army included soldiers from Bavaria, Württemberg, and Baden, men who spoke more than ten different dialects and resented the Prussians. "In many ways I deplore the fact that it has fallen to my lot to command the South Germans," he confided to his diary, expressing his concern that the southerners were "ill disposed towards us" and "quite untrained in our school." The best he would be able to do with them, he reasoned, was to maintain them as a "reserve force"—hardly an attractive prospect for an ambitious soldier.

"It is a dreadful position for him . . . ," Vicky wrote Queen Victoria, "but . . . the King and the generals could entrust this most difficult task to no one but Fritz!" The British Attaché agreed, commenting that Fritz's was the "hardest" assignment, "but one that no other man could so well fulfill."

The First Army was under the command of the seventy-four-year-old General Steinmetz, the last fighting veteran of the campaign against Napoleon I (1813–14) and strategist for Fritz's crucial victory at Nachod (1866), which had laid the stage for Königgrätz. Before the campaign, Colonel Walker, who was again attached to Fritz's headquarters, asked Steinmetz his opinion of the Crown Prince. "He described H.R.H. as I know him," said Walker, "cool, thoughtful, considerate of the opinions of others, ready to give them free hand in the first instance and full credit afterwards, without a spark of jealousy. A noble fellow, and a future blessing to his country. 'Thank God [said Steinmetz] that I shall close my eyes with the feeling that the country will one day be safe in such hands.' "

HAVING AGREED with Vicky that saying good-bye would be too painful, Fritz slipped out of the Neues Palais at dawn on the morning of July 26 before she awoke. She had sat up very late the night before waiting for his return from Berlin, but, still weakened from childbirth, had fallen asleep before he came back. Next morning she found a note saying that he was on his way to the front and wanted to spare them both a difficult parting. "The thought was so kind," she wrote her mother, "and yet now I feel as if my heart would break—he is gone, without a kiss or a word of farewell, & I do not know whether I shall ever see him again!"

CHAPTER
THIRTY-TWO

"All the French should be shot and stabbed to death, down to the little babies."

JOHANNA VON BISMARCK

*T*HE MOST SURPRISING THING about the Franco-Prussian War—to everyone outside the Prussian high command—was that when it finally came to pass, the victor was determined within the first thirty days of fighting.

Napoleon III's disordered troops provided little competition for the clockwork precision of the Prussian armies. With full mobilization completed in just sixteen days, the Prussians surged over the French border into Alsace in early August, outfought the French in three places, bottled up the main part of their army at Metz in Lorraine, and roundly defeated what was left at the decisive Battle of Sedan on September 1. After that, the Prussians took up positions around Paris, to which they laid siege for over four months. But by then, the war was essentially over.

Of the five decisive battles of the Franco-Prussian War,* the Crown Prince's oddly assorted Third Army won the first two and was a deciding factor at the last.

When he had first arrived in southern Germany, however, Fritz was distressed at the awkwardness of the young and overweight Bavarian soldiers. He was not alone. "I never saw such a dawdling sloppy people in my life," said Colonel Walker. "Their clothes look as if they belonged to some one else . . . and they march as if they had peas in their shoes." Pleasantly surprised by the enthusiasm of his reception, Fritz was amused at twenty-five-year-old King Ludwig of Bavaria, who asked him whether it was "still customary in the Prussian Army for every soldier to take his doxy [whore] on service with him!"

Starting out from the town of Speyer, in the western part of Germany, Fritz moved his army into Alsace, engaging the enemy for the first clash of the war at the border town of Weissenburg, a French fortress on the banks of the Lauter River northeast of Strasbourg. Utilizing both Bavarian and Prussian soldiers to launch a two-pronged advance, Fritz quickly overwhelmed the French. The attack was, according to Colonel Walker, "a brilliantly conducted

---

* *Weissenburg, Wörth, Saarbrücken, Metz, and Sedan.*

affair. . . . I . . . have never seen anything more perfect than the Prussian advance to take the heights." It was the first Prussian victory over France in over half a century. "God be praised . . . ," the Crown Prince wrote when it was over; "our men's confidence is already much enhanced."

Two days later, now well within French territory, the Crown Prince and his men gained another major victory, at Wörth. Fritz had expected to be able to give his soldiers a two-day rest between battles, but when the enemy began shooting, he engaged them immediately, remarking "almost nonchalantly" that he was prepared to send every last man to secure the heights. By dusk, the French had been completely routed. The Crown Prince made his traditional appearance on the battlefield to console the wounded and thank his soldiers. "It is impossible to realize the enthusiasm and joyful excitement of the troops at the sight of their beloved commander," said his Chief of Staff, Blumenthal, "and from this day forward he was called Unser Fritz* everywhere."

More than nine thousand Frenchmen were taken prisoner in the Battle of Wörth, and over ten thousand Germans and eleven thousand Frenchmen were killed or wounded. Even for one familiar with battlefields, it was a horrifying scene. "I detest this butchery," the Crown Prince told Gustav Freytag, a writer attached to his headquarters. "I have never striven for military honours; I should have left such glory without envy to any other, and it has become my fate to be led out of one war into another, from one battlefield to another, and to wade in human blood before I mount the throne of my forefathers. That is a hard lot."

His Chief of Staff felt differently: "In a few days the Prince had become the idol of his army. Assurance and unconditional mutual confidence inspired as with an electric spark the army which had just been formed from the most varied elements, and henceforward no task seemed too difficult for it."

"The Crown Prince is by no means inclined to treat the South Germans with undue graciousness, as if he was anxious to ingratiate himself with them," said one of the Bavarian officers under Fritz's command.

> On the contrary, he has expected the utmost from them, and has not spared their commanders with his criticisms. But it is just this calm demeanour and spirit of justice that won our complete confidence. . . . it is to him above all others that we owe the brotherly comradeship among the troops, and that the Bavarian like to walk arm-in-arm with the Prussian. . . . Even the privates are devoted to him body and soul; he does not speak to them "condescendingly" or "graciously," but with . . . obvious personal interest and good-fellowship.

"Pray say, if you are asked," Colonel Walker wrote home, "that the gallantry of the French has been as great as can be conceived, but they have always been out-manoeuvred, and both on the 4th [Weissenburg] and 6th [Wörth] completely outflanked by the skilful leading of the Crown Prince."

* *Our Fritz. Frederick the Great was called Old Fritz.*

"The Battle of Wörth was a tremendous one . . . ," Vicky wrote pridefully to her mother.

I was thankful that dear Fritz was the victor. I know how harrowing and dreadful war is to him. . . . on the other hand I know that he is considered our best leader, and more thought of than Fritz Carl or Steinmetz! . . . that it was not thought necessary to give him the best officers on his staff whereas they were kept for Fritz Carl, so great was the confidence on the part of Moltke & the King in Fritz's genius. He is always quiet & self possessed & determined, having no personal ambition he only thinks of what is best, not of what makes most effect.

That was the trouble. The combination of Fritz's self-effacement and Bismarck's determination to keep his political foe from becoming a war hero robbed the Crown Prince of the military reputation he deserved. It was his cousin Fritz Carl, overbearing in person if unsure on the battlefield, who snagged the laurels due the Crown Prince. According to General Alfred von Waldersee,* who served on the general staff during the Franco-Prussian War, Fritz Carl was a man of "slow understanding" who made up in dogged memorization of military history what he lacked in intellect. Determined to succeed in his chosen career, he was hampered by being a "nervous horseman" and a timorous strategist. Primarily known for "great prudence," Fritz Carl was, in Waldersee's words, "a fortunate, rather than a great, military leader."

This fortune was helped along by Bismarck. While the British Military Commissioner complained about Fritz Carl's "horrid blunder" in sending "an inferior force" to attack the fortress of Metz, and military historians point to his "headstrong conduct" during the early part of the war, the Bismarck press hailed him as a *"Bayard sans peur et sans reproche,"*† after two minor victories. These papers, of course, said little or nothing about Vicky's husband. Even the French soldiers, beaten at Wörth by the Crown Prince, asked him at the end of the battle, "Are you Prince Charles [Fritz Carl]?"

Although Fritz answered with humor, he was hurt. "I see plainly enough how at home the old, familiar game is again being played of mentioning my name as seldom as possible, and always giving merely the number of the armies instead," he wrote in his diary after one of his major victories. "Other commanders of high rank are invariably indicated by name, which after all is the shortest way, but one that in my case appears to be intentionally avoided."

It was not only Bismarck but the King who downplayed his son's military prowess. Angry at his politics and jealous of the adoration of his troops, Wilhelm, whose entire life had been devoted to the army, could not accept the fact that Fritz, trained by his mother in liberal ways, rivaled his father's prowess in

* *Later Field Marshal; he became chief of the general staff after Moltke.*

† *The French knight Pierre Terrail Bayard (1473–1524) was known as the knight "without fear and without reproach."*

battle. Professor Hans Delbrück, a historian of the day and a tutor in the royal house, confirms what he calls Wilhelm's "monarchical jealousy" of his son. According to Delbrück, Fritz was only too aware that this jealousy kept him from being appointed Commander-in-Chief of the army.

After Wörth, the Crown Prince was given the choice of taking his army straight to Paris or north to help a newly formed Fourth Army under the Crown Prince of Saxony cut off the forces of the French general, MacMahon. Fritz chose the second alternative, and, after fourteen hours in the saddle, arrived in time to take "a prominent part" in the decisive battle of the war at Sedan.

Fritz's Third Army reached Sedan on August 31. Located just north of the province of Champagne, Sedan was then a small town on the River Meuse with a tiny seventeenth-century fortress. It was protected to the south and west by the river valley and to the north by hills sloping upward. MacMahon had chosen it as a place to reorganize his troops after having failed to reach the army of General Bazaine, under siege at Metz.

At 4:00 A.M. the day after his arrival, the Crown Prince set out to find the enemy. Hidden by a dense fog, he gained a position at the top of a hill, where he remained throughout the ensuing battle, frustrated by orders that prevented him from joining his men on the field below. By noon it became apparent that the bulk of the French army, attacked in both the front and the rear, would be forced to yield to the Prussians. "[E]verywhere we saw men of all arms bolting headlong for Sedan," the Crown Prince wrote in his diary; "each quarter of an hour increased the number of the fugitives, who in ever denser masses crowded into the steep sunk-ways leading up to the fortress . . . as they realized that not a chance was left them now to avoid being taken prisoners."

"I saw half a French regiment of hussars swept away as a mower cuts down grass," said Colonel Walker. "Never was so complete a victory since war invaded the peaceful earth." It was, according to Blumenthal, Fritz's decision to move his Third Army to Sedan "which alone had rendered so magnificent a result possible."

The result was even more magnificent than anyone dreamed. Within the fortress where French soldiers were raising white flags was the Emperor Napoleon III himself, who had joined MacMahon and was now a prisoner of war. A few hours later his formal surrender arrived in the form of a note to King Wilhelm:

> My dear brother,
> Not having been able to die in the midst of my troops, it only remains to me to surrender my sword into Your Majesty's hands. I am, Your Majesty's good brother,
>
> Napoleon

Wilhelm and Fritz "threw" themselves "into each other's arms," and Fritz congratulated Moltke and his own Chief of Staff, Blumenthal. It was to them, he said, that "our Army owes an enduring debt of gratitude." When the King tried to present his son with the Iron Cross, Fritz refused to take it unless he decorated Blumenthal in the same manner.

Although the German papers virtually ignored the decisive role of the Crown Prince in the victory of Sedan, the King promoted his son to the rank of field marshal on the spot. He did the same for Fritz Carl. This rank had never before been conferred on a prince of the House of Hohenzollern—a break with tradition that disturbed Fritz, although he said he was pleased that his "gallant Army should see in this promotion . . . a token of recognition of their exploits." Fritz Carl, whose comment on hearing of his promotion was "At last," immediately assumed the title "the Prince Field-Marshal," thus implying that he was the sole bearer of this distinction.

At Fritz's suggestion, Wilhelm met Napoleon III at the country house of Bellevue, thus saving the French Emperor "the humiliation" of surrendering his sword in public. During the private ceremony, Wilhelm praised the French for their bravery. Napoleon agreed, but added that his soldiers "lacked the discipline that so highly distinguished" the Prussian troops.

When Napoleon saw the Crown Prince, he thanked the son for the kindness of the father with tears running down his face. "I cannot deny that at this moment I pitied the Emperor and was grieved to think how swift was the punishment that had overtaken him for his insane arrogance," Fritz wrote in his diary, remarking as they rode away at how the "glittering new uniforms" of the French "formed a strange contrast with ours, worn threadbare in war service."

The Crown Prince of Prussia gave vent to his own brand of reverse snobbism. He had raised an eyebrow at the paraphernalia of war left behind by fleeing French officers—gourmet delicacies, toilet articles, and women's clothing—and was similarly surprised by the line of imperial carriages and wagons drawn up in front of Bellevue. The members of the defeated Emperor's household, he noted in his diary, were still dressed in "rich liveries"; even the postilions, who rode outside the carriages, were decked out "in gala dress and powder as if for a pleasure trip to the Longjumeau racecourse."

Vicky's comments on Napoleon III concurred with those of her husband. "Poor Emperor—his career has ended and he brought his fall upon himself. . . . ," Vicky wrote Victoria after Sedan. "He has done the best thing he could for himself under the circumstances. . . . he has of his own free-will surrendered to his equal, which is not so humiliating as being driven from throne and country by an infuriated populace. Such a downfall is a melancholy thing, but it is meant to teach deep lessons. May <u>we</u> <u>all</u> learn what frivolity, conceit and immorality lead to!"

Queen Victoria drew even harsher conclusions from the Battle of Sedan. The fall of Napoleon III, she said, seemed like a "judgment from heaven" and the collapse of the French army, "a just retribution on a very guilty government and a very frivolous vain-glorious people." It was, she told Vicky, "the fulfillment of beloved Papa's most earnest wishes!"

It was, of course, Prince Albert who had taught his family that discipline was the basic requirement of kingship and that other accoutrements—ostentatious courts, frivolous pleasures, flattery of the monarch—led to disaster. These fripperies, developed to a fine degree and practiced by French dynasties from Bourbons to Bonapartes, had surely brought on the reckoning they were witnessing but that "dearest Papa" had not lived to see.

"It is a great satisfaction to me to see how Prussian character, discipline, habits, etc., is now appreciated and seen in its true light, its superiority acknowledged with pleasure and pride . . . ," Vicky wrote Victoria. "Gay and charming Paris! What mischief that very court and still more that very attractive Paris has done to English society . . . what harm to our 2 eldest brothers [Bertie and Affie]—and to the young and brilliant aristocracy of London! . . . Our poverty, our dull towns, our plodding, hardworking, serious life has made us strong & determined—is wholesome for us. I should grieve were we to imitate Paris and be so taken up with pleasure that no time was left for self-examination & serious thought."

One can imagine the amount of teasing the Prussian Crown Princess had endured from Bertie and Affie over the years to produce such priggish nonsense. The Queen of England answered her daughter in the same spirit of moral rectitude:

"Your 2 elder brothers unfortunately were carried away by that horrid Paris, beautiful though you may think it, & that frivolous & immoral court did frightful harm to English Society (that Papa knew & saw) & was very bad for Bertie & Affie. The fearful extravagance & luxury, the utter want of seriousness & principle in everything—the many crimes in France all showed a rottenness which was sure to crumble & fall."

In spite of their clucking, both ladies were moved by the plight of their old friend Eugénie. The Empress, who had taken over as Regent while her husband was in battle, had tried to exhort the nation to superhuman deeds of courage and valor. But on hearing of the French defeat at Sedan and the Emperor's captivity, the Parisians revolted and proclaimed a republic on September 4, 1870. With the city in chaos, Eugénie barely escaped from the Tuileries, and like her predecessor, Louis Philippe, fled to England. Victoria told Vicky that she had sent the former Empress a message of consolation. Although she knew that her Prussian enemies would probably use her mother's actions against her, Vicky wrote back that Victoria was "so right" to do it.

"What else can one have but pity and sympathy for her [Eugénie] in her misfortune," Vicky said.

She whose grace and beauty, charitableness & kindness of heart ought to have endeared her to the French . . . has been cast aside as one would an old and useless garment. . . . I fear the French are so fickle, corrupt & ignorant, so conceited and foolish that it is hopeless to think of their being sensibly governed. . . . as for a constitution or a parliament or real solid liberty they do not even understand what it means, and this republic seems as wretched a thing as can be imagined. I fear they are incurable as a nation though so charming as individuals.

This could have been written by Prince Albert.

THE "INCURABLE" NATION, however, surprised the German victors. By mid-September, with the Emperor in captivity, the Empress in flight, the Crown Prince of Prussia on the march to Paris, and Strasbourg and Metz under siege, the French people refused to recognize defeat. The new government called for recruits from the provinces, and guerrilla partisans, called *francs-tireurs,* sprang up behind German lines, prowling through the villages, sniping at soldiers, and taking prisoners of their own. This led to swift reprisals. If the shots could be traced to a particular home, the owner was often flogged. Towns suspected of harboring partisans were forced to pay heavy fines; to guarantee the payments, hostages were taken. In the worst cases, whole villages were sacked and burned, like the town of Châteaudun, which had housed some seven thousand people.

Frustrated by French resistance, Bismarck complained that the French were not being made to "feel" the impact of the occupation. The Chancellor resented the fact that Prussian generals often refused to make war against noncombatants and was furious when soldiers or guerrillas were taken prisoner instead of being shot, complaining that they only added to the burden of occupation. On being told of sixteen hundred new prisoners of war taken in a battle on the Loire River, he said he would have been "better pleased, if they had all been corpses." As for African soldiers, like the Zouaves and Chasseurs d'Afrique from the French colonies, he considered them subhuman. "If I had my way," he said, "every soldier who made a black man prisoner should be placed under arrest. They are beasts of prey, and ought to be shot down."

The Crown Prince thought differently. "Germany is at war with the Emperor of the French, not with the French people," he told the residents of Nancy. "The population need fear no hostile measures—I trust that business and trade will revive, and that the authorities will remain at their posts." Fritz, who reached Versailles on September 20 and took up the command of the siege of Paris, disapproved of Bismarck's attitude toward French civilians who came out of the city walls to dig for potatoes in the fields. With French infantry concealed in the trenches, the potato diggers (including men dressed as women) approached the Prussian outposts, begging the soldiers to allow them to forage. "Naturally our fellows find themselves in a painful fix," said the Crown Prince, "as it is impossible under such circumstances to fire either on the defenceless wretches or on the marksmen lying in ambush behind them."

Fritz's gallantry did not go unappreciated by the French. "The Crown Prince has left the memory of countless traits of kindness and humanity in the land that he fought against . . . ," one French journalist wrote. "When he was present, no excess remained unpunished. . . . No human life was uselessly or lightly sacrificed, and no oppression was permitted. . . . Versailles owes to him in great measure the order observed during the period of occupation."

On October 5, the King joined the Crown Prince at Versailles. He was accompanied by Bismarck, Moltke, and Roon, as well as various courtiers who disgusted Fritz with their quantities of luggage. Wilhelm's reader arrived in his own carriage, as did Police Commissioner Stieber, anxious to dig up plots against the King. Fritz's uncles Prince Charles and Prince Albrecht came to give advice. There was also Augusta's brother, the Grand Duke of Saxe-Weimar, and Prince Ludwig of Bavaria.

At Versailles, the King followed the same schedule as in Berlin. Huge dinners were served at 4:00 P.M., followed by tea in the evening at nine o'clock in the company of all the military personnel and whatever princes had attached themselves to the royal headquarters. Wilhelm was nonetheless bored, and the high point of his day occurred at 11:00 P.M., when the generals appeared for the nightly war council. Moltke laid out every detail soberly and quietly, while Roon spat "copiously" and shrugged his shoulders if anything sounded strange to him—a "pantomime" that Fritz found impressed his father more than "Moltke's admirable clarity."

As the siege of Paris dragged on, the differences between Bismarck and Moltke became a serious problem. The Chancellor believed that the army was there to serve political ends, and he expected the military to submit willingly to his decisions and timetables. Moltke and his subordinates retaliated by excluding the Chancellor from their nightly war councils, thus frustrating his efforts to find a way to end the fighting.

With the continuation of French resistance, Bismarck had the additional problem of finding a responsible government that could negotiate the peace. In his usual fashion, the Prussian Chancellor kept all his options open, dangling the possibility before Napoleon and Eugénie of returning to power in exchange for suitable secessions of territory. Like everyone else at Prussian headquarters, Bismarck knew that the French, especially the upper classes, were far more frightened of the republic within the city than the German armies without. In a memorable interview held with Jules Favre, the representative of the new French republic, the imperious Chancellor, dressed in the blazing white uniform of a colonel of the Cuirassiers, demanded impossible terms, pointing to a door behind which he claimed was waiting the representative of Napoleon III with whom he was negotiating a Bonaparte restoration!

These theatrics had one end in view—to create a demand for annexation of the provinces of Alsace and Lorraine, whose inhabitants had lived as Frenchmen since the days of the French Revolution. Bismarck's desire to acquire these provinces dated back to the beginning of the war, perhaps even before it.

On July 21, five days after mobilization and before the Germans had even crossed into France, Bismarck had planted an article in a Bavarian paper urging the Germans not to lay down arms "until Alsace and Lorraine are again German and the Rhine is Germany's river, not Germany's frontier." During the early weeks of the war, there were constant references to annexation, and at the end of the first month of fighting, Bismarck ordered his new press secretary, Moritz Busch, to write an article for an official paper, adding a nationalistic slant. "[I]t must not be forgotten," Busch wrote, "that this territory which we now demand was originally German and in great part still remains German, and that its inhabitants will perhaps in time learn to feel that they belong to one race with ourselves."

The Germans readily embraced this explanation. All Alsatians and some Lorrainers spoke a German dialect, and there were legitimate military reasons for annexation, involving the location of the military fortresses of Strasbourg and Metz. Moltke, who agreed with Bismarck on little else, believed in annexation. Wilhelm, a great believer in the spoils of war, was easily convinced of the rightness of his claim. Even the Crown Prince, who started the war "extremely averse" to taking the provinces, came to believe that the "annexation of Alsace, and perhaps of a part of Lorraine, is surely well earned by the sacrifices Germany has made."

"Voices are loud every where in all classes, in defence of Germany regaining her old provinces of Elsass [Alsace] & Lothringen [Lorraine]," Vicky wrote her mother. "I cannot say I think it a good thing but I do not see how the Government are to resist the resolute determination of the German nation to wrest them back at all hazard!"

This demand for Alsace and Lorraine was the element that most contributed to the length of the war—a problem Bismarck proposed to solve with a precipitate bombardment of Paris. Fritz disagreed with this, as did Moltke and most of the generals.

"Apparently it is becoming a perfect mania in Berlin, this eagerness for the bombardment of Paris," Fritz wrote in his diary at the end of November, "and I even hear that Countess Bismarck-Schönhausen points me out to all and sundry as more particularly the guilty cause of its postponement. And she is quite right, for above all things I do not wish fire to be opened till in the opinion of professional gunners and experts the necessary ammunition . . . for an effective, uninterrupted bombardment is there on the spot."

Fritz's stand caused problems for his wife. "In Berlin," he wrote two weeks later, "it is now the order of the day to vilify my wife as being mainly responsible for the postponement of the bombardment of Paris and to accuse her of acting under the direction of the Queen of England. Countess Bismarck-Schönhausen and . . . a lady of the Court of the Dowager Queen Elisabeth, have repeated the scandal quite openly."

The source was Bismarck. Unable to budge the Crown Prince in his determination to wait for ammunition, Bismarck told his guests at dinner on November 28, "The assertion of the generals that they have not enough ammunition is untrue. They do not want to begin because the Heir Apparent does not wish it. He does not wish it because his wife and his mother-in-law are against it." Anonymous items appeared in two papers, claiming that the "real cause" of the postponement was "the influence of very highly placed ladies" and "freemasons," a reference to the Crown Prince's well-known membership in the Masonic Order.

The bombardment of Paris did not get under way until after the beginning of 1871, and even then it did not bring about the desired results. French forts held, and the shells falling within the city did limited damage, mostly in the wealthier sections. Peace seemed just as elusive as before, only more lives were being lost.

"Everything has fallen out differently from what we seemed justified in expecting . . . ," Fritz wrote on the last day of 1870.

> Both the two contending nations in this bitter struggle have come to regard it as a point of honour not to give in. . . . It may be the governments of both countries are equally open to the reproach that they have called up spirits they cannot now lay, and heedlessly given currency to watchwords that public opinion has now appropriated for its own. . . .
>
> The longer this struggle lasts, the better for the enemy and the worse for us. . . . We are no longer looked upon as the innocent sufferers of wrong, but rather as the arrogant victors . . . no longer content with the conquest of the foe, but fain to bring about his utter ruin. . . . we are neither loved nor respected, but only feared. . . . Bismarck has made us great and powerful, but he has robbed us of our friends, the sympathies of the world, and—our conscience.

CHAPTER
THIRTY-THREE

"There is nothing which history will not justify."

ANTON CHEKHOV

WHILE HER HUSBAND AND OTHER MEN WERE at the front, Vicky was left in Potsdam with what she referred to as a "large convent of melancholy and excited women." The Crown Princess felt sorry for her mother-in-law, whose well-known French sympathies made her very unpopular during the war, but resented the fact that the Queen, nominal head of the ambulance and hospital services, took so little interest in them. Vicky herself monitored the construction of new medical facilities and oversaw the linen depots in the Berlin town hall and the Victoria Bazaar, where soldiers' wives and society volunteers made up bandages, bedding, and other hospital necessities.

The Crown Princess had long been involved in improving care for the wounded. During the Schleswig-Holstein conflict, she had started an army nursing corps, and in the spring of 1869 she attended the meetings of the International Congress in Aid of the Wounded, urging Queen Victoria and the English government to give the Congress their support as well. "If wars are to continue and their art to be studied," Vicky said, "surely all the ingenuity the human mind possesses ought to be set to work to mitigate its horrors."

With war now raging between France and Prussia, the Crown Princess again turned to her mother for help, sending a list of requirements to the Queen, who voiced concern about the "difficulty of sending anything" in light of England's neutrality. "I know how difficult your position must be. . . ," Vicky wrote back, "though I should have imagined you could have sent either to the Empress of the French, or to me—without appearing partial. A wounded man," she said, "has ceased to be an enemy."

The Queen of England agreed to furnish "some old linen & oilcloth," provided that her name not be attached to the shipment. Vicky was delighted. "I hear they are going to send out Drs & nurses from England. I wish a very few of them could come here to me as I am forming a separate staff and am much in want of them. I have borrowed money and given some of my jewels in trust to be able to do this."

But whether it was her foreign birth, her revolutionary ideas about fresh air in the wards, or the jealousy of Queen Augusta, the Crown Princess's efforts to improve medical care were not appreciated in Berlin. "My wife is going to Homburg with the object of establishing a model hospital there and inspecting those on the Rhine, which are in a sad state," Fritz wrote in his diary on August 23. "In Berlin and Potsdam all her endeavours and offers of help in the matter of tending the sick were contemptuously rejected!"

Vicky arrived in Homburg in early September. Her sister Alice, about to give birth to another child, was with her, and the Crown Princess shuttled between her family and the hospital. After the baby's birth, Alice had trouble with her milk, so Vicky, who was still nursing four-month-old Sophie, helped nurse her sister's child as well.

"I am having a hut built at my own expense and the large barracks done up also at my expense and by my directions . . . ," she wrote Victoria shortly after her arrival. "The hospitals in the villages around which I visit of an afternoon are very bad—mostly the people are so touchingly kind to the wounded, but do not understand how to take care of them and are dirty beyond description."

Plagued by her daughter for more supplies, Victoria sent some "splendid cases" of old linen to Homburg. The Crown Princess had these made into handkerchiefs, compresses, and pillowcases, making sure that people knew that the source of their comforts was the Queen of England. "I returned yesterday evening from a most fatiguing tournée to Wiesbaden, Bieberich [Biberach], Bingen, Bingerbrück, Rüdesheim and Mayence[Mainz] . . . ," she wrote toward the end of the month. "At all these places I went over the hospitals. . . . Some were good, but very few, others tolerable and the rest wretched. . . . Everywhere the population is doing to the utmost of its power & abilities & means . . . but it is often very ill done."

At military headquarters at Versailles, Fritz heard that Vicky's efforts were finally being "properly appreciated" and that the local doctors were "astonished at the wide range of her knowledge." He was very proud. "It gives me infinite pleasure to hear in all quarters repeated expression of the high respect my wife's quiet but strong and efficient activity evokes. In Homburg she has created a perfect model hospital . . . ," the Crown Prince wrote in his war diary. "I communicated to His Majesty much of what I had learned, but without hearing one word of commendation in reply."

Like her husband, Vicky engendered disapproval for the very skill with which she performed her duties. She was too smart by half, too independent, too innovative, and far too energetic. Such a daughter-in-law made Queen Augusta look bad in comparison. Vicky had been in Homburg for only a little over a month when she was informed of the imminent arrival of the Queen—a daunting prospect. In having to dance attendance on Augusta, Vicky knew her hospital work would be curtailed and she would have far less time for Alice and their babies. Moreover, the Queen carried on her social life as if there were no war. "My mother-in-law comes the day after tomorrow morning! . . . ," she wrote Victoria on October 9. "She brings between thirty and forty people with her—and is only a single person. I have the same number with six children."

Vicky's concern was justified, although she did not understand the real reason for Augusta's visit. Misled by the fact that her mother-in-law was "very kind and amiable," the Crown Princess entertained the Queen daily for dinner and tea. "[I]f I can be of any use or comfort to her," she wrote her own mother, "I am only too glad, for nothing gives me greater pleasure than when she is happy and satisfied."

It never occurred to Vicky to connect her mother-in-law with a "very unkind" letter she received a few days later from the King. Ordering the Crown Princess back to Berlin, Wilhelm insisted that he had never given his consent for her to take her children with her to Homburg, that "traveling was bad for their health and education," and that she obviously did not understand her duties as Crown Princess. Although she tried to get permission to stay on until her thirtieth birthday on November 21, she was told that she must be in Berlin that day for the Prussian people

Vicky returned as ordered, but no one except Augusta came to see her. Fritz, who had celebrated his wife's birthday in Versailles with a luncheon, a dinner, and a display of the famous fountains, was mortified when he heard how she had been treated in Berlin. In Homburg, on the other hand, there had been a large display of "genuine and grateful affection." Bismarck's anti-English propaganda in Berlin had done its work.

Nevertheless, back in the capital, Vicky continued on her self-appointed rounds of the hospitals. She also managed to see the Queen every day. "I think she has got to like coming and seeing the children which I am very glad of," Vicky wrote Victoria. But Augusta also demanded her social due—the visits and calls she expected Vicky to make with her in spite of the war. "[I]t is a superhuman strain on one's temper," the Crown Princess wrote her own mother, "& 1870 had decidedly not improved mine, which never was a first rate article."

WHILE VICKY STRUGGLED with problems at home, the siege of Paris dragged on. Although Bismarck had not been able to bring his war to a timely conclusion, he did use the ongoing strife to accomplish his primary goal—German unification. In this he was aided by the Crown Prince. Fritz's experiences in commanding Württembergers and Bavarians had convinced him that the old liberal dream of unity was an "urgent and indispensable" sequel to the fighting, and he used his considerable prestige with the southern Germans to help Bismarck bring them into the North German Confederation.

There were four south German states outside the confederation—Baden, Hesse-Darmstadt, Württemberg, and Bavaria. Baden, the domain of Fritz and Vicky's liberal brother-in-law, Grand Duke Fritz of Baden, had for years been in the forefront of the movement for unification. The Grand Duke of Hesse-Darmstadt had no choice but to go along, since half of Hesse was already in the North German Confederation, and his people were strongly in favor of unification. Württemberg had been thrown into the nationalist camp by the war, and Bavaria, the largest and most important southern state, was eventually won over by major concessions. These included an independent railway, postal, and telegraphic system, the right to be represented at peace negotiations, and the right to maintain its army as "a self-contained unit" under the command of the King of Bavaria except in time of war. "The girl is very ugly indeed," the liberal Eduard Lasker said about Bavaria's demands, "but nevertheless she must be married." By the end of November 1870, treaties had been signed with the south German states, and the German Empire was a *fait accompli*.

All that remained was to convince Wilhelm to accept the title Kaiser (Emperor) of the German Empire. But Wilhelm had always balked at the idea of any national entity taking precedence over Prussia. Believing that the other German monarchs would never allow just another king the powers they would freely give an emperor, Bismarck turned to the Crown Prince for help.

Dubbed by one contemporary "perhaps the most convinced Imperialist in the whole of Germany," Fritz agreed with Bismarck that his father must accept the title of Kaiser in order to achieve unification. He tried to explain this to Wilhelm. But while Fritz helped Bismarck, the Chancellor disparaged him behind his back, claiming that he sought unification purely for the sake of imperial pomp. "The Crown Prince," he said, "is the dumbest and vainest of men; he's crazed again by the Kaiser madness."

The person the Chancellor finally found to persuade Wilhelm to accept his new title was the twenty-five-year-old King Ludwig II of Bavaria. An impractical dreamer, already showing signs of the insanity that would eventually destroy him, Ludwig belonged to the venerable House of Wittelsbach, a dynasty even more ancient than the Hohenzollerns. Having incurred heavy debts by indulging his passions for art, music, and fantastic castles, Ludwig was now in need of money.

Ludwig's equerry, Count Max von Holnstein, arrived in Versailles two days after the conclusion of the last of the treaties with the south German states and returned to Munich with the draft of a letter written by Bismarck that Ludwig was instructed to copy and send to the King of Prussia. It invited Wilhelm I to "re-establish a German Reich [empire] and the German imperial dignity"—a request from a fellow sovereign that Bismarck knew the King could not refuse. In payment for this letter, Ludwig was provided with an annual income of £15,000. A ten percent commission was paid to Holnstein. The money came from Bismarck's Reptile Fund, stolen two years earlier from the King of Hanover.

Although Wilhelm finally agreed to accept the title of Kaiser, he sulked throughout the Christmas season and the weeks preceding the ceremony of German unification. On the day before the celebration, he erupted in a temper tantrum, declaring that as Kaiser, he would be no better than a common everyday "President." He then broke down sobbing. Fritz tried vainly to soothe his father with a recitation of the changes in Hohenzollern titles over the years, but Wilhelm refused to be consoled. "Delivering the imperial baby was a difficult case," Bismarck wrote his wife, Johanna. "At such a time, kings—like women —have strange longings."

The ceremony celebrating the founding of the new German Empire took place in the Hall of Mirrors at Versailles at noon on January 18, 1871. For the occasion, the new German Kaiser chose to wear the Russian Order of St. George, while the Crown Prince wore the English Garter. In spite of some thirty German princes fanning out on either side of Wilhelm in colorful uniforms, sparkling with orders, medals, and swords, the event was uninspiring. Wilhelm and Bismarck were furious with each other. The latter read his speech "in the grimmest of humours," after which the Grand Duke of Baden, Wilhelm's son-in-law and the highest-ranking nonroyal prince present, lifted his right hand and proclaimed, "Long life to His Imperial Majesty the Kaiser Wilhelm!" The new Kaiser then descended from the dais to greet the various officers and men in attendance, passing by Bismarck without a word or a handshake.

"I have just come back from the emperor-charade," Wilhelm wrote Augusta. "I cannot tell you what nervous (!) emotion I have been in during these last few days, partly because of the high responsibility I have now to undertake, partly and above all to see the Prussian title supplanted!" It was not until she received this letter that Augusta realized that she was now Kaiserin (Empress) of Germany, since, as Vicky explained, her father-in-law was "so averse to the whole change that he did not like it spoken of beforehand, & no one else took the initiative of informing us here of what was going to be done!"

But for Fritz, January 18 was the culmination of the dream of unification. "I have witnessed Coronations, Oaths of Allegiance and many unusual ceremonies, but I have known none either so august or so well contrived and so incomparable in external significance," said the Crown Prince of the new German Empire.

Vicky was as pleased as her husband, though neither had any illusions about the kind of empire Bismarck had created. "I am convinced that he [Prince Albert] would have rejoiced over recent changes," Fritz wrote Vicky the following year. "However, he would not have approved of the methods whereby unification was achieved any more than you and I."

The declaration of the German Empire was the catalyst for peace. Paris capitulated to the German siege ten days later, on January 28, 1871. "Although tomorrow is my day for writing I cannot resist doing so today," Vicky wrote Victoria on January 30, "as our hearts are all so full of joy and gratitude at the news from Versailles. . . . I have hung out all my flags, and were I a Roman Catholic, I should burn wax tapers on the altars of the churches—as I am not, I have given vent to my feelings in sending a great bucket of spiced, hot ale to the guardhouse for the men."

The following month, Adolphe Thiers, who represented the new French Republic, arrived at Versailles to discuss peace terms with Bismarck. Excluded from the war councils during the fighting, the Prussian Chancellor now retaliated by conducting the peace talks without the generals. Observers noted that he was intentionally rude and overbearing, bullying and shocking Baron Alphonse de Rothschild, who attended the financial negotiations as the French counterpart to Bismarck's German banker, Gerson von Bleichröder.

One reason for Bismarck's unpleasantness may have been that his campaign for Alsace and Lorraine had taken on a life of its own, and though he now felt that Lorraine would be politically detrimental to the new German Empire, he had no choice but to satisfy the national frenzy he had set in motion. "Everyone is firmly convinced that the French will wish to begin another war again as soon as they possibly can to wipe out the stain of 1870 on their military glory!" Vicky explained to her mother. "For this reason it is argued we must take a part of Lorraine and Alsace, so that when they do begin again, our frontiers may be a better protection to us. . . . I share this opinion and I find it universal both among soldiers, statesmen & the public at large."

But Vicky, like many others, was appalled by Bismarck's demands for the peace. She could not believe the first reports she heard, insisting to her mother that they were simply "invented by a German newspaper correspondent." The terms were as reported: Germany took all of Alsace and northern Lorraine plus a five-million-franc indemnity. To guarantee payment, a German army of occupation was left in France to live off the land until the debt was paid off.

It was suggested that Bismarck had an ulterior motive for this extremism, i.e., that by mutilating France and turning her into a vengeful neighbor, he was creating an excuse for maintaining the army at full force and Germany in a constant state of armed preparedness. The Crown Prince was disgusted by the terms, predicting that the "whole non-German world" would condemn them, which it did.

The English, whose distrust of Napoleon III had prejudiced them in favor of the Prussians at the beginning of the war, now realized that one European danger had been substituted for another, and Disraeli, now leader of the opposition, claimed that the balance of power in Europe had been "entirely destroyed." Vicky's old friend Robert Morier, hitherto a great Germanophile, expressed his fears that the "absolute power that the German nation has acquired over Europe" would "modify the German national character, and not necessarily for the better. Arrogance and overbearingness are the qualities likely to be developed in a Teutonic race under such conditions."

Disapproval made the Germans defensive. When Queen Victoria opened parliament on February 9, referring to Germany and France as "two great and brave nations," Augusta accused her old friend of expressing "unconcealed sympathy" for the French. Wilhelm agreed with his wife, and the Bismarck press whipped up the German people. "[T]he excitement against England is very great just at this moment . . . ," Vicky wrote in early February. "How I suffer from all this I cannot say. . . . Popular opinion is like the sea—it is easily lashed up into a fury."

"The feeling here towards Prussia is as bitter as it can be," Queen Victoria wrote Vicky a few weeks later. "It is a great grief to me—& I can do nothing! . . . To see the enmity growing up between 2 nations—which I am bound to say began first in Prussia, & was most unjust & was fomented & encouraged by Bismarck—is a great sorrow and anxiety to me—& I cannot separate myself or allow myself to be separated from my own people."

45. Otto von Bismarck, 1863, the year after he became Prime Minister.

46. Johanna von Bismarck in 1873, at the age of forty-nine.

47. Bismarck with Kaiser Wilhelm I in the Kaiser's study.

48. Vicky and Fritz, December 1860, one month after her twentieth birthday.

49. Vicky in the uniform of her Regiment of Hussars, 1861.

50. Napoleon III.

51. Empress Eugénie as sketched by Queen Victoria at Osborne.

52. Duke Friedrich of Augustenberg ("Fritz Holstein"). Bismarck dispossessed him of the duchies of Schleswig and Holstein. One of his daughters married Wilhelm II.

53. Cartoon of Wilhelm I during the Franco-Prussian War.

BY DIVINE WILL MY DEAR AUGUSTA
WE'VE HAD ANOTHER AWFUL BUSTER
10.000 FRENCHMEN SENT BELOW
PRAISE GOD FROM WHOM ALL BLESSINGS FLOW

54. Entry into Berlin of the victorious Prussian Army, June 1871. Led by Wilhelm I, the parade has just passed through the Brandenburg Gate.

55. Count Helmuth von Moltke. A cosmopolite and intellectual, he reorganized the Prussian Army and commanded it during the Austro-Prussian War.

56. Fritz on the battlefield during the Franco-Prussian War, from a painting by Camphausen.

VICKY—PAINTINGS AND DRAWINGS

57. Watercolor of the Neues Palais, her home in Potsdam, 1874.

58. Painting of her son Henry in his naval uniform.

59. Sketch of Fritz in Highland dress, the required uniform for Queen Victoria's sons-in-law during visits to Balmoral, probably 1863.

60. *The Field of Battle*, 1855. Vicky was fifteen when she painted this picture of a fallen soldier in the Crimean War.

61. Fritz and Vicky's home in Berlin, the Kronprinzenpalais on Unter den Linden.

67. Family group, August 1875. Left to right: Henry, Vicky, Fritz holding Mossy, Moretta (seated in front), Sophie, Waldemar, Willy, and Charlotte.

68. Vicky and Willy, fifteen years old, February 1876.

69. Willy at sixteen, 1875.

OPPOSITE, COUNTERCLOCKWISE:
62. Count Götz von Seckendorff, Vicky's loyal Court Chamberlain, 1877.

63. Friedrich von Holstein, 1879, in a drawing by Anton von Werner.

64. Herbert von Bismarck.

65. Prince Alexander of Bulgaria in the mid 1880s.

66. Count Hugo Radolinski, the diplomat put in Fritz's palace to get rid of Seckendorff.

William Prince of Prussia 1884.
„ *I bide my time* "

71. Willy and Dona, 1880, the year of their engagement.

72. Four generations of Hohenzollern men, with Wilhelm I holding Willy's eldest son.

OPPOSITE:
70. Willy in 1884, at twenty-five. "I bide my time."

73. Members of Fritz and Vicky's household grouped around Ernest von Bergmann. Left to right: Dr. Bramann (Bergmann's assistant, who performed the tracheotomy on the Crown Prince), Major Kessel, Major Lyncker, Hedwig Brühl, Count Radolinski. The last four were appointed by Bismarck and/or were spies for Holstein.

74. Morell Mackenzie.

75. Fritz at work after he became Kaiser, sometime between March and June 1888.

76. Fritz in the white uniform he wore for Queen Victoria's jubilee, June 1887.

77. Willy dressed as his idol, Frederick the Great, 1897.

78. "Dropping the Pilot"—the famous *Punch* cartoon by Sir John Tenniel (illustrator of *Alice in Wonderland*) about Wilhelm II's dismissal of Bismarck, March 1890.

79. Bismarck in the country with his dogs, June 1886.

80. Vicky and Bismarck in the 1890s.

81. Willy in October 1888, four months after he became Kaiser, with Bismarck.

82. Vicky with her children at Friedrichshof, May 1900. Left to right: Sophie (Crown Princess of Greece), Moretta (Princess of Shamburg-Lippe), Willy (Kaiser Wilhelm II), Vicky (Dowager Empress of Germany), Charlotte (Princess of Saxe-Meiningen), Henry (Prince of Germany), Mossy (Princess of Hesse-Kassel).

83. Friedrichshof, the home Vicky built for herself in Kronberg.

84. Friedrichshof, the entry hall.

85. Vicky and Victoria, 1889.

86. Bertie (later Edward VII of England), from a painting, Bad Homburg, 1896.

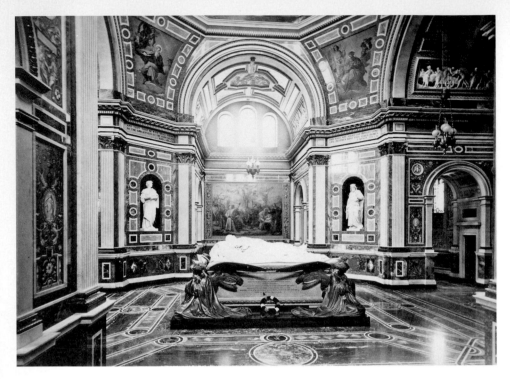

87. Victoria and Albert's crypt in the mausoleum of Frogmore at Windsor.

88. Vicky and Fritz's crypt in the mausoleum of the Church of Peace at Potsdam. On her trip to the newly united Germany in 1992, Queen Elizabeth visited this crypt. Vicky was her great-great aunt.

Vicky agreed. Although she had looked forward to visiting her mother once the war was over, she told the Queen that Fritz was afraid that "we Germans will not be able to show our faces in England for a long time to come, as we are so hated."

THE NEW GERMAN KAISER, the Crown Prince, the Chancellor, other royalties and officials, and their suites arrived home in Berlin in the middle of March 1871. The first to appear was Bismarck, now promoted to the title of Prince, a distinction he professed to disdain. "It was contrary to my desire that his majesty made me a prince," he said. "Earlier I was a rich count, now I am a poor prince." Hardly. Along with his new title, Bismarck received the property of Friedrichsruh, a richly timbered estate near Hamburg valued at one million thalers, from a grateful sovereign, his own railway car from the Association of German Railways, and 2.3 million marks from the Prussian House of Lords.

But these expressions of appreciation seemed only to make Bismarck more difficult. One conservative deputy and intimate was convinced that he had undergone a personality change. "He no longer tolerated contradiction," Gustav von Diest observed; "he was accessible to flattery; even the smallest, alleged disregard for his ego and his position exasperated him." Prince Chlodwig Hohenlohe, an old friend and one of Bismarck's successors, said that Bismarck now treated everyone "with a certain arrogance" and was "the terror of all diplomatists."

The day after Bismarck's arrival, the Crown Prince returned with his father and the other royal princes. "The next week will be one of constant going out," the Crown Princess wrote her mother. For the first time since the fighting started, she began to complain of sore throats and coughs, fatigue, and all the ailments that had vanished when she was working in the hospitals and going to bed early. Fritz, too, was dismayed by the schedule, commenting that his first week at home "tried him more than the whole campaign."

Three months later, on June 15, 1871, the victorious Prussian army made its formal entry into Berlin. A "swarm of greats" (Vicky's words) had descended on Berlin for the victory parade, symbol of the rise of Germany to the status of a major European power. Unter den Linden had been decorated with huge banners, garlanded flagpoles, and triumphal arches; hundreds of cannon, taken from the French, had been lined up along both sides of the street; and three enormous plaster-of-Paris statues had been erected at the beginning, midpoint, and end of the route—a personification of the city of Berlin, a female Victory bearing smaller statues of Strasbourg and Metz, and "Germania receiving back into her arms Alsace and Lorraine." The American Minister to Berlin was impressed. "[T]he *via triumphalis* was about three miles long," he wrote, "through streets as wide and in some places thrice as wide as Broadway."

With one million people crowding the parade route, Kaiser Wilhelm I of Germany, preceded by Bismarck, Moltke, and Roon, and followed by the Crown Prince and his son, the future Wilhelm II, rode out to meet forty thousand soldiers of the Prussian army and escort them into the city. The ceremony took place at the Brandenburg Gate, the beginning of Unter den Linden, where an enormous red-and-gold canopy had been stretched over four gold columns, each supporting a figure of Victory. Waiting under the canopy were the mayor of Berlin and other dignitaries of the city, along with the inevitable covey of maidens in white, one of whom had to get through a seemingly endless poem before the King and his party could ride off. In their procession down Unter den Linden, they were joined by over thirty mediatized* German princes, who appeared to have made up for their loss in political power with the resplendence of their uniforms, medals, plumed helmets, and polished swords.

The sun was "positively broiling," and any number of riders could be seen "falling in a faint" and "pitching from the saddle." The Kaiser's younger brothers, Prince Charles and Prince Albrecht, both collapsed in the heat, and Albrecht apparently suffered a mild stroke. Nevertheless, according to Vicky, it was "the greatest fête Berlin, and I may say Germany, has ever seen." After the parade, the royal family attended the unveiling of a statue of Wilhelm's father, Friedrich Wilhelm III, which was accomplished with a flourish of the Kaiser's sword and accompanied by the thunder of cannons, music, and cheers. Decorating the steps at the bottom of the memorial were fifty-six captured French flags and eagles.

The person who seemed to enjoy all of this the most was Fritz and Vicky's son Wilhelm, who rode behind his father and next to his uncle, Grand Duke Fritz of Baden, on a small dappled horse. A slight adolescent with acne, Willy had had trouble learning to ride because of his useless left arm, but he "sat his horse remarkably well all through" the celebrations, according to his proud father. As they advanced along the avenue, a man in the cheering crowd called out, "Wilhelmkin, Wilhelmkin, long life to you!" The twelve-year-old refused to acknowledge his well-wisher. "I laughed to myself," he wrote later, "and rode on." He was, however, very proud when his grandfather laid a hand on his shoulder as he rode by, acknowledging the boy as the eventual heir to the new German Empire.

The future Wilhelm II, said Wilhelm I, "will never forget this day!"

---

* *Princes whose properties had been annexed to Germany, but who were left with their titles and other privileges.*

PART FOUR

Empire

CHAPTER
THIRTY-FOUR

> *"But for me three great wars would not have taken place, eighty thousand men would not have been killed and would not now be mourned by parents, brothers, sisters, and widows."*
>
> OTTO VON BISMARCK

*I*N THE SUMMER OF 1871, Fritz and Vicky traveled to England to see her mother. It had been three years since their last visit. The Queen was living in total seclusion at Osborne on the Isle of Wight, the kind of private existence that suited Vicky as well. Mornings were spent outdoors—breakfasting, writing letters, and walking. Lunch was a family meal, as was tea, taken in the garden at five, followed by a drive and more reading and writing. There was almost no social life—a blessed relief to Vicky, although she and her siblings were aware of the danger that the Queen's continuing isolation posed to the English monarchy.

Vicky's father had been dead for ten years, and during that time her mother had retreated further and further from the English people, not only during vacations but during the times she should have been visible. There was considerable criticism of Her Majesty—a constantly resurging wave that threatened to engulf the throne, but which the Queen's ministers seemed incapable of bringing home to her. The Franco-Prussian War, which resulted in the overthrow of Napoleon III and the establishment of another republic in France, had only added to the more strident antimonarchical voices in England.

Vicky discussed the problem with Prime Minister William Gladstone* and her brothers and sisters during her stay, and in August she wrote a "splendid" letter, signed by the entire family, appealing to "Beloved Mama" on behalf of them all to let her subjects see her. The letter expressed the family's concerns over the perils to the monarchy and the dynasty caused by their mother's withdrawal. "We have each of us individually wished to say this to you . . . but we refrained from a fear of offending. . . . Had not the conviction come upon us all (moving as we do in different circles), with an alarming force, that some danger is in the air, that something must be done . . . to avert a frightful calamity."

Her efforts were not appreciated by the Queen, who complained that the

---

* *The Liberals were in power at the time. Gladstone was Prime Minister four times during this period: 1868–74, 1880–85; 1886; and 1892–94.*

Crown Princess of Germany had become willful and domineering and was no longer a "congenial" companion.

Vicky's self-assurance and courage in advising the Queen on political affairs did not extend to their personal relationship. Now thirty-one, the Crown Princess was still like an adoring but respectful suitor, tiptoeing around her mother. "Our drive last night was delicious," she wrote during her stay at Osborne. "I enjoyed it so much, seeing the lovely country & having you all to myself was a great treat. Might I lunch with you? Might I bring the children?" When the Queen left Osborne for Balmoral Castle in Scotland, Vicky wrote that she and her family "roamed with tearful eyes and heavy hearts. . . . I took one last look at your rooms, and one turn through the deserted corridors . . . which still seemed to be haunted by your voice!"

Vicky's strong attachment to Victoria was based largely on her need for the Queen's approval. Unlike Albert, Victoria had never been quite so taken with their eldest daughter, and Vicky still chased an affection that sometimes eluded her. Having left her childhood behind when she moved to Prussia at seventeen, the Crown Princess needed a loving adult—a role that neither of her in-laws was fit to play. For Vicky, Queen Victoria and England remained the ultimate refuge in a life dominated by disapproving relations and dynastic jealousies.

For her part, the Queen bowed to her daughter's superior education and frequently sought her advice on such things as artists and monuments, but was furious when Vicky refused to follow her edicts in matters of court etiquette (mourning) and health (nursing). Nor did Victoria ever hesitate to disparage Vicky's basic optimism—the resilience that buoyed her up in spite of the frustrations of her life.

Protocol dictated that as soon as she got back to Germany the Crown Princess had to call on the older members of the royal family. Making the rounds from the Queen Dowager to Prince and Princess Charles was, as she wrote Victoria, "what I hate most of all. . . . I think there is nothing so irksome [as] to smile and appear delighted when one is the very reverse! One feels such a humbug!"

A touch of the humbug certainly would have smoothed Vicky's path. Incapable of even the most self-protective pretenses, she managed to alienate not only the members of the royal family who were politically disposed to fear her, but possible supporters as well. When it came time to celebrate the first anniversary of the Battle of Sedan, fought on September 1, 1870, but not conceded in writing until the next day, the Crown Prince and Princess celebrated alone on the anniversary of the battle itself, explicitly ignoring the flags and guns and boycotting the church services on the official day of celebration, September 2. It is hard to know why they engaged in such futile gestures, unless they felt that the real heroics had occurred on the battlefield and that it was only Bismarck's foreign policy they were acknowledging by celebrating the day of formal capitulation. According to Walpurga (Hohenthal) Paget, who visited Vicky about this time in Berlin, the Crown Prince and Princess were currently "boiling over with irritation against Bismarck."

Fritz and Vicky's refusal to join in the official commemoration of the Battle of Sedan must have added to Wilhelm's irritation over their recent trip to England, and his determination to make them pay came close to endangering the health of the entire family. With a smallpox epidemic raging half an hour from Potsdam in Berlin—three hundred children dead within ten days—Vicky and Fritz telegraphed Wilhelm to ask his permission to take the family to Castle Wilhelmshöhe in Kassel, away from the danger of contagion.

But to Wilhelm I, a smallpox epidemic was no excuse for decamping. In response to their request, the Crown Prince and Princess received a wire informing them that Potsdam was "very healthy," and, if they insisted upon leaving, the Kaiser must have a written statement to the contrary issued by the court doctor. "By all this I see the Emperor considers our stay in England the only change we are to have in the year," Vicky wrote Victoria. "Just think of Fritz at 40—being treated like a boy of 6. . . . It is a tyranny which I consider quite insupportable."

To underscore his irritation, the Kaiser sent a new watchdog to Fritz and Vicky's palace. "A general is put about our children against our will with orders from the Emperor & our house turned topsy turvy . . . ," she wrote her mother. "I feel in a perfect rage."

Wilhelm finally gave permission for them to go to Kassel for "a short while" but "not on grounds of health as that was a ridiculous excuse." The Crown Prince, who never stopped trying to see the best in his father, was "very much hurt and very angry."

Because of the epidemic, Fritz and Vicky and their children spent the greater part of late summer and early fall of 1871 at Wilhelmshöhe. The elaborate schloss, built by the Princes of Hesse at the beginning of the eighteenth century, was set in the middle of a park with Greek temples, rockeries, waterfalls, and a 230-foot statue of Hercules.* Since the Austro-Prussian War, when Prussia took over northern Hesse, Wilhelmshöhe had become a Hohenzollern showplace, a symbol of the sort of excess that the Hohenzollerns claimed to scorn but had expropriated with pride. The irony was not lost on Vicky, who said that there was "too much art, too little nature," and too many examples of the "bad means" by which the Electors of Hesse, among the most repressive of the petty German monarchs, had "enriched themselves." Still Kassel was more to her taste than Baden-Baden, where they were expected for Augusta's sixtieth birthday at the end of September.

Vicky referred to Baden-Baden, the most popular spa in Europe, as "the most odious haunt I know." Unlike other royalties, she loathed the perpetual round of luncheons, dinners, teas, receptions, and soirées—all those social obligations that seemed to her to abuse the body and destroy the soul. Worse were

* Nelson's monument in London is 170 feet tall.

the "scenes at the Emperor's"—the incessant bickering and fights that she and Fritz were forced to witness between her in-laws. On her mother-in-law's birthday—a "dreaded" yearly celebration—everyone had to be dressed formally by 9:00 A.M., the women in low-cut gowns, the men in evening coats, white ties, and orders. The Crown Prince and Princess spent the day running "backwards and forwards" between two courts—the Neues Schloss, on a hill overlooking the town, where Wilhelm stayed, and Miramar House, the villa favored by Augusta.

Vicky's aversion to the frantic social pace of the resort was more than just a matter of temperament. As a child, she had been indoctrinated against this sort of frivolity by her father. Ever since his death, she had tried to maintain a reasonable middle ground between her mother, who avoided as much contact with society as possible, and her mother-in-law, who ran to every party in youthful frills and outlandish wigs.

A letter from the English Queen enclosing an article on the conspicuous consumption of the *beau monde* gave the German Crown Princess a chance to state her case: "It is indeed sad to think of the frightful waste of money on dress & luxury of all kinds when there is so much poverty around . . . ," she wrote Victoria. "I think it is a pity when Queens and Empresses set the example of over done élégance. . . . Simplicity is quite compatible with beauty." But as Vicky knew, nothing would change her mother-in-law's taste for inappropriate finery.

Although Fritz and Vicky managed to escape Baden-Baden after several days, their departure was "neither a peaceful nor a pleasant one." Vicky empathized with her husband's distress over ugly scenes with his father, who resented their leaving. "I think it very hard upon Fritz," she wrote Victoria, "not to speak of my own feelings, when I see my father-in-law so violent."

They did not return to Berlin for some weeks, stopping in Weimar, where Augusta had gone to see her family. "No member of the family has increased in beauty since I last had the pleasure of seeing them," Vicky commented to Victoria about Augusta's relatives. The Crown Princess was particularly irritated with her mother-in-law, who had had the poor taste to inform her mother, before she herself chose to do so, that once again she was pregnant.

IN EARLY 1872, Vicky's thirty-three-year-old cousin Feo died of scarlet fever, and the following month Queen Victoria paid a visit to Feo's mother, her bereaved half-sister Feodora, in Baden-Baden. She stayed for close to two weeks. Anxious to console Feodora, Queen Victoria seemed to have slighted Vicky, who lived only a day away, but was not allowed to travel because of her pregnancy. The Queen, as Vicky did not hesitate to remind her, had never spent one night under her roof in the thirteen years she had lived in Germany. "Some day in later years perhaps when we are established in some very pretty, quiet and wholesome spot, you may be tempted to come and visit us!" the Crown Princess wrote the Queen.

There was more than one reason for Vicky's pique. Although she had continued to produce children at a rapid rate, she had become "horribly afraid of the event" facing her in April. Countess Blücher, her mainstay during confinements, had recently died, and she needed maternal support. "I am very nervous about it," she wrote Victoria, "as there is nothing I can do in the way of walking or diet or anything to make me have an easier time, and those very hard ones such as with Waldemar & Sophie are really dreadful." When Vicky wrote Victoria about how "immensely wretched" she was feeling, however, she elicited a minimum of sympathy.

"I am sorry to see you are not well," the Queen replied. "But I am not surprised at it, & I only hope & pray you will be satisfied when you have 7 [surviving children]—& not go on exhausting your health & strength so precious to all you belong to & so necessary to your husband & children & to your adopted country."

Vicky's mother-in-law was no more responsive to Vicky's needs than her mother. She had promised the Crown Princess that she would wait to see her through the birth of the baby, but had already started pressing her daughter-in-law to help her secure an invitation to visit Queen Victoria in England. "May I ask a question without being indiscreet?" Vicky wrote her mother. "You did speak once of favoring the Queen's [i.e., the Kaiserin's] great wish of going to England during the summer. . . . She has not asked me again, but I hear second hand that she is still extremely anxious for it. Would it be possible for you to ask her in the month of June when you are at Windsor? That would I am sure be what she would like best."

Victoria replied with an invitation for early May, which elicited another appeal from Vicky to change the date from May to June, along with assurances that Augusta would stay no longer than a week. Her mother-in-law, the Crown Princess said, would "prefer to alter her plans . . . than lose the opportunity of going to England altogether."

The result of Vicky's efforts on Augusta's behalf was that the Kaiserin, promises forgotten, left her daughter-in-law in the middle of April, when the baby was due, in order to visit Victoria in England. "I took leave of the Empress yesterday, who was very kind," Vicky wrote Victoria, "in fact the whole winter through she has been most kind to me, and we have got on very well in spite of little rubs. . . . it is not in her nature to enter much into the feelings of others or show any consideration for their necessities,—so life can never be easy either to her or with her but I am always most thankful when we are on loving and cordial terms, delighted when I can be of use to her and grateful for any kindness she shows me."

"I am so glad that you have got on so well with the Empress Queen," Victoria answered. "Don't you think it is rare that people do understand the necessities, feeling and wants of others? No one suffers more from this than I do—for I suffer from excitement and fatigue and none will (even of my own children) understand my wants! Towards me the Empress Queen has always been most considerate and kind."

■

VICKY'S LAST CHILD was born on April 22, 1872. The Crown Princess was disappointed that it was not a boy, although, as she wrote her mother, "for myself alone a little girl is much nicer." She did not really want any more children after this one—"what one has to endure is too wretched"—but still felt she owed Germany another son. "Though you take no interest in babies," she wrote Victoria, "I may mention that this one has got an immense lot of dark hair, which I am sorry to think will not remain." As predicted, the hair fell out quickly, and by the time the infant was christened, her head was covered with short hair like moss, from which she acquired her nickname, Mossy.

"I don't dislike babies," the Queen answered, "though I think very young ones rather disgusting, & I take interest in those of my children when there are 2 or 3 . . . but when they come at the rate of 3 a year,* it becomes a cause of mere anxiety for my own children & of no great interest. What name is this 4th daughter to have?"

The child was named Margaret Beatrice Feodora, and Margaret, the Crown Princess of Italy, was asked to be a godmother. "I suppose you don't mean to ask Beatrice [Vicky's fifteen-year-old sister] to be sponsor? . . . ," Victoria wrote in response to this piece of information. "I was [a] Godmother . . . when I was only 11 . . . & as you ask Catholics & so many sponsors it would not imply any responsibility."

"We did not venture to ask Beatrice to be sponsor much as we wished it, we were afraid you would not like it . . . ," Vicky wrote back. "We shall be too delighted if you will allow us to do so, and I shall write to dear Beatrice today."

Ever since Fritz had attended Margaret of Savoy's wedding to Crown Prince Humbert of Italy, Vicky had been exposed to the "raptures" of her husband and other men who had met Margaret, and she was wildly curious to see her. When the Crown Prince and Princess arrived for the baby's christening, she agreed that the twenty-year-old girl was "a very charming graceful creature." "I wish you had seen her . . . ," she wrote Victoria; "everybody here is charmed with her. She is so amiable."

High on the list of those who were delighted with the pretty and lively young woman was Vicky's father-in-law, the Kaiser. Her mother-in-law, on the other hand, had gone to Baden-Baden during the christening in order to avoid meeting the Italian Crown Prince and Princess. Recent events in Italy had caused further polarization of the pro- and anti-Catholic forces in Germany. Augusta was definitely not on the side of the Italian royal family, which had finally succeeded in wrenching the last bit of Italian territory from the Pope in order to complete the nation of Italy.

It was the onset of the Franco-Prussian War that had forced Napoleon III to withdraw his French troops from Rome, where they had been guarding the papal domain. In August of 1870, only twelve days after the French defeat at Sedan, the Italians had entered Rome, annexed it to Italy, and made it their capital. Although they granted Pius IX royal honors and prerogatives, including

* *Vicky, Alice, and Helena all had children in 1872.*

diplomatic rights, immunities, and an income of 3.25 million lire to offset the income from his former land, he insisted on styling himself "the prisoner of the Vatican." Among his most vocal supporters was Augusta, who urged her husband to support the Holy Father against the Italians—a policy that would have thrown Italy with France against Germany. Unable to get her way, Augusta carried on a vendetta against the Italian royal family.

Augusta's Catholic bias put her in the opposite camp to Bismarck, who believed that the Catholic Church was out to destroy Germany. The Chancellor was now at the political epicenter of Europe, sending shock waves that reverberated through England, France, Russia, Austria, and the other smaller nations. In contending with his enemies—or those he labeled as such—Bismarck's actions would assume a different character after 1871. As one historian put it, the Iron Chancellor felt that what he had gained "by violence" now "had to be protected by coercion."

These wars to win men's minds would distress Vicky at least as much as Bismarck's earlier campaigns on the battlefield.

CHAPTER
THIRTY-FIVE

"In Berlin everyone whistles the same tune. Everything is depen-
dent on Bismarck and on Bismarck alone. Never was the rule of
one single man so exclusive, not only from fear but also from
admiration and voluntary subordination of men's minds to
him."

LOTHAR VON SCHWEINITZ, *German Ambassador to Russia*

IN FORGING HIS EMPIRE of blood and iron, Bismarck had made France
into an enemy whose desire for revenge would influence the policies not only
of Germany but of all Europe for the next forty years. Because of this, the
Chancellor needed to isolate the French as they made a quick recovery from
the settlements exacted from them after the Franco-Prussian War.* One of the
factors that most helped Bismarck was the political chaos in France that followed her military defeat. Napoleon III had been sent into exile in England,
and another (the third) republic of France had been established.

Bismarck knew that nothing guaranteed solidarity among the monarchical
set more than the specter of republicanism. Only a few days after the Battle of
Sedan, he had warned the Czar of the necessity for a common platform in "view
of the elements, not only republican but distinctly socialist, that have seized
power in France."

Indeed, the Chancellor worked very hard to keep those dangerous republican elements in power. In the face of a strong movement toward restoration of
a French monarchy (although there was some disagreement as to *which* monarchy—Bourbon, Orléans,† or Bonapartist‡), Bismarck supported Adolphe
Thiers, Napoleon III's conservative opponent, who was elected first president
of the Third Republic, and was infuriated when Thiers fell in the spring of 1873.
Thiers was followed into office by Marshal Marie Edmé MacMahon, a soldier
and monarchist elected to prepare the country for a restoration. But the Count
of Chambord (representing the Bourbons) and the Count of Paris (representing
the Orléans) could not come to terms with each other, and MacMahon was

---

* *By September of 1873, only two years after the war, France had already paid off her war*
reparations, thus ridding the land of the German army of occupation.

† *The house of Orléans was a branch of the house of Bourbon.*

‡ *The possibility of a restoration of Napoleon III did not last long. Preparing for what he*
believed would be a triumphal reentry into Paris, Napoleon underwent a series of operations for
bladder stones and died in January 1873.

elected president for seven years. In 1875, a new constitution established a permanent republican form of government in France.

If one of the main objectives of Bismarck's postwar foreign policy was the isolation of France, the most crucial element of his policy, the underlying *sine qua non* was Germany's friendship with Russia. It was this relationship, cemented by family ties, on which the Chancellor counted to keep Germany from the peril of enemies both east and west. Prussia had supported Russia when the Russians broke the Crimean War treaty,* in return for which Czar Alexander II had warned Austria not to join France against Prussia in the Franco-Prussian War. "Never will Prussia forget that it is due to you that the war has not assumed extreme dimensions," Wilhelm I had wired his nephew the Czar.

Bismarck's foreign aims also included good relations with Austria. Not wanting to rely exclusively on the Russians, Bismarck needed an understanding with the Habsburgs. Such an alliance would not only free Germany of dependence on Russia, but forestall an entente between Austria and France.

Austria needed Germany as well. After their defeat in 1866 at the hands of the Prussians, the Habsburgs had lost much of their power to the Hungarians, and since 1867, the Austrian Empire had been known as the Dual or Austro-Hungarian Empire. Unable to break the strong ties between Russia and Germany and eager to prevent an exclusive alliance between them, Franz Joseph set out to ally Austria with them both. In the summer of 1872, he invited Wilhelm to his shooting box at Ischl. Willhelm immediately returned the favor with an invitation to visit Berlin in the fall.

Now it was the Czar's turn to worry. Concerned that the monarchs of Austria and Germany might join in an alliance against *him*, Alexander II promoted an invitation to Berlin for himself. Lord Odo Russell, the new British Ambassador to Berlin, commented that Bismarck would no doubt "readily turn" this unexpected confluence of emperors to the advantage of Germany.

Because of such fluctuating alliances, one of the major duties of nineteenth-century royalties was paying state visits abroad and receiving royal visitors at home. Whether these were official events, which included large diplomatic suites, welcoming parades, and all the formal paraphernalia of court life, or private family reunions, there was always a great deal of thought and preparation given to impressing the visitors—some of whom the Crown Princess of Germany welcomed more sincerely than others.

"I pity you indeed to have to be at Berlin . . . for that week of Emperors . . . ," Victoria wrote. "<u>How</u> ever will you manage between the Kaisers as to rank? . . . every Sovereign <u>is</u> <u>alike</u>—& no one yields to the other . . . what <u>will</u> happen? I should really be amused to hear."

Vicky, who nursed Mossy between events, complained that the meeting of Franz Joseph, Alexander II, and Wilhelm I (aged forty-two, fifty-four, and seventy-five, respectively) was "more like an immense bivouac than anything else." She might not have been so put off had the Czar, who came to Berlin

---

* *This treaty prohibited Russia from maintaining a fleet in the Black Sea.*

bearing dozens of medals and honors, not presented the uniform of an elite regiment of grenadiers to Willy, age thirteen. As it was, both the heir to the throne and his ten-year-old brother were swept up in the general glorification of men-in-arms, parading at the rear of the first platoon of a regiment led by their father in an enormous military review.

"It gave me even more pain that it can give you to see my poor children made victims to an absurd & obsolete tradition to which their grandfather so strictly adheres," Vicky wrote her mother. "It does them harm and it makes a very difficult education more difficult still. No one wishes more than I that every compliment possible . . . [be] shown to our splendid, heroic and glorious army. . . . But . . . What was natural 200 or 600 years ago is now not only absurd but mischievous in more than one respect, and now it is high time such customs were abolished."

The very things that annoyed the Crown Princess helped impress Germany's guests. Although there was no announcement made at the time, the meeting of Wilhelm I, Franz Joseph, and Alexander II was followed the next year with a pact in which the three Emperors expressed their solidarity against subversive republicanism and agreed to resolve any future quarrels in the interests of the monarchical principal. A minor piece of paper, the Three Emperors' League was the precursor of more significant alliances in 1879 and 1882. Odo Russell had been right when he predicted that Bismarck would turn fortuitous happenstance to Germany's advantage, and the Chancellor was delighted with his achievement. "It is the first time in history that three Kaisers have sat down to dinner together for the promotion of peace . . . ," he told Russell. "I wanted them to stand in a silent group and allow themselves to be admired, but I was determined not to allow them to talk . . . because they all three think themselves greater statesmen than they are."

IF THE MEETING of the three Emperors demonstrated the best of Bismarck's preventive diplomacy, his five-year campaign against the Catholic Church and its party in the German Reichstag exemplified the worst. Launched at the end of the Franco-Prussian War, the *Kulturkampf,* as this campaign was known, was also an attempt by Bismarck to solidify his personal power—an undertaking to which he applied himself with characteristic force but without his usual success. The word *Kulturkampf*—cultural struggle—was originally coined by Rudolf Virchow, a professor of pathology and progressive member of the Prussian Chamber of Deputies, who hoped to free education from all religious influence, Protestant as well as Catholic. Many Germans saw it as a struggle between modern culture and medievalism.

In attempting to undermine what he claimed was the Catholic threat to the Protestant majority in Germany and the German Parliament, Bismarck was supported by the National Liberals, formerly his enemies, but after unification his staunch allies and the most powerful party in the Reichstag. Most liberals felt that in following Bismarck's lead, they were joining the great nineteenth-century march toward progress in science, education, and humanism in general.

"The joy and enthusiasm of the national [National Liberal] party at Prince Bismarck's declaration of war to the Church," said Odo Russell, "are even greater than the joy and enthusiasm which preceded the wars with Austria and France."

As to the Church itself, there was some cause for alarm. Aware that it was losing out both ideologically and financially to a new order, Catholicism had split into two camps—liberals, who believed that traditional religion and nineteenth-century advances could coexist, and "ultramontanes," who felt they must solidify the Church's authority by reinforcing old dogma. From the Vatican, Pius IX led the retrenchment.

In 1864, the Pope had published the "Catalogue of the Principal Errors of Our Time," a document censuring such nineteenth-century "errors" as nationalism, socialism, and the freedom to exercise one's own conscience against Church dogma. It was considered by German liberals a declaration of war and was followed in July of 1870 by the proclamation of the dogma of papal infallibility, a decree that raised the authority of the Church above that of the state. Opposed by every German bishop at the Vatican Council of 1869 (who were nonetheless required to support it), the doctrine caused particular consternation in Germany, home of the Reformation.

Bismarck had always feared and despised the ultramontanes, who he believed were conspiring to raise a Catholic coalition against Germany and change the political order in Europe. Germany had been divided since the Reformation, with each German state professing its preference for Protestantism or Catholicism. Catholicism, once a minor factor in the Prussian Chamber of Deputies, became a major consideration after the Franco-Prussian War and the addition of the largely Catholic south German states. Catholics were represented in the Reichstag by the Center Party.

Second only to the National Liberals in number of delegates, the Center boasted as its leader one of the best politicians in Germany, Ludwig Windthorst. A hunchback from Hanover with an acerbic tongue, Windthorst was loathed by Bismarck for the brilliance of his opposition, around which Bismarck knew that other Catholics—south Germans, Poles, Alsatians, and Lorrainers—might rally their disparate forces. "Everybody needs somebody to love and somebody to hate," said the imperial Chancellor. "I have my wife to love and Windthorst to hate." Other delegates to the Reichstag respected Windthorst for his gentility and civility.

Initially, the German Chancellor tried to establish his authority over the Center Party through the Pope. Asked to protest Italy's expropriation of papal lands and offer asylum to Pius IX, Bismarck refused the first request—a country in the process of unification could not deny the same satisfaction to its southern neighbor—but was quite willing to grant the second. "If we give asylum to the Pope," he said, "he must do something for us in return." But when Pius IX refused to order the members of the Center Party to support the Chancellor's policies, Bismarck declared war on the Church.

In June of 1871, the month the victorious Prussian army returned to Berlin, the Chancellor published an article claiming that the Center Party had tried to prevent the unification of Germany, that it was still trying to do so, and that the German government must therefore take the offensive against the Catholic Church "abroad as well as at home." He removed the head of the Catholic Department of the Ministry of Education and Religious Affairs, a ministry that had always operated through both Catholic and Protestant divisions, and placed the entire agency under a Protestant. Eight months later, he saw to it that the Catholic order of the Jesuits was outlawed in Germany.

Bismarck threw himself into this project with calculated outrage, turning what was essentially an attempt to control the Center Party in the Reichstag into a contest between church and state. Since education came under the individual states rather than the Reich (empire), the major struggles took place in the Prussian Chamber of Deputies. Stringent laws ("May Laws"), enacted in 1873 and 1874, sent two archbishops to prison and drove over one thousand priests from their parishes.

In the fall of 1873, Pope Pius wrote the Kaiser to protest this "destruction of Catholicism," adding that he had heard that Wilhelm himself did not approve of "the harshness of the measures." Pius was right. As the pressure of Bismarck's campaign intensified, the Kaiser, torn between his anti-Catholic Chancellor and his pro-Catholic wife, grew agitated and sick. Her father-in-law, Vicky explained to her mother, was not "seriously ill . . . only sitting about the room with a cap on his head, looking very depressed and uncomfortable."

While the Kaiser suffered, the Catholics dug in their heels. Often choosing jail over submission, they closed their seminaries rather than accept secular supervision, left ecclesiastical positions vacant rather than submit their candidates to government approval, and repurchased confiscated church properties. Worse for Bismarck, in the elections of 1874, the Center Party increased its seats in the Reichstag by nearly fifty percent.

The Chancellor reacted to defeat with renewed persecutions, complaining that his Minister of Education and Religious Affairs, a popular reformer named Adalbert Falk, was not carrying out his orders with sufficient force. But the Crown Prince, who disliked the ultramontanes and had approved of Bismarck's early attempts to decrease the power of the Church, objected strongly to what he referred to as "Bismarck's personal brand of justice."

In the summer of 1874, Bismarck was shot by a young Catholic worker, who said he was reacting to the May Laws and the Chancellor's hostility to the Center Party.* Although the man obviously acted alone, Bismarck seized on the incident to try to prove that there was a Catholic conspiracy against him. "You may try to disown this assassin," the Chancellor said in an attack on the Center Party in the Reichstag, "but he is clinging to your coattails all the same!" Fritz

---

* *Bismarck kept this pistol and one from another would-be assassin loaded on his desk. They were part memorabilia—he loved to tell the stories of his near-escapes—and part protection, for his wife, Johanna, was convinced that there was a plot to murder him.*

was afraid that Bismarck would try to use this attempt on his life "as a pretext for harsher measures."

The *Kulturkampf* turned out to be one of Bismarck's least successful undertakings—a venture doomed to backfire because of the nature of the victim. The fact that the Chancellor's own religion had been the maidservant of his early political success may explain why he did not comprehend the dedication of the forces his aggression brought to the surface. "I fancy that Bismarck utterly misunderstands and underrates the power of the Church," Odo Russell reported to London. "Thinking himself more infallible than the Pope, he cannot tolerate two Infallibles in Europe. . . . The German Bishops who were politically powerless in Germany and theologically in opposition to the Pope in Rome—have now become powerful political leaders in Germany and enthusiastic defenders of the now infallible Faith of Rome, united, disciplined, and thirsting for martyrdom, thanks to Bismarck's uncalled for and illiberal declaration of War on the freedom they had hitherto peacefully enjoyed."

The Crown Princess agreed. Her objection to Bismarck's campaign put her in opposition to her husband, her father-in-law and her mother. "[A]ll over Europe there is an attempt made to resist authority & to defy it, by the Priesthood," Victoria wrote Vicky in 1873. "I do not think they [Roman Catholics] can be treated as people of other religions."

Vicky made no attempt to conciliate her mother. Brought up to distrust the Catholic Church, she might look askance at the Catholic rites she had seen in Rome—the elaborate garb of the priests and the speed with which they repeated the Latin liturgy—but she still preached religious freedom, even for Catholics.

When Queen Marie of Bavaria* converted to Catholicism in 1874, Victoria berated Vicky for not feeling as she did. "I must say I am greatly shocked for it is a complete surrender of your intellect—& individuality to another. . . . one can't understand anyone who has been a Protestant ever submitting to this. Tell Fritz that I share his and the Emperor's feelings being as dear Papa was—a fervent Protestant & hating all that approaches Catholicism. . . . But I know you don't feel as I do—& have not that love for the very simplest, purest faith as near to our Saviour's precepts as possible."

Vicky refused to be chastised. "I do not quite see with what right you say that I do not care for a pure faith approaching the precepts of Christ as I fancy it is the very contrary—the purer the teaching from these precepts is, the better I like it—but one of them is tolerance, & if other people are not of my way of thinking I can regret it, & think them difficult to understand but I do not blame them!"

The Crown Princess was not surprised when Bismarck's campaign began to fail. "I dare say he is beginning to see that it is not so easy a matter to fight the Church of Rome as he fancied," she wrote her mother in 1875, "and that he

---

* *Wife of Maximilian II of Bavaria and a first cousin of Wilhelm I of Prussia.*

has underrated her power of resistance and overrated the power of the government in the strife which he has <u>purposely</u> brought on, <u>why</u> I do not know!"

Far too idealistic and impractical to understand Bismarck's method of neutralizing the political opposition before it could become dangerous, Vicky regarded the *Kulturkampf* as just another example of the fact that there was too much power resting in one unprincipled man. Her husband had expressed this concern to Queen Victoria immediately after the Franco-Prussian War. "He [Bismarck] is no doubt energetic and clever," said the heir to the throne, "but bad, unprincipled, and all-powerful; in fact he is the Emperor."

CHAPTER
THIRTY-SIX

*"You have not seen war! If you had seen it, you would not utter
the word so calmly. I have had experience of war, and I must tell
you that it is the greatest of all duties to avoid war whenever
possible."*

CROWN PRINCE FRIEDRICH WILHELM OF PRUSSIA

*B*Y ALL HISTORICAL INDICATORS, the 1870s should have been a period of
relative calm and contentment for the Crown Princess of Germany. She had
survived childbirth seven times, lost only one child to illness, and was still in
love with her husband. Her father's great wish and the reason for her marriage
—the unification of Germany—had been accomplished, albeit by means other
than Vicky or Albert would have chosen. The new German Empire was the
strongest force in central Europe, a potential Protestant ally for her native
England, and a counterbalance to Catholic Austria and France, Orthodox Russia, and Muslim Turkey. As the future Kaiserin of this vital young country,
Vicky could look forward to a day, probably in the near future (her father-in-
law was well over seventy), when her husband would be in a position to dismiss
Bismarck and bring parliamentary reform to the empire.

But whatever it should have been, the decade of the seventies was particularly frustrating for the Crown Princess, as Bismarck's reputation, defying the
laws of political gravity, continued to soar. After 1871, German citizens proudly
compared their Chancellor to a force of nature—"a ruler of the great Germanic
type, lionlike in temperament . . . dangerous to enemies and allies, demoniacally
defiant in his strength, crushing, pitiless. . . ."

Conditioned by hundreds of years of toadying to arrogant princes and
petty bureaucrats, untouched by the salutary humor of the English or the skepti-
cism of the French, Vicky's fellow Germans seemed to fall naturally into self-
prostration. As historian Erich Eyck put it, they "had to idolize" Bismarck,
"because unless he was a truly great man there was no excuse for their submission to him and for their acceptance of his manners."

In a letter to her mother written in the middle of the 1870s, Vicky offered
a logical (if somewhat patronizing) rationalization for her countrymen:

> The Germans must be excused at having lost their heads a little and having
> accepted Prince Bismarck's code of right & wrong—as they have for years
> been misgoverned, as personal & political liberty has been smothered &

kept down. . . . A glance at German history will show . . . how little they have been <u>fitted</u> <u>by</u> <u>degrees</u> to fill the place they <u>ought</u> to occupy in the world! Now it has come all at once, & the public at large enjoy it immensely. . . .

The idea that Bismarck has made us <u>great</u>, has made us <u>feared</u>, and therefore he is <u>perfectly</u> <u>infallible</u> is the prevailing one! . . . I do <u>not</u> wish to depreciate Bismarck's talent and merits, his energy and his quickness, but I <u>do</u> consider him & his principles & his policy a misfortune & the means . . . he uses <u>most</u> . . . dangerous.

As to Bismarck himself, success had not brought him peace of mind, and his health, buoyed or calmed by stimulants and depressants, had become a focal point of his life. Retreating for months at a time to the country, the Chancellor usually took refuge at his estate of Varzin in Pomerania, where he spent the days tramping through the woods and fields with his ever-present dogs, worrying about himself, and feeding his gargantuan appetites. Plagued by neuralgia, rheumatism, and gout, he was subject to migraines and digestive ailments. Although the doctors counseled moderation, meals at the Bismarcks included six heavy courses—hot beef with potatoes, cold venison, and fried puddings—plus dessert. Supper was served at midnight, just before going to bed.

"The first time I dined at the Bismarcks [1875]," recalled Christoph von Tiedemann, one of the Chancellor's personal assistants,

> he complained about not having any appetite. Then I watched with growing astonishment as he devoured a three-man serving of every course. He preferred heavy and indigestible foods, and the princess supported this inclination. If he suffered from an upset stomach at Varzin or Friedrichsruh, she had nothing more pressing to do than to telegraph the restaurant Borchardt in Berlin for a shipment of *pâté de foie gras* of the larger size. When this was presented at table the following day, the prince would open a large breach in it with the first stroke. As it was passed around the table he followed it with jealous glances. . . . When the dish came back to him, its volume only slightly diminished, he devoured all that remained.

Bismarck drank as much as he ate. A Bavarian diplomat who spent an evening at his home noted that the Chancellor downed "several litres" of bock beer, Jamaica rum, champagne, and port without being noticeably affected. Even during a time of professed illness, he was seen imbibing between a quarter and a half bottle of cognac.

This kind of consumption, coupled with an obsessive temperament, led to chronic insomnia. "I can't sleep at all, regardless of what I try . . . ," he complained in the early 1870s; "when I can't sleep, I recall all the vexations I have had —and in increased measure—never anything pleasant. I find excellent replies to utterances that have annoyed me. This wakes me up all the more."

Two of the chief objects of these nocturnal furies were the Kaiserin and the Crown Princess, and during the 1870s, the relationship between Bismarck and the two most important women in the royal family, never good, deteriorated even further. "One of Bismarck's more notable characteristics," according to a minister of his cabinet, "is the tendency to harbor deep thoughts of revenge or retaliation for injustices he has suffered or presumes to have suffered. In his pathological excitability he conceives many things to be unjust that others probably do not intend to be such."

Comfortably astride the German colossus, the Chancellor knew he held all the reins of power but one. That one, however, depending as it did on the tenuous life of a man as old as the Kaiser, made him nervous, irritable, and dangerous to his enemies. His sense of insecurity can be measured by remarks he made in the spring of 1873 about Augusta and Vicky to Lord Odo Russell, the British Ambassador to Germany.

The German Chancellor had spoken to the Kaiserin only twice in the two years since the Franco-Prussian War. He pointedly refused an invitation to dine at the British Embassy because protocol decreed that he would have to sit next to her, and he constantly attacked what he called her political "influence" on her husband, on which he blamed the failure of his *Kulturkampf*. Bismarck told Russell that Augusta had "the advantage" of eating breakfast with the Kaiser and going over the morning papers with him. He claimed that during these morning tête-à-têtes, she fought "the battle of the clericals"—whom he referred to as her "spiritual and political directors"—thus undermining Wilhelm's confidence in his Chancellor, "whose services His Majesty had unhappily never appreciated."

After this conversation with Bismarck, the Ambassador's wife wrote Queen Victoria to say that her husband was worried about what Bismarck would do to ruin Vicky's position with the public. Referring to the Chancellor's "unscrupulous" manipulation of the press that he used "to undermine his political enemies," Emily Russell quoted Bismarck as saying he "is able to agree with the Crown Prince, but he fears that will never be possible with the Crown Princess."

These are rather strange words, coming as they did from the most powerful statesman in Europe about a thirty-four-year-old woman, and they say more about both the Crown Princess and the Chancellor himself than he probably intended. What is remarkable is the older man's sense of bewilderment. Why, Bismarck apparently wondered, could he not sweep Vicky along in his political wake, as he had most other liberals? Why, seeing that his policies had proved so successful while her moral quibbles were so unpopular, did she not simply accept the empire he had forged and which she would some day help rule? Why were means so much more important to her than ends?

ONE DOES NOT have to look far, however, to find the sort of governmental adventuring that Vicky deplored. An extreme example—certainly the most damaging to Germany's image—was the so-called War-in-Sight scare, a Bismarck-engendered crisis that broke over Europe in the spring of 1875. A time of diplomatic and financial turmoil that frightened a continent, its origin and meaning are still unclear. Often blamed on Bismarck's poor state of health, the war scare may well have been no more than a diversionary tactic on the part of the Chancellor, aimed at turning the attention of the German public away from the ongoing failure of the *Kulturkampf,* a depressed economy, and shifts in the political balance of the Reichstag. It was not uncommon for Bismarck to use the fear of foreign devils, real and imaginary, to keep a lid on domestic problems.

Four minor events led up to the near hysteria:

The first, which came perilously close to a scene from comic opera, involved a Belgian Catholic boilermaker who wrote to the Archbishop of Paris offering to kill the German Chancellor for the sum of sixty thousand francs. Warned by the Archbishop, Bismarck demanded that the man be punished in spite of the fact that there was nothing in the Belgian legal system to deal with someone who had only proposed a crime. His harshly worded protest to Brussels, sent to other governments around Europe, flabbergasted the recipients.

A second and third incident soon followed. Hearing that the French were trying to buy ten thousand saddle horses from Germany, presumably for their army, Bismarck slapped an embargo on the sale. One week later, when the French Parliament voted to increase the size of their infantry, the German Chancellor claimed that this was an indication of France's warlike intentions.

After the fourth event—a meeting between King Victor Emmanuel of Italy and Emperor Franz Joseph of Austria, whose business, Bismarck claimed, was directed against Germany—the Chancellor ordered the German press to broadcast an alarm.

Three articles, published in different places in Germany, disrupted a peaceful Europe. The first, which appeared in Cologne, criticized the meeting between the Italian and Austrian monarchs, spoke of a current threat to European peace, and pointed to the French army reform as preparation for war. A second, more sensational article appeared in the Berlin *Post.* Entitled "Is War in Sight?," it speculated on the possibility of a French alliance with Catholic Italy and Austria against Germany—the so-called Catholic League of Bismarck's nightmares and one of the objectives of his failing *Kulturkampf.* A third article, published in the Chancellor's own mouthpiece, the *Norddeutsche Allgemeine Zeitung,* said that although there was no danger from Italy or Austria, France was a different matter.

This was vintage Bismarck, and Europe was not slow to react. Nervousness destabilized stock exchanges all over the continent, and the French Foreign Minister, Louis Décazes, issued memos to France's foreign embassies warning them of the possibility of German attack. Although Décazes was accused of using the situation to rally the other Great Powers around France—a tactic of which he was more than capable—he would have been derelict in his duty if he had not reacted to what looked like the kind of Bismarckian propaganda campaign that had preceded Prussia's three recent declarations of war.

When the Kaiser asked Bismarck for an explanation, the Chancellor denied his role in the uproar, suggesting that the article in the Cologne paper might be a maneuver on the part of French bankers, the Jewish Rothschilds, to manipulate stock prices. Bismarck's explanation satisfied Wilhelm, who often preferred not to know what his Chancellor was doing. "Somebody wanted to poison our relations," the Kaiser told the French military attaché. "It was all caused by the nonsense written in a couple of newspapers, but now it is over and done with."

Hardly. On the same day the Kaiser dismissed the matter so lightly, his Chancellor sent a report from the head of the German army, Field Marshal Moltke, to the German Embassy in London. The architect of Germany's success in the Franco-Prussian War, Moltke had atrophied into a seventy-five-year-old Teutonic prophet of doom, an old soldier with a single theme: France intended to declare war on Germany at the first opportunity in order to recapture Alsace and Lorraine. This was the gist of the report sent to London.

Up until this point, Bismarck had himself engineered this war of nerves. But on April 21, Joseph Maria von Radowitz, a high-ranking German diplomat known to be close to the Chancellor, told the French Ambassador to Germany that although the crisis between their countries was over, some Germans felt that if France continued to foster the idea of revenge for Alsace-Lorraine, Germany would be better off making a preemptive strike. "Why should we wait so long?" Radowitz asked. "Would it not be better if we anticipated it?" Not too surprisingly, the French Ambassador sent a frantic dispatch to his chief in Paris, Foreign Minister Décazes, warning that Germany might in fact be planning a surprise attack on France.

The effect of Radowitz's statement was intensified by Bismarck, who told the Austrian Ambassador that it was "the duty of the German Government to take the initiative" against France. And knowing how inflammatory Moltke could be, the Chancellor sent him to see the British Ambassador. Moltke told Odo Russell that it was not the country who took up arms that was responsible for war, but the country that provoked such a response!

The final salvo came in early May of 1875, when Bismarck instructed his Ambassador to Paris to warn French Foreign Minister Décazes that he believed France was preparing to make war on Germany.

But Décazes caught Bismarck at his own game. First, he ordered copies of Radowitz's statement sent to the other European powers with the comment that Germany ought to be carefully watched. The Czar responded with assurances that if Germany was planning to declare war on France, he, Alexander II, would personally warn the French in advance. The English reacted sympathetically as well. London dispatched a carefully worded warning to Berlin, and, more significantly, exchanged reports with Russia over the possibility of German aggression.

Décazes then called in the Paris bureau chief of the London *Times,* to whom he showed all the pertinent dispatches. The result was a devastating piece exposing Bismarck's manipulations. Entitled "A French Scare," it was reprinted all over Europe.

Two days after this article appeared, Alexander II of Russia arrived in Berlin. Originally planned as a polite stopover on the way to a cure in Bad Ems, the Czar's visit became the focus for peace hopes all over Europe. Even Queen Victoria sent a letter to be delivered on Alexander's arrival in which she expressed the "firm hope" that he would use his "great influence to keep the peace and to dissipate the profound alarm which the language issuing from Berlin has aroused throughout Europe."

Occasionally the close relationship between the houses of Hohenzollern and Romanov worked for the benefit of Europe. With Fritz by his side, Wilhelm assured his nephew* that nothing could be further from his mind than war with France. At the same time, the Russian Foreign Minister extracted a promise from Bismarck that Germany was not planning an attack on France.

The War-in-Sight crisis was an embarrassing public defeat for the German Chancellor. In a letter to the Kaiser, however, Bismarck blamed it on "the Ultramontanes and their friends [who] have attacked us both secretly and openly in the press, accusing us of wanting to begin war very shortly, and the French Ambassador who lives in these circles."† In a speech to the Reichstag, he denounced "inexperienced diplomatists" and the "drawing-room influences of highly-placed personages"—an attempt to shift his failure onto the Kaiserin.

He then retreated to his estate of Varzin, where he remained from June to November of 1875, unavailable to his ministers, who carried on the workings of the German government without him. Like a great wounded beast—angry, roaring, and dangerous—Bismarck remained in his lair, striking out periodically at his enemies. "Behind our backs, Bismarck raves like a maniac," commented Odo Russell.

To this day, the question of whether Bismarck really intended to precipitate war in 1875 is a subject of disagreement. It seems fair to conclude that he was probably trying to frighten France into quiescence and at the same time assert his personal power, seriously damaged by the failure of the *Kulturkampf*. Had his campaign against the Catholics showed more success, perhaps there would have been no need for this brandishing of arms. Bismarck probably did not tell Radowitz what to say, but given the opening by his underling, pursued it to see how far it might take him toward his goal of neutralizing France.

Whether premeditated intimidation, pragmatic jockeying, or some combination of both, the War-in-Sight scare of 1875 damaged both the Chancellor and Germany. Bismarck's actions opened the door to a closer understanding between Russia and France and, at the same time, demonstrated that those archrivals and superpowers of the day, Russia and England, could and would work together against Germany to keep the peace. They also branded the new and powerful German Empire as a blustering political adolescent—a potential vacuum of responsibility in the center of Europe.

In addition, the War-in-Sight crisis showed how Bismarck looked for a scapegoat when things did not go his way. Usually it was the Kaiserin. Some-

---

* *Alexander II was the son of Wilhelm's sister Charlotte.*

† *In his memoirs, Bismarck claimed that the crisis had been invented by Russian Foreign Minister Gorchakov and the French Ambassador, the Viscount of Gontaut-Biron, who had the original conversation with Radowitz and whom the Chancellor hated. But by then (1899), everyone knew it was Bismarck.*

times it was a member of her household, like the Kaiser's House Minister or Augusta's personal reader. These people, according to Bismarck, formed a clique with the Crown Prince and Princess that preyed on the Kaiser, especially when he was ill, undoing all the efforts of his hardworking Chancellor. To bolster this argument, Bismarck claimed that Wilhelm had suffered a stroke at the end of 1873, thereafter falling completely under the pernicious influence of his wife. Other observers mentioned only an intermittent fever and depression, traceable to Wilhelm's anguish over the *Kulturkampf.*

Another object of Bismarck's resentment was the head of the Admiralty, General Stosch. An independent man who resented Bismarck's attempts to interfere in his command, Stosch, who had served as Fritz's Chief of Staff and was a regular at Augusta's teas, clashed frequently with the Chancellor, who accused him of being "an intriguer and spy who does not open his mouth in cabinet meetings, but then tells everything to the Crown Prince and to his majesty." Having convinced himself that Stosch was the head of a mythical "shadow" cabinet lying in wait to take over when the Crown Prince ascended the throne, Bismarck attacked him on the floor of the Reichstag and in the official press. The head of the Admiralty hung on for two weeks, then offered to resign. When his offer was refused by the Kaiser, Bismarck tendered his own resignation, but Wilhelm refused to let him go either. Besides, as Vicky wrote Victoria, Bismarck was "too fond of power ever to give it up."

After the Stosch incident, Bismarck withdrew to Varzin as he had done two years earlier after the War-in-Sight scare. His chronic bad health improved during his ten-month absence, but his anger and resentments did not. It is a measure of Bismarck's state of mind during this hiatus in the country that he inadvertently killed his favorite dog, Sultan. The mastiff had apparently disappeared for a few hours. When he returned, Bismarck beat him so severely that he died from internal injuries. "He accuses himself of having a violent temper, of being brutal, and of giving pain to everyone who comes in contact with him," said Friedrich von Holstein, Privy Counselor for Foreign Affairs, who was visiting at Varzin. "Then he again reproaches himself for mourning so long and deeply the death of an animal."

From Varzin, Bismarck also took out his fury on Augusta, whom he dubbed "the traitoress." He ordered Moritz Busch to write articles accusing both the Kaiserin (a certain "exalted lady") and the Catholic Church ("Ultramontane poison out of the sewers of Rome") of causing the Chancellor's poor health. Called by one historian "the most libelous attacks ever leveled at a queen," the articles incensed Vicky, who begged her father-in-law to come to his wife's rescue. He refused. The Kaiser, she told her mother, was "very nice—but also very calm about it!" The seven "friction" articles, as they were called, also pointed a finger at recalcitrant diplomats and ministers who, according to the Chancellor's press agent, "made opposition, conspired and intrigued . . . against the greatness [i.e., Bismarck] which overshadowed them."

Bismarck's accusations did not exclude the Crown Prince and Princess. "[I]t is an abominable system of his," Vicky wrote Victoria, "trying to pull down the royal family in the eyes of the public to appear a martyr! It is wicked, disloyal and ungenerous . . . and the German public are so blind in their adoration of Bismarck that they would believe anything bad of us, if it came from him or was sanctioned by him."

ONE OF THE REASONS for Bismarck's ongoing frustration was the economic and political situation within the empire itself, where the Chancellor had yet to settle on a domestic agenda and find the elements in the Reichstag necessary to support it.

Up until the mid-1870s, Bismarck had paid little attention to domestic problems. Having unified Germany during a time of prosperity, he had been able to leave economic policy to his Finance Minister, Otto von Camphausen, and his Minister of the Interior, Rudolf Delbrück. It was not until his withdrawal to Varzin in 1875 that he began to contemplate the shaky finances of his nation.

During the years of unification, Delbrück had instituted a program of regulatory changes aimed at simplifying life in the disparate states under Prussian domination. Thirty-three state currencies had been replaced by the German mark; uniform weights and measures were inaugurated; a central bank was established; and joint stock companies were legalized. These and other measures had helped Germany develop from an agricultural state into an industrial nation. With the advent of the railways, accelerated by the exigencies of war, Berlin had grown into a financial center and Germany had become a major player in the industrial revolution of the nineteenth century.

Victory in the Franco-Prussian War and a postwar boom, augmented by an economic flood of five million francs in French indemnities, added to the prosperity. But industrial growth, which reached an apex in the three years after 1870, brought with it unbridled greed. Rich and poor alike speculated in the stock market, which crashed in the fall of 1873, bringing a whole spectrum of society—shopkeepers and porters, upwardly striving bureaucrats and professional men, even old-line aristocrats like Fritz and Vicky's friend Prince Putbus—to financial ruin.*

---

* *A typical example of a promotional scheme gone awry centered on a converted Silesian Jew named Strousberg, whose consortium to build railroad lines in Romania collapsed. Bismarck described the fiasco to the French Ambassador: "Our greatest lords and our bootblacks believed that Strousberg would present them with a gold mine, and a great many risked the best part of what they possessed. . . . All that is buried now in the Romanian mud, and, one fine day, two dukes, one general who is an an aide-de-camp, a half-dozen ladies-in-waiting, twice that many chamberlains, a hundred coffeehouse owners and all the cabmen of Berlin found themselves totally ruined. The Emperor took pity on the dukes, the aide-de-camp, the ladies-in-waiting, and the chamberlains, and charged me with pulling them out of the trouble. I appealed to Bleichröder who, on condition of getting a title of nobility, which as a Jew he valued, agreed to rescue the Duke of Ratibor, the Duke of Ujest, and General Count Lehndorf; two dukes and an aide-de-camp saved—frankly, that is worth the 'von' bestowed on the good Bleichröder. But the ladies-in-waiting, the cabmen, and the others were left drowning" (Pflanze, Vol. III, pp. 15–16).*

Financial debacles led to a wave of anti-Semitism, spearheaded by the Prussian Junkers, who had used the Jewish banks to see them through hard times but had always resented the bankers. The Junkers launched an attack on Bismarck in the summer of 1875 for what they called the Bleichröder-Delbrück-Camphausen era. "Jews actually govern us now," they said, ignoring the fact that although the Chancellor's personal banker, Gerson Bleichröder, was Jewish, his Finance Minister, Camphausen, and his Minister of the Interior, Delbrück, were not. (Delbrück, however, was the author of the legislation that had brought about the rise of the bourgeois industrialists, whose financial success was deeply resented by the Junkers.) While correct in their assumption of corruption in government, the Junkers were wrong about its authors, especially Delbrück and Camphausen, both honest and dedicated workhorses.

"I am no real expert in these fields," Bismarck said in 1875, "but my present advisers, however well-qualified they may be when it comes to routine business, have no creative ideas. I have to count upon myself to think up plans for reform and to pick up the instruments for their implementation. . . . " Minister of the Interior Delbrück took the hint and immediately resigned.

"Germany wants rest, peace and quiet," Vicky complained to Victoria in the summer of 1875; "her commerce and the development of her inner resources are not progressing as they should!" But Bismarck—ill, angry, devastated by the attacks of his old conservative cronies, and intent on keeping his own name out of the financial scandals—emerged from his retreat at Varzin only to demand stronger laws for his *Kulturkampf* or to engage in foreign skirmishes like the War-in-Sight scare of 1875.

Certainly, the German economy was not recovering as quickly as it should have from the stock market crash of 1873. The railroads were still running at a loss a year later; scandals continued to surface; and the Krupp factories laid off four thousand workers between 1874 and 1876. Alfred Krupp had to mortgage his empire to qualify for a bank loan; since this empire included his armaments plants, panic surged through the German military establishment.

Ninety percent of the budget of the German Empire was used to support the German army. When the military budget—or "iron" budget, as it was called—came up for renewal in 1874, Bismarck presented a bill that precluded the Reichstag from a say in either the size or cost of the army for an indefinite number of years. Faced with the Chancellor's threats to resign and the prospect of asking voters to deny military appropriations three years after Germany's victory over France, the National Liberal Party compromised on a seven-year budget (the Septennate). Shortly thereafter, however, it split over a bill involving the German judiciary system. Refusing to accept a code of justice that allowed the government to open private mail and officials accused of violating legal rights to be tried in special courts, the left-wing Progressives bolted, leaving the centrist liberals without a viable coalition.

One way for Bismarck to build a new coalition was to bring these centrists into a working coalition with conservatives. To do this, he tried to coopt a leader of the National Liberals, Rudoph von Bennigsen, by offering Bennigsen a unique position in the two governments over which he presided—Prussia and the German Empire.

Up until that time, union had been invested only in two people—Wilhelm I, who was both King of Prussia and Kaiser of the German Empire, and Bismarck himself, who served as Minister-President of Prussia and Chancellor of the empire. Bismarck offered to appoint Bennigsen Minister of Finance in both governments, thus making him vice president in charge of domestic affairs. By doing this, the Chancellor hoped to assure the support of the National Liberals in the Reichstag, rid himself of the responsibility for domestic economics, and forge further bonds between the Prussian tail that wagged the German dog.

It was an irresistible offer, and Bennigsen accepted. To pave the way for Bennigsen, Bismarck publicly disavowed his current Minister of Finance, Otto von Camphausen, humiliating him in front of the Reichstag and forcing him to resign in disgrace. Shocked at the way Bismarck treated a loyal minister, Bennigsen immediately withdrew as a candidate for the dual office.

The import of the Bennigsen "fiasco" lies in the tragic alienation of the National Liberal Party, which, according to historian Erich Eyck, "represented at this time the loyal and patriotic middle class of Germany more strongly and more completely than any party has ever done since then." Certainly these moderate liberals were Germany's one hope of a viable opposition, the last brake on autocracy and militarism in the empire.

It has to be added, however, that in the Bismarck political constellation, the position of the National Liberal Party had never been a particularly bright one. Unlike their counterparts elsewhere, German liberals had always been forced to maneuver within the narrow political corridor left by an autonomous Kaiser and an autocratic Chancellor. Because of this, they were limited to the traditional choice of compromising their beliefs to remain in power or sticking by their principles and functioning purely as an oppositional party.

Had the National Liberals or their left-wing colleagues, the Progressives, ever reached out to the lower classes, the history of Germany might have been very different. But, as Otto Pflanze said, even the Progressives "lacked . . . the social comprehension and political imagination" necessary to spread their wings over uneducated agrarian peasants and factory workers. Throughout these formative years of the empire, the liberals had remained an elite group of middle-class men who, for all their principles feared the unknown dangers from the left more than they feared the familiar, almost familial dictatorship of the right.

The Bennigsen incident coincided with a resurgence of the ultraconservative elements in the Reichstag. Seeking a broader appeal for voters, the Junkers launched a new "German Conservative Party" in 1876—a slightly updated version of all the conservative parties of the past. Although it managed to change its image, its members remained, as Bismarck put it, nothing more than the "old feudal party of the Kreuzzeitung in disguise." They were still large landowners, bureaucrats, and army officers; over half the delegates they sent to the Reichstag were aristocrats. But when the liberal coalition fell apart, the Chancellor looked back to these men, his earliest supporters, for support in the Reichstag.

The renewed cooperation between Bismarck and the ultraconservatives signaled the unmistakable triumph of everything against which Vicky and Fritz had been fighting, and it put the stamp of certainty on the Crown Princess's anxieties about the future of the empire under Bismarck.

CHAPTER
THIRTY-SEVEN

> *"The most important point to bear in mind when considering Bismarck's career is not that for a number of years he made war and then stopped, but that he cheated and made mischief all his life."*

> EDWARD CRANKSHAW

*I*T IS AN UNFORTUNATE FACT of history that rumors about well-known figures, repeated often enough and with sufficient conviction, eventually find their way into the common pool of knowledge from which chroniclers and biographers draw their information. Because of this, a whole range of fallacies —from political propaganda to backstairs gossip—has been elevated over the years to the status of truth. It would be hard to find many historical figures who have suffered more from this phenomenon than the Crown Prince and Princess of Germany.

The primary instigator of the stories about Fritz and Vicky was Bismarck. In his determination to seize control of the mind of Germany, the Chancellor used every weapon in a well-stocked arsenal to undermine the credibility of those who questioned his methods or views. To the expediency of discrediting his political opponents, Bismarck added a personal vindictiveness so pronounced that it distressed his most ardent admirers. "Even the puniest attack excited him to defense," said one of his secretaries. "He was always prepared to repay a pin-prick with a knife thrust."

There is little doubt that Bismarck's rancor toward anyone who crossed him robbed Fritz of his rightful reputation as a military commander. Called "the leader in two wars"* by Baron Hugo von Reischach, a Hussar who served Wilhelm I, Fritz, and Wilhelm II, Fritz was a better general than his vaunted cousin Fritz Carl,† and as dedicated to the army as his father. But by distorting the Crown Prince's misgivings over the arrogant militarism of the Prussia of his day—apprehensions that history has certainly justified—Bismarck managed to cast this man with a conscience as a German Hamlet, unworthy of the Hohenzollern mantle.

---

* I.e., the Austro-Prussian War of 1866 and the Franco-Prussian War of 1870–71.

† In Who's Who in Military History, *Fritz Carl is cited as "the last of the Hohenzollerns to show the military skill by which the family had risen to pre-eminence." The Crown Prince is not mentioned (Keegan and Wheatcroft, pp. 130–31).*

Crown Prince Friedrich Wilhelm was a brave man. Far less confident than his wife, he clung to personal integrity in the face of Bismarck's ridicule, accusations of disloyalty, adverse public opinion, and family tradition. It would be hard to estimate what it must have cost this son of the army to disobey the orders of his Commander-in-Chief—who was also his father, the King of Prussia, and the Kaiser of Germany.

Fritz was nonetheless devoted to the family image. Accused of being overly conscious of his lineage, he wrote an extensively researched history of the Hohenzollerns, sections of which he sent off periodically to historians for comments and changes. "His estimate of his ancestors," Professor Hans Delbrück wrote, "was absolutely unbiased. . . . he was quite free from . . . pseudo-patriotism . . . [and] a false idealization of the past. He desired no floweriness and no concealment, but the simple historical truth." At the same time, the Crown Prince had a healthy respect for the power of the press, creating a sensation in caste-ridden Berlin by receiving reporters and editors at the palace and talking to them at official functions.

He was also the major force behind excavations at Olympia in Greece and Pergamon in Asia Minor. These digs eventually led to two of the most extraordinary exhibits in any western European museum—the life-sized Greek temple and Babylonian victory walk at the Pergamon Museum on Museum Island in Berlin.

"The Prince . . . inspired confidence . . . ," said one contemporary; "he was . . . Lohengrin . . . with a noble character, always ready to rush to the defense of those who were ill-treated or trodden upon, and to interest himself in every worthy cause."

Fritz openly favored the advancement of women and supported a petition, sent to the Reichstag in 1872, demanding that they be allowed into such bastions of male bureaucracy as the postal, telegraphic, and railway services. Without his approval, Vicky would never have been able to start the Victoria Lyceum, a place where girls, still barred from universities, could attend scholarly lectures.

Fritz's position on women, unique among Hohenzollerns, was due to his relationship with his wife. Vicky gave him advice and support and kept up his spirits when he was seized by his periodic depressions. But in an aggressively patriarchal society where wives were expected to limit their activities to *"Kinder, Kirche, und Küche"* (children, church, and kitchen), this kind of acknowledged partnership left both the Crown Prince and Princess vulnerable to Bismarck's denunciations.

Having taken advantage of Vicky's English birth to cast aspersions on her loyalties, Bismarck used her uncommon intelligence to satirize her as a domineering wife—a tactic that also enabled him to lampoon Fritz as a henpecked husband. "I am English, foreign . . . and I dominate you . . . ," Vicky wrote Fritz in 1879. "I don't take the position . . . considered proper and suitable for a princess at the Berlin court. . . . A kind of higher lady . . . who dresses well, looks pretty . . . is a doll in her own house . . . does not have the cheek to deal with her household or her children, and thus does not spoil the children's 'Prussian upbringing.' "

The Crown Princess was an anomaly outside the court as well. A young woman with political ideas, inflexible principles, and an advisory relationship with her husband was incomprehensible to the average *Herr* and his *Hausfrau*. As she complained in a letter to Fritz, a woman in Germany was "not the partner, friend and <u>helper</u> of her husband . . . does not have the same educational level as <u>he</u>. . . . If . . . a wife lays claim to this status . . . she is considered dangerous, domineering, ridiculous, peculiar. . . . In England, every woman participates in conversations on politics, reads the newspapers, knows what's going on, etc. . . . <u>No</u> Englishwoman," the Crown Princess said, "would accept and adjust to the lowly and not very dignified status of a German wife."

Unable to fathom such a woman, such a prince, and such a relationship, Archduke Albrecht of Austria, returning from a visit to Berlin, wrote Franz Joseph his assessment of Vicky in the mid-1870s:

> After a big dinner with many civilian guests I visited the Crown Princess, who returned to Potsdam the following morning. The better you get to know her, the more puzzling she appears to be. So many indications of real womanly feeling, a good mother, and then again such contrariness and eccentricities, a great desire for undisturbed domesticity and then an inordinate lust for power! Spoilt in England as the Princess Royal, she needed an iron hand to control her, instead she entirely dominates her husband, has remained completely English and her parents-in-law have no idea how to deal with her.

Criticized by the all-powerful Chancellor, distrusted by Fritz's relatives and her peers around Europe, Vicky blossomed in the confines of her own home. "How different was the atmosphere at the Crown Prince's Palace!" said one courtier. "Nothing rigid or severe or motheaten to be found there, thanks to the progressive thought, the liberal broad-mindedness of 'Our Fritz' and his cultured wife."

In Berlin, where aristocratic drawing rooms remained closed to the banker, the professor, the artist, and the Jew, Fritz and Vicky's was the only palace where, as one young member of the British Embassy put it, "love of art, a real sympathy with the intellectual movement and a wider liberal outlook on life prevailed." This intercourse with intellectuals and artists was life-giving to the Crown Princess, who loved to debate ideas, often for the sheer joy of the argument. "I invariably take the side of the absent," she told one of her entourage, explaining why she praised England in Germany and "always fought Germany's battles" in England.

Throughout the 1870s, Vicky continued to pursue her reading and studies —political, scientific, and literary—as well as music, sketching, and painting. She studied with Angeli, produced large portraits of both Willy and Charlotte, and did numerous sketches and watercolors. To develop her eye, she made pilgrimages to the museums of Italy.

Describing a trip to Venice he took with the Crown Princess in the 1870s, Anton von Werner, a well-known genre painter of the day, said that she "studied, drew, and painted indefatigably" in the museums and the city, "quite alone and incognito, or else she painted studies of heads in Passini's studio with the rest of us. . . . I . . . was surprised at her unerring taste . . . and the ease and accuracy with which the object was represented, no matter in what medium." More than Vicky's "technical powers," which were not great, Werner responded to what he called her "artistic comprehension."

IF MUCH OF THE LITERATURE on the Crown Princess of Germany focuses on Bismarck's role in her life, while she is only fleetingly mentioned in biographies of him, it is because she was almost too easy a mark, scarcely worthy of the highly developed propaganda machine the Chancellor used to destroy her. In his attacks on the Crown Princess, Bismarck was perhaps most successful in the realm of motherhood, where he managed to convince his countrymen that this earnest young woman with a mission was a heartless, driving harridan.

There is no question that the Crown Princess was a demanding parent, impossible to please. Raised by a perfectionist father who had sent her to Prussia to produce a generation of reformers, Vicky believed it her godgiven duty to instill in the future Kaiser of Germany and his siblings the qualities she had been told were necessary for moral and political leadership. Taught never to be satisfied with herself, Vicky could not stop trying to improve those in her care.

But whereas Vicky and her siblings had been purposefully kept away from court life with its dangers of toadyism and flattery, the Crown Princess was required to raise her offspring in a semifeudal society that favored self-importance and accepted the silliest obsequiousness as its due. Taken on a trip to England when she was eleven, Charlotte was with her grandmother Victoria when the Queen's gillie, John Brown, was ushered into the room.

"Say How de do to Brown, my dear," her grandmother told her.

"How de do."

"Now go and shake hands."

"No, that I won't. Mama says I ought not to be too familiar with servants" was the reply that was repeated to Vicky by the irate Queen, causing "no end of a row" between them.

Since Vicky was as democratic in her manners as Victoria—her father always accused her of too great familiarity with servants—Charlotte's behavior clearly stemmed from the atmosphere of servility that permeated the Prussian court. Unlike her parents, Vicky did not control the world of her children, and she was constantly undermined by her in-laws.

A particular area of disagreement was travel. "I hope we shall be allowed to send our Willie all over the world," the Crown Princess wrote her mother when her eldest son started school, "but we are in a difficult position as Fritz's parents interfere so much in all we do with the children, and the King dislikes all innovation as most people about court here do, think that where the children are born, there they are to grow up and never go away for fear of their becoming estranged from their country. . . . This is the place of 'tradition.' . . . What never has been done never is to be done, and all people who think differently are unpatriotic."

Health was also an issue. Stuffed into swaddling clothes, baby binders, and what Vicky called "the rest of the antediluvian aparatus [sic]," infant Prussians were kept smothered in heat, far away from the dangers of fresh air. Royal babies who survived grew up to inhabit hot, unaired palaces, where primitive plumbing helped breed constant winter infections and worse.

Vicky worried constantly about childhood illnesses—and with good reason. Pneumonia, scarlet fever, diphtheria, typhoid, and measles were only some of the sicknesses that regularly carried off a high percentage of the young. "I always feel nervous when our dreadful winter is at the door," she wrote Victoria in 1873, "so many months of it and shut up in town is really very formidable for young children with all the catching diseases of the throat and chest about, the awfully unwholesome undrained condition of Berlin & the treacherous climate!" The Crown Princess constantly begged the Kaiser and Kaiserin to allow her to take her children away in the winter, but since the most dangerous months for disease coincided with the social season, she rarely succeeded.

In matters of health care, the Prussian Crown Princess clung to English training and prejudices. Having been consigned to the hereafter by the German doctors during her first confinement, it is not surprising that she had little faith in them and imported English doctors for future births. She also consulted with the old family physicians about her children when they were in England. Her anxieties were increased by the death of Sigi, whose meningitis had gone unrecognized. After that, she herself tried to keep a careful watch on things that the doctors might not catch.

Unlike most of her royal peers, Vicky was an ever-present parent. She bucked tradition and court prejudice to nurse her last five babies and cared for her children herself when they were ill: "I had a great fright last night," she wrote Victoria in the spring of 1869, "as Waldy was suddenly seized with the croup about midnight. . . . I made him a hot bath, gave him a teaspoonful of Ippecacuhana* wine, & wrapped him up in hot blankets so that he was much relieved by the time the Potsdam Dr. arrived. Wegner came in the morning and now the dear child is all right again, but he was frightfully ill for half an hour he could not get his breath. I am quite knocked up, having never left him all night."

As for appearances, Vicky's children were not good-looking even by royal standards, which were not particularly high. Queen Victoria and her family were always amazingly blunt in discussing looks, and none of them ever hesitated to speak of a beloved child as ugly. When Alice told Vicky that her daughter Irene was not pretty, Vicky "comforted" her by saying that she was "not a 3rd so plain as my poor Henry, whose ugliness is a grief to me."

The fatter the baby, the prouder the nineteenth-century parent, since chil-

---

* *Ipecac, an emetic or purgative.*

dren with a surfeit of weight had more to draw on when they took sick. Vicky's letters to Victoria were filled with lamentations over the thinness of her brood. Compared to their Hohenzollern cousins, Fritz and Vicky's children were decidedly puny. The Crown Princess was extremely sensitive to criticism along these lines, and there was plenty to keep her bristling. Above all, there was Willy's withered arm. According to Fritz's cousin Fritz Carl, "a one-armed man should never be King of Prussia."

While life in the Hohenzollern clan was rife with petty jealousies, the atmosphere within Vicky and Fritz's home was apparently quite happy. The parents and their brood of seven followed a regular pattern with winters in Berlin, summers in Potsdam, and a family vacation in July or August. Like Vicky, her children could not wait for the annual migration to the country. In Potsdam, the children rode horseback with their mother in the mornings and, on holidays, took long walks with their father. When he was not away soldiering, the Crown Prince took his sons rowing or swimming. When they were older, he took them hunting.

Wherever they were, in Berlin or in Potsdam, the children breakfasted with their parents. In later years, the younger ones always arrived in their parents' room promptly at 7:00 A.M. and sat on their bed while they had their tea and toast.

"My mother, with her many children, was always active and very busy . . .," said Moretta. "But she never neglected her children. Every moment that she could spare away from the various duties which devolved upon her was spent with us. She carefully supervised and watched our upbringing both in the nursery and the schoolroom."

Poultney Bigelow, the son of an American diplomat brought into the palace to play with Willy, remembered being both pleased and distressed by this attention. "[N]o parents could have shown more interest in their children than the . . . Crown Prince and Princess," he later wrote, explaining that Willy's parents were usually there with "a smile and kind word" when their children ate supper, although he also recalled that the Crown Princess "had a keen eye for napkins not properly tucked in or any breach in nursery manners."

While their children were still very young, Vicky and Fritz bought a farmhouse in the village of Bornstedt, a mile outside Potsdam. A run-down property discovered by Vicky when her coachman took a wrong turn, Bornstedt required years of work to get it and its inhabitants into shape. Before the Crown Prince and Princess took over, the peasants who lived there slept in their clothes and boots and rarely washed. None had ever seen mattresses, sheets, or blankets. Meals were eaten anywhere they were working—in the stable, the yard, or sitting on the staircase in the house.

Fritz and Vicky bought the farm in 1863 when they had only three children; by the time it was fit for habitation, their family had increased to five. Meanwhile, Vicky had purchased two cows, installed a dairy, and turned the garden into a playground with swings, seesaw, and a cricket field. Later she added chickens and ducks and moved the children's ponies there.

In cleaning up their new property, Fritz and Vicky also transformed the local village. They rebuilt the church, reordered the graveyard, and established a trade school, where local girls learned needlework. They started a new village school, where Fritz liked occasionally to take over classes.

The Crown Prince adored the role of country squire and was popular with the villagers. He managed the planting and harvesting of the crops, while Vicky supervised the dairy. Although Bornstedt probably cost more than it earned, it was a place where the entire family could live what passed for a simple country life among nineteenth-century royalties and Fritz could spend more time with his children.

Because of his military duties, the Crown Prince was more often than not away from his growing brood, who, as Vicky said, "seem to look upon it as a matter of course that Papa is very seldom at home." This was one reason why Vicky felt responsible for educating and disciplining their children. "[I]t is sad to do and settle every thing without Fritz who is so much away that every thing in the house and about the children's education falls upon me," she wrote Victoria during the Franco-Prussian War. "It is more responsibility than is quite fair."

THEORIES OF CHILD REARING in the middle of the nineteenth century were far different than they are today. Witness the following passage, written by a German doctor named Daniel Schreber, whose books went through forty printings. It was first published in 1858, the year before Willy's birth:

> The little ones' displays of temper . . . should be regarded as the first test of your spiritual and pedagogical principles. . . . Once you have established that nothing is really wrong . . . you . . . should proceed . . . by quickly diverting its attention, by stern words, threatening gestures, rapping on the bed . . . or by appropriately mild corporal admonitions repeated persistently at brief intervals until the child quiets down or falls asleep. This procedure will be necessary only once or at most twice, and then you will be master of the child forever. From now on, a glance, a word, a single threatening gesture will be sufficient to control the child.

Compared to this, Vicky was a loving and empathetic parent, whose demands were primarily intellectual. This does not mean that the sons and daughters of the Crown Prince and Princess were spared the formalities of life in a nineteenth-century palace. They were required to sit "stiffly upright" at meals and were not allowed to speak unless spoken to. As in other royal households, they were required to stand in the presence of their parents and kiss their hands when bidding them good morning or good night.

But family life does seem to have been more pleasant and relaxed with fewer of the empty rituals demanded in other palaces. At the age of three, Moretta, who had been taken to see her paternal grandmother and had behaved extremely well throughout the visit, was severely reprimanded by Augusta for running out of the room. "Come back," the Queen ordered the toddler. "You walk out of my presence, you do not scamper."

Unlike both her mother-in-law, who had refused to have more than two children, and her mother, who had resented each new pregnancy, Vicky welcomed every addition to her family. Queen Victoria worried about this. "Believe me, children are a terrible anxiety . . . the sorrow they cause is far greater than the pleasure they give." The Queen thought her eldest daughter was riding for a fall. "[W]hen one idolises one's children, as you do, what will you suffer when you have quite to give them up & feel how little they care for you and all your care & anxiety."

If Vicky adored her children, she was also obsessed with preparing them for great deeds. In 1866 she asked her mother for copies of memoranda written by her father and old Baron Stockmar to use as a guide in setting up an educational plan like the one used at Buckingham Palace. Her immediate problem was Charlotte's French governess, who, she felt, had usurped her maternal prerogatives. In rearranging her nursery, Vicky flew in the face of Hohenzollern tradition:

"I cannot and will not abandon all right of interfering with the children's education and must reserve to myself to judge of what they are to learn & who is to teach them . . . ," she wrote her mother. "This is very difficult here as the Princesses were given up hand and foot to a Countess or Baroness who had the unlimited control over everything, lessons, meals, dress, walks & all, and answerable to the Sovereign whoever he might be. This is the precedent here & I never could get it out of Sophie's [the French governess's] head."

Unlike other German princesses of her day, Vicky did not exhibit an all-consuming interest in clothes, and after eight years of complaints about the money wasted on gowns and accessories, she also dispensed with the services of the maid who had accompanied her to Berlin to supervise her wardrobe. "[S]he had grown so grand & fine and difficult to manage, & my money went at such a rate with the expenses of my toilette that I thought it better to keep her no longer," the Crown Princess explained to her mother.

The palace nurseries were not immune to similar domestic upheavals, and governesses, nurses, and nursery maids came and went with some regularity. With six children in the first ten years and eight born over a fifteen-year period, it was not easy to keep an adequate staff that got along with the children, their employers, and the other employees in the household. In a situation where everyone—tutors, nurses, governesses, and maids—vied for status, there was always a quarrel to be settled or a place to be filled. To get some idea of the constant hiring, firing, and shuffling required, one has only to note that when traveling in Germany with her children, the Crown Princess's entourage numbered between thirty and forty people.

HAVING ACQUIRED the daughter-in-law she wanted, it would have been logical for Augusta to help Vicky along what was not an easy road. But the Kaiserin had little or no love for Vicky or her children. Time and again, the Crown Princess complained that Augusta paid no attention to her grandchildren, even ignoring their birthdays. Although their grandfather was fond of them, his enthusiasm did not extend to presents either.

It was Queen Victoria who never let an occasion or a birthday slip by, sending off all manner of elaborate gifts, some of them clearly aimed at the future (silver candlesticks, jewelry), others more immediately practical (ponies for Willy and Charlotte). "I always say you are like a Fairy Godmother who showers down beautiful gifts on your grandchildren," Vicky wrote after Victoria sent some flat silver to Waldemar for his second birthday. "They will have lovely souvenirs from you to keep all their lives and transmit to their descendants!"

When Charlotte turned three, Queen Victoria sent her a dress. "I kiss your dear hands for it," Vicky wrote her mother. "Her grandparents here have not taken the slightest notice of her birthday. . . . neither the King or the Queen ever give her anything, so you see your gifts are a double pleasure, dear Mama."

Queen Victoria also welcomed visits from her grandchildren with or without their parents. Both Willy and Henry were sent to England for their health, and all Vicky's children spent periods of time there. These trips were invariably preceded by lengthy discussions about the number of servants who were to accompany them, with Victoria stipulating how many she was prepared to house and Vicky responding that it was not enough, since her father-in-law routinely required at least one "watchdog" (usually a German army officer) in attendance.

Vicky always worried about her children's behavior when they were with her mother. It was vitally important to her that the Queen approve of her children, and she fretted over the fact that one or another looked poorly, might not appear intelligent, or might not behave according to Victoria's exacting standards.

Nevertheless, her children grew up loving England nearly as much as she did. "Our whole family were the guests of my grandmother, sometimes at Buckingham Palace, sometimes at that splendid Castle of Windsor, or at Osborne . . . ," Kaiser Wilhelm II wrote in later years. "We were treated as children of the house, and we looked up to our grandmother, Britain's great Queen Victoria, with affectionate awe. The Queen was always particularly kind to me from the very first."

This did not mean that Victoria was blind to an unfortunate self-importance developing in her eldest grandson, a tendency she hastened to call to his mother's attention during the five-year-old's sojourn in England in the summer of 1864. Willy, it seems, had refused to ride backward in his grandmother's carriage, since that seat indicated a lesser position in the family.

"We have often observed that tinge of pride in Master Willie which you speak of and tried to correct it . . . ," the Crown Princess answered; "the servants & everybody in the house only tend to encourage it, and he is very fond of ordering people about, thinks a great deal of his own importance. . . . I make him sit backwards in the carriage on purpose & get in last etc., but the footmen are always ready to put him in before me, and to do all he chooses."

Vicky tried to counteract the attitude displayed by the court toward young Willy, but it was a losing battle. From England, the Queen continued to caution her daughter: "[B]ring him [up] simply, plainly, not with that terrible Prussian pride & ambition, which grieved dear Papa so much."

CHAPTER
THIRTY-EIGHT

"[I]t is the task of the tutor to grasp hold of the soul of his pupil."

GEORGE HINTZPETER

*I*N 1864, WHEN THE FUTURE Kaiser Wilhelm II was five years old, Vicky wrote her mother that she hoped they would "make no mistakes in his education or do him harm in any way. . . . One can in fact do very little and one must study the child itself, as it is and then judge what is best for it, instead of making for oneself an ideal . . . & then being provoked with the child for not coming up to one's wishes; I often feel I am in danger of running into this fault from mere zeal and ambition that he should turn out like dear Papa and become a great man, a second Frederick the Great."

Resolutions to the contrary, the Crown Princess failed to curb her aspirations for Willy. Moreover, she hired a tutor who made things worse.

History is full of disastrous royal tutors—none more carefully chosen nor more painstakingly vetted than George Hintzpeter, a Calvinist doctor of philosophy and classical philology who entered the Crown Prince and Princess's household in 1866, when Willy was six, and remained for more than a decade. Thirty-nine years old at the time, Hintzpeter had impressive bearing, lofty ideals, and a great shortage of common sense. He was found by Vicky's old friend Robert Morier, with whom he shared a belief that the strength of a nation lay in the well-being of its working class—a noble and innovative precept for Germany at the time, but hardly a recommendation of pedagogical talent. Even the mild-mannered Ernest von Stockmar, a friend of Morier who usually agreed with him, was put off after a conversation with Hintzpeter:

"He is a very superior man," Stockmar wrote Morier,

> but I have my doubts whether he is the right man. . . . he . . . is a hard Spartan idealist. And as to his ideals I am afraid they are somewhat unpractical. He says that a king is doomed to live a solitary life, a life entirely devoted to duty, and among the conclusions drawn from this proposition are the following: That he [Willy] is not to be brought up with other boys; that he is not to have drawing or music lessons, because that sort of thing does not belong to kingcraft. . . .

I am afraid he is crotchety. . . . he maintains that a boy ought not to go to the Zoological Gardens to see an elephant unless he should already know that elephants don't lay eggs. . . . He says a boy ought never to see the model of a weaver's loom, that would be perfectly barbarous, he ought to see the weaver at his loom in his torn jacket. . . . Now this is confounding two obviously different things: if you want to study weavers then you must see the torn jacket . . . but that has nothing to do with the mechanism of the loom. . . . I see a tendency to push things, true in themselves, to an extreme.

Nonetheless, Hintzpeter was engaged in the fall of 1866, and he quickly settled into a position of authority. According to Hohenzollern tradition, Willy had already been removed from the care of women and put under the tutelage of a military governor. Within a year of Hintzpeter's arrival, the governor was gone. When Fritz and Vicky wanted to take Willy with them to England and France when the boy was eight, Hintzpeter protested against the interruption of his lessons. Vicky seldom questioned Hintzpeter. Her eldest son, she said, was "just beginning to get into the way of learning—and behaving well."

Hintzpeter was deemed by the Crown Princess to be "a pearl" and "a treasure." "We feel so great a confidence in his judgement and can confide our boys to him with perfect security. . . . I often think how dear Papa would have delighted in him," Vicky wrote Victoria when Willy was nine and Henry six. "We may consider ourselves very fortunate in having found Dr. Hintzpeter," she reiterated three years later.

Her sons might not have agreed.

"Hintzpeter was an able man, thoroughly well educated," Wilhelm II said in later life. "His knowledge was extensive and his interests wide. . . ." But, according to the pupil, Hintzpeter's "educational system was based exclusively on a stern sense of duty and the idea of service; the character was to be fortified by perpetual 'renunciation.' . . . When our Meiningen cousins came on a visit, I had, as host, to offer them cakes, but must take none myself; 'Renunciation' was the word. Dry bread for breakfast. . . ."

Worse than dry bread was the absence of praise. In Hintzpeter's educational system, there was no place for encouragement. "The impossible was expected of the pupil in order to force him to the nearest degree of perfection," said Wilhelm II. "Naturally, the impossible goal could never be achieved; logically, therefore, the praise which registers approval was also excluded."

This approach was a logical extension of Hintzpeter's strict Calvinism. Although the tutor made it a point never to discuss religion with his pupils, his personal belief in predestination,* an implacable God, and a chosen elite cannot help but have infected his educational and moral outlook. It is remarkable that

---

* The Calvinists believed that the soul was predestined for heaven or hell, and that the chosen could be identified through their lives and their manner of living.

Vicky and Fritz, whose religious attitudes were considered dangerously tolerant for their day and caste, did not realize the implications of Hintzpeter's rigidity.

At the same time, there must have been something good about Hintzpeter —an innate sincerity perhaps, apparent in person but not available to the historian—that made his pupils fond of him. "[D]espite the hard school he put me through," said the ex-Kaiser in 1926, "I have never lost my sense of grateful respect for all he did for me. . . . I never lost touch with him; up to his death I saw and corresponded with him."

Hintzpeter's arrival coincided with that of a new governess, Mlle. Darcourt, whom he eventually married. Seemingly two of a kind, they took over both nursery and schoolroom. Vicky, who had been struggling with toadying servants who refused to back up her discipline, was grateful. "Children's faults often proceed from the people about them . . . ," she wrote Victoria shortly after the changeover in personnel. "A mother is . . . too apt to be too quick & impulsive, because the children's faults aggravate her much more than other people, as she is more ambitious for them and feels responsible for their dispositions. . . . I think you would find me much more gentle and sensible with the children than I was. . . . I have no need of acting the policeman now."

But by putting unrealistic demands on her children, the Crown Princess seemed to reinforce the Hintzpeter message. No achievement was ever enough —either in scholastics or character—to satisfy her. After leaving her sons in Cannes with their tutor during the winter of 1870, Vicky wrote to thank Willy for a letter, which was apparently the first he had ever written without Hintzpeter's guidance. (Vicky's children wrote to her in English.) "[I]t is so pleasant to be independent and feel one can do things without help," Vicky told her son, "and then never to be satisfied with what one does but always to try and do better still."

She seemed incapable of giving the boy a compliment without a criticism or a prod: "It is a great pleasure to me to get letters from you . . . ," she told the eleven-year-old a few weeks later, but added, "I cannot compliment you dearest boy on your writing, the hand and the spelling are both bad, there was hardly a word without a mistake or a letter left out." To remedy this, the Crown Princess frequently returned Willy's letters with her corrections.

SOMEWHAT BEFORE HINTZPETER'S arrival, Willy had begun a course of daily gymnastics, inaugurated by his mother over the objections of Doctors Wegner and Langenbeck, who apparently disapproved of this simple attempt to overcome the boy's handicap. The exercises seemed to Vicky to do her son a great deal of good, more than the unpleasant "galvanization" treatments (electric stimuli applied to his useless arm) that had been prescribed in England by Queen Victoria's doctors.

By the time he started gymnastics, Willy had already had two operations to straighten the line of his head by separating muscles in his neck. The first was performed shortly after his sixth birthday. "I cannot say how I dread the thought of another operation," Vicky wrote Victoria shortly before the second, "but I see that it is necessary, the former operation having already done so much good."

Ramrod posture was considered essential in the military society in which young Willy grew up, a world where parades were important public manifestations of the power of the state. "It was impossible to think of the capital of Prussia without soldiers and regimental bands," he himself said later. "The midday changing of the guard was part of the picture of the city." If Willy was one day to assume his rightful place at the apex of this pageantry, he must look the part. This meant not only straightening his crooked upper body, but also teaching him to ride horseback. Vicky understood the symbolism. "He must become as good as the best riders in Prussia, and I will not be satisfied short of that," she wrote Fritz when their son was four, adding that the boy was making "good progress in riding." The progress was not enough for Hintzpeter.

"When the prince was eight and a half years old," he wrote,

a lackey still had to lead his pony by the rein, because his balance was so bad. . . . So long as this lasted, he could not learn to ride: it had to be overcome, no matter at what cost. . . . Therefore, the tutor, using a moral authority over his pupil that by now had become absolute, set the weeping prince on his horse, without stirrups, and compelled him to go through the various paces. He fell off continually: every time, despite his prayers and tears, he was lifted up and set upon its back again. After weeks of torture, the difficult task was accomplished: he had got his balance. These morning exercises in the alleys of the Park were a nightmare to everyone: worse for the torturer than for the tortured.

Perhaps. But one would be more inclined to believe in Hintzpeter's personal agony if the rest of his tutoring did not bear such a strong resemblance to the heartless riding lessons.

"Prof. Hinzpeter, a stern, serious, hard-working man . . . was very strict with my brother," said Willy's sister Moretta. "Not a minute of the day would be lost. All the time would be taken up in serious study or in necessary exercise. . . . There were times when I would hear Hinzpeter shouting at the top of his voice and using what I took to be a cane. He was in the next room to us with William. The noise of the cane distressed me greatly. I was certain it was being used on William, and I taxed Mademoiselle Darcourt about it, but she refused to say a word against her fiancé, hotly denying that he ever raised a finger to his pupil."

Schoolwork began at 6:00 A.M. in the summer, 7:00 A.M. in the winter and lasted for twelve hours with two breaks—for meals and physical exercise. The curriculum included Latin, English, arithmetic, history, and geography. "But you begin too early with Latin," Victoria cautioned her daughter. "Our boys only began at 10—& Willy is not 9." Before Hintzpeter's arrival, Vicky, who taught the children English and beginning chemistry herself, would have agreed. Now she gave way in the face of Hintzpeter's assumption of superiority. By the time he was twelve, the future Kaiser had read all seven books of Caesar's *Gallic Wars* and had begun to study Greek.

Hintzpeter's educational theories were also aimed at giving Willy and Henry a taste of life in the workplace. Twice a week their tutor took them to a factory, workshop, blacksmith's, or foundry to acquaint them with the processes of manufacturing and expose them to life among the laboring classes. Upon arriving at the factory, the boys were required to approach the manager, take off their hats, and offer suitable thanks for allowing them to visit. "We saw the miserable housing conditions of the workers and their families, and the grim poverty, often, of their homes," said the ex-Kaiser over fifty years later. "Worst of all was the soul-destroying power of the machine, in which the worker was the tiniest cog in a gigantic clock. . . . This was . . . Hinzpeter's greatest contribution to my real education."

Lessons like these, however, were not allowed to interfere with the cult of the military. At the age of ten, Willy, like his father and grandfather before him, was given a commission in the Prussian army and invested by his grandfather in the Order of the Black Eagle, the highest Prussian honor, presented to him on a huge solid-gold plate. His mother disapproved.

"Tomorrow will be trying to me . . . when I see William seized upon and all sorts of nonsense talked to him, which I have carefully kept from him till now . . . ," she wrote Victoria on the eve of his tenth birthday. "The King and whole family are delighted. They fancy the child will be quite one of them from that day forth. Of course Willie is as proud and excited as possible to think he is really going to enter the ranks of the army & have his name put down in the lists. I think of how absurd he looks dressed up in his uniform & all his orders, etc. You can imagine that the household pays him no end of compliments etc., however it cannot be helped & I must just put the best face I can upon it."

A few months later, Willy took part in his first military parade, celebrating the anniversary of one of Prussia's victorious battles. The entire royal family, Vicky included, marched or rode in these parades, which took place several times a year. Although Vicky wrote Victoria that Willy had "marched past very well" in his first attempt, she had clearly communicated her displeasure over his participation to her son. Writing his grandmother, who also disapproved of his early induction into the military, the ten-year-old said, "There were lately two parades where I marched before the King; he told me that I marched well, but Mama said I did it very badly."

Willy's passion for the army surfaced early. Vicky first noticed it during the Schleswig-Holstein War, when he ran around chattering "constantly" about battle sites with no idea of what he was saying. Hintzpeter encouraged this interest, and during the Franco-Prussian conflict expected Willy and Henry to follow the progress of the German armies, pointing out their relative positions on a huge map as part of their daily lessons.

As an alternative to this "too engrossing military passion," the Crown

Princess encouraged her sons' interest in ships. Their grandmother had the mast and rigging of a British man-of-war copied for them; it was installed on the lawn at Bornstedt, where they could study the ropes and learn to climb. In planning a family trip to England, during which Hintzpeter had arranged edifying trips to manufacturing centers like Manchester, Liverpool, and Birmingham, Vicky interspersed visits to Portsmouth and Southampton—outings that thrilled her sons.

But there was more to Vicky's emphasis on the navy than even she realized —a subtle way of comparing England to Germany and making sure that England came out better. "Many thanks for your letter . . . which was written with more care and tidiness . . . ," she wrote Willy during his winter in Cannes.

> What a pretty sight it must have been to see the English yacht run into the harbour. . . . it is always a special object of pride and delight to me to see an English ship. The neatness, cleanliness and order which are so far superior to American, German, or French, Italian or Portugese ships always strikes me afresh and I say to myself (quite inwardly), "Britannia rules the waves!" However you being a little German boy are not supposed or expected to feel this, and some day when you grow up I am sure you will feel as proud and grateful to be a German as I am to be an Englishwoman, at least I hope so with all my heart.

Willy had his first glimpse of a German ironclad during a family trip to the island of Nordeney in the North Sea. The thrill of seeing the *König Wilhelm*, then the largest battleship in the world, never left him. "What impressed me most, after the massive rigging, was the long tier of guns with their heavy polished muzzles," he said.

On his twelfth birthday, the Crown Princess sent her mother an assessment of her son and her role in his education:

> "I am sure you would be pleased with William if you were to see him. . . . He is not possessed of brilliant abilities, nor of any strength of character or talents, but he is a dear boy, and I hope & trust will grow up a useful man. He has an excellent tutor, I never saw or knew a better, and all the care that can be bestowed on mind and body is taken of him. I watch over him myself, over each detail, even the minutest, of his education."

"I am sure you will watch over your dear boy with the greatest care," Victoria answered, "but I often think too great care, too much constant watching leads to those very dangers . . . which one wishes to avoid. It is a terrible difficulty and a terrible trial to be a prince. No one having the courage to tell them the truth or to accustom them to those rubs and knocks which are so necessary to boys and young men." Willy's English grandmother worried about the effect on her grandson of the German preoccupation with rank. In answer to a warning from her mother, the Crown Princess had this to say:

> You need not fear that he will be brought up in a way to make him proud and stuck up. . . . Willy is very shy by nature and that often makes him

look proud. The ladies and gentlemen who tried to nurture a mistaken pride in the idea that it was <u>patriotic</u>, are no longer about him. . . . His companions are chosen without <u>any</u> regard to rank or family, and the continual contact into which <u>our</u> <u>princes</u> are brought with <u>soldiers</u> (there is not a more democratic institution in the world than our army . . .) is a safeguard against their growing up in ignorance of the wants and interests of the lower classes.

Whether Vicky recognized it or not, the Prussian army was one of the most elite organizations of nineteenth-century Europe. Officers were nearly always of noble birth, uniforms were a fetish, and men still fought duels for the fun of it. Contrary to what Vicky hoped, the army was the last place to instill any sort of democratic principles in her eldest son.

THERE WAS ANOTHER INFLUENCE on Willy, one that turned out to be stronger than that of either parent and that, like the army, reinforced the boy's sense of caste. This was his grandfather, Wilhelm I, whose belief in the divine right of kings was fed to his heir along with champagne and tales of old battles during cozy tête-à-tête dinners in his palace. A gentleman who believed himself to be a sincere servant of his people, Wilhelm I still rose before daylight and slept in an iron camp bed, a relic of his last campaign, in a dark, airless room on the palace courtyard. Hidden from an outer chamber by a green curtain, this alcove represented the essence of Willy's grandfather. Aside from the wooden crucifix over his head, there was a case containing his decorations, a stand for his swords, and a rack with ribbons and streamers from old wreaths. Next door was Wilhelm's dressing room, in which he had refused to install a tub, preferring to have one lugged over from the neighboring Hôtel de Rome when he wanted to take a bath. Nevertheless, Wilhelm I was always correctly dressed. He might open his coat indoors, but he quickly buttoned it up and added his order Pour le Mérite when he heard the band coming for the changing of the guard. "Once or twice," an observer noted, "I saw him come out of the Palace at seven o'clock in the morning on a raw, wet winter's day, when it was so dark that the street lamps were still alight, and stand on the muddy pavement until the troops had gone by."

The room known to his subjects from pictures and photographs as the Kaiser's room was actually the third in his suite. There were many Germans who recognized at a glance the famous writing table, clustered with family pictures, and above it, shelves with a bust of Friedrich Wilhelm III, portraits, medallions, and reference books—army lists, drill books, lists of orders, law books, dictionaries, and the report from his general staff on the Franco-Prussian War. It was here, on a rickety green card table set up in a corner, that grandfather and grandson were served their dinner. These were wonderful evenings, in which the two developed an "extremely intimate" bond, the kind of relationship that should have smoothed out some rough spots for the child and given him a refuge from the excessive demands made on him at home. In this case, however, it served mainly to keep an impressionable boy aware of his future as God's anointed.

During the Franco-Prussian War, Vicky complained to Fritz that Willy had grown "very haughty, exceptionally self-satisfied and pleased with himself." To counteract this, the Crown Princess reminded her son of his infirmity. As she wrote the boy's father some years later, "When William was still a child and frequently talked and acted and carried on in such a complacent fashion, I always said to him, in order to tease him, none will take you, with your black finger, etc., and he would insult me back." It became a "frequent bantering exchange" between them.

Aware that his continual absences from home were having an adverse effect on the boy, Fritz wrote that at Willy's age, he had emulated his father and that "contact with me would be very useful just now. . . . I am always worried that the 'prince' affects him more deeply than we believe, and I would love to know if the Emperor thing is already going around in his head too."

Nevertheless, both parents were sanguine about their influence on their son on the eve of his teens. "Thank God there is between him and us, his parents, a simple, natural, cordial relation, to preserve which is our constant endeavour, that he may always look upon us as his true, his best friends," Fritz wrote on January 27, 1871, in his diary from military headquarters in Versailles.

His sentiments were echoed in a letter written by Vicky to Victoria the next day from Berlin. "I am happy to say that between him and me there is a bond of love and confidence, which I feel sure nothing can destroy."

OF ALL VICKY'S CHILDREN, her eldest daughter, Charlotte, was the most difficult for her. Born just nineteen months after Willy, Charlotte showed signs of agitation as a toddler—biting her nails and pulling at her clothes. Forced to wear gloves or stand with her hands tied together, she stopped at age five, but only briefly. "Tell Charlotte I am so shocked to hear of her biting her things & that Grandmama does not like naughty little girls," the Queen wrote Vicky.

More disturbing than Charlotte's nervousness was her seeming inability to learn—a big problem to an ambitious mother. "Stupidity is not a sin," Vicky wrote about her, "but it renders education a hard and difficult task."

Vicky's worries about Charlotte were not helped by Dr. Hintzpeter and Mlle. Darcourt, who continually told the Crown Princess that they had never encountered "more difficulties" than with this strange little girl. "Alas, she is an unsatisfactory child, poor little thing . . . ," Vicky wrote when Charlotte was seven, "but with so excellent a governess, so perfect a master . . . I trust she may yet be all we can wish, if a means can be found to develop her intelligence and her affections and give her a sense of duty. She is in very good looks, and much admired."

The acknowledged favorite of Wilhelm and Augusta, young Charlotte was deemed pretty by the royal family—a judgment that can be explained only by her strong resemblance to them. They spoiled this troubled child, who eventually grew into a troublemaking young woman, eager to show that she knew everything better than everyone else—proof perhaps that Charlotte's inability to learn was nothing more than passive resistance, an unconscious weapon against a mother who so desperately valued intelligence and scholastic achievement.

Vicky's third child and second son, Henry, was a fretful baby who suffered a long, weakening bout of dysentery during his third winter. Dr. Wegner blamed the Crown Princess, who, he said, kept the child too cool. The doctor ordered the windows of the nursery closed, sent Henry out to play "smothered" in flannels, and put him to bed at night with hot packs tied around his stomach. By late spring Henry's health had improved, but he had changed from an active, independent toddler into a hestitant one, unsteady on his legs, crying to be carried around, or just crying. The next year, when he was sent off to spend the winter in England with his grandmother, Vicky felt she must warn her mother what manner of grandchild she was getting: "You do not know how much trouble we have had with Henry. . . . He never spoke the truth, roared by hours together if the <u>least</u> <u>thing</u> was refused him . . . bit, kicked and scratched the maids if they did not instantly do what he chose. . . ." Nevertheless, Vicky was still sure her mother would "like the poor child; he cannot help being so ugly, and he is really not stupid and can be very amusing."

Two years later, Henry was moved out of the nursery and started on his lessons. Hintzpeter, hired the previous year, complained that this child, too, was "very backward & slow." In spite of Queen Victoria's warnings, Vicky allowed Hintzpeter to proceed with his lessons. "He <u>must</u> begin to know his letters, to hold a pen and to count—he has done nothing <u>at</u> <u>all</u> till <u>now</u>, not even learned to speak French, & he is past 5 years old, he is more ignorant than any other little child of his age here, as on account of his health we hitherto left him his entire liberty."

Victoria issued another warning three years later. "You need not be afraid that Henry is forced or pushed in any way . . . ," Vicky responded. "I trust you will . . . make the acquaintance of their excellent tutor who is indeed a treasure, which I cannot be thankful enough for, it is so difficult to find the <u>right</u> person."

THE CHILDREN OF the Crown Prince and Princess are usually divided into two groups, with the first three—Wilhelm, Charlotte, and Henry—forming a little family unto themselves. By 1872, the Crown Princess had given birth to eight children, seven of whom survived. Of the four youngest—Moretta, Waldemar, Sophie, and Mossy—two were wartime babies: Moretta had been christened the day before Fritz left for the Austro-Prussian War, and Sophie had been born during the diplomatic joustings that preceded the war between Prussia and France.

Vicky seldom complained about Fritz's long absences from his family, but she was upset by this aspect of their lives. When her husband returned in the spring of 1871, she noted that the baby was "very shy of her Papa" and hoped that with Germany united and the wars at an end, Fritz would be home more. But, as Vicky well knew, the Hohenzollerns were a clan of warriors, and it was this that had created the new German Empire. Moreover, it suited both Bismarck and Wilhelm I to keep the Crown Prince occupied with his troops—away as much as possible from the liberal influence of his wife.

CHAPTER
THIRTY-NINE

*B*Y THE TIME SHE WAS in her thirties, Vicky's complaints to her mother about life in Germany in general and her ailments in particular had assumed a fairly consistent pattern. They started in the winter, coinciding with the social season, and subsided in the late spring, when she left for Potsdam and comparative freedom. "Oh the expense of the toilettes & the fatigue!" she had written Victoria when she was still in her twenties, "11 balls await us!!—none over before 3 o'clock . . . then 2 fêtes with trains, an innumerable quantity of small soirées and concerts besides the theatre and audiences. I consider it far worse than the treadmill, it is just as much a punishment to me!"

There were both physical and social reasons for Vicky's misery. In the first place, she had inherited her father's inability to stay awake late. Her biological rhythms, like his, dictated early rising, intense activity, and early bedtime—a problem in a court in which the Kaiser and Kaiserin insisted on long, drawn-out parties every night. "I fear I am more sleepy of an evening than even dear Papa was—it is quite a misfortune as it makes one so unamiable, & is such misery to oneself."

Added to the physical discomfort was the atmosphere of disapproval surrounding the Crown Princess. Vicky was well aware that from her first day in Germany the ladies of the court considered it "a pity their future King had married one so plain and so unornamental for society." They, in turn, bored her witless. "[I]t makes me feel so stupid talking about the weather etc. that I get quite absent, & nearly go to sleep . . . ," Vicky wrote Victoria after a day of female audiences. This was explained by Baron Hugo von Reischach, who served Wilhelm I and became Vicky's Lord Chamberlain many years later. The Crown Princess, he said, "possessed a virtue which distinguished her from other princesses: she had an open mind."

She was no happier in the ballroom. Short, inclined to be stout, with skin that flushed red in the intense heat (salons were kept at over eighty degrees in the winter), Vicky was ashamed of her "hideous self" and felt far more comfortable with people who did not judge her on her looks. "I fear I cut a sorry figure at balls, as my eyes invariably close with fatigue—& I have to make such faces to keep them open!" For a girl who loved cool, fresh air, the stale odors of heated bodies, heavy gowns, and uniforms were slow torture, and she usually left the ballroom with a pounding headache.

Vicky had always suffered from what one member of her household called "an almost inconquerable shyness," and making small talk was an enormous effort. "Everybody noticed how cordial and charming Her Imperial Highness was here last Monday," Emily Russell, wife of the British Ambassador, wrote Queen Victoria in 1877, "and how graciously she went round and talked to everybody. . . . the people to whom she only says a few words are at once charmed . . . but they complain . . . that the Crown Princess will not give herself the trouble to speak much to them. . . . in consequence she is not as popular as she might be but all those who know her and have the privilege of talking to her are devoted to her."

Unlike Victoria, who shared her daughter's distaste for court gatherings, Vicky was not in a position to determine her own schedule, and at the end of April 1873, she agreed to attend the opening of another international exhibition, this one in Vienna. Emperor Franz Joseph and Empress Elisabeth had invited fourteen-year-old Willy as well, and a few weeks before they were due to leave, Vicky wrote to tell Victoria that her eldest son would accompany them. The Queen, who dated Bertie's moral decline from his introduction to Paris at the same age, was not pleased.

"I am rather sorry you take dear Willie as I fear it will make him old before his years & bring him too forward," she warned. Vicky hastened to answer the Queen's concerns. "[L]et me say Willy is quite incognito: at Vienna, does not appear at dinners or parties but goes to bed quite early as he does here. We do not wish to bring him forward in any way; he is only to have the treat of seeing the Exhibition."

Willy, whose treats seem to have been few and far between, had been enjoying the temporary absence of Dr. Hintzpeter during which he led what his mother called "quite a dissipated life for him, going with us to see pictures [i.e., museums] etc." It was probably Hintzpeter's absence that gave Fritz and Vicky the courage to include their son in the Vienna trip; in a letter to a former employer, Hintzpeter criticized the Crown Prince and Princess for not being able to resist the temptation to show him off.

This was Vicky's third international exhibition, and she did not look forward to it. "It is the dressing & undressing which fatigues me and which I hate most of all! I dread Vienna so much, the Exhibition interests me immensely but I am so sick of ceremonies, etiquette, dress, show, fatigue & waste of time," she said.

Met at the station "with all ceremony possible" by Franz Joseph, a quantity of archdukes, and brothers Bertie and Arthur, the Crown Prince and Princess of Germany and their son were escorted to the castle at Hetzendorf, a small, comfortable rococo building with a lovely garden behind the famous Schönbrunn Palace, where they could walk in the royal park.

While his parents attended social events, Willy and the German general sent to watch over him spent their time with Crown Prince Rudolph, heir to the Austrian Empire. Rudolph and his suite of gentlemen took Willy on excursions into the countryside around Vienna and through the city itself, where the heir to the German throne reveled in the jewels of the old Holy Roman Empire and the Ambras collection of armor and weapons. The boys ate their meals together and were occasionally invited to visit at the table of their elders.

Willy was particularly impressed with Rudolph's mother, the Empress Elisabeth, whom Vicky had once described to her son as "the most beautiful woman in Europe." When they arrived in Vienna, the teenage heir to the German throne was so "completely carried away" with Elisabeth's beauty that he forgot to kiss her hand. A few days later, he was called down to the garden at Hetzendorf and instructed to carry the Empress's train while the ladies walked together. As he wrote later in his memoirs, he "observed with devotion and wonder the stateliness of the Empress's carriage and her beautiful gliding walk. It could be literally said of her what an old-time injunction of Court etiquette demanded: she did not sit down—she took a seat; she did not stand up—she rose; she did not walk—she wended her way."

If Willy's short, pudgy, and quick-moving mother was a contrast to the graceful Elisabeth, he was also thrown into relief against the charming heir to the Habsburg Empire. "Willie is a good bit taller and twice as broad as the little Crown Prince Rudolph, who is a slight graceful boy with very nice manners," Vicky reported to Victoria when she arrived. "I fear Willy seems rather a bear or a schoolboy beside him."

Accorded the honor of leading the procession into the exhibition hall on the arm of Franz Joseph, the Crown Princess compared the opening of the exhibition, held in a pavilion large enough to accommodate the dome of St. Peter's in Rome, with that of the great exhibition in London in 1851. "The ceremony was grand and imposing but my thoughts were far away & I recalled the brilliant & touching scene 23 years ago . . . ," she wrote Victoria, "you standing on the Hautpas [podium] and darling Papa looking so beautiful & reading that never-to-be forgotten speech! I saw it all . . . and the reality before me seemed gloomy and matter of fact compared with that! Others who cannot share these precious recollections no doubt were much impressed with the immense size of the building and the crowds (mostly seen in morning dress) which filled it."

Although she spoke gratefully of the kindness and attentions of Franz Joseph and Elisabeth, the Crown Princess soon tired of the other royal guests. She and Fritz left for a short tour of northern Italy before the arrival of her mother-in-law, described by one Austrian nobleman as a "ridiculous, florid, garrulous dolled-up creature, with the voice of a corpse." Of all the royalties present, Vicky had most enjoyed her own brothers. "You can imagine what a delight it is to me to see Bertie . . . so irresistibly kind & good-natured," she wrote their mother, passing along Bertie's apologies for not writing himself.

"It gives me so much pleasure to hear you speak so lovingly of dear Bertie for he deserves it . . . ," replied Victoria, who had nearly lost her eldest son to typhoid eighteen months earlier. "I am also very glad to see how much you like the Emperor & Empress of Austria—& Willie the young Archduke Rudolph," the Queen of England added. "It will be of <u>such</u> use."

QUEEN VICTORIA WAS NOT the only one who believed in the political efficacy of friendship and marriage between rulers—a common nineteenth-century fallacy to which even Bismarck was prone. In that regard, Alix and her sister Dagmar, wives of the heirs of the British and Russian thrones, respectively, had promoted a match between Vicky's brother Affie (Alfred) and Czar Alexander II's daughter, the Grand Duchess Marie. Queen Victoria was strongly opposed, partly because of religion (the Romanovs were Orthodox), partly because of politics, but mostly because the Czar had not jumped at the chance to marry his only daughter to the Queen of England's second son.

The Crown Princess of Germany was of two minds about her brother's choice. She distrusted the Russian royal family, but had been impressed with the Grand Duchess on the few occasions they had met. Marie was Vicky's kind of girl—highly intelligent and relatively unaffected. She was not, by any stretch of the imagination, pretty, but Vicky made every effort to look at her good points—a clear complexion and nice forehead, an unaffected and outspoken manner, and a fortune that would go far in the duchy of Coburg, which Affie was due to inherit from his father's childless brother, Duke Ernest. Besides, Affie was already twenty-eight years old, dangerously late for a royal brother to be marrying and starting a family.

Vicky decided to attend her brother's wedding. Queen Victoria was not overjoyed at the news. "I hope the cold at St. Petersburg will not be too much for you," she wrote. "I shall feel not being present for the first time at the marriage of one of our children, but at the same time I dislike <u>now</u> witnessing marriages <u>very</u> <u>much</u>, & think them sad & painful."

The wedding of the Czar's daughter to the Queen of England's son took place on January 23, 1874, in the splendor of the Winter Palace. It was celebrated in two parts to conform to the Orthodoxy of the bride and the Anglican religion of the groom. The Russian ceremony was by far the more picturesque, with the bride and groom circling the altar of the imperial chapel carrying lighted candles. A few days later, the company moved on to Moscow, where there were more luncheons and dinners and balls, including a party given by the bridal couple a week after their wedding.

It was a lavish wedding, even by royal standards. Augusta Stanley, wife of the dean who officiated at the English service, wrote home to say that although she had borrowed diamonds from everyone she knew before leaving England, she still made a poor showing next to the Russian Grand Duchesses, who were "literally covered with them—belts, trimmings, skirts, bodies, heads—gigantic stones—and emeralds, and other stones besides." Another English lady complained bitterly about the lack of personal hygiene among these well-jeweled ladies, whom she accused of smelling no better than the muzhiks who served them.

Vicky spent less time in the Czar's palaces than the other ladies. She was out, seeing and sketching this exotic new world, which she described in a letter to Victoria after her return:

> Anything to be compared with Moscow as a sight—and as a picture I never saw. . . . the grandness of those 300 churches with their golden green & blue domes, the mighty fortress walls with the beautiful little towers with glazed, green tile roofs and strange columns some Byzantine, some Norman and some Mauresque—all this with the beautiful glittering snow and the black crows circling round this forest of proud towers & steeples was too magnificent. . . .
>
> I am very glad I went to Russia, though profoundly thankful I am not a Russian and need not spend my days there. . . . over the whole of Russia there seems to me to hang a dull, heavy, silent melancholy very depressing to the spirits! I do not talk of Petersburg as those who like to live in a whirl of excitement & frivolity can do so just the same as at Paris or Vienna, and have no time to . . . reflect of the world beyond the brilliant salons, and the luxe écrasant of the Palaces & the frantic extravagance of so great a Court.

Nothing more than a few weeks of expensive royal celebrations came of this matrimonial thaw between England and Russia. The marriage of Prince Alfred of England and the Grand Duchess Marie of Russia, which looked promising at the beginning of 1874, was not a happy one. Nor did it, as had been hoped, improve relations between their countries. It was, in fact, little more than a political irrelevancy—a union that did nothing to alter the alignment of powers so carefully arranged by Bismarck.

CHAPTER
FORTY

"To prefer . . . a bad Christian to a good Mohammedan seems to me so utterly mistaken."

CROWN PRINCESS VICTORIA OF GERMANY

*E*VER SINCE THE EIGHTEENTH CENTURY, the great nations of Europe had been watching the disintegration of the once mighty Ottoman Empire, contemplating what each stood to gain or lose by its inevitable collapse. Brought on by mismanagement, interior corruption, and the rise of nationalism, the demise of the "Sick Man of Europe" began to accelerate toward the end of the nineteenth century. This splintering off of pieces of the Sultan's territory was of particular interest to Germany's partners in the loosely binding Three Emperors' League—Austro-Hungary and Russia.

To the Austrians, fragmentation implied danger. Would the Slavic minorities who were starting to fight for independence from the Turks encourage their brothers under the Austro-Hungarian Empire to do the same? To the Russians, primarily the influential group around the throne known as the Pan-Slavs, the breakup of the Ottoman Empire was an opportunity to expand Russian influence into the Balkans and drive the Turks out of Constantinople. For hundreds of years, the Russians had coveted that fabled city of mosques and minarets guarding the waterway from the Black Sea to the Mediterranean—gateway to warm waters and easy trade with the west.

The three other great European powers—France, England, and Germany —had less at stake. Least concerned was France, since she was primarily focused on recovering Alsace-Lorraine and her dignity. England, especially her Queen, was vociferously pro-Turkish, because it was the Turkish Empire that had always prevented Russia from expanding too far in Asia, Asia Minor, and the Balkans. The principal interest of the British Empire was the port of Constantinople, which she was determined to keep from falling into Russian hands. If Russia took the Turkish capital, which she so desperately wanted, she would then be a dual threat to India—from the Suez Canal on the south and Afghanistan on the north. Britain dreaded the possibility of Russian warships appearing in the Mediterranean, threatening her position in the Middle and Near East.

Germany, in the person of its Chancellor, was anxious to avoid being sucked into a war in which his new and still tenuous empire would be forced to choose between its two allies, Austria and Russia. One of the basic tenets of Bismarck's foreign policy was the preservation and strengthening of the Three Emperors' League of 1873. Already damaged by the war crisis of 1875, this rather toothless expression of monarchical solidarity was threatened when Russia and Austria began to compete with each other over the Turkish spoils.

This (in very broad terms) is how matters stood when the Christians in the Turkish provinces of Bosnia and Herzegovina revolted against the inhuman treatment of their Turkish masters in July of 1875. The insurgents' cause was immediately supported by the neighboring Serbs, who hoped to acquire Bosnia and Herzegovina and unite the southern Slavs into a great Serbia. It also was taken up in Russia by the Pan-Slavs, who saw Mother Russia as the supreme protector of the Slavic Christians, and by ambitious members of the military who saw a chance to acquire Constantinople. Attempts to mediate the conflict by the powers* elicited only halfhearted promises of reform by the Sultan— improvements in religious freedom and taxation that he was unwilling or unable to enforce on his provincial satraps.

At the beginning of 1876, Bismarck approached the British Ambassador, Odo Russell, to suggest close cooperation between Germany and England in the interests of preserving the peace. Germany itself, Bismarck asserted, was "territorially saturated" and had no interests beyond keeping Russia and Austria from fighting each other or, on the other hand, becoming "too intimate" behind Germany's back. Prime Minister Disraeli, who had come into office two years earlier vowing that England would take a more active role on the European continent, thought the Anglo-German understanding a good idea as did Queen Victoria, who based her concurrence on old loyalties and family ties. Although she noted in her journal that "one can never trust Bismarck," the Queen told her Foreign Minister, Lord Derby, that since the Chancellor was apparently sincere, it was "of the utmost importance that we should accept the proffered aid of Germany, a strong state whose interests are the same as ours."

Ever since the peace deliberations at the end of the Franco-Prussian War, the German Chancellor had been flirting with a British alliance. Queried by Russell at the time about Germany's traditionally close relationship with England's enemy Russia, Bismarck insisted that there was nothing between Germany and Russia beyond a "national and family alliance of friendship and gratitude for past services," a link that Bismarck considered his "duty to maintain" until "more advantageous alliances" presented themselves.

But Bismarck's offers of friendship were rejected by the British. Having just purchased the majority of stock in the French-financed Suez Canal from the economically ailing Khedive of Egypt, the British government was nervous about too close a relationship with France's worst enemy, Germany. Moreover, the Foreign Office rightly assumed that Bismarck, the master schemer, was seeking to embroil England in Germany's ongoing fight with France.

---

* *Germany, England, Russia, Austria, France, and Italy all took part in one or more efforts at keeping the peace during this period.*

Rebuffed by the English, Bismarck turned back to the Russians, suggesting that perhaps they and the Austrians might come to some agreement as to how to divide the Balkans between them. But the Russians, who suspected Bismarck of trying to involve them in a fight with Austria and maybe with England as well, put his suggestion aside.

Neither the English nor the Russians misjudged the German Chancellor. If Bismarck's first priority was to maintain the peace, his second was to exercise as much control as he could over the potential peacemakers. Therefore, in May of 1876, he joined with the Foreign Ministers of the other two countries in the Three Emperors' League (Austria and Russia) in the preparation of the Berlin Memorandum, a convention calling for Turkish reforms and peace in the region. Accepted by France and Italy, it was rejected by Britain because she had not been consulted in its drafting, because she "refused to put a knife to Turkey's throat," and because it was impossible to get the British cabinet to act on anything over a weekend.

Dismayed that her dream of an Anglo-German coalition had been summarily dismissed, Vicky remonstrated with her mother over England's refusal to join in the Berlin Memorandum. "Every wish is shown here to go with England. . . . the fault does not rest with our Government that England did not take part in the Conferences," she wrote.

Vicky's passionate desire for a rapprochement between England and Germany was well known in the German Foreign Ministry. Having used her relationship with Victoria to vilify the Crown Princess within Germany, Bismarck now exploited it in order to set up an informal line of communication with Disraeli. A willing conduit, Vicky was anxious for England and Germany to step into the Balkans quickly in the interest of saving lives.

"Fritz had a long conversation with Prince Bismarck 2 days ago," she wrote Victoria on June 13, "and I was to tell you, that Prince Bismarck said it was his wish that England should entirely take the lead in the Oriental Question, and that he was quite ready to follow and back up whatever England proposed. This I thought very nice, and hope that the opportunity may be seized of the two countries acting in concert, England making proposals for what is to be done."

But by this time, the revolution in Bosnia and Herzegovina had been followed by uprisings in Bulgaria—revolts that were put down by the Turks with particular ferocity. Stories of the Bashi-Bazouks, gangs of Turkish vigilantes who savagely murdered twelve thousand Bulgarian Christians, swept through the capitals of Europe. With the Balkan blaze spreading rapidly, the Pan-Slavs stepped up pressure on the Czar to declare war on the Turks. While Alexander II hesitated, the Serbs, still dreaming of a great Slavic nation, declared war on the Turks on June 30, 1876.

Both those devoted Russophobes, the German Crown Princess and the Queen of England, blamed Russia for the Serbian action. "I . . . fear the Russians have stirred it up & set it going," Victoria wrote Vicky the month after the fighting began. "Alas, you say right, I fear . . . ," Vicky answered; "one can almost say it has been the Russians fighting in Serbian dress!" She was not totally wrong. The Serbian army fought the Turks under the command of a Russian general. Still, it was roundly defeated by the end of the summer.

Under ever-increasing pressure to enter the war, the Czar of Russia appealed to his uncle the German Kaiser for assistance in the event of open hostilities. "I count on you, Sir, as you can always count on me," the Czar wrote in a not-so-subtle reference to Russian neutrality during the Franco-Prussian War. Faced with the precise situation he had hoped to avoid, Bismarck replied that in the event of war between Russia and Austria, Germany would remain neutral and would intervene only to keep either country from being destroyed by a coalition of European powers. As was to be expected, this response was considered less than satisfactory in St. Petersburg.

In England, former Prime Minister Gladstone, who had emerged from retirement to demand that the British government cease supporting the repressive Turks, published his famous pamphlet "The Bulgarian Horrors and the Question of the East." Called by one historian "the finest invective of the century," it sold 240,000 copies in three weeks, gave birth to large anti-Turkish rallies all over London, and, like its author, drew down the wrath of the Queen of England. Desperate to find a rationale for the Turks, Victoria's convoluted reasoning on the cause of the war supplies one of the few sources of humor in a bloody and tragic time. In a wondrous upheaval of logic, the Queen managed to shift the responsibility for the Turkish horrors onto the subjects of the Czar, writing Disraeli that "Russia instigated this insurrection, which caused the cruelty of the Turks."

Faced with the same incontrovertible evidence of Turkish atrocities, Vicky also managed to redirect the blame—leading one to wonder if she was trying to curry favor with her mother in order to push England into taking a stand. "The Russians can not be trusted," she wrote. "It is they who urged on the Serbs, they who fought, and they, who it seems to me are responsible for giving the Turks an opportunity of displaying their barbarity towards the so called Christians."

Unlike Queen Victoria, however, Vicky did not take into account the fact that Germany's friendship with Russia on her northwestern flank provided the Czar with enough security to aggressively pursue his dream of dominion over the Balkans and Constantinople to the south. In response to a letter to that effect from her mother, she defended Bismarck's policy.

> You say "Germany is with Russia." . . . It is sorely against Prince Bismarck's will and liking, I am sure, as he does not care for a Russian alliance; but an alliance he must have, being in the disagreeable position of having always to be on his guard against France. This spring he would have given anything for a hearty response to his overtures [to England]! . . . he got no answer . . . so that he said to himself, as indeed all Germany does, "Oh! there is no use in reckoning on England or going with England; she has no policy, will do nothing, will always hang back, so there is no help for it but to turn to Russia." . . . The only strong Power willing to stand by

Germany when she is in a pinch is <u>Russia</u>, therefore we must . . . keep on the best terms with her and serve her, so that she may serve us, as she did in 1870.

Surely Prince Bismarck is not to be blamed for this; it is only common prudence and good sense to make sure of having a strong friend. . . . If Lord Derby had spoken out in the spring, and if the Berlin Memorandum had been accepted, matters would now stand differently. Bismarck wanted <u>England</u> alone to decide in the Eastern Question, play the first part and have the <u>beau</u> <u>role</u>. . . . I think it is not too late now, to come to a satisfactory and close understanding with Prince Bismarck, as at any moment Russia may go even a step further than Germany can quietly agree to.

In her enthusiasm, the Crown Princess allowed herself to be duped by Bismarck, going so far as to call his motives "simple and honest." Mistaking Bismarck's policy of aggressive self-preservation for a new and healthy antipathy to Russia, Vicky wrote that the German Chancellor "dislikes & distrusts the Russians, & feels that they are very dangerous neighbours for us."

But Queen Victoria, less idealistic and better advised than her daughter, saw through Vicky's words to Bismarck's schemes. It had become clear that the German Crown Princess was no match for Bismarck—a political swordsman with whom even the most sophisticated statesmen in Europe found it difficult to thrust and parry, knowing that his weapons were always tipped, if not with instant death, surely with slow, inexorable poison.

EARLY IN in 1877, Russia and Austro-Hungary did sign a secret convention, as suggested by Bismarck, defining their areas of interest in the Balkans, were Russia to declare war on the Turks. In return for Austria's promise of neutrality, Russia agreed to forgo setting up a large client state (Bulgaria). Austria was to be allowed to occupy Bosnia and Herzegovina when she chose. With Austria defanged, Russia was free to declare war on Turkey, which she did on April 24, 1877.

The war lasted into early 1878, allowing both Vicky and Victoria ample time to indulge in condemnations of Russian aggression. Even so, the Queen of England called her daughter to task more than once for not expressing sufficient hatred for the Russians or enough approval of Disraeli and the supporters of Turkey in England. "It is a very anxious time & <u>we</u> <u>must</u> & <u>will</u> take some <u>marked</u> line to show that Russia is <u>not</u> to have all her <u>own</u> way . . . ," the Queen wrote her daughter shortly after Russia declared war. "You never answer when I constantly tell you this—as if you thought the <u>Liberals</u> & that madman Gladstone <u>must</u> be <u>right</u> & the <u>Government</u> <u>wrong</u>!"

Meanwhile, Vicky kept up her losing campaign for cooperation among the Great Powers, lobbying for England to take the lead in bringing Germany, Austria, Italy, and France into a political consortium strong enough to frighten the Russians into settling with the Turks. In spite of little tiffs with her mother over who was more barbaric—Turks or Russians, heathen Muslims or misguided Christians—Vicky's great concern was the tragedy of war itself, the lives wasted and the cruelties inflicted. "What a good thing it would be if France, England, Italy, Germany & Austria simultaneously proposed to negotiate a peace & stop these horrors! If only the rest of Europe would hold firmly together," she wrote in the fall of 1877. Time and again she begged the Queen to take a firmer stand, send in the British fleet, put an end to the bloodshed.

Fritz, who was convinced that the Russians were motivated by jealousy of Germany's military successes and "the re-establishment of our national power," was impressed with the bravery of the Turks, hampered as they were by "palace intrigues at Constantinople." It was generally known that the Sultan's orders, based on the whims of his favorites, frequently led to ill-advised changes in the high command and operations of his army, and the Crown Prince pitied the soldiers doing the fighting. "It is with a feeling of horror that I notice the approach of winter—whilst the thinned armies of Russia and Turkey are still opposed to each other . . . ," he wrote his mother-in-law in the fall of 1877. "Since I have been fated to witness three wars, I feel myself a real horror whenever I hear of fresh campaigns."

But the killing continued, and by the end of 1877, a victorious if exhausted Russian army had advanced nearly to Constantinople. In March of 1878, the Czar imposed the Treaty of San Stefano on the Sultan. It was a one-sided settlement that defied Austria by creating a large Bulgaria and placed virtually the entire Balkan peninsula under Russian domination. Furious, the British sent a fleet of six battleships into the Sea of Marmara. This frightened the Russians into calling their soldiers to a halt six miles outside Constantinople.

Vicky, who had been longing "for one good roar of the British Lion," was pleased. "Except among the sworn friends of Russia, I think there is universal approval of England's step and England's views," she wrote Victoria, "and everywhere a feeling of relief that at last England should have come forward. . . . I cannot help thinking that the Russians will draw back and give way."

They did. To avoid what seemed like imminent hostilities between England and Russia—proliferation that no one wanted—Russia withdrew, and Austria proposed a European congress to be held in Berlin in the summer of 1878 to settle the so-called Eastern Question. The choice of Berlin was significant. A nod to the new and upgraded stature of Germany, it also verified the central position of her Chancellor in European affairs.

THE BERLIN CONGRESS began to debate the fate of the Turkish Empire on June 13, 1878. Between the armistice and the peace conference, however, Bismarck had become deeply involved in Germany's domestic affairs and was anxious to get the work of the Congress over as quickly as possible.

The German Chancellor had reluctantly agreed to assume the presidency of the Congress. It was said that he had tried to avoid taking a position that he knew would bring him nothing but resentment and had accepted it only because the Czar insisted. Although most of the terms were decided in secret before the

Congress convened, he and his country were, as he predicted, held accountable for its decisions.

The formal deliberations took place in the Radziwill Palace in the Wilhelmstrasse, a building in the French style recently purchased by the government and presented to Bismarck as his official residence. The first session was opened at two o'clock in the afternoon, with the delegates in "golden coats and glittering stars" stopping for port and biscuits on their way. Germany's Chancellor, who was suffering from nerves and shingles, complained about his health. "Bismarck, with one hand full of cherries, and the other of shrimps, eaten alternatively, complains he cannot sleep and must go to Kissingen," said Disraeli.

There were innumerable dinners, banquets, and receptions during the month of the Congress, with the powers trying to outdo each other in lavish soirées and the delegates rushing off to the theater or the Tiergarten between diplomatic events. "It is absolutely necessary to go to these receptions," Disraeli complained in a report to Queen Victoria, "but the late hours try me. I begin to die at ten o'clock and should like to be buried before midnight."

Bismarck, who fell quickly under Disraeli's "spell"—"Der alte Jude, das ist der Mann!"*—entertained the British Prime Minister a number of times during the course of the Congress. Disraeli used these occasions to encourage Bismarck's confidences. "I dined with [Bismarck] alone, i.e., with his family, who disappear after the repast, and then we talked and smoked," Disraeli wrote. "If you do not smoke under such circumstances, you look like a spy, taking down his conversation in your mind. Smoking in common puts him at his ease."

At the Chancellor's dinner for sixty, Disraeli was seated to the right of his host, who held forth on the "duplicity . . . universal among sovereigns." "He impressed me never to trust Princes or courtiers," the British Prime Minister wrote Queen Victoria, "that his illness was not, as people supposed, brought on by the French War, but by the horrible conduct of his Sovereign, etc., etc."

"Bismarck soars above all," Disraeli wrote another correspondent: "he is six foot four I should think, proportionately stout; with a sweet and gentle voice, and with a peculiarly refined enunciation, which singularly and strangely contrasts with the awful things he says: appalling from their frankness and their audacity. He is a complete despot here, and from the highest to the lowest of the Prussians, and all the permanent foreign diplomats, tremble at his frown and court most sedulously his smile."

All except Disraeli himself, who got exactly what he wanted for England from the Congress. Queen Victoria was "very triumphant" when she was notified of the terms of the peace: independence from Turkey for Serbia, Romania, and Montenegro; occupation of Bosnia and Herzegovina by Austro-Hungary; Bulgaria split in two; Cyprus awarded to England; and France allowed to occupy Tunis.

If the British were pleased with the provisions of the treaty, the Russians

---

* *"The old Jew—he is the man!"—referring to the most important person at the Congress.*

complained bitterly that the Powers had deprived them of the rightful spoils of victory. Anxious to deflect the resentment of the ultranationalistic Pan-Slavs from himself, the Czar did nothing to contradict this assumption. The anger of the Russians, who found a scapegoat in Bismarck, subsequently formed the kernel of what George Kennan called an "almost hysterical embitterment against the Western Powers, above all against Germany." This Russian rancor, which paralleled the fury of the French after the Franco-Prussian War, eventually drew these two nations closer together.

Although the Congress of Berlin was regarded as a success at the time and Bismarck himself came out with heightened status, Europe emerged from the deliberations with another problem, one noted by the German Crown Princess: "The Congress has ended its labours!" she wrote Victoria on July 13. "I am only so afraid that the hurry to get over the work has been too great, and that the durability may suffer; it has been driven on with such desperate haste by Prince Bismarck, and that is not good! These matters are too serious to stand a hasty treatment."

Indeed, the cavalier attitude of the members of the Congress to the peoples of the Balkans, who were settled into states and provinces with little thought for ethnic loyalties or nationalistic yearnings, left unresolved, deep-seated conflicts that would would plague Europe until the outbreak of World War I and well beyond.* Bismarck was not displeased by this. Four months after the peace treaties were signed, he told the Crown Prince, "It would be a triumph for our statesmanship if we succeeded in *keeping the Eastern ulcer open* and thus jarred the harmony of the other Great Powers in order to secure our own peace."

But the great intriguer himself was also outfoxed by the events of 1876–78. If the cornerstone of Bismarck's foreign policy was Germany's tie with Russia on its eastern flank and his bugaboo was a resurgence of a vengeful France on the west, his major aim was to keep these two nations, Germany's best friend and its worst enemy, from forging a bond. The Russo-Turkish War—and particularly the Congress that ended it—opened cracks in Bismarck's carefully constructed fortress of diplomatic alliances, fissures that would lead eventually to a real break in the German-Russian axis on which he had built Germany's foreign policy.

---

* At this writing (1995), the Serbs are engaged in "ethnically cleansing" the Croats and Muslims out of Bosnia and Herzegovina.

CHAPTER
FORTY-ONE

> *"Only Prince Bismarck has been able to understand and awaken, as no statesman before him, the national feelings of the people and direct them under his leadership."*
>
> OTTO VON BISMARCK, *1880*

*T*HE CROWN PRINCESS OF GERMANY'S concern over the "desperate haste" with which the German Chancellor had concluded the deliberations of the Congress of Berlin was not ill placed. As Vicky realized, Bismarck had cut short the diplomatic sessions in order to pursue a new domestic agenda, suddenly made possible by unexpected events. Just before the Congress was due to convene, two attempts had been made to kill the Kaiser. For Bismarck, seeking support in the Reichstag and an answer to economic problems in the nation as a whole, these assassination attempts, perilous though they could have been for his position, provided an opportunity for political gain.

The first occurred in May, when a penniless plumber named Hödel fired at Wilhelm I while he was out driving. The shots hit only the Kaiser's carriage. Questioned about his political affiliations, Hödel, who had been expelled from the Socialist Party for eccentric behavior, said he had none, but Bismarck tried to use the incident to promote a bill against "Socialist outrages." It was defeated. None the worse for his ordeal, the Kaiser appeared in his box at the opera that evening.

Less than a month later, on June 2, another, more successful attempt was made on Wilhelm's life, this time by a middle-class economist named Nobiling. Firing from the second-story window of an inn, Nobiling hit Wilhelm in the cheek, throat, shoulder, and right hand, with which he was saluting. Bullets grazed the Kaiser's forehead through his helmet. He began to hemorrhage.

From England, where they were visiting her mother, Fritz and Vicky hurried back to Berlin. The Crown Prince was "in floods of tears" on the way home, while his wife remained remarkably calm. Questioned by her lady-in-waiting, who found her sangfroid somewhat unnerving, Vicky replied that it was "necessary for Fritz." They arrived in Berlin late at night and went straight to her in-laws' palace. The Crown Princess said that her mother-in-law was "more calm & natural" than she expected "& certainly far more reasonable than all the others who seem to have lost their heads."

Next morning they saw the Kaiser. His blood-soaked, bullet-ridden cloak was still in the room, as was his helmet, studded with pellets. His head and arms were bandaged, his face swollen and bruised, and he was without his false teeth. But he told them that he had no pain and was starting to move the fingers of his left hand again.

To his daughter-in-law, Wilhelm I looked miserably uncomfortable in his narrow camp bed with its torn covers. With the permission of the doctors, Vicky moved "2 nice English brass bed stands" from her sons' rooms to the Kaiser's palace. The Kaiser, she wrote her mother, "wants a good nurse but no one may go near him except his valets!"

The question of what position her husband would take during his father's incapacitation concerned the Crown Princess. Fritz had come home prepared to assume a regency, a position that would have entitled him to act on his own during his father's recuperation. But Wilhelm insisted that the government "be carried on in accordance with my views, and everything remaining as it is." Much to Fritz's distress and Bismarck's delight, Fritz was merely deputized for his father.

"The Crown Prince has an almost impossible task before him," Charles Anton Hohenzollern commented; "he is obliged to carry on the Government in accordance with his father's ideas, and very often has to act against his most cherished convictions." Honor bound to carry out Wilhelm's policies, the Crown Prince was forced to sign, among other things, a decree that condemned Hödel to death.

As soon as she returned to Berlin, the Crown Princess received a letter from her mother with advice for her father-in-law. "The Emperor," Queen Victoria said, "must go away for a time from Berlin and not drive in such a low open carriage. . . . These socialist atheists are awful! Believe me when there is no respect for God—no belief in futurity—there can be no respect or loyalty to the highest in the land. Authority of some kind does come from Above, and if that is trampled under foot and if the clergy—narrow-minded through they be—are ridiculed and abused everything will go down! Philosophy without religion will bring the nation down. . . . Do remember that."

The Queen's unquestioning assumption that it was atheistic socialists who were behind the attempts on the Kaiser's life is indicative of the witch-hunting climate Bismarck quickly succeeded in creating in Germany. Neither of the Kaiser's would-be assassins had any viable connection with the Socialist Party, but this information was suppressed by the state's attorney investigating the cases as Bismarck set out to destroy the liberal parties.

The Chancellor was on his estate at Friedrichsruh when the Kaiser was shot. The telegram bearing the news of the condition of the old man, who was at first not expected to survive, was given to Christoph von Tiedemann, Bismarck's personal secretary, who set out across the estate to find his chief.

"As I stepped out of the park," Tiedemann recalled,

I saw the Chancellor walking slowly across the field in the bright sunshine, with his dogs at his heels. I went to meet him and joined him. He was in the best of tempers. After a while I said: "Some important telegrams have arrived." He answered jokingly: "Are they so urgent that we have to deal with them out here in the open country?" I replied: "Unfortunately, they are. The Kaiser has again been fired at and this time he has been hit. His Majesty is seriously wounded."

With a violent start the Prince stopped dead. Deeply agitated, he thrust his oaken stick into the ground in front of him and said, breathing heavily, as if a lightning flash of revelation had struck him: "Now we will dissolve the Reichstag!" Only then did he enquire sympathetically after the Emperor's condition and ask for details of the attempt.

WHAT BISMARCK HAD IMMEDIATELY understood was that fate, in the persons of Hödel and Nobiling, had handed him a triple opportunity: to gain a majority in parliament, smear the liberal delegates opposed to his policies with guilt by association, and force antisocialist laws on the Reichstag. But he knew he had to act quickly before the public realized that the socialists had had nothing to do with the assassination attempts. Socialism and its representatives in the German Reichstag, the Social Democrats, had become an obsession with the Chancellor, who was determined to roust them out of parliament and get their supporters out of Germany.

On June 4, Bismarck called a meeting of his cabinet. He told his ministers that he had been considering resignation, so disheartened was he when the Reichstag had voted down an antisocialist bill after the first attempt on Wilhelm's life. After this second attempt on the life of their Kaiser, however, he would stay in office in order to pursue passage of an even more stringent bill. With that in mind, he planned to dissolve the Reichstag.

The Crown Prince was not invited to this all-important meeting. Had he been there, he would have voted with the three ministers who objected to the dissolution, assuring Bismarck that there was no need to hold new elections, since the current delegates would surely vote with the government in light of the recently averted tragedy. Fritz, now acting for the Kaiser, was furious at Bismarck for not including him in the deliberations, and they apparently quarreled. The Crown Prince must have suspected the truth—that the Chancellor was lying when he told him that the cabinet had agreed *unanimously* that the Reichstag must be dissolved. Under the circumstances, however, there was nothing he could do legally besides agree to order the dissolution.

"I was certain," Bismarck wrote later in an attempt to deny the rift,

that the Crown Prince would accept my view, even if all my colleagues had been of a different opinion. . . . I intended to keep my post, because, if the Emperor were to recover from his severe wound . . . I would not forsake him against his will. I also regarded it as my duty, if he should die, not to refuse to his successor, unless he wished it, those services which the confidence and experience I had acquired enabled me to render him. . . . As to the latter's relations with me . . . to the end of his life he maintained the same confidence in me as his father.

This was, of course, untrue.

Anxious to seize on the general anxiety to maximize his personal control, Bismarck demanded that martial law be imposed on Berlin with one thousand extra policemen and six regiments in the capital to "impress the mob." He wanted new passport regulations issued to keep immigrants out of the city. When the Crown Prince and the cabinet refused to agree to these measures, he complained about "cowardice," "irresolution," and "obstructionism."

In line with this manufactured hysteria, Vicky wrote Victoria that the royal family was "continually told that there is a plot to murder . . . all of the family, & that we shall not escape our doom." Although she admitted to occasional concern when out driving, the Crown Princess told her mother, "I cannot believe this quite, & do not feel afraid. . . . we will make no change in our habits."

Vicky's reaction to the antisocialist propaganda was hardly typical of a nineteenth-century royal princess. Unlike other members of reigning families, who barricaded themselves mind and body inside their palaces, or even Queen Victoria, who immediately assumed that attempted murder was a natural corollary to atheism, the Crown Princess was curious about socialism and sent out for a copy of Karl Marx's *Das Kapital** Fascinated by what she read, she asked a friend, Sir M. E. Grant Duff, a member of Parliament, to find Marx in England, where he had been living since he was expelled from Prussia in 1849, and send her his impressions. She received the following report from Duff in early 1879:

He [Marx] is a short, rather small man of sixty-one, with grey hair and beard. . . . The face is somewhat round, the forehead well shaped and filled up, the eye rather hard but the whole expression rather pleasant than not, by no means that of a gentleman who is in the habit of eating babies in their cradles—which is, I daresay the view the police take of him.

His talk was that of a well-informed, nay, learned man . . . very positive, slightly cynical, interesting and often, as I thought showing very correct ideas when he was conversing of the past or present, but vague and unsatisfactory when he turned to the future.

He looks, not unreasonably, for a great and not distant crash in Russia; thinks it will begin by reforms from above which the old bad edifice will not be able to bear and which will lead to its tumbling down altogether. Next he thinks that the movement will spread to Germany, taking there the form of a revolt against the existing military system. . . .

---

* The first volume, which was published in 1867. The subsequent two volumes were finished by Engels and published posthumously, in 1885 and 1895, respectively.

"But supposing," I said, "the rulers of Europe came to an understanding amongst themselves for a reduction of armaments which might greatly relieve the burden on the people, what might become of the Revolution which you expect it one day to bring about?"

"Ah," was his answer, "they can't do that. All sorts of fears and jealousies will make that impossible. The burden will grow more and more as science advances, for the improvements in the art of destruction will keep pace with its advances, and every year more and more will have to be devoted to costly engines of war. It is a vicious circle—there is no escape from it." . . .

In the course of the conversation Karl Marx spoke several times both of Your Imperial Highness and of the Crown Prince, and invariably with due respect and propriety. Even in the case of eminent individuals of whom he by no means spoke with respect, there was no trace of bitterness or savagery—plenty of acrid and dissolvent criticism. Altogether my impression of Marx, allowing him to be at the opposite pole of opinion from oneself, was not at all unfavourable, and I would gladly meet him again. It will not be he who, whether he wishes it or not, will turn the world upside down.

UNLIKE VICKY'S CORRESPONDENT, Bismarck had always had a healthy respect for the power of the socialist message, particularly when it came to the political exploitation of the lower class. As far back as 1863, he had sought out a disciple of Marx, Ferdinand Lassalle, for secret conversations on how to attract proletarian votes and loyalties.

Although Bismarck referred to Lassalle as "one of the most clever and attractive men with whom I have ever talked," their conversations had bogged down after a few months. Both men became disillusioned—Lassalle because he realized with the onset of the Schleswig-Holstein War that Bismarck preferred external adventures to internal reform, and Bismarck because he decided that Lassalle was more theorist than pragmatist. "What could Lassalle offer and give me?" he asked, referring to the paucity of supporters the socialist leader left behind when he died in 1864 after a duel over a love affair. Fourteen years later, in 1878, the German Chancellor was looking for a way to destroy those followers —now a major political force.

As Bismarck conceived it, the primary domestic problem in the decade following the founding of the German Empire had been to bind together the diverse states, each with its own customs and traditions, and instill in the new citizens of the Reich some sense of pride in belonging to what was in many ways an enlarged Prussia. In accomplishing this, he had been helped by the fantastic growth of the German economy, which had brought German industry on a par with that of its European competitors.

But unification and accelerated industrial growth had raised new economic and social divisions. These breaks in the social fabric of the empire had been further strained by proindustrial legislation, particularly a law removing barriers to internal migration. After 1867, anyone could settle in another German state, engage in business, or own property. Lured by a life free of restrictions on their jobs and families—some Prussian farmworkers had not even been allowed to marry without the consent of their Junker landlords—unskilled labor began moving to the cities.

That the factory worker was disappointed with what he found in the urban environment is a cliché of the nineteenth-century industrial revolution. "[Bismarck] has done nothing for the working people," the inheritors of Lassalle complained. "He has not made our lives easier, only more sour year by year, because of the effect of the economic laws passed with his help." With no sympathy or solutions forthcoming from the government or existing political parties, labor had followed the lead of the Socialist International and in 1863 founded its own political arm, the German Workers' Union.

The establishment of a workers' party led to an outbreak of strikes—for better pay, improved working conditions, and shorter hours. Management, which usually fired or threatened the protesters, was frequently assisted by the government. German labor unions did not gain much of a following, and individual workers audacious enough to claim to represent the interest of the proletariat were summarily jailed.

The most active socialists in Germany in the late nineteenth century were Wilhelm Liebknecht, a passionate disciple of Marx, and August Bebel, the first socialist in the Reichstag. Both men had voiced their objections to the Franco-Prussian War; both were arrested while serving in parliament and imprisoned in 1872 as enemies of the state for libeling Bismarck. Freed in 1874, they joined the followers of Lassalle, incorporating the German Workers' Union into a new Social Democratic Workers' Party the following year. Their goals were universal suffrage, civil liberties, freedom of association, and social reforms. Although the party's program specified working for labor "within the framework of the existing national state," they rapidly eclipsed the Catholic Church as Bismarck's primary *bête noire*.

From 1871 to 1874, the Social Democrats doubled their strength in the Reichstag to nearly seven percent, and thereafter almost quadrupled the number of their newspapers (from eleven in 1875 to forty-two in 1877). Although Bismarck tried to suppress socialism in every way he knew, it was not until the spring of 1878 that he thought he had found the key. Not only did he hope to use legislation to destroy the socialists and left-wing Progressives in the Reichstag; he also saw an opportunity to use the same currency of fear to buy his way out of the economic quagmire that had been threatening to swamp his government.

In 1878, the depression—brought about by a general European recession, increased military spending, and decreased revenues—was already five years along. The mood of the public was bad, and Germany was in the grip of economic paralysis. Sick and more ill-tempered than usual, Bismarck was having difficulty attracting ministers into his cabinet, since no one wanted to follow

Otto von Camphausen to public ignominy and political extinction. To solve his fiscal problems, the Chancellor had been trying to find a way to raise new taxes without letting the Reichstag tie them to constitutional reforms. Suddenly the solution presented itself. Even Bismarck's liberal opponents in the Reichstag referred to the Chancellor's "incredible luck."

It was only eleven days after Nobiling's attempt on Wilhelm's life (June 13, 1878) that the Congress of Berlin opened. Two days later, in the middle of the diplomatic sessions, the Chancellor dissolved the Reichstag. The subsequent election was a nasty one. Claiming that the left-wing Progressives had paved the way for socialism, Bismarck set out to cast their associates and his former parliamentary allies, the National Liberals, as the enemies of law and order. In the elections, which took place at the end of July, both National Liberals and Progressives suffered severe defeats, ending liberal domination of the Reichstag and leaving the parliamentary body divided among three factions of approximately equal strength—liberals, Catholic centrists, and conservatives. Bismarck still needed the liberals to get his legislation passed, but a shift to the right within the party itself, along with the drubbing its members had just received at the polls, made them more amenable to his call.

On July 30, 1878, Vicky wrote her mother about the significance of the new face of the Reichstag and the fact that the socialists had fared better than anyone expected:

"Here the elections have shown how large the 'Social Democratic' Party is! I am not afraid of what they will do,—only of the frantic mistakes the government will not cease making . . . the reactionary measures they will take . . . leading to an abuse of authority which only makes authority hated & despised!"

In that regard, Bismarck's antisocialist bill passed the Reichstag in October of 1878. It outlawed organizations whose activities were deemed disruptive to "harmony between the social classes." This infinitely elastic criterion enabled the government to fine and/or imprison landlords, proprietors of inns, and taverns—anywhere people might gather to voice their discontent—as well as owners of publishing houses, bookstores, and libraries, where they might publish or read complaints. Within eight months, over 250 publications were closed down.

Limited martial law was imposed on Berlin. Sixty-seven prominent socialists were arrested and expelled. Bismarck tried to imprison two Social Democratic deputies to the Reichstag, who returned after the expiration of martial law to resume their seats in the parliament; in this, however, he was thwarted by their fellow deputies. Less fortunate individuals and organizations were persecuted by the police.

For all its severity, this law was not as harsh as the one originally proposed by the Chancellor and overwhelmingly rejected by the Reichstag. It was the Crown Prince who worked with the liberal delegates in the Reichstag to effect a compromise.

■

IN THE SAME LETTER to her mother in which she condemned the "abuse of authority" of the antisocialist law, the Crown Princess deplored "the protectionism" into which Bismarck's government was, as she put it, "so stupidly driving" Germany. The two movements, in fact, went hand in hand, and, as Vicky predicted, the rise of conservatism in political life brought with it a campaign for protective tariffs.

Up until the late 1870s, German financial policy had been one of free trade. But ongoing economic depression had strengthened the protectionists, who lobbied for tariffs similar to those of their neighbors in Austria, France, and Russia.

The power of the Reichstag was limited to indirect taxation—duties on consumer goods like tobacco, beer, and sugar—while only the individual states were allowed to levy taxes directly. Decreasing revenues and increasing outlay had, by the late 1870s, forced the German government into deficit spending. Faced with fiscal crisis, Bismarck decided that the time had come to find new sources of revenue, change the tax equation, and make the individual states dependent on the empire for money. First he tried to raise funds through nationalization of the lucrative railway system—an attempt in which he was strongly supported by the Crown Prince. When that failed, he turned to a general campaign to raise imperial revenues through a wall of tariffs. Along with the money to make up fiscal shortfalls, Bismarck believed that tariffs would build a bridge between the industrialist and the Junker, the bourgeois and the aristocrat—new money and old.

The Junkers, who refused to soil their hands in trade, had left industrial development to the middle classes. Once an entrepreneur became successful, however, he looked for his reward in estates and ennoblement, which the aristocracy resented. One of Bismarck's tasks after 1871, as he saw it, was to bring these two groups together. Protectionism offered their first common economic ground.

Germany, the Chancellor asserted, had become the junkyard of Europe, the place where other European countries, protected by their own tariffs, dumped their excess grain and timber. "The work and production of the Fatherland," he said in a speech labeled by Bennigsen a "demagogic masterpiece," deserved protection from those who "prospered from German gold." Under Bismarck's skillful direction, protectionism and greed acquired the shiny veneer of patiotism. What he did not say was that the new tariff on grain raised the cost of bread for the common German laborer, who could ill afford it.

The Protective Tariff Act of 1879 added a powerful consortium of big business, agriculture, and banking to the old Prussian tripod of Kaiser, army, and bureaucracy. If Bismarck's avowed task during the 1870s had been to unite the new Germans, he had succeeded in promoting and integrating the *material* interests of the new aristocracy, Junkers and industrialists—while silencing the complaints of the lower class.

Under the new economic and political conservatism, greed and repression became the state-sponsored handmaidens of the old Hohenzollern ideals. As the Crown Princess wrote Queen Victoria two weeks after the passage of the Protective Tariff Act, "[T]he great man is ruining Germany as fast as he can, and his abuse of authority <u>can</u> only lead to the spread of communism and revolutionary tendencies! I see it quite clearly but am not believed by those amongst whom we move."

CHAPTER
FORTY-TWO

"To see one's child totally independent & constantly wishing to go quite contrary to their parents' wishes, convictions & kind advice is very dreadful"

QUEEN VICTORIA

*D*URING THE LATE 1870S, while the new German Empire was settling into a new, more conservative mold, its Crown Princess was passing from young adulthood to middle age. Barred from the inner sanctums of power, Vicky sought outlets where she could—too often in the lives of the next generation. As the limitations of her three eldest children became more apparent, Vicky, raised on the heady wine of brilliance acknowledged, became disillusioned. "The 3 eldest are such complete Prussians. . . . ," she wrote Victoria in 1877, "in tastes etc. we are completely different. . . . William (my especial favorite) is hard and cold by nature."

Bright but insecure and unstable, Vicky's eldest son was the confused product of an absent father, ambitious mother, insatiable tutor, and indulgent grandparents. By his teens, when few boys inclined toward piety, Willy thought of himself as extremely religious and resented the intrusion of anyone between God and himself, the person who would one day be anointed by the Almighty to temporal power. "I gained nothing from him that was of use to me," he said of the clergyman engaged to prepare him for his confirmation. "The really elevating initiation of that period I derived from our Lord's teaching . . . not from any doctrine of human origin." But according to Hintzpeter, Willy's knowledge of religion was superficial, he had no personal faith, and, when asked to write his beliefs, stated them in an unsuitably "sermonizing tone."

"Your Imperial Highness's harsh judgment of Prince Wilhelm's creed is unfortunately only too correct," Hintzpeter wrote the Crown Prince after showing him the results of his son's efforts to commit his faith to paper.

> The whole thing is hard, and hard is also the Prince, very hard. Even if he does not kick his feet at his sister any more when she touches his toys, even if nowadays he sometimes forgoes the sinister pleasure of denouncing his brother in order to get him into trouble and have him punished, indications of positive goodwill towards anyone are nevertheless as rare with him

as those of heartless egotism are frequent. . . . Phrases of the beauty and necessity of love, gratitude and goodwill are not at all lacking with him, because unfortunately hypocrisy is not alien to his character. . . . Whether he can ever be helped partially to overcome his almost crystal-hard egotism, only time can tell; it forms the innermost core of his being.

Hintzpeter's solution to Willy's problems was to send him to a real school, where he would be humbled by being measured against his peers. "[I]t is to be hoped that such wholesome humiliation will awaken the ambition in the Prince to acquire that superiority which he is so wrong in thinking he possesses," the tutor wrote Willy's father.

In 1874, the future Kaiser was sent off to the gymnasium (high school) in the town of Kassel with his brother Henry. It was a major victory for the boys' parents, but a shocking break with Hohenzollern tradition. The Crown Prince and Princess incurred "the censure of everyone at court & in society." She was accused of being "very dangerous and heretical!"

If Willy was upset at the prospect of having to compete, as he put it, with "strange boys in a public school . . . and, to come out lower in the list!" the idea of excusing him from military duties and putting him on an equal footing with boys his own age was anathema to Wilhelm I. The Kaiser, whose concept of education began and ended with military maneuvers, never resigned himself to his grandson's scholastic career, and during Willy's years at Kassel there were quite a few "violent" scenes between the generations. At one point, unbeknown to his parents, Wilhelm I ordered his teenage grandson invested with the Spanish Order of the Golden Fleece, sent by the King of Spain. "[C]eremonies of this kind," Vicky wrote Victoria, "are not good for a schoolboy."

Like many of Hintzpeter's educational schemes, the basic idea of sending Willy and Henry to Kassel was good, but the execution was excessive. Having used the journey for an instructive walking tour in the Harz Mountains, the indefatigable moralist arrived with his charges, aged fifteen and twelve, at their new home tired and hungry. To quote Hintzpeter's diary for September 12, 1874:

We entered Kassel in . . . deliberate antithesis to the public imagination. We cheerfully sat in the enclosure for yeomen on the bowling-green of a coachman's beer-house, partaking of sour beer and hard bread. It was raining, and I held my umbrella over the lunch to prevent the beer becoming still more watery, for we needed strengthening after a hard march. Then we heard the whistle of an engine, and by this knew that at that moment the Emperor [Kaiser] was arriving in Kassel in triumph,* in a comfortable saloon-car, honoured, extolled, well-dined, in complete enjoyment of a hard-earned position after a lifetime's work; while Prince Wilhelm, having quite insufficiently breakfasted, with tired legs and empty stomach, walked to Kassel, and entered Kassel in the true manner of a

---

* *Wilhelm had gone to Kassel for the annual autumn maneuvers.*

traveling student. And this moral sermon was fully exemplified in word and deed. So as not to be with the Emperor in Kassel, we wander about in the surrounding country, obtain, with difficulty, a cup of coffee in some pleasure grounds, wherein we blissfully soak a pocketed crust of bread, in a yeoman's enclosure, and finally move on to our *Fürstenhaus* [palace] . . . where the porter, in gala array, is only with difficulty persuaded that we represent the expected company.

Since silly exercises like these were not accompanied by the one thing that might have helped democratize Willy—social intercourse with his peers—the lesson failed to take root. True to his deepest self, Hintzpeter encouraged his charge to maintain an "ever tactful reserve which forbade all familiarity" with his schoolmates.

The main thrust of the gymnasium education was classical, and history was slanted toward the ancients. This did not please Germany's future Kaiser. "The history of Germany was presented in the most general way, without any attempt to arouse enthusiasm for the national idea . . . ," he wrote fifty years later; "there was absolutely no adequate basis for 'Germanism' . . . such as I awoke later in the German people."

Willy had to "work very hard" at Kassel. The average schoolday for a student in a nineteenth-century gymnasium started at five or six in the morning and lasted ten or twelve hours, with at least two hours of homework. It was worse for the heir to the throne, who had additional daily lessons with Hintzpeter, as well as French and English tutors. No matter how hard he worked, Willy was unable to please Hintzpeter, who wrote his father even before classes started:

"The effect of the school on the Prince is . . . merely skin-deep, his new life interests him but only superficially as usual; his books, his notebooks, his school hours and even his cap—anything is more important to him than learning. . . . his entire tenure in Kassel . . . will all be for naught unless his character improves. . . . He performs his tasks slowly; the results are hardly brilliant."

This is not what Willy told his mother:

"I get on very well with my studies hoping to please by the good report I shall bring back, especially I get on well in the mathematics in obedience to the wish you expressed in one of your letters."

But Hintzpeter wrote that Willy was showing "so little talent and so little disposition" for mathematics that his efforts usually resulted in "scenes of flustering embarrassment and towering rage." His mother wrote him accordingly, presumably in response to this and a poor progress report from his teachers:

"I am so sorry to hear that you are so bad at your mathematics & so behindhand compared with other boys! I fear you fancy yourself far more perfect in <u>many</u> things than you really are, and you will have to find out by experience how little you really <u>do know</u>, compared with what you ought to aim at. . . . It must be your <u>own</u> effort and your <u>own energy</u> which makes you get over these difficulties, no one can do it <u>for</u> you. I hope . . . that you will not disappoint us, and remember besides how well it is to be <u>modest</u>. . . . You fancy yourself wonderfully accomplished . . . <u>we</u> think you far behind what you might be."

"I get on very well in school," he answered. "I perceive how the teachers love me & I again like them. The boys are all very kind to me & very polite. . . . in my class I have already a certain position for the boys very often, when they have found a difficulty, come to me . . . before the Latin or Greek lesson & beg me to explain it to them . . . which I of course willingly do."

It is at this point in his life that one begins to see the future Kaiser's separation from painful reality. Although there is no indication that Willy had yet begun to suffer from the grandiosity or breakdowns that punctuated his years on the throne, it is clear that he already had emotional problems. Sometimes these manifested themselves sexually. One has only to read his more personal letters to his mother:

"I have got a little <u>secret</u> . . . for you alone . . . ," Willy wrote Vicky six months after he started the gymnasium.

> I dreamt last night that I was walking with you & another lady. . . . you were discussing who had the finest hands, whereupon the lady produced a most ungraceful hand, declaring that it was the prettiest and turned us her back. I in my rage broke her parasol; but you put your dear arm round my waist, led me aside, pulled your glove off . . . & showed me your dear beautiful hand which I instantly covered with kisses. I wish you would do the same, when I am at Berlin, alone with you in the evening. Pray write to me what you think about the dream.
>
> I have again dreamt about you, this time I was alone with you in your library, when you stretched forth your arms & pulled me lower to your chair so that my head rested on your left arm. Then you took off your gloves . . . & laid your hand gently on my lips, for me to kiss it. . . . I instantly seized your hand & kissed it; then you gave me a warm embrace & putting your right arm round my neck got up & walked about the rooms with me. In 8 days we will come to Berlin & then what I dreamt about we will do in reality when we are alone in your rooms without any witnesses. This is the second <u>secret</u> for you. . . . write to me what you think about it & promise to do so really as you did in my dreams to me, for I do <u>love</u> you. . . . this dream is only <u>alone</u> for <u>you</u> to know. I wrote it to you to show how my thoughts are dwelling with you.

There is nothing to indicate that Vicky ever tried to seduce her son or encourage his fantasies. She acknowledged the dreams briefly in her letters, kept her responses light, and in one instance tried to deflect his ardor by bringing up the beauty of his cousins, Alice's daughters. Still, she relished the power she held through his love. "Your little secret is indeed very drole [droll]," she wrote at one point, "& I will keep it <u>quite</u> to myself of course. It gives me great pleasure to think that your old Mama who thinks <u>so</u> much of you, and who loves you <u>so</u> much, is <u>often</u> in your thoughts, and also in your dreams as you are in mine! A <u>better</u> friend you will not have in your whole life than your old Mama, who is <u>always</u> ready to hear all your thoughts, wishes, doubts & fears, to help you where she can & make you as happy as it is in her power, the more you confide in her, the happier it makes her of course!"

The dreams continued through Willy's sixteenth year. "Again have I been dreaming about your dear, soft warm hands & I am awaiting with impatience the time when I can sit near you & kiss them. But pray keep your promise you gave me at Berlin . . . the last evening we drove together <u>always</u> <u>to</u> <u>give</u> <u>me</u> <u>alone</u> the soft <u>insides</u> of your hand to kiss, but of course you keep this as <u>secret</u> for yourself."

"You never answered anything about my dream & about my request, my dear Mama," Willy wrote some weeks later. "I hope I have not hurt your feelings? But perhaps you do not like those dreams about your hands? I can't help that for I very often dream about them."

"I did not answer about your dream. . . . But it did not hurt my feelings in any way, it only made me laugh," she responded. "About my poor hands, I can only say they are very clumsy and mostly concerned with paint or ink when they are not on the piano, or spinning or scrubbing the little ones!" she added when queried on the same subject the following summer. "Therefore what I think of them is that I wish they were more useful and better worth having."

IN JANUARY OF 1877, two days before his eighteenth birthday, Willy graduated from the gymnasium tenth in a class of sixteen. He returned home to be invested with the highest Prussian order, the Black Eagle, receiving from his father the floor-length red mantle on his shoulders and from his grandfather the gold chain around his neck. On the same day, he was also invested with the Order of the Garter, the highest English honor, sent by his grandmother from England.

Queen Victoria had originally proposed sending her grandson the Order of the Bath, advising Vicky that since Willy was not yet the heir apparent, he was not eligible for the Garter. But Willy raised a fuss, and Vicky wrote back saying that since the Czar of Russia, the Emperor of Austria, and the King of Italy had already sent him their highest orders, anything less from England would be taken amiss in Germany. "Willy," she lied, "would be satisfied with the Bath, but the nation would not."

Willy's graduation from the gymnasium marked the end of George Hintz-peter's long reign in the Crown Prince and Princess's household. It had been a harsh decade for both Willy and Henry and little better for their mother, who had grown progressively disillusioned with her sons' tutor. Hintzpeter's conde-scension had poisoned the atmosphere, his "silence, distant reserve, peevishness and . . . sour, morose face" had ruined mealtimes, and his "dry and disdainful" attitude had been adopted by her eldest son.

"I bore with Dr. Hintzpeter for these many years," she wrote Victoria, "because I respected him & thought him in <u>many</u> ways a <u>great</u> great blessing for Willy, though I knew all the while Dr. H. detested me, and it often wanted <u>superhuman</u> patience to . . . smoothe the quarrels his violent temper got him into with almost every one he came near. I feel that Willy will never know how much I have done & suffered for him, but after all, it does not matter if only he becomes good and useful & happy."

What Vicky had not taken into account was the effect Hintzpeter had on her and her husband's relationship with Willy.

"Dr. Hintzpeter," according to Vicky's friend Frau von Stockmar,

deliberately undermined the prestige of the parents in their son's eyes, made fun of their views and insinuated charges of insincerity and pompos-ity against them. My husband* on several occasions warned the Crown Princess Frederick, but she said, "It is quite possible—I have suspected it more than once—but I am making the sacrifice because Hintzpeter is the only man capable of making William concentrate and pushing him on." That is the Empress Frederick all over. Intellectually right, yet entirely mistaken. At that time, Prince William admired his mother. . . . But Hintz-peter's influence soon became apparent. He and Charlotte began to criticise their parents. . . .

Hintzpeter had blamed the boys' parents for the demands placed on them, retaining the role of defender for himself and eventually convincing Willy that even his ghastly riding lessons "must be attributed" to his mother. It was Hintz-peter, however, not the Crown Prince or Princess, who had filled carefree journeys with morality lessons, insisted that Vicky's sons keep to their books on vacations, and complained constantly about their laziness and inability to learn. From the time he entered the home of the Crown Prince and Princess, Hintz-peter made Fritz and Vicky feel that their offspring were wanting. The only children in the family who seemed to have a relatively normal attitude toward their parents and their studies, regardless of basic aptitude, were the ones who were too young to fall under the influence or tutelage of George Hintzpeter.

IN THE FALL OF 1877, Willy, like his father before him, entered the university at Bonn. Although he had an easy grasp of superficialities, Willy found it nearly impossible to sustain his attention on any topic—a failing that the indulgences of power had already begun to exaggerate. In Bonn, he lived with his entourage in a large, handsome villa, where he was taught privately by his professors. "In this way it was possible for me, whose time was so much more fully occupied than that of my fellow-students, to have more leisure for my studies," he com-mented. His uncle, the Grand Duke of Baden, offered another interpretation. Willy, he said, was "exclusively devoted to pursuing his own pleasure and pays so little attention to public lectures that it is impossible to discuss them with him afterward."

"[H]e is very young, very childish, and unformed [for] his age, but a dear good boy, if he will only remain so . . . ," Vicky wrote Victoria that year. "You say, dear Mama, it was not your lot to have dear beloved Papa there to guide

---

* *Ernest von Stockmar, Vicky's onetime private secretary.*

his sons at an age at which they most want their father. . . . Thank God that Fritz is there & can watch over the boys. His very existence & presence I hope will prevent their getting into mischief."

Mischief was not the problem. Although Willy joined "the most swagger" of the student clubs, the Borussia, to which his father had belonged, he was shocked by the "heavy drinking" of his fellow students. "I tried hard to check this pernicious habit while I was there, and even after I had left," he said.

During his first year at the university, Willy began an adolescent revolt against his parents, particularly his mother. His father was baffled. "I cannot imagine how he could find anything at fault with his own parents' home," Fritz wrote Vicky in answer to her complaints that Willy, who was serving in Potsdam with the army, no longer came by to see her; "there is nothing in it which even most remotely resembles the tortured atmosphere with which I was faced at his age!"

Vicky did not understand what was happening. When Willy stopped writing, she began to complain. "I never leave my dear Mama without 2 letters a week, & I have still more to do than you have," she said a few months after he entered the university. "I should feel so ungrateful and undutiful if I did not write twice a week & sometimes oftener—this I have done for 19 years ever since I left home! Sons that love their mothers write as often as they can."

But Willy was in the throes of furious rejection—all the more pronounced for the intensity of the love that had preceded it. "Certainly if you like it, when I am photographed again, it shall be as you wish it, but a black kid glove would not come out prettily at all, I am afraid," Vicky wrote in pre-Freudian bewilderment the summer after her son's first year in university.

To visitors to the court, Willy's repudiation of his parents appeared merely as bad manners. He was, according to the Second Secretary of the British Legation, "a hot-tempered intolerant youth, whose rudeness to his mother before strangers shocked" observers. "Never would he play at tennis on the same side as his mother, and if he was beaten, he invariably lost his temper and flung down his racket."

During his student days, Willy often visited Darmstadt, where he spent Sundays in the cozy, English-chintz home of his aunt Alice and her family. None of Alice's children liked their cousin. According to Meriel Buchanan, daughter of the British Chargé d'Affaires at Darmstadt, the future Kaiser "would want to go rowing, then it would be riding, or a game of tennis, always eager to show how proficient he was in spite of his crippled arm. He would rein in his horse, or throw down his racket in the middle of a game, and order them all to come and listen to him reading the Bible."

Willy fell in love with Alice's daughter Ella, and there was talk within the family of a match between the cousins—discussions that came to a head during his first year at Bonn. In the fall of 1878, Vicky received a letter from Queen Victoria, indicating that her son's suit had been refused. "I could not but think with regret of what might have been," the Queen wrote Vicky a year and a half later.

Like his grandmother, Willy never got over Ella's refusal; even after they were both married, he kept his distance from her. "Questioned as to this marked avoidance of his cousin," said Meriel Buchanan, "he sometimes refused to reply, or if he did, said harshly that he could never forget how much she had meant to him in the past and how much he had loved her."*

Except for his unrequited love for his cousin, Willy was not a romantic. Happiest soldiering in Berlin or Potsdam, his only unconventional desire before settling down after university was to travel to Egypt, a project vetoed by the Kaiser. Willy reported for active service in the fall of 1879 and quickly fell into the mode of what one courtier called "the typical narrow-minded and arrogant Prussian officer."

Starting in the First Regiment of Foot Guards, of which he was given command a year after entering the army, he soon transferred to the cavalry—a challenging move for a man with a useless arm. His success as a Prussian Hussar, culminating in a presentation of "galloping squadrons" before his grandfather, was one of the great triumphs of his life.

Willy loved the intimate camaraderie of the elite Prussian officers. He relished the constant activity and bright new uniforms. The ribald humor of his fellow officers appealed to what one secretary of the British Embassy called Willy's "boisterous geniality. . . . It might gratify a certain mentality to be smitten from behind with a tennis racquet by a future emperor," the secretary said, "but on the other hand such gratification was qualified by the fact that the blow could not be returned."

IF ELLA WOULDN'T HAVE the heir to the German Empire, there was one young woman to whom Willy looked like the proverbial rescuing knight. This was Princess Augusta Victoria, called Dona, the rather plain, uninteresting daughter of Fritz and Vicky's old friend Duke Friedrich of Schleswig-Holstein-Sonderburg-Augustenburg. Dona and Willy had played together as children, and they renewed their acquaintance in 1878.

Everyone was surprised that Willy had not fallen for Dona's prettier sister, known in the family as Calma. But the heir to the throne, rejected once, wrote his tutor that he "had never seriously contemplated the possibility that a lady would find an interest in me" because of his withered arm. He probably felt less threatened by Dona, who was, as everyone kept repeating to everyone else, a fine young woman with nice manners, an acceptable figure, and dignified bearing. "Calma is the prettiest but Victoria [Dona] has a sweet, winning smile," said Queen Victoria, who had difficulty resigning herself to her grandson's unprepossessing fiancée.

It was not Dona's appearance but her lineage that raised eyebrows in the Prussian royal family. Dona's mother was a daughter of Queen Victoria's half-

---

* *During the Russian Revolution, he would try unsuccessfully to save Ella, who married Alexander III's brother, Grand Duke Serge of Russia, from a ghastly death at the hands of the Bolsheviks.*

sister Feodora, but one of her grandmothers was a mere countess, and her father was the man from whom Prussia had stolen the duchies of Schleswig and Holstein. As the Queen wrote Vicky, "people often dislike those they have ill-used." Members of the family still suffered from the stories spread about them, and Vicky worried that it would be "very difficult to overcome the prejudices which have taken root from constant misrepresentation of fact." But since it was clear that Dona was Willy's choice, his parents set out to make the marriage possible for him.

"[C]ould you only make Grandpapa believe how warmly I adore her, how everything I do & think is always in connexion with her!" Willy wrote his mother from Bonn in April of 1879. The following month, he wrote begging the Crown Princess to use her "diplomatic talent" to bring matters to a happy conclusion. "Could you not speak with Grandpapa? Now that I know through Uncle Fritz's* letter that the sweet one loves me . . . you must work on the Emperor a little," he said a few weeks later.

But permission for Willy to marry Dona did not proceed as quickly as the bridegroom-to-be had hoped. Wilhelm I put off giving his grandson an answer until he could study a memorandum on the subject to be prepared for him by his Chancellor. Bismarck procrastinated. His wrist was so painful, he said, he could not write and had to go to a spa. It was not Dona, he claimed, but her sister Calma who wanted to marry Willy. When that ruse failed, he turned to politics, alleging that Dona's father, the Duke of Augustenburg, had announced that he "would still certainly live to reign in the Duchies." Clearly enjoying himself at the expense of Willy's parents, anxious for their son's happiness, Bismarck dallied for months.

Meanwhile, the Duke was dying of cancer. "It seems cruel of me to say it, for you cannot help it, but this uncertainty about Dona's future is killing him," Vicky's sister Helena, the wife of the Duke's younger brother, wrote Vicky in December of 1879. It was not until February of 1880, nine months after he had asked the Chancellor for a memorandum on the subject, that Wilhelm I finally gave his permission for Willy to marry the Duke's daughter. It cannot have been a coincidence that the decision was handed down two weeks after the death of the bride-to-be's father—another triumph for Bismarck over a man he had set out to destroy.

Fritz, who attended his old friend's funeral, was surprised when Willy showed no emotion over the Duke's death, sent no word of condolence to Dona, and did not apparently "wish to hear how his future bride was faring" after her loss. When questioned, the heir to the throne would only say that Dona was "not yet a bride" and that he had to wait until the Kaiser "had spoken." Fritz could scarcely believe his ears. "You can imagine how much his replies and his surprised self-assured attitude hurt . . . ," he wrote Vicky. "Only now do I recognize in him an icy, self-centered character."

---

* *Fritz was Dona's father, the Duke.*

A month after her father's funeral, Willy and Dona became engaged, and Willy wrote his father a note thanking him for the past year of efforts on his behalf. "I cannot find words enough to tell you how grateful I am for the great and extensive trouble which you have taken upon yourself on my account, and the number of struggles which you have fought and the difficulties you have overcome," he said.

"[A] brilliant 'parti' in the eyes of the world it certainly is not!" Vicky wrote Victoria, "and that will wound the inordinate parvenue pride & vanity of the Berlin people, who since 1871, think themselves the only great people in the world."

Neither the public nor the court took the news of Willy's engagement well. Prince Charles, the Kaiser's most social brother, asked his nephew Fritz how it happened that Willy was marrying the daughter of a parvenu, and Charlotte could not wait to tell her father how the Prussians were "turning up their noses" at the Princess from Schleswig-Holstein. But when Dona came to Potsdam for the formal announcement, the Kaiser was unexpectedly kind. His attitude may be explained by a comment he made in a letter to one of his sisters. "Two of my generals," Wilhelm I wrote, "to whom she talked for a long time . . . were enthusiastic about her."

"Willy is very busy with his military duties," Vicky wrote Victoria after Dona had gone home to prepare for her wedding, "& full of zeal . . . almost too much . . . here it has the effect on people for narrowing their minds . . . and imparting harshness to their character!" The Crown Princess was appalled at her son's reaction that summer when a gamekeeper, who was given a little money for shooting cats, shot one of the household pets, hung it on a tree, and cut off its nose. "I am very silly perhaps," Vicky wrote Victoria, "but I cannot help crying! . . . People are so brutal here with poor dogs & especially cats, they think nothing of ill using & killing them, & I cannot bear it!" Willy, his mother said, "thought it was laudable zeal . . . as cats might harm pheasants."

The Crown Prince and Princess hoped that Willy's future mate, a seemingly innocuous girl who bolstered his ego, would help him overcome this need to appear tough. Before they were officially engaged, Vicky had written Fritz that her "only hope for the arousal and development of feelings of consideration, gratitude, compassion—sensitivity—is geared to the influence of a gentle, sweet wife—perhaps she will suppress in him that crass, cold, hard egotism which . . . is his natural disposition." This seemed to be the case. "If he is alone in the room without her," Fritz wrote Vicky after the engagement, "he assumes that certain gruff air of self-confidence, his old, slightly condescending way of being—probably to give himself countenance and to hide his inner emotion."

Ironically, it was the very quality that Fritz and Vicky most cherished in Willy's fiancée—her accepting admiration of her future husband—that would eventually cause them both, particularly Vicky, a great deal of pain. Before her engagement, Dona had told Vicky's sister Helena that she would "do all in her power to be a comfort" to the Crown Princess in order to "prove . . . <u>how</u> grateful" she was for Vicky's "great love and kindness to her." But she quickly forgot her promise. In a life that had already had more than its share of disillusionment, Dona was not the peacemaker Vicky hoped she would be.

CHAPTER
FORTY-THREE

*"If I were going to be married and had to go through all the
ceremonies which attend the marriage of a German princess, I
think I would remain an old maid."*

LILLIE DE HEGERMANN-LINDENCRONE, *wife of the
Danish Ambassador to Germany*

WHILE THE CROWN PRINCESS played a large role in finding an appropriate wife for her eldest son, she had nothing to do with her daughter Charlotte's choice of husband. Charlotte, who was married three years before Willy, had become engaged to Prince Bernard of Saxe-Meiningen in 1876, when she was sixteen. Bernard was an intelligent, weak-willed army officer, obliquely related to Queen Victoria's half-sister Feodora.* He was an amateur archeologist—an interest not shared by Charlotte, an angry teenager with an aversion to things of the mind. Their romance is said to have started on a private railway on an island in the Havel River. When Willy, who had been driving the engine, suddenly sped up, his sister grabbed hold of Bernard and promptly fell in love. True or not, this kind of instant, temporary passion for some person, place, or thing fits with Charlotte's reputation among her relatives for a changeable temperament and underscores one court intimate's assessment of Vicky's eldest daughter as a "foolish, frivolous little Princess."

"How differently the younger generation expects to be treated from what we were," Vicky wrote her mother during Charlotte's engagement. "Fancy that Charlotte <u>never</u> tells me when she writes to Bernard or when he writes to her. . . . They <u>resent</u> the slightest restraint put upon them & Bernard thinks they ought to <u>do just</u> as they like."

"I think there is a great <u>want</u> of <u>propriety</u> & <u>delicacy</u> . . . in at <u>once</u> treating your bridegroom as though (<u>except on one</u> point) he were your husband . . . ," the Queen wrote back. "Here now they have lost all modesty for not only do they go about driving, walking & <u>visiting</u>—everywhere <u>alone</u>, they have also <u>now</u> taken to go out everywhere together in society . . . & make a <u>regular</u> show of themselves. . . . In short young people are getting very American, I fear in their views and ways."

Ignoring Victoria's warnings that she would find her daughter's marriage a "great trial," Vicky plunged eagerly into assembling Charlotte's trousseau.

---

* *His stepmother was Feodora's daughter.*

"How well I remember all the trouble you took about mine," she wrote Victoria, "and how it touched me that you should see into each little detail yourself."

Dressing Charlotte was not easy. Oddly proportioned with a long waist and neck, "immense" arms and breasts, and very short legs, Vicky's eldest daughter looked tall when seated and top-heavy when on her feet. In spite of the usual nineteenth-century program of posture and dancing lessons, Charlotte, who "trundle[d]" along with her elbows stuck out, remained awkward in a day when grace was considered one of a woman's major assets.

The wedding took place in February of 1878. "After the fackeltanz * I took her to her room . . . ," Vicky wrote Victoria. "I helped her to undress & get ready for going to bed, and with an aching heart left her, no more mine now— to care for & watch & take care of but another's. . . . Forgive my paper being so blotted, but I cannot help shedding a few tears. When I came back last night & I looked into her little empty room & empty bed where every night I have kissed her before lying down myself . . . I felt very miserable. . . . I have thought more of you—than ever in my life. . . . Mothers do not † lose their daughters if all love their Mothers as much as I do you."

NEXT TO HER MOTHER, the relative to whom Vicky was closest was her sister Alice, whose family was hit by diphtheria in the fall of 1878. Within two weeks, Alice's four-year-old daughter May was dead, but the rest of the family seemed on the way to recovery. "How good it would be if in a week or 2 they could all go to a warmer climate . . . after all they have gone through! . . . Do you not think so too?" Vicky wrote Victoria, lobbying as usual for the Queen to help Alice with finances.

But Vicky's hint was in vain. Worried about breaking the news of his baby sister's death to her ten-year-old son, Ernie, Alice softened the blow with a maternal kiss. For Alice, as Disraeli said, it was literally "the kiss of death." Weakened from nursing the rest of the family, she contracted diphtheria and died a week later, on the anniversary of her father's death, December 14, 1878, at the age of thirty-five.

"If I only could know how you are! . . . ," Vicky wrote Victoria in a forty-one-page letter. "Our darling!—I can hardly bear to write her dear name—was my particular sister. . . . I think of the dear house now so desolate and empty. . . . It was the only place in Germany except Coburg where I loved to go, & which seemed a bit of home!"

---

* *The* Fackeltanz *("torch dance") was the main feature of German royal weddings. At midnight, two rows of ministers carrying torches entered the White Hall and walked around it in time to stately music, bowing before the bride and groom. The bridal couple, attended by ladies carrying her train, stepped down from a dais to follow the torchbearers around the room. The bride then took the Kaiser by one hand and her nearest male relative by the other, while the groom took the Kaiserin and the bride's mother. All walked slowly around the room. This continued until the bride had paraded with all the princes and the groom with all the princesses, each group making their obeisances to the Kaiser and Kaiserin.*

† *Underlined three times in original.*

Due to the fear of infection, Vicky was "forbidden" to attend her sister's funeral and wrote Victoria that she thought it "a cruel deprivation not to be allowed to fulfill a last and sacred duty to the beloved one!" She was also hurt by Willy's "coldness and indifference" to his aunt's death, but pleasantly surprised by what she saw as an outpouring of sympathy in other members of the court. Even "the dear Emperor shows feeling in his way. . . . he loved & admired her so much! Telegrams & letters rain & people crowd to say a kind word & express their sympathy."

Vicky would have been less pleased had she been privy to a conversation held at one of Augusta's tea parties about a week after Alice's death. Augusta had always resented the fact that Vicky and her sister did not share her enthusiasm for the Catholic Church. When someone mentioned the premature death of the Grand Duchess, the Kaiserin was unmoved. "Perhaps it is just as well for her children that she has died," Augusta said, "because, like all English Princesses, she was a complete atheist!"

The Crown Princess had no sooner begun to recover from the death of her sister than her third son, eleven-year-old Waldemar, also came down with diphtheria. Waldemar, the most appealing of Vicky's sons, promised to be everything his brothers were not.

"He is such a dear child, & although rather more spirited than is easy to manage, he is so trustworthy and honest . . . ," Vicky had written Victoria on his eleventh birthday. "If Heaven spares him I am sure he will be liked & trusted everywhere."

Six weeks later, Waldemar's servant came to his mother's room to say that the boy was ill. "I do all I can for him, feed him, look to his throat etc. but do not stay very long in the room . . . ," Vicky wrote Victoria. "You can imagine my anxiety & who & what are continually in my thoughts, but I do not fear contagion myself the least in the world! I gargle, & put on a mackintosh over my clothes while I am with the dear child."

"I have washed him today with hot vinegar & water . . . ," Vicky reported the next day when her son seemed better, "& changed his linen & his shirt, popping it all into a pail of carbolic acid. . . . I keep a flannel jacket on the dear boy,—& the windows wide open in the next room with the doors wide open, & a good open fire,—so that the air is excellent! I myself change my clothes, & have carbolic acid sprayed over me before I go to the others. . . . The doctors feel quite cheerful about him, but of course all cause for anxiety is not yet over!"

Around nine o'clock that evening, the doctors called the Crown Princess to her son's room. His breathing was worse, and sometime after midnight he died.

Fritz and Vicky buried their son covered by one of his mother's nightgowns, with his father's handkerchief over his face. The Crown Princess invited the household staff with their wives, her son's schoolmasters, and the parents of his friends to a private funeral service in their home. The next day was the official funeral, which Vicky did not attend. Later on, she visited the tiny chapel in the Friedenskirche (Church of Peace) in Potsdam, which now held the tombs of both her dead sons. The boys lay in white marble sepulchres under a dome painted with angels and inscribed *Lässt die Kindlein zu mir kommen.** Vicky had executed much of the painting herself.

There were those in Germany, undoubtedly influenced by the Bismarck press, who took satisfaction in her tragedy. The official papers always painted the Crown Princess's maternal qualities in the blackest ink, and one minister said that he hoped that Prince Waldemar's death was a trial sent by the Almighty as divine retribution for Crown Princess Victoria's hard heart.

On the evening of Prince Waldemar's funeral, Bismarck hosted a party for members of the Reichstag.

SLIGHTLY OVER A MONTH after Waldemar's funeral, Charlotte gave birth to a daughter, Vicky's first grandchild. Having done her duty by the dynasty, the eighteen-year-old Princess declared that she would have no more children and returned quickly to society, taking her place at the head of the young matrons of Berlin who rode, skated, and gossiped while their husbands went out shooting. A favorite of the Empress Augusta, Charlotte was a welcome addition to the faction at court that denounced her parents. Her criticisms, "inspired by the friends of the Empress Augusta," were, according to one intimate, "passed from mouth to mouth and whispered and passed on."

Meanwhile, the thirty-eight-year-old Crown Princess struggled through the first weeks of mourning in physical shock. She confided her worries about her own body to the Queen, begging her to "scratch out with your pen" the carefully couched details. It seems that Vicky had started menstruating "rather violently" during the day of Waldemar's death, but that the blood had ceased just as suddenly within a few hours.

Hormonal upsets were followed by giddiness, neuralgia, and rheumatism. Dr. Wegner recommended winter in a warm climate. "[T]he Empress will never allow this I am afraid," the Crown Princess wrote her mother, explaining that her mother-in-law felt that if the Crown Princess's health was poor, "it must just remain so, as hers is not good either." Augusta was in fact too busy preparing for the many celebrations surrounding the golden anniversary of her miserable marriage to pay attention to her daughter-in-law's grief.

Unable to arouse sympathy in her in-laws, the Crown Princess slipped into martyrdom, eyeing everything through the lens of her loss. In this she differed from Fritz, who tried to be philosophical, writing the Prince and Princess of Romania, who had lost their only daughter, "We endeavour to bear God's decree with resignation, but we cannot even now become reconciled to the loss of another son . . . a son . . . who justified our highest hopes, and already displayed character at an early age."

Vicky's tendency to seek the tragic mode, formed in her mother's court, was intensified by the callousness of the Hohenzollern family, who were equally

---

* *Let the little children come unto me.*

determined to downplay what Vicky had been taught was appropriate mourning for those left behind. Seething over their indifference, Vicky's physical ailments multiplied, and she began to complain of faintness and giddiness. Soon there were more telling symptoms—perpetual noises in her head, uncontrollable shaking in her hands, and feelings of suffocation. In early September of 1879, the doctors sent her to a spa in the Tyrol, where the local physicians diagnosed anemia, debilitating rheumatism, and severe depression. It was clear that Vicky was in the throes of a breakdown. She was sent to Italy for the winter. After a fight with her in-laws, she was allowed to have her three young daughters join her.

From October to May, away from the temperature and torments of the capital, her mind and body slowly improved, her chronic rheumatism disappeared, and she even removed her mourning. "I hate myself for taking it off, & yet I feel it ought to begin . . . ," she wrote Victoria over seven months after Waldemar's death. "Of course I wear <u>all</u> black and shall do so for some months longer. I tell you this little detail as you . . . have the same feeling as I about the mourning one wears for those one loves best! It all seems a sacred thing to me!"

Like her mother after Albert's death, Vicky came dangerously close to settling into perpetual mourning over her dead son—a state at least partly caused by an odd sense of loyalty, common to Victorians, that seemed to require the living to hold on to their grief in order to prove the depth of their love. She also shared another personality quirk with her mother—a seemingly unconquerable need to compare the virtues of the dear departed with the deficiencies of those left behind. Just as the Queen of England never hesitated to criticize the ways of her two elder sons in contrast to the unblemished life of their sainted father, Vicky could not stop comparing the qualities of nascent manliness already evident in eleven-year-old Waldemar to Willy's lack of humanity and Henry's maddening apathy.

Like Victoria, Vicky was honest to the point of insensitivity about her children. It was a family failing, and it helped estrange the German Crown Princess from her second son, Henry, a sweet, uninteresting child who adored his mother but grew into an ineffectual man, easily swayed by the opinions of others. Where Henry was concerned, Vicky's comparisons were not limited to Waldy, but encompassed Henry's older brother as well.

"Willy is so forward in <u>every way</u>. Henry is <u>awfully backward</u> in <u>every</u> thing . . . is <u>hopelessly lazy</u>, <u>drole & idle</u> about his lessons—but <u>such</u> a good natured boy—everybody likes him, though he is dreadfully provoking to teach from being <u>so</u> desperately slow!" she had written Victoria when Henry was eleven.

Deemed incapable of intellectual pursuits, Henry had been put into the navy. At sixteen, he left Germany for a two-year cruise on a warship, arriving home in the fall of 1880. His ship docked in Kiel, where he was to pursue his naval studies. "It was an agony to me to see Kiel again," Vicky wrote Victoria, the place I had been to with my beloved Waldie. . . . Dear Henry is looking very well indeed. . . . We spent the afternoon and evening on board his ship, talking over so many sad things, & shedding many tears, yet so thankful to see him safe & well, and especially as pure—& innocent as when he left us. . . . Herr v. Seckendorff* has watched over him like a mother. . . . Of Henry's abilities little is to be said as you know! . . . It made my heart ache to breaking when I thought of the other precious one, my pride and my hope—gone!!

Henry, whose purity may have been laudable but whose homecoming sounds less than enjoyable, raised himself in his mother's estimation by telling her how "lost" he felt without his younger brother in the palace. Henry, Vicky wrote her mother, "is good & affectionate. I wish I could make him a little prettier, & I wish still more I could give him more brains. That, alas, is not in my power!"

ONE OF VICKY's great regrets had always been her own looks, which had not improved with age or the shock of Waldemar's death. In the spring of 1879, she sent her mother a photograph of "your oldest & ugliest daughter," and just before her fortieth birthday the following year, wrote that she was "growing very unsightly . . . have lost almost all my hair, & what remains has turned very grey; my face is full of lines and wrinkles especially round the eyes & mouth, and having no good features to boast of, I really am an annoyance . . . when I look at myself in the glass."

Her husband, however, had not married her for her beauty, and she must have continued to attract him for, unlike most royalties, they still shared a bedroom.

In Vicky's eyes (and others as well), the Crown Prince remained the epitome of an old-fashioned German prince—tall, handsome, gallant, and romantic. A young British attaché, Sir James Rennell Rodd, never got over the "vivid impression made upon me" when he saw Fritz for the first time "approaching the tennis ground with his four Italian greyhounds, a splendid figure of dignified manhood, radiating kindliness with a friendly smile." Vicky's letters to her mother confirm her deep love for her husband, and, on occasions like anniversaries, overflow with appreciation to her parents for arranging her marriage.

The Crown Princess had seen enough of royal marriages to realize that they were almost never love matches and that the wife usually suffered doubly —first, from having to submit sexually to a man she found unappealing, and secondly, having to endure the humiliating infidelities that inevitably followed. A mutually satisfactory bond, both physical and intellectual, was a distinct rarity in royal circles, the only other one she had ever known (probably the only other one to be found in her time) being that of her parents.

---

* *Henry's military governor, not to be confused with Count Götz von Seckendorff, a member of the Crown Princess's household.*

According to the young secretary to the British Ambassador, "Few women have exerted greater charm without really good looks" than the Crown Princess, and by the age of forty, she had learned to be more outgoing with those on the perimeter of her life. Society ladies, who had once complained that she did not "give herself the trouble to speak much to them," were impressed with her, although it remained clear that the Crown Princess still disliked having to deal with the empty social life of Wilhelm and Augusta's court.

But this situation did not seem as if it would last much longer. Given the natural course of life (and death), it looked as if Fritz and Vicky would soon take over from Wilhelm and Augusta and bring their own people to court. The probability frightened Bismarck, who recognized privately what he refused to admit to publicly—that both the Crown Prince and his wife were people of incorruptible character, generosity, and humility. In a revealing conversation that took place on February 23, 1879, with his press chief, Moritz Busch, Bismarck spoke about the Crown Prince and Princess as compared to the Kaiser and Kaiserin.

He [the Crown Prince] is more human, so to speak, more upright and modest. . . . He does not say: "I have won the battle, I have conducted the campaign," but "I know that I am not capable of doing it; the Chief of my general staff has done it, and he therefore deserves his rewards." The Most Gracious [Wilhelm I] thinks quite differently. He also cannot tell exactly an untruth, but he will have it that he has done everything himself; he likes to be in the foreground; he loves posing and the appearance of authority.

The Crown Princess also is unaffected and sincere, which her mother-in-law is not. It is only family considerations that make her troublesome . . . but she is honourable and has no great pretensions.

Probably this is why Bismarck thought it so necessary to destroy the Crown Prince and Princess in the eyes of the German people.

CHAPTER
FORTY-FOUR

> *"In trying to deal with its worst nightmare—an alliance between France and Russia—Germany made this alliance inevitable. As German defense policy was geared to coping with a two-front war, it presented an increasing threat to all its neighbors. A Germany strong enough to deal with its two great neighbors jointly would surely be able to defeat them singly. Thus Germany tended to bring on what it feared most."*
>
> HENRY KISSINGER, 1968

*F*OR THE FIRST TIME since her marriage over twenty years earlier, the Crown Princess of Germany was out of the political picture for eight months—from September of 1879 to May of 1880. It was during her absence that Bismarck embarked on the first of the famous secret alliances with which he hoped to defend Germany—a treaty with Austria that brought him into a pitched battle with the Kaiser.

A few weeks before Alice's death, Wilhelm I had made a triumphal reentry into Berlin to celebrate his recovery from the assassination attempt that had nearly killed him. Ramrod-straight, mustaches bristling, the eighty-one-year-old appeared to his physician to have actually benefited from the gunshot wounds. "The old blood has been drawn off," explained the doctor, "and he looks much better now than earlier."

Just before his own death, Nobiling, Wilhelm's would-be-assassin, explained why he had pulled the trigger. He had, he said, tried to eliminate the Kaiser so that Crown Prince Friedrich Wilhelm, who was "more independent and less easily influenced" than his father, could ascend the German throne. Perhaps Nobiling's remark was repeated to the old Kaiser. Perhaps the recent reminder of his own mortality had brought him up short. Something clearly happened to change Wilhelm's attitude, and the man who had always followed his Chancellor's lead with a minimum of fuss now balked at a new twist in Bismarck's foreign policy.

For some time, Bismarck had espoused a doctrine geared to maintain Germany's position in the center of Europe, surrounded as it was by other powerful nations, especially a vengeful France. Called the "Kissingen dictation,"* the Chancellor's theory was summed up in his phrase, "When there are five, try to be *à trois.*" Based on the premise that there were five so-called Great Powers that controlled Europe—England, France, Germany, Austria, and Russia—Bismarck believed that Germany's only security against France lay in being one

* *He had committed it to paper while taking the waters at Kissingen.*

of a coalition of three of the others. The specter of an anti-German alliance among Germany's neighbors, France, Russia, and Austria, a "nightmare of coalitions" as he called it, haunted his dreams.

Bismarck's original consortium, the Three Emperors' League, signed in the fall of 1873 by Wilhelm I of Germany, Alexander II of Russia, and Franz Joseph of Austria, was a vague, nostalgic document, currently threatened by the rivalry between Russia and Austria in the Balkans. Based on the collective nervousness of the signators, but not binding on their governments, the Three Emperors' League had also been weakened by several blows to Russo-German friendship —the war scare of 1875, during which Russia made it clear that she would not sacrifice France to Germany; the economic depression that hit Europe in the mid-1870s, prompting Russia to raise protective tariffs that threatened German business; and the territorial results of the Congress of Berlin (1878), for which the Russians continued to blame the Germans. Added to these real and perceived threats was a sharp enmity between Bismarck and the Russian Foreign Minister, Prince Gorchakov, a sulky old man on the verge of senility.

The Czar believed that Russia had been purposefully duped at the Congress by a European coalition led by Bismarck, and the Russian press took up this anti-German theme after the war. Angry at being criticized for something that was not his fault, Bismarck withheld German support from Russia in various international commissions established at the Congress, raised tariffs on Russian goods, and, hearing that there was a plague in the lower Volga, closed the Russian-German border. In accounting for his actions, he blamed the Czar, whom he called "an autocrat without the capacity to rule"; the Czar's adored mistress, who had to be, like Augusta and Vicky, a bad influence on the man in her life; and, of course, old Gorchakov. The Chancellor ordered articles written for the German press critical of the Russian Foreign Minister, and he even went to the trouble of writing one himself. He also sent an envoy to warn Alexander II that relations between Germany and Russia could not improve while Gorchakov remained in power.

But the sort of Bismarckian blitzkrieg that did away with inconvenient ministers at home had little or no effect in St. Petersburg. As tensions mounted between the two countries, it became increasingly clear that the Three Emperors' League could not be saved. In line with the Kissingen dictation, Bismarck moved to set up an alliance elsewhere. "Austria," he instructed his subordinates, "is more certain, because her people favor such an alliance. Besides, she brings England along with her, and she becomes vulnerable to hostile influences, if she finds no support with us."

The Chancellor had not reckoned with the Kaiser.

Wilhelm I had always been devoted to his Russian family—his now-deceased sister, the former Czarina (wife of Nicholas I), and his nephew, Czar Alexander II. To the Kaiser, who embodied the best and the worst of royal conservatism, the friendship between Germany and Russia was more than a political convenience; it was, as he put it, a "sacred legacy." Moreover, Wilhelm's first recollections of military glory dated from the days when the Prussians had joined the Russians in defeating Napoleon I. That was back in 1813, when he was a young officer, still in his teens. Over half a century had elapsed since then, but time had only brightened the significance of that alliance in the mind of the old soldier.

In early August of 1879, Czar Alexander II sent his uncle Wilhelm a letter condemning Bismarck's current anti-Russian policies, which he blamed on the German Chancellor's personal animosity to Gorchakov. He told his uncle of the "fears" that preoccupied him, "the consequences of which could be disastrous for our two countries." When Wilhelm showed this somewhat ill-considered letter to Bismarck, the Chancellor easily turned it into a rationale for the Austrian alliance. "I was compelled by the threatening letter of Czar Alexander (1879)," Bismarck claimed in his memoirs, "to take decisive measures for the defence and preservation of our independence of Russia." The idea of a defensive treaty between Germany and Austria appalled Wilhelm I of Germany, who told Bismarck that such a concept ran "contrary to his principles."

While Bismarck was marshaling his arguments to prove to the Kaiser that the road to German security lay through Vienna, Wilhelm sent an envoy to Alexander II. The Czar responded with an invitation for Wilhelm to meet him at Alexandrovo, on the border between Russia and Germany. There, Alexander apologized for his unwise letter, nephew and uncle quickly smoothed over their difficulties, and the Kaiser informed Bismarck that he would abdicate rather than agree to a defensive alliance with Austria against Russia.

During the following month, September of 1879, there ensued what George Kennan called "a conflict of epochal dimensions" between the German Kaiser and his Chancellor. Up until this time, Wilhelm had always been able to rationalize Bismarck's policies as means to an end he understood, namely, the preservation of himself and the House of Hohenzollern. Now, Bismarck was asking him to act in a manner that ran contrary to his deepest beliefs and came perilously close to dishonoring the family code. He refused.

By indicating to the Crown Prince that the exclusion of Russia would mean the inclusion of England in the alliance, Bismarck found "a strong advocate" for his policy, and Fritz undertook to convince his father that a treaty between Germany and Austria was a good thing. Fritz and Vicky both believed that an Anglo-German alliance would not only keep the peace but would help reverse the conservative trend of policies within Germany itself. "[I]f Germany truly allies with Austria, England, France and Italy, I fail to see how world peace can ever be disturbed," she wrote him. "Such a union will bring great advantages and blessings . . . and commercial differences [i.e., protective tariffs] will disappear." Not too surprisingly, the Crown Prince's support for Bismarck's alliance did nothing to change the Kaiser's mind.

Unable to budge Wilhelm, the Chancellor simply went ahead with his negotiations, shuttling between Gastein and Vienna for talks with the Austrian Foreign Minister, Count Andrassy. Letters and messages flew back and forth between Chancellor and Kaiser, but neither would give way. Intent on getting his agreement through while the pro-German Andrassy was still in power (he was due to leave soon), Bismarck threatened to resign. "Bismarck is more necessary than I am," Wilhelm admitted, caving in a month after his meeting with the Czar.

The Dual Alliance, which was kept secret, was dated October 7, 1879. The linchpin of Germany's foreign policy, it remained in effect until the demise of both the German and Austrian empires, guaranteeing mutual support in case either should be attacked by Russia or another power supported by Russia. But if the French attacked Germany and were *not* supported by Russia, Austria was bound only to neutrality. This meant that Austria's greatest danger, an attack by Russia, was covered in all instances, but Germany's greatest fear, an attack by France, was not.

Wilhelm I reluctantly signed, adding next to his signature, "Those men who have compelled me to this step will be held responsible for it above [i.e., to God]." When he asked that the Czar be informed of the terms of the secret document, Bismarck refused. At Fritz's suggestion a compromise was effected, whereby Alexander II received a letter representing the new alliance as a resumption of the old ties between Germany and Austria, dissolved in the breakup of the German Confederation at the time of the Austro-Prussian War. The Czar accepted this explanation, writing his uncle that he would like "to see the return of that perfect entente of the three emperors." To facilitate this, Alexander II appointed a man whom Bismarck liked as his new Ambassador to Germany.

While he was still struggling with the Kaiser and some three weeks before negotiations were completed with Austria, Bismarck began sounding out the possibilities of adding England as the third party to his treaty, sending the German Ambassador to the Court of St. James's, Count Münster, to ask Disraeli "what Britain's policy would be if Germany fell out with Russia." Count Münster was, in Vicky's words, "<u>not</u> a clever man nor a great statesman, but a thorough gentleman." According to Disraeli, Münster said that "Bismarck proposed an alliance of Germany, Austria-Hungary and Great Britain." Disraeli answered that he would consider Bismarck's proposition, and the delighted German Ambassador wired Berlin the positive results of his mission.

Bismarck wired back that he was not satisfied. Disraeli, he complained, had not answered his question, "What will Britain do if we are involved in a dispute with Russia over the Eastern Question?" Münster was instructed by his chief to break off negotiations.

Like many factors in the German Chancellor's international balancing act —a performance in which he seemed to keep the other European nations in perpetual motion—the proposed agreement with England, which Bismarck used to enlist the help of the Crown Prince, was purely a matter of expediency. In between the time Bismarck ordered Münster to see Disraeli and the time Münster actually met with the Prime Minister (who was on vacation), the Czar had sent two emissaries of peace, thus obviating the necessity for the English connection. Their visit left Bismarck gloating. "I knew that the Russians would come to us," he said, "once we nailed down the Austrians."

Bismarck had, of course, paved the way for the Czar's return to the fold by intimating to Russia that the Dual Alliance was only the first step on the road to reestablishing the Three Emperors' League. At the same time, he had informed the English and French that his alliance with Austria was a bulwark against the dangers of Russian Pan-Slavism. The brilliance of his maneuvering lay as much in these explanations as in the alliances themselves. "It will not do to accept any one of Bismarck's statements as the true exposition of his policy," historian William Langer said. "What he aimed at was rather a system of checks and balances . . . at holding the balance between West and East and at upholding the commanding position of Germany by playing off the one against the other."

With the Dual Alliance signed and the Russians panting to be let in, Bismarck was again on his way to resuscitating the defunct Three Emperors' League, which he claimed constituted "the only system offering . . . maximum stability for the peace of Europe." But he was in no hurry to conclude the treaty with Russia, now that she was anxious to join the others, and dawdled along for six months, teasing the Czar, varying the pace and temperature of the negotiations from fast to slow, from ardent to cool, in order to teach Alexander II a lesson. Sure of ultimate compliance, Bismarck played the indifferent lover, lacing his proposals with petulant complaints about Gorchakov and rumors of a Franco-Russian entente. In February of 1880, he told one important general that he preferred Britain to Russia as the third member of his proposed trio.

Bismarck's role of reluctant suitor changed quickly to that of determined seducer, however, when Disraeli and the Conservatives lost the English elections to Gladstone and the Liberals in the spring of 1880. Overnight, the German Chancellor found not only his alliance but his role as the prime mover on the European stage threatened by Gladstone, who had again emerged as an outstanding voice in European affairs, promoting peace through such un-Bismarckian concepts as mutual cooperation among nations and self-determination for ethnic groups. This last precept brought Gladstone into conflict with the Austrians. Where the traditional hostility between the English and the Russians had seemed unresolvable, both England and Russia now found common cause in supporting the self-determination of nationalistic groups suffering under the repressive weight of the Habsburg Empire.

These shifts in the winds of foreign policy reached Vicky, now on the road to recuperation in Italy. "Prince Bismarck . . . [is] . . . convinced that the Gladstone Cabinet are enemies to Germany & friends of France which makes him inclined to lean again towards Russia," she wrote Victoria; "he has no interest in interfering with any design of Russia's on Constantinople—his only aim and interest is not to be isolated in case of France making war upon Germany! If he finds he cannot make sure of England's & Austria's support . . . of course he must turn to Russia, & if he is to obtain a Russian alliance he can only do [so] by letting the Russians do what they like in the east. . . . I own I think with horror of such a combination! Nothing is morally so bad for Germany as an intimate friendship with despotic & military Russia."

The Crown Princess's major concern about the ongoing deterioration of the Ottoman Empire was still Constantinople, which she felt must at all cost be kept out of Russian hands. In that regard, she mentioned to her mother the possibility, neither new nor original to her, of setting up a separate state that would include Constantinople and be led by her brother Affie, the future Duke of Coburg who was married to the daughter of the Czar. "It does sound very wild,—I own, & formerly I thought it preposterous," she wrote her mother, "but now I ask myself <u>what</u> is to become of the East if the present state of things cannot & will <u>not</u> last & the Turkish Gov't <u>cannot</u> be kept on its legs. . . . Surely England <u>never can</u> stand by to see the Russians at Constantinople?"

Vicky's Russophobia, which often carried her far afield, was partly based on knowledge of the very real dangers for Germany inherent in another alliance with the Czar. But the Russian conservatism that repelled the German Crown Princess was just what attracted Bismarck, who believed that hard-line autocracies like Russia made far more reliable allies than constitutional monarchies like England. News of the change in the English government only served to confirm this belief, and he hastened to conclude his triple alliance with the Czar. The idea of bringing Russia into the alliance delighted Wilhelm I, who agreed to terms painstakingly worked out during the winter of 1880.

All that remained was to get Austria's approval to the triple agreement—a task made more difficult by the new Austrian Foreign Minister, who was determined to make no concessions to the Russians. A colorless figure with the stubbornness of the insecure, Baron von Haymerlé was so wary, according to Bismarck, that he said "no" three times each morning on awakening "for fear of having undertaken some commitment in his sleep." Negotiations dragged on throughout 1880 and into the summer of 1881.

MEANWHILE, TWO ROYAL EVENTS occurred that would influence the Russo-German alliance.

The first was Willy's marriage to Dona, which took place on February 27, 1881. Willy, who had recently celebrated his twenty-second birthday and had just been appointed Captain of the Body Guard, escorted his bride on her entrance into Berlin the day before the wedding. As he led his company to the palace to receive her, one of Dona's attendants remarked that the groom seemed "more concerned with the appearance of the Guard than of the bride." *

Dona's marriage to the heir to the throne only encouraged Willy's militarism and his desperate need to show off. A provincial young woman whose horizons were limited to home and church, Dona clung fervently to her family and never expressed anthing but acceptance and admiration for her young husband. Her primary duty, as she saw it, was to bolster Willy's fragile ego. It was the heir to the throne's need to express this ego in obvious and flamboyant

---

* The validity of this observation is born out by a chapter of Wilhelm II's autobiography called "Marriage and Friendship," in which he devoted two pages to his wife and eleven and a half pages to his friendships with several men, mostly generals.

ways that would at first strengthen Bismarck's alliance with Russia—and then destroy it.

The second event, which occurred two weeks after Willy and Dona's wedding, was the assassination of Czar Alexander II. On March 13, 1881, a Nihilist threw a bomb that blew up Alexander's carriage. Unconscious and bleeding profusely, the Czar was carried back to the palace, where he died almost immediately in the arms of his beloved mistress, Catherine Dolgorukaya.

"One is so horror-struck, that one really does not know what to say!" Vicky wrote Victoria.

> Poor dear Emperor Alexander! . . . with all his faults and failings he was so amiable and charming and lovable, so kind-hearted and well-meaning. . . . Too many cruelties, too much severity had been shown by the Government . . . for a spirit of revenge not to spring up. . . . The saddest part is that it should be wreaked out on so well intentioned and kind hearted a Sovereign —who was not the tyrant the others had been before him, though he had a little of it in him at times, as mostly all Czars must have! . . . Despotism is a demon . . . and must sooner or later lead to such terrible things, which then usually fall on the innocent.

Alexander II had always been well liked by the elite brotherhood of European monarchs in spite of his irregular personal life, which centered on Catherine and their two children. The object of frequent assassination attempts, fearful of what might happen to his mistress if one of them should succeed, Alexander II had shown tragic foresight by marrying her within weeks of the death of the Czarina.* Eight months later, he himself was dead, and his son was on the throne.

The new Czar was very different from his father. A huge, heavyset man with nervous hands the size of hams, Alexander III was known for physical strength, moral puritanism, and mental sloth. In his mid-thirties when he inherited the crown, he subscribed to fidelity in marriage and ultraconservatism in affairs of state. Sasha, as he was known in the family, believed that repression, not compromise, was the appropriate response to civil unrest.

Alexander III did not have the same ties to Germany as Alexander II. Wilhelm I was only his great-uncle, a distant figure, and the new German Empire was arrogant and overbearing. Moreover, Alexander III's wife, the new Czarina, was a daughter of the King of Denmark and the younger sister of Alix, Princess of Wales. Like Alix, she hated Bismarck for stealing Schleswig and Holstein from her father.

One of Alexander III's most significant traits, however, was a curious indolence when it came to making decisions, and it was this passivity that led him

---

* *Originally Princess Marie of Hesse-Darmstadt. A pretty, intelligent young woman, the Czarina had been Alexander's adored wife and confidante until he fell in love with Catherine. Marie spent the last years of her life suffering from tuberculosis and a broken heart, and died early in the summer of 1880.*

to follow the road laid out before his accession and accept a treaty for which he personally had little enthusiasm. Two months after the death of his father and some twenty months after the signing of the Dual Alliance, negotiations were finally brought to a conclusion, and the new Three Emperors' League was signed.

Dated June 18, 1881, this treaty, unlike the 1873 agreement among monarchs, was binding upon the participating governments for a period of three years. It provided that if any one of the three signators—Germany, Austria, or Russia—declared war against a fourth country, Turkey excepted, the others would remain neutral. Beyond this, however, the treaty outlined possible scenarios for the future. It stated that Austria might annex Bosnia and Herzegovina whenever she chose; in exchange for this, Germany and Austria agreed not to oppose an eventual union between Bulgaria proper and the south Bulgarian province known as Eastern Rumelia, currently under Turkish control—thus defying the Congress of Berlin's intention to keep Bulgaria from becoming a Russian client state.

Due to the nature of the treaty itself and particularly the agreements involving Bosnia, Herzegovina, Bulgaria, and Eastern Rumelia, the Three Emperors' League had to remain a secret. It did—for nearly forty years, until 1919. While bureaucrats in the foreign offices of Germany, Austria, and Russia pursued policies thought to be in line with official positions, there was a document which, if it had come to light, might have required a whole other train of action. As George Kennan said, the Three Emperors' League was a "very solemn and significant instrument, affecting profoundly the behavior of the three monarchs and their most intimate advisers, but affecting it in ways of which they could give to the wider public no adequate accounting."

The following year, in 1882, Bismarck supplemented the Dual Alliance in still another direction. Italy, which had lost Tunisia to France and continued to fear French intervention in Vatican politics, needed powerful allies and joined Germany and Austria in May of 1882 to create what became known as the Triple Alliance.* This alliance guaranteed that Germany and Austria would come to Italy's aid if she were attacked by France, and that Italy would do the same for Germany. If any of the three countries were attacked by two other Great Powers, i.e., France and Russia, it would be supported by the others. Primarily an attempt to isolate France, the Triple Alliance was also Bismarck's way of neutralizing Italy, since he believed that the Italian army was basically worthless in time of war.

THE CHANCELLOR'S REJECTION of England in favor of Russia as the third member of the Three Emperors' League had been a serious blow to the Crown Prince. Seeing his chances to be an effective liberal leader cut out from under him—first with the reversal of domestic policy, then with the realignment of Germany with her ultraconservative neighbors to the east—Fritz apparently fell

---

* *Romania also signed on in 1884.*

into one of his periodic depressions and told Vicky that he was ready to withdraw from public life. But she urged him to continue to speak out for his principles and recommended that he "arrange some meetings" with liberals who could enlighten him about "the things which are being covered up in official circles!"

Unlike her husband, the Crown Princess did not give up. There was, as she realized, a great deal of discontent within Germany, which she hoped would bring Bismarck eventually to heel. What she could not foresee were the lengths to which the Chancellor would go, not only to deal with that unrest, but to undermine the future reign of her husband.

CHAPTER
FORTY-FIVE

"History as a weapon is an abuse of history."

ARTHUR M. SCHLESINGER, JR.

*B*ISMARCK'S SUCCESSES in foreign relations in the early 1880s were not repeated at home, where his plans to capitalize on political conservatism and economic protectionism failed to materialize. Domestic politics continued to be a problem for the Chancellor. The acknowledged European master at manipulating the interests of other nations to the benefit of his own, he did not seem to comprehend the enormous social changes that rapid industrialization had wrought within Germany itself.

Bismarck understood only two classes of people—the landed aristocracy from which he came, and the former peasants who depended for their livelihood on the local seigneur. "There is no worker who, when I come, does not meet me at the threshold, extend his hand trustingly, invite me inside, wipe off a chair and invite me to sit down," the Chancellor boasted to the members of the Reichstag. "Hence I know the opinion of the workers rather well."

Seemingly unaware that this bucolic fantasy had nothing to do with a new class of urban worker whose frustrations were being channeled into a major political force, Bismarck's attempts to appease the socialists with one hand (two social insurance acts passed in 1876 plus an industrial code in 1878) and repress them with the other (the antisocialist law of 1879) had not produced the effect he expected. During the 1880s, socialism continued to thrive, albeit underground, and the Social Democratic Party held its own in the Reichstag.

Nor did the wall of protective tariffs erected in 1879 return the German economy to the elusive climate of boom and hope, so seductive in the early 1870s. Tariff revenues had to be used to balance the budget, and an upsurge in industrial production only led to intense competition, a decline in prices, and the failure of small businesses.

Agriculture also hit hard times. Ever since the 1870s, Germany had consumed more food than it could produce, but farmers who tried to compete with imports of wheat could find little unused farmland left to plow.* Junkers were

* *Modern farm machinery and fertilizers were not introduced into Germany until after 1890.*

often forced to abandon what Max Weber scathingly called their "lordly aristo-cratic existence." According to Frederick Engels, the Junker of the 1880s was in much the same pickle as Mr. Micawber, trying to figure out how "to have an annual income of say 20,000 marks, an annual expenditure of 30,000 marks and not make any debts."

As farming grew less profitable, more and more sons of the landed nobility turned to the bureaucracy to support themselves. At the same time, ambitious scions of the new industrial magnates joined the officers corps of the army or purchased ailing Junker estates in a frantic quest for titles and prestige. This resulted in the emergence of a new ruling class combining the swagger of the old aristocracy with allegiance to a new industrial god.

Vicky was not the only person to question the conventional ethos of the day as promulgated by the Chancellor. Up until 1880, liberals like Eduard Lasker, the leading defender of parliamentary power and civil rights, had felt compelled to swallow the compromises of the National Liberal Party on the grounds that Wilhelm I was elderly and his son, who would soon ascend the throne, shared their belief in parliamentarianism. But in March of 1880, after the increase in the military budget and the passage of the antisocialist law, Lasker resigned from the National Liberal Party. He was followed by twenty-five other important liberals, including Fritz's friend Max von Forckenbeck. A former president of the Reichstag, known for his skills in mediation, Forcken-beck had also reached the limit of political tolerance. "The Bismarck system," he said, had created "the politics of popular impotence."

In August of 1880, the defectors started a new party, the Secessionists, dedicated to the promotion of political liberalism, laissez-faire economics, tax relief for the lower classes and human rights. At the same time, the Progressive Party, led by Eugen Richter, also began an assault on the status quo. Mean-while, the old National Liberals remained the common ground for large farm-ing interests, industrialists, professional men, and teachers—men who had traded their ideals for material benefits and protection from the blue-collar class. Freed from the miseries of voting against their principles, the Secessionists and the Progressives gained political momentum.

On election day in October of 1881, Vicky wrote Queen Victoria that she had never seen the German people so excited about domestic politics. "Usually," she commented, "they are <u>utterly</u> indifferent. Alas! had they not been so we should not have an all-powerful Bismarck. . . . If he succeeds in carrying out his plans Germany will one day be the prey of <u>communism</u>."

The election of 1881 dealt Bismarck an enormous blow. In spite of system-atized government intimidation of the voters and an appeal to anti-Semitism, over two-thirds of the seats were won by men opposed to Bismarck, those whom the Chancellor had labeled *Reichsfeinde*—enemies of the state.

Frightened by the election, Bismarck launched a campaign against the liberals and the Crown Prince. Conducted in the official press and private memos to the Kaiser, Bismarck hinted that Gladstone and the English radicals were looking forward to Fritz's accession because he would surely encourage comparable democratization in Germany. He drafted a royal edict for Wilhelm to issue as King of Prussia, proclaiming the king's right to personal control over the politics of members of his government. "Everyone who is not with us is against us," Bismarck declared, combing the records of government employees for "harmful and unworthy elements."

"Have you read the Emperor's Proclamation to his Ministers?" Vicky wrote Victoria. Bismarck, she told her mother, had arranged for word to be "spread every where here . . . that Fritz was a party to it," when in fact "he first read it in the newspapers and was horrified." To alienate her husband's liberal supporters and soil his image with the public, articles were planted in the government press asserting that the Crown Prince was "quite satisfied" with Bismarck's policies and that it was only "his English wife" who disapproved.

Bismarck's determination to force the Crown Prince into line reached into the core of Fritz and Vicky's palace. Aided by the heads of the military establishment, who replaced Fritz's longtime comrade and aide-de-camp General Mischke with an ultraconservative, General Winterfeldt, the Chancellor set out to remove Karl von Normann, one of the Crown Prince's most trusted courtiers.

Shortly after the election of 1881, Fritz had asked Normann to arrange a secret meeting for himself with the leader of the Progressive party, Eugen Richter. The Crown Prince always read at least one radical paper on the assumption that he knew "full well what the Government thinks," but wished "to know what other people think as well." Now he asked to meet personally with Richter in order to hear for himself the ideas of the men who now made up the second largest party in the Reichstag. Normann knew he was endangering his position if his efforts should ever be revealed, but arranged the audience in his personal apartments in the palace annex.

The following year, Fritz promoted Normann to the position of Chamberlain of his Court. But by then, word of the secret meeting had leaked out. Convinced that Normann was plotting a "joint attack on his position" with the Crown Princess, the Kaiserin, and Normann's friend General Stosch, Bismarck had Normann named Minister to the tiny state of Oldenburg on the North Sea, well on the other side of Germany. There was nothing the Crown Prince could do, since Bismarck was head of the Foreign Ministry. "Once I am Emperor," Fritz assured Normann, "you will be the first whom I will recall."

To replace Normann, Bismarck appointed Count Hugo von Radolinski, an intimate of Friedrich von Holstein, the most powerful man at the Wilhelmstrasse. A bachelor with no interests outside his work, Holstein had, according to one contemporary, "one great ambition: to know everything about everybody and to rule everybody through fear of the disclosures which he could make were he at any time tempted to do so." To accomplish this, Holstein had developed a vast spy network into which Radolinski fit nicely.

A career diplomat, Radolinski was brought into the Crown Prince's palace from Weimar, where he had been serving as Prussian Minister. His new job was presented to him by Bismarck as "an act of political self-sacrifice," a position he need fill for only six months to a year before being rewarded with a highly desirable posting,* even if the Chancellor "had to kill someone to make room" for him.

Ostracized by the other members of the court as Bismarck's spy, Radolinski managed nonetheless to make "a splendid position for himself." Smooth and elegant, he ingratiated himself with Vicky, who asked Queen Victoria to receive him when he visited England. Privy to the details of life inside Fritz and Vicky's palace, Radolinski repeated everything to Holstein and Bismarck, invariably adding some damaging tidbit, often fabricated, to be used in the corridors of the Foreign Ministry or the salons of Berlin as evidence of Vicky's failure as a wife and Crown Princess.

In his new position of Court Chamberlain to the Crown Prince, Radolinski —usually referred to by Holstein as "dear Rado" or "good old Radolinski"— was given specific orders: to get rid of his counterpart, Vicky's Court Chamberlain, Count Götz von Seckendorff. Seckendorff, called by Odo Russell "one of the most amiable and agreeable of Prussians I know," shared a liberal political outlook with the Crown Princess, along with a love of painting and sketching, in which he was apparently reasonably gifted. His loyalty to the Crown Princess was unshakable.

Shielded from these intracourt machinations set in motion by his Chancellor, Wilhelm I expressed pleasure in what appeared to him to be "a favourable turn in the political opinions of Fritz and Victoria." The Kaiser was not the only one unaware of the Byzantine network Bismarck had constructed to thwart the Crown Prince and Princess. As Lady Ponsonby wrote her husband Henry, Queen Victoria's secretary:

> I don't think the Queen realizes what an extraordinary state of things exists in Germany in the way of espionage and intrigue. They, the Foreign Office, which means Bismarck, wanted to put a man of their own about the Crown Princess so as more effectually to control the Crown Prince when he becomes Emperor. Seckendorff refused to play the spy, and would not lend himself to this intrigue. They began by dismissing his brother, after twenty years' service, from the Foreign Office without any reason being given. Then they appointed Radolinsky . . . with orders to get rid of Seckendorff. Radolinsky . . . then began the undermining of Seckendorff.

The campaign to discredit Seckendorff was highly successful, according to his friend and court intimate Princess Catherine Radziwill.

> A great deal of untruth has been told and written about him [Seckendorff] . . . I was always struck by his broadmindedness, his lofty views, his high intellectuality. . . . When he was made the subject of most unjustifiable, even dastardly attacks, it was not so much he that was being aimed at as the Crown Princess. The greatest reproach that could be leveled at Seck-

* *Radolinski would eventually serve as Ambassador to Turkey, Russia, and France.*

endorff was that he sometimes failed in tact. . . . his strong English leanings and sympathies alone would have singled him out among the crowd of flatterers and sycophants that surrounded the old Kaiser, the Empress Augusta, and . . . the great Bismarck. . . . he had always refused to act the spy, and this alone would have been sufficient to ostracize him in those Berlin drawing-rooms where a particular pleasure was found in gossiping about the Crown Princess.

THE EFFORT TO ENFORCE CONFORMITY within palace walls was a reflection of the atmosphere outside, where clamorous chauvinism had taken the place of patriotism and Bismarck had become a national icon—the man whose prescience had enabled Prussia to fulfill its godgiven destiny. "No doubt he is quite patriotic & sincere . . . ," Vicky wrote Victoria. "He thinks a great central power is necessary, & that one will must decide. . . . I do not like this state of things but most Prussians & conservatives do,* & our two sons think it perfection and every other country miserably governed. There is no disputing or discussing these points with them."

Both Willy and Henry, who always followed his brother's lead, subscribed enthusiastically to the prevailing historical revisionism that cast the Chancellor as a demigod and Wilhelm I as the resolute hero whose refusal to bow to parliament in 1862 had brought this remarkable person to power. To rationalize their glorification of the pragmatic, Vicky's sons and other Teutonic tub thumpers pointed to the successes of the Prussian army in three wars, the unification of Germany, and the nation's current position of dominance in western Europe. The lessons to be learned were obvious: the good of the state superseded ordinary concepts of right and wrong; the dictatorial powers of the crown and the military had been proved correct; and those who objected to the extra constitutional functioning of the German government should be written off as obstructionist or unpatriotic.

Misleading in itself, this political philosophy was far more dangerous when combined with a burst of national xenophobia, fanned by an irate Chancellor fighting liberalism. The chief victims of this witch-hunt were the Poles and the Jews.

Ever since the end of the Napoleonic Wars, Poles had been slipping over the border into Prussia in search of work or escape from compulsory military service. They labored in the fields and factories, taking the place of the German peasants who had moved westward looking for a better life. For years the Polish immigrants, who had resisted Bismarck's attempts at Germanization, had been a source of frustration to the German Chancellor, who saw them as the chief carrier of the virus of Catholicism.

By the middle of the 1880s, there were over two million Poles living and working in Germany. Some were recent immigrants, but many were second-generation property owners, men with serious careers. Regardless of status or

---

* Underlined three times in original.

achievements, Bismarck ordered the expulsion in 1885 of all aliens from four border provinces. "The border jumpers of impeccable conduct, who appear to be a burden neither to the police nor to society, are often the most dangerous politically," he said, justifying his actions on the grounds that it was this group that spawned revolutionaries. Even ordinary workers "untouched by political agitation" were guilty of upsetting the "state organism by polonizing the border provinces, whose Germanization is the state's task."

Over the vociferous objections of the majority of the members of the Reichstag, who condemned the government for "unjustified" expulsions, over half the aliens* residing in Germany were deported by the spring of 1886. Bismarck also established a Prussian state fund of 100 million marks to purchase estates from Polish landlords in order to lease them to Germans. In spite of Wilhelm I, whose conscience began to bother him, the Polish language was prohibited in schools, and Polish officials and soldiers who were left were transferred to the West to "learn the blessings of German civilization."

While the Poles suffered from state-sponsored bigotry, the Jews fell victim to another sort of persecution that, although not inaugurated by the government, was readily accepted by it. Anti-Semitism was surely nothing new in Germany, where Jews had been exiled from Brandenburg until the time of the Great Elector.† Although the army of Frederick the Great had one Jewish general, Frederick himself did not like Jews, saddling them with economic burdens such as a law decreeing that Jewish couples had to buy a specified amount of porcelain from the royal porcelain factory, which the King was trying to save from ruin, before they could obtain permission to marry.‡ Life for Germany's Jews improved under Frederick's nephew and successor, Friedrich Wilhelm II, and during the time of the reformers, laws were enacted declaring that Judaism was a religion like any other—a change in attitude that allowed seventy thousand Jews to become citizens of Prussia.

Thus, for half a century, anti-Semitism had lain relatively dormant in the small German villages and towns, while in larger cities like Berlin, Jews had been assimilated into the intellectual community, rising to positions of political and financial leadership, intermarrying or discarding their old orthodoxy for a faith that allowed them to get ahead economically if not socially in a Christian world. (The Junkers were notorious anti-Semites.) The crash of 1873 had changed all this, and the search for a scapegoat on whom the disgruntled could blame their financial losses brought the submerged currents of distrust and hatred out into the open.

While the crash devastated big investors, the depression that followed hurt the small storekeepers, workers, and artisans who made up the bulk of the German lower and lower-middle classes. Suspicious by nature, these people

* *Approximately twenty-seven thousand of an estimated forty-four thousand.*

† *The beginning of the fifteenth century.*

‡ *Ironically, this eventually resulted in Jews owning some of the best porcelain collections in Germany.*

were easily convinced that it was the Jews who were responsible for a failed economy. In 1873, a journalist named Wilhelm Marr published a pamphlet, "The Victory of Judaism over Teutonism," in which he predicted that the Jews would supersede the Germans unless the latter girded themselves for a major attack on the infiltrators. The next year another writer, Otto Glagau, published a book entitled *The Stock Exchange and Founding Swindle in Berlin,* in which he claimed that it was the Jewish capitalists who were destroying the middle class and killing German idealism.

But the man who was ultimately responsible for the engulfing wave of hatred that swept through Germany in the 1870s and 1880s was the chaplain of the court, Adolf Stöcker. A vigorous preacher with a sonorous voice and a talent for demagoguery, Stöcker was an evangelical whose anti-Semitic rhetoric, launched as a handmaiden to his personal political ambitions, developed into a major national movement.

In his position as Chairman of the Berlin Mission, Stöcker had come face to face with the misery of the lower class and its growing adherence to socialism and the Social Democratic Party. Because of this, he founded in 1875 what he called the Christian Social Labor Party, a militantly Christian organization aimed to appeal to the workers of Berlin. But Stöcker's call for social reforms based on Christian faith and love of the Kaiser failed to seduce the workers. The German Protestant Church had no record of helping the workingman, and it was obvious even to the uneducated that Wilhelm I was against giving labor a voice in parliament. Stöcker did not give up.

In 1880, partly to gain a constituency and partly to punish the Jewish journalists and politicians who had criticized his previous bid for power, the court chaplain dropped the word "Labor" from his party's name, added a large dose of anti-Semitism to its political platform, and set out to capture the votes of small businessmen and petty bureaucrats, men whose livelihoods had been damaged by the ongoing recession and whose jobs might be perceived to be threatened by an influx of Jews coming out of eastern Europe.

Stöcker's self-promoting oratory, along with written assaults on the Jews by Henrich von Treitschke, a leading historian and member of the Reichstag, released a great, noxious miasma of anti-Semitism lying just beneath the surface throughout Germany. Treitschke, who believed it was his duty to promote nationalism through his historical books, labeled the Jews Germany's "national misfortune," an unassimilable group "devoted to huckstering and usury."

Bismarck saw no need to stop the anti-Semitic groundswell of 1880, which he believed would help him defeat the liberals at the polls the following year. Not only did the government do nothing to prosecute those accused of anti-Semitic violence, but it was said that Bismarck's Reptile Fund* secretly financed some of the hate-mongering newspapers that appeared on the scene. The combination of Stöcker and Treitschke, unopposed (at the very least) by the man

---

* *The money Bismarck expropriated from the King of Hanover at the end of the Austro-Prussian War.*

holding the highest office in the nation, gave anti-Semitism patriotic credibility in the eyes of the average German citizen.

Vicky, whose religious intolerance was confined to a somewhat petulant impatience with the formal rites of the Catholic Church, clearly did not approve of this politics-by-hatred. Some years earlier, she had written her mother, "If you want to read anything perfectly cracked you should see Richard Wagner's new pamphlet called 'Jewish Influence in Music.' I never read anything so violent, conceited or unfair. It is very much talked about here in Germany."

Now there was far more cause for concern, as demonstrations took place, riots broke out, and Jewish homes and a synagogue were burned. "The disturbance about the Jews is going on . . . people are so violent & excited," she wrote Victoria from Wiesbaden in December of 1880. "It is most painful & disagreeable in a town where the Jews do all for the public, as at Berlin & are so generous and charitable! I own one is shocked and disgusted with this movement." Two weeks later, she wrote from Berlin on Christmas Day about the "deplorable" state of German political life in which the "poor Jews" were being "infamously used" and "insulted in every way!" To show her personal feelings on the matter, the Crown Princess accepted the honorary chairmanship of an orphanage for Jewish girls founded in Berlin, and stepped in when she heard about persecuted individuals.

But the anti-Semitic wave, once set in motion, did not abate. It was kept alive by Wagner in Bayreuth and writers like Paul Lagarde, a biblical scholar and guru for many educated Germans. In 1881, the League of German Students was founded with the express purpose of disseminating nationalistic and anti-Semitic propaganda in the universities. The Russian pogroms, which began in 1881, sent thousands more Jews westward into Posen (German Poland) and Germany. Once there, the immigrants worked hard, prospered, and incurred the jealousy of both German and Polish workers. Treitschke claimed that these new Jews were less civilized than their assimilated brethren, that they were possessed of what he called a "dangerous spirit of presumptuousness," and that their children and grandchildren would one day try to dominate the newspapers and stock markets of Germany. Wilhelm I told his Secretary for Foreign Affairs that although he did "not approve of the action of Pfarrer [Pastor] Stöcker . . . the noise is of use in making the Jews rather more modest." Bismarck's official mouthpiece, Moritz Busch, added his bit. Jews were not members of a religion, he claimed, but "a race"—one that could never become German.

The Crown Prince, like his wife, was strongly opposed to the kind of virulent scapegoating that pervaded the court and the upper reaches of society. "Fritz considered the anti-Semitic movement . . . terrible," Vicky wrote after his death. "As a modern civilized man, as a Christian and a gentleman, he found it abhorrent. . . . He tried to counteract this monstrosity as and where he could by action and free expression of his opinions and feelings."

Fritz had started opposing anti-Semitism when he was young. An ardent Freemason, he had insisted that Jewish Masons from England be allowed to visit Prussian lodges, from which they had traditionally been barred. Trained by his mother, whose Catholic sympathies did not preclude tolerance for Jews, the Crown Prince fought anti-Semitism both personally and symbolically. "I so greatly admire dear Fritz's speech about the poor, ill-treated Jews," Queen Victoria wrote Vicky in January of 1881 during the anti-Semitic riots. During the violence the Crown Prince also attended a service in a Berlin synagogue in full dress uniform and made sure that he was seen attending a university lecture on the evils of anti-Semitism.* He helped at least one Jewish professor secure tenure and, on the social side, tried to save young Fräulein von Bleichröder, daughter of Bismarck's Jewish banker, embarrassment at her first court ball.

Seeing that no one was dancing with the young woman because she was a Jewess, Fritz ordered two of his officers to do so. "The Crown Prince was well aware that I, like him, regarded anti-Semitism as a stain on the escutcheon of German culture," said the first, Count Bernstorff. The second was not so gallant. "By the command of His Imperial Highness, the Crown Prince, I ask you to dance with me," he said, thus humiliating the young woman, who fled the ballroom and never again appeared at court.

Ostracized from the policymakers, laughed off by the social element at court, there was little Fritz or Vicky could do to staunch the onset of the campaign of hatred that would culminate sixty years later in the Holocaust. Begun by one politically ambitious demagogue, it was carried to the final extreme by another.

ONCE BISMARCK REALIZED that his campaign to suppress the socialists had, like his attack on the Catholic Church, done little more than solidify the determination of his opponents and improve their representation in the Reichstag, he embarked on a more practical method of wooing the working class— through social reform. Health, accident, and old-age insurance were to do for the loyalty of common laborers what high tariffs and protectionism had done for their betters.

Although Bismarck's plan was a groundbreaking one, decades ahead of its time, it failed to weaken socialism or co-opt malcontents. What Bismarck did accomplish, however, was even more significant. By instituting fundamental, prototypical safeguards for the working man—protective buffers that other countries did not adopt for many years—Bismarck broke political barriers and established precedents that outlived his government, the monarchy he served, and the terrible effects on Germany of his concept of service.†

* These appearances were made against the advice of others, who warned of how they might be used against him. After both Fritz and Vicky attended a concert in a synagogue in Wiesbaden, Stockmar wrote that "it would be best for your Highnesses to abstain from anything which might appear to be a demonstration for one side or the other, thus preventing that your persons might become involved in a struggle among factions, a struggle which is frequently conducted with sordid means and raising a lot of dirt" (J. C. G. Rohl, Wilhelm II, p. 415).

† "The bold reform programs of the thirties and forties and fifties and beyond . . . ," Daniel Patrick Moynihan wrote in 1973, "have consisted to a dispiriting degree of ideas Lloyd George borrowed from Bismarck" (Pflanze, Vol. III, p. 171).

The first was health insurance. Established on a local basis with the cost divided between employers (one-third) and workers themselves (two-thirds), the Medical Insurance Act of 1883 provided thirteen weeks of support at three-quarters of the sick or disabled laborer's normal salary. It aroused a great deal of public interest and parliamentary support, breezing through the Reichstag with a vote of better than two to one.

Accident insurance was a different case. Although Bismarck introduced accident before health insurance, it failed to pass the Reichstag three times before becoming law in July of 1884. This was probably due to the fact that the Chancellor had another more pressing agenda. "Accident insurance in itself is for me a secondary consideration," he told one of his legislative assistants, who promptly resigned in protest. "My chief consideration is to use this opportunity to . . . establish the basis for a future representative body . . . either as a substitute for, or as a parallel body to, the Reichstag."

For some time, the Chancellor had been exploring the idea of replacing the Reichstag with an economic council composed of what would essentially be chambers of commerce—groups of men who kept their politics in their pocketbooks, who would be less idealistic and more easily manipulated by materialistic considerations. The Accident Insurance Act of 1884 was only one in a series of his aborted attempts to bypass parliament. Not too surprisingly, the legislation passed only after the Reichstag divested it of the administrative infrastructure geared to facilitate Bismarck's coup.

After the passage of the health and accident acts, Bismarck lost interest in social reform. Old-age and disability insurance, introduced in 1883, was not even brought to the floor of the Reichstag until 1889, and by then the Chancellor had turned back from domestic to foreign affairs. He had obviously failed to prove to the lower class, as he put it, that "the state is not to be regarded as an institution invented merely for the protection of the better situated classes of society." This was because, as Lassalle had recognized some twenty years earlier, it was simply not true.

Bismarck lost interest in bettering the lot of the laboring class when the results of the election of 1884 showed that he no longer needed to court the liberals in the Reichstag. Shortly before that election, the two left-wing parties, the Secessionists and the Progressives, merged into a new German, Liberal, or Freethinkers, Party. This was done in order to give the Crown Prince—sure to inherit the throne in the very near future—a parliamentary bloc on which he could rely, as Bismarck now counted on their former cohorts, the National Liberals. But in their first election, the amalgamated party won only about two-thirds of the seats they had captured as separate parties, thus reversing what looked like the liberal trend of 1881. Their loss of support can be explained partly by the problems inherent in the new so-called Freethinkers Party itself and partly by Bismarck's manipulation of the death of a political opponent.

The consolidation of the two left-liberal parties took place in March of 1884, only ten weeks after the death of Germany's leading liberal statesman, Eduard Lasker. The most respected liberal of his era, Lasker was known for his effectiveness as a speaker and for his refusal to bow to Bismarck—traits that had earned him the Chancellor's outspoken hatred. No bill ever seemed to reach completion without an amendment from the man Bismarck referred to as that "dumb Jew boy" or the "disease-bearing louse." According to a fellow member of the Reichstag, Karl Braun, "Whenever anything goes wrong somewhere, whenever someone has corns or suffers from a badly made shoe, he is told Lasker is the cause of it. He made those bad laws under which you suffer." In an attempt to get rid of Lasker, Bismarck had even run his elder son Herbert against him in the elections of 1878, but Herbert had been roundly defeated.

Lasker died suddenly at fifty-five of a heart attack while visiting the United States. The U.S. House of Representatives sent an official resolution of condolence to the German Reichstag, an encomium to "the eminent German statesman Eduard Lasker . . . [whose] . . . firm and constant exposition of and devotion to free and liberal ideas have materially advanced the social, political, and economic conditions of . . . lovers of liberty throughout the world."

Interpreting this message as critical of his style of government, Bismarck refused to pass it on to the Reichstag. He sent the condolence back to the House on the grounds that Lasker did not deserve the tribute. When one of the dead statesman's friends protested, Bismarck delivered a vicious attack on Lasker on the floor of the Reichstag, calculated to strengthen the old National Liberal Party at the expense of the splinter Freethinkers, or, as it was now being called, the Party of the Crown Prince. He succeeded in undermining confidence in the liberals and blackening the name of an old opponent.

The historian Erich Eyck points to a comparison between Bismarck's diatribe in the Reichstag against Lasker and Lord Salisbury's posthumous praise in parliament of his "lifelong antagonist Gladstone" as a "great Christian statesman." This, according to Eyck, is an example of the difference in political tradition between Germany and England. To others, it may say less about the gallantry of English statesmen in general than about Bismarck's personal inability to let pass any opportunity for revenge, even on a dead man. It was an ugly passion that did not play itself out with Lasker, but eventually wreaked havoc on the reputations of the Crown Prince and Princess as well.

CHAPTER
FORTY-SIX

"If all is well with dear England, all is well everywhere."

CROWN PRINCESS VICTORIA OF GERMANY

*F*OR OVER A QUARTER OF A CENTURY, the Crown Princess had tried to be a good German, to follow the precepts instilled by her father and old Baron Stockmar as the proper basis for a life of public service. But her belief in Germany as a center of culture and rationality had been trampled—first by the ultraconservative Prussian court, then by Bismarck, and finally by the German people themselves, who seemed all too easily led to believe the worst of *die Engländerin.* Knowing herself to be untrusted and unloved in her adopted country and temperamentally unfit to pay lip service to principles she loathed, Vicky began to turn back to England. This change in attitude can be traced in her letters to her mother; in the early 1880s, the word "we," which formerly referred to the Germans, now meant the English.

It is not a coincidence that Vicky's realignment occurred just as the new German Empire began to challenge decades of British imperial supremacy by entering the colonial race. At this point, her priorities clashed, and Germany came out the loser. During the early stages of German overseas expansion, the Crown Princess began to write long, passionate letters to Victoria in which she espoused schemes like a British railway through the Euphrates Valley to the Persian Gulf—a plan that would thwart the colonial dreams of other empires like Germany—and descriptions of new weapons like Mauser rifles, which England should consider adding to her arsenal. In these recommendations, she was fulfilling Bismarck's early predictions of irreconcilable conflict. But it was the Chancellor himself who had created the climate for Vicky's disaffection.

By the early 1880s, Bismarck had succeeded in cutting the Crown Prince and Princess out of the information loop that ran through the government and the court. The price of exclusion ran high. While Fritz continued to ask members of Bismarck's government embarrassing questions, to which they were instructed to give evasive answers, Vicky began to withdraw. The end result of Bismarck's campaign to isolate the heir to the throne and his wife, destroy their reputations, and render them politically powerless was alienation. Bismarck's accusations of divided loyalties aimed at Germany's future Kaiserin for twenty-five years had finally become a self-fulfilling prophecy.

GERMANY WAS THE LAST great European power to achieve unification, and for that reason, the last to establish colonies around the world. For nearly twenty years before Germany entered the colonial race, the Foreign Ministry had been receiving requests for colonies from commercial interests around the country, especially the Hanseatic port cities, ancient home of the import-export trade. Four arguments were offered by the merchants of Hamburg and Bremen, who wanted protection for their foreign adventures: overseas colonies would consume Germany's excess production, provide raw materials and foodstuffs, serve as a place to invest German capital, and be a "safety valve" for political and religious deviants, an alternative to the United States, where most German emigrants were taking refuge.

Bismarck himself had always disdained the colonial adventure. "I don't care for colonies at all," he had asserted back in 1871, insisting that for the infant German empire, colonies would be "like sable coats worn by Polish noblemen who don't have shirts." Nine years later, in 1880, Bismarck's Secretary for Foreign Affairs, Prince Hohenlohe, brought up the subject again. "He will not hear of colonies, now as at other times," Hohenlohe wrote. "He says we have not an adequate fleet to protect them, and our bureaucracy is not skillful enough to direct the management of them."

None of these conditions had changed when Germany began to establish colonies in 1883–84. But by then, Bismarck needed a way to destroy the Crown Prince's liberal supporters in the Reichstag and divert the attention of the general populace from economic problems. Colonialization appealed to the richer members of parliament—Conservatives and National Liberals who found the black-white-and-red flag of German nationalism a convenient wrap for their commercial interests and those of their constituents. It was not popular with the Freethinkers, who reasoned that Bismarck's belated interest in overseas expansion was bound to bring Germany into conflict with other countries who were already there. However valid this argument, Bismarck knew that the Freethinkers were vulnerable in an election to accusations of a lack of national pride. As Vicky wrote her friend Lady Ponsonby, "I am almost certain that the whole agitation about colonial enterprise would not have been cooked up if it were not a useful handle for the elections."

But there was another, more Machiavellian reason behind the Chancellor's about-face. By the time Germany entered the colonial race, England, France, Spain, Portugal, Belgium, and the Netherlands had already staked out most of their claims, leaving only southwest Africa and the South Sea islands open to further settlement. In both these areas, England had arrived first—with her Cape Town colony in South Africa and Australia in the South Seas. In 1883, Wilhelm I of Germany was eighty-six years old. By embracing colonialism at that time, Bismarck could steer Germany into competition with England and undermine the imminent reign of the next Kaiser and his English-born wife.

In 1890, Herbert von Bismarck, Otto's elder son, who served as his father's special envoy to England during these years and later became Germany's Secretary of State, explained his father's sudden conversion to colonialism as a preparation for the accession to the throne of the Crown Prince. "During this reign," Herbert said, "English influence would have been dominant. To prevent this, we had to embark on a colonial policy, because it was popular and conveniently adapted to bring us into conflict with England at any given moment."

The Chancellor was extraordinarily proud of his cunning. In September of 1884, at a meeting of the Emperors of Austria, Russia, and Germany, he boasted to Czar Alexander III that "the sole object of German colonial policy was to drive a wedge between the Crown Prince and England." Although this was the sort of remark Bismarck knew would please the Anglophobic Czar, it was also the truth.

UP UNTIL THE 1880s, Bismarck had enjoyed watching the competition over colonial possessions between other European governments. With his penchant for stirring the international pot, he had encouraged the British to occupy the Turkish sultanate of Egypt in order to promote hostility between England and France; as his conduit to Whitehall and Buckingham Palace, he had used the Crown Princess:

"I foresee so much good . . . both for the unhappy ill-used [Egyptian] population who deserved better government, better masters and better treatment, and for the development of agriculture, of trade," Vicky had written Victoria at the start of the Russo-Turkish War, lobbying the Queen for British occupation of Egypt.

Neither Victoria nor her Prime Minister had been fooled. Detecting the fine hand of the German Chancellor, Disraeli had remarked that if "the Queen of England wishes to undertake the government of Egypt, Her Majesty does not require the suggestion, or permission, of Prince Bismarck."

The Crown Princess had quickly backed off. All she wanted was for "England's influence" to be "paramount" in Egypt, "both for the benefit of England's interests and for the happiness of an oppressed and unfortunate people." Many Englishmen had voiced this idea before, and because it happened to coincide with a proposal of Bismarck's, it should not be dismissed out of hand.

Vicky's unshakable faith in an improved life for the oppressed under the British Union Jack was one of the recurrent tenets of her political philosophy. Like many others born in the British Isles, she believed that it was England's duty to spread its civilizing influence over the politically, religiously, and financially deprived, and if this advanced Britain's trade and economy at the same time, so much the better.

What the Crown Princess did not realize was that the Egyptians resented the Europeans, who had loaned them the money (at enormously high interest rates) to build the Suez Canal. Desperately in debt, the Egyptian Khedive* had

---

* *The semi-independent Viceroy of Egypt, appointed by the Turks.*

sold his shares in the Suez Canal Company in 1875 to the British government, making England the largest shareholder as well as the biggest user of the canal. Five years later, a law requiring that surplus funds in the Egyptian treasury be used to service her debt led to the formation of an Egyptian nationalist movement, which demanded relief from foreign control.

In 1882, the Khedive appealed to the European powers for help against the nationalists. British and French squadrons appeared at Alexandria, and riots broke out in the city in which about fifty Europeans were killed. (Some said that the riots were started by the Khedive in order to get England and France to intervene on his behalf.) As a conference was being called in Constantinople to settle the crisis, the German Crown Princess began to deluge her mother with letters of advice. Her ardor for England was increased by the fact that Bismarck had just launched another anti-English campaign in the German press.

"The German newspapers are more than rude against England . . . ," Vicky wrote Victoria in late June of 1882. "My opinion is that Prince Bismarck would be too glad to play us a trick now. . . . I do not wish the British Lion to cut any unnecessary capers, but I wish he would rise up and give a good roar now and then."

Vicky did not have long to wait. In retaliation for the deaths of the Europeans, the British bombarded the city of Alexandria, an attack in which the French refused to take part. "You will rejoice at the success of the bombardment which was inevitable though one regrets the loss of life of innocent people deeply," Victoria wrote her daughter.

"The bombardment . . . was not only an inevitable but a wise step to take, horrible as all bloodshed, destruction, violence & strife always must be," the Crown Princess wrote back, adding that England must "occupy Egypt, return order & peace, and once for all secure for herself the Suez Canal! . . . It would be for the good of Europe and all Europeans who may hereafter again settle in Egypt; it would also be good for the Sultan, who can never hope to govern the Egyptians. . . . The German Press & public are very anti English now, but England's true friends . . . rejoice. . . . It is a great blessing for our prestige in the whole of the East."

Needless to say, Europe was not as sanguine about England's role in the Middle East as the German Crown Princess. France was particularly unhappy, refusing to join England as she began landing soldiers to protect the canal. By the middle of September of 1882, the British had occupied Cairo, causing serious friction with the French—exactly what Bismarck had tried to bring about through Vicky five or six years earlier. Meanwhile, the Chancellor had effected a significant change in Germany's own relations with France.

For nearly a decade after the Franco-Prussian War, the French republic had nurtured its hostility toward the conqueror. But in 1880, Jules Ferry, an impassioned imperialist, had been named to the position of Premier. Unlike his predecessors, Ferry was willing to deal with the Germans in order to extend France's colonial empire, and Bismarck was only too happy to help the French thwart the English.

By the end of 1882, two of the elements Bismarck wanted in place before entering the colonial race were there. The first—France's hostility toward England—he had tried and failed to bring about five years earlier, but had now been handed as a by-product of England's occupation of Egypt. The second—Germany's new friendship with France—he had engineered himself.

A master at taking advantage of any political situation, the German Chancellor turned to colonialism in 1883–84 as he had previously turned to war. Germans who had reacted well in the 1860s and 1870s to the annexation of Schleswig-Holstein, Bavaria, and Alsace-Lorraine might now be diverted from domestic woes through the romance of new acquisitions in Africa or the South Seas. A shrewd politician could guess that proud citizens, given an excuse to wave the flag, and powerful financial interests, provided with new markets, were likely to show their appreciation at the polls.

GERMANY ENTERED the colonial race through negotiation with a tobacco importer from Bremen named Adolf Lüderitz. In 1882, Lüderitz applied for, but was denied protection for, a trading post he planned to establish on the coast of South-West Africa. The following spring, he got an entirely different reception when he returned to the Foreign Ministry to complain that he had encountered a British trader who had challenged his right to acquire property on the Bay of Angra Pequena from a Hottentot chieftain.

This time, Bismarck ordered an inquiry into British sovereignty, informing the German Consul in Cape Town and the German Ambassador in London that Lüderitz had "a claim on the protection of the German Reich for his holdings." To intensify the pressure on England, the Chancellor attacked her Egyptian policy. "Here the newspapers have as usual found an opportunity for abusing England in which the public heartily join," Vicky wrote Victoria in the summer of 1883, "i.e. the cholera in Egypt which is attributed to British selfishness, & will, it is said, spread to Europe through England's fault!"

Encouraged by Lüderitz's success, other German traders acquired rights to large chunks of land in the Cameroons and Togoland—possessions that were promptly affirmed by a Consul General dispatched in a gunboat to conclude treaties with the natives and raise the German flag.

The British, astonished by this sudden development in German foreign policy, were besieged with requests from their own traders, missionaries, and African chiefs, nervous about what would happen to them under German rule. "This German colonisation and hoisting of German flags has perfectly enraged our colonies who protest in every direction," Victoria wrote Vicky. Local concerns multiplied as Germany expanded her claims up the coast of Guinea, across Africa to the east coast and parts of Zululand, and into Kenya. "The acquisition of land is very easy in East Africa," Bismarck said. "For a couple of guns one gets a piece of paper with several Negro crosses."

As word of German activity in Africa reached London, the British government decided to implement Australia's earlier demands for the annexation of eastern New Guinea, thus far only a limited British protectorate. Formally notified of Britain's intentions, Bismarck dispatched a rival expedition, and Britain's intended colony was soon flying the German flag. Joseph Chamberlain, the father of Neville and a member of the Gladstone cabinet, summed up the attitude of the British government: "I don't care about New Guinea, and I am not afraid of German colonization," he said, "but I don't like to be cheeked by Bismarck or anyone else."

Vicky was not so cool. "I think it a great shame that the German flag has been hoisted in New Guinea," she wrote Victoria in December of 1883. "I do so wish we [Britain] had taken the whole, 3 years ago, before colonizing had become the rage & fashion here! People are too foolish here about it & will make a fine mess of those so called colonies as you will see."

Although Bismarck was clearly baiting Gladstone, whom he loathed, the British Prime Minister and his Foreign Secretary, Lord Granville, were, unlike the Queen's eldest daughter, difficult to rile. Unable to provoke Britain by normal methods, Bismarck resorted to diplomatic chicanery.

Claiming that he had sent the British Foreign Office written notification in May of 1884 that Germany intended to "further our interests in cooperation with other powers [i.e., France]," the Chancellor accused the British government of thwarting German colonial policy by refusing to answer this dispatch for eight months. Lord Granville, who had never seen such a document, ordered an immediate search of Foreign Office records. When nothing turned up, he called in the German Ambassador, Count Münster, to whom Bismarck claimed he had consigned the dispatch. "He was frightened out of his wits," Granville told Gladstone, "and went home to consult his archives. He found the famous dispatch, but also a telegram not to act upon it. He begged me to keep this secret."

Münster had, in fact, acted in a timely fashion on Bismarck's *primary* instructions in the missing dispatch, which were to ask Britain to cede to Germany the tiny island of Heligoland off the coast of Schleswig-Holstein. But no sooner had Münster started talks about Helgoland than he received a second wire from Berlin ordering him to stop negotiations and never mention the island again.

It seems that the Crown Prince had grown suspicious of Bismarck's machinations against England and asked the Secretary of the Foreign Ministry about Germany's colonial policy. The Secretary referred him to Bismarck's note (the one the British never got) with its implied threat to the British government. When the Secretary told Bismarck about Fritz's inquiry, the Chancellor ordered him not to mention Helgoland to the Crown Prince and sent the wire to Münster, instructing him to drop the subject. The historian Erich Eyck attributes this bizarre behavior to the fact that Bismarck was afraid not that the negotiations would fail but that they might succeed, thus laying the groundwork for improved relations with England during what looked like Fritz's imminent reign.

Eight months later, in January of 1885, faced with Bismarck's accusation of malevolence, Granville took the floor of parliament to say that he had never received official notification of Bismarck's colonial intentions. In a state of undiplomatic pique, he informed the House of Lords that Bismarck had also advised England "to take Egypt." Furious at being caught, Bismarck denied the charge, published a series of newspaper articles accusing the British Foreign Secretary of a breach of confidence, and gave a speech on the floor of the Reichstag, called by Eyck "perhaps the most vehement attack made by the Minister of one state on the Foreign Minister of another in time of peace." Many people thought it was intended to provoke a diplomatic break with Britain.

But Bismarck, who rarely did what was expected of him, sent his son Herbert to London to smooth things over. Gladstone made it clear to Herbert that he was prepared to extend himself to meet Germany's colonial claims, but that he would not be treated in such high-handed fashion. Because of Gladstone, negotiations on South-West Africa were satisfactorily concluded, and Herbert returned in triumph to Berlin. "To discuss with Mr. Gladstone the essence of the foreign policy of a great state is useless," the thirty-five-year-old son of the Chancellor said of the seventy-five-year-old Prime Minister, "because he is quite unable to understand it."

Bismarck tried to draw England into conflict in other ways. At an international conference called in London in the summer of 1884 to settle the foreign debts of the now nearly bankrupt Egyptian government, the English proposed reducing the interest on the Egyptian debt and using surplus revenues to pay for a campaign against the Sudanese, who were fighting the Egyptians. This suggestion was rejected by the French, egged on by Bismarck.* When asked about his role in the proceedings, the Chancellor claimed that his support of France was entirely due to Britain's attempt to undermine German colonial expansion.

England and Germany did eventually settle their colonial differences. In 1885, Herbert arranged for the partition of eastern New Guinea between England and Germany, the German part being called Kaiser Wilhelm Land and the Bismarck Archipelago. Britain also acceded to new German colonies in the Cameroons and Tanganyika.

But the budding Franco-German entente, conceived by Bismarck to needle the English, was very short-lived. An agreement signed at the end of 1885 had barely settled French and German colonial boundaries before the French, reminded by their rightist press of how much they hated the Germans, stopped cooperating with the country that had robbed them of Alsace and Lorraine.

As BISMARCK ORIGINALLY FEARED, Germany's entry into the colonial game turned out rather badly. The Chancellor, who said that he differed from other European imperialists in that his goal was "the governing merchant and not the

---

* *Egypt's finances were finally resolved in the spring of 1885 at another conference, but by then, General Gordon and his garrison, who had gone to Khartoum to effect an evacuation of the Egyptians, had been massacred, and the Dervishes were well on their way to complete control of the Sudan.*

governing bureaucrat," was unable to effect this policy. Men like Lüderitz were neither qualified nor equipped to oversee large areas in exotic lands nor to fund huge capital ventures, and they inevitably turned back to their governments for assistance. In order not to lose face at home, Bismarck was forced to produce German troops to protect the colonies, civil service officers to administer them, and consortiums of bankers and industrialists to buy them out when the going got rough. At one point, Lüderitz, unhappy with the price offered by a German group, threatened to sell his mineral holdings to Britain.

Matters were even worse in East Africa, where German interests were in the hands of an egotistical adventurer named Karl Peters. Peters founded the German East Africa Company, which settled Tanganyika; like Lüderitz, he had to be kept from selling out to the British. To get rid of him in order to attract funding from bankers and industrialists, Wilhelm I himself had to put up half a million marks. Even then, the German East Africa Company got into trouble when African natives and Muslim traders revolted, sending company employees fleeing to the safety of German gunboats anchored off the coast. Faced with a native uprising, Bismarck needed an appropriation of some ten million marks from the Reichstag to fund a military expedition. To do this, he had to win the Catholic Center Party over to colonialism.

During the 1880s, while other European countries took a stand against the African slave trade, the German Chancellor, who despised blacks, had ordered the members of the Foreign Ministry to sidestep the issue. But in 1888, realizing that the campaign against slavery could be used to revive public interest in Germany's overseas territories and bring the antislavery Catholics into the pro-colonialist bloc in the Reichstag, Bismarck ordered the fires of public opinion stoked with tales in the press of enslaved blacks. "Can't we scare up some vivid details about inhuman treatment?" he asked members of the Foreign Ministry.

With the necessary monies voted by concerned members of the Reichstag, Bismarck sent mercenaries to reestablish the German protectorate of Tanganyika. The German press made much of the fact that the soldiers had saved the colony from the tragedy of slavery, but Bismarck knew that it had, in fact, never fought slave traders—slavery had already been formally abolished in the area—but Muslims in revolt against German rule.

In the end, colonialism did not solve any problems for Germany. Although over one million people emigrated from Germany between 1887 and 1906, less than seven percent chose to make their homes in the colonies. Only a minuscule percentage (.13 percent) of imports came from colonial territories, and scarcely more (.17 percent) were sent out as exports. Of these last, the major items were weapons, gunpowder, and liquor. When Britain and Belgium proposed to limit the export of spirits to the natives, Bismarck, who owned a distillery in Pomerania, demurred.

For the German Empire, the great adventure turned into what the Chancellor called the "colonial swindle." Bismarck kept Germany's colonies because England kept hers, but by 1886, he had begun to tire of colonial problems. "Your map of Africa is certainly very beautiful," he told one explorer, who wanted to extend German territory into the heart of the continent, "but my map of Africa lies in Europe. Here lies Russia and there lies France, and we are in the middle. That is my map of Africa."

After three years of far-flung adventures, Bismarck did need to turn his attention closer to home, to the old problem of the Balkans, where the situation in Bulgaria was causing trouble between Russia and Austria and threatening the Three Emperors' League, on which the Chancellor counted to protect Germany. With France again bent on revenge, Bismarck could no longer afford to taunt England. This new disposition, however, did not make him any more amenable to the Crown Princess. The Bulgarian crisis, in fact, brought Vicky into perhaps her worst clash with Bismarck—this time, through one of her daughters.

CHAPTER FORTY-SEVEN

"It is no fun being Prince of Bulgaria."

ALEXANDER OF BATTENBERG, 1884

E VER SINCE THE MIDDLE of the fourteenth century, the Bulgarians, like other peoples of the Balkan peninsula, had been unwilling subjects of the Otto- man Empire. Although they revolted no less than seven times during the first three-quarters of the nineteenth century, wresting permission in 1870 to estab- lish a Bulgarian branch of the Orthodox Church, they continued to struggle under religious oppression and heavy taxation, while the Muslims got the best jobs and benefited from the corruption of the Porte.

In 1875 and again in 1876, the Bulgarians joined the Christians of Bosnia, Herzegovina, and Serbia in the general uprising against the Turks that preceded the Russo-Turkish War. Crushed with ghastly severity by the Turks, they were abandoned by the Congress of Berlin, which drew postwar borders with far more regard for the great nations of Europe than the ethnic origins or national- ist yearnings of the Sultan's former subjects. In order to thwart Russia's plans for a large satellite state, the countries at the Congress split Bulgaria into two separate entities—the principality of Bulgaria north of the Balkan mountains, and a Turkish province called Eastern Rumelia to the south nearer Constantino- ple. Disraeli told Vicky that without Eastern Rumelia (the name used to dis- guise the fact that the province was actually southern Bulgaria), Bulgaria would remain stable for seven years at best.* The Czar of Russia did not plan for it to last that long. He sent one of his generals to Eastern Rumelia with eighty thousand guns. "Russia has done what she could to help you; she is not to blame for this separation," said the Czar's emissary. "Accept these rifles, learn to use them and help yourselves later."

As in other small Balkan countries spun off by the protracted death of the Ottoman Empire, the new (northern) principality of Bulgaria needed a ruling prince to help it climb out of the slough of corruption and underdevelopment left by five hundred years of Turkish rule. The most promising candidate was an energetic young German with close ties to several of the ruling dynasties of

---

* *He was right, almost to the month.*

Europe, Prince Alexander of Battenberg. The history of the Battenbergs is a classic example of the ways in which royal prejudices influenced European politics.

IN 1841, AT THE AGE of twenty-three, the future Czar Alexander II of Russia had fallen in love with and married a German princess, Marie of Hesse.* Scarcely sixteen at the time of her marriage, Marie was accompanied in her move across Europe by her young brother, also named Alexander, who joined the Russian army and made a place for himself in the St. Petersburg court. After an abortive love affair with the Czar's daughter—Nicholas I did not consider a prince without a throne an appropriate son-in-law—Prince Alexander of Hesse fell in love with Countess Julie Haucke, a pretty lady-in-waiting to his sister Marie. The Romanovs were outraged.

Julie was the daughter of a Polish general descended from commoners, who had lost his life serving the Czar in the Polish revolution of 1830. In recognition of her father's heroism, Julie had been invited to serve as lady-in-waiting to the young wife of the heir to the throne, but she was not expected to fall in love with a member of the family. As fastidious about birth as the Habsburgs and Hohenzollerns, the Romanovs blamed Julie for presumption and Alexander for placing personal happiness above the dictates of caste.

Forced to leave the Russian court, Alexander of Hesse joined the Austro-Hungarian army and married Julie in 1851. Because the marriage was regarded as morganatic,† neither she nor their children were allowed to carry the royal name of Hesse. Julie was given the title Countess of Battenberg‡ after a small town named for a branch of the Hesse family that had died out. Alexander and Julie eventually moved to Darmstadt, where they enlivened the provincial Hessian court, home of Vicky's sister Alice, her husband, Louis, and their family.

The Battenbergs had always been very popular with the English royal family. When Alice's first child was christened at Windsor, it was Alexander who was sent to represent the Hesses; he charmed Queen Victoria, who said that it was the "first time" since her husband's death eighteen months before that she found "someone of our own rank" with whom she enjoyed conversing. Alexander also remained on intimate terms with his brother-in-law, now Czar Alexander II of Russia, facilitating the marriage in 1874 between the Czar's daughter, Marie, and Queen Victoria's second son, Affie.

Alexander and Julie had five children—a daughter and four tall, handsome sons. (Among the generally unattractive European royal families, the Hesses

---

* *The royal family of Hesse, which was divided into two branches, Hesse-Kassel in the north and Hesse-Darmstadt in the south, occupied an important position in European royal circles, owing in large part to the brilliance of their marriages.*

† *Out of the line of succession to titles and property.*

‡ *The Battenbergs became allied in marriage with the English royal family. During World War I, the name Battenberg was anglicized to Mountbatten, just as the English royal family's official name was anglicized from Saxe-Coburg and Gotha (formerly Hanover) to Windsor.*

were noted for good looks.) The eldest, Louis of Battenberg,* entered the British navy. The second, Alexander, known as Sandro, volunteered for the Russian army during the Russo-Turkish War; he was encouraged in this by his father, who believed that Czar Alexander II would prove helpful to his son's career. But the Czar's eldest son, Sasha, the future Alexander III, looked down on the young man when he arrived at court, referring to him variously as his "morganatic cousin" or "the German." Perhaps this was because Alexander III's wife, a former Danish princess, had hated the Germans ever since the Schleswig-Holstein War. Perhaps it was that Sandro was lean and dashing, while Sasha was unattractive and fat.

An excellent soldier, Sandro fought in the front lines of the Russo-Turkish War with the victorious Russians, Romanians, and Bulgarians. During the Congress of Berlin, Sandro's father heard that the Congress had raised the status of northern Bulgaria to a principality, which meant that they would appoint a prince to rule it. Since the Congress had decided not to allow any member of a reigning dynasty to take the position, Alexander of Hesse hurried to Berlin to lobby for his son.

The throne was considered a good one, and there were several willing candidates. Sandro, however, had the edge. His father had ties to all three empires: he was the brother of the Czarina of Russia; he came from the ruling German House of Hesse; and he had served in the Austrian army. Sandro himself had served in the Russian army but was not Russian; therefore, his appointment would not anger the English, would likely please Bismarck and the Austrians, and would look to the Russians as though they were getting someone whom they could manipulate. Over the opposition of his aunt, the Czarina, who adored Sandro and feared that nothing good would come from the appointment, he was named Prince of Bulgaria at the age of twenty-two.

The Czarina's concerns were valid. Sandro's new subjects were totally unversed in the basics of parliamentary government, and the new Bulgarian constitution had been prepared under the direction of a resentful Russian, Prince Dondukov-Korsakov, who had himself expected to be named Prince of Bulgaria. Although the Czar refused to force Dondukov-Korsakov to change the unworkable constitution, he offered his nephew five million French francs, presumably for the bribes that oiled Balkan governments. Sandro naïvely declined, asking that the money be set aside until he needed it to marry and establish a court. Alexander II agreed and gave the penniless Prince a small advance so that he could undertake a series of courtesy visits around the capitals of Europe before assuming his new position.

In Vienna, the new Prince of Bulgaria promised to respect the dictates of the Congress of Berlin as long as it was possible, for no one could presume to keep Bulgaria divided forever. He tried the same tack in Germany, but Bismarck demanded that he observe strict conformity to the peace terms as drawn. When

* *Father of Earl Mountbatten of Burma, the last Viceroy of India, and grandfather of Prince Philip, the current Duke of Edinburgh.*

Sandro offered to resign in the face of such an impossible task, the Chancellor closed the door of the room. "You do not leave this room till you have promised you will go to Bulgaria!" he said. When Sandro asked what would then happen if he failed, Bismarck told him that he would "at all events take away a pleasant recollection with you."

Bismarck's cavalier attitude toward Sandro's future was balanced by the genuinely warm welcome he received from Vicky, who found the handsome young man "very nice, charming . . . so pleasing & amiable, natural, frank & . . . full of the best intentions!" Worried only that he might be a "Russian vassal," Vicky recommended Sandro to her mother. "I do not think Sandro a bit Russian," Queen Victoria said after their meeting. Just as taken with her visitor as Vicky had been, the Queen wired her Foreign Secretary to offer "any help and encouragement we can give" to the new Prince of Bulgaria.

After a frigid interview with the Sultan—in which the leader of one of the cruelest empires in the world admonished Sandro to be "kind and just" to his subjects—the Prince of Bulgaria traveled to his new home. Hailed by the populace, he took an oath to uphold the constitution.

Like other Europeans arriving in the Balkans, the new Prince of Bulgaria was disappointed in what he found. Sofia, the capital of Bulgaria, was a town of miserable mud hovels, deteriorating public buildings, and poorly paved streets. His "palace," a one-story edifice started as a residence for the Russian Dondukov-Korsakov, had been finished hastily and sloppily when it was discovered that another was destined to live there. The interior walls were made of dried mud. The roof became so waterlogged that the ceilings of three rooms fell in, and a wooden scaffolding had to be erected over the Prince's bed to protect him.

But Sandro was a soldier, used to life without creature comforts. What bothered him most was what dogged every European ever sent to rule in the Balkans—the system of *baksheesh* (bribery), which in this case had been eagerly adopted by the Russians from the Turks. When they were not enriching themselves on the backs of the Bulgarians, the Russians, mostly officers of the Czar's army, amused themselves by playing one political faction off against another, disrupting parliamentary processes in open defiance of the law. "The Russian scoundrels are my worst enemies, and I can trust no one," Sandro wrote home, discouraged by the first of many failed attempts to get the Czar to call off his dishonest envoys.

"[I]t is obvious that every Russian who comes to Bulgaria must choose whether he will serve the Panslavist Minister for War . . . or me," Sandro told an Austrian diplomat.

> Naturally the choice goes against me, for what have I to offer him beyond his post? On the other hand, if he does his work to the satisfaction of his Russian superiors, he can safely count on promotion and privileges of every kind in Russia itself.
> It is impossible to rule with this senseless Bulgarian Constitution, for

it is immaterial whether the Conservatives or Liberals are in power. . . . The Opposition are only concerned with changing places with the Government in power, so that they can find posts for their own people. . . . I cannot turn my back on Russia, because I am too weak and too dependent and would lose all support if I sought elsewhere for help.

Sandro's future looked even less promising after Alexander II was killed by a nihilist's bomb in March of 1881, and his unfriendly cousin, Alexander III, mounted the Russian throne. Stopping in Berlin on the way home from the funeral, Sandro met with Bismarck, who suggested a remedy for his constitutional problems: "Why not risk a *coup d'état*, Highness, if you can rely on your troops?" The Austrians agreed with the German Chancellor, and, in May of 1881, Sandro presented the Bulgarian Parliament with an ultimatum—extraordinary powers to introduce reforms or abdication. His victory frightened Alexander III, who saw himself losing control of his puppet.

Pressed by his new countrymen for an heir, Sandro explored the marriage market—a German duchess recommended by his mother, a young relative of the Queen of Romania, an exceedingly rich Yusupov princess from Russia— but as of April of 1882, his prospects were diminishing in direct proportion to the increasing difficulties of his position. "Good Lord," he remarked to his anxious relatives, "how can you expect anything of a man who never knows in the morning whether he will not be murdered before evening."

This was only a mild exaggeration. The Bulgarians were agitating for independence, and Sandro found his position of mediator between his Russian sponsors, to whom he owed his position, and the Bulgarian Parliament, to whom he owed his allegiance, dangerous and nearly impossible to maintain. Alexander III's envoys, who understood that it was to their advantage to portray the young Prince as an ungrateful wretch paid by Austria to destroy the Czar's position in Bulgaria, tried to engineer a palace coup while Sandro was in Moscow for the coronation of Alexander III.

Although the coup failed, Sandro managed to worsen his relationship with Alexander III by forcing his way into the august presence during his visit to Moscow. Perhaps it was this breach of etiquette or Sandro's absence from his quarters when Alexander III paid the requisite return call; perhaps it was the Czar's embarrassment over his envoys' failed coup or Sandro's lack of tact that rubbed his cousin the wrong way—whatever it was, during his stay at the Kremlin, Prince Alexander of Bulgaria, never popular with his cousin, managed to arouse what George F. Kennan calls "a hatred and resentment . . . for which there seems to have been no parallel" in the life of Alexander III, "an unreasoning and uncontrollable emotional fixation" against the Bulgarian Prince.

In Berlin, Sandro was castigated by Bismarck and the Kaiser for incurring the Czar's wrath, and Wilhelm I accused him of not treating Alexander III with sufficient humility. He was, however, received with open arms by Vicky, whose mother had recommended Sandro as a possible match for Vicky's second daughter, Moretta.

Not by any stretch of the imagination a pretty girl, Moretta was described by Mary Ponsonby as "a kind of wild, Scandinavian woman, with much of her mother's impetuosity and a streak of her brother Willy's eccentricity." Just seventeen, Moretta caught her mother and grandmother's enthusiasm for the beleaguered Prince of Bulgaria and promptly fell in love. Kept abreast of the goings-on by his spies in the palace, Bismarck announced that he disapproved of the romance.

On his return to Sofia, Sandro was ordered by the Czar to dissolve the Bulgarian Parliament and surrender his powers to the Russians in his government. Soldiers from the Bulgarian army were commanded to demonstrate against the Prince, who hastily moved his residence to a tent in the middle of a military encampment outside Sofia. He was rewarded with a vote of confidence by the Bulgarian Parliament. "All my efforts are now directed towards arousing Bulgarian national feeling, and using it as a protective rampart against Russian aggression," Sandro wrote Fritz in the fall of 1883. "Russia nearly brought about my downfall once, but she will not be able to do so a second time."

Vicky's explanation of the Czar's behavior reiterated a well-worn theme: "the old idea of the Russians possessing themselves of Constantinople is by no means abandoned . . . ," she wrote Victoria. "The Russians wish to keep a firm hold on Bulgaria for this reason, & to prevent this State from developing itself independently or its ruler from establishing himself well and having a secure position!"

In that regard, Queen Victoria said that England's objective must be "to prevent Russia" from forcing Sandro to resign and seeing him replaced by "a Russian vassal." In a letter to her Foreign Secretary, the Queen enumerated Sandro's accomplishments. "Standing quite alone without help from any of the Powers, he has freed the Bulgarians from the pressure of those irresponsible Russian generals, has reconciled the two hostile political parties, has been enthusiastically acclaimed by the Chamber and is therefore helping his people to make themselves independent of Russia."

This was certainly an impressive record for a man of twenty-six, one that was bound to focus attention on the Prince of Bulgaria. "My poor Vicki [Moretta] is in despair," the Crown Princess wrote her mother in 1883. "She always thinks that he [Sandro] will meet some Princess whom he will like better. Do you think he can wait?"

Having received a letter from the Prince of Bulgaria regarding her daughter, Vicky did not quite know what to do. Her husband, who did not consider Sandro royal enough for his daughter, had forbidden her to pursue the matter. But, as she wrote back, she hoped that Sandro's position would soon be more secure, that he would be less likely to be overthrown by Russia, and that her husband, who adored his daughter, might then acquiesce to an engagement.

But Vicky was living on dreams. In November of 1883, the Russian Foreign Minister arrived in Berlin to strengthen Russo-German relations, and Bismarck agreed to give the Russians a free hand in Bulgaria. A few months later, a plan surfaced to marry Moretta's younger sister, fourteen-year-old Sophie, to

Alexander III's son Nicholas (later Czar Nicholas II). Set in motion by Herbert Bismarck, currently serving in the German Embassy in St. Petersburg, it was clearly an attempt on Herbert's part to ingratiate himself with Wilhelm I, who would have been delighted with another match between the Houses of Hohenzollern and Romanov.

The Bismarcks knew that the Crown Prince and Princess did not see eye to eye when it came to royal marriages. Raised in a far more open-minded court, Vicky believed that certain delicate issues of blood might be shaded or overlooked—only in the case of certain families, of course, and only up to a point. Her husband, on the other hand, stuck to the Hohenzollern code, which did not permit marriages between royalties and anyone with nonroyal blood. However much he liked and admired Sandro personally, Fritz did not consider him an appropriate son-in-law.

The Crown Prince did not approve of another marriage about to take place between Sandro's older brother, Prince Louis of Battenberg, and Princess Victoria of Hesse, the daughter of Vicky's deceased sister, Alice. The celebration in Darmstadt in April of 1884—a major royal event, owing to the presence of Queen Victoria—was treated by the Kaiser and Kaiserin as a royal calamity, since the Hesses were closely related to the Hohenzollerns. When, on the evening of his daughter's wedding, the widowed Grand Duke Louis secretly married a pretty divorcée, the Kaiserin ordered all the Hohenzollerns at the wedding to leave Louis's "contaminated court" immediately and return to Berlin.

Even though Louis bowed to family pressure and had his marriage annulled, the scandal at her uncle's court did not help Moretta's desire to marry Sandro. A wave of indignation against the Battenbergs, spearheaded by Willy, surged through Hohenzollern ranks. Willy had known and admired Sandro when they were both at the gymnasium in Kassel, but he now threatened to "club the Battenberger to death" if he engaged himself to his sister. Willy insisted that his opposition to Moretta's romance was based purely on the fact that "the well-being of the Fatherland was at stake"—a form of snobbery parading as patriotism that infuriated his mother.

"Alas, we have had to go through many disagreeables on account of poor Sandro," Vicky wrote Victoria the month after the wedding of Louis of Battenberg and Victoria of Hesse. During that month, Bismarck's press office had been churning out stories of Sandro's bad debts and his women.

<u>Willy</u> behaved <u>most</u> unkindly and spoke in terms of Sandro which made it difficult for his <u>Papa</u> to keep his temper! He said he could not imagine how such a person could <u>dare</u> to think of his sister—the Emperor's granddaughter—how impertinent everyone thought it! And then he repeated all the usual accusations—& when Fritz said they were unfounded . . . William said—how can one believe a word Sandro says—Prince Bismarck & the Foreign Office know the truth. . . . Then I had the same story over again from Henry & from Charlotte. They quite <u>cut</u> poor Vicky [Moretta]. . . .

I own it is a great comfort that Fritz has taken a liking to Sandro. . . . He admitted to me that when he once is Emperor he will allow it rather than make her unhappy—but at present he must abide by the Emperor's decision. . . . The poor child is <u>wretched</u>, & the Emperor has not been kind about it, & the Empress still worse.

Having ranged the royal family on his side, Bismarck advised the Prince of Bulgaria to make his peace with the Czar and "marry an Orthodox millionairess *. . . for ruling in the East means bribery and that requires money.*" A marriage with Moretta, Bismarck told Sandro, would "interfere with my political interests. This I will not permit and I have informed His Majesty that so long as I am Chancellor, this marriage will not take place." Sandro's appearance in Berlin after his brother's wedding in Darmstadt caused an enormous row between the Kaiser and the Crown Prince. Wilhelm forbade his granddaughter from seeing Sandro; in defiance of his father, Fritz gave a formal dinner for the diplomatic corps in Sandro's honor.

Retaliation followed swiftly. The St. Petersburg court was about to celebrate the coming of age of the future Nicholas II, and Fritz had assumed that he would represent his father at the festivities. But during one of her mother-in-law's Thursday dinners, the Kaiser's Court Chamberlain congratulated Vicky on Willy's appointment as the Kaiser's representative. When she asked her father-in-law about what she had heard, he answered with some embarrassment that he had just made up his mind that morning. Why then, she said, had neither she nor her husband been informed before the other members of the court? The Kaiser lost his temper and replied, rather too loudly, that he had "good reasons for everything he did, and would brook no interference" with his decisions. Guests at the palace that evening noted that Vicky's eyes were filled with tears when she sat down for dinner.

Carefully coached by Bismarck, twenty-five-year-old Willy traveled to St. Petersburg, where he told Alexander III that Russia, Germany, and Austria "should stand together as a three-sided bastion against the furious onslaught of anarchy and liberal democracy." Assuring the Czar that there could "never be any question of marriage" between his sister and the Bulgarian Prince, Willy elaborated on the difficulties Sandro was causing the German government, his ungratefulness, and his dishonesty. "The man is no good," the heir to the throne concluded. Delighted, Alexander III told Willy that he could in the future use the familiar form of *"Du"* when speaking with him.

On his return to Berlin, Willy began posting letters to his new best friend. "I only beg one favour of you," he wrote the Czar. "On no account trust my English uncle [the Prince of Wales]! You know him, he loves being contrary and is under my mother's thumb and she, in turn, is guided by the Queen of England and makes him see everything through English eyes." "I assure you the Emperor [Kaiser], Prince Bismarck and I are of one mind, and I shall not cease to regard it as my highest duty to consolidate and support the Three Emperors' Alliance."

This promise was followed some weeks later by a letter carrying a description of a fight Willy had had over the Prince of Bulgaria with his father.

> Altogether, dear cousin, the Prince of Bulgaria—by fair means or foul—has got my mother in his pocket and consequently my father too . . . but these English have not taken me into account. . . . We shall see the Prince of Wales here in a few days; we are not at all pleased at this unexpected appearance—pardon, he is your brother-in-law *—with his duplicity and love of intrigue he will doubtless try either to encourage the cause of the Bulgarian—may Allah banish him to hell, as the Turk would say—or discuss politics with the ladies behind the scenes. I shall do my best to keep an eye on them but it is impossible to be everywhere.

Willy was better than his word—informing Alexander about the movement of English and Indian regiments on the subcontinent and warning him about other English preparations for war against Russia. "Although Friedrich was denounced in Germany for representing the interests of another country," one historian † notes, "it was actually Wilhelm who, in his correspondence with the Tsar . . . acted like the agent of a foreign power."

While Willy busied himself on the Czar's behalf, the Russian government tried to destroy the reputation of the Prince of Bulgaria, suggesting that there were sexual as well as political reasons why the German Kaiser had refused to allow him to marry his granddaughter. It was variously hinted in the Russian press that the Bulgarian Prince had contracted a venereal disease or implied that he had "Turkish tastes" (i.e., was homosexual). This sort of rumor-mongering was obviously aimed at keeping Alexander of Bulgaria from marrying anyone at all.

It was becoming increasingly clear, even to Vicky, that the Moretta issue was being used by Sandro's enemies to destroy him. "I see there is <u>nothing</u> <u>to</u> <u>be done</u>!" she wrote Victoria in early 1885, adding that Morretta "sees it too—and deeply as she is attached to Sandro she will <u>not</u> stand in the way of his interests! He <u>must</u> think of his country and as Prince Bismarck <u>insists</u> on swelling out the question to one of <u>high</u> <u>political</u> <u>importance</u> . . . we must think of it <u>no</u> more!"

Vicky was, however, deeply worried about her daughter. In a letter marked "Private To Be Burnt," she told Victoria that the girl "cannot & will not believe that there is no chance left—she says she would try to die!" The Crown Princess asked the Queen to write to Moretta "to have courage & hold her head up. Every word you say she listens to . . . because she loves you so devotedly & believes you wish her really well."

The appeal to Victoria was a sensible one. Moretta had recently written to the Queen saying what "a comfort" it was to have "one Grandmama who loves one & to whom one can tell everything. . . . Oh! if I could but only get a

---

* *Alexander III and the Prince of Wales were married to sisters.*

† *Thomas Kohut.*

glimpse of him, so low in spirit I am & there seems no hope, if beloved Mama were not there to rouse me up perpetually, really I do not know what would become of me."

Like Moretta, Sandro was prey to self-pity, but of a different kind. "As a private individual I had chances of a far better marriage than I have in my present position . . . ," he wrote a friend.

> I might even at one time have become engaged to the friend of my child-hood, Beatrice of England,* had not Bulgaria's remoteness, the Princess's love of her home and the Queen's reluctance to be parted from her daugh-ter formed insuperable obstacles. Much the same was the case with Princess Hilda of Nassau whose father . . . could hardly be expected to allow his daughter to marry into Bulgaria. Then there was my cousin, Theresa of Hesse . . . whom I would have liked most of all, but here there were money difficulties.
>
> You will certainly have read in the Press . . . that I asked for the hand of Princess Victoria of Prussia; but I have never done so and have never been a suitor for her hand. The suggestion came from the German Crown Princess after we had both been attracted to each other in Darmstadt last year. But that came to nothing through the refusal of Emperor Wilhelm to give his consent. I believe that Emperor Wilhelm would not have been opposed to the marriage so strongly had he not been influenced by the Empress Augusta who is bitterly prejudiced against an alliance between a Hohenzollern and a Battenberg on the grounds of inequality of rank.

Was Sandro telling the whole truth? Probably not. At the same time, it is clear that in her enthusiasm Vicky had built her daughter's future on a fragile attraction and maternal dreams. Whatever had passed between Moretta and Sandro, as of the spring of 1885 their romance was officially over, and in March the Prince of Bulgaria signified this in a formal letter of renunciation, demanded by the Kaiser.

ONE OF Vicky's problems in the Battenberg affair was that she did not seem to recognize the difference between what her mother, the Queen of England, and she, the mere Crown Princess of Germany, might do and say vis-à-vis a Balkan prince under Russian sponsorship. Russia was England's enemy, and the Queen could express herself in any way she pleased, so long as she only recommended her preferences to her discreet and usually placative ministers.

This was patently not true in the case of Vicky. The same words coming from her were in direct opposition to German foreign policy, however wrong-headed the Crown Princess believed that policy to be. For Bismarck, Vicky was providing another transgression to wave under the Kaiser's nose to discredit both herself and her husband. For her son Willy, looking for a platform on which to assert himself against his parents, it was a blunder from heaven.

---

* *Vicky's youngest sister.*

In time, Vicky's excessive involvement with the embattled Prince caused other friends and admirers to withdraw. As one of the younger court intimates put it,

With all my admiration for the Crown Princess, I cannot help regretting her attitude in this Battenberg affair, inspired as it so largely was by her dislike and distrust of Russia. It compromised her in the eyes of the old Emperor, and gave Prince William a pretext once more to represent her as not caring for German interests, but playing England's game even in family matters. In fact, it created between mother and son a breach which was never healed, and put into the latter's hands a weapon which he used to the uttermost.

CHAPTER
FORTY-EIGHT

"None of the obstacles that restrain and thwart the other sovereigns . . . exist for the Emperor of Russia. What he dreams of at night he can carry out in the morning."

FRIEDRICH VON GENTZ, *German diplomat*

ONE OF THE TRUMP CARDS used by Bismarck in his crusade against Sandro of Battenberg was the seemingly irreversible Hohenzollern bias against anyone of diluted royal blood. The shock caused in the court of Berlin by the marriage of Vicky's niece Princess Victoria of Hesse and Sandro's older brother, Prince Louis of Battenberg, was redoubled in December of 1884 when Queen Victoria announced that her youngest daughter, Beatrice, was engaged to Sandro's younger brother, Prince Henry of Battenberg. Beatrice's attraction to Liko, as Prince Henry was known in the family, had become apparent during his brother's wedding the previous spring at Darmstadt. Since that time, Queen Victoria had done everything she could to discourage the marriage—not for reasons of blood, but of convenience.

Princess Beatrice was the last daughter at home, her mother's full-time companion, secretary, and general factotum. As the Queen wrote Vicky, "[Y]ou who are so fond of marriages which I (on the other hand) detest beyond words, cannot imagine what agonies, what despair it caused me . . . when I first heard of her wish! It made me quite ill. For long I could not hear of it. . . . But alas! she was so determined that her health would have suffered if I had not relented." What the Queen did not say was that for six months she had refused even to discuss the marriage with Beatrice and agreed to it only under the proviso that her daughter's future husband agree to live in his mother-in-law's court in England.

Beatrice's hard-won happiness offended the German royal family. As Wilhelm I, who had given up the great love of his life to dynastic purity, wrote Bismarck: "We were absolutely startled last evening by a telegram from the Queen of England announcing the engagement of her youngest daughter to the third Battenberg son. . . . To such depths has the Queen of an old and powerful dynasty descended to keep her daughter in the country (as a secretary). . . . My son [i.e., Fritz] says, 'It was somewhat difficult to have to recognize the eldest Battenberg [Louis] as a nephew, but to have the third as brother-in-law is too much!" Augusta was so shocked that she simply stopped writing to Victoria.

Unlike her husband and in-laws, Vicky supported the Battenbergs. "I saw you take the right view of darling Beatrice's engagement with Liko," the Queen wrote her eldest daughter. "There is no kissing, etc. (which Beatrice dislikes) which used to try me so with dear Fritz. But the wedding day is like a great trial and I hope and pray there may be no results! * That would aggravate everything. . . . Now I must tell you how very unamiably the Empress and even dear Fritz have written to me. . . . Dear Fritz speaks of Liko as not being of the blood—a little like about animals. Don't mind my saying this."

Worse than Fritz or his parents were Vicky's three older children. Queen Victoria was infuriated by the "extraordinary impertinence and insolence" exhibited by Willy, Charlotte, and Henry on the subject of the Battenbergs. "Willie, that very foolish undutiful and—I must add—unfeeling boy . . . I wish he could get a good 'skelping' [beating] as the Scotch say and seriously a good setting down. It is very wrong of the Empress to spoil him so much. The atmosphere he lives in is very bad for him," the Queen wrote Vicky. "As for Dona [Willy's wife], a poor, little insignificant Princess raised entirely by your kindness to the position she is in, I have no words."

The wedding of Beatrice of England and Henry of Battenberg was celebrated at the end of July 1885. Vicky was hurt not to be invited. The Queen may have been subtly punishing her for her husband's attitude. The Crown Prince of Germany, as Victoria had written her personal secretary some years before, was "absurdly proud, as all his family are, thinking no family higher or greater than the Hohenzollerns. Not proud to those below him that is, to the people, but proud & overbearing to other Princes." The reason given for Vicky's absence, however, was that Queen Victoria thought it would be unseemly due to the presence of the groom's brother Sandro.

SHORTLY AFTER Sandro returned to eastern Europe from his brother's wedding in England, the people of Eastern Rumelia revolted against the Turks and proclaimed union with the Bulgarians. The movement toward unification had been secretly encouraged by the Russians, who immediately withdrew their support when the revolutionaries invited Sandro to become the first leader of a united Bulgaria. While English and Austrian diplomats rejoiced over a newly enlarged buffer to Russian expansion, the Czar ranted and fumed, stripping the Prince of Bulgaria of his rank in the Russian army, his Russian decorations, and his honorary regiment.

"Russia behaves and has behaved shamefully," Queen Victoria wrote her Foreign Secretary. "Her anger against Prince Alexander is merely because her plan of deposing him and uniting the two countries under a Russian Prince or one who would be a creature of Russia's . . . failed. . . . Prince Bismarck ought to remember that he forced Prince Alexander to go there and shut the door behind him . . . and now he has deserted him ever since!"

Vicky agreed and sent Sandro a twenty-eight-page letter of congratulations

* *There were four—three sons and a daughter, who became Queen Ena of Spain.*

from Venice, where she had taken Moretta to revive her spirits. Poor Moretta. Not only had her first cousin, who was German, been permitted to marry Sandro's older brother, but now her aunt, who was English, had just married the younger one. Moretta, the Crown Princess wrote Sandro, was "only sorry that in this decisive and momentous hour she cannot be at your side to share all the danger and excitement." Her daughter, she told him, "wears your pearls and your first letter sewn up in a handkerchief close to her heart. Be of good courage. He who does his duty, is loyal, honest and courageous, always wins through."

Sandro certainly needed encouragement. Bulgaria's neighbors, Greece and Serbia, reacted to the unification of Bulgaria by demanding commensurate increases of territory to preserve the balance of power. Angered that Russia had supported Bulgarian rather than Serbian interests at the Congress of Berlin, the Serbs turned to Austria for support. Two ambassadorial conferences were called to solve the Balkan question, but no agreement among the various countries could be reached: Russia wanted to remove Sandro before acknowledging a unified Bulgaria; Austria backed the Serbs; Germany was determined to retain the status quo; England supported Sandro and the union of Bulgaria; and Turkey, sure that Russia and Austria would go to war against each other, refused to commit itself at all.

In the middle of November of 1885, Serbia invaded Bulgaria. All of Europe expected a Bulgarian defeat. Not only was the Serbian army far more experienced, but Alexander III had recalled all the Russian officers of the Bulgarian army (some two or three hundred men) just six weeks earlier in an attempt to show the Bulgarians how much they still needed Russia. But Sandro, who was a far better soldier than diplomat, took command of the army and led his soldiers to an astonishing victory—a virtual rout of the Serbs. The Germans, who admired military prowess above all things, were impressed by the young Prince of Bulgaria. The extent of their admiration can be gauged by the fact that Bismarck complained that the Battenbergs were bribing the German press.

The Serbian army was, in fact, saved from annihilation only by the intervention of Austria, who insisted that the border between Bulgaria and Serbia remain as it was before the war. Although this was a disappointment to the Bulgarians, they were proud of the success of their army and their Prince and pleased when the union of Bulgaria and Eastern Rumelia was accepted by the great powers in April of 1886. The Sultan, however, refused to grant Prince Alexander more than the title of Governor General of Eastern Rumelia, thus limiting the two Bulgarian provinces to personal unification.

For his part, Bismarck was delighted with the situation. What better bone of contention between England and Russia could there be than Queen Victoria's protégé who had just bested the Czar? Like Vicky, Bismarck had allowed the Moretta-Sandro affair to become a symbol of personal success or defeat. As Bulgaria joined the list of autonomous Balkan countries, it became clear that the German Chancellor had more riding on its future than Germany's relationship with Russia or the appeasement of the Czar.

■

THE MONTH AFTER the unification of Bulgaria, Vicky visited Queen Victoria. She had planned to take Moretta, but Wilhelm and Augusta refused to allow their granddaughter to go anywhere she might come in contact with Sandro's Battenberg brothers or their wives—Liko and Beatrice or Louis and Victoria. "I think it insulting to me, to Fritz, and to the poor child, who is in a dreadful state of mind, has not left her room nor ceased crying!" Vicky wrote Victoria. Still harboring dreams of Moretta's marrying Sandro, the Crown Princess decided not to "make a row about it! . . . As the Emperor is <u>so</u> obstinate, I had better not make him <u>worse</u>. . . . It might make him still more difficult to bring round later . . . <u>now</u> is not the moment!"

While Vicky fantasized about her daughter's future with the brave Prince of Bulgaria, the Russians were doing everything they could to topple him from his throne. Special Russian agents were sent to Bulgaria to ferret out disgruntled army officers to man a conspiracy against him.* Two attempts were made on his life. When these failed, a band of officers abducted him from his palace, hustled him out of the country, and put him in a boat headed down the Danube River.

The coup, exemplifying what George Kennan called "that wonderful mixture of extreme danger and high comedy which the Balkans alone seem able to provide," failed almost immediately. The conspirators were swiftly arrested, and the nationalists sent a wire to Sandro asking him to return to Bulgaria. Urged to do so by Queen Victoria and the Crown Princess of Germany, the Prince went back, barely escaping death when someone discovered a block of wood placed across the tracks to derail his train. In Sofia, he was cheered by the people and carried in triumph on the shoulders of army officers back into his palace.

Russia's embarrassment was a diplomatic windfall for the British Foreign Office, and Queen Victoria hailed Sandro as "one of the bravest [and] wisest of rulers. . . . The Queen," she told her ministers, "is much attached to the dear, brave, and so cruelly used Prince of Bulgaria. . . . we must stand by him." To Sandro himself, she wrote that his own parents "could hardly have felt greater anxiety and fear" for his life, and that "no one rejoiced more than I did when . . . the news of the counter-revolution arrived."

But Sandro made a fateful mistake. Purposefully misled by a Russian diplomat as to Alexander III's reaction to his return, he wired the Czar thanking him for his vote of confidence, saying that he looked forward to future good relations between them, and, in a gesture of princely generosity, offered to voluntarily relinquish his throne, if at any time Alexander III wished him to do so. "As Russia gave me my Crown I am prepared to give it back into the hands of its

---

* These were not too difficult to find, since Sandro had been forced to pass over a number of deserving Bulgarian officers, filling the posts that would normally have been theirs with newly inducted Eastern Rumelians in order to assure the Rumelians' loyalty in his hastily amalgamated army.

Sovereign," he wrote in what he conceived of as a "golden bridge" to reconciliation with the Czar.

Unmoved and unimpressed, Alexander III wired back that he did not approve of Sandro's return to Bulgaria. He published the Prince's confidential wire in the Russian papers and publicly accepted Sandro's purely ceremonial offer of abdication. The Prince's supporters were appalled. "I am speechless and entreat you to cancel this step," Queen Victoria wrote him. "After such triumphs this was unworthy of the great position you had won. You are being blamed for having telegraphed to the Czar instead of asking advice here first."

But Sandro was exhausted and disheartened. He appointed a three-man regency and left Bulgaria on September 8, 1886, never to return. Not too surprisingly, it was nearly a year before the regents could find another prince willing to undertake the job.

WITH SANDRO OFF the throne of Bulgaria, Bismarck no longer had any reason to stop his marriage to Moretta. Although he had previously said that he would not object to the match if Sandro was merely a German officer, articles labeling the former Prince of Bulgaria as an ongoing danger both to Germany and the peace of Europe now began to appear regularly in the official German press.

The attacks are easy to explain. Prince Alexander of Battenberg had proved himself a genuine, self-sacrificing hero, exhibiting not only military prowess but the kind of public appeal noticeably lacking in Bismarck's elder son, Herbert, the Chancellor's candidate as his eventual successor. Recognizing Sandro's potential danger as a political alternative, Bismarck presented Wilhelm I with a long memorandum about the Battenberg Prince within a few weeks of his return to his home in Darmstadt. Along with a laundry list of personal faults, the Chancellor claimed that if the Prince of Battenberg was given a commission in the German army, which he wanted, he would eventually propose himself as a candidate for the post of Chancellor representing the oppositional parties hostile to Wilhelm I. "As Imperial Chancellor the Prince would be supported by the majority of the present Reichstag," Bismarck claimed. Frightened by his Chancellor, the Kaiser barred Sandro from coming to Berlin or joining the army.*

The Sandro affair had split the German royal family down the middle, and the Crown Prince and Princess were made to pay once again for their support of the Battenberg Prince. In the fall of 1886, Vicky was "rather horrified" to hear that her son Willy had attended a meeting at Gastein between the Kaiser and Franz Joseph of Austria and was on his way once again to see Alexander III of Russia. Asked why the Crown Prince was not invited to Gastein instead of his son, one of the Kaiser's aides-de-camp explained that Wilhelm I "did not care to be bothered again with this Battenberg affair." When the gentleman was asked how the Kaiser knew that the subject would come up, he replied, "Oh,

---

* *Bismarck never got over his fear of Alexander of Battenberg and continued to publish articles against him in the official press long after he was out of the public eye.*

Prince Wilhelm had warned his grandfather that the Crown Princess intended to attack him on the subject."

Unaware of her son's self-promoting machinations, Vicky was hurt for Fritz and concerned about the way Bismarck was using Willy. "It stands to reason that you could not go and curry favour with the Czar after that knavish trick that he had caused his rascally officials to play on a German Prince . . . ," she wrote her husband; "it would be impossible for a decent man to shake hands with him. That they have chosen our son for this is hardly complimentary to him; that he undertakes it, does him no credit."

Willy went off to St. Petersburg, prepared to share all the newest gossip about his parents and their English relations with the Czar. Since his last visit, however, Alexander III had developed a new perspective on the heir to the German throne, whom he referred to as *"un garçon mal élevé et de mauvais foi."* * When the twenty-seven-year-old delivered what he thought would be a *coup* of friendship and mutual Anglophobia, i.e., a message from Bismarck stating that Germany would not mind if Russia took Constantinople from the Turks, he was shocked at Alexander III's reaction. "If I want it I shall take it when it suits me," he told Willy. "I do not require the permission or consent of Prince Bismarck."

Confused by the change in Alexander's attitude, Willy consulted an old Russian general, who blamed the Czar's coolness on the Congress of Berlin, which, he said, had "destroyed the old friendship" between Russia and Germany. "[W]e are now forced to depend on this damned French republic which hates you and is full of revolutionary ideas," the general explained, confirming the fact that Bismarck's policy of appeasing the Russians, which included the political and personal destruction of the Prince of Bulgaria, was proving ineffectual in his greater struggle to keep Russia and France from allying with each other against Germany.

This was something Vicky had understood from the beginning:

"The fear here, of France & Russia joining hands to attack us, is very great and universal," she had written her mother just before Sandro's removal, "& has the result of making the Chancellor humour Russia too much. . . . It is certain that neither of these powers would attack us without being instantly joined by the other; but it would seem to me that for this very contingency, it would be so important to have a Bulgaria as strong as possible. . . . The great man is so anxious to have peace, & naturally enough so afraid of a war, that I fear he rather overlooks this."

* *"An ill-mannered boy of bad faith."*

CHAPTER
FORTY-NINE

"Treaties of alliance were for Bismarck the sort of conjuring trick that battles had been for Napoleon I—they would get him out of every difficulty."

A. J. P. TAYLOR

*I*N SPITE OF Bismarck's efforts to placate the Russians, the Bulgarian crisis had made Germany's position vis-à-vis Russia and its Czar far more precarious. A man whose huge, unwieldy bulk and skewed personality seemed an apt metaphor for the size and paranoia of his country, Alexander III continued to blame his partners in the Three Emperors' League, Germany and Austria, for his Balkan frustrations.

In 1886, nearly a decade after the Russo-Turkish War, the Czar was still wavering between two schools of political thought. The first, led by his Foreign Minister, urged him to continue to support the Three Emperors' League. The second, spearheaded by an influential anti-German journalist, M. N. Katov, claimed that by sticking to the league, Alexander III was binding himself to his major territorial rival in the Balkans (Austria) and accepting as the chief arbiter of Russian foreign policy the all-powerful Chancellor of Germany. Germany's military success (this argument continued) would not have been possible without Russia, which had served as a "crutch" throughout its series of aggrandizing wars. The time had come for Russia to stop predicating her foreign policy on the solidarity of monarchs and look elsewhere for allies.

Slow-moving and slower-thinking, Alexander III was incapable of recognizing or resisting sophistry, certainly not a distortion of facts that meshed so completely with his innermost fears. As Vicky wrote Victoria at the end of 1886, "So called <u>absolute</u> monarchs are <u>always</u> dupes. . . . while yielding to their own caprices . . . they are pushed by those who know how to excite them! Tyrannical & violent as he [Alexander III] is, I suppose he is the tool of the panslavists, and of all the lying officials in his service."

For corroboration of Vicky's opinion, we have a letter written a week later by Bernhard von Bülow,* German Chargé d'Affaires in St. Petersburg, to a friend: "For some time, now, no one has dared any longer to oppose the emperor [Czar] in political matters, or even to tell him the truth. . . . In this

---

* *Later Chancellor of Germany (1900–1909).*

way the Emperor sews himself into wholly false imaginings and expectations; when these fancies are destroyed by confrontation with the facts, a dull fury overcomes him, as though someone had done him great injustice. Thus, he is now, without rhyme or reason, angry at Germany, because the Bulgars will not give up."

Although the Crown Princess of Germany understood certain principles of global power, she invariably failed to take into account Bismarck's brilliant use of foreign instabilities and the domestic concerns they aroused to further his political agenda. A prime example is the way in which the Chancellor now undertook to manipulate Russia's animosity over Bulgaria and the appearance in 1885 of a chauvinist leader in France to raise Germany's military budget and change the character of the Reichstag.

The French, having disavowed the imperialistic Jules Ferry in the elections of October 1885, were currently suffering from economic depression, disenchantment with their conservative republican government, and a desire to avenge themselves on the Germans. In need of a leader to rally their spirits, they found one in their new Minister of War, General Georges Boulanger.

A blond, bearded blowhard with shrewd political instincts, Boulanger started his ministry by bringing French soldiers home from overseas and instituting military reforms at home. On Bastille Day of 1886, he appeared astride a prancing black circus horse at the head of his newly enlarged and invigorated forces, making himself into an instant national hero. Searching for ways to promote himself, he soon became a tool of the far right, the rifle clubs and ultrapatriotic groups looking to ally France with autocratic Russia.

When diplomatic relations between Russia and France, broken off since the beginning of 1886, were resumed in October of that year, the Germans grew nervous. Although their Ambassador to Paris assured Bismarck that France remained peaceful, the Chancellor used Boulanger's increased military expenditures, the construction of new barracks for the French army near the German border, and the resumption of Franco-Russian ties to push through some legislation of his own. "I could not invent Boulanger," he admitted much later, "but he happened very conveniently for me." Capitalizing on the public mood, Bismarck appeared in the Reichstag on November 5, the first day of the 1886–87 session, to ask for a renewal of the military (iron) budget for seven years.

The current appropriation was not due to expire for nearly a year and a half, but Bismarck pushed the date forward to create an issue over which he could dissolve the Reichstag, still controlled by his opponents. Worried that the liberal deputies would soon have a new kaiser (Fritz) behind them, the Chancellor had determined to try to change the character of the parliament before it was too late. First he made a dramatic plea for his seven-year military budget (*Septennat*), warning that anyone who opposed the bill was assuming responsibility for the disintegration of the empire. When the deputies approved only a three-year budget, he read Wilhelm's order, previously prepared, to dissolve the Reichstag.

A new election was set for February 21, 1887. Called the *Septennat* election, it was fought on the phony issue of patriotism and won by a cartel put together by Bismarck from the parties favoring his seven-year appropriation—new and old conservatives and National Liberals. The main losers were the new Free-thinkers party and the Social Democrats.* In February of 1887, Vicky summed up the political situation for her mother:

"[T]he moderate liberal party [Freethinkers party], the best we have, has been paralyzed & crushed, and the Socialists increased," she said, noting that "the fear of war has driven all the rest into Prince Bismarck's camp. As his Home policy is very bad, I regret this; though perhaps for the moment the peace of Europe will profit by it, a thing to be thankful for."

"It is a sad pity that some reconciliation or understanding cannot be ef-fected between Bismarck & the Liberal [Freethinkers] party," she wrote a few weeks later. That the real butt of Bismarck's cartel was her husband, Vicky had no doubt. "There is a blind war being waged against all that is liberal, both socially & politically here now," she told Victoria, "with the thought that if the Liberal Party can only be ruined in the eyes of the people & the government always be strong enough to have a majority against them, Fritz would someday be prevented from going with them or recruiting ministers from their ranks."

Which was precisely the point. Bismarck not only got his *Septennat* appro-priations passed shortly after the election, but succeeded in maneuvering the electorate into electing a pliant majority in the Reichstag that would not be likely to join the Crown Prince to defeat his bills.

ALTHOUGH BISMARCK USED the fear of war to increase military spending and change the complexion of the Reichstag, he remained uneasy about Germany's relations with Russia and France, and in 1886 began early negotiations to extend the Triple Alliance of Germany, Austria, and Italy, due to expire in May of 1887. Since Austria balked at the idea of supporting Italy against France in the Mediterranean, the Chancellor had to supplement the Triple Alliance with a separate treaty between Germany and Italy in which the Germans agreed to back the Italians against French aggression in North Africa. The Triple Alliance was then renewed on February 20, 1887, enabling Bismarck to use Italian rivalry with the French to expose France to the possibility of a two-front war—against Germany on the east and Italy on the south.

As was usual during periods of coolness between Germany and Russia, Bismarck looked across the channel to England, suggesting that the English, who had come up against the French in Egypt, ally themselves with the Italians against French expansion in North Africa and with the Italians and Austrians against Russian aggression in the Near East. Germany, he told the British, was all for these defensive pacts, but could not risk taking such a position itself.

In this way, the German Chancellor promoted the First Mediterranean Agreement—an informal understanding acknowledged by an exchange of notes

* *Although they gained in the popular vote.*

in the spring of 1887 among England, Italy, and Austria* to preserve the status quo in the Mediterranean, Adriatic, Aegean, and Black Seas. Two months later, Spain signed on to the agreement, and Bismarck could congratulate himself on having isolated France by surrounding her with defensive treaties. He had also removed pressure on Germany to support Austria against Russia in the Balkans by shifting the responsibility to England and had managed to push some of the onus of Russian resentment onto England as well.

When the Three Emperors' League came due for renewal in the summer of 1887, however, the Czar, now in open territorial competition with Austria, refused to extend it, and Bismarck was forced to negotiate a separate treaty with Russia in its place. Known as the Reinsurance Treaty, it was the Chancellor's proudest achievement in a proliferation of treaties.

Signed in the middle of June 1887, the Reinsurance Treaty guaranteed neutrality on the part of both Germany and Russia if either should "find itself at war with a third great power." (If war was started by Germany against France or Russia against Austria, the treaty did not apply.) They agreed to maintain the status quo in the Balkans and Russia's "preponderant and decisive influence in Bulgaria." In an "additional and ultrasecret" protocol, Germany agreed to oppose the restoration of Alexander of Battenberg to the Bulgarian throne† and accept any candidate backed by Russia. Germany also promised to give "moral and diplomatic support" to whatever the Czar might deem necessary to defend "the key to his empire," i.e., Russia's outlet from the Black Sea. "We have absolutely nothing against Russia's going to Constantinople and taking the Dardanelles," Bismarck declared.

In negotiating this successor to the Three Emperors' League, Bismarck was agreeing to support Russian aggression. At the time, the promise seemed to cost him nothing, since he knew from his own efforts in encouraging the First Mediterranean Agreement that both England and Austria were now bound to oppose it. Hardly compatible, the two protocols (First Mediterranean Agreement and Reinsurance Treaty), one signed by Bismarck and the other promoted by him, did protect Germany and keep France and Russia apart—for the time being.

Vicky pointed to Bismarck's acquiescence in Russia's Bulgarian designs as the one area in which the Chancellor "can easiest oblige the Russians without sacrificing anything he cares about! I only think that all this obliging is no use & of no avail, & that the Russians will do just what they please, & ally themselves with the French whenever they think convenient," she warned.

There is no question that the Crown Princess had become too emotionally involved in the Bulgarian issue through her fondness for Sandro of Battenberg.

* Austria joined six weeks after England and Italy.

† The Bulgarians had continued to work for the return of the Battenberg Prince, even offering the throne to Sandro's father, Alexander of Hesse, so that the son might inherit it. But Sandro refused to go back.

But Bulgaria had also become a symbol in Vicky's mind—and not an inappropriate one—for the dangers of realpolitik as practiced by Bismarck. It was the Chancellor, she reminded Victoria, who had advised Sandro to accept the Bulgarian throne in the days when France was still weak.

> [Now] he [Bismarck] considers France strong, and very well armed, & he knows how easily a Franco Russian alliance could be made!! He is right therefore in not offending Russia. . . . Where he seems to me to be wrong, is in thinking that he can buy her friendship by any sacrifice he could make! He is also wrong in allowing her to strengthen herself . . . via Bulgaria. Europe has been very shortsighted, since she seems to think that by dropping the Bulgarians altogether, & leaving them to their fate, she can prevent awkward questions from being raised & can avert war, this seems to me a miscalculation.

IN SPITE OF Bismarck's efforts to appease the Czar, the rift between Germany and Russia, opened during the Congress of Berlin, had continued to widen during the 1880s. The ongoing depression added to diplomatic strains, as Alexander III, struggling to pay for the Russo-Turkish War, demanded tariff payments in gold rather than paper currency, thus subjecting the Germans to a rise of between thirty and fifty percent in import duties. By 1886, Russia had built up an enormous national debt, her chief creditors being German financiers who had infused vast sums into Russian industry. Russian securities fell on the Berlin stock exchange at the end of 1886, both countries engaged in another round of tariff hikes during 1887, and political tensions continued to be underscored by economic ones.

Although the loudest proponents of militant nationalism in Russia and France both disappeared from the public scene during 1887—Boulanger was ousted from the French cabinet in May, and Katov died in Russia in August—the danger of an entente between Germany's neighbors did not diminish. The election by the Bulgarian Parliament of an Austrian army officer, Prince Ferdinand of Saxe-Coburg-Kohary,* to the Bulgarian throne in July of 1887 added another fractious element to the struggle for Balkan hegemony between Austria and Russia. Bismarck's refusal to support Ferdinand's candidacy was not sufficient in the eyes of Alexander III, who expected Germany to take a more active role in unseating the man he viewed as an Austrian puppet. Pressed by the Czar, Bismarck turned to his fallback ally, Austria.

In August of 1887, Wilhelm I met Franz Joseph at Bad Gastein, where the German Kaiser assured the Austrian Emperor that he now favored the Austro-German alliance he had so strongly opposed eight years before. Since Bismarck had prompted Wilhelm to say this, it is odd that he also arranged for the Kaiser to be accompanied to Gastein by his pro-Russian grandson Willy. Perhaps Bismarck included Willy as a reminder to Franz Joseph of Germany's Russian

---

* *A distant cousin of Vicky's.*

obligations, i.e., his excuse for not supporting Austria against Russian aggression in the Balkans.

Hearing that Bismarck was seeking a rapprochement between Germany and Austria but that the parties disagreed over Bulgaria, Vicky wrote her mother that Bismarck

> admits the possibility, though not the probability of all his lovemaking to Russia being fruitless, so he is looking about in other directions . . . for allies . . . Had this policy been adopted a year ago . . . we should . . . have perhaps Sandro King of a united & independant [sic] Bulgaria. . . . If Germany had made fast her other alliances, she might have defied Russia & France. . . . now much time has been wasted in running after Russia and trying to buy her good graces, by sacrificing Sandro & Bulgaria, it was both wrong & shortsighted. . . . An enormous deal now depends on the influence England . . . can gain over the Sultan!

The value of the English vis-à-vis the Turks was one area where Bismarck agreed with Vicky, and he now set about to encourage the expansion of the First Mediterranean Agreement into a second one between Germany's allies Austria and Italy, and England. Signed in December of 1887 and aimed at shielding the disintegrating Ottoman Empire from Russian aggression, this new document, agreed to by England, Austria, and Italy, outlined the status quo in the Near East and reiterated the importance of keeping Turkey free of foreign domination. It was agreed that the Sultan would not give up any of his rights in Bulgaria or the straits. If he failed to resist encroachment, the signators would be justified in occupying Turkish territory. Like most previous treaties, this one had to be kept secret.

Along with promoting this second anti-Russian alliance, Bismarck also took some direct steps to discourage Russia from military action. Embittered by the Russian press, which continued to blame Germany for Ferdinand's appointment, he ordered the Reichsbank to stop using Russian stocks as collateral, thus cutting the floor out from under the Russian security market, destroying the value of Russia's state bonds, and undermining the Czar's financial ability to wage war.

In teaching Russia a lesson, however, Bismarck failed to take one major factor into account. Forced to look around for another source of capital, Russia found it in France. Parisian financiers welcomed a new and profitable source of income, and French politicians who had long believed in a Franco-Russian entente rejoiced at an economic bridge that might well precede a political one.

IN NOVEMBER OF 1887, one day after Bismarck issued his fateful order to the Reichsbank, Alexander III arrived in Berlin on his way home from a visit to his wife's family in Copenhagen. He remained only eleven hours, just long enough to visit Wilhelm I, meet with Bismarck, and attend a state dinner. During separate conversations with the Kaiser and his Chancellor, the Czar promised to call off the German-baiting Russian press. He assured Bismarck that Russia would never attack Germany, had no intention of allying itself with France, and, in any case, would never deal with "that animal Boulanger." *

This was all very well for the Czar to say, but earlier that fall, in response to the appointment of Ferdinand to the Bulgarian throne, the Russians had begun massing troops along the Austrian frontier. Taking foreign relations into their own hands, a group of German generals, headed by Quartermaster General Alfred von Waldersee, recommended a preventive winter campaign to stop what they said were Russia's plans to wage war in early 1888. On December 17, 1887, the generals, who had not been told of the Reinsurance Treaty between Germany and Russia, invited Willy to join them for a meeting with the Kaiser to outline the Russian danger. The future Wilhelm II, as his close friend Count Waldersee said, was "very keen on the idea of war." Although Wilhelm I refused to believe that the Russians really intended to go to war, he agreed to the discussions. Needless to say, the Crown Prince was angry when he heard about the meeting.

It is not too surprising, considering the participants, that the talks moved rather quickly from defensive to offensive war. Irate at the generals for usurping his prerogatives, Bismarck had his own plans to exploit the national concern over Bulgaria. This involved securing the passage of a bill adding 600,000 soldiers to the German army in the event of war. In a major address to the Reichstag, announced a week in advance and attended by the largest crush of spectators anyone could remember, Bismarck said that Bulgaria was not worth war between Germany and Russia. Germany, he said, would not begin a war, but if anyone else did, the army would be prepared. "We no longer ask for love, either from France or from Russia," the Chancellor declared. "We Germans fear God and nothing else in the world!"

The speech created a sensation. In the exultant aftermath, Moltke wept, the military bill passed the chamber unanimously, and it took five policemen on horseback as well as Herbert Bismarck's elbows to clear his father's way back to the chancellery. As a token of his appreciation for Bismarck's restraint, the Czar sent the Chancellor a large barrel of fresh caviar. Even Willy temporarily repudiated his warmongering. "God preserve me from such criminal frivolity," he told an audience in Brandenburg; "I reject such accusations with indignation!"

With his unerring instinct for seizing the political moment, Bismarck had undercut the generals, muzzled the hawkish young heir to the throne, and increased his own power. It was a brilliant performance.

But for Vicky, Bismarck's triumphs did not justify his means. "I do love honesty & plain dealing—fairness & simplicity . . . ," she wrote Victoria during the speculation preceding the Chancellor's speech.

* Although Boulanger lost his position as Minister of War in May of 1886, he continued to be extremely popular with the French people, who tried to stop his transfer to the Auvergne by blocking the train with their bodies. From his new posting, he continued to agitate for and attract financial and political support from antirepublicans.

One is <u>so</u> sick & weary of a system which stoops to <u>means</u> which are <u>so</u> low!! even be it wielded by ever so great a man, and be its <u>success</u> <u>&</u> <u>brilliancy</u> <u>worshipped</u> by a <u>crowd</u> of shortsighted blind admirers, whose national vanity being <u>flattered</u>, fancy themselves great patriots, while the standard of national sentiments & aspirations is being <u>lowered</u> & <u>deterio-rated</u>. . . . Prince Bismarck's power & prestige are greater than ever, the poor dear Emperor is but a shadow, & Willy Prince Bismarck's willing tool and follower!

Just how willing, the Crown Princess was about to find out.

CHAPTER
FIFTY

"[I]t is better to fall into the hands of God than of men."

OTTO VON BISMARCK, *1887*

*E*VER SINCE THE BEGINNING OF 1885, Wilhelm I had been in bad health, suffering from kidney disorders, blood loss, and little strokes. He seemed to be nearing his end, an eventuality that made Bismarck and his subordinates at the Foreign Ministry extremely uneasy about the future of Germany. It is probably not coincidental that within a few months of the start of the Kaiser's decline, Bismarck said that the Crown Prince "summoned" him to Potsdam to ask him to stay on as Chancellor after his father's death. Bismarck said that he promised to remain in office "under two conditions—no parliamentary government and no foreign influence in politics." The Crown Prince, he claimed, agreed to these stipulations.

Although the meeting certainly took place, there is no apparent corroboration of any such agreement from either Fritz or Vicky. The only information we have comes from Bismarck himself (who never hesitated to alter his memories to support his image), his publicist, Moritz Busch, and Holstein at the Foreign Ministry, who was desperate to bring about a rapprochement between the Chancellor and the Crown Prince.* Holstein, who dismissed the heir to the throne as weak and his wife as unpatriotic, believed it imperative that Bismarck remain at the helm "as an insurance against the follies which the Crown Prince would otherwise commit."

Since Holstein and Radolinski were extremely close, it must have been Radolinski who prompted the members of Vicky's entourage to present her with a picture of the dangers to be faced if her husband dismissed Bismarck after he became Kaiser: "[I]f the Chancellor sits sulking in Varzin and Prince Wilhelm deserts to his camp with beat of drums and flourish of trumpets—as he undoubtedly will," she was warned, the combination "would be stronger

---

* *The man who helped Holstein bring about the meeting, Fritz's private secretary, Lieutenant Colonel Sommerfeld, demanded cash payment from Holstein—a fact that says something about the kind of men Bismarck and Holstein had put in the Crown Prince's household (Holstein, 2, p. 214).*

than Your Imperial Highness' government." Faced with reality, Vicky agreed that Fritz should retain Bismarck, providing certain important changes were made.

Wilhelm I and Bismarck, she wrote in a memorandum to her friend, Minister of Justice Friedberg, had "created a unique and wondrous structure," but "the structure has its weaknesses." Her husband, she said, would retain what was good about the old empire—its strength and industry—but give the German people the kind of education that would prepare them to make their own political judgments. The central government would have to cede some of its power to the people. "The strong hand of a Prince Bismarck will no doubt be capable of building these bridges that will safely enable us to cross into a new era that will crown his lifetime achievements . . . ," she said in an attempt at compromise. "Perhaps if Prince Bismarck would see me more often, he would see that I am not the disruptive and dangerous person that I am considered to be. . . . he has never had the opportunity to see for himself that the opposite is true."

Toward that end, Vicky offered to meet with Bismarck in order to "thrash things out" in person with him. He refused.

"We've had no quarrel needing to be settled," he told Holstein. "The only thing I reproach the lady with is that she's remained an Englishwoman and exerts a pro-English influence on her husband. She's got no feeling for Germany."

"And no religion either, none whatever," Holstein added.

"Well that's her own affair," Bismarck said. "All I object to is her bad political influence." Vicky's "sole aim," according to the Chancellor, was to "trap him" into looking as if he was "clinging to his position." Nevertheless, prodded by Holstein, he agreed to call on the Crown Prince and Princess in Potsdam in July of 1885 in order to come to an understanding with them.

He was met at Wildpark Station by Radolinski. On the way to the palace, the Chancellor told Radolinski what he intended to say to the Crown Prince and Princess: he disapproved of the "English influence" Vicky brought to Germany; he objected strenuously to the Battenberg marriage; and he saw great advantages in marrying Moretta to a Prince of the Portuguese royal family. (The Catholic King of Portugal had asked for Moretta to convert and marry his son.) By saying all this in advance to Radolinski, who he knew would repeat it to Vicky, Bismarck managed to rile her and get her out of his way. Vicky jumped into the trap. She avoided speaking with the Chancellor any more than necessary during the visit and sent for the carriage to take him back to the station as early as possible. Meanwhile Bismarck met with the Crown Prince alone—with no one to weigh in on the side of liberalism and no one to contradict his version of their discussions.

They talked for half an hour after lunch in the garden of the Neues Palais. In his memoirs, Bismarck said that Fritz "told him that he must of course stay on." When the Chancellor held forth on the "misfortune" of the English influence and the Battenberg marriage, Fritz, according to him, merely pursed his lips. Bismarck claimed that this gesture constituted agreement, which Fritz dared not state because of his wife.

This was the conversation on which Bismarck based his subsequent claim that Fritz had agreed there would be no parliamentary democracy in Germany and no tilt away from Russia toward England. Unfortunately for Fritz and Vicky, when the time finally came for them to take over, they were no longer in a position to counter Bismarck's story, which was placed, unquestioned and unqualified, into the history books.

A YEAR AND A HALF LATER, in January of 1887, the Crown Prince began to be bothered by a pronounced and persistent hoarseness, assumed to be the result of a cold, an inclement winter, and many speaking obligations. By early March, when winter had turned into spring and his voice had not improved, Dr. Wegner called in a professor of clinical medicine from the University of Berlin, Karl Gerhardt. Gerhardt discovered a swelling on the lower part of Fritz's left vocal cord. He said he could remove it in ten days, although the treatment would be painful. Every day, morning and evening, the doctor poked a wire snare down the patient's throat and fished around, trying to catch hold of the lobular mass. When that failed, he resorted to a circular knife. This was also unsuccessful, and by the middle of March, Gerhardt was cauterizing the mass with red-hot platinum wire. But for every swelling the doctor burned off, a new one appeared. There were thirteen of these agonizing treatments.

In April, the Crown Prince, Crown Princess, and Dr. Wegner left for the spa at Ems, where the heir to the throne could take inhalations and rest his voice. His cough improved, as did his spirits. But on his return to Berlin in the middle of May, Gerhardt noted that the left vocal cord was not moving properly and that the tumor was larger. He called for a consultation with Ernst von Bergmann, professor of surgery at the University of Berlin and president of the Association of German Surgeons. There were six doctors at the consultation. They decided that the growth was cancerous and that Bergmann should perform a laryngotomy (incision in the larynx) to remove the growth. Bergmann assured Vicky that the procedure would be "no more dangerous than an ordinary tracheotomy."

In his career, Bergmann had performed seven laryngectomies—with less than encouraging results. In cases involving total removal of the larynx, two patients had died within two weeks and three within six to eighteen months; in two cases of partial removal, one had died in three months, though the other survived. Later, when the Crown Princess complained that she was not warned of the risks, she was told that Bergmann and the other doctors were afraid that neither she nor Fritz would have been willing "to consent & submit to it" had they been told the truth.

But when Bismarck learned that plans were underway for an operation to be performed on the heir to the throne without the knowledge of the Kaiser, the Chancellor, or the patient himself, he told Wilhelm I, who stopped the procedure and ordered further consultation. After some discussion, the German doctors decided that of the three throat specialists in Europe at the time, Morell Mackenzie, an Englishman whose textbooks were used in German medical schools, should be summoned from London.

"The doctors have only told him [Fritz] that before deciding how to treat his throat <u>now,</u> they would like to consult Dr. <u>Morel</u> <u>McKenzie</u> *[sic]* of London (Harley St) and hear <u>his</u> opinion," Vicky wrote Victoria. "He is considered the <u>best</u> with the exception of one at Petersburg. . . . The celebrated surgeon Prof. Bergmann is for operating . . . & you can imagine that <u>this</u> is <u>not</u> an <u>easy</u> operation nor a small one! . . . Of course Fritz is, as <u>yet</u>, not to know a <u>word</u> about this. He is at times so <u>very</u> <u>depressed</u> . . . that it is especially necessary . . . to . . . keep him in a calm & cheerful state of mind. He now often thinks his father will survive him, etc.! & I have fine work to make these passing sad thoughts clear away."

A cable was sent to Morell Mackenzie by the German doctors, asking him to come immediately. Bergmann told Vicky that "he would not decide on performing the operation <u>before</u> Morel *[sic]* Mackenzie has given his opinion, but that <u>if</u> M.M. viewed the case exactly as he did, the operation would take place at <u>once</u>!"

"Oh how I hope & pray it may <u>not</u> be necessary," Vicky wrote Victoria,

as I know the voice could never return. I spent a <u>terrible</u> day yesterday, it is so difficult to appear unconcerned when one's heart is so torn! And it is so important he should eat & sleep & feel well—up to the moment! I have quickly arranged some rooms in the top storey of the Berlin house in the hopes that there will be less noise & dust & more air. . . . <u>all</u> the doctors say that Fritz has been <u>quite</u> <u>rightly</u> treated till now, & are satisfied that no time has been lost . . . & that Prof. Gerhardt <u>was</u> the <u>right</u> authority to go to.

The next day, Bismarck came to see Vicky. He was, she reported to her mother, "really very nice! He said his wife sent me word I was <u>not</u> to <u>allow</u> such an operation. I said I had nothing to allow, what the responsible authorities decide as the best, we should have to submit to, & that we were bound to follow their advice."

ON THE AFTERNOON of May 20, 1887, Morell Mackenzie, a fifty-year-old specialist of Scottish descent, arrived in Berlin. The eldest son of a general practitioner who had died when he was fourteen, Mackenzie had struggled hard to achieve his worldwide reputation. Ambitious medically and socially, he lived on Harley Street in London in lavish style. His caricature, as drawn by Spy in *Vanity Fair,* shows a slight man of medium height with his hands clasped behind his back—all the energy of a hardworking intellect focused in his prominent beaklike nose, sharp chin, and deep-set, intense eyes.

Founder of the Throat Hospital of London, Mackenzie had published many books and articles, among them, an "epoch-making" treatise on abnormal growths of the larynx and a two-volume text, *Diseases of the Throat and Nose.*

Claimed by some to have "the largest and most important" roster of patients in the world, he was criticized by his enemies for an autocratic manner, praised by his friends for the number of people he treated free of charge (especially actors), and seemingly adored by his patients. Inquiries made by Queen Victoria had elicited the information that although "certainly . . . very clever," Mackenzie was greedy for money and honors and disliked by others in his profession. "I only mention this that you may know whom you are dealing with," she warned Vicky.

Not too surprisingly, Mackenzie was impressed by his new patient. "His Imperial Highness received me most graciously," he later wrote, "apologising with the charming *bonhomie* which endeared him to all who knew him, for all the trouble which his throat was causing to other people, and in particular for the long and fatiguing journey which it had entailed on me. He spoke in English with scarcely a trace of foreign accent, but his voice, though perfectly intelligible, was little better than a gruff whisper." Although Fritz offered to submit to an examination immediately on the specialist's arrival, Mackenzie said that he should first meet with the doctors who had sent for him.

Mackenzie's estimation of his German colleagues, written later when he became the centerpiece of a medical controversy, was anything but complimentary. He said he had known Professor Gerhardt personally and professionally "as a physician who, in the midst of his labours in other departments of medical science, had found time to give some attention to diseases of the throat." As to the surgeon Bergmann: "I had never . . . seen him mentioned in laryngological literature, save as a somewhat unfortunate operator in a few cases of extirpation [removal] of the larynx." The others, he felt, were equally mediocre.

"I confess that I felt some surprise that among those with whom I was invited to take counsel in a case of such importance there was not at least one of the leading German specialists in throat diseases," he said. "Every laryngologist could, without any difficulty, name several men in Germany whose reputation is not confined to their own country; their absence here seemed to me so significant that I rather hastily concluded that the Crown Prince must be suffering from some obscure disease of which the laryngeal affection was only an accidental complication."

On examining Fritz, Mackenzie discovered "a growth about the size of a split pea" on the back of the left vocal cord. He recommended that the German doctors put off any decision to operate until a biopsy could be done and suggested that one of the gentlemen remove a piece of the growth for that purpose. Gerhardt declined the honor. Neglecting to mention his earlier failures with the wire snare and circular knife, he merely said that he could not "operate with forceps." Dr. Tobold, an elderly specialist, also refused on the basis that he no longer operated.

"These replies increased the surprise which I already felt at a case of such a nature having been entrusted to the hands of these gentlemen," Mackenzie wrote, "for a throat-specialist who cannot use the forceps is like a physician who cannot use the stethoscope, or a carpenter who cannot handle a saw." Mackenzie said he would remove a piece of tissue himself. It was agreed to send the tissue to Professor Virchow, the founder of modern pathology, whom Mackenzie called "the greatest living authority on all matters pertaining to morbid anatomy."

Working under the watchful eyes of Bergmann, Gerhardt, and Tobold, Mackenzie removed a small fragment of the tumor. Both Gerhardt and Tobold, he reported, greeted his success with looks of "annoyance and disappointment."

After the operation, Fritz and Vicky invited Mackenzie to return with them to Potsdam, where the Crown Prince said that he had run into a friend at Ems who said he was "grieved to hear that Gerhardt says you have cancer." Fritz wanted to know if Mackenzie thought Gerhardt should have sent him to Ems if he knew he had cancer. He also asked if it was appropriate for physicians to give "other people" a diagnosis "when the patient's own wife" was not told of it. The Crown Prince was clearly very upset. It appears that while Vicky was putting on a good face for Fritz, he was doing the same for her.

Virchow reported that he could find no evidence of malignancy in the tissue submitted to him, but wanted a larger piece to examine. Mackenzie tried to cut another piece off the tumor, but failed. He did not try a second time, he said, because Fritz's throat was congested and irritated, a condition that he blamed primarily on the way in which Gerhardt had "burnt" the patient's larynx.

When Mackenzie declared that he could not excise another piece of the tumor and laid down his forceps, Gerhardt asked to examine the larynx himself. No sooner had the German doctor put the mirror in Fritz's throat than he pulled it out with what Mackenzie called "a highly artistic expression of horror and alarm" and accused the Englishman of having wounded the Crown Prince's right (healthy) vocal cord. This started a major feud between the Englishman and his German colleagues.

"I assured the Professor that his fears were quite groundless," Mackenzie wrote, "and showed him that with my forceps it would be difficult, if not impossible, to wound a healthy cord, even if one tried to do so. The blades would cut away anything *projecting from* the cord, but not a smooth surface." Moreover, according to Mackenzie, "a wound of such severity as that described by Professor Gerhardt could hardly have been inflicted without the patient's suffering some inconvenience from it afterward . . . smarting at the seat of injury . . . great irritation in the larynx. . . . Above all there would have been the objective symptoms of blood being coughed up." But, according to Mackenzie, "not one of these symptoms was present."

Mackenzie laid the accusation down to jealousy on the part of Gerhardt, who made sure that his charges were repeated to the Crown Prince. "Did any accident occur during your operation, as Professor Gerhardt looked so very much alarmed?" Fritz asked Mackenzie as soon as the cocaine anesthetic wore off. Although the Crown Prince said that his throat felt "quite comfortable" after the procedure, Gerhardt refused to drop the matter. In the middle of another consultation two days later, lowering his voice significantly to "a tragic whisper," he asked Mackenzie whether he might inform the other physicians of "a certain event" that had taken place. "We are among colleagues, and with closed doors," he assured the specialist.

Bergmann and Tobold then examined the Crown Prince and announced that Gerhardt was right, that the right vocal cord had been injured. Gerhardt added that he could even see "a vegetation already sprouting from the wounded spot," adding, "It will be interesting to observe whether the new growth (!) will prove to be malignant." Mackenzie retorted sarcastically that this would be "an event of the greatest interest, as such an occurrence would revolutionize everything that was thought to be known in pathology."

VICKY'S STATE OF MIND throughout these procedures can well be imagined. "Of course the suspense is very trying to me," she wrote Victoria after the first biopsy, "but I own the hope held out is a very great relief, & as I am sanguine by nature, I easily cling to it. . . . I cannot bring myself to believe the worst, it seems too cruel!"

Alternating between optimism and despair, trying to keep Fritz's spirits up while hiding the "horrid preparations" the doctors told her to make in case they decided to operate, she was "touched to tears" by her mother's letters of "love & sympathy"—the kind of support she did not receive from the members of Fritz's family. "Dear Louise of Baden questions & talks me to death till I nearly turn rude!" she complained to Victoria.

Her sister-in-law had arrived in Berlin in the middle of March to direct the festivities for the Kaiser's ninetieth birthday and had stayed on, ostensibly to take care of him, after her mother's departure for her annual vacation in Baden. But Louise paid little attention to her father. She had been far too busy consulting with the doctors and acting as press agent for the court. "How all the details about Fritz's throat have come out, & found their way into the public, & the press, I do not know . . . ," Vicky complained to Victoria at the end of May; "gossip & inventions are rife. . . . Louise of Baden has articles put into the *Reichs Anzeiger** without ever asking or consulting us."

Louise had also taken up the matter of the Battenberg marriage. Although the former Prince of Bulgaria had been barred from Berlin and Moretta had been prohibited from visiting Darmstadt, where he now lived, Louise and Augusta fretted that Moretta might still disgrace the Hohenzollerns by marrying him. To prevent this, Augusta had prepared a codicil to the Kaiser's will stating that he disowned his granddaughter if she married the Battenberg Prince. When she left town, she put Louise in charge of getting her father's signature.

"I know not whether the Emperor will or will not sign . . . ," Vicky wrote Victoria when she found out what was going on behind her back. "You cannot interfere in any way, as it is a private matter of the Emperor & Empress & their private fortune they can leave to whoever they like!" What Vicky did ask her mother to do was earmark a "little separate fund" for her to give Moretta in

---

* *A daily newspaper.*

case the young woman was disinherited by her grandfather. The Crown Princess deeply resented Fritz's mother's and sister's interference. "They are . . . so convinced that <u>they</u> <u>alone</u> are right & <u>have</u> to <u>enforce</u> what is <u>proper</u>."

IN EARLY JUNE, Mackenzie succeeded in removing a large portion of Fritz's tumor, which was sent to Virchow for analysis. A "grand consultation" followed, during which the pathologist's lengthy and obtuse report was discussed. According to Virchow, there was "nothing present . . . which would be likely to arouse the suspicion of wider and graver disease."

In other words, good news. But Virchow the pathologist was also Virchow the politician, a liberal member of the Reichstag (Bismarck had once challenged him to a duel) and a friend of the Crown Prince and Princess. "Virchow," as Mackenzie noted, "knowing that his report would come under the eyes of the patient, was naturally anxious to make it as favourable as he could consistently with truth. . . . Nevertheless . . . the report could not fail to be highly encouraging. . . . It is true that the evidence here was merely negative, and did not positively disprove the existence of malignancy, but it made it very improbable."

After this report, the German doctors decided to turn the Crown Prince over to Morell Mackenzie for treatment. If the Crown Prince had cancer, which they believed he did, they knew it would be far better for them if he died under the care of a foreigner. Mackenzie returned to London, where the Crown Prince planned to follow him to have the rest of the tumor removed and take part in the festivities surrounding Queen Victoria's jubilee, celebrating her fiftieth year on the English throne.

"I think we may be quite easy about Fritz now," Vicky wrote her mother the day after Mackenzie's departure,

> although I see that the German doctors refuse to be so, & want to make out that Dr. MacKenzie contradicts himself etc. But Virchow's report bears out completely all he has said. . . . Of course one must carefully avoid criticizing them . . . or irritating them. . . .
>
> Fritz asks me to beg you, if <u>possible</u>, to obtain 2 cards of admission to some corner in Westminster Abbey for the 21st to be given to Dr. McKenzie—a card for him & one for his wife! It seems it is the wish of his heart. . . . I cannot refuse to mention it, as I feel that <u>if</u> he had <u>not</u> come, we . . . should certainly not have the chance we are looking forward to so much, of being at the jubilee.

The opportunity to attend Queen Victoria's jubilee, anticipated with great enthusiasm by both Fritz and Vicky, also offered an additional benefit, one the Crown Princess had mentioned in a previous letter home. "I must ask a favour of you!" she wrote her mother on June 3. "Under the <u>present</u> circumstances & <u>for</u> <u>the</u> <u>present</u>, it would be the greatest relief to us, if we could bring <u>over</u> <u>all</u> <u>our</u> <u>private</u> <u>papers</u> to England. Would you allow them to be locked up in <u>the</u> iron room leading out of dear Papa's library at Buckingham Palace?? We should feel <u>much</u> <u>happier</u>. I can explain <u>more</u> when we meet."

CHAPTER FIFTY-ONE

"She [the Crown Princess] has been the guardian angel of my existence, and she has helped me to bear all its sorrows and dark hours. She is perfection itself as a woman."

CROWN PRINCE FRIEDRICH WILHELM OF GERMANY

*T*HE THREE IRON-BOUND BOXES of papers referred to by Vicky in her letter to Victoria belonged to the Crown Prince, whose concern over their safekeeping was not unwarranted. With the old Kaiser fading, their household infiltrated with Bismarck's spies, and Willy growing more aggressive by the day, Fritz realized that events might overtake him quickly, before he had a chance to put his affairs in order. Judging from his conversation with Mackenzie, he must have guessed that his chances of survival were slim. That meant preparing for all contingencies.

At the age of ninety, Wilhelm I was deteriorating rapidly, the victim of many little strokes with attendant aphasia and memory loss. Even layers of royal insulation could no longer hide his infirmities. "It seems to me the old Emperor cannot live much longer," Crown Prince Rudolph of Austria reported home from Berlin during the festivities surrounding the Kaiser's ninetieth birthday; "he looks terrible and seems very feeble."

The problem for Fritz and Vicky was not Wilhelm I, however, but their son, the future Wilhelm II. For some time, the young heir to the throne had been taking advantage of his grandfather's weakness to bypass his father in the royal hierarchy and thrust himself into second position. When it was a question of representing the Hohenzollerns at ceremonial functions, Willy appealed directly to Wilhelm I or the all-powerful Chancellor. When it came to politics, he promoted himself by accusing his parents of a lack of patriotism—a pattern of behavior encouraged by Bismarck and his son Herbert.

Willy and Herbert, nine years his senior, had become friends in 1884, when the former was sent to represent his grandfather at the coming-of-age celebrations of the Czarevitch in Russia and Herbert was working in the German Embassy in St. Petersburg. Herbert's career in foreign affairs had begun after an aborted love affair with a divorcée; her political connections had so enraged Bismarck that he persuaded Wilhelm to change the law, making it impossible for men who married divorced women to inherit entailed estates. Since Herbert's acquiescence, Bismarck had been grooming him as his successor. The Chancellor's elder son had remained in minor positions for only a few years before being catapulted in 1886 to the highest position in the Foreign Ministry, Secretary of State. On assuming his new post, he suggested to his father that the heir to the throne be brought into the ministry for training.

"Considering the unripeness and inexperience of my eldest son, together with his leaning towards vanity and presumption, and his overweening estimate of himself, I must frankly express my opinion that it is dangerous as yet to bring him into touch with foreign affairs," the Crown Prince protested to Bismarck. But the Chancellor counted heavily on that "vanity and presumption" to undermine Willy's parents. With the consent of the Kaiser, Vicky's elder son was given an office in the Foreign Ministry, where he reported twice a week to listen to discourses on foreign policy as interpreted by Herbert. Herbert felt that Willy could not "be stirred up enough" against the land of his mother's birth, and the heir to the throne soon announced that "one cannot have enough hatred for England."

"William is used as a tool by the Government & conservative party—& by the Emperor's Court," Vicky wrote Victoria in the spring of 1887, while her husband was undergoing treatments by Dr. Gerhardt. "We want him to have a Regiment in the provinces, but all these people will not allow the Emperor to let him go! & he fancies himself consequently of enormous importance & that he is of more use to the country than his Papa, who, in his eyes, does not keep up Prussian traditions enough & is suspected of a little leaning toward a more liberal & modern tendency!"

It did not take long, however, for Herbert to lose patience with his protégé. The Secretary of State complained to Holstein that he "had no staying power —he simply wanted to be amused." Even Willy's well-known passion for the army was only skin-deep: "all that really interested him in army life was wearing a handsome uniform and marching through the streets to music." Willy, in Herbert's words, was "as cold as a block of ice. Convinced from the start that people only exist to be used . . . after which they may be cast aside."

Whatever they said behind his back, the Bismarcks made sure to flatter the heir to the throne in person. Bismarck Sr. invited him to intimate evenings in the Bismarck home, during which the Chancellor—lying on his sofa after a huge dinner—dispensed political bons mots. Bismarck Jr. tried to draw Wilhelm into his social circle.

But Willy soon became disillusioned with Herbert. He disapproved of drinking, and Herbert was well on his way to becoming an alcoholic. Willy was also a sexual prude, and guests at the Secretary of State's home loved to tell about the evening the future Kaiser took a belligerent stance *outside* the door to Herbert's salon, making it clear that he disapproved of the suggestive lyrics of a female singer his host had hired to entertain the all-male company within.

Nor was Herbert the best guide for the young heir in matters of diplomacy. Detailed to greet Alexander III of Russia on one of his visits to Berlin, the Secretary of State found himself some distance from the Czar's railway carriage when the train pulled into the station. As the story was told, Herbert ran down the platform, elbowing two members of the Czar's suite aside in order to be in place when Alexander descended. "Pardon me," he said. "I am Count Bismarck."

"That is an explanation," one of them was heard to remark, "but not an excuse."

High-handed with visiting dignitaries, Herbert von Bismarck was known within the Foreign Ministry itself for his ill temper, and even Willy was surprised by what he called the Secretary of State's "rudeness towards his subordinates." The heir to the throne was also smart enough to notice that other trainees were "taught nothing" beyond carrying out the orders of the Chancellor. As the future Kaiser put it (in a somewhat unfortunate simile), "The Prince [Bismarck] bulked there like a huge granite boulder in a field; roll it away and you find beneath it little but vermin and withered roots."

In Vicky's opinion, Bismarck was a "very dangerous" role model for her son, although she freely admitted that he was "a genius." As she wrote Victoria, Bismarck himself might be a

> great man, but his system is a pernicious one, which can only do young people harm. . . . his blind followers & admirers & the many who wish to rise by a servile and abject pandering to his every wish & whim are a bad lot. . . . These are all William's friends now, & he is on a footing of the greatest intimacy & familiarity with them! . . .
> William's judgment is being wharped [sic] & his mind poisoned. . . . He is not sharp enough or experienced enough to see through the system nor through the people. . . . He is so headstrong, so impatient of any constraint except the Emperor's, & so suspicious of every one who might be only a half hearted admirer of Bismarck's that it is quite useless to attempt to enlighten him. . . . The malady must have its course, & we must trust to later years & changed circumstances to cure him! Fritz takes it profoundly "au tragique," whilst I try to be patient, & do not lose courage. It is after all a very natural consequence of the Emperor having enforced the contrary of all we wished & thought salutary for William, & the natural consequence of Bismarck's omnipotence.

Bismarck and his son were not the only ones who played on Willy's need for self-importance. There was also his wife, Dona. Vicky had overestimated the common sense and goodwill of the Duke of Augustenburg's daughter, lifted out of the ignominy of a ruined family to marry the heir to the throne. The power and position that might have broadened Willy's wife had only made her aggressively ordinary. Bigoted, not very bright, Dona fulfilled her husband's belief that "women were to marry, love their husbands, have lots of babies, bring them up well, cook nicely and make their husbands [sic] home comfy for them." She gave Willy unqualified approval and four healthy sons * during the first six years of their marriage. "Clothes and children are . . . the only things

---

* *She eventually gave birth to six sons and a daughter, all within ten years.*

she thoroughly understands," complained the English-born German princess, Daisy of Pless.

A limited young woman of unlimited prejudices, Dona rushed to condemn the unfamiliar. She praised everything German, despised anything foreign, particularly English, and played a significant role in widening the breach between Vicky and her elder son. Egged on by the Kaiserin, who did not share Dona's narrow point of view but adored intrigue, Willy's wife was, according to one young intimate of the court, "one of the persons who did most harm to her mother-in-law."

It is not surprising that Queen Victoria, who strongly disapproved of Willy and Dona, had not planned to invite them to the jubilee, celebrating her fifty years on the throne. She gave Vicky three reasons: "first because Fritz & you come, & second because I must lodge them & thirdly because you know how ill he behaved, how rude, to me, to Liko [Henry of Battenberg] . . . & how shamefully he calumniated dear, excellent, noble Sandro & how shamefully he behaves to you both. . . . Bertie wants me to invite William & Dona, but . . . I fear he may show his dislikes and be disagreeable. Tell me what you think."

"[W]e most decidedly think he ought to come," Vicky wrote back; "he need only stay a very few days, but as your eldest grandchild, he ought to be present." The Crown Princess knew how her son loved pagentry and hated being left out of anything. Willy, she assured his grandmother, would be on his best behavior. Nor would it do to give the Chancellor and his party ammunition to use "against you & Fritz & me."

Vicky admitted that Willy was "young, green, & fanatical, imprudent, believes anything & everything he is told by the flatterers . . . amongst whom he lives!" But, she insisted, "He means no harm, fancies himself of immense importance & service to the state, to his country, thinks he is indispensible [sic] to Bismarck and the Emperor! . . . he is not aware of the mischief he does & the game that is played with him. Personally he is quite nice & amiable to us, & so he would be to you & all his relations."

The Crown Princess was poorly repaid for her intercession. A few days after Fritz's first biopsy, Willy appeared at his parents' palace to announce that his grandfather had "ordered" him to attend Queen Victoria's jubilee as the official representative of the German court. "Fritz has not given up the idea of going to your Jubilee yet," Vicky wrote her mother; "therefore William has no right to supersede his father without knowing whether he wishes it. . . . I do not think it very nice of William to allow himself to be put forward before he knows what our wishes & plans are."

Willy had, in fact, already telegraphed Queen Victoria that he was coming to London "by the Emperor's orders" to represent him at the festivities, and it was not until the forgetful Kaiser was reminded that the Crown Prince also planned to go to England that he reversed himself. This did not stop Willy. In her invitation, Queen Victoria, who was hard-pressed to house all the visiting royalties, made it a condition that her eldest grandson bring only two gentlemen-in-waiting. Starting a pattern that was to alternately annoy and amuse his relations for the rest of his life, Willy, who said that he was "hurt and offended" by the limits imposed by his grandmother, wired back that he could do with no less than four.* Throughout the weeks preceding her jubilee, the future Wilhelm II continued "bombarding" his grandmother with telegrams questioning his father's ability to travel and demanding a larger suite as befitted his status. Once again, Vicky assured her mother that Willy "meant no harm whatever."

"I trust you will not be angry with William!" she wrote. "He did not mean to be impertinent, but it is only his rashness, his want of reflexion, & tact, & discretion which make him do such foolish things as to telegraph right & left, and announce the Emperor's wishes & orders, before he half knows what is going on!"

Willy, who would ignore his grandmother's wishes by bringing four gentlemen-in-waiting to the jubilee, apparently did not receive the special treatment he felt he deserved, for he and Dona "sulked" throughout the celebrations, causing his ailing father and worried mother considerable embarrassment. According to Hedwig von Brühl, Vicky's lady-in-waiting and one of Holstein's spies, "he [Willy] only saw his grandmother a couple of times, at Court functions; she [Dona] was always placed behind the black Queen of Hawaii!! Both . . . were in no doubt as to the quarter which had intrigued against them."

THE CROWN PRINCE AND PRINCESS of Germany arrived in England in the middle of June 1887. Fritz was unable to take part in any of the jubilee festivities except the grand parade of kings and princes that accompanied the Queen to her thanksgiving service at Westminister Abbey on June 21.

It was a sunlit day. Triumphal arches, festooned with crowns, shields, and evergreens, marked the parade route, and greenery interlaced with flags and banners hung from balconies and reviewing stands. The Queen's procession was led by the Prince of Wales's Hussars, the Horse Guards, and Life Guards with drawn swords, flashing in the sun. She was preceded by her aides-de-camp and equerries on horseback, six carriages of relations, a phalanx of military leaders, six more carriages bearing members of the royal family, the Master of the Horse, and a parade of seventeen princes on horseback—three sons, five sons-in-law, and nine grandsons.

Of the royal gentlemen on horseback, by far the most impressive was the Crown Prince of Germany. Dressed in the pure white uniform and silver breastplate of the Pomeranian Cuirassiers, a steel, eagle-winged helmet on his head, the Order of the Garter slashed across his chest, and his gold-inlaid field marshal's baton in his hand, Fritz, according to an English brother-in-law,†

---

* *Years later, Willy's cousin Queen Marie of Romania would write about the "embarrassingly numerous suite composed of embarrassingly huge gentlemen in blazing uniforms" that the short-statured Kaiser Wilhelm II had insisted upon bringing to her wedding, thus outshining both the bride and the groom.*

† *Princess Louise's husband, Lord Lorne.*

looked like "one of the legendary heroes embodied in the creations of Wagner." Of all the members of the procession except Victoria herself, he garnered the greatest outbursts of applause and the loudest cheers. Most people had heard of his illness; some even commented on his thinness; but everyone, including the Queen herself, thought him the most beautiful person in the parade.

Victoria had adamantly refused to travel in a glass coach or wear the crown and state robes, but she had agreed to an open landau pulled by six of her famous cream-colored horses. Dressed in her usual black, spruced up for the occasion by a bonnet trimmed in lace, diamonds, and white feathers, she had specified "Bonnets and Long, High Dresses without Mantel [sic]" for the other ladies as well. In the Queen's carriage, dressed as ordered, were the Princess of Wales and the Crown Princess of Germany.

After a slow and solemn entry up the aisle of the abbey, Victoria took her place on the five-hundred-year-old coronation chair, surrounded by her forty closest relatives on gilt chairs, separated from the rest of the congregation by a gilt railing. At the end of the service, when the princes and princesses stepped forward to kiss the Queen's hand and be embraced by her, it was Vicky whom she held the longest. And when the Queen stepped down from her coronation chair and found Fritz standing near her, she embraced him a second time, holding onto his arm an extra moment or two in a sign of deep and concerned affection.

THE CROWN PRINCE AND PRINCESS stayed in a hotel outside London in order to spare Fritz all but that one important appearance; other days, he went to Morell Mackenzie's office for treatment. On June 28, one week after the jubilee parade, Mackenzie managed to remove all that remained of the growth from his vocal cord, which was sent to Virchow in Berlin. Again, Virchow found no evidence of malignancy.

After a period of recuperation, Fritz, accompanied by a surgeon from the London Throat Hospital, went to Scotland. He was noticeably better, and when he visited his mother-in-law at Balmoral, she was delighted to hear him speak in what she called his "natural voice again." Mackenzie told his patient that his "sufferings" were "at an end," although he still "required special care with rest and silence for a long time in order to avoid a relapse." In accordance with Fritz's wish, the Queen conferred a knighthood on the specialist.

With his treatments over, the Crown Prince was urged to return to Berlin and the care of the German doctors. But Mackenzie prescribed rest, and it was decided that Fritz would go to Toblach in the Italian Tyrol with Mackenzie's assistant, Mark Hovell, and Gerhardt's assistant, Dr. Landgraf. Fritz had great confidence in Hovell, but did not like Landgraf, a young doctor who appears to have been neither skillful nor gentle. Just before leaving for Scotland, the normally stoical Crown Prince, suffering from Landgraf's rough awkwardness, finally voiced his objections, and the young doctor was warned by Dr. Wegner to approach his patient with more care. To cover himself, Landgraf sent reports back to Berlin, claiming that the Crown Prince was being kept away from his (Landgraf's) ministrations because Morell Mackenzie was trying to conceal from the other doctors the patient's "<u>dangerous state</u>."

WHILE FRITZ was in Scotland and Vicky was taking a cruise on her mother's yacht to Portsmouth and Cowes, Count Radolinski, who had accompanied them to England, took Queen Victoria's private secretary, Sir Henry Ponsonby, aside to tell him that the Crown Princess and her Court Chamberlain, Count Seckendorff, were having an affair. "He goes everywhere with her—he is complete master," Radolinski said. Vicky, he intimated, had prevented the doctors from performing an operation on her husband so that he would remain alive just long enough for her to become Kaiserin; after that, he would die, leaving her with a lot of money and her beloved Seckendorff.

It was a clever ploy, for Seckendorff was not popular with the Queen or her court. Several years earlier, Vicky had arranged for him to accompany the Prince of Wales to India. Bertie felt put upon, and the incident had left bad feelings all around. Now Radolinski, still trying to fulfill his mission of getting rid of Seckendorff, appealed to Queen Victoria.

"I flattered her terribly," he boasted in a letter to Holstein, detailing how he had told the Queen that she was "the only person" to whom her daughter listened. "She smiled sweetly like a blushing girl and was really completely charming. For three days in succession she invited me to dine with her with an intimate group. . . . I am <u>very</u> <u>satisfied</u> with my campaign."

The Queen was not fooled, merely advising her daughter to send Seckendorff away for a month in order to "calm" Radolinski. "As you said in your letter," she wrote Vicky, "Count Radolinski was the tool in the hands of the set at the Foreign Office, who were anxious to . . . overthrow Count Seckendorff."

Radolinski's tales received a more enthusiastic reception at the Foreign Ministry. The following extract from Holstein's diary was written in late September of 1887:

> The Crown Prince is in a poor way. . . . The Crown Princess's behaviour is typical. Gay and carefree, with but one idea—never to return to Prussia. I persist in my view, which is now shared by others, namely that from the very beginning she accepted the idea that the worst would happen. Judging by all I have heard of her in recent months, I am tempted to call her a degenerate or corrupt character. . . . She has always despised her husband. She will greet his death as the moment of deliverance.

What is more amazing than Holstein's rancor or Radolinski's belief that he could manipulate the Queen is the Crown Princess's naïveté regarding Radolinski. Having been won over by Fritz's urbane Court Chamberlain, she never accepted the fact that he was her enemy. Instead of demanding Radolinski's resignation on the spot, she found excuses for his behavior.

"I am <u>so</u> <u>thankful</u> to <u>you</u> for having given me this correct information about Count Radolinsky's conversation at Balmoral. . . . ," Vicky wrote her friend Mary Ponsonby, wife of the Queen's private secretary.

> My friends say . . . that of course Count Seckendorff has enemies! It is these who have got hold of Count Radolinski and taken advantage of Count Radolinski's credulity, of his excitability and of his irritation against Count Seckendorff. . . . Count Radolinsky is sincerely attached to us, but he quite forgets it is not his business to take our affairs out of our hands and try to settle them as he thinks right and fit (out of devotion) behind our backs and against our will! If he has let himself be persuaded that it is for our good, he will dash violently into a thing, and use the least fair of means to accomplish his ends without hesitation. . . .
>
> I had a long conversation on board the yacht with Count Radolinski. . . . He said he had never spoken to any members of the English court on the subject, but they had asked him so many questions, and had forced the subject upon him. He had found so great a dislike and indignation against Count Seckendorff at the English court that he had not needed to add his own impressions; it had only been a proof more to him of how widely spread Count Seckendorff's bad reputation was!
>
> I gave Count Radolinsky a piece of my mind, but whether I shall thereby stop him in his insane endeavours to get rid of Count Seckendorff I do not know. Count Radolinsky has been to Prince Bismarck about it, and has also begged Herbert Bismarck to work on his father and on our son William in this sense!!! Old Prince Bismarck does not go out or mix in the world and is thoroughly dependent on the tales that are carried to him by his satellites, which he always implicitly believes.

Like most of the propaganda spread by Bismarck and his subordinates, the rumor of an affair between the Crown Princess and her Court Chamberlain was ultimately effective, so much so that it became the generally accepted view— one of those politically inspired canards repeated to this day as proven truth by descendants of the Chancellor and at least one-well known German historian.

BY THE FALL OF 1887, there was tremendous pressure from Berlin for the Crown Prince to return home, where he could be treated by the German doctors and take over if his ailing father should die. It was obvious to everyone by now that Wilhelm I was nearing the end of his life. What would happen if he were prevented from fulfilling his duties and the Crown Prince were out of the country? The affairs of state could not be left to chance or his grandson.

"It would be madness to spoil Fritz's cure, while he is in a fair way to recovery, but not well yet!" the Crown Princess wrote her mother at the end of August, explaining that they were following Mackenzie's advice by staying out of Berlin. "I know the life there. . . . He would never cure his voice, what gain would that be!! The Emperor, the Empress, & Bismarck wish Fritz to be cured first. . . . It seems to me sacrificing the future to the present."

Ignoring the pressure from Berlin, Fritz and Vicky spent two weeks in the Italian Tyrol, then moved south to San Remo on the Italian Riviera, where they rented a home, the Villa Zirio. Their continued absence from Berlin increased the attacks on Vicky. "It is very unfair and ungrateful & unkind to abuse me at Berlin for having an English doctor for Fritz," Vicky wrote Victoria, "& even going so far as to abuse me for bringing Fritz to an English house instead of a German one in Italy."

Shortly after their arrival at the Villa Zirio, Dr. Hovell found a fresh swelling in a different spot in the Crown Prince's throat. It looked malignant to him, and he sent for Morell Mackenzie.

"Sir M. arrived this morning. . . . ," the distracted Crown Princess wrote her mother in early November,

> & is not satisfied with the look of this place, it has a malignant character about it, & symptoms which do not please him! . . . The doctors have communicated their fears to Fritz, which has depressed him very much. We have let the Emperor & Empress, our three eldest children and Prince Bismarck know of this out of pure prudence & conscientiousness. Two other doctors will come to consult with Mackenzie, but not those who made such a mistake this spring. . . . This sudden & rapid change in his state has taken us very much aback.

Fritz, who asked Mackenzie bluntly if he had cancer and was told he did, thanked the doctor for his frankness. "I have lately been fearing something of this sort," the Crown Prince admitted, taking hold of Mackenzie's hand with what the Englishman called "that smile of peculiar sweetness, which so well expressed the mingled gentleness and strength of his character. In all my long experience I have never seen a man bear himself under similar circumstances with such unaffected heroism," Mackenzie said.

Only later, when he was alone with his wife, did the Crown Prince break down. "To think that I should have such a horrid, disgusting illness! that I shall be an object of disgust to everyone, and a burden to you all! I had so hoped to be of use to my country. Why is Heaven so cruel to me! What have I done to be thus stricken and condemned! What will become of you? I have nothing to leave you! What will become of the country?"

Vicky did what she could "to console & pacify" her weeping husband. As she wrote her mother, she used everything she could "think of which was comforting & reassuring, though consistent with the truth! I said we must leave the future in God's hands &—not trouble about it, but fight this illness as well as we can, by remaining cheerful & hopeful, taking care of health."

With her beloved husband dying and her life's purpose crumbling about her, there was little else the Crown Princess could say.

CHAPTER
FIFTY-TWO

"I cannot and will not give up hope."
CROWN PRINCESS FRIEDRICH WILHELM, *November 1887*

*T*HE DIAGNOSIS of the Crown Prince's cancer in November of 1887 let loose all the jealousies and schemes for self-advancement lying beneath the surface of the German court and government. Only the ultimate reckoning of a long-term change of power had kept Fritz's political opponents in check. Now, with the crown destined to go from conservative grandfather to conservative grandson—with only a short detour, if any, into liberalism—the establishment could afford to defy or simply ignore the man and his wife who had waited so long to change the course of German history.

The leader of the pack was Willy—charging forward under the banner of his grandfather's authority, brandishing threats concerning the medical mistreatment of his father. His posturing, which seesawed wildly between chauvinism and maudlin sentimentality, could have passed for farce onstage. But of all the criticism aimed at the Villa Zirio, none hurt the Crown Princess as much as his. Even Herbert von Bismarck, who despised the Crown Prince and Princess, began to speak of the heir to the throne's behavior as "heartless, superficial," and "vain."

As soon as the new growth on Fritz's larynx was discovered, Willy "begged" his grandfather for permission to go to San Remo "in order at last to clear the matter up." Brimming over with self-importance, he arrived at his parents' villa, planted himself at the bottom of the stairs, and demanded immediate access to his father's room. When his mother, who was on the upstairs landing barring his way, suggested they first take a walk together, he replied that he was "too busy—he had to speak to the doctors." The doctors, she told him, reported to her, not to him. But Willy said that he had come on "the 'Emperor's orders'" to insist upon the right thing, to see that the doctors were not interfered with, and to report to the Emperor about his Papa." Vicky replied that this was unnecessary, as they themselves "always reported" to Wilhelm I.

There were other people present at this unfortunate exchange, during which the heir to the throne apparently stood with his back half turned to his mother, playing to the onlookers. Disgusted, she walked away, saying she would report his behavior to his father and ask that he be refused entry into their home. Willy then sent Count Radolinski to apologize on his behalf and beg her to say nothing to his father, although he added that "it was his duty to see that the Emperor's commands were carried out." Vicky was mollified, Fritz came out of his room to see what all the fuss was about, and Willy raced up the stairs and threw himself into his father's arms.

After this, the visit took a more reasonable turn. Vicky reported that she and Willy took "many a pleasant little walk & chat together," while he said later that he and his father "came in spirit very close to one another . . . during the heavy days that followed."

The Crown Princess guessed that her son had arrived "with the <u>intention</u> of <u>insisting</u> on this <u>terrible</u> operation being performed." Willy, she told Victoria, was "too young and inexperienced" to understand that he was being used by the faction in Berlin that wanted the Crown Prince operated on, the quicker to dispense with him. Vicky felt (not without reason) that an operation at that stage "would simply have assassinated Fritz." *

Whatever Willy did or did not understand, he had been convinced by Herbert and an "anonymous" article in Bismarck's official paper, the *Norddeutsche Allgemeine Zeitung,* that there was a plot between Mackenzie and his mother to keep his father's cancer hidden for fear that the Crown Prince would abdicate if he knew the truth. Vicky deeply resented Willy's intrusion, based on little more than a desire, conscious or not, to take over as quickly as possible. His sudden extravagant concern for his father's welfare was particularly galling after his previous attempts to turn the Crown Prince into a dynastic and political cipher.

But Willy, too, had a point. The fact was that, whatever his failings, the heir to the throne was twenty-eight, and his parents, particularly his mother, continued to treat him like a child. Although he disagreed with her politics, he was about to become Kaiser over some forty-six million German souls, and she would have been better off giving him a modicum of respect. But this she was unable to do. His arrogance, his conservatism, worst of all his sanctimony set her teeth on edge.

As noted by their contemporaries, there were also great similarities between mother and son. Holstein thought that Wilhelm II had the "same character as his mother, but with a greater contempt for mankind." Willy's closest friend, Philipp zu Eulenburg, was kinder. "He was so similar in character and temperament to this unusually clever, highly educated, and interesting woman, that these two headstrong individuals with their autocratic outlooks simply *had* to collide with one another."

■

---

* *Felix Semon, Edward VII's physician and a sharp critic of Mackenzie, wrote about the high mortality rate of laryngectomy and "the deplorable, even suicidal, mental state" of patients who survived it at the time (Stevenson,* Morell Mackenzie, *p. 97).*

HAVING VERIFIED the presence of the new growth on the Crown Prince's larynx, Mackenzie had called two specialists to San Remo for consultation—Professor von Schrötter from Vienna, an expert in the treatment of respiratory illnesses, and Dr. Krause from Berlin, whom Mackenzie called "one of the leading laryngologists in Germany." Schrötter agreed that the Crown Prince was suffering from cancer and recommended that the larynx be removed; Krause said cancer was highly probable, but suggested that potassium iodide be given to rule out any chance that the disease was an indication of an earlier bout with syphillis.*

The doctors drew up a gloomy prognosis, which they presented first to Vicky, then to Fritz. "They read to me their Protocol—cruel indeed it sounded, I hardly expected _much_ else, still . . . it gives one an awful blow! I would not break down before them of course . . . ," she wrote her mother. "My darling has got a fate before him which I dare hardly think of! . . . William has just arrived, not by _our_ wish & just at present is rather in the way."

In his memoirs, Wilhelm II says that he and his siblings were not in the room when the physicians gave his father the fatal news, because, as he put it, "it would have taxed our strength too high." Nonetheless, the heir to the throne wrote letters to his grandmother Victoria and his tutor, describing the scene as if he himself had been there. It was his mother who remained, so that the doctors might not, in her words, "put their opinion in _too plain_ language & give Fritz a terrible shock."

The Crown Prince greeted the phalanx of medical men with a kindly nod and a slight bow, making it clear that he preferred to remain standing while he heard the news. He appeared to be perfectly calm and listened stoically with no visible sign of emotion. Dr. Schrötter said that it was the most affecting scene that he had ever witnessed. Only Dr. Schrader, the old Kaiser's physician, who had arrived with Willy, broke down into "convulsive sobbing."

Having presented the patient with the facts and probabilities, the physicians left him to make up his own mind between excision of his larynx and eventual tracheotomy when he could no longer breathe. Within a few minutes, the Crown Prince sent them a note saying that he did not want his larnyx removed, but would submit, when necessary, to a tracheotomy.

"I have thought back over the many difficult and dangerous days in which I saw the Prince and remembered how I always marvelled at his total calm and cold-bloodedness . . . ," Admiral Stosch wrote Normann when he heard the news. "May the Prince have a speedy end and keep the reputation of a courageous and fine man. He was always a handsome and lovable person, and he will remain one to the end."

"And so I suppose I must set my house in order," Fritz wrote in his journal that evening before he went to bed.

One of his first concerns was to get his war diary to a safe place. It had not been among the original papers he had taken to England earlier that year. A

* *Before the Wassermann test, potassium iodide was used to determine the presence of syphilis.*

three-volume record of his role in the Austro-Prussian and Franco-Prussian wars, the diary was important because it detailed the day-to-day events in a career systematically belittled by the Bismarck press. Watched carefully as he was by Bismarck's men, especially Radolinski and a nursing orderly installed by Bergmann, Fritz had to find another way. It was Mackenzie's assistant, Mark Hovell, who came up with a plan.

Hovell suggested that the volumes be placed in plain sight on a table in the drawing room of the Villa Zirio. Late one evening, the doctor claimed he had received an emergency message calling him home to England. As he left the villa, he passed through the drawing room and picked up the volumes, which he hid under his coat. When Bismarck's agents discovered that both the English doctor and the diaries had disappeared overnight, orders went out to watch all the routes to England, stop Hovell, search his luggage, and seize the diaries.

Neither Hovell nor the diaries were found, and three days later the doctor returned to San Remo. He had taken a train to Berlin, where he arrived in the early hours of morning, awakened the British Ambassador, and left the diaries with him to be forwarded to England by diplomatic courier. The enormous effort made by Bismarck to find and waylay these volumes testifies to their authenticity concerning the Crown Prince's role in the unification of his country.

MEANWHILE, the German doctors brought in for consultation had returned to Berlin and prepared a short written statement of the Crown Prince's condition for the aged Kaiser, who wrote Fritz at the Villa Zirio, praising him on his "Christian submission" to the will of God. The doctors had pledged absolute secrecy as to the contents of their findings, but within a day or two of their arrival in the capital, their report confirming the presence of a malignancy was published word for word in a Berlin newspaper. It may or may not be significant that one of the two men charged with swearing the doctors to silence was Count Radolinski.

Another doctor, Moritz Schmidt of Frankfurt, had also been brought to San Remo by Willy at the Kaiser's request. Like Krause, Schmidt thought that syphilis had to be ruled out. Returning to Frankfurt, he profited from his royal consultation by introducing the case of the Crown Prince into one of his university lectures. The Paris press picked up the story, reporting that the Crown Prince of Germany was suffering not from cancer but from syphilis. The reports, which made titillating copy, never completely disappeared from the welter of misinformation surrounding Fritz's illness.

Schmidt also thrust himself into the political arena, advocating that Wilhelm I be succeeded on the throne by his grandson. "[T]here is an idea being ventilated now, which I think monstrous," Vicky wrote Victoria the week after the consultation; "it was expressed here by Dr. Schmidt, whether put in his head by Willy or vice versa I do not know, but General von Winterfeld* seems

---

* *Fritz's aide-de-camp, appointed by Bismarck.*

to agree with it: i.e. that if the Emperor dies, Fritz shall not accept the succession but pass it on to William!!" Fritz was as upset as Vicky, telling Radolinski that he was "in deep grief that his son could barely await his end" and was "already putting on airs of being the Crown Prince."

When the Crown Princess objected to Schmidt's idea, she was accused of greed, since everyone knew that Wilhelm I kept Fritz on a short financial tether. "Do not think I am complaining on interested grounds, I am really <u>not</u>!" she told her mother. "If Fritz succeeds, he can provide for his daughters & for his wife! If he does <u>not</u> succeed, he can do <u>nothing</u> for us! This is however <u>not</u> my motive!! But I <u>think</u> it would be such a satisfaction to Fritz to be able to be of use to his country, nation, army & to Europe, if only for a limited time! If he felt too ill to discharge business later on, <u>he</u> could then institute a Regency!"

"The <u>interference</u>, the attacks, the <u>advice</u>, continue to pour down upon us from Berlin, i.e. upon <u>me</u>, because we trouble Fritz as little as we can!" Vicky wrote her mother two days later.

> The newspapers are filled with absolute lies. . . . You know there <u>is</u> a party who <u>have</u> their representatives at this moment even at our court, who . . . <u>insist</u> that <u>I</u>* am at the bottom of all the mischief!—prevented the operation in May, <u>forced</u> Sir M. Mackenzie on Fritz, & have kept everyone else away! They also say that this horrible operation would <u>kill</u> or <u>cure</u> Fritz and that I have prevented both . . . they think William would <u>be</u> better than an Emperor suffering from an incurable malady. . . . They say I try to hide the gravity of the situation from him, that he ought to feel more what danger he is in . . . that <u>I</u> buoy him up with <u>false</u> <u>hopes</u>, which is <u>also</u> not true, as I carefully avoid speaking of the future in order not to be obliged to say what I do not think!

Most of these stories originated in the Crown Prince and Princess's entourage, now dominated by Bismarck's and Holstein's men. "The Crown Princess and her democratic adherents are spreading barefaced lies about the Crown Princes' health," Holstein wrote in his diary after receiving a letter from Radolinski. "The aim is to prevent the Crown Prince from being made to renounce his claim to the throne on the ground of incapacity." Like other conservatives, Holstein feared that "a dying monarch with the Crown Prince's character, completely dominated by his wife, could . . . destroy or severely damage the monarchy."

In league with the Crown Princess, according to this scenario, was the Englishman Mackenzie, who was accused of lying to the German public about his patient's condition. It was asserted that Mackenzie had purposely taken the section of tissue for analysis by Dr. Virchow from the healthy rather than the diseased portion of the larynx, thus fulfilling the Crown Princess's desire to trick the German doctors into keeping her dying husband alive long enough to inherit the throne, instead of allowing the operation that would have saved his

* *Underlined three times in original.*

life. Returning from San Remo, Willy added to the furor, accusing Mackenzie of purposefully misdiagnosing his father so the Crown Prince "should not be declared incapable of assuming the government!"

Fed by Bismarck and the conservatives, the press dragged the Queen of England into the controversy, forcing the usually conciliatory British Ambassador, Sir Edward Malet, to take a stand. When an article appeared in Bismarck's paper, the *Norddeutsche Allgemeine Zeitung,* insinuating that the Crown Princess of Germany and the Queen of England were responsible for bringing Mackenzie in on the case, Malet, who had known the Bismarcks all his life, wrote Herbert:

> Now as a matter of fact, of which I am sure you are aware, the Crown Princess had nothing to do with calling in Sir Morell Mackenzie, still less the Queen. The report that the Crown Princess sent for him originally is doing her great injury and is devoid of truth. Would it be possible . . . to state authoritatively in the same paper . . . that Mackenzie was called in by decision of the physicians attending the Crown Prince, and that the Crown Princess was not even consulted and that certainly the Queen of England had nothing to do with it? I am sure that your chivalry will make you feel as I do about these statements.

Needless to say, Herbert did nothing to stop the story, which fed so conveniently into his and his father's anti-British foreign policy.

But two weeks after Willy's visit, Vicky was able to report to Queen Victoria that at least the plot to operate on her husband had been foiled. "They have not been able to tear Fritz out of the hands of Sir Morell, Dr. Krause and Dr. Hovell, nor to drag Fritz to Berlin, put him under incompetent doctors, and force the operation on him, which would either kill him or reduce him to the most awful existence you can imagine. They cannot therefore force Fritz to resign as they wanted, nor get rid of me!"

IF THE CROWN PRINCE or Princess had any illusions left, they were shattered by a visit from their son Henry toward the end of November. "Henry maintains that his Papa is lost * through the English doctors & me, & the Germans would have saved him with the operation!!" Vicky wrote Victoria.

Henry, who was acting as his brother's errand boy, arrived bearing a letter from Willy saying that he had been appointed to sign all official papers instead of his father in the event his grandfather should become incapacitated. Conceding that he was temporarily unavailable in Italy, the Crown Prince wrote Bismarck that he was nonetheless "painfully affected" when the power of signing official documents was given to his son "without informing me . . . or of obtaining my views." Vicky added her objections, which Bismarck answered in "quite a civil & pleasant" way, claiming he was not responsible for the order and could not have stopped it.

* *Underlined three times in original.*

But it is obvious that neither this order nor any of the agitation in Berlin against the Crown Prince and Princess would have been possible without Bismarck's approval. The Chancellor had encouraged his son and the Foreign Ministry in their efforts to bypass the Crown Prince in the succession, and he was certainly the force behind the removal of the Crown Prince as the signator of official papers. His aim was not, as might be imagined, to unseat Fritz, but rather to send him to the throne in a state of insecurity beyond that brought on by his illness. It was the Chancellor's way of establishing firm control over the future Kaiser and particularly his wife, when they finally came to power.

To do this, Bismarck needed to have Fritz and Vicky look on him as their sole protector in a jungle of predators. "The conviction that those who opposed an over-hasty operation were in fact right, is seldom disputed now," Bismarck wrote Vicky in early December, "for not only was the success of an operation . . . always uncertain but even if successful it would hardly have been acceptable to the illustrious patient. Moreover six months of life were gained. . . . if I were in His Imperial Highness's place I would rather expose myself to the dangers of the disease than to those of an operation."

It was a cynical letter even for Bismarck, and it succeeded in allaying Vicky's suspicions. In this, as in all the controversies surrounding her husband's illness, the Crown Princess—distraught, beleaguered, and in need of a champion—was easy prey for the Chancellor.

CHAPTER
FIFTY-THREE

*"Press, Jews & mosquitoes . . . are a nuisance that humanity
must get rid of in some way or another. I believe the best would
be gas?"*

KAISER WILHELM II *of Germany, 1927,
letter to an American correspondent*

*D*URING THE WEEKS following the diagnosis of her husband's cancer,
the Crown Princess struggled between reality and hope. Faced with the inevitable end of love and her life's work, she took refuge in the slim possibility that
the doctors had made a mistake. Meanwhile, she tried to make Fritz more
comfortable.

When the swelling in his throat was worse, he sucked ice cubes and wore
bags of ice around his neck. During these times, Vicky stayed in his room,
eating her meals there and leaving him only to take long, restorative walks.
Because of her care, the Crown Prince, who suffered from depression under the
best of circumstances, seemed amazingly cheerful. He kept busy reading and
writing, and preparing himself to take over from his father. Fritz was also
buoyed up by Mackenzie, who sounded hopeful by never committing himself.
His favorite words when relaying news of his patient's health to Victoria's
doctors were "satisfactory" and "favourable."

One of Vicky's biggest aggravations in San Remo was the press. The
Villa Zirio, built on a mountain slope above the Riviera road, was inadequately protected from outsiders by its walled garden of palm and olive trees,
and the Hotel Victoria, temporary home of an ever-increasing horde of
reporters, stood diagonally across the street. Even Willy complained about
the great number of journalists and photographers who "made their presence felt in a most disagreeable fashion by their pushful curiosity and their
spying. The majority of them," Willy claimed, "consisted of Mackenzie's
creatures!"

If that had been so, life would have been a good deal easier for Willy's
mother, who was developing the siege mentality of a general under bombardment. "The less details are made public the <u>better</u> . . . ," she wrote Victoria
in early December of 1887 about the latest developments in the Crown
Prince's illness. "The newspaper reporters dogg [*sic*] us & hunt us & follow
us, & manage to get into the house without our being able to prevent it."

"Letters are not safe either & as for telegrams, they are <u>all</u> copied . . . here, in France & in Germany," she added a few days later when two of her personal letters had been intercepted and published.

"[Y]ou must have traitors in the camp who telegraph behind your back . . . ," Queen Victoria wrote back. "I wish you would try & find out. For everything is known. Any telegram to Sir M. Mackenzie is immediately known. . . . I fear Sir M.M. is not reticent enough."

Flattered by the confidence placed in him by the Crown Prince and Princess, Mackenzie was not above using his position of intimacy in the royal household for his own ends. But the English specialist was less of a concern for Vicky than the German members of her household, who knew that the way to ingratiate themselves with the future regime was to disparage the current one. This attitude extended even to the dying man's body servants, who had been co-opted by Bismarck's and Willy's men in his father's household, General von Winterfeldt and Gustav von Kessel.*

"I cannot tell you how that woman gets on my nerves," Baron von Lynkar, another member of Fritz's household who became a favorite of Wilhelm II, reported to the Foreign Ministry.

Now, when it is so bitterly cold that all our teeth are chattering with the frost . . . she . . . has the windows opened. . . . During our walks she runs ahead like a mad thing until the Crown Prince comes to a standstill, exhausted, and says: "I can't go any further. My wife is racing ahead again." I stay with him then, but the Princess just walks on, saying with a soft upward glance: "You will walk really slowly, won't you, dear Fritz, so that you don't get too hot?" . . . I cannot bear to see that everlasting smile on her face—the woman has driven every good genius out of her house with that smile.

It was an unfortunate smile—the outward manifestation of a forced cheerfulness Vicky believed it her duty to project for the sake of her husband. That no one realized how much it cost her to keep up this front is a telling commentary on the effectiveness of the government's campaign to portray her as an unloving wife and the predisposition of the men placed in her household to believe it. Even Radolinski wrote Holstein that he wished Vicky "did not always appear so smiling before the world," because it made her look as if she "does not have any deep emotions," which, as he said, was "not true."

Mary Ponsonby, Queen Victoria's former maid of honor and Vicky's old friend who visited the Villa Zirio over Christmas, wrote the Queen that there was "not a soul on earth" to whom the Crown Princess could "speak openly." "If she does it is always taken with a twist, with suspicion, misrepresented, exaggerated and turned against her. Whatever faults (and I perfectly see them) Count Seckendorff may have," Lady Ponsonby said, "there can be no manner of doubt that the advice he gives the Crown Princess is always sensible, honest, open and fearless. . . . Princess Victoria [Moretta] is a great comfort to her

---

* Both serving as aides-de-camp to the Crown Prince.

mother and has, I think, a great deal of character. The Crown Princess is, however, very very lonely."

Writing to her husband, Lady Ponsonby was more specific.

I declare I think the unfairness about the Crown Princess is unbearable. The German press all adopt the tone that the real truth is kept back, and if she quotes Dr. Krause (the German doctor here who works with Hovell) they say that he has been won over. Bismarck (the old one) and the Emperor and Empress are kind, which helps her. The Crown Prince trusts implicitly in her . . . but the wagging of heads of the children . . . and the significant looks of Brühl* irritate me. . . .

Yesterday was the first day she, the Crown Princess, broke down before me. . . . it was too much to find him [the Crown Prince] reading a recapitulation of the doctors' former opinion with a paragraph pointing out the difference between this and the present bulletins. . . . The poor Crown Prince turned to her and said, "Why will they take every ray of hope away? What good is done by this?" . . . She was quite cheerful to him and then came into the next room where I was and cried. She is so wonderful generally that it fills one with pity.

Along with an inquisitive press and defecting courtiers, Vicky had to cope with an endless parade of relatives who began flocking to the Italian Riviera. For the first time in her life, she refused her mother's offer to send one of her sisters for comfort. There were too many people in the house already, she said —some well-meaning, others downright troublesome. Her younger son Henry fell into the latter category.

"The boy is as foolish as he is obstinate & pigheaded," she wrote Victoria, "it is no use discussing with him and I avoid it, as he becomes so rude & impertinent that I can really not stand it!!" It was not until Vicky's sympathetic brother-in-law, Grand Duke Louis of Hesse, arrived, that Henry, who always believed the last person with whom he had spoken, stopped accusing his mother of killing his father. Henry had become engaged to Louis's daughter Irene, and as his future father-in-law, Louis had some influence on him.

Back in Berlin, Willy was causing other problems. At the end of November, Willy and Dona had attended a meeting called to launch the Berlin City Mission founded by the court chaplain, Adolph Stöcker, in other cities around Germany.† It was held at the home of Willy's close friend, Count Alfred von Waldersee, Quartermaster General of the German army. The Crown Prince and

---

* *Countess Hedwig von Brühl, the Crown Princess's lady-in-waiting, one of Holstein's spies, referred to by Queen Victoria as "that odious Hedwig" (KHH: QV to V, 2/16/88).*

† *It will be remembered that Stöcker's mission was an attempt to pry the workingman away from socialism through monarchical authority, conservative Christianity, and anti-Semitism.*

Princess resented Waldersee's influence on their elder son, as did Bismarck, who correctly assumed that Waldersee coveted his job. But Countess von Waldersee was related to Dona, and the young ladies were great admirers of Pastor Stöcker. As was Willy, who described the court chaplain as a "second Luther." Willy and Dona had saved Stöcker from being fired from his post by Wilhelm I a few years earlier and had insisted that the pastor take part in the christenings of their children.

Introduced by Stöcker at the Waldersee meeting, Willy delivered a speech pointing to religion as "the most effective protection" for the throne and lauding the court chaplain's mission as a particularly useful way of getting the working class "to recognize the authority of their legal superiors and the need for loyalty to the Monarchy." He concluded his remarks by saying that he had obtained his grandfather's and his father's permission to lend his name to Stöcker's cause—a total fabrication. The Crown Prince wrote a letter of protest to the Minister of Justice and sent Count Radolinski to Berlin to speak to his elder son. "Wilhelm," he said, "does intentionally what he knows is disagreeable to me."

It took very little time for the liberal press to jump on the political implications of the Stöcker meeting. Hurt by the adverse publicity, Willy defended Stöcker by claiming that the public outcry was purely the result of Jewish control of the papers. "When I have the say, I will not allow Jews to operate in the press!" he announced. Advised that such a decree would violate the constitution, Willy responded, "Then we shall repeal it."

Bismarck was nearly as appalled by the future Wilhelm II as his parents were. The Chancellor was no admirer of Stöcker, whom he considered a threat to his own social programs. He sent Willy a letter outlining the dangers of his activities and had articles published in the official press attacking the religious conservatives for using him. "For the sake of the Chancellor," Willy wrote his old tutor, Hintzpeter, "I have (so to speak) for years locked myself out of my parents' house. So I did not deserve such treatment."

Bismarck also made it clear that he disapproved of Willy's unseemly eagerness to ascend the throne. Anticipating the deaths of both his grandfather and his father, Willy had already drawn up exact plans for the transition of power to himself; orders "down to the tiniest detail" had been recorded and placed in his desk drawer by the end of November 1887. He was currently drafting his accession proclamation, which Bismarck advised him to burn.

IN JANUARY OF 1888, Fritz began to have great difficulty breathing, and on February 9, Bergmann's assistant Dr. Bramann performed a tracheotomy. Seven doctors were in the operating room, while Vicky, Moretta, and Vicky's brother-in-law Louis waited in the room next door. "Thank God the operation was carried out well and all went straight," Vicky wrote Victoria after it was over; "dear Fritz is dozing & I am at his bedside. Of course, he <u>cannot</u> speak! He breathes quite well now, but the sound of the air through that canula [sic] is of course very horrid! . . . I own I was in terror & agonies. . . . Poor dear, he was so good & patient & made no fuss, & I did my best to make none either! . . . Henry & Charlotte were very nice to me today." Willy, informed of his father's operation, immediately paid a call on Bismarck to ask him to be as loyal a servant to him as he had been to his grandfather.

Two days later, Dr. Bergmann arrived at the Villa Zirio with Count Radolinski, who informed the Crown Princess that "all Berlin was in the state of the wildest excitement & alarm." He himself, he said, had not expected to find the Crown Prince alive. Angered by Vicky's efforts to keep up appearances for Fritz, Radolinski told her in no uncertain terms that her husband was "irrevocably lost, that at Berlin no one thought of reckoning with him, and that he was already considered as belonging to the past!"

"I fear Count Radolinski is not acting as he ought & yet I think he is much attached to you both . . . ," Victoria wrote Vicky; "my blood boils at the infamous behaviour of those who ought to stand by & help you."

Radolinski wrote his friend Holstein at the Foreign Ministry, complaining that the Crown Princess had greeted him

> smiling as if nothing had happened. I approached her in a very serious manner and let her see very clearly that I was not pleased by her cheerful behavior. She told me that the operation was not serious, that anyone could perform it, and any child undergo it. . . . He would be completely cured in a short time since it was now quite certain that it was not cancer but a simple perichondritis,* which was not in any way malignant, and though it certainly called for much care, it was not fatal. . . . It is very easy to understand why the Crown Princess clutches at every straw, and continues to hope.

The Crown Princess's withdrawal into unrealistic optimism was supported by Mackenzie, who, Radolinski claimed, told him that the symptoms of cancer apparent in November had disappeared and that "cancer was now only a remote possibility." In early March, however, with Virchow unavailable, a second pathologist was called in, malignancy was unequivocally diagnosed, and Mackenzie admitted that he "no longer had reason to doubt" the presence of cancer. While admitting to Victoria that "it may be" cancer, Vicky refused to give up hope. Her determination to believe that Fritz still had a chance to survive, which communicated itself to him, continued to infuriate those around them, particularly the German doctors. Although we now know that a positive attitude can have a beneficial effect on the quality and length of the lives of cancer patients, this was not a popular view in Germany in the late 1880s.

One major source of friction between Mackenzie and the German doctors was a large cannula inserted after the operation into Fritz's trachea. Although it caused severe hemorrhaging, intense discomfort, and sleeplessness, the German

---

* *Inflammation of cartilage.*

physicians refused to replace it with a thinner version recommended by Mackenzie. This disagreement typified the difference in the English and German doctors and goes far toward explaining why Fritz and Vicky infinitely preferred the former, who tended to be gentler with their hands and their pronouncements. Unwilling to admit that they could have made a mistake, the German physicians insisted that the blood was coming from Fritz's lungs, going so far as to call in a lung specialist from Strasbourg, who found nothing wrong. "Surgeons have made a muddle and want to find excuse," Mackenzie reported in cryptic telegraphese to London.

On March 6, Dr. Bergmann issued a disclaimer regarding the treatment of the Crown Prince. Signed by four German doctors plus Mackenzie and Hovell, it stated that the "sole responsible treatment" for the Crown Prince "is now, as it was before the operation [biopsy], in the hands of Sir Morell Mackenzie."

The reaction of Berlin society was, according to the Secretary to the British Ambassador, "nothing less than brutal in its criticisms of the Crown Princess. It was she who had brought the English doctor, whose diagnosis had been incorrect, and had had the German doctors set aside; it was her influence which had prevailed at the outset to stop an operation which would have saved the Prince's life."

Needless to say, neither the German doctors nor the Bismarcks enlightened Vicky's accusers.

ON MARCH 8, 1888, two days after word of the Crown Prince's cancer was official, Fritz received a wire from Willy warning him that the Kaiser was very weak. The Crown Prince sent for Mackenzie.

"Would it be dangerous for me to return to Berlin at once?" he asked the doctor.

"Yes, Your Imperial Highness, it would certainly be rather dangerous."

"There are occasions when it is a man's duty to expose himself to some risk. . . . I shall go back the day after tomorrow."

But before Fritz could leave, Wilhelm I was dead. He died at eight-twenty on the morning of March 9, 1888, sitting up on his narrow camp bed in the presence of his wife, his daughter, and the future Wilhelm II.

Special sessions of the Prussian and German parliaments were called. Robert von Puttkamer, the ultraconservative Prussian Minister of the Interior and Vice President of the State Ministry, had the task of announcing the death of the Prussian King to members of the government of Prussia. His failure to follow this with an announcement of the accession of Friedrich III—followed by a similar omission by the president of the Prussian House of Deputies—was taken as an ominous sign by the liberals.

The announcement was handled far better by Bismarck: "It is my sad duty to report to you officially what you actually already know," the Chancellor told the Reichstag, "that this morning at half-past eight His Majesty Kaiser Wilhelm passed away to his fathers. As a result of this event the Prussian crown and . . .

the imperial title have passed to His Majesty Friedrich III,* King of Prussia."
At one point in his speech, the Iron Chancellor's voice broke, and he began to
sob, wiping the tears away with his hand. "One saw many serious men with
tears on their cheeks," the leader of the National Liberal Party, Johannes Mi-
guel, later reported. "We all maintained our silence. And . . . we departed, with
the awareness that a serious time could now be beginning."

AN HOUR OR SO EARLIER, Fritz, who was just starting his morning walk in the
garden of the Villa Zirio, had been handed a telegram from his elder son,
addressed to "His Majesty the German Emperor and King Friedrich Wilhelm."

"So now I have ascended the Throne of my Fathers and of the German
Emperors!" Fritz, age fifty-six, wrote in his diary. "God grant me his help in
fulfilling my duties conscientiously and for the benefit of my native Prussia and
the whole of Germany."

Members of the household of the Villa Zirio quickly gathered to greet the
new Kaiser and Kaiserin when they came into the drawing room. The man who
would now be known as Friedrich III sat down at a small table, as was traditional among Hohenzollern rulers, to write out the announcement of his own
accession. He then invested his wife with the highest honor he could bestow,
the Order of the Black Eagle. Unable to speak, he drafted the following statement, which he gave to Morell Mackenzie:

"I thank you," the new Kaiser of Germany wrote, "for having made me
live long enough to recompense the valiant courage of my wife."

---

* Fritz had always dreamed of taking the title Friedrich IV from the Holy Roman Empire. "I
alone created the German Empire," he had explained to a friend the previous year. "My father
considered it a matter of secondary importance and still treats it like that. I intervened; when
Bismarck spoke to me after Sedan . . . I bound to him the idea of the German Empire" (Patricia
Kollander, The Liberalism of Frederick III, p. 243). But Bismarck objected to the title on the
grounds that there was no connection between the Holy Roman Empire and the new German
Empire, and Fritz agreed to Friedrich III. Vicky shared Bismarck's view.

CHAPTER
FIFTY-FOUR

"The Emperor is dead, long live the dying Emperor!"

Saying in Berlin, spring 1888

MY OWN dear Empress Victoria . . . may God bless her! You know how little I care for rank or titles, but I cannot deny that after all that has been done and said, I am thankful & proud that dear Fritz & you should have come to the throne," Queen Victoria wrote Vicky on March 10, 1888, the day after Wilhelm I's death. Although the Queen acknowledged that her son-in-law must "feel deeply" the loss of his father ("my kind old friend"), she was delighted to see her middle-aged children relieved of what she called the "extraordinary & incomprehensible thraldom & tyranny" under which they had been living for thirty years. "I know how kind & good and forgiving you are," she warned Vicky, "but I beg you both to be firm & put your foot down & especially to make those of your children, who were always speaking of the Emperor and Empress to remember who they are now!"

The new Kaiserin had already reached Berlin when she received this letter. Traveling by special train—three coaches, two salon cars, one sleeping and three baggage cars—Fritz and Vicky arrived on Sunday night, March 11, 1888, shortly after 11:00 P.M. Their train pulled into the Westend station, the one closest to the palace of Charlottenburg where they had decided to live.

Citizens of Berlin had been gathering for hours, braving a heavy snowfall and icy winds that roared through what was in those days the outskirts of the city to take up positions around the railway station and along the road leading to the palace. The bad weather delayed the train by nearly half an hour, but, as the newspaper *Kreuzzeitung* (pro-royal if not pro–Friedrich III) reported, few of the thousands waiting were willing to go home. "We are not leaving here even if it takes until early morning and we can see the imperial carriage only in the distance," one stalwart was quoted as saying. "Our Fritz *[unser Fritz]* deserves that we should get our feet cold and wet for him," said another.

A pavilion had been erected to protect the sick man from the storm. Lined in red and laid with rugs, it had been decorated with palms and flowers, lit with candelabra, and furnished with gilded chairs bearing the imperial eagle. Willy and Dona, Charlotte and her husband, Bernhard, and Henry had all arrived at the station an hour ahead of time. When the train finally pulled in, they boarded it to greet their parents.

Wearing a long gray army coat with fur collar and a cap on his head, a gaunt Friedrich III of Germany stepped off the train and hurried through the tent to a closed carriage, which drove him to Charlottenburg. The imperial carriage was preceded and followed by soldiers on horseback from the Gardes du Corps. The people in the crowd took off their hats, waved them in the falling snow, and cheered.

Although Vicky said that she was "glad to think that my beloved Fritz has the satisfaction of feeling that he is at home," she told Victoria that the journey had been a "great risk and a great fatigue." Fritz had spent a bad night on the train, and the doctors ordered him to stay in bed the next day. The lovely eighteenth-century palace of Charlottenburg had been chosen over their home in the heart of Berlin because it was larger and more out of the way. Or, as Vicky put it, "the people cannot look in at the windows."

EVEN BEFORE his arrival in Berlin, the new Kaiser had begun consultations with Bismarck and the ministers of his father's cabinet, whom he had asked to meet his train in Leipzig. Curious citizens standing in the Leipzig station noted that the Chancellor entered the imperial carriage first, and, since the windows had no curtains, they could see Friedrich III step forward to greet his old foe, whom he kissed three times. The ministers were then asked in for a short conference, during which the Kaiser, unable to speak, wrote his remarks on a pad of paper. These gentlemen later told how disturbed they were by the sound of their monarch's breathing as it gurgled and whistled through the cannula in his neck. After they returned to their own train, which took them back to Berlin, Bismarck and Herbert remained with the new Kaiser and Kaiserin.

Frederick III handed the Chancellor copies of a proclamation and a letter, the first addressed "To My People" the other to the Chancellor himself. Published in the paper the next day, these two "beautifully written" (Bismarck's description) documents had been drafted nearly three years before, in 1885, at the time everyone expected Wilhelm I to die. They were the work of several of Fritz's personal advisers: General Stosch; Baron Roggenbach, liberal counselor to Fritz's brother-in-law, the Grand Duke of Baden; Heinrich Friedberg, Minister of Justice and a personal friend of the new Kaiser; Ernest von Stockmar; and Heinrich Geffcken, a friend of Fritz's since university days and an outspoken critic of Bismarck. The Chancellor asked the monarch for time to study them.

But, as Bismarck soon discovered, there was nothing in either the proclamation or the letter to cause him alarm. Originally drafted when the future Kaiser thought he had plenty of time to effect reforms, replace ministers, and change the underlying philosophy of the government, they were aimed at conciliating Bismarck and the princes of the other German states, many of whom were notorious reactionaries. Now Fritz was a dying man, and the documents, which acknowledged the necessity for continuity in government and Bismarck's enormous contributions to Germany, read less like a soothing prelude to reform than a tragic irony.

Expressing his gratitude to Bismarck as "the faithful and brave adviser who gave shape" and "realisation" to his father's policies, Friedrich III said that the Chancellor had "a right to know" certain principles that would guide the new regime—respect for constitutional law, the welfare of the general public as the basis of government, and adherence to the doctrine of religious tolerance for all Germans, regardless of "religious community or creed." These concerns were unusual for a Hohenzollern monarch, but no more so than Fritz's personal credo, stated in the last sentence of his letter to the Chancellor: "Not caring for the splendor of great deeds, nor striving for glory, I shall be satisfied if it be one day said of my rule that it was beneficial to my people, useful to my country and a blessing to the Empire."

Vicky, who thought the documents "very good, & prudent," explained to her mother that circumstances were "so peculiar" that her husband could not "come forward with a 'profession de foi' [profession of faith, i.e., liberal faith] as he would if he were well!" She was considerably amused at Bismarck's surprise when Fritz presented the proclamation and letter to him and believed that they "produced the right impression." Clearly they did.

"I feel relieved of the great concern I had that I would have to fight with a dying man against inappropriate intentions even to the point of demanding my release from office," Bismarck told his cabinet two days later. "In view of his earlier utterances in younger years, there was reason to fear he would pursue all kinds of deviant aims—but I do not fear that any more!"

In spite of this statement, Bismarck continued to claim that his decision to stay on as Chancellor after the death of Wilhelm I had been based on Fritz's promise made in the summer of 1885 not to press for a more democratic domestic government or a pro-English foreign policy. Had the Chancellor really extracted a promise of business as usual from Fritz at that time, there would have been no need for the apprehension he expressed before reading the documents. The one thing that Bismarck and everyone else knew about Friedrich III was that once he had made a promise, however distasteful, he would never go back on it.

What distressed Vicky now was the painful contrast between her dying husband, aged fifty-six, and the Chancellor, who at nearly seventy-three seemed amazingly healthy. Although Bismarck had taken his personal physician with him to the meeting in Leipzig, Vicky observed a few days later that the Chancellor was "not a bit shaky. I never saw him looking stronger . . . hale . . . rosy in the face. . . . He seems well disposed," she told her mother, "& we do all we can to keep him so."

Bismarck had little reason not to respond in kind. The day after Wilhelm I's death, he had asked Dr. Bergmann how long Friedrich III had to live. Bergmann replied that he would not survive the summer. Faced with what Bismarck described to the French Ambassador as "a feminine interregnum of a few months," he must have decided not to antagonize the dying man and to cover long-standing enmities with a civilized veneer—at least for a while. The same could not be said of his son Herbert, the Secretary of State, who told his close friend at the Foreign Ministry, Bernhard von Bülow, "The Emperor's fate . . . affects my father deeply, but I on the contrary regard his death as good fortune. The influence his wife has over him and her totally English outlook would, if the Emperor were to reign long, bring us to dependence on England and that would mean the greatest possible disaster for our foreign and, especially for our internal policy."

Herbert was not the only person in Berlin who could scarcely wait for the ailing Kaiser to die. "It is very evident that all sorts of intrigues were going on before he [Fritz] came back . . . ," Vicky wrote Victoria; "most people supposed Fritz would return merely to resign! Underlying everything is the belief that the present reign will only last a very few months."

FUNERAL SERVICES for Wilhelm I did not take place until a week after his death. Meanwhile, he lay in state in the Berlin cathedral, an ugly building far too small to accommodate the thousands who came to pay their respects. Insufficient space plus jurisdictional disputes among court authorities, police, and the military made it difficult to determine who qualified for admittance. Taking their cue from Crown Prince Wilhelm, now in conspicuous ascendance, officers of the army demanded priority, claiming precedence over ordinary citizens, nonmilitary organizations, and some 400,000 pilgrims from around the empire. Things got so muddled that members of the Reichstag, having made arrangements for entrance with the Court Chamberlain, were unceremoniously turned back by the police in order to make way for an insignificant group of soldiers. Once having gained admittance to the area, people were dangerously crowded, making it difficult to breathe freely or move one's arms. Mourners were also forced to defend themselves against a small army of professional pickpockets who had descended on the cathedral from around Europe.

The citizens of Berlin voted to spend 600,000 marks on decorating their city for the last rites of Germany's first Kaiser, and the route of the cortege down both sides of Unter den Linden through the Brandenburg Gate was lined with burning torches set on top of black pillars connected with festoons of black crepe and evergreens. Leading the procession were eight squadrons of cavalry, a body of infantry, and three military bands. The carriage bearing Wilhelm's casket was drawn by black-draped horses and protected by a black-embroidered yellow silk canopy held aloft by twelve army generals from the Franco-Prussian War. Following the casket was the traditional riderless horse, the widowed Empress Augusta (long since confined to a wheelchair), and, in place of his father, Crown Prince Wilhelm. Wearing the uniform of a general, Willy led more than one hundred other princes, German and foreign—including his uncle the Prince of Wales (later Edward VII), the Czarevitch of Russia (later Czar Nicholas II), and Crown Prince Rudolph of Austria—plus members of the diplomatic corps, parliament, universities, and other institutions, all protected from the spectators by the "rather over-zealous" Berlin police.

Once it had filed down the snow-covered Unter den Linden and under the Brandenburg Gate, the cortege proceeded through the Tiergarten to the mausoleum at Charlottenburg. It passed under the Kaiser's window, where Friedrich III, wearing a general's dress uniform and the Order of the Black Eagle, stood at attention. "That is where I ought to be now," Fritz told Morell Mackenzie, who watched at his side.

"On account of the bitter weather Fritz could not leave his room" Vicky wrote Victoria, "& I was unable to be with him at the sad moment. When the hearse passed close under his window he quite broke down. . . . Directly afterwards we went to him & he was calm again and is now resting a little in bed."

IN THE TRADITION of Hohenzollern rulers, one of Friedrich III's first acts was to reward with titles and decorations those who had made special contributions to Germany and/or shown particular loyalty to him. He offered Bismarck the chance to become a duke and Herbert a prince, both of which the Chancellor refused. "Sure, and if I had two million thaler, I should have myself made pope!" Bismarck remarked to his ministers. Still, the Kaiser raised Herbert to the status of minister, much to the irritation of the cabinet. "At the moment, whenever the big bowwow is not actually attending a session, we can at least grouse to our hearts' content," one explained. "But that will have to stop if his son is listening."

The Kaiser also raised his Court Chamberlain, Count Radolinski, to the status of prince. Radolinski's relationship with Fritz and Vicky continued to be an ambivalent one. At the same time that the Court Chamberlain reported everything the Kaiserin did to Holstein, his spymaster at the Foreign Ministry, he let it be known that he had inserted a clause in his will stipulating that if his own son did not survive him, Fritz and Vicky's son Henry was to inherit part of his estate.*

Fritz also conferred the rank of field marshal on his Chief of Staff during the Franco-Prussian War, General von Blumenthal. It was a generous act, considering that Blumenthal had, in a letter to his wife that had been published, claimed all the credit for Fritz's accomplishments in the war.

Having bestowed on Vicky the Order of the Black Eagle immediately on his accession, Friedrich III also offered the same honor to Minister of Justice Heinrich Friedberg, an adviser for over a quarter of a century. Conservatives and members of the court were appalled, for Friedberg was a commoner and a converted Jew. Moreover, since commoners could not receive the Black Eagle,

---

* According to Holstein, Willy resented the bequest and told Radolinski that his brother would be "a rich man in any case, but he, Wilhelm had nothing to live on." Therefore Radolinski ought to "bequeath everything to him" (Holstein, Vol. II, p. 355).

Friedberg had to be ennobled by adding the all-important "von" before his name. The same was true of Dr. Eduard Simson, who had served as president of the Frankfurt Assembly in 1848, first president of the Reichstag, and was currently the presiding judge of the supreme court.

One of the new Kaiser's most vociferous critics was Willy's friend General von Waldersee. Waldersee disapproved of the conferral of the Black Eagle on the new Kaiserin, but managed to shrug it off: "Like the bestowal of all Orders on women," he said, it "is a matter of mere trifling." The ennoblement of Friedberg, however, carried sinister implications for the Fatherland. "He is regarded by the Liberals as one of their own men, and he is of Jewish origin; I believe indeed he has remained a Jew. The bestowal therefore suggests a programme: it is an open attempt to win favour with the Liberals and the Jews."

Waldersee's reaction was typical of the ultraconservatives, who referred among themselves to their new Kaiser as "Cohn I, King of the Jews." Slurs like this were not echoed in the Bismarck press, which for once, according to a leading Berliner, seemed to have "more tact and feeling of decency . . . than the upper ten thousand." At the same time, Bismarck used the Kaiser's honors list to pillory the Kaiserin with the already nervous members of his cabinet, waving it before them as an example of how their new Kaiser's wife was pulling strings to undermine them, their policies, and their positions. This was not the last time during her husband's reign that Bismarck would use Vicky to his own advantage without her being aware of what he was doing.

At the beginning, however, Bismarck made certain to appear as the dutiful servant of her dying husband, welcoming Friedrich III in the official press as the noble embodiment of "the national idea of the empire," a true Hohenzollern who had "struggled manfully with and heroically withstood the insidious disease" and had done his duty by returning immediately to Berlin. As to the new Kaiserin, the Chancellor told his Minister of Agriculture, Robert Lucius, that he was treating her "like an infatuated graybeard."

An extract from Vicky's memoirs proves that Bismarck was successful. Grateful that he was careful not to overtax a dying man, she later wrote that Bismarck "was particularly kind and pleasant . . . came to see Fritz often and was considerate and easy to associate with."

This was at the beginning.

But sometime between March 13, when Bismarck told the ministers of his cabinet, "Everything is going easily and pleasantly with his majesty," and March 22, when he frightened them by saying that under the new regime their positions were "most seriously in question," Bismarck must have decided that Fritz and Vicky, particularly the latter, would be more useful to him in an adversarial position. One historian ascribes this reversal to Fritz's refusal to rubber-stamp Bismarck's requests. Another points to political rumblings beneath the surface, to problems Bismarck was just beginning to comprehend vis-à-vis Willy. Both are correct, but neither takes into account how Bismarck purposefully destroyed what little was left of Vicky's reputation to serve his own ends. As his biographer, Otto Pflanze, observed:

The tension that developed between palace and chancellery during the short reign of Friedrich III cannot be dismissed as the work of his wife. Nor can Bismarck's effort in the public press to establish a contradiction between the good German Kaiser and the bad English Kaiserin be accepted as anything but a caricature. That Victoria may have tried too hard to shield her dying husband from unnecessary distresses and burdens is probable. But there is no evidence that she did not interpret or relay correctly her husband's wishes. Nor can it be assumed that Kaiser Friedrich, had he been blessed with a longer reign, would have been able to retain Bismarck for long as chancellor. . . . the Bismarck government could not have lasted with Friedrich on the throne.

The immediate causes of disagreement between Kaiser and Chancellor were two bills that had been passed by the Reichstag during Wilhelm I's reign but did not come up for the monarch's signature until after his death. The first was an extension of the antisocialist law, aimed at expelling the Social Democrats from parliament. The second was a constitutional amendment changing the period between elections from three years to five, thus retaining the current conservative, pro-Bismarck coalition in the Reichstag for another two years. Many liberals, notably Minister of Justice Friedberg, thought these bills had been rammed through the Reichstag with undue coercion. Both undercut the last hope of liberalization entertained by the new Kaiser and his wife. With a pathetically small amount of time left to change the course of German history, Fritz tried to find some legal way around signing them.

The most logical argument, the one put forward by the liberal press, maintained that since these bills, like all legislation in Prussia and Germany, rested on the authority of the sovereign and began with his name—"We, Wilhelm, by the Grace of God King of Prussia and German Kaiser, do proclaim . . ."—they ceased to be valid on the death of the stated authority and had to be brought up again for debate. On the strength of this, Fritz requested time to think over his position before committing himself.

Bismarck, who had encountered minimal opposition from Wilhelm I, was not pleased by this expression of independence from his successor. On March 21, he drove out to Charlottenburg, where he was received by Vicky. "I had a special opportunity of experiencing the Chancellor's claws!" she wrote later about their encounter, during which Bismarck threatened to resign if her husband did not sign the two bills. Bismarck started the discussion by telling the Kaiserin that the Kaiser "had no right to refuse" and was "exceeding his prerogatives." When that line of reasoning failed, he pulled out his trump card —the future Wilhelm II—and explained at some length what might happen to Willy and Germany "if the Government resigned, which it would have to do if the Emperor [Friedrich III] refused his signature."

Frightened by visions of the volatile, warmongering Willy marching at the head of a German Empire unrestrained by Bismarck, Vicky capitulated. If Fritz's "signature has to be given according to the Constitution, it would doubtless be given immediately." She suggested that Prince Bismarck explain to her husband "how the matter stood," and she was sure that "it would be put right at once."

On that same day, Bismarck also managed to obtain Fritz's signature to a document authorizing Crown Prince Wilhelm to sign certain bills for his father. In Prussia almost everything down to the least army promotion had to be signed by the king, and since the death of Wilhelm I, less than two weeks earlier, over five hundred official documents had accumulated for signature. Fritz had worked his way through one hundred of these on the train from Leipzig to Berlin, but the doctors could already see how the first few days of constant decisions and endless audiences had "quite exhausted" the dying man.

The question of finding a deputy to sign less important papers for Friedrich III had been raised earlier, and Vicky had offered herself as the logical choice. Although Bismarck made no objections in her presence, he disparaged her behind her back, agreeing with Prince Henry that "Hohenzollern Prussia and the German Reich must not allow themselves to be led by a woman." The new Kaiserin was difficult to convince, however, and it was not until her brother Bertie, in Berlin for Wilhelm I's funeral, told her that she must not press the issue that she acquiesced in favor of her elder son.

The deputization, as finally written, was a face-saving one, stating that it was important for the Kaiser to familiarize the Crown Prince with affairs of state and that the choice of papers passed on to him would remain with his father. Still, as one chronicler* of the day astutely pointed out, for the Kaiser to give up his signature even on minor papers like army commissions and civil promotions was a sign of defeat in a hierarchical society where royal appointments were front-page news and every new preferment and nonpreferment was carefully studied for its political and social implications.

"I think people in general consider us a mere passing shadow, soon to be replaced by reality in the shape of William!" Vicky wrote Victoria the week after her husband's accession. "I may be wrong, but it seems to me as if the party that opposed & ill-treated us so long hardly think it worth while to change their attitude except very slightly, as they count on a different future."

The centerpiece of that future was Crown Prince Wilhelm, who spoke about his father only to criticize him or use him as a springboard to self-aggrandizement. Henry, who lived in his brother's shadow, supported Willy, as did Charlotte, anxious to assume a more powerful place in the sun. "I have no words to express my indignation & astonishment about the conduct of your three children," Queen Victoria wrote her daughter at the end of March. "This must not be allowed. . . . I think you ought to send for them and threaten strong measures if it goes on! William with his odious, ungrateful wife should be sent to travel. Send them . . . to see the world. Henry I should send to sea."

But Willy, backed by Waldersee and an ever-burgeoning coterie of ambitious position-seekers, was left in Berlin, where he waited breathlessly to assume his father's place and denounced his mother, who, he told a friend, had "be-

* *J. Alden Nichols, in* The Year of the Three Kaisers.

smirched" Germany and "brought [it] to the brink of ruin." When Willy showed Waldersee the cable he had received from his father after Wilhelm I's death, the two agreed that Friedrich III's words were proof of the new Kaiser's utter disregard for his son. "In deep grief over the death of my father, at which it was not granted to me, though it was to you, to be present," Friedrich III had wired the new Crown Prince, "I express my confidence, on coming to the throne, that you will be an example to all of fidelity and obedience!" This cable, according to Waldersee, passed "beyond all bounds in its frigidity."

It was Willy's wife, Dona, who constantly encouraged Waldersee to "help" the Crown Prince with his counsel. Both Dona and Waldersee knew that the road to Willy's heart lay in attacking Willy's parents. The day after Wilhelm I's death, Waldersee told Willy that whereas they had all assumed that "it would be a misfortune" if Willy's father survived his grandfather, they may have been wrong. The new Kaiser and Kaiserin, Waldersee assured his friend, "would do so many foolish things that the ground would be prepared" for Willy "in the best way." All the Crown Prince needed to do was bide his time and remain in the background.

But making himself unconspicuous was hardly Willy's forte. On April 1, Bismarck celebrated his seventy-third birthday. The Crown Prince, who had invited himself to the Chancellor's party, had prepared a toast to the Chancellor that was a direct insult to his father. Comparing Germany to an army corps "that has lost its commanding officer [Wilhelm I] on the battlefield and whose first officer [Friedrich III] is badly wounded," Willy raised his glass to the man he called the bearer of the German flag—"our illustrious prince, our great chancellor." It was to Bismarck, Willy said, that "46,000,000 true German hearts turned in anxiety and hope. . . . He goes before us, we follow him!"

"Well," said the editor of the *Norddeutsche Allgemeine Zeitung,* "and isn't Friedrich then also the commanding officer? . . . it is not nice for the son to emphasize his father's severe illness that way." The Kaiser himself was clearly hurt. "You have probably not considered how lacking in loyalty it sounds to describe the minister, at the expense of the monarch, as the only active force in the government," he wrote his elder son. It was said that Bismarck helped Willy doctor the official printed version released after the fact so as to change the offensive insinuation, but, as the Chancellor knew better than anyone, the implication had taken root and the damage had been accomplished.

Riding high and enjoying himself immensely, Bismarck continued to believe he could keep Crown Prince Wilhelm under control. Meanwhile, he took every opportunity provided by the dying Kaiser and frightened Kaiserin to frustrate their wishes and manipulate them for the preservation of his personal glory. As one member of the British Embassy staff put it, "There was . . . through all this grim period . . . a conspicuous absence of chivalry at Berlin."

CHAPTER
FIFTY-FIVE

"For him [Bismarck] politics was a game in which the greatest mistake consisted in not using and abusing the advantages which the clumsiness of one's adversary had put within one's reach."

PRINCESS CATHERINE RADZIWILL

*I*F THERE WERE minor skirmishes between Vicky and Bismarck during the early days of Fritz's reign, the major battle that pitched the Kaiserin against the Chancellor in a prolonged crisis of conflicting egos was the still unresolved question of the Battenberg marriage. Within days of Wilhelm I's death, it was clear that Vicky had been waiting only for her husband to accede to the throne to force the marriage through. As in the past, the Battenberg match was a poor place for the new Kaiserin to take a stand.

In the first place, Sandro had lost interest in Moretta. Denied a commission in the German army, he had settled in Darmstadt a year and a half before Friedrich III's accession and had fallen in love with a young opera singer. When he received a letter from Vicky, written immediately after Wilhelm I's death, saying that she was planning to ask her husband to settle his marriage to Moretta, he was horrified.

The situation had changed, Sandro wrote back. Four years ago he had been a ruling prince with a respectable income; now he was a poor man with no position. Moreover, as the Kaiserin knew better than anyone, a union with Moretta would be opposed by the future Wilhelm II, who would destroy his sister's life if she married him. Along with this letter to Vicky, Sandro wrote his brother Liko, Queen Victoria's son-in-law, asking him to get the Queen to point out to her daughter the difficulties of a marriage opposed by the future Kaiser. Victoria complied:

I can understand how, with the painful uncertainty which dear Fritz's health causes you, you should wish to settle and arrange everything that is of importance, but do <u>not</u> <u>too</u> suddenly alter things and above all do not carry out anything which is in <u>direct</u> opposition to the poor departed Emperor's wishes, I mean for instance the projected marriage of Moretta with Sandro. Above all do <u>not</u> even contemplate such a step <u>without</u> the <u>perfect</u> <u>acquiescence</u> of William. You <u>must</u> <u>reckon</u> <u>with</u> <u>him</u>, as he is Crown Prince, and it <u>would</u> <u>never</u> do to contract a marriage which he would not agree to. It would simply bring misery on your daughter and Sandro.

But Vicky would not give up. Frustrated in all her other dreams—the dismissal of Bismarck, the establishment of parliamentary democracy, revenge over those who had treated her so badly for so long—she convinced herself and Fritz that Moretta's heart would be broken if she could not have her Sandro. On March 31, 1888, the Kaiser informed the Chancellor that he intended to give Sandro an army command and that the former Prince of Bulgaria was coming to Berlin in a few days to become engaged to his daughter Moretta.

Hardly surprised by this news (General von Winterfeld, Friedrich III's aide-de-camp and one of Bismarck's informants, had already told him), the Chancellor met with the Kaiser and told him that the marriage was "impossible!" If Friedrich III reversed his position on the match, Bismarck said, it would look as if Germany was changing its foreign policy vis-à-vis Russia. If His Majesty persisted in making Sandro his son-in-law, Bismarck would be forced to resign.

"What to do?" Fritz wrote on his pad.

"Telegraph him not to come," Bismarck answered.

Fritz wrote out the telegram and gave it to Radolinski to send. As he was giving the Court Chamberlain his instructions, Vicky, who had apparently been outside waiting for Bismarck to leave, came into the room. Her husband, she said with tears in her eyes, must not break their daughter's heart.

Fritz apparently tried to calm Vicky, but she would not be assuaged. They may or may not have argued. It was alleged by one courtier that the Kaiser "jumped up in great agitation, tore the bandage from his throat and tried to speak, but only the words 'Leave me alone!' were clear." In another's version, he "stamped his foot and pointed to the door, at which the Kaiserin retired as white as a sheet."* After she left the room, he wrote his instructions for the Chancellor on his pad: "Battenberg will not come now, submit memorandum [i.e., a memorandum on the Battenberg marriage], discuss the matter with my wife."

Back at the Foreign Ministry, Holstein chortled over the contretemps. "The Battenberg struggle is in full swing . . . ," he wrote in his diary. "I am not particularly impressed by the Kaiserin's behaviour in this affair. On the other hand the danger of such a marriage so far as Russia is concerned is not so great

---

* The reports on this scene come from Holstein's diaries, meaning that they originated with Radolinski and Holstein's other informers at court. In Radolinski's version, Vicky grew "more and more violent," while Radolinski begged her "to think of the Kaiser's health" and the Kaiser "rent his clothes, wept, tore his hair" and "gasped for breath"—an unlikely performance from a monarch who prided himself on preserving his sangfroid in the presence of others (Holstein, Vol. II, p. 366). There was certainly a disagreement, possibly even an argument, although neither Fritz nor Vicky would have considered it proper to fight in front of others, and there is no indication of their having done so at any other time. Holstein himself said that the "accounts I was given by Bismarck and by informants at the Court . . . certainly did not tally; to say the least, they diverged rather widely" (Holstein, Vol. I, p. 141).

as the Chancellor makes it appear. The Chancellor wants to use this opportunity of winning back the position of trust he formerly enjoyed with the Crown Prince [Willy], before the Stöcker affair."

Holstein was right on both counts. In the first place, Russia no longer cared what happened to Sandro. When queried, the Russian Foreign Minister said that the marriage would in no way endanger the relationship between the two countries, while the Pan-Slav press claimed that the match between the former Prince of Bulgaria and the German Princess would actually *help* the Russians by keeping Sandro out of Bulgaria. The Russians were, if anything, amused by the discomfiture of the German Chancellor.

Bismarck's insistence on preventing the marriage was, as Holstein accurately pointed out, primarily an effort to impress Willy. This must have been obvious to Vicky, who also knew that the Chancellor was playing for time— until Fritz was replaced on the throne by her son, who hated Battenberg. Frustrated beyond reason, she wrote "a crazy letter" to Sandro, in which she talked of a secret marriage, a flight from Germany, and a commission for Sandro in the Austro-Hungarian army. She summoned Radolinski to tell him that Moretta and Sandro's engagement would take place the following week and that he should make the necessary arrangements. Radolinski contacted Willy.

"I will make things unpleasant for my mother," the Crown Prince said; "I will take it out of my parents for this." He went to Bismarck, who dictated a "very biting" letter for him to sign, aimed at frightening Sandro off. "I shall regard everyone who works for this marriage not only as an enemy of my House but also of my country, and will deal with him accordingly," the future Wilhelm II warned the Battenberg Prince.

Willy was obsessed with Sandro's morganatic lineage. "The worst thing," he wrote his friend Philipp zu Eulenburg, "is the feeling of deep shame for the sunken prestige of my house, which always stood so gleaming and unassailable! But yet more intolerable is that our family escutcheon should be bespotted and the Reich brought to the brink of ruin by the English princess who is my mother!"

Meanwhile, in response to the Kaiser's request for a memorandum on the subject, Bismarck marshaled thirty pages of arguments against the marriage, starting with his own threat of resignation, elaborating on all the old reasons that the match would jeopardize Germany's relations with Russia, and adding two new scenarios to frighten the Kaiser: first, that Sandro would return to Bulgaria to march at the head of the Bulgarian army;* second, that he would be called to eastern Europe as a candidate for the throne of Poland! In both, marriage to the daughter of Friedrich III would force Germany to take up arms against Russia. The memorandum concluded with a postscript saying that if Friedrich III and his wife received Sandro at court, it would be viewed as a political statement in support of England.

---

* *Sandro had repeatedly refused to return to Bulgaria, and Ferdinand of Coburg had been on the throne for nearly a year.*

Bismarck next saw Vicky. But in this meeting, held at Fritz's request, the Chancellor took an entirely new tack. He did not reject the idea of a marriage between Moretta and Sandro, only spoke vaguely about arranging something in the future. He told the Kaiserin that although he was forced to take an official position against the match, he personally did not care if the young couple married or not. All he asked from her was to agree to a postponement. As a gesture of reconciliation, he offered to get nine million marks released from Wilhelm I's estate to settle on Fritz and Vicky's three younger daughters for their dowries.

As Bismarck well knew, Wilhelm I had kept his heir in a position of complete financial dependence and had refused to provide for the three younger princesses, using money as the ultimate control and threatening to disinherit Moretta if she married Sandro. Fritz's major worry since the onset of his cancer had been what would happen to his wife and younger children if he died before his inheritance from his father could be settled.

Presented with a way to marry Moretta to Sandro, give her two younger daughters a chance to marry whomever they chose, and settle Fritz's mind regarding their future, Vicky agreed to postpone the issue. She asked Fritz to add a clause to his will, instructing Willy to acquiesce in the marriage—which he did. "I count on you to fulfill your duty as my son by complying with my wish," Friedrich III wrote the future Wilhelm II.

This conversation between the Kaiserin and the Chancellor should have ended the controversy over the Battenberg marriage, but it did not. Having come to an understanding with Vicky—the Chancellor boasted to a journalist that the Kaiserin was "enchanted" with him—Bismarck now told her that they must appear before the outside world to continue their quarrel. Misled by his apparent sympathy, Vicky agreed to do as he asked—in essence giving him carte blanche to cast her as a villain.

That same day, Bismarck had an item inserted in one of the Berlin papers saying that there was a rumor that the Chancellor was "about to hand in his resignation" over what was coyly referred to as a "secret conflict." The next edition of the paper narrowed the mystery down to questions of "a family nature." A follow-up article reported that there was a great excitement in "diplomatic circles" due to Prince Bismarck's intention of resigning over the possibility of a marriage between Moretta and the Battenberg Prince. According to a "reliable source," both Battenberg and Queen Victoria were planning to come to Berlin, where the Queen would act the role of "matchmaker." Germany, the article continued, must preserve her disinterest regarding Bulgaria and thus the trust of both Russia and Austria. "This trust would naturally be destroyed with a single blow . . . if the most hated personal enemy of the tsar became the son-in-law of the German Kaiser." This fact must be evident to "any German who loves his fatherland."

Once he had set the public press in motion, Bismarck turned to his private propagandist, Moritz Busch. "I would suggest to you to take the present opportunity of . . . showing how England has at all times sought and still seeks to influence us for her own ends. . . . always emphasize the fact that it is foreign influences that are working against me; not the emperor, but the reigning lady and her mother."

There were several political benefits Bismarck hoped to extract from this carefully orchestrated crisis over his bogus resignation. First, there was the strengthening of the Reichstag cartel, currently under attack by the Conservative and Center parties over a bill that would strengthen state schools at the expense of the churches. What better way to bring these elements back into the fold than by dangling the possibility of a new liberal chancellor before them?

A second and greater benefit was increased tension between Germany and England. To keep the friction going the Chancellor cabled his Ambassador in London that the "Battenberg marriage project with our princess is again being more actively promoted from the English side and personally through Her Majesty Queen Victoria." He instructed his representative to warn Lord Salisbury* that if the marriage took place, Germany would alter her policy "necessarily and permanently" toward Russia and against England. He had Herbert warn the British Ambassador that Germany believed Queen Victoria could stop the marriage and if she did not do so, her refusal would be looked on as "an unfriendly act" toward Germany.

"I am very sorry not to be able to comply with Prince Bismarck's wishes," Salisbury replied. "But he asks me to assist him in thwarting the wishes of his Emperor and my Queen, in order to gratify the malignant feelings of the Emperor of Russia. This would be certainly inconsistent with my duty; and if German cooperation cannot be had except at this price, we must do without it."

Warned by the British Ambassador not even to risk a proposed visit to Berlin to see her dying son-in-law, Victoria refused to be intimidated. Bismarck, she said, was "really disloyal, wicked and really unwise in the extreme! . . . Russia really <u>cannot</u> care a <u>straw</u> about Prince Alexander's marriage. . . . How Bismarck and still more William <u>can</u> play such a double game it is impossible for us honest, straightforward English to understand."

On April 4, the Prince of Wales, who deplored the "great hubbub in the press," received a letter from the British military attaché in Berlin, saying that the upper echelon of German bureaucrats were behaving "as if the last spark of honour and faithful duty had gone. . . . It seems as if a curse had come over this country, leaving but one bright spot and that is where stands a solitary woman doing her duty faithfully and tenderly by her sick husband against all odds. It is one of the most, if not <u>the</u> most, tragic episodes in a country and a life ever recorded in history."

Six days later, Mary Ponsonby received a letter from her husband, Victoria's private secretary, which adds a new and curious element to the situation: "So many conversations go on about this marriage affair that one gets bothered . . . ," Henry Ponsonby complained;

---

* *Gladstone's successor, serving as both Prime Minister and Foreign Secretary.*

rumour at Berlin said that old Bismarck had for some time been bored with the love story till he discovered that Herbert was in love with Princess Victoria [Moretta]. He was rather pleased with the idea. Herbert tells everyone he intends to marry Victoria and the Empress having heard this is determined to get the marriage with Sandro completed. Herbert therefore stirred up Crown Prince William, has managed to drag in the Russian Scare, and has met the Empress' move by telling the newspapers that his father will resign if the marriage takes place. . . . Sandro's love had certainly cooled. But he won't stand being insulted by William or cut out by Bismarck, so he is now full of fire again.

Vicky, led down the garden path by Bismarck, wrote her mother on the same day: "I do not wonder that you should have been startled and alarmed . . . by the senseless, ridiculous and violent storm in the press. . . . If you knew why all this row was made, you would see more clearly that the reason was a futile one! Our relations with the Chancellor never have been more cordial or agreeable." Three days earlier, she had also written the Queen to "pay no attention to the newspapers—there is no Chancellor Crisis—All this row is made for a purpose, & is really very silly."

What purpose? What could Bismarck possibly have said to Vicky to give her this false sense of security in the face of such a carefully crafted campaign of hate? Surely it was not the financial settlement on her daughters, which he had only accelerated, or the specter of Herbert, an unlikely candidate for Moretta's hand.

There are two more compelling explanations for Vicky's complicity in allowing the Chancellor to prolong the crisis that was so damaging to her personally. The first was the fear of a regency, which would have taken the heart out of her dying husband. This was an ongoing threat brandished by the conservatives, who continued to insist that a kaiser without a voice is no kaiser at all. Bismarck would not have scrupled to use it any more than he hesitated to play the Willy card in the matter of the Kaiser's signature on the Reichstag bills.

A second explanation is Vicky's concern about her elder son. Although we will never know for certain, we can guess that Bismarck may well have told the Kaiserin that he must appear to oppose the marriage in order to keep the Crown Prince on his side, away from his pious, warmongering friends like Waldersee and Stöcker. If the Chancellor allowed himself to appear to acquiesce in the matter of the marriage, Willy would turn permanently to the extreme right for support, and Germany would be lost. The one way for Bismarck to seduce the future Wilhelm II to the side of reason was for him to publicly oppose Battenberg. It would have been an extremely persuasive argument.

In line with this explanation is the fact that one of Friedrich III's earliest acts, apparently set in motion by Bismarck, was to order the chief of the military cabinet to get Willy's hawkish friend Waldersee out of Berlin by appointing him to a command in Hanover. Although the plan was thwarted by Moltke, the fact remains that the Chancellor and the Kaiserin did have one common concern—

the volatility and bellicosity of the man who would soon be in a position to plunge Germany into war. An awareness of her son's instability would surely have made Vicky acquiesce to almost anything Bismarck suggested.

By making an issue out of the Battenberg marriage project and convincing the Kaiserin to allow him to maintain it at crisis level, Bismarck managed to keep all the disparate elements of the German court and government under his control—the Kaiser and Kaiserin, the Crown Prince, the conservatives, and the members of the Reichstag. The price was one he was only too happy to pay— the reputation, both with her contemporaries and with history, of the unfortunate Kaiserin.

CHAPTER
FIFTY-SIX

"I must get well. I have so much to do."

FRIEDRICH III OF GERMANY

O N THE NIGHT OF APRIL 12, *1888*, Vicky's husband took a turn for the worse. Tormented by incessant coughing, he wrote in his diary that he began to notice a "peculiar sound" in his throat, which felt as if it had contracted. The difficulty was apparently caused by cancer cells that had begun to grow around the inside end of the cannula, narrowing the space through which he could breathe. Before inserting a new cannula, Mackenzie sent for the Kaiser's official surgeon, Ernst von Bergmann. From this point on, there are two opposing versions of the story.

Bergmann said that he arrived to find the Kaiser "in a state of suffocation." A rasping sound caused by the obstruction "could be heard in the next room," according to the surgeon, who said that Fritz's cheeks and lips had turned blue and that it seemed to him the Kaiser would die "in a few minutes."

Showing Mackenzie the apparatus he had brought—"large blunt hooks" that he claimed Mackenzie "specially admired"—Bergmann held open the Kaiser's trachea while his assistant inserted a new cannula. According to Bergmann, Friedrich III expressed his immediate relief by "joyful movements and by grateful pressure of our hands." There was moderate bleeding attached to the procedure.

This was Bergmann's story.

Mackenzie's was different: After a bad night, during which Dr. Hovell had adjusted the Kaiser's cannula several times, Mackenzie said he wanted to try a tube with another kind of curve. Since this constituted a change in treatment, he called Bermann out of medical courtesy, asking him to come "as <u>soon</u> as possible." The surgeon, who was "in a state of great excitement," did not arrive until late afternoon.

They found the Kaiser in his study "engaged in writing." Although his breaths were "distinctly audible," there was "not the slightest indication of any difficulty in breathing." At this point, Mackenzie said that Bergmann took over without asking anyone and tried twice—"with considerable force" but unsuccessfully—to insert two different tubes. Each attempt was followed by a "violent fit of coughing" and streaming blood.

"To my consternation," Mackenzie said, "Professor von Bergmann then pushed his finger deeply into the wound, and on withdrawing it tried to insert another tube; he again failed . . . and again the attempt was followed . . . by most distressing coughing and copious bleeding." Bergmann finally called for his assistant, who inserted a cannula into the opening "with the greatest ease." Not only was Bergmann clumsy with the patient, Mackenzie said, but, according to Hovell, the German doctor did not even wash his hands before touching the wound.*

Before the Kaiser retired for the night, he called for Morell Mackenzie: "Why did Professor von Bergmann put his finger into my throat?"

"I do not know, sir."

"I hope you will not allow Professor von Bergmann to do any further operations on me."

"After what I have seen to-day, sir, I beg most respectfully to say that I can no longer have the honour of continuing in attendance on Your Majesty if Professor von Bergmann is to be permitted to touch your throat again."

Mackenzie's version of the story may have been exaggerated, but Fritz was clearly distressed by his rough treatment at the hands of the German surgeon, who, he said, "ill treated me." Although he never spoke against Bergmann in public, he refused from then on to be touched by him. "Bergmann for consultation," he wrote in his journal that day, "but he immediately took Mackenzie's place and with brutal strength forced in another cannula. Respiration easier but was very worn out after this business and stayed in bed that afternoon."

The incident was reported in the conservative German papers, which, as a matter of course, took Bergmann's part. One reported that the German surgeon was brought in because Mackenzie "knew not what to do." Another claimed that Mark Hovell had injured the Kaiser's trachea while trying to adjust the cannula during the night. Even the London *Times*, picking up the story from the Berlin press, reported that the new tube had been "deftly" inserted by Bergmann himself. Mackenzie and Hovell tried to counter this with letters to the editor, but were unsuccessful, primarily because the editor of the *Times* bore Mackenzie a grudge for not telling him some months earlier that the Kaiser had cancer. As one member of the British Embassy observed, "The battle between the doctors continued, to the infinite disgust of decent people."

It was not until many years later, after the other doctors were dead, that Mark Hovell explained what had happened. "There was no doubt whatever in his mind," Hovell told Mackenzie's biographer, "that von Bergmann had been drinking and that he swayed from side to side as he tried to insert the cannula." Within hours of the operation, Fritz's temperature began to rise, and the

---

* *Bergmann disputed this, claiming that he touched Fritz only after disinfecting his hands in a basin of carbolic lotion.*

irritation in the trachea spread into the bronchial tubes. Three days later, he was running a fever of 103. Mackenzie suspected the presence of an abscess, "attributable solely to the injury" caused by Bergmann's "random stabbing" with the cannula. On April 18, Mackenzie wired England that the Kaiser's prognosis was "very serious." Two days later, the abscess (or abscesses) erupted, releasing what Mackenzie called a "large quantity of pus."

Meanwhile, word of the Kaiser's precarious condition radiated throughout Berlin. "[E]verywhere groups of people stood together whispering, for the news had spread quickly that the Kaiser had a bronchial infection, that is, the beginning of the end had come," Baroness Spitzenberg, an intimate of the Bismarck household, wrote in her diary. Willy told Waldersee that the situation was "hopeless," and that "the physicians gave the Emperor hours only, some of them gave him a day."

"In the opinion of the doctors the Kaiser has only a few days to live," Holstein echoed from the Foreign Ministry. "Professor Bergmann, who recently explored the tubal aperture with his finger, discovered that the aesophagus was also affected, and so he thinks an early death as a result of an affectation of the lung would be the best thing. The way the English doctors treat the Kaiser defies description."

Holstein noted that the latest gossip from the palace, relayed by Radolinski, had Willy ordering dinner for himself, Henry, and Charlotte at one end of Charlottenburg while his mother dined with his three younger sisters at another. Primed for his accession, the Crown Prince had already issued secret orders to the commandant of Charlottenburg: "The moment you hear the news of the Kaiser's death, man the entire castle and let no one go out, without exception."

But just as Willy was giving these instructions to the commandant, his father appeared at a window of the palace, and the crowds of people, who had come by foot, carriage, and train to stand outside, began to cheer.

THE KAISER'S near death prompted Queen Victoria to hasten a trip she had been planning to Charlottenburg. She arrived on April 24. In an unexpected turnabout, Bismarck told the British Ambassador that Germany would welcome Victoria, even if her son-in-law died before she could get there, and requested that she bring a minister with her. Aimed at expanding the Queen's visit into the political arena, the Chancellor's invitation was a pointed reminder to the Czar that Germany could always look across the channel for a friend.

The Chancellor also revised his contention that Queen Victoria was responsible for the scheme to marry Sandro to Moretta. "Her Majesty never supported the marriage project with the Battenberg prince," one semiofficial government paper claimed, adding that "even if Queen Victoria had taken a different position. . . . The Berlin population is too morally cultivated to greet the mother of the German Empress other than with respect." The apogee of this new praise-the-Queen campaign was a flowery welcome, which blossomed on the front page of the *Norddeutsche Allgemeine Zeitung:* "All German hearts," it said, were grateful that the Queen was coming "to the sickbed of our dearly beloved Kaiser" and thereby sharing "in our heavy trouble and great concern."

Before her arrival, Victoria had been warned to approach her grandson Willy with care. "It appears that his head is turned by his position . . . ," Prime Minister Salisbury wrote, explaining that Bismarck and the Foreign Ministry were "afraid" that if Crown Prince William "acted so as to draw any reproof from Your Majesty, he might take it ill . . . [and] . . . hinder the good relations between the two nations. . . . it is . . . true—most unhappily—that all Prince William's impulses, however blameable or unreasonable, will henceforth be political causes of enormous potency; and the two nations are so necessary to each other that everything that is said to him must be very carefully weighed."

By the time Victoria reached Berlin, Fritz was over the worst of the post-operative crisis. "He was lying in bed," the Queen wrote in her journal, "his dear face unaltered; and he raised up both his hands with pleasure at seeing me and gave me a nosegay. . . . afterwards Vicky sat talking with me for some time in my room. She is very sad, and cried a good deal, poor dear. Besides her cruel anxiety about dear Fritz, she has so many worries and unpleasantnesses. The whole dreadful bother about poor young Vicky [Moretta] had been purposely got up, and they had never had a quarrel with Prince Bismarck."

It was during this conversation that Vicky must have tried to explain to her mother why she had allowed Bismarck to inflate the so-called Chancellor Crisis. The Queen also tried to convince her daughter that Sandro was no longer interested in Moretta. But Vicky refused to accept this. (A month later, the Queen was still begging the Kaiserin to let the young man off the hook: "I was the first person who mentioned the project to you, five years ago, when I thought it would bring happiness to both," she wrote.)

The meeting next day between the sixty-nine-year-old Queen and the seventy-three-year-old Bismarck, bruited around Berlin with considerable apprehension, passed off extremely well. Both were determined to avoid conflict, and both were experienced in the subtler forms of expressing their opinions. The Chancellor, observed by the Queen's private secretary to be "almost nervous" at the prospect of the audience, was brought into the Queen's room by the Kaiserin, who left him alone with her mother. He remained about forty-five minutes. Victoria later said she was "agreeably surprised" to find him "so amiable and gentle."

He spoke a great deal . . . of his great object . . . to prevent war . . . of Russia not being dependable. . . . I expressed my satisfaction that there was no idea of a regency as I knew it would upset dear Fritz dreadfully, and he assured me that there would be none. Even if he thought it necessary, which he did not, he would not have the heart to propose it. I appealed to Prince Bismarck to stand by poor Vicky, and he assured me he would, that hers was a hard fate. I spoke of Prince William's inexperience. . . . Prince Bismarck replied that [William] knew nothing at all about civil affairs, that he could, however, say "should he be thrown into the water, he would be able to swim for he was certainly clever."

"What a woman!" Bismarck is quoted as saying as he emerged from the audience—a reaction he quickly modified, reporting to a colleague that "Grandmama behaved quite sensibly at Charlottenburg."

The audience had clearly been a good one. "Prince Bismarck . . . ," Ambassador Malet wrote his Prime Minister, "has said that if the action of England should correspond with the sound sense and practical character of the views held by Her Majesty, the danger of a European war would be minimised."

Malet watched the Queen and the Chancellor carefully at dinner that evening. He was amused when Bismarck chose a large candy with Vicky's picture on it, and, calling Victoria's attention to what he was doing, "unbuttoned his coat and placed it next to his heart."

Before she left, Victoria had a last conversation with her daughter. "Vicky took me back to my room and talked some time very sadly about the future," the Queen wrote, "breaking down completely. Her despair at what she seems to look on as the certain end is terrible. I saw Sir M. Mackenzie, and he said he thought the fever, which was less . . . would never leave dear Fritz, and that he would not live above a few weeks, possible two months, but hardly three!!"

After their talk, Vicky took her mother to the railway station. "[I]t was terrible to see her standing there in tears, while the train moved slowly off, and to think of all she was suffering and might have to go through. My poor poor child, what would I not do to help her in her hard lot!"

But as Vicky wrote her, the visit itself had raised her spirits. The Queen's appearance in Berlin had more than made up for all the times she had been unable to visit her eldest daughter. With the weight of her authority as monarch of the most venerated power in Europe, Victoria had stamped out, however briefly, the overt political backbiting surrounding her daughter, even causing a temporary hiatus in the anti-British outpourings of the Bismarck press.*

Everyone seemed pleased by the visit except the Crown Prince. Willy was so resentful of his grandmother's attentions to his parents that he announced after she left Berlin that it was "high time the old lady died."

A MONTH AFTER his mother-in-law's departure, the Kaiser was well enough to put in an appearance at the wedding of his second son, Henry, to Princess Irene of Hesse. Through some mix-up in arrangements, he had not been told where to go for the ceremony and arrived late. The proceedings had just started when

---

* Five days before Victoria's arrival, an article appeared in the Bismarck papers attacking "Foreign Influences in the Reich," i.e., Queen Victoria's interference in German foreign policy through her support of the Battenberg marriage. Four days after her departure, Bismarck publicly denounced this "notorious" article. When Busch, who had written the original attack according to Bismarck's specifications, ventured to mention it, the Chancellor only smiled. "The article," he told his publicist, "was really quite first rate" (Nichols, The Year of the Three Kaisers, pp. 252–53).

he entered "in full uniform, with all his Orders," carrying a cane for support. "[H]e looked so handsome and dignified but so thin and pale . . . ," Vicky reported. "I kept back my tears with difficulty and felt with bitter sorrow that we should never again see him attending such a festive gathering as Emperor!" As Friedrich III emerged from the chapel, Field Marshal Moltke turned to one of his friends. "I have seen many brave men," he said, "but none as brave as the emperor has shown himself to-day!"

After the ceremony, Bertie spoke with Herbert von Bismarck, who told him that a monarch who could not talk should not be allowed to reign. "If I had not taken into consideration that good relations between Germany and England were essential I should have thrown him out," the Prince of Wales later told his mother.

Seeing his chance to change the course of Germany ebbing away with his life, Fritz had become progressively more despondent about the conservatives, the military clique and the Bismarcks, who, he told Vicky, "had control of weapons which were not 'fair' "—particularly "the new weapon of chauvinism which they called patriotism!" He despaired not only about what they might do to Germany, but to his family. "I dare not die, I cannot leave you," he told Vicky in May. "Who would protect you and the poor girls? What would happen to Germany?"

Of all his parents' anxieties, the most distressing was their son and heir. "William fancies himself completely the Emperor—and an absolute & autocratic one!" Vicky wrote her mother on May 12. Willy did everything he could think of to affront his parents, even inviting Bergmann to dinner "as demonstratively as possible" as soon as he was dismissed from his father's case. The German surgeon, she explained to her mother, had been "a most convenient tool" for their enemies, both inside and outside the household. "We have no difficulties amongst the doctors now," she said, adding with remarkable generosity that although Bergmann was "not the right person" medically, he had done "his best and meant well."

Vicky was also still trying to make excuses for Willy. "He is in a 'ring,' " she wrote Victoria, "a coterie, whose main endeavour is as it were to paralyse Fritz in every way. William is not conscious of this!"

"I am indeed grieved to hear that you have still so much annoyance," Victoria answered. "But I must always repeat that you should not allow it. You are the masters & as long as you are, you must be determined & not allow it."

Even Holstein at the Foreign Ministry was disturbed by the lack of respect shown the dying Kaiser and his wife. "I am not one of the Kaiserin's adherents —rather the contrary," he wrote in his diary in the middle of May. "But I am bound to admit that her unpopularity is now used by many as a pretext for turning away from the Kaiser and towards his successor. It is shocking for royalists to see how completely powerless the Kaiser is. . . . Their Majesties are actually the object of a wanton sport."

To defend her husband and herself, the Kaiserin sought the advice of

Ludwig Bamberger, a liberal leader brought to her by her close friend, Frau von Stockmar. Bamberger was an excellent choice of mentor—the first and last Vicky ever found in Germany. After a successful career in international finance, he had achieved prominence in the National Liberal Party before following Lasker in a revolt to the left. A gifted writer and orator, Bamberger was also a political realist. He found Vicky's current reading of the Chancellor as a sympathetic ally beset by difficult ministers "droll" to say the least, but stopped short of trying to disabuse her about Bismarck's loyalty, since a change of chancellors was impossible in light of the Kaiser's illness.

Of all the members of the current government, perhaps the one who most antagonized Friedrich III and his wife was Robert von Puttkamer,* Prussian Minister of the Interior. A corrupt hardliner, Puttkamer would have been forced under ordinary circumstances to hand in his resignation after Wilhelm I's death, but was being encouraged by his conservative friends to hang on until Wilhelm II came to power. A great friend of Willy's, Puttkamer was one of those who talked about removing Friedrich III on the grounds that he could not speak.

Fritz had "been waiting for an opportunity" to get rid of Puttkamer when he heard that Bismarck, concerned about Puttkamer's influence on the Crown Prince, wanted him out, too. The Chancellor, however, said he could not "take the initiative" because of "collegial, family† and party considerations." So as Vicky put it later, "Bismarck . . . transferred the odium of the dismissal to the Kaiser, as he indeed always understood how to unload the odium of what he did onto other people."

Two months after Fritz became Kaiser, Puttkamer presented him with a bill for his signature extending the term of the delegates to the Prussian Parliament from three years to five—the same bill Fritz had been forced by Bismarck to sign against his will in the German Reichstag. With his signature, the Kaiser sent Puttkamer a letter saying that the bill carried with it an obligation for government officials to protect the voters from corruption—a pointed allusion to Puttkamer's well-known attempts to thwart electoral reform through redistricting in order to save his brother's seat in parliament.

No sooner had Friedrich signed the bill than Bismarck told him that if he did not want the bill to go into effect, he should simply refuse to have it published. Unaware that he was being set up by the Chancellor, Fritz followed his advice. Three days later, having provoked a crisis between the Kaiser and the Prussian Parliament and having raised an enormous hue and cry in the press, Bismarck reversed his position.

Meanwhile, Puttkamer had replied to the Kaiser's letter with a false report denying malfeasance in his department. Bamberger advised Friedrich that if he answered this report in an "ungracious" manner, Puttkamer would have to

---

* *The man who announced Wilhelm I's death in the Prussian Parliament but neglected to mention Friedrich III's accession.*

† *Johanna Bismarck's maiden name was Puttkamer; Robert was her cousin.*

resign. The Kaiser's answer—meticulously composed, probably by Radolinski with Bismarck's knowledge or advice—was sent to the Interior Minister, who was forced to tender his resignation.

Bismarck, who had kept out of the debates by sequestering himself in the country, had taken care to spread rumors of how worried he was "that the Kaiserin might carry out some sort of coup" while he was out of town. On his return, he released a number of "confidential" reports naming the Kaiserin as the source of Puttkamer's dismissal. Everyone believed him—including Puttkamer.

"Mama and she alone, in league with the German liberals, overthrew Puttkamer," the Crown Prince wrote his uncle Fritz of Baden. Willy claimed that his mother would bring down the other ministers of the cabinet as well. They "no longer feel secure," he said. Bismarck had, in fact, been using the Puttkamer affair to keep the others in line. According to Lucius, his Minister of Agriculture, "He . . . elaborated on the bad handling that Puttkamer had received, as if that could yet happen to others too."

The ousting of Puttkamer achieved exactly what Bismarck had intended at no political cost to himself—the removal of Willy's dangerous friend and a lesson for the Crown Prince about what could happen when a Kaiser overreached his authority without the support of his Chancellor. For the moment, Willy became "very careful and sensible." He even assured Bismarck that he would not try to reinstate his friend Puttkamer after his accession, that he would abandon the extremists on the right, and that he would try to rule like his grandfather.

Insofar as Vicky was concerned, even this temporary improvement must have been worth the price. "Fritz has after much difficulty & some diplomacy got rid of Puttkamer . . . ," she wrote Victoria. "He will be able to carry all sorts of other things if he can break through the wall of opposition . . . in which William is so deeply involved—he would be different to us, I am sure, when these people & influences have gone, that use him for their purposes against us!! He would be much more amenable & reasonable then I am sure."

However she misjudged her son, Vicky had preserved some sense of humor concerning the situation. In answer to Bismarck's tongue-in-cheek lamentations about the trouble she had caused him over Puttkamer, she replied, with equal playfulness, that if he really wished to have his Minister of the Interior reinstated, she thought she could get the Kaiser to sign the order!

But when Bismarck reported this conversation to his cabinet, he told it quite differently. He said that when he informed the Kaiserin that he was being accused of bringing about Puttkamer's downfall, she immediately asked, "Do you want him reappointed? The Kaiser will do it right away!" This, he told his ministers was "proof of Her Majesty's fickleness and complete lack of political understanding."

CHAPTER
FIFTY-SEVEN

> "No one will ever be able to say how Friedrich would have ruled
> the German Empire if fate had given him good health and the
> normal span of life. But one thing is for certain: he was a man
> of liberal and humane ideas. . . . He would have bridged a gap
> in the development of the Reich, which, as things turned out,
> proved a crucial one and has made itself felt right up to the
> present day."
>
> ERICH EYCK, 1944

ON JUNE 1, Vicky moved Fritz on their new yacht, the *Alexandra*, to the Neues Palais in Potsdam. In spite of stormy weather, thousands had gathered to see the dying Kaiser, and as the ship left the dock, they broke through the police lines and ran cheering along the banks of the Spree Canal and the Havel River. There were flowers, flags, and the usual complement of girls with blossoms in their hair. Even the boats in the harbor were decorated. Vicky tried to use the cheerful atmosphere to talk to Willy, who was in command of their yacht, but since each blamed their inability to get along on the entourage of the other, they docked at Potsdam without making much progress toward an understanding.

When the Kaiser and Kaiserin arrived at the Neues Palais, which Fritz had renamed Friedrichskron, Vicky put him in a room on the ground floor so he could go outdoors without climbing stairs. Like most of the rooms of the palace, this one had (and still has) a magnificent ceiling traced in gold-leaf vines, but its marble fireplace and red-and-white Meissen tiles spoke more of grandeur than of comfort. Across from the Kaiser's bed, which was placed in a niche, hung a huge picture of his father's coronation, painted in 1861,* with Vicky as one of the principles in the center of the canvas.

Back in Berlin, the denizens of the Wilhelmstrasse criticized the decampment to summer quarters. "God damn this whole abominable Potsdam!" Herbert fumed. His sister's husband, Count Kuno von Rantzau, who had worked as his father-in-law's secretary and was now Minister to Bavaria, complained that it would take him three hours to attend an audience with the Kaiser. "Heaven knows that monarchs should not get sick or not meddle in affairs," he said.

But most people who spent time in the palace were impressed with the

---

* The picture was painted by Adolph Menzel before the advent of Bismarck, who was added later when he became Prime Minister, and was moved around a few times before the artist settled on an appropriate spot.

Kaiser's gallantry. Even Bismarck Sr. spoke of Friedrich III's "imperial dignity," and "composure of soul" in the face of his own demise. The Chancellor was particularly impressed that the Kaiser, no matter his suffering, always rose and showed him to the door of his room after an audience. "One day, as he was walking with me through the room, I noticed that he was shaking with pain and weakness, and had already stretched out my arm, as I thought he was about to fall, when he managed to seize the door-knob and steadied himself. Yet he uttered no complaint and bore his pains in manly silence."

But like his son and son-in-law, Bismarck was growing impatient for the Kaiser to die, and a week after the move to Potsdam he sent again for Bergmann. "I have to give in to the Emperor a great deal," he told the physician, "and the daily struggle to keep him in check is too great for my seventy-three years. But I wish to conserve them for the successor to the dying man. Consequently I must know how much longer I have to bear this." Bergmann stood by his initial prognosis: the Kaiser would be dead by the end of summer. Bismarck did not have to wait that long.

Ever since the middle of April, Friedrich III had been visibly slipping away. Entries in his diary, which he had kept regularly through most of his life, now consisted of one or two lines at best, more often scribbled notes. A few days were left entirely blank. Often Vicky made his entries for him. On June 11, he asked her, somewhat pathetically: "What will become of me? Do I seem to improve?"

The next day, the Kaiserin wrote her mother that things were "not going well! I have not much hope left, but how long our precious one will be left to us I do not know . . . it cannot be for very long!" She was upset when Fritz insisted on receiving King Oscar of Sweden on June 12, standing in full dress uniform, helmet in hand. The strain taxed him considerably. After the King's departure, Vicky ordered her husband's bed moved into a salon, where he received Bismarck.

The Chancellor had finished his business and was about to leave when the Kaiserin entered the room. They stood on opposite sides of the Kaiser's bed. As Friedrich III gave Bismarck his hand, he took hold of his wife's as well and laid it in that of the Chancellor. According to Radolinski, who was in the room, the Kaiser "sealed their hands together with his and held them for quite a long time with his left hand, while with the right he touched the shoulder of the Chancellor, patted it, showing that he was thereby entrusting the beloved Empress to the Chancellor's care." Bismarck kissed the Kaiser's hand. "Your Majesty may rest assured that I shall never forget that Her Majesty is my Queen" was his noncommittal response.

Vicky, who had broken down in tears at what Radolinski called "one of the most touching and important scenes" he had ever observed, gathered herself to accompany the Chancellor out of the room. She could not help noting the scarcely concealed elation of her old enemy. "[H]is face expressed neither sorrow nor sympathy!" she said.

On the contrary he was strong, full of life and stood up straight—I fancied I saw a quick look of triumph, of relief and joy in his eyes, as if a painful period were now at an end, as if he had been set free . . . and now he could press on full speed to the new task of guiding a young Master, who was his pupil and an enthusiastic and fanatical admirer. . . . To me it was like a stab in the dark, but I could not take it amiss; it was only natural for a man like him. Fritz, after all was finished, so why waste time in sentimental lamentations! . . . I shook hands and let him go.

Vicky had accurately gauged the mood of the Chancellor. The next evening, Herbert gloated to friends, "Our day will soon begin again."

"I hardly leave Fritz's room, or the one next door, only going upstairs to sleep," Vicky wrote her mother on June 14. "He suffers <u>no pain</u>, & indeed hardly any discomfort. . . . What it is to me, to see my poor darling <u>so</u> changed! He is a perfect skeleton now, & his fine thick hair is quite thin! His poor throat is such a painful & shocking sight, that I can often hardly bear to look at it, when it is done up . . . I have to rush away to hide my tears. . . . It is very difficult to keep the air pure in the room, so it is a great comfort that the weather permits his being on the terrace!"

It is not surprising that Vicky found Fritz's throat an unpleasant sight. The silver of the cannula had corroded, the wound was red and suppurating, and the smell, according to the doctors, was dreadful. Although she was blamed for not letting others near her husband, Vicky struggled through his last few days and hours trying to preserve Friedrich III's dignity before the world.

That afternoon, she made an entry in his diary for him: "I am not supposed to sleep now." Fearful of not waking again, the Kaiser took off the chain he always wore around his neck, hung it on his wife, pushed "a special little key" down the front of her dress, pointed to a black cash box containing family papers, nodded, and smiled. "He knew," Vicky later wrote, "that the rest of his things were in safe keeping."

She was awakened at 3:00 A.M. that night by Mackenzie. Her husband's pulse was weaker, his breathing more rapid, his fever high. Vicky got up, but, fearful of alarming him, went no farther than the door to his room. He was restless, tossing about in his bed, coughing every fifteen minutes or so. His manservant stood by, fanning him constantly.

At seven the next morning, someone brought the dying Kaiser the bouquet of flowers he had ordered for his daughter Sophie's birthday. He had planned a family celebration, a boating picnic on the Havel. But Vicky scarcely left his side that day, writing out his whispered fears when he could not do it himself: "What is happening to me?" "Are the doctors content with me?"

She sent for Henry and Irene and Charlotte and Bernhard. Willy and Dona arrived, giving orders "left and right" and generally taking "possession of the palace." That night, Vicky slept in a chaise longue just outside her husband's door, where she could watch him without his knowing.

He began to die at ten o'clock the next morning. His children came into the room. Vicky sat on his bed and kept talking softly to him. When he was thirsty, she gave him white wine on a sponge to suck. She asked if he was tired. "Oh, very, very!" he replied. He himself wrote out the last entry in his diary— "Victoria, me, the children . . ."—before lapsing into unconsciousness.

"Gradually his dear eyes took on a different . . . look!" Vicky wrote later. "We held a light up . . . but he did not blink at all; I raised his dear hand and he let it drop of itself!" Moretta knelt by his bed in tears. "He no longer seemed conscious," Vicky said, "coughed hard once more, took a deep breath three times, then gave an involuntary jerk and closed his eyes tight and convulsively as if something was hurting him! Then everything was quiet!"

Friedrich III died shortly after 11:00 A.M. on June 15, 1888, in the palace in which he had been born fifty-six years before. His wife reached up for a withered laurel wreath hanging on the wall, the one she had given him when he came home from the Franco-Prussian War in 1871. She placed it on his body along with his sword.

As soon as he was sure that his father was really dying, Willy ordered a cordon of soldiers to take up preassigned positions around his parents' palace. As the royal purple standard was being lowered and raised again at half-mast, they sprang into action. Men from battalions stationed in Potsdam approached on the double through the park, some galloping on horseback, others on foot. Red-coated Hussars, waiting for a signal, suddenly "appeared unmounted, with rifles in their hands from behind every tree and every statue."

The order had been given that no one was allowed to enter or leave the palace, not even ministers or court officials. Soldiers were stationed at strategic points in the palace itself to prevent members of the family from entering the telegraph office. No one was allowed to contact the outside, and the servants were prevented from wiring Berlin for the usual black crepe and mourning. When the distraught Kaiserin came out on the terrace to cut roses to place on her husband's body, she was stopped by an army officer, who took her arm to propel her—unceremoniously and not very courteously—back into the palace.

General Winterfeld, Friedrich III's aide-de-camp who had been placed in his position by Bismarck, immediately "flung himself" on the dead man's writing table, tearing out the drawers and rifling through them. Wilhelm II, garbed in the full-dress uniform of the Hussars, saber at the ready, apparently conducted the search of his mother's room himself, while his adjutant, Colonel Gustav von Kessel, was observed running back and forth, insisting that there were " 'papers' which had to be confiscated" and that some documents had already disappeared and "must be found!"

Most people ascribed this frantic and unseemly search to Wilhelm II's desire to confiscate the truth about his parents, but Willy managed to blame the Chancellor. "The measures taken were severe, but necessary," he claimed years later. "The object of isolating the palais was to prevent State or secret documents being conveyed to England by my mother, a possibility of which Bismarck had warned me." The Chancellor must at least have encouraged the search, because Johanna von Bismarck, an ever-accurate barometer of her husband's current line, was quoted as saying that at least one chest of papers was discovered in the "shrubbery" around the palace.

But, in fact, nothing was ever found. "In spite of all assertions to the contrary . . . ," the disappointed young Kaiser told his friend Waldersee later that day, there was "nothing in writing to be seen, everything has been done away with."*

In his eagerness to ferret out plots and conspiracies, Wilhelm II had planned to detain Morell Mackenzie, but was finally convinced by the Minister of Justice that this would be against the law. Mackenzie had antagonized nearly everyone with whom he came in contact, primarily by arranging for a number of second-rate correspondents whom he knew to obtain access to the palace. But at the time of Friedrich III's death, the new Kaiser's soldiers could find only one journalist to arrest—a Mr. Bashford of the London *Daily Telegraph*, who was held in custody until evening. The gentleman later protested to his consulate that he had been given nothing to eat throughout his detention.

If Wilhelm II could not find grounds on which to arrest Morell Mackenzie, he did the next best thing—ordered an autopsy of his father's body in order to prove malfeasance on the part of the English doctor. Bergmann, Winterfeldt, and Bismarck had asked Mackenzie to issue a final report on the case immediately after Friedrich III's death, hoping that he would incriminate himself by saying that his patient did not die of cancer. But Mackenzie's report agreed with the postmortem.

Vicky, who had originally acquiesced to the idea of an autopsy, was distraught when faced with the reality and begged her son not to go through with it. But Bergmann said that "German medicine must have the opportunity to vindicate itself against Dr. Mackenzie's skullduggeries." He told Wilhelm II that the postmortem was required by law—it was not—and when Vicky appealed to Bismarck, the Chancellor claimed that he was too busy to try to stop it. "I was mad with sorrow, anger, and agitation," she wrote Victoria, "that they dared to touch his dear, sacred mortal remains."

The lying-in-state and funeral arrangements were made exclusively by Wilhelm II, who wanted to dispose of his father's body as quickly and unceremoniously as possible.† "The dead man was very hastily dressed in his uniform,"

---

* *Wilhelm II later claimed that "important state papers did reach England and were made public there, to the detriment of the German Reich." But the state papers to which he referred were his mother's personal letters to his grandmother, detrimental only to his own reputation (Kürenberg, The Kaiser, p. 81).*

† *A year and a half after Friedrich III's death, his widow received a sealed letter containing the dead man's wishes about his funeral and his remains. She was told that it came from a box which the head of Wilhelm II's household had "forgotten to open" at the time of his death (RA: Z 48/3, V to QV, 12/6/89).*

Willy's friend Eulenburg said, "just as hurriedly the [Jasper] gallery was emptied of its contents, while the coffin, surrounded by workmen plying their hammers . . . stood on the floor like a tool chest."

Unlike the services honoring Wilhelm I three months earlier, the funeral of Friedrich III took place within seventy-two hours, leaving scarcely two days for the traditional viewing of the body. Wilhelm II invited no foreign heads of state to his father's funeral, nor did Bismarck see fit to attend. A thin cortege, winding its way across the royal park in Potsdam from the palace to the church, was a pathetic contrast to the massive gathering of princes, soldiers, prelates, and dignitaries that had marched down Unter den Linden through the Brandenburg Gate to the palace of Charlottenburg bearing the body of Wilhelm I. To discourage onlookers, the new Kaiser had the route of his father's funeral procession cordoned off by soldiers. Waiting for the body at the little Church of Peace in the park, the clergymen "stood around laughing and chattering." It is not surprising that Vicky refused to attend this travesty, retreating with her three younger daughters to Bornstedt, where she held a private service of her own.

In spite of the speed with which the ceremonies were hurried along, the Prince and Princess of Wales managed to get to Berlin. "Try, my dear George, never to forget Uncle Fritz," Bertie wrote his son, the future George V. "He was one of the finest and noblest characters ever known; if he had a fault he was too good for this world."*

Bertie and Alix were infuriated by Willy's behavior and the attitude it engendered around the court, particularly the young Kaiser's treatment of his mother. "Instead of William being a comfort and support to her," the Princess of Wales wrote later, "he has quite gone over to Bismarck and Co. who entirely overlook and crush her. It is too infamous." Wilhelm II, according to Bertie and Alix, was no better than an "immature bad boy."

Still, Bertie urged his sister to try to maintain her ties with her son in order to provide an alternative to the Bismarcks. "Prince Bismarck is like Mephistopheles behind W. urging him to do things which must be painful and distasteful to you, and bolstered up by the son Herbert Bismarck and many others no doubt, and when one knows that the Official Press is the mouthpiece and in the pay of the Wilhelm Strasse, it is doubly galling and bitter for you to bear. Still I would urge [you] . . . not to quarrel with W. whatever happens."

While Wilhelm II tried to negate the meaning of his father's life, others spoke about the tragedy of Friedrich III's death and their hopes for a more democratic Germany. Baron Roggenbach, the liberal adviser to the Baden court, called the death of Friedrich III "the saddest catastrophe that ever happened in history," and the *Vossische Zeitung* mourned this "Siegfried . . . this knightly prince . . . snatched away by malignant death." While conservatives openly rejoiced in the brevity of his reign, the *Frankfurter Zeitung* contended that the dead man had not lived in vain: "The good that he did, the greatness that he strove for . . . remains a living thing for his family, for the nation, and

---

* *Bertie's second son would become heir to the throne after the death of his older brother in 1892.*

for the world." And in England, Gladstone referred to the fallen Hohenzollern as "the Barbarossa* of German Liberalism."

Although his life and character had been impressive, the reign of Friedrich III had been more symbol than substance. Perhaps the most articulate testimony to that life came from Vicky's old friend, Robert Morier, now British Ambassador to Russia. "[H]aving had the great privilege of personal intercourse with His late Majesty during the long period of thirty years . . . ," Morier wrote,

> I would fain . . . bear my humble testimony to the character of a man so great, where the greatest have proved themselves so small, so valiant a soldier yet so filled with the horror of war, so conscientious a workman in the task of building up his country's glory, yet so callous to all personal sense of glory, so conspicuous a figure in all the great battles of the age, yet of so steadfast a faith in those higher national tasks which cannot be realised on the field of battle . . . in a word, so pre-eminently human in an age so preeminently one of blood and iron.

---

* *Friedrich Barbarossa, or Red Beard, a twelfth-century king. The physical ideal of a Teutonic knight with flowing strawberry blond hair and beard, he was a leader of great charisma who ruled over Germany and parts of Italy.*

PART FIVE

Mother of the Kaiser

CHAPTER FIFTY-EIGHT

> *"It is too dreadful . . . to think of Willy & Bismarck & Dona
> being the supreme head of all now! Two so unfit & one so
> wicked."*
>
> QUEEN VICTORIA, *1888*

WILLIAM II SUCCEEDS WILLIAM I . . . the sooner he [Friedrich III] is
forgotten the better, therefore the sooner his widow disappears, the better also,"
Vicky wrote her mother shortly after the death of her husband.

From the beginning of his reign, Wilhelm II made clear his intention of ex-
cising Friedrich III from the consciousness of Germany. The twenty-nine-year-
old Kaiser buried the recent past in his speech at the opening of the Reichstag
by dubbing his grandfather "Wilhelm the Great" and promising to "follow the
same path" as the first Kaiser of the German Empire. As he said in his *Memoirs*,
"I became the successor of my grandfather. . . . I skipped a generation."

"I close my eyes & ears to the official world," Vicky wrote Victoria, "and
find it the only way not to feel the profoundest irritation with William. I am
only too ready to make all allowances for him, when I think of the deplorable
friends he has had, & of all the nonsense with which his head has been so
sytematically stuffed!!"

Preening in the admiration of supporters like General Waldersee, who
claimed that with the accession of Wilhelm II Germany had "recovered from a
bad sickness," the young Kaiser kept his distance from his mother. The new
Dowager Empress saw nothing of the Chancellor either. "Prince Bismarck has
not asked to see me to take leave, or condole!" Vicky wrote Victoria nearly
three weeks after her husband's death.

Queen Victoria, who had just seen Wilhelm II's envoy and Friedrich III's
former aide-de-camp, General Winterfeldt, was not surprised. Willy had sent
Winterfeldt to announce his accession to the throne to his grandmother. After
Winterfeldt's audience, the young Kaiser complained about the "cold reception"
his envoy had received.

"The Queen is extremely glad to hear that General Winterfeldt says he was
received coldly . . . for such was her intention," Victoria replied. "He was a
traitor to his beloved master, and never mentioned his name even, or a word of
regret, and spoke of the pleasure which he experienced at being chosen to
announce his new master's accession."

In his maiden speech as Kaiser, Wilhelm spoke about his personal friend-ship with Alexander III of Russia, and a month after his accession sailed off to St. Petersburg. Her son, Vicky said, was acting "as if he could not wait to show himself, to amuse himself . . . to enjoy the outward honours of his position." She was equally dismayed by the political implications of the trip. "I think the first visit he pays in the position which he alas now fills ought to be to you!!" she wrote Queen Victoria.

The Queen, who called her grandson's trip "sickening," wrote to suggest that the twenty-nine-year-old Kaiser honor his father's memory and refrain from immediate travel. Willy replied that his journey was being made in accordance with Bismarck and in the interests of "the peace of Europe . . . I would have gone later if possible, but state interest goes before personal feelings, & the fate which sometimes hangs over nations does not wait till the etiquette of Court mournings has been fulfilled. . . . I deem it necessary that monarchs should meet often & confer together to look out for dangers which threaten the monarchical principle from democratical & republican parties in all parts of the world."

"Trust that we shall be very cool, though civil, in our communications with my grandson and Prince Bismarck, who are bent on a return to the oldest times of government," the Queen wired Salisbury after Willy's letter.

The night before he left on his tour, Willy stopped to say good-bye to his mother, who took the opportunity to try to get his approval for the marriage between Sandro and Moretta. In spite of the directive in his father's will, the Kaiser refused. A few months later Sandro married his opera star. "All one can now pray & wish for is that she should be good enough for him & make him happy," Vicky wrote Victoria when she heard the news.* But she continued to worry about twenty-two-year-old Moretta, now plunged into depression and self-loathing.

The Kaiser's visit to St. Petersburg was not entirely satisfactory. Accompa-nying Wilhelm II was Herbert, who tried to impress the Czar with tales of dangerously democratic Friedrich III and the political warfare in Berlin. Alexan-der III may have resented hearing about family fights from a nonroyal; perhaps he had heard it all before from Willy; possibly he was no longer willing to put up with anyone named Bismarck. Whatever it was, he remarked rather acidly about members of the Kaiser's suite washing the Hohenzollerns' dirty linen in public.

While her husband was cruising in the Baltic, Dona gave birth to the fifth of their six sons. "William is overjoyed that it is a boy . . . ," Vicky wrote Victoria. "He was afraid it might have been 'only' a girl!! She is pleased too."

Vicky, who had visited her daughter-in-law daily while the Kaiser was away, was hurt that the child was not named after her. "The last one, I was told must be named 'August' on account of the Empress Augusta, & this one, I am told can only be called 'Oscar' after the King of Sweden, who is after all no

---

* *Sandro died less than five years later, at the age of thirty-six. He was buried, at the request of the Bulgarians, in Sofia.*

relation—surely *I* might have been considered first, & out of five grandsons one might be called 'Victor' as well as Oscar. It is really not kind," she wrote Victoria, adding untruthfully, "& I wished for 'Victor' on account of you."

After the christening festivities, the Dowager Empress wrote her mother that by "some mistake" she had "missed all the royal visitors." Although she herself seems to have thought nothing of this, it is fairly obvious that she had been kept away from the guests by her son and daughter-in-law.

No sooner had Wilhelm II returned from Russia than he began plans for his next trip—to Austria and Italy. "Since our terrible loss—not two days have been devoted to mourning, or to quiet, or a little bit to his mother!" Vicky complained to Victoria. "It has been one whirl of visits, receptions, dinners, journeys, parades, manoeuvres, shooting & entertaining."

Vicky was not alone in commenting on her son's frenetic pace. The wags of Berlin began to speak of the three German Kaisers of 1888 as *"Der greise Kaiser, der weise Kaiser, und der Reise-Kaiser* [the Old Kaiser, the Wise Kaiser, and the Traveling Kaiser]."

ONE OF VICKY's first problems as a widow, an issue that dominated her life for months after her husband's death, was finding a place to live. Shortly after the funeral, Wilhelm informed his mother that she must give up her home of thirty years in Potsdam, Frederick the Great's old palace that she and Fritz had restored. "I am to leave Friedrichskron," she wrote Victoria at the end of June. "I would have liked Sanssouci*—it was curtly and rudely refused. . . . They would like me to go right away, for fear I might gain some influence over William, remind the public of Fritz . . . and possibly retain some connections with the Liberal Party and give them support."

Victoria, who had by now heard from Bertie of the "terrible intrigues" surrounding Vicky, had written Wilhelm II to try to persuade him to give his mother a decent home in Potsdam. When he failed to answer, she was annoyed, but wrote a second time:

"I am naturally very much occupied with poor dear Mama's future home," the Queen told the young Kaiser.

> She feels probably a certain awkwardness . . . to ask for anything, where so lately all was her own. . . . Would you not . . . offer her to stay, at any rate for the present let her have Friedrichskron, or else Sans Souci? Uncle Bertie told me you had mentioned the Villa Liegnitz,† but that is far too small & would not do I think for your mother, who is the first after you & who is the first Princess after Aunt Alix in Great Britain. . . . Mama does not know I am writing to you on this subject, nor has she ever mentioned it to

---

* *Frederick the Great's jewel of a palace in the Potsdam park, where Frederick William IV had lived out the end of his life.*

† *A small villa in the royal Potsdam park, the former home of the morganatic wife of Friedrich Wilhelm III, briefly occupied by both Henry and Charlotte.*

me,* but after talking it over with Uncle Bertie he advised me to write direct to you.

This time Willy wrote back, rationalizing his failure to answer Victoria's first letter on the "enormous amount of work" he had to do because of what he called "the complete stagnation" of the government at the end of his father's reign. For three weeks, he said, he had been working almost around the clock just to get through the "heaps of unsigned orders, papers, patents, etc."

The young Kaiser told his grandmother that he was doing his "uttermost to fulfill" his mother's desire for a country home. "[W]hen I found out that the capital she wanted was not free because it is meant as a legacy for us children after her death, I at once renounced for my part once for all, & promised to bring my sisters to do the same." Sanssouci, he said, was needed for "strangers coming to see us"; his mother herself "adores" the Villa Liegnitz; and all the other palaces in Potsdam belonged to his grandmother Augusta. He had, he said, given his mother permission "to stay at Friedrichskron for this year."

Although Wilhelm II sounded generous on paper, his treatment of Vicky seems to have been calculated to make her unhappy and uncomfortable—perhaps enough to leave Germany. In comparison with his father's largesse toward Augusta, Willy's settlements on the new widow were stingy and unchivalrous. Wilhelm I's widow had been given three palaces—in Berlin, Potsdam, and Coblenz—with the upkeep paid by the crown, plus four million marks.† Vicky was given her palace in Berlin and (very briefly) the Villa Liegnitz and expected to pay for their upkeep out of an inheritance less than one-sixth that willed to her predecessor. Once again, she had to fall back on her English dowry, which had helped cover household expenses during Fritz's lifetime. "Capital I have none, Vicky wrote her mother, adding a week later, "Had Fritz been spared to us longer, he would have been able to leave more, of course!"‡

This was a large part of the trouble. During her husband's lifetime, when Vicky criticized Willy for joining the Foreign Ministry against his father's wishes, he had answered that "it's the Kaiser [i.e., Wilhelm I] who pays me, not my father." And long after his parents were both dead, Wilhelm II said that the reason he had always been closer to his grandfather than his father was because "My father never once gave me a single penny."

In March of 1888, immediately after becoming Kaiser, Friedrich III had signed an order specifying that the living allowance for both his mother and Vicky after his death should be increased, since the monies provided for Augusta's predecessor in 1861 would be insufficient for their comfort. When this

---

* This is not true.

† Around $1 million. From these figures we can estimate that Wilhelm II gave his mother around $165,000.

‡ From this we can assume that the income from the crown estates came to whoever was kaiser and that Friedrich III was not on the throne long enough to build up any capital to leave her. During his reign, Wilhelm I managed to save twenty-two million marks.

order was published after his death, however, the normal proviso—that the salaries of Vicky's entourage should be paid by the crown—was missing.

"I do not wish to suggest . . . any possible perpetrator of this trick played on the Empress [Vicky]," said Baron Reischach, head of Vicky's household. "I am perfectly certain that the . . . Chief of the Council for the Royal Household [i.e., Wilhelm II's household], was incapable of such an underhand action, but I could not help quoting . . . a verse from Schiller's play *Wallenstein,* when the Croat general remarks after the banquet in which Wallenstein was betrayed: 'I read differently before dinner.' "

As Lord Chamberlain of the Dowager Empress's household, Reischach asked the head of the Privy Council to suggest to Wilhelm II that he provide a living allowance for his mother proportionate to that allotted his grandmother. "But he always had some excuse," Reischach said, "and claimed that inasmuch as the Emperor was spending enormous sums on his visits to all the Courts, and on the upkeep of his forty-eight castles . . . he could not be expected to increase the allowance." Nor, said Reischach, could the Dowager Empress ever be "induced to make any claim upon her son's munificence."

Vicky began looking for a country home as soon as Willy told her that she must leave Friedrichskron. She eventually located an estate near Frankfurt, in Kronberg, which she was able to buy and rebuild, thanks largely to the generosity of a friend, the Duchess de Galliera.

Within days of this purchase and less than three months after Willy's soothing letter to his grandmother, Vicky was told that she must also give up the Villa Liegnitz in Potsdam so that Wilhelm II's gentlemen-in-waiting would have a place to stay when they were in attendance on him. This left her with no home in or near the royal park, where all the other members of the German royal family owned huge properties and spent their summers. Reduced to her insignificant farmhouse in the outlying town of Bornstedt, which she was allowed to occupy although she was told that it now belonged to the state, Vicky was informed that she might stay in the old palace in the town of Potsdam, but must ask special permission each time. Moreover, the money Willy had promised her was now withdrawn on the grounds that the crown could not afford it. "William did not even say he regretted it," she wrote Victoria.

Vicky moved out of Friedrichskron in September of 1888, three and a half months after Fritz's death. During the years it took to build her home in Kronberg, she spent summers in the royal castle at Bad Homburg, the dower house* granted her when she married Fritz. Vicky was annoyed that her son had not sent anyone to clean it up for her. "I never saw anything so dirty!" she complained to her mother when she arrived; "the weeds grow up to the front door, just in front of which was a hole, in which the horses might have broken their legs!" Her servants scrubbed off the filth, but there was no heating, no proper drainage or indoor plumbing—no sinks, no baths, no toilets—and no permission to put them in. "[T]hey refused everything one asks for, even a few

---

* *The house a widow was allowed to use during her lifetime, but which she did not own.*

paving stones . . . in front of the stable door! They say they want every penny for the Emperor for the Schloss & for Friedrichskron . . . and that if I am not satisfied I can remain in my home at Berlin!"

The Kaiser was currently spending large amounts of money on his own grandeur, and within five months of his accession, he had demanded an increase of six million marks* to his annual income. He had commissioned the conversion of a warship into a new yacht, the *Hohenzollern*, and was refurbishing the palace of Friedrichskron, commandeered from his mother. In spite of a letter left by Friedrich III saying that the palace should continue to "bear the name of Friedrichskron in honor of its creators,"† Wilhelm II officially renamed his parents' summer home the Neues Palais immediately upon taking it over. "[I]t is so unkind . . . ," Vicky wrote Victoria, "now that this name is so associated with Fritz & that he was taken from us under that roof. . . . I cannot say how bitter it makes me!"

EVEN THE DIPLOMATIC community was stunned by Wilhelm II's eagerness to disavow his parents. "When a young and strong Monarch who probably had a long reign before him, can hardly wait until his father and predecessor is cold in his grave before starting in great haste to reorganize, dismiss and pension off," the Austrian Ambassador to Germany remarked, "this is prone to arouse serious misgivings."

"It pains me to see that William has changed & upset so many things that Fritz had so carefully arranged for the army . . . ," Vicky wrote Victoria six weeks after Friedrich III's death. "William has even forbidden Fritz's own regiment to keep the name 'Kaiser Friedrich'."

But Wilhelm II was a novice compared to Bismarck. One of the first ways in which the Chancellor tried to discredit Vicky was to accuse her of stealing state papers. The fact that nothing incriminating had been found in her palace must have embarrassed him, for within a few days of Friedrich III's death, Herbert von Bismarck, General Winterfeldt, and Colonel Kessel began spreading word around Berlin that the Dowager Empress had "purloined the papers of Kaiser Friedrich and sent them abroad to publish them there." The accusations were repeated in the official press.

"State papers there were none, that Fritz did not instantly return to the different offices," Vicky wrote Victoria five days after her husband's death. "I never had one in my hands. He wished my private correspondence & his to be safe from the ruthless hands of people who were traitors to him & to me!"

Shortly after her mother's visit, Vicky had, in fact dispatched the last box of her husband's papers to England, including two volumes of his diary. "Never never give them up please, even if they try to make you!" she wrote Victoria. "You can deny having such or say what you like. . . . Besides they cannot & do

---

* *Approximately $1.5 million.*

† *I.e., Frederick the Great, who built it (and probably Friedrich III, who restored it).*

not know what was there, or where it is now. Fritz tore up & burnt heaps both at Charlottenburg here, Baveno, San Remo—& before we left for England last year."

Two weeks later, however, the Dowager Empress was forced to reverse herself. A visit from her friend, Minister of Justice Friedberg, convinced her that she must prove to the government that she had not removed German state property. "[A]s Friedberg is thoroughly devoted to Fritz & to me, it is perhaps better the things should come back here, I can have him & the House Minister here and show them that the things belong to me! They will then . . . say it to the other ministers & will be able to defend me better. . . . Therefore please dearest Mama, send me all and everything you have of ours, tin boxes, black box & all."

Friedrich III had left his papers to his wife, and, after looking them over, the Minister of Justice confirmed that they were not state documents, but personal papers to do with as she wished. Nevertheless, after this experience the Dowager Empress wrote to suggest that Queen Victoria keep her letters to her eldest daughter at Windsor: "[I]n case I died suddenly, I should not like them to be put in the German Archives, and if they found them after my death they would be sure not to allow them to be taken to England."

Vicky wanted to collect material for a life of her husband, and in that regard sent her mother a secret memo. Unlike her husband and mother, she said, she had never kept a journal, and her letters to the Queen, along with her letters to Fritz, were the "only documents of the 30 years of our married life that exist." She hoped her mother might designate a discreet surrogate to extract "the political events, also matters of the court & our life here, etc. with a view to my having selections made & translated. . . . I must not let the matter rest," she told Victoria. "I may die any day, & the truth which is being so systematically smothered & twisted must be put down some where, no matter whether it be published in my life time or no!"

Vicky's anxiety to set the record straight was partially due to the much-heralded appearance of a pamphlet on Fritz's illness. Written by the disgruntled Professor Bergmann with the help of his colleague Dr. Gerhardt, the sixty-two-page, black-bordered pamphlet was ordered by Wilhelm II and published by the German government less than a month after Friedrich III's death. "Scarcely an objective scientific work," according to the Austrian Ambassador, it accused Mackenzie of malpractice by not insisting on an immediate operation on the Kaiser, which, Bergmann contended, "was no more dangerous than that of inserting a tube."

This was hardly true.

On the day of publication, Bergmann was giving a demonstration lecture to a class at the University of Berlin. "Gentlemen," he said to his students, "I have the honour to present to you a sick man whose case is exactly the same as that of His Majesty Emperor Friedrich, who unfortunately was in inexpert hands. . . . We will now proceed with the operation which alone could have saved His Majesty's life and Throne—the removal of the affected part, possibly the whole of the larynx. In its way it is an historic act, namely the justification of German science, which I now have the opportunity of demonstrating . . ."

This speech, recalled in the memoirs of a pupil of Bergmann who was present in the operating theater that day, was followed by a description of the operation: "They began and it continued for a long time. . . . After an hour and a half there were whispers around the operating table. Then there was a respite; Bergmann straightened up and said: 'Gentlemen, we were mistaken. It is not carcinomatous but tuberculoma. I am discontinuing the operation.'

"After two hours the man was dead."

Eight years later, a German nobleman, exhibiting symptoms similar to those of the Crown Prince, was also operated on by Bergmann. "The operation lasted 2 hours," Vicky wrote one of her daughters, "and yesterday the poor victim died. . . . They tell me that poor Count. S's state _after_ the operation, with half his throat gone, was so dreadful that to die was a mercy and a relief."

THE BERGMANN PAMPHLET was only one of several efforts on the part of Bismarck's government and the young Kaiser to politicize the death of Friedrich III. Within two weeks of his demise, an article appeared in a government paper alleging that Friedrich III had stated that *"he would not assume the Government [i.e., throne] if it were placed beyond doubt that he was incurably affected by cancer."* The article, which originated in the Foreign Ministry, claimed that there were people who tried to "deceive" Friedrich III "as to his real condition." Among these, of course, were Mackenzie, who had taken it "upon himself to seek to intervene in deciding the destiny of the German Nation," and the Kaiser's English-born wife.

But, as the secretary to the British Ambassador said in his memoirs, "[I]t was not the Crown Princess who was responsible for the original summons to Mackenzie. It was Bismarck's intervention which prevented the contemplated operation. Nevertheless the general public in Germany in 1887 and 1888 assumed that the selection of Mackenzie was due to the Crown Princess, and Bismarck, who knew the truth, did nothing to put public opinion right."

Mackenzie's official answer to Bergmann, a book called *The Fatal Illness of Frederick the Noble,* appeared in England three months after Bergmann's pamphlet. Thirty-four German publishers bid for the rights to the translation, and the top bidder printed 100,000 copies, all of which were confiscated by the German police. "They have _no_ right to _do so!_" Vicky complained. "It is a perfectly despotic proceeding worthy of St. Petersburg!" In spite of the government's attempt to suppress Mackenzie's side of the story, another 100,000 copies of the book were sold in England, and American and French editions appeared in the bookstores.

But the book did its author no good. Mackenzie was accused of indiscretion and attacked for his hostile tone, although few of his detractors had read the German pamphlet that he set out to refute. His most outspoken critics came from the Royal College of Physicians and the Royal College of Surgeons. His fellow physicians, who had never liked him and resented his penchant for publicity, now demanded his resignation. He died three years later of pneumonia at the age of fifty-four with a cloud still over his reputation. It seems that old Baron Stockmar had been right when he refused to assist at the tragic confinement of Princess Charlotte of England nearly three-quarters of a century before: a doctor attending a member of a royal family in a country not his own ran risks that were hardly worth the honor of the assignment.

By encouraging Bergmann to publish the original pamphlet, Wilhelm II and Bismarck hoped to complete the political assassination of Friedrich III and his widow. Had the German doctors been able to prove that the Englishman—in collusion with the patient and his wife—purposefully misdiagnosed the Crown Prince's cancer in order to allow him to mount the throne, they would have succeeded in destroying the reputation of Friedrich III, his widow, and his liberal supporters. But neither their pamphlet nor Mackenzie's book proved the other wrong, and the question continued to be argued for years. Meanwhile, other pressures were brought to bear on the Dowager Empress, for, as Bismarck had long ago discovered, one of the ways to keep the brash, young Kaiser on his side was to harass and discredit his mother.

CHAPTER
FIFTY-NINE

> *"Nothing was so striking among the German people as their identity of thought on all public matters."*
>
> ANNE TOPHAM,
> *governess in Wilhelm II's household*

O<small>N AUGUST 6, 1888</small>, eight weeks after Fritz's death, Vicky reminded her mother that it was the anniversary of the Battle of Wörth, one of the early battles of the Franco-Prussian War won by the army under Friedrich III's command. "His dear old horse 'Worth' came to me this morning," she wrote, adding that someone in the household had placed a laurel wreath around the animal's neck. "How fond of it he [Friedrich III] was!" she recalled. "At Charlottenburg it came into the garden, & licked his hands; even now, when any one imitates the sound of his footstep in the stables, the old creature pricks up its ears, neighs, & turns round & thinks it hears its master coming! How proudly it carried him <u>all</u> day (this day 18 years ago) and at Sedan."

Vicky was one of very few people left in Berlin who dared speak or write about her husband's role in the Franco-Prussian War or its aftermath, the unification of Germany. According to the Wilhelmstrasse, the German Empire had been entirely the work of Bismarck. Therefore, the publication of excerpts from Friedrich III's war diary in a monthly magazine, the *Deutsche Rundschau*, erupted into a political firestorm.

Appearing in late September, a little over three months after the Kaiser's death, these excerpts testified to Friedrich III's major contribution to the creation of the German Empire. According to the day-by-day records, some of the credit taken by Bismarck clearly belonged to Fritz, who, aided by his brother-in-law the Grand Duke of Baden, had championed the idea of the empire and convinced Wilhelm I—over the old man's violent objections—that it must be created. In his diary, Friedrich had, in fact, gone so far as to criticize Bismarck for not being aggressive enough with the other German princes.

"The Marmor Palais [home of Wilhelm II] & Berlin are in a state of fury & excitement about the publication of Fritz's diary . . . ," Vicky wrote Victoria on September 24.

William was in a rage & called it "high treason" and theft of State papers!
. . . I was much surprised and also annoyed at the publication which is

extremely injudicious & indiscreet! Of course it is <u>all</u> <u>true</u>. . . . The part that Fritz played at Versailles in January 1871 is of course not known by the public! The German Empire is supposed to have been called into existence by the Emperor William & Prince Bismarck—whereas it was Fritz who got it done! Therefore this comes in the light of a revelation!

I cannot imagine how it got into the <u>Rundschau</u>. Fritz had several copies <u>lithographed</u> and gave them to his more intimate friends. . . . Everyone now thinks <u>I</u> have done this . . . to play Prince Bismarck a trick to revenge myself. . . . Of course, this is all a mischievous lie! in order to excite his party, William, etc. against me.

The Chancellor's immediate reaction was to declare the writing a forgery, claiming that the Crown Prince could not have known these things since he, Bismarck, had never had Wilhelm I's permission to speak about matters of state with the heir to the throne. In a report released to the press, Bismarck said that he was "not allowed by King Wilhelm to discuss the more confidential aspects of our policy with the Crown Prince, because His Majesty feared indiscretions leaking out to the English Court, which was full of French sympathisers."

To his propagandist, Busch, however, who had read the extracts and informed the Chancellor that he considered them to be "genuine," Bismarck told an entirely different story: "I myself consider the diary even more genuine than you do," Bismarck said, instructing Busch that this was all the more reason to deny its authenticity: "First assert it to be a forgery, and express indignation at such a calumny upon the noble dead. Then, when they prove it to be genuine, refute the errors and foolish ideas which it contains, but cautiously, and bearing in mind that he was Emperor and father to the present Emperor."

While Bismarck planned his press campaign, Vicky tried to track down the source of the excerpts. "The Diary is <u>perfectly</u> & <u>completely</u> <u>genuine</u>, word <u>for</u> word . . . ," she wrote Victoria; "the original is . . . in the <u>archives</u> of the Haus Ministerium [Ministry of the Royal Household], and was among the papers I gave <u>up</u>! . . . On the one hand I am now terrified that if William hears where it is he will have it burnt because Prince Bismarck has officially said it is 'apocryphal.'

"I have <u>not</u> published this Diary, nor had anything to do with it!" she wrote two days later. "I fear it was Dr. Geffcken who did it,—it was imprudent and indiscreet, but I <u>will</u> stand up for every word that is <u>said</u>. Mischke, Blumenthal, Stosch & many others can testify to the absolute <u>historical</u> truth of all it contains, but I certainly should <u>not</u> ask them to come forward, as they & <u>all</u> <u>our</u> <u>friends</u> are suspects to the government & might be treated '<u>à la</u> <u>Arnim</u>.' "*

Vicky was right about the danger. As soon as Geffcken—a professor of law and government, old friend and former adviser to Friedrich III—announced that it was he who had published the extracts, he was charged by Bismarck with "high treason" and imprisoned. "There is not a doubt that Prince Bismarck only

---

* *Harry Arnim had been Germany's Ambassador to France. Worried that Arnim could unseat him because of his close ties with the court, Bismarck had sued him for stealing state documents and ruined him.*

puffs up Geffcken's misdeed . . . as much as he can, in order to . . . terrorize all people who might be inclined to speak a word of truth . . . ," Vicky wrote Victoria. "Independent people are silent, cowed into holding their tongues! The whole machinery of the press is in Bismarck's hands—in Berlin alone the Government employés are 33,000 people; all of these have no other opinion than what he orders them to have!"

Even Vicky, however, did not fathom the depths of emotion in Bismarck stirred by the publication of the diaries. This only came out several months later in a conversation between Bismarck and the wife of the British Ambassador. The Chancellor had come to pay his respects to the Ambassador on Queen Victoria's birthday. Since the Ambassador was out, Bismarck asked to see Lady Malet. After the usual courtesies, the Ambassador's wife reported that the Chancellor's "manner changed," his face grew "angry and almost malignant," and he delivered his real message:

"I want him [Ambassador Malet] to know and I want your country men to know that it was I and only I who alone made this German empire. It was my sole work. And how do you think I accomplished this? How did I succeed in triumphing over every obstacle and in crushing every man who stood in my way? I will tell you. All this I achieved through . . . cunning. I set one man against another, and again and again I broke them."

Given the strength of the Chancellor's feelings, it is not surprising that "poor old Geffcken" was kept in jail for over three months, until January of 1889, when the Supreme Court dismissed the charges against him for lack of substantiation.* Bismarck's reaction was to dismiss Minister of Justice Friedberg for not having won the case for him. And in spite of all proofs to the contrary, Wilhelm II continued to insist that his mother was responsible for the publication of the excerpts from his father's diary and that she had arranged for everyone in England to read it.

In another, less successful attempt to discredit the dead Kaiser and his widow through their friends, Bismarck reopened charges of espionage against Sir Robert Morier, currently Britain's Ambassador to Russia. Morier, who had been accused six months earlier by Herbert von Bismarck of passing information to the French during the Franco-Prussian War when he was Minister to Hesse, had obtained a categorical denial from Marshal Bazaine, the French commander with whom he was said to have been in contact. According to Bazaine, the charge was no more than a "clumsy invention."

When the Chancellor floated this story for a second time at the end of 1888, Morier sent Bazaine's denial to Herbert, requesting that "as a gentleman and man of honor" he issue a public repudiation to save Morier's good name. In a curt, two-line note, Herbert refused. To retaliate, Morier released his correspondence with both Bazaine and Herbert to the press. Never much liked, the smart,

---

* *Geffcken, who was in his sixties and in frail health, became addicted to the barbiturates sold to him in prison for insomnia. He died one night a few years later when he upset an oil lamp in a drugged stupor, suffocating in the fumes and setting fire to himself.*

fat Morier suddenly found himself the darling of St. Petersburg, where hostility to Bismarck was becoming fashionable. A small matter of personal vindictiveness, the Morier matter turned into a major public relations debacle for the Bismarcks.

Perhaps the most insidious campaign launched by the Bismarck forces against Friedrich III and his widow, however, was the rumor that Vicky married her Court Chamberlain, Count Seckendorff, shortly after her husband's death. An attempt to undermine the picture of the happy home life of Friedrich III and turn him into a cuckold, it was eagerly accepted by the gossips of Berlin,* but denied by those who knew them. To quote the head of Vicky's household, Baron Reischach, who also served Wilhelm I and Wilhelm II: "I must here authoritatively deny an allegation which was frequently made in the press, namely, that the Empress married Count Seckendorff after the Emperor Friedrich's death. I well remember that the Empress said to me in 1888 or 1889, when Count Seckendorff was very ill, 'We must look round for a successor to Count Seckendorff, for he will be unable to continue his service and will have to be pensioned off.' "

Another man who served Wilhelm II, Bernhard von Bülow, who became Wilhelm's Chancellor in 1897, also said that the story was "completely" false. "The allegation that Empress Friedrich married Count Seckendorff secretly, after her husband's death," he said, "is one of the silliest lies ever invented."

Still, a few years after Fritz's death, Marie von Bunsen, a young friend of Vicky's from a German diplomatic family, wrote in her diary that "so many well-informed people had told me definitely of a secret marriage, contracted a few years previously, that on my journey here [to visit Vicky in Cronberg] I believed in it. I do not do so now," she added after two months of living with the Dowager Empress and Seckendorff.

Vicky's friend Mary Ponsonby urged her "resolutely to abstain from listening" to these assaults. But, as Lady Ponsonby admitted to Queen Victoria, "It seems almost more than human nature can bear to know that misrepresentation & lies are freely circulated & yet to take no notice."

Wilhelm jumped at any chance to discredit his mother. When his adjutant, Colonel Kessel, could not find Friedrich III's cipher, which had been used for secret correspondence, he claimed that Morell Mackenzie had stolen it from Fritz's room to give to a foreign government. While the official press accused the Dowager Empress of indirect responsibility for its disappearance, Wilhelm instituted an official inquiry. For three months, Vicky's household lay under a cloud of suspicion; all the servants were called in for questioning, and depositions were taken. Suddenly Kessel found the code in a drawer in his own table.

"Gustav von Kessel, with a wickedness & audacity I could hardly have credited even in him, now swears . . . that the cypher . . . was not there when he last looked through the table drawers & insinuates that it has been put there by someone in this house!! . . . ," Vicky wrote Victoria; "the whole time I

* *It is repeated to this day.*

thought it <u>must</u> be amongst his things, & said it was sure to come to light; but William preferred the cock & bull story which Kessel spread about everywhere! Now he does not like to own it was his own <u>fault</u>, so he invents this in order to cast blame & suspicion on others!"

Insults to his mother were always welcomed by the Kaiser, for, as Lady Ponsonby said, the Dowager Empress still remained "a very powerful personality in Europe." To prevent a political party growing up around her, Wilhelm lashed out with attacks that were often primitive. When he ridiculed her to the King of Italy as "that fat, dumpy little person who seeks influence," his remarks, like those about his parents to the Czar, met with "great surprise, but not admiration."

Wilhelm did not reserve his complaints for his fellow monarchs, and Vicky soon discovered that he was telling anyone who would listen (in Germany everyone listened to the Kaiser) that " 'an English doctor killed my father, and an <u>English</u> doctor <u>crippled</u> my arm & this we owe to my mother who would not have Germans about her!' "*

She was enraged.

"<u>You</u> know, dear Mama, that if I <u>had</u> been under the care of an enlightened English doctor, William's arm would <u>not</u> have been injured & I should not have suffered such tortures! It was <u>Martin</u> who treated me! You <u>also</u> <u>know</u> that we should have lost our beloved Fritz a year sooner or 6 months sooner had it not been for Sir Morell! . . . such lies ought <u>not</u> to go down to history to make out 'a case' as it were against me, as what my own son says, who alas is Emperor, every ignorant person believes."

BY THE FALL OF 1888, Vicky had reached the nadir of her widowhood. Like her mother before her, she resented the cheer of others, angry at them for forgetting her and Germany's loss. Feeling she had "<u>nothing</u> to hope for," except that "perchance" one day the truth about Fritz might come out, she wrote Victoria, quite rightly, that "suffering makes one selfish." The reality of her physical loss often overwhelmed her as well. "How I pine & long for him, & for his kind words & looks & for a kiss!!" she wrote on September 29, the anniversary of their engagement thirty-two years before. "Day by day I feel more lonely & <u>unprotected</u>," she added. "<u>No</u> one to lean on, and the difficulties I have to face alone are really too terrible. Yesterday I felt very <u>near</u> <u>putting</u> <u>an</u> end to myself!"

Utterly frustrated with the government, her son, and his court, Vicky found some sense of self-worth in her philanthropic activities. The citizens of Berlin gave her a gift of 57,500 marks in honor of her late husband's birthday to use for whatever charities she deemed appropriate. "Some of the kind gentlemen from the town said they hoped I would look upon this as a silent protest against

---

* *The Kaiser's accusation that it was an Englishman, not a German, who had delivered him was repeated so often that when this author started research, most texts claimed that Eduard Martin, the German chief of obstetrics at the University of Berlin who was hired by Wilhelm I to deliver his grandson, was an Englishman sent to Berlin by Queen Victoria to attend her daughter's confinement.*

all that had been said & done to hurt & pain us . . . ," she wrote her mother in October. "Of course they cannot proclaim it on the housetops, but they said they were ready to . . . support whatever Fritz would have liked! The town authorities have always been so nice to us, & also to me, independently. I am much touched by this!"

Outside Berlin, however, in the conservative provincial courts, there was a notable absence of compassion for the Dowager Empress. Even Vicky's brother-in-law, the once liberal Grand Duke of Baden, deserted her and his principles in rushing to pay court to his nephew. He has "completely changed in politics," the Dowager Empress told Victoria, adding philosophically, "It is in his <u>interest</u> to do so." Vicky had never expected any support from the Grand Duke's wife (Fritz's sister, Louise), and she got none. Louise, she told Victoria, "says William behaves <u>so</u> wonderfully well in every way," because he "walks in the way of his grandfather."

Of all the defectors, the most damaging to Vicky's public image were her uncle, Duke Ernest of Saxe-Coburg, and Gustav Freytag, a well-known writer under the patronage of the Duke. Infuriated by Uncle Ernest's toadying to Bismarck,* Vicky was convinced that two anonymous pamphlets attacking Fritz and her were written by him. The first, published in 1886 during Fritz's lifetime, had accused them of collusion with the enemy during the Franco-Prussian War. The second, which appeared the year after Fritz's death, vilified the Dowager Empress and Queen Victoria.

Uncle Ernest's desertion to the enemy camp was particularly galling, since Vicky had always avoided speaking ill of her father's brother. Certainly, the Duke's amorous life had been a source of trouble to his entire family, leaving relatives like Vicky to look after his discards like Hélène Reuter, an illegitimate daughter of the Duke, and her children, whom Vicky had rescued from poverty in the 1870s. An intelligent rake and wily ruler of his small duchy, Vicky's uncle sought the kind of power unavailable to enemies of the current regime.

A few intrepid statesmen spoke out against the Duke's pamphlets, and one brave man, a Dr. Harmening, whom Vicky did not know, wrote a rebuttal. Charged by Duke Ernest with libel, the doctor was sentenced to prison.

"The result is, that Uncle . . . escapes free, whereas the man who boldly defended Fritz & me & you . . . is sent to prison for six months and has to pay the costs!" Vicky wrote her mother. "[I]t is pretty well known now everywhere that he <u>is</u> the author and that Dr. Harmening . . . was not able to prove it. . . . I <u>could if</u> I liked, but of course would not & could not do such a thing against Papa's own brother, & also for Alfred's† sake. . . . <u>Uncle</u>, <u>knowing</u> all this, allows the man to be condemned for libel." Although Vicky did not have the

---

* *Frederick Ponsonby, Friedrich III's godson who later edited some of her letters, called Duke Ernest's memoirs "one long eulogy" of Bismarck (Ponsonby,* Letters of the Empress Frederick, *p. 366).*

† *Vicky's brother Alfred was due to the inherit the duchies of Saxe-Coburg and Gotha from Duke Ernest.*

courage to stand up for a stranger against the family name, she never spoke to her uncle again.

Just as destructive to the reputations of Friedrich III and his wife was a book by the Duke's protégé, Gustav Freytag, published in the spring of 1889 under the title *The Crown Prince and the German Imperial Crown*. Fritz and Vicky had been introduced to Freytag early in their marriage by Uncle Ernest. The first book they read aloud together was by Freytag; the author had become a family friend; and during the Franco-Prussian War, Fritz had allowed Freytag to accompany him to army headquarters to gather material for a novel. Since then, Freytag had changed his politics, and his book gave the impression that important secrets relating to the deployment of the German army during the war had reached the French through Vicky's and Alice's letters to their mother in England.

The charges were patently false. Both girls were working in hospitals in Germany at the time, and Freytag would never have been allowed to see their intimate letters. But in the current political climate in Berlin, his derogatory innuendos were accepted as the truth. Referring to Princess Alice as "a brave German woman," Freytag implied that Vicky's loyalties lay elsewhere, and he claimed that Fritz's "subordination" to his wife was "absolute." It is said (probably correctly) that Freytag submitted his book to Bismarck for the Chancellor's approval before publication.

All this made the love and support of Vicky's brother-in-law, the Grand Duke Louis of Hesse,* more meaningful. Finding it "quite incomprehensible" how the country had been turned so quickly against Friedrich III, Louis assured Vicky that his political principles had remained the same. "When I can do anything to propagate Fritz's views I will do so," he told her, adding, however, that he "must be very careful" not to do something that would bring reprisals on his duchy. After his death in March of 1892, Vicky wrote Victoria that it was "only Louis to whom I could talk, & who understood & who could share many of my feelings & fears."

One of the most painful aspects of Vicky's new life was the speed with which almost all her husband's relatives except a few cousins had lined up on the side of power. Her mother-in-law was the first to renounce her liberal principles—the tenets over which she had spent a lifetime fighting with her husband—to fall in behind Wilhelm II, kowtowing to him in ways she knew would earn his love. The Empress Augusta, Willy proudly told Waldersee, never left Berlin to go to her home in Coblenz without first asking his permission, "thereby showing him that she considered him as the head of the house."

Augusta carried on a normal social life during the summer of 1888 in spite of the recent death of her son. Ensconced in her home at Babelsberg, she continued her audiences and dinners, flying the royal standard at full height, never mentioning Fritz, and rationalizing her need for constant amusement on

---

* *Alice's widower.*

the grounds that mourning "interfered" with her "duty not to change former customs and habits."

Augusta had always spoiled Wilhelm, who now returned the favor. Describing the "continual intercourse" between the Kaiser's palace and his grandmother's home, Vicky complained that Willy and Dona "ask the Empress Augusta about everything. This house," she added, "does not exist! William never comes, & I am taken no notice of!" In a society that lived on hierarchical nuances, Vicky suddenly found herself several rungs down the royal ladder. "It seems to be more & more adopted that I am the third here at court! . . . I am quite ready to give way to the Empress Augusta on account of her age . . . but to have to knock under to my own daughter in law besides, makes it rather trying & almost ludicrous sometimes."

Used to life at the seat of power, Vicky resented living in a primarily female household. Her home, she complained, was "really like a convent . . . nothing but ladies, & only two gentlemen, sometimes only one, and at other times (though rarely) none!! Formerly it used to be principally gentlemen and so many coming and going, people wanting to speak to one every minute, carriages driving up & away, etc. . . . Now all is silent. . . . The bees seem to have deserted this hive and flown to the new one."

This was certainly true of the Dowager Empress's eldest daughter, Charlotte, who, according to her mother, "fawns on William." Even Charlotte's husband, the complaisant Bernhard, had become a loud and chauvinistic advocate of his brother-in-law. Anxious to remain in favor, Charlotte and Bernhard went around Berlin saying that it was Vicky's fault that "William & Dona had not taken their right place" at Queen Victoria's Jubilee the year before because Vicky "had prevented William from representing his grandfather." "These last accusations," Vicky explained to her mother, "are not Charlotte's invention but William's & it is believed that part of his behaviour towards me is the revenge he is taking for having had to submit to his own dear father going before him on every occasion last year."

Henry and Irene got along much better with the Dowager Empress, who moved in with them to see Irene through the birth of their first child, a son, the winter after Fritz's death. When she arrived at their home in Kiel, Vicky was shocked to find that her daughter-in-law* wore no shawl or scarf "to hide the 'shadow' cast by 'coming events.' " "As to you, it is to me utterly incomprehensible why & how the young ladies of the present day like to go about . . . ," Vicky wrote Victoria. "I think it quite embarrassing & would never have dreamed of doing so, especially before gentlemen & children & strangers." The Dowager Empress was more disturbed to discover that neither her second son nor his wife ever read a newspaper. Staying with them in Kiel, she said, was like being "in Russia," where the royal family lived in nearly total seclusion and ignorance of the outside world. "I am so unaccustomed to think & talk only of the little

* Irene was also Vicky's niece, one of the daughters of her deceased sister Alice.

trifling occurrences of every day life that I feel it very suffocating," she wrote Victoria.

Although the refrain was a common one among the wives of dead monarchs, the situation was more poignant for Vicky, who had lived for so many years on the expectation of power, which had come and gone with dizzying speed. Most women in her position had at least a few years to satisfy their ambitions before being forced to give way to the next generation. Certainly, no royal woman of her day had been more meticulously prepared for a throne—or more quickly deprived of it.

EVER SINCE Fritz's death, Queen Victoria had been urging Vicky to come home for a restorative visit. Prime Minister Salisbury, however, worried that the trip would undermine Anglo-German relations even further and wrote the Queen giving reasons why it would be "more prudent" for the visit to be postponed.

"Letter received," Victoria wired her Prime Minister. "Intention doubtless well meant, but it would be impossible, heartless, and cruel to stop my poor brokenhearted daughter from coming to her mother for peace, protection, and comfort. She has nowhere to go to; everyone expects her to come, and wonders she has not come before. It . . . only encourages the Emperor and the Bismarcks still more against us. You all seem frightened of them, which is not the way to make them better. . . . Please let no one mention this again."

There was trouble from Berlin as well. "Bernhard goes about saying he hopes they will not let me go to England, as I only want to intrigue against the German Government! . . . ," Vicky wrote Victoria. "I must be run down & annihilated, as I am a relic of that fabric of hopes & plans he [Bismarck] wishes to destroy <u>once</u> and <u>for</u> <u>all</u>! He fears that William <u>might</u> some day fall under my influence, & therefore, <u>this</u> must be prevented . . . by making me out a danger to the state & an enemy to the Government."

Apparently, Bismarck still feared the widow of Friedrich III. "The Empress Friedrich is a decided embarrassment for Emperor Wilhelm, for, to his regret, she refuses to live abroad, but is obviously engaged in forming a Court for herself which may well become the centre of oppositional elements," said the German Ambassador to Austria, Prince Reuss.

"The Clique wish to frighten & drive me out of the country," Vicky told Victoria a few months after Fritz's death. But Vicky could not give up the mission she had been sent to Germany to perform. As she explained to her mother, "[I]t would be foolish and wrong & undignified to allow oneself to be frightened away or bullied out of the country for which one has toiled . . . for 30 years."

CHAPTER SIXTY

"[I]t is so bitter to see the tide of life & business pass by & leave one standing on the bank, hardly a spectator even!"

THE DOWAGER EMPRESS, *July 1888*

*A*CCORDING TO THE NEW REGIME in Berlin, Kaiser Friedrich III was an aberration of German history, an atypical Hohenzollern who had fortunately died before he could exert any influence on the nation. His misapprehension of Germany's role in the world had been largely the fault of his English wife and his mother-in-law, who had lured him away from Germany's longtime ally, Czarist Russia, toward Britain, thus trying to corrupt a proud military autocracy and turn it into a toothless constitutional monarchy.

Behind the official line, conceived by Bismarck and Son and eagerly adopted by Wilhelm II, was Willy's desperate need to establish himself as an Emperor of Consequence and show the world that he was not under the thumb of his English relatives. An opportunity to do this and put Uncle Bertie in his place as a mere heir apparent presented itself to the young ruler less than three months after his accession.

In early September of 1888, the Prince of Wales wrote his nephew to thank him for the attentions paid some British officers in Germany and to say that he was on his way to Vienna, where he looked forward to seeing the Kaiser, who, he had heard, was planning to visit Franz Joseph at the same time. If given the date and time of Willy's arrival, Uncle Bertie said, he would be more than happy to arrange to meet him.

Wilhelm did not answer the letter. He waited until the Prince of Wales was already in Vienna, then wired Franz Joseph that since he, the German Kaiser, was coming on "affairs of state," it would be wiser not to have any other royalties present. As intended, the wire created "a scandal."

Thrown into an impossible situation—Austria could not afford to offend Germany—Franz Joseph was forced to let the Prince of Wales know that his nephew the Kaiser did not wish to see him. Bertie immediately withdrew to Romania, where he stayed throughout Willy's visit. In Vienna, the young Kaiser chortled over his victory, quipping to friends that he preferred his "uncle's rooms to his company."

It was not until two weeks later that Vicky heard about her son's "gross insult" to her brother. "You know, dearest Vicky, how I have taken his part & stuck up for him in the family," Bertie wrote her, explaining how it pained him to have to tell "all this" to her. "I am so ashamed and so "indignant . . . ," she wrote their mother, "& feel it more than any rudeness to me, as, alas, I am used to that."

Willy was more than rude. When Queen Victoria asked him for an explanation, he said he knew nothing about what had happened. He would have been happy to see his uncle, he said, intimating that it was a matter of policy for which Bismarck was responsible. Required to produce an excuse, the Chancellor explained somewhat lamely that the Czar of Russia might have taken offence if the Prince of Wales had been at a meeting between the monarchs of Germany and Austria. Moreover, Bismarck added, Bertie continued to treat Willy as his nephew, rather than as Kaiser of Germany.

Victoria would have none of it:

"[I]t is simply absurd," she wrote Prime Minister Salisbury, "that the Emperor of Russia, the Princess of Wales's own brother-in-law should have been angry at the uncle and nephew meeting . . . as regarding the Prince's not treating his nephew as Emperor; this is really too vulgar and too absurd. . . . We have always been very intimate with our grandson and nephew, and to pretend that he is to be treated in private as well as in public as his Imperial Majesty is perfect madness! . . . If he has such notions, he better never come here. . . .

"As regard the political relations of the two Governments, the Queen quite agrees that that should not be affected (if possible) by these miserable personal quarrels; but the Queen much fears that, with such a hot-headed, conceited, and wrongheaded young man, devoid of all feeling, this may at ANY moment become impossible."

To cover the Kaiser's foolishness, the Bismarck press presented an entirely different version of the incident: "Here Bertie was blamed for . . . having left Vienna, in order not to see William, & to be purposely uncivil to him!" Vicky informed Victoria.

Four months later, however, in January of 1889, Bismarck needed a rapprochement with England. The situation in France had suddenly changed. Boulanger, the chauvinistic general who had been exiled to the French provinces, won a seat as a member of the Chamber of Deputies, returned in triumph to Paris, and was expected to declare himself dictator of France. Frightened of what might happen if Boulangism again took hold in France, Bismarck executed a complete reversal in foreign policy by proposing a defensive Anglo-German alliance. The alliance was refused by the British, who did not feel currently threatened by France and trusted neither Bismarck nor the Kaiser. Vicky was not displeased.

"I believe thoroughly that Prince Bismarck & William wish to be on good terms with England, & that it is in their interest," she wrote Victoria, "but they consider themselves lords & masters of the universe. . . . The rest of Europe will have to teach them manners."

The British Prime Minister looked at it differently. Although he suspected that Bismarck's overture was partially due to the fact that Germany's relations with Russia were "less satisfactory" than usual, Salisbury told Queen Victoria that if Germany wished "to be received back" into England's favor, it was in the Queen's "interest to make his penitential return as easy . . . as possible."

At the same time that Bismarck proposed an alliance, Willy wrote his grandmother, inviting himself to England. "William must not come this year," Victoria wrote Bertie, "you could not meet him and I could not after all he has said and done." To Salisbury, Victoria explained that the Kaiser must make "some sort of apology" to the Prince of Wales for the incident at Vienna before being accepted back into the good graces of his English relatives. Nonetheless, the Prime Minister convinced Queen Victoria to invite the Kaiser to come with his fleet during the summer to Osborne, where she could treat him to a naval review. (Everyone knew how Willy loved parades.) Vicky heard of the invitation through her son Henry.

> William yesterday informed Henry (in his own childish, inflated & bumptious style) that you had invited him (William) to Osborne in July, and that he was going to have a glorious reception, great preparations would be made for him, a naval review would be given in his honour, & he would bring his fleet, etc. I suppose Lord Salisbury wished it, it is also, I suppose & believe, very right & proper & necessary. But you can imagine what a stab it gives me! The thought that W. who has so trampled upon me, & on his beloved father's memory, should now be received . . . in my own dear home! . . . W. has no 'delicatesse de coeur.' To announce triumphantly to his brother what he cannot take the trouble to mention to me, is only one of the 1000 insults which I ought to be used to, but which always wound me.

A week later, after an apologetic letter in which the Queen said she could not refuse to receive Willy, Vicky was more resigned. "I quite understand about William's visit . . . ," Vicky answered. "I know you could not do otherwise, but I am sure you will also understand what my feelings must be! No amends have ever been made to me for all I have been made to suffer, no explanations offered —nor excuses, and I cannot forget what has passed."

Nor could Bertie, who requested an apology from his nephew for the Vienna incident. But the Kaiser claimed that the snub had been nothing more than an "invention" of others. In that case, Bertie replied, why could Willy not just write "a few lines saying he regretted that I was under the impression that he was averse to seeing me at Vienna."

The Kaiser still refused. He hinted that the blame lay elsewhere, with the Foreign Ministry or his friend Prince Reuss, the German Ambassador to Austria. No one could budge him. Not even Queen Victoria, who decided to accept his disclaimer but wrote to ask "if he could enquire how the mistake occurred." Wilhelm's answer, according to the Queen's private secretary, made "matters worse than ever by accusing the Prince of Wales . . . of inventing the Vienna story!"

The Queen tried again. She offered to make Willy an Admiral of the English Fleet in honor of his visit. The honor, however, carried a price tag: Wilhelm II could best "show his gratitude to the Queen" by writing to her "how glad he will be to meet his uncle the Prince of Wales, and how sorry he was that there should have been a misunderstanding."

The Kaiser refused to pay. "Her Majesty wrote to me ten days or so ago that she was thankful for my information concerning the Vienna affair and considered the whole as <u>closed</u> and <u>finished</u> to her satisfaction! . . ." he wrote Christian of Schleswig-Holstein, who was serving as intermediary between the two courts. "So you see <u>all is right</u>."

But it wasn't—not with anyone but Willy. The Kaiser went to England without a proper apology, and the Prince of Wales was, in the words of his private secretary, "sacrificed by Lord Salisbury to political expediency."

As was the Dowager Empress of Germany. "I hope to hear as little as possible about William's visit to England," she wrote her mother. For nearly thirty years, Vicky had incurred accusations running the gamut from mere disloyalty to actual treason for trying to promote the friendship that had now been usurped by her enemies, who laughed openly at her frustration. "To think that you will have to receive all the people about William who have behaved <u>so</u> disgracefully & abominably & <u>treacherously</u> to Fritz & to me gives me <u>great</u> pain. . . . They <u>revel</u> in the thought that it is a fresh humiliation for me!"

In spite of her feelings, there was no question that the Dowager Empress submitted fully to the royal code. "Wronged and persecuted as I have been, I could have appealed to you & all my brothers and sisters to seek redress for me . . . ," she wrote her mother. "But this I could <u>not</u> do in my position. England <u>must</u> appear to ignore what are affairs of the German Court & see that the relations between the two great countries be not disturbed or affected by family affairs! . . . my brothers—English Princes—cannot be as outspoken with the Emperor of Germany as if he were someone else. Alfred, Christian & Louis have interests of their <u>own</u> in Germany,* & cannot risk giving offence by . . . speaking truths which give offence!"

The thirty-year-old Kaiser, who boasted "I can do with my grandmother anything I wish," arrived at Spithead on August 1, 1889, on board the *Hohenzollern,* the sleek, powerful warship that he had had trimmed with gold and fitted out as a pleasure yacht. Wearing the bright new uniform of a British admiral, he and Henry were received with all due pomp by the Prince of Wales, who escorted them to see the Queen. The young Kaiser was, according to his grandmother, "very amiable," kissing her "very affectionately" on both cheeks when he arrived two and a half hours late.

Wilhelm was given the promised naval review, in return for which he presented his grandmother with a parade of men from the German navy who

---

* *Her brother Alfred was due to inherit the duchies of Saxe-Coburg and Gotha; her brother-in-law Christian (married to Helena) was from Schleswig-Holstein; and her brother-in-law Louis (Alice's widower) was the Grand Duke of Hesse.*

had accompanied him to England in a showy escort of twelve men-of-war. Victoria thought that Willy's sailors were "fine-looking," noting in her journal that they "marched beautifully, though in that peculiar Prussian way, throwing up their legs." During the visit, however, there were rumors that Wilhelm II had already started talking about building up a great fleet of his own to rival that of his grandmother, causing the *Times* to speculate on the wisdom of giving him such a complete look at the British navy.

But Prime Minister Salisbury was satisfied. He prevailed upon the Queen to give Bismarck a portrait of herself and congratulated her on "the admirable effect produced upon the mind of the Emperor and those who were with him." Back in Germany, the Bismarcks could scarcely wait to trumpet their success to Willy's mother. Not too surprisingly, she resented "the triumphant and defiant tone" in which they told her that "no Sovereign was ever so fêted."

"All these demonstrations of friendship of the present regime are right & proper . . . ," Vicky commented, "but they are little in accordance with what has been said & done, written & professed both last year & before! They no doubt suit the moment & the situation."

Which was precisely the case. Bismarck's newfound enthusiasm for England lessened when he heard that Salisbury could not get the parliamentary majority needed to carry through an Anglo-German entente. And it evaporated at the news that General Boulanger had failed to take over France,* where the republicans had rallied their forces. Vicky still had the capacity to be shocked by the machinations of the most pragmatic politician in Europe. Her son Wilhelm II, on the other hand, never took the trouble to understand them, preferring to accept without question the military pomp that he could now call upon to buttress his ego.

AMONG THE FEW JOYS that the Dowager Empress counted when she reviewed her widowhood were her three younger daughters—Moretta (Victoria), Sophie, and Mossy (Margaret). Aged twenty-two, eighteen, and sixteen at the time of their father's death, the three young women remained loyal to their mother in the face of Willy's and Charlotte's defection and Henry's lack of concern.

In October of 1889, some sixteen months after her father's death, Sophie married Prince Constantine, the heir to the throne of Greece.† Tino, as he was known in the family, was not very bright, but, as Queen Victoria wrote Vicky, "a good heart and good character . . . go far beyond great cleverness." When the time came, it was a wrench for Vicky, who dreaded sending Sophie so far from home. She also worried about Moretta, who, as an unengaged young

* *Charged with treason, Boulanger fled France and committed suicide two years later in Brussels on the grave of his mistress.*

† *The Greek royal family was descended from the Danish. Alix and Dagmar's brother had ascended the throne of Greece in 1863 as George I; he had married the Grand Duchess Olga, niece of Alexander II of Russia; Constantine was their eldest son.*

woman, now had to endure the humiliation of walking behind her younger sister at functions of the court.

There were religious complications as well. Queen Olga of Greece did not want her son to marry a non-Orthodox Princess, and Dona did not approve of Sophie's joining the Orthodox Church. A religious fanatic, Dona had fired all the palace servants who were not evangelical Christians when she became Kaiserin. She spoke about his sister to Willy, who announced that he would not allow Sophie back in Germany if she gave up the Protestant faith. Matters were temporarily resolved when it was decided to hold Protestant and Greek Orthodox services.

The wedding between the Kaiser's sister and the son of the King of Greece was an occasion for a large gathering of what Queen Victoria referred to as the "royal mob." Much as she disapproved of the Greek Orthodox religion, Dona had decided to attend the wedding. It was only after the Dowager Empress was on the steamer en route to Athens,* however, that she found out how her pious daughter-in-law had dealt with the religious question.

"On arriving here on board, I got a letter from Dona saying that they had "forgotten to tell me" that they were taking Kögel† to Athens to perform the marriage ceremony," Vicky wrote Victoria.

> This they announce . . . without <u>asking</u> or consulting <u>me</u> or Sophie!!! Kögel they <u>know</u> that Fritz & <u>I</u> particularly disliked, & we have made all arrangements months & months ago that the King of Greece's German chaplain, Dr. Peterson . . . was to perform the Protestant ceremony!!! They have had a <u>years</u> [*sic*] time to think & talk this over. . . . Most likely Dona <u>knew</u> that I & Sophie would <u>object</u>, therefore it was done behind my back. . . . I am only afraid Willy [King George] of Greece will be much hurt, at never having been told or consulted either!

This may have been why King George of Greece did not come to Piraeus to receive the Kaiser personally—a slight for which Wilhelm never forgave him. Whatever the excuse, Herbert von Bismarck was rude to the Greek ministers, Wilhelm II's court behaved poorly, and Vicky was "considerably relieved" when Willy left Greece. As was the Prince of Wales, who had arrived in Athens with Her Majesty's Mediterranean squadron, thus giving his nephew the Kaiser an opportunity to strut about in the uniform of a British admiral and offer unsolicited advice on the size and armaments of the British fleet. Willy's exhortations did not stop when he left Greece. He continued to send his grandmother letters filled with suggestions for improving her navy—"the humble notion of a simple Admiral of the Fleet," as he put it—from his palace in Berlin.

From Greece, the Kaiser paid a state visit to the Sultan of Turkey, thoroughly upsetting the German Foreign Ministry, which was committed to Tur-

---

* *Before leaving, Vicky sent Queen Victoria some letters and personal papers for safekeeping. It was clearly unsafe for her to leave anything behind when she herself was not there to guard it.*

† *Dr. Kögel was a particularly conservative court chaplain.*

key's enemy, Russia. A few weeks earlier, Alexander III had asked Bismarck for assurances that he would remain in office during the reign of Wilhelm II. "I certainly have full trust in you, but unfortunately your Kaiser gives others his ear, especially General Waldersee, who wants war," the Czar said. Bismarck tried to reassure him that neither the Kaiser's recent trip to England nor his projected journey to Turkey was aimed against Russia.

Willy, who never failed to be impressed by lavish royal trappings,* enjoyed his visit to the Sultan and was distressed to find Bismarck speaking "quite disdainfully" of the Turks on his return. "I thought I might inspire him in part with essentially more favourable opinions, but my efforts were of little avail . . . ," he later wrote. "Prince Bismarck and Count Herbert were never favourably inclined towards Turkey and they never agreed with me in my Turkish policy—the old policy of Frederick the Great."

Wilhelm, who loved to compare himself to his illustrious ancestor, was growing restive under the tutelage of the old Chancellor and was no longer the abject Russophile Herbert had taught him to be. His trip to St. Petersburg the previous year and the Czar's disinclination to return it had wounded Willy's pride. In spite of family pleasantries, the Kaiser believed that Alexander III was plotting against him, and he looked forward to the inevitability of war between them.

Unmindful of Bismarck's *tour de force* diplomacy, Wilhelm II based his foreign policy solely on the unpredictable quirks of royal relationships and the efficacy of his own charm. To quote Wilhelm II's peer, the ill-fated Archduke Rudolph of Austria: "The Kaiser is likely to cause great confusion in Europe before long. He is just the man for it; energetic and capricious, firmly convinced of his own genius."

---

* One of the things Wilhelm II loved about Eastern monarchs and their underlings was their elaborate presents—"priceless treasures" that he "carried off from the houses of those Arab and Turkish officials whom he delighted to honour by visiting them in their homes." During a visit to Syria, he apparently received an entire suite of ivory inlaid furniture in exchange for a life-sized portrait of himself (Townley, Indiscretions of Lady Susan, p. 165).

CHAPTER
SIXTY-ONE

*"How one does bless a constitution like a British one, when one
sees a young man totally without knowledge & experience playing the despot."*

THE DOWAGER EMPRESS, 1890

I NEVER remember the outlook having been as dark as it is now . . . ,"
Vicky wrote her mother in the fall of 1889, just after her son's return from
Turkey. "The enormous sacrifice the nation is called upon to make for the Army
creates a deep-seated discontent in the masses of the people, of which William
is totally unaware & for which Bismarck cares nothing."

Vicky was right when she said that Bismarck was not overly troubled by
agitation in the lower classes, but her assessment of her son's attitude was
inaccurate. It was not that Wilhelm II was unaware of domestic discontent, but
rather that he disagreed with the Chancellor about how to deal with it. Their
rift had come to the fore a few months earlier, when a miners' strike set off a
series of walkouts affecting eighty percent of the German mining force and
crippling the economy, just recovering from the long depression. The strike—
the greatest work stoppage in the history of Germany—started on May 3, 1889,
with the coal miners of the Ruhr Valley of Westphalia. Although the demand
for coal had risen, they had received no increases in pay. They were fined for
refusal to work overtime (up to sixteen hours underground) and found that
when they tried to leave the mines, the elevators stopped operating. In response
to their demands for an eight-hour day, a fifteen percent pay increase, and
better working conditions, the Governor of Westphalia called in the army. Nine
people were killed.

Fundamental differences between Bismarck and Wilhelm II as to how to
handle the emergency surfaced immediately. The Kaiser told the Governor of
Westphalia that the owners of the mines in his area must increase workers'
wages or the army would be withdrawn. But the Chancellor was not all that
anxious for the strike to end. The fear of rampaging workers, he felt, provided
an excellent backdrop for the renewal of the antisocialist law, due to expire
the following year. Bismarck laid out his position during a meeting of his
cabinet shortly after the strike began. Much to his surprise, Wilhelm II himself
appeared at the next cabinet meeting, uninvited, unannounced, and in obvious
disagreement with his Chancellor. After he left, Bismarck told his ministers

that it was "necessary to protect" the young monarch from his own "excessive zeal."

Within a few days, the Kaiser met with both owners and miners. To the former, he preached a sermon on their duty to their employees and the state. To the latter, he threatened that if they had anything to do with the Social Democratic Party, "I will have you all shot down."

"I was more than horrified at William's speech . . . ," Vicky wrote Victoria. "It is just like him! He . . . thinks himself very grand! I think such words in the mouth of a sovereign & so young & inexperienced a man, most brutal & unbecoming."

Despite Wilhelm's bluster and an attempt by the National Liberals to mediate the dispute, walkouts in a number of other industries—building, metallurgy, and textiles—as well as in the coal mines took nearly 300,000 workers out of the workforce over the next year. During this time, the gulf between Wilhelm II, whose sympathies were with the workers, and Bismarck, who supported the owners, deepened, widened, and finally became unbridgeable.

Bismarck did not believe there was anything seriously wrong in the condition of the working class in Germany. "The efforts of workers to obtain ever more pay for ever less work has no limits," he told the young Kaiser. But Wilhelm blamed the factory owners. "Not all industrialists are like Krupp and Stumm, who take good care of their workers," he said. "Most exploit workers ruthlessly and ruin them. . . . The corporations don't care for their workmen; many are foreign-owned."

To arrive at this conclusion, the Kaiser had consulted a variety of sources, starting with the court painter, August von Heyden, who had been a miner thirty years earlier, and a rich industrialist, Count Hugo Douglas, who had given a speech praising the young Kaiser as a ruler of both rich and poor. Wilhelm's most influential adviser was his old tutor Hintzpeter, who had prepared a memorandum on the labor question, saying that if the Kaiser took up the subject, he would find in it "a mine of popularity for himself."

Hintzpeter's report, along with two other explorations of the question,* represented a serious challenge to Bismarck's authority. There was, in fact, a tantalizing vacuum developing at court. Bismarck was rarely in Berlin during this period, spending most of his time at his estate in Friedrichsruh, near Hamburg, leaving the hyperactive Wilhelm to Herbert. In the spring of 1889, Bismarck Sr. told the Dowager Empress that "he had comparatively very little to do," since her son had "unlimited confidence" in Herbert. By the end of the year, he was not so sure. "If I was younger and able to be with him every day, as I did with the old emperor, I would twist him around my finger, but as it is he lets himself be influenced by individual people, by adjutants, especially by the military."

Along with a fundamental difference in their attitude toward labor, there

* One requisitioned by Holstein at the Foreign Ministry and another prepared by the Kaiser's closest friend, Philipp zu Eulenburg.

was another potential source of friction between the Kaiser and the Chancellor —the antisocialist law, which Bismarck presented to the Reichstag for permanent renewal in October of 1889. The Reichstag cartel, made up of National Liberals and extreme to moderate conservatives, supported the law, although the parties disagreed on whether police should be allowed to expel agitators from their homes. Believing that the ongoing strikes would frighten the public into demanding even more stringent legislation, Bismarck refused to negotiate a compromise, even at the risk of destroying his valuable cartel on the eve of elections, due to be held in February of 1890.

On January 24, Wilhelm II called for a crown council to discuss "my ideas on the labor question." Bismarck hurried back from Friedrichsruh for two preliminary meetings—the first with his cabinet, during which he ordered his ministers to temporize with Wilhelm II on the matter of social reform, and the second with the Kaiser himself. There are no records of their tête-à-tête, but observers say it ended in a "very tense mood." Ten men—the Kaiser, the Chancellor, and eight ministers—then seated themselves around the table for a crown council.

Wilhelm II started off by announcing that he had called the council on this particular day because it was the birthday of Frederick the Great. He himself, he said, wanted to be the "King of the Beggars."* In that regard, he had important labor reforms he wanted to effect—restrictions on Sunday, night, female, and child labor; provisions for arbitration; and workers' committees. He said he intended to make a public proclamation on the subject that very day. Then and only then did he ask Bismarck for his opinion.

Furious at his former pupil for taking control of the meeting, the Chancellor insisted that these topics needed to be studied before any royal declarations were made. The tense mood grew electric.

Wilhelm then turned to the subject of the antisocialist bill, which he asked Bismarck's ministers to accept without the expulsion provision in order to save his newest enthusiasm, the cartel that held the majority of seats in the Reichstag. The cartel had wooed and won Wilhelm II with flattery, comparing him to "his distinguished ancestors, holding the reins of government with unflagging zeal and untiring attention to duty." Wilhelm urged Bismarck's ministers to preserve both the cartel and the antisocialist bill. "If his majesty has a different opinion on such a weighty question, then I am obviously no longer the right person for my position," Bismarck threatened.

It was obvious to Wilhelm and the members of his cabinet that the Chancellor was trying to provoke a crisis. If a harsh new antisocialist law brought about demonstrations, it would give Bismarck an excuse to call in the army, force even more repressive legislation through the Reichstag, and prove his own irreplaceability—all in one stroke. This was vintage Bismarck. But for the first time in his career, it failed to produce the desired result. Unlike his grandfather

* *"Le Roi des Gueux."*

and father, Wilhelm II did not retreat. "That puts me in a dilemma," he said, looking around the table for support. "I beg these gentlemen for their opinion."

The ministers did not dare join him against his Chancellor in the latter's presence. No votes were taken, nothing was resolved, and Wilhelm II left the crown council "boiling." "They are not my ministers," he said in fury, "but Bismarck's." Two days later, Bismarck admitted that he had "gone too far." His ministers agreed. "We parted with . . . the feeling," one reported, "that an irreparable breach had occurred between sovereign and chancellor."

Events now marched toward a dénouement. Wilhelm published a proclamation announcing labor reforms and proposing an international conference on labor problems to be held in Berlin. Bismarck tried to get the Kaiser's conference boycotted by Switzerland and France. Both the Chancellor's antisocialist law, which was rejected by the Reichstag, and her son's plans for a labor conference concerned the Dowager Empress:

> My beloved Fritz was so much against the passing of the [original] Socialist Law! He foresaw what the Liberal party always foresaw & which has now happened, i.e., it would only encourage the growth of Socialism and teach the Socialists to organize themselves into a body secretly. This is now done. They have grown with extraordinary rapidity even since last year, & all the miners who sent a deputation to William last year have since joined the Socialists. . . . Prince Bismarck, whose fault the present situation is . . . counts upon William getting into a dreadful mess . . . & his then being appealed to to put everything . . . straight again! . . . William . . . is perfectly delighted with himself, & the flattery which is continually lavished upon him makes him think himself a genius!!

Vicky was particularly dubious about Willy's European labor conference, which, she felt, he had not thought through: "There is too intimate a connection between economic questions & the Labour question to be able to solve one quite without the other! . . . ," she wrote Victoria, placing the blame for the ills of Germany's workers on Bismarck's policy of protectionism.

> It is true the Labour question exists in every country alike, but still under very different conditions. . . . One must be a very great authority on these subjects, or possess a vast experience to venture on such a step as a proposal to settle this question. To stir it up without arriving at some very striking, important & satisfactory result . . . raises expectations doomed to be disappointed & excites the masses instead of calming them, which . . . will lead to a struggle here—to coercion—& perhaps violence—and then reaction. Prince Bismarck sees this most likely—does he wish it or not?

Victoria understood her daughter's concern, but replied that her grandson's interest in labor was still "a move in the right direction, & shows a will to do something for the working & often suffering classes"—just what Vicky and her beloved Fritz had "always been so anxious to do. Could you not just say a word to him in that sense?" she suggested.

But Vicky could not get past her own hurt feelings. Willy, she said, had "never mentioned affairs or politics" to her since his father's death. "[T]o take the initiative would be a great mistake on my part and a want of proper pride —and that is the last thing one clings to when all else is taken from one."

Her son, she said, "fancies he is gifted with supreme wisdom. . . . The adulation and flattery which is heaped upon him you would hardly believe! His mother is the only one who will not stoop to this. . . . There are so many who are anxious to get rid of me . . . that it is only [by] remaining perfectly quiet & passive that I can be safe from their accusations, their attacks & intrigues."

Things were better, she said, but only because she no longer gave her enemies any ammunition with which to attack her. "[T]hey see that I want nothing and do not care to have so-called 'influence.' . . . they . . . think me harmless and sans conséquence, which of course makes William & Dona less suspicious. . . . The 'modus vivendi' between the other court & myself is quite smooth—outwardly & that for the present & under the circumstances is all I can expect."

WHILE VICKY was enjoying a period of relative calm, the tensions between Wilhelm II and Bismarck continued to mount. The young Kaiser's arrogance, fed by the Bismarcks, had finally come home to haunt the Chancellery itself. The issue was no longer Wilhelm's labor conference, his proclamation, or even the defeated antisocialist bill. It was now the political survival of Bismarck.

Hoping to produce the same panic and capitulation he had always aroused in Wilhelm I, Bismarck announced at the end of January 1890 that, owing to differences of opinion with the monarch, he intended to resign his Prussian titles, retaining only his position as Chancellor and Foreign Minister of the Reich. Expecting the usual hue and cry, the old man was disappointed. No one came forward to beg him to stay, and the National Liberals said that this would be good for the Prussian Ministry. Still, Bismarck waited ten days before presenting his resignation to the Kaiser, and when Wilhelm asked him to support the military appropriations due to come before the Reichstag, he quickly withdrew it.

But the Chancellor's power was obviously slipping away. Sensing the need for support, he turned to old adversaries. He dropped in unannounced on Waldersee, who was not at home, and Moltke, who kindly urged him to remain in office. On February 19, he paid a call on the Dowager Empress. He brought along his wife, Johanna, for support. It was the moment for which Vicky had been waiting for twenty-eight years:

"Prince Bismarck, you come to me when you know what you have done between me and my son. I cannot help you," she said.

"I want only sympathy," he answered.

She agreed to listen.

Bismarck spoke about her son's labor proclamation, complaining that "he could not keep pace with innovations so suddenly resolved and carried out in such a hurry and on the advice of people he thought in no way competent to give it." He told her that he had tried and failed to "dissuade" Wilhelm from his rashness and was now simply trying to limit the damage.

"So far, I think Prince Bismarck was very wise, & acted very loyally towards William," Vicky wrote Victoria,

> & I could only agree with him! Of course, he did not discuss principles of policy . . . with those you know I could not agree. But I certainly think the advice he gave William in this case was prudent and sensible & practical and I am very sorry it was not taken.
>
> I thought Prince Bismarck looking remarkably strong & well & inclined to take things very philosophically. He is exceedingly fond of William and he never was of Fritz (this is quite natural), but I fancy he is uneasy at the very great self-confidence and the naiveté with which he exercises his will & takes responsibilities, and also at the curious people who have access to him & are listened to.

As so often happened, the Dowager Empress had misjudged the Chancellor. Hardly philosophical, Bismarck was frantic at the idea of being pushed out by the brash, independent young Kaiser.

The following day, which was election day (February 20, 1889), Bismarck's cartel suffered a major defeat, as the beleaguered Social Democrats attracted over twenty percent of the voters, more than any other party. It was a moral rather than a political victory, since districting gave the Social Democratic Party only thirty-five delegates to the Reichstag. Nevertheless, Bismarck used their gains to try to convince Wilhelm II that he must remain in office long enough to hold off "the socialist menace."

Towards that end, the Chancellor presented a militant spring agenda, geared to appeal to the aggressive young Kaiser. Would His Majesty agree to order out the army in case of uprisings over the antisocialist bill? If so, the Chancellor would ask the Reichstag to pass both it and the new military appropriations. There would probably be many dissolutions of parliament before they —Kaiser and Chancellor together—prevailed. In a scene reminiscent of one he had played out nearly thirty years before with Wilhelm I, Bismarck announced "No surrender!" shook hands vigorously with Wilhelm II, and strode out of the room. "The Kaiser is ready to fight. . . . ," he announced on his return to the Foreign Ministry; "I can remain at his side."

But it was obvious at a meeting of the crown council the next day that Wilhelm and Bismarck were still on opposite sides when it came to labor reform and that the ministers, who invariably came down on the side of power, were now with the Kaiser. After a difficult session, Bismarck was seen wandering through the Ministry of Interior "like a ghost, his expression blank, without apparent purpose, opening a door here and there and looking inside." Lowly clerks, "startled" by the appearance of the great man in their midst, "moved respectfully out of his way." From Interior, Bismarck moved on to the Ministry of Foreign Affairs, where he vented his frustration with the Kaiser on the *éminence grise* of the ministry, Friedrich von Holstein. Holstein was not surprised. He had been in contact with Waldersee, who was advising Wilhelm, and with Prince Reuss, the German Ambassador to Austria and the Kaiser's old friend. "[T]he breach can no longer be healed . . . ," Reuss said. "I had not expected the moment to come so soon when he [Wilhelm II] would wish to be his own Chancellor."

With four out of every seven votes having been cast for parties hostile to himself, Bismarck floated the idea of a new consortium of princes empowered to dissolve the Reich (empire) without consulting the people. Wilhelm balked. Nor would the Kaiser support Bismarck's new, harsher antisocialist bill. Faced with a distinct lack of confidence from the monarch and the electorate, Bismarck should have offered to resign. Calculating that the military appropriations would be enough to dissolve the Reichstag, he merely withdrew the antisocialist bill.

On March 12, 1890, Bismarck tried one last desperate parliamentary maneuver: he invited his old enemy Windthorst, head of the powerful Center Party, to talk about forming a new cartel. But neither conservatives nor National Liberals would join the Catholic Center. "I have just left the deathbed of a great man," Windthorst remarked to a friend when he took his leave of his old opponent.

Two days later, Bismarck sent a message requesting an audience with the Kaiser to discuss his conversation with Windthorst. Wilhelm's answer did not arrive until after Bismarck had retired for the night. Hastily awakened at eight-thirty the next morning, Bismarck was told to expect a visit from the Kaiser in thirty minutes. Now it was Wilhelm's turn to wait while Bismarck dressed himself. Neither was in a good mood when the audience finally began.

The Kaiser said he had already heard that Bismarck had seen Windthorst. He was irate, as under German law he had the right to be informed before his Chancellor attempted to form a new majority. He demanded that Bismarck speak with him before entering into negotiations with party leaders—a directive the Chancellor angrily refused. He also told the Chancellor to rescind an order, passed in 1852 during the reign of Friedrich Wilhelm IV, which prevented the monarch from dealing directly with his cabinet ministers, since, as Wilhelm put it, Bismarck was "in Friedrichsruh most of the time." Bismarck refused that, too. Lastly, Wilhelm informed the Chancellor that he wanted military appropriations reduced to a point at which they could pass the Reichstag, thus effectively removing Bismarck's last means of provoking a dissolution.

In a desperate show of power, Bismarck brought up the subject of foreign affairs. He told Wilhelm that he should give up another projected trip to Russia, saying that he had received a report that the first visit had not been particularly successful. Wilhelm demanded that Bismarck show him the source of his information. In what can only have been a deliberate gesture, Bismarck started to cover some papers lying on his desk. The Kaiser naturally asked to see them. Bismarck refused. Wilhelm grabbed one. It was the famous dispatch from Alexander III in which the Czar referred to Wilhelm II as "an ill-mannered boy of bad faith." As the outraged Kaiser left the room, both men knew that they could never work with each other again.

To avoid the opprobrium attached to dismissing the leading statesman in Europe, Wilhelm tried to force Bismarck to resign. Prodded by Waldersee, he sent a messenger to the Chancellor telling him he must rescind the Decree of 1852 or appear at the palace that afternoon, resignation in hand. "I am not well enough to go to the Palace" was Bismarck's response. "I will write." He met with his cabinet instead.

During the meeting, a messenger arrived at the Chancellery to inquire why, if the Chancellor could not deliver the paper in question, he did not have it sent to the palace. Bismarck replied that he needed time to put his resignation in publishable form.

It was not until the next day, March 18, 1890, after General Leo von Caprivi had already taken up duties as the new Chancellor of Germany, that Bismarck finally delivered his resignation. In it, he claimed that he could not continue to run foreign affairs in light of the Kaiser's attitude toward the Russians, and that Wilhelm's refusal to abide by the Decree of 1852 was a return to domestic absolutism. It was a masterful document in which the old man managed to absolve himself of any wrongdoing and accuse the young Kaiser of destroying the work of his life. Wilhelm refused to allow it to be published.

In place of Bismarck's statement, the Kaiser printed his own, in which it appeared that he had merely acquiesced to Bismarck's request to be relieved of his duties for reasons of age and poor health. It was with "deepest emotion" and a "troubled heart," Wilhelm II said, that he had accepted the Chancellor's resignation. Enumerating Bismarck's contributions to the Fatherland, he bestowed on him the equivalent of the rank of field marshal, a large sum of money, and a new title, the Duke of Lauenburg. Along with these honors, the Kaiser gave the Chancellor a life-sized portrait of himself.

Bismarck refused the money and announced that he would use the title of Duke of Lauenburg only when he wished to travel incognito.* From that day forward, whenever he used coins, Bismarck turned the side with the Kaiser's likeness downwards. In this way, he explained, he did not have to look at "that false face."

Wilhelm II rushed to justify his action with other European monarchs. He wrote Franz Joseph of Austria that Bismarck had "tried to degrade" him.

The man . . . for whom I had endured in my parents' home a moral persecution like the pains of hell, the man for whom, after the death of the Emperor William, I had thrown myself alone into the breach in order to retain him, bringing upon myself the anger of my dying father and the inextinguishable hatred of my mother,† was looking on all this as nothing

---

* Royalty usually traveled under aristocratic pseudonyms when not on state visits.

† A falsehood. Neither the dying Friedrich III nor his wife ever considered letting Bismarck go.

. . . because I was not ready to bow to his will. His boundless contempt of humanity . . . even those who were working themselves to death for him, did him a bad turn here, when he took his master for a nobody.

To Czar Alexander III of Russia he wrote a letter in the same vein and received a predictable response: "You were entirely right," the Czar assured him. "The Prince, though a prince, was after all only your minister, your servant. As such, his first duty was to obey you. His disobedience to his Emperor brought his fall. In your place I should have done just the same."

Wilhelm II also spoke with the British Ambassador, asking him to inform Queen Victoria of the "train of circumstances" that had brought about Bismarck's resignation: Bismarck's constant withdrawal to the country, his refusal to compromise on the antisocialist bill, the "complete subjection" of his ministers who "dared not" support the Kaiser's social reform, his eagerness to call out the army, his efforts to undermine the Kaiser's labor conference, and above all, the fact that Bismarck treated Willy "like a schoolboy."

These arguments may have garnered sympathy with monarchs around Europe, but not with the Kaiser's mother. "I cannot approve of the way in which Prince Bismarck's resignation came about . . . ," Vicky wrote Victoria. "The love of playing the despot . . . is very great." Bismarck, the Dowager Empress said, had been ousted for all the wrong reasons, at a time when his "genius and prestige . . . might still have been useful & valuable for Germany & for the cause of peace." Vicky would have been even more annoyed if she had heard her son tell his journalist friend, Poultney Bigelow, that one of the reasons he let Bismarck go was "the manner in which the late Prime Minister spoke of . . . [his] . . . mother and . . . permitted the treatment given to her by his official press."

"Prince and Princess Bismarck came and took farewell . . . ," Vicky wrote Victoria on March 25, 1890, saying that the former Chancellor "did not exactly complain, but . . . feels very deeply that he has not been treated with the consideration due to his age & position. We parted amicably & in peace, which I am glad of, as I should have been sorry—having suffered so much all these long years under the system—that it should appear as if I had any spirit of revenge, which I really have not."

Four days later, Bismarck left the German Chancellery after twenty-eight years in the service of the Hohenzollerns. It seemed as if all Berlin had turned out to say good-bye. "Like a flood the crowd surged toward the carriage, surrounding, accompanying, stopping it momentarily, hats and handkerchiefs waving, calling, crying, throwing flowers," ran a contemporary account of the scene. "In the open carriage, drawn by the familiar chestnut-colored horses, sat Bismarck, deadly pale, in his cuirassier uniform and cap, Herbert at his side, before them a large black mastiff—all three covered with flowers, to which more were constantly being added."

Passing through an honor guard at the railway station, Bismarck was met by Chancellor Caprivi, all the important Prussian and German ministers, members of the diplomatic corps, and officers of the army. The national anthem was played. Bismarck walked to the train, climbed into his carriage, and with tears in his eyes, shook hands with Germany's new Chancellor. "The Emperor shall see me again," he muttered as he got into his carriage. The train pulled slowly away. It was, the former Chancellor observed bitterly, "a state funeral with full honours."

OF ALL THE MEMBERS of the Hohenzollern family, only one distant cousin* was present at Bismarck's departure. Kaiser Wilhelm II did not see fit to put in an appearance. Two days earlier, however, he had written his grandmother Victoria an astonishing letter:

> Yesterday Prince Bismarck said goodbye to me & we parted under tears after a warm embrace. I hope & trust that the woods of Friedrichsruhe will do him good. . . . I spoke to his doctor two days ago, who assured me, that if the Chancellor had kept on a few weeks longer, he would infallibly have died of apoplexy. . . . The nights he could not sleep, & in daytime . . . even sometimes, when he worked with me, he suddenly would break down, with crying fits. After this had gone on for a month I became afraid of the consequences & after much discussion & with deep regret, I resolved to part from him, in order to keep him alive.
>
> I look upon the Prince as an international European capital, which I must try to keep going as long as possible, & not use him up in the guerilla warfare with the Reichstag. It was a very hard trial, but the Lord's will be done. . . .

---

* *Prince Max of Baden, a young nephew of Wilhelm's uncle Fritz of Baden.*

CHAPTER
SIXTY-TWO

"I always knew he [Wilhelm II] had not much heart (if any) but he appears to have no head either!"

THE PRINCE OF WALES
(later EDWARD VII), 1891

*A*T THE BEGINNING OF 1890—the year of Bismarck's dismissal—Vicky was in Rome, where she had taken her two unmarried daughters after Sophie's wedding to spend the winter. Greeted by the King and Queen of Italy with the kind of loving welcome she no longer received at home, the Dowager Empress was awaiting instructions from the German Embassy about visiting the Pope when she heard that the seventy-eight-year-old Empress Augusta was suffering from influenza. "Louise of Baden says the fever has left her & she passed a good day yesterday!" Vicky wrote Victoria on January 6. Two days later, Augusta was dead.

In spite of the old woman's hostility, Vicky vowed to honor her mother-in-law's memory. "She was my darling's <u>mother</u> . . . a remarkable woman. <u>How</u> gladly one would have loved her, if she had only shown affection & sympathy & kindness. But now I shall only remember what was good & bright, her virtues & her sufferings, & forget all the bitterness I endured!" she wrote hopefully and unrealistically to her own mother. She regretted throwing away Augusta's last letter, received just the day before, but, as she explained, "it was so distant & freezing that it pained me. I am sure it was kindly meant though."

Vicky did not like returning to Berlin for her mother-in-law's funeral—"3 weary winter months of imprisonment . . . in my sad empty House where my sorrow is always staring me in the face!" She also realized that for a cost-conscious ex-empress, there would not be too many other opportunities to escape the frigid Berlin weather, climatic and political. A winter in Rome, she rationalized, "would have been so good for the girls, and the King & Queen are such kind true friends.!"

The Empress Augusta was sent on to the next world in the same state of overdress that she had fancied in this one. "You would have thought she was just going to a fête, or a soirée! . . . ," Vicky wrote Victoria after viewing the body. "Her false hair in ringlets on her brow, the line of the eyebrows & eyelashes carefully painted as in life . . . an ample tulle veil . . . flowing & curling about her head & neck & shoulders, hiding her chin. . . . I felt that if she could have seen herself she would have <u>been pleased</u>." Vicky's visits to her mother-in-law's bier only served to remind her that she was a pariah in the Hohenzollern family. I "felt <u>so</u> lonely, so helpless among them all. . . . No one took me up or down stairs. . . . one feels <u>so</u> set on one side, so forgotten. . . . Dona means quite <u>kindly</u>, I suppose, but her grand condescending airs aggravate one so much."

Augusta, who always resented the fact that her predecessor Queen Elisabeth* had left her jewels to Vicky, took her revenge by leaving nothing to her daughter-in-law or Vicky's daughters. "The Empress left a very large fortune," Vicky wrote Victoria. "Part goes to William, part to Henry . . . the largest part to Louise of Baden, & some to Vicky† of Sweden. . . . I think what went to William, who does <u>not want</u> it [need it], might have been parted amongst my 4 daughters & Henry's son! But I did not expect we should be remembered."

With Augusta no longer around to foment intrigue, Vicky hoped that intrafamily hostilities would be eased and that her position in the royal hierarchy would improve. In this, as in all intercourse with the young court, she was disappointed. "I have only seen William and Dona at the funeral ceremonies," she wrote her daughter Sophie in Greece, "but neither of them, have taken any notice of me since." Vicky was particularly hurt by Willy, who "often drives past me when we are walking, but he never stops the carriage to ask how I am or to speak to me."

The most blatant affront to the Dowager Empress, however, was the transfer of the Empress Augusta's honorary titles directly to the current Kaiserin. The German Red Cross and a patriotic group known as the Fatherland Women's Association had been organized under Augusta, who served as nominal head of both organizations. After her death, the honor and titles that should have gone to Vicky—the only one of the three Kaiserins who worked seriously in that area —passed directly to Dona, who, as her mother-in-law said, "knows nothing of taking care of the sick and wounded."

Vicky was devastated. Not only had she been cut out, she had never been forewarned. On her arrival in Berlin, she naïvely told Willy that she was "ready now to take over these 2 Societies."

"You need not trouble yourself about it," he answered; "<u>my wife arranged with the Empress Augusta a year ago that she would take her place</u>."

"I have for years taken trouble to prepare everything for this . . . ," Vicky wrote Victoria in despair. "I wrote to Louise of Baden about it last year. . . . I‡ who helped the Empress Augusta with the sick and wounded in 1864, 1866 & 1870–1871, & since then I have continued to study the subject. . . . You see how I am treated, dearest Mama, & how much the assurances of William are worth when he says he wishes to do everything to please me!"

---

* *The widow of Friedrich Wilhelm IV.*

† *Louise of Baden's daughter, Augusta's granddaughter.*

‡ *Underlined three times in original.*

Told that these organizations "could <u>only</u> be under the patronage of the reigning Empress," Vicky asked why they had then remained under the Empress Augusta during the three months when she herself was on the throne. "Of course it is easy for them to find <u>excuses</u> . . . ," she wrote Victoria. "I am the only lady of that position in the family who is passed over, & has <u>never</u> had, even for ever so short a time, the opportunity of <u>helping</u> others in an <u>official</u> <u>capacity</u>, as, whatever I do now, is purely private, out of my own pocket!"

The insult was not gratuitous. It was done, Vicky realized, to "prevent my having a work which would . . . give me a certain amount of influence!" As she wrote Victoria, "I am well aware that a large & powerful party are determined that I should have <u>nothing</u> in my hands, which could cause people to look to me, or apply to me. After I have waited here for <u>30</u> years, & <u>not</u> had an easy life, it does seem hard."

After Augusta's death, Vicky extended herself to be kind to her grieving sister-in-law, Louise of Baden. She suggested that Queen Victoria offer the Order of Victoria and Albert, conferred on Augusta and due to be returned to England on her death, to Louise instead. "I think it would be considered a compliment to the Empress's memory, & be much appreciated by Louise . . . ," Vicky wrote, "though she might . . . act differently toward me & might have saved me much trouble & sorrow . . . yet she is sorely stricken & feels her mother's death very much; so I venture to plead your giving her her mother's order."

Vicky might not have been so thoughtful had she known at the time—she discovered it two years later—that Louise had been one of the people who had helped persuade Augusta to deprive Vicky of her rightful role as head of the two most important German charitable societies.

The Dowager Empress did not attend the "great ceremony" honoring the Kaiserin's succession to the chairmanships of the Red Cross and the Women's Association. "[U]nder the circumstances," she wrote Victoria, "I should have felt <u>too</u> foolish." Still, she had to appear at other official occasions to chaperone her two unmarried daughters. Now the ultimate arbiter of society, Dona required that her young sisters-in-law attend all functions of the court and made "a <u>most</u> disagreeable row" if they were not present.

Although she had no official title, the Dowager Empress continued on her charitable rounds—laying the foundation stone of a home for nurses built with money pledged in honor of Fritz's and her twenty-fifth anniversary; starting a children's hospital with the sum given her in Fritz's memory by the citizens of Berlin; and lending her name and presence to the ever-popular fund-raising bazaars. She gave a "little present" to four nurses who had volunteered to work in the cholera wards in Hamburg. In staffing her wards, Vicky ignored the religion of the nurses. "We have Catholics and a Jewess," she wrote Victoria. This of course is "not approved of" by the "Low Church Clique to which Dona [and] Louise of Baden belong."

Charity was the only outlet the Dowager Empress approached with any enthusiasm after the death of her husband. She seemed to avoid personal pleasures and resented the amusements of others—those who enjoyed themselves in spite of her (and their) loss. In this, she was following the lead of the most conspicuous widow in history. Like her mother, the Dowager Empress seems to have believed that by never removing her black mourning (or only reluctantly, on occasions like christenings that demanded gray), she was proving the intensity of her love for her dead spouse. But Vicky's position was vastly different from that of the Queen. Unlike Victoria, who was a reigning monarch, she was a displaced foreigner, virtually ostracized by her son and the royal family, who considered her anything but an asset to Germany. Her very name—the Empress Frederick—was indicative of her lack of status.

Vicky's determination not to be consoled can be partly attributed to her desire to keep Fritz's name and ideals before the public. In this she seems to have succeeded. Five years after his death, she heard that there was "a perfect pilgrimage" to the mausoleum she had built to house his remains and those of their two dead sons. Wreaths had been sent from all over Germany. "He is not forgotten yet!" she reported in triumph to Queen Victoria.

Beyond the dead Kaiser, the Dowager Empress obviously wanted it known that she was in mourning for Germany itself—for the country that might have been and the dream that never had a chance to be realized. To take off black would have signified an accommodation with Germany as it was, not as she wished it to be.

On a personal level, Vicky also wanted to remind Willy how much he was making her suffer. One feels that if the Kaiser had allowed even minimal expressions of respect for his father, his mother would have eventually passed through her period of mourning. But he gave her nowhere to go, and her vulnerability only encouraged him to humiliate her further.

As to Vicky herself, she held as tightly to her martyrdom as any masochist in history. She had only to look at the example of the once-liberal Augusta to see how just a little elasticity in the more meaningless forms of court etiquette would have eased her way. But having been forced for nearly thirty years to conform to the court of Wilhelm I, she had grown too old and too proud to lend her name to anything that smacked of autocracy from her own son. Willy's silly pomposities were all too symptomatic of a philosophy and style of government that she believed would eventually destroy Germany. And so she continued to suffer—angrily, volubly, and demonstrably. Like a pin poised over the Kaiser's balloon, the Dowager Empress remained a constant reminder of the insecurities he concealed inside—and therefore a voice that had to be silenced, a presence that had to be shunned.

WHILE SHE WAS STILL recovering from hurt over the charity issue, Wilhelm dealt his mother another blow. The citizens of Berlin had raised money to build a large equestrian statue of Friedrich III, but when they applied to the Kaiser for permission to erect it, he refused.

"[I]t is the first time they have done so for one of their sovereigns!" Vicky told Victoria.

They have the money already! They informed me of this and I told them how <u>much</u> it touched me . . . much more than a monument ordered, executed & paid for by Government.* They sent in their plans & have been waiting over 4 months for an answer, & now William has refused to grant them the permission & says that the state will do it! . . . such a spontaneous demonstration of respect . . . is a <u>very</u> different thing from a state order, which is just as one would order a bridge, or new barracks. . . . The town of Berlin said the monument should be made according to my wishes. Now, of course, all is spoilt!

"[I]t <u>again</u> appears as if William did <u>not</u> wish historical evidence of Fritz's <u>popularity</u> to go down to posterity!" she wrote Victoria ten days later. "As history books for all the schools in Prussia are <u>arranged</u> by the Ministerium,† his <u>life</u>, his <u>character</u>, his <u>views</u> & short reign can be made as little of as is thought advisable, and all can be coloured as the present Government please! as they did about his illness & his Diary."

For a brief time after Fritz's death, Vicky had believed it might be possible to appeal to her daughter-in-law to mitigate the harshness of the Kaiser's edicts. Another woman, she thought, might more readily understand her sorrow and needs. But the young Kaiserin's primary function, beyond breeding sons, was to keep Wilhelm II's fragile ego intact—a job that seemed to require trampling on the mother-in-law who had helped her gain her position.

Asked by Queen Victoria why she had sponsored the marriage in the first place, Vicky replied, "Dona seemed to me the most likely to make an excellent wife & mother. We had a great affection & esteem for her father.‡ I <u>then</u> hoped and thought she might be grateful & affectionate to me. . . . in <u>that</u> my hopes have been <u>completely</u> disappointed. She has <u>quite</u> forgotten, or does not like to remember, or really does not understand what she owes me. . . . She has a great sense of duty, but she does not seem to see <u>what</u> her duty towards <u>me</u> is!"

The young Kaiserin's duty, as she herself saw it, was to impose her personal values on the members of the court. Her daughter-in-law, Vicky contended somewhat feebly, "means to be very kind to me, but she has something condescending & patronizing which irritates me, & rubs me up the wrong way." Vicky was not the only person who found Dona's manner off-putting. Royal cousins visiting Wilhelm II frequently complained of his wife's heavy sense of superiority, social and moral.

The Dowager Empress rarely saw Willy's children. "Dona keeps them away from me, purposely as much as she can . . . ," she complained; "they are inclined to be fond of me—most likely that is the reason." To Vicky, who adored children, this was real deprivation. When Wilhelm and Dona had their sixth

---

* *Wilhelm II had already arranged for the state to erect a statue of his grandfather Wilhelm I.*

† *The Ministry of Education and Religious Affairs.*

‡ *Duke Friedrich of Augustenburg.*

and last son, Joachim, she offered to hold the baby during his christening, "as the Empress Augusta or the Emperor William held all mine." She was turned down by her daughter-in-law, who told her, "William does not wish it as you are not the godmother."

Vicky spent quite a lot of time, however, with her other grandchildren. Charlotte was delighted to leave her daughter, Feo, with her grandmother, as this gave her freedom to move from place to place. "Wherever William & Dona go," Vicky wrote Victoria, "she likes to be, especially when there is anything going on." The Dowager Empress also saw a lot of Henry and Irene's infant son. A hemophiliac like Vicky's brother Leopold,* the child caused his parents and grandmother no little worry.

Another ongoing concern was Vicky's daughter Moretta. Already in her mid-twenties, Moretta was growing perilously old for an unmarried princess. Friendly and easily attracted to the opposite sex, Vicky's second daughter was not, as her mother put it, "cut out for an old maid," and Vicky worried that she could not keep Moretta confined and virginal much longer. In a letter to Victoria, she said that she lived "in dread" of the young woman's "becoming attached to a person she might meet who was not of her rank . . . as William would not hesitate to cast off his sister altogether." Before her death, the Empress Augusta had threatened to take Moretta away from her mother if she again became involved with an inappropriate man like Sandro of Battenberg. Under these circumstances, Vicky felt that "the only protection" for her second daughter was a "suitable marriage" to someone acceptable to the Hohenzollerns.

The first candidate—Prince Charles of Sweden—was suggested by Bertie. But Charles, whose brother had married Moretta's first cousin,† wanted nothing more to do with women from the Hohenzollern family. To get Moretta over yet another disappointment, Vicky sent her to visit Victoria in England. A grand duke from the Romanov family had been mentioned as a possible husband, and Vicky planned for Moretta to meet him while she was there. When the prospect of the Russian grand duke also fell through, Moretta was devastated. "I shall never marry . . . ," she wrote her mother from England, "all my relations, sisters, friends do except my stupid self, nobody will have me, nothing but disappointment is my lot in life. . . . I am too ugly, that is the reason!"

"I think we must go [no] further," Queen Victoria cautioned. "You have had now 3 direct failures. Moretta has expressed a strong wish not to marry now & I own I think you should let it alone for the present. Let her see people, but pray don't force . . . or press her to marry for marrying's sake. . . . I think it hardly right or dignified for you to go about trying to marry your daughter & getting refusals. I had something of that kind to go though with Louise‡ & it was very painful."

---

* *Prince Leopold, the Duke of Albany, was the eighth child and fourth son of Victoria and Albert. He suffered from hemophilia and died at thirty.*

| *Louise of Baden's daughter.*

‡ *One of Vicky's younger sisters, who married the Marquis of Lorne.*

"I should never never press her to marry for marrying's sake! . . . ," Vicky wrote back. But the Queen, she said, did not understand the problem.

> You living in England & being quite your own mistress cannot . . . see . . . the great difficulties and drawbacks of the existence of a young unmarried Princess who is no longer a child! especially at a court like the Berlin one. . . . I cannot give Moretta the liberty & independence she would like, as everything is criticized, commented upon, & twisted against us! Therefore, I think it my duty to . . . let her make the acquaintance of people who might suit. . . . It is intensely repugnant to me . . . to be looking about without success. . . . Still I must consider & weigh what chances there might be for her, so that she may not later reproach me.

In June of 1890, Moretta accepted a proposal of marriage from Prince Adolf of Schaumburg-Lippe, the fourth son of a provincial German prince. The decision had been a hard one for the young Princess. "In her depression & discouragement, feeling that the happiness she had hoped for is not to be hers, she accepts this," Vicky wrote Victoria. "I hope it is a wise step, but it made my heart ache to think it is not what she had dreamt of. . . . William wishes this marriage particularly. . . . I am glad she should have a home of her own & someone to protect her in case I die."

For Moretta and Adolf, there were none of the lengthy rituals usually attendant on Hohenzollern weddings. Not only was Adolf of insufficient rank to warrant them, but the Kaiserin was pregnant again, and shorter ceremonies were better for her. After their wedding, the couple left for an extended honeymoon in Egypt and Greece. A few weeks later, Vicky received a "frantic telegram" from Sophie, saying that Moretta and Adolf had arrived in Athens, but stayed "only a few hours" before rushing back to Germany. The reason was an early miscarriage, after which Moretta was never able to conceive again.

EARLIER THAT SAME summer, Vicky's daughter Sophie, now Crown Princess of Greece, had given birth to her first child—a confinement that caused the Dowager Empress no little anxiety. The Balkans were not known for the quality of their doctors, and royal mothers whose daughters provided heirs to the so-called Eastern thrones usually arrived well before the due date—doctors, nurses, and anesthetic in tow. Unfortunately for the Dowager Empress of Germany, the Greek royal family would brook no interference in what was considered a national event. Having tried but failed with a barrage of letters to Sophie's in-laws, King George and Queen Olga of Greece, as well as the King's parents, the King and Queen of Denmark, Vicky was forced to acquiesce. Sophie, she was told, would be attended by a Greek doctor, recommended by a Viennese physician whose lectures on childbirth he had attended.

"I feel it cruelly that for the sake of a national susceptibility, my own precious child's health & even life may be endangered," Vicky wrote Victoria. "What earthly good can it do the Greek nation or the King's dynasty, if she is made to suffer more than she need because the <u>best</u> advice is not to be provided!"

Told that the baby was due on August 8 but that the doctor had predicted it would not arrive before August 17, Vicky was on board her mother's yacht, steaming slowly toward Gibraltar, when a telegram arrived announcing the birth of a son to Sophie on July 19. Either by design or accident, the Dowager Empress had missed presiding over the event.

When she got to Greece, she discovered that her worries about Sophie's care were more than justified. Had the Dowager Empress not installed a London-trained midwife masquerading as a maid in Sophie's household, her daughter and the baby might well have died. It seems that the presiding Greek doctor had been recommended by the Viennese physician because he had procured a decoration for the physician's son. He had not practiced medicine for years and knew little about childbirth. Asked by the midwife to assist in removing the umbilical cord, which had wound itself around the baby's neck, the doctor "took off his coat, folded his arms, and told her to wash her hands." He himself, however, "caught hold of the Princess" with dirty hands and "tried to tear the afterbirth away from her." By the time he was hustled out of the room by Sophie's husband, Tino, the damage had been done. Sophie began to run a high fever accompanied by periods of delirium. She did not recover her health for some time.

When Sophie's brother Wilhelm heard about his sister's confinement, he wired the King of Greece that he was sending "a skilled doctor" to Athens. Having had a taste of the Kaiser's overbearing style at the time of Sophie's wedding, the Greek royal family would have nothing to do with him or his doctor. "William is only the brother, & neither very affectionate nor one that has ever been intimate with his sisters," Vicky wrote Victoria; "<u>therefore</u> . . . it is <u>not</u> put down to his solicitude on her account!"

The Kaiser's interest in Sophie did not stop with her medical treatment, but extended into her religious life as well. The question of religion was a ticklish issue for the scions of European dynasties, sent off to rule Balkan countries where the non-Muslim citizens belonged to Eastern Orthodox churches. Raised as Protestants or Catholics, the imported royalties usually christened their children in the local religion and sometimes themselves converted. This was the case with Sophie, who told her family of her decision to convert to the Greek Orthodox Church on a subsequent visit to Berlin.

No sooner had she made her announcement than she was summoned to the palace by the Kaiserin. "I hear you are thinking of changing your religion," Dona said. "We shall never agree to that. If you have no feeling about it yourself, William, as Head of the Church and of your family, will speak to you. . . . You will end up in hell."

"That does not concern anyone here and I do not need to ask anyone," Sophie retorted. "William? I know him better than that, he has absolutely no religion. If he had, he would never have behaved as he did. Whether I go to hell or not is my own affair and I must beg you not to concern yourself about it."

Not used to being crossed, the Kaiserin appealed to her husband, who appeared at the Dowager Empress's palace the next day in full regalia. "If my sister does anything like that, I will forbid her the country," he threatened his mother, his sister, and his brother-in-law, the future King of Greece.

Shortly thereafter, on December 17, 1890, the Kaiserin gave birth to her sixth son, a healthy child whose two-weeks' prematurity Willy blamed on Dona's argument with his sister. It was his mother, he told everyone in Berlin, who was responsible. "The version here . . . is that I made a scene to Dona," Vicky wrote Victoria, "announcing to her that Sophie had turned Greek, and in consequence, Dona had fallen ill, & the baby had been born too soon."

In spite of Willy and Dona, Sophie entered the Greek Orthodox Church the following Easter. "I trust nothing more will be written or done to distress her, offend her family & annoy me . . . ," Vicky wrote Victoria after a long winter of family hostilities. "Of course it gives me rather a pang to think of my child no longer belonging to our Church in which she was christened & confirmed . . . but I cannot blame her or think it wrong, and can only hope she will feel happy sharing her husband's faith & that in which her child is to be brought up in the country which is now her home."

Queen Victoria agreed and told the Kaiser that "one has not the right" to interfere "where another person's conscience was concerned." Willy tried to justify himself with his grandmother:

"Sophy made poor Dona—in the highest state of expectancy—an awful scene in which she behaved in a simply incredible manner like a naughty child which has been caught doing wrong," the Kaiser wrote Queen Victoria. "My poor wife got ill and bore too early and was for two days at death's door. . . . I had an interview with her as Head of the Church, at which Mama and Tino assisted. In this Sophy entirely refused to acknowledge me as the Head of her Family or Church. . . . If my poor Baby dies it is solely Sophy's fault and she has murdered it." (The child was, at the time of this letter, five months old.)

Queen Victoria refused even to reply.

In response to an appeal from her mother, Sophie made one last attempt toward family peace, composing a letter to her brother in which she carefully outlined the reasons for her conversion. But Wilhelm II refused to rescind his edict of banishment.

Shortly thereafter, the Dowager Empress received the following telegram from Athens—sent uncoded through the regular postal service for all to see:

RECEIVED ANSWER. KEEPS TO WHAT HE SAID IN BERLIN. FIXES IT TO THREE YEARS. MAD. NEVER MIND. SOPHIE.

CHAPTER
SIXTY-THREE

"What kind of a jackass would dare to be Bismarck's successor?"

COUNT LEO VON CAPRIVI

O N NOVEMBER 21, 1890, Vicky turned fifty. Her birthday was marked by a luncheon at the Kaiser's palace, hurried along because the gentlemen in attendance were anxious to get to another court event.

"How much I thought of you . . . ," Vicky wrote Victoria. "I am always pleased to think that I was the first on whom you bestowed a mother's kiss & affection. 50 years that love has not failed me, and it has supported me in the dark & terrible days of bitter trials, the shadow of which will forever hang over my saddened life!"

"It does indeed seem strange to me that now I am 50, I am completely cut off from the official world . . . ," she wrote a few weeks later. "I might be buried alive. . . . I have not the faintest ambition to play *un rôle* in the present regime . . . but it is impossible to lose one's interest in the affairs of this country, and in the course of peace & progress in the rest of the world."

For all her complaints, with Bismarck out of power and out of Berlin, the Dowager Empress had begun to enjoy a somewhat better relationship with the government, if not with her son. Soon after the Bismarcks called to say goodbye, the new Chancellor, Leo von Caprivi, came to pay his respects.

"I thought him extremely sensible and only hope he may succeed," Vicky wrote Victoria, "but . . . if William means (as he says sometimes) merely to have people who 'obey him' and 'carry out his orders,' I fear he will find it very difficult, almost impossible, to fulfill all the duties of his office."

A man whose great size and stern Teutonic expression reminded the London *Times* of no one so much as Otto von Bismarck, Caprivi was in fact the opposite of his predecessor. A Spartan military gentleman—unassuming, unmarried, and ascetic—Caprivi belonged to no political party and hoped to create a ministry responsible to the German people. He had never approved of Bismarck's one-man rule or his tactics of setting one faction against another. At the same time, he was an uncompromising monarchist. Honest about his own abilities, he was loath to assume the position left vacant by Europe's most adroit statesman, but had agreed to take on the job because he believed he could not refuse anything his Kaiser asked of him.

Caprivi certainly seemed an improvement to Vicky. She was concerned, however, when she heard that her son wished to retain the services of Herbert von Bismarck as Secretary of State—and was delighted when Herbert refused. By this time, Herbert's reputation was in shreds. Over at the Wilhelmstrasse, they were saying that their chief had lost all interest in foreign affairs beyond using inside information for financial speculations. Vicky heard that he was "rarely sober" anymore in the evening.

The Kaiser, who thought that he could eventually persuade Herbert to return, replaced him with a man of no experience in international diplomacy, Baron Marschall von Biberstein. The Baron's lack of qualifications were of little concern to Wilhelm II, who believed he could manage Germany's foreign affairs himself. "I, not my Ministers," he told the English, "direct German policy."

An opportunity to prove this arose sooner than he expected.

BEFORE HE LEFT OFFICE, Bismarck had succeeded in surrounding Germany with his wall of secret treaties, erected to protect the Fatherland from Russia and France. On the day that Wilhelm II demanded Bismarck's resignation, Russia had asked Germany to renew the most important of those agreements, the so-called Reinsurance Treaty. Although he no longer liked or trusted Alexander III, Wilhelm assured Shuvalov, the Russian Ambassador to Germany, that he would follow the path laid out by Bismarck and renew the treaty. Shuvalov and Giers, the Czar's Foreign Minister, were delighted. Their pleasure was short-lived. The Kaiser had not thought to consult his new Chancellor before committing himself to a program about which he knew nothing.

Caprivi, who had as little knowledge of foreign affairs as Wilhelm II, relied for advice on his friend Holstein at the Foreign Ministry. Holstein had long believed that the Reinsurance Treaty between Germany and Russia was incompatible with the Triple Alliance signed by Germany, Austria, and Italy; if discovered, Holstein contended, it was bound to damage Germany's relationship with Austria. And who could be sure that Bismarck, now out of power, might not disclose it in a fit of pique? Moreover, with Bismarck gone, there was no one in the Foreign Ministry capable of handling such contradictory policies.

Much of Bismarck's diplomatic success had rested on his ability to preserve all his options at one time. Balancing alliances, he offered everyone a glimmer of hope, but gave no one his word. While others got mired in the quicksands of ideology, Bismarck had never allowed loyalties to concepts or people to hamper him. And if he occasionally got backed into a political corner, he had no compunction in lying his way out. "A man such as yourself can juggle five balls at the same time," Caprivi had once told him, "while other people do well to limit themselves to one or two balls." Caprivi's assessment was seconded by the German Ambassador to Russia. "If Bismarck were still at the helm, I would advise that the [Reinsurance] Treaty be renewed," he said. "Under the changed circumstances, it would be dangerous to pursue such an ambiguous policy."

Thus advised, the Kaiser reversed himself. His about-face, coupled with recent strains and the Czar's uneasiness about the stability of Germany under Wilhelm II, put an end to long-standing Russo-German friendship. Typically, Willy found a way to blame someone else:

"I am very sorry that Prince Bismarck plays such a sorry part in Europe . . . ," he wrote his grandmother Victoria two months after the old man's dismissal. "Especially his perpetual leaning & pointing towards Russia . . . shows how right I was in not trusting him. . . . Great is the number of people who now are beginning to understand the dangers I had forseen, & who are thankful that the Prince is no more in a responsible position."

Wilhelm, who also accused Bismarck of secretly plotting with Russia "against me, my government & the Triple Alliance," apparently forgot that he had written his grandmother only weeks before that the reason he let Bismarck go was to save the old man's life. But the thirty-one-year-old Kaiser, who had destroyed his father's reputation and his mother's life on the grounds that friendship with England was anti-German, had suddenly decided to woo the English lion, possibly even as an additional member of the Triple Alliance.

Two days after Bismarck's dismissal, the Kaiser had arranged for the Prince of Wales, arriving in Berlin for his international labor conference, to be greeted with the fanfare usually accorded a reigning monarch. But Uncle Bertie, who was required to stay in the royal palace with his nephew, refused to be co-opted. He attended a dinner given by Vicky and even paid a call on the disgraced Bismarck, who could scarcely wait to disparage the young Kaiser to his uncle. Bertie also allowed his entourage to accompany the British Ambassador to a dinner at the Bismarck residence, while he himself accepted an invitation for lunch with Herbert von Bismarck.

When Queen Victoria arrived in Germany the following month on her way home from the south of France, Willy hastened to Darmstadt to pay court to her, making sure that his wife followed and did her bit by taking Victoria for a drive. In Darmstadt, Wilhelm explained his dismissal of Bismarck to the Queen on the grounds that Bismarck had been "intriguing with Russia behind his back." In this interpretation of events, the Kaiser was seconded by his uncle, Fritz of Baden, conveniently seated on the other side of the Queen at a family luncheon.

Convinced that Wilhelm II genuinely wished for friendship with England, Prime Minister Salisbury concluded an agreement whereby England exchanged the useless island of Heligoland in the North Sea off the coast of Germany for sizable German territories in East Africa—an arrangement that looked to Europe as if Germany was trying to buy English goodwill.

A few months later, in August of 1890, Willy arrived at Osborne for the Cowes regatta on his yacht, the *Hohenzollern*. He enjoyed himself thoroughly, and from then on was a yearly participant in Regatta Week, which took place every August close to Queen Victoria's home at Osborne. He soon bought an English yacht, complete with captain and crew, and began to race against his uncle Bertie. Having acquired the title of Admiral of the British Fleet from

Victoria in 1889, he constantly hinted for new honors and their appropriate outfits—a childish practice his grandmother Victoria referred to as Willy's "fishing for uniforms."

He also continued to talk about an alliance between Germany and England —the realignment of Germany's foreign policy away from Russia that Vicky had always wanted. But for whatever reasons—a lack of common interests, the realities of geography, the ambivalence of Wilhelm II himself, profound differences in political philosophy—friendship between Germany and England failed to materialize. Unlike Bismarck, who always made sure he had potential allies waiting in the wings, the Kaiser was unable to fill the Russian void.

AT THE SAME TIME as he was making overtures to England, the Kaiser tried to improve Germany's relationship with France. Having alienated Russia over the Reinsurance Treaty, Wilhelm now faced the imminent danger of an anti-German alliance between his eastern and western neighbors. The French and the Russians were, in fact, already known to be engaged in preliminary talks.

The Kaiser himself had never liked the French. Their effortless elegance annoyed him, and their lax regard for sexual morality shocked him. Worse, they had not paid enough attention to him on his first and only visit to Paris in 1878. He refused to allow his mother and sisters to visit Queen Victoria in Aix-les-Bains in 1890, saying that he was "bound to uphold" a law passed by Wilhelm I in 1887 "which strictly forbids any Prince or Princess of the Prussian house to cross the French frontier." It was, he wrote his grandmother, "quite out of the question to make any exceptions."

But Wilhelm II was a great believer in the efficacy of personal over professional diplomatic exchanges. He himself could not return to France—a German Kaiser might attract hostility if not actual attack—but his mother had often visited Paris, where she was known as a cosmopolite, an intellectual, and a great supporter of the arts. She could be his weather vane, an indicator of sunshine or storms on the other side of the Rhine.

Approached by her old friend Count Münster (now German Ambassador to France), Chancellor Caprivi, and her son, the Dowager Empress eagerly accepted the mission to Paris, where she was told to contact French artists to participate in an international art exhibition in Berlin. No longer cast aside, chosen in fact for the very virtues that had been denigrated at court, Vicky felt that she could be of use once again. She was informed that she would be traveling incognito but staying at the German Embassy—thus blurring the lines between a personal and semiofficial visit. From France, she planned to go on to England, but she cautioned her mother to say nothing about her first stop. "I am especially anxious that the private visit to Paris should not be known at present, so is William & Caprivi also! I would go to the German Embassy and only have Mossy, a Lady & Gentleman with me."

The Dowager Empress and her entourage arrived in Paris on February 19, 1891. Greeted at the Gare du Nord by Ambassador Münster and a good-sized contingent of police, Vicky and her eighteen-year-old daughter, Mossy—the latter pronounced by *Le Figaro* "very blond, very svelte, and thoroughly charming"—were met by a respectful crowd of onlookers before being whisked off to the Embassy, a former home of Eugène de Beauharnais,* furnished with treasures from the era of Napoleon I.

Up and out by 10:00 A.M. every morning, the Dowager Empress was a major topic of interest in the French papers, which detailed her tours around the city. The weather was good for February. Vicky had already visited a number of artists in their studios and picked a "good many pictures" for the exhibition in Berlin, when two pleasure excursions—to the gardens of St. Cloud and the palace of Versailles—put an untimely end to her visit.

The rightist Boulangists, out of power for over a year since the exile of their leader, General Boulanger, had been eagerly scanning the Dowager Empress's schedule for a cause. They found what they were looking for in her trips to these two national sites and spun them into political capital. By visiting St. Cloud (site of the palace where Vicky had stayed with her parents when she was fourteen, later destroyed by the Germans in the Franco-Prussian War) and Versailles (scene of the crowning of Wilhelm I of Germany), the Dowager Empress, they claimed, had gone out of her way to offend the French. "Vive Russia! Down with the allies of the Germans!" they shouted at a meeting held to protest these affronts to national pride.

It was a good story, and the local press took it up, praising the painters who refused to go to Berlin and claiming that those who would allow their works to be shown in Germany were dishonoring France. These unfortunate artists now began to receive anonymous letters and threats. "Without the hullabaloo from the newspapers," one reporter said, "it could be affirmatively stated that the visit of the Dowager Empress of Germany to Paris would not even have been known by the French public."

The German press was easily drawn into the fray. The Cologne paper claimed that France owed satisfaction to Germany for insulting their great Kaiser and his noble mother. In spite of a letter from Vicky begging him not to do it, Wilhelm II ordered the renewal of repressive passport requirements for those who lived in Alsace-Lorraine. Moderate voices, like that of the paper in Frankfurt, soon reestablished calm, but by then the Dowager Empress had been advised to leave France.

She got out on the morning of February 27, her train pulling away from the Gare du Nord a full hour and twenty minutes before the time given to the press. Police had been stationed on both sides of the street every hundred yards between the German Embassy and the Gare du Nord. When the German Ambassador expressed surprise at the politeness of the large crowd at the station

---

* *Eugène de Beauharnais (1781–1824), son of Josephine and her first husband, Alexandre de Beauharnais, served as Viceroy of Italy under Napoleon I, married a Bavarian Princess, and was named by Napoleon heir apparent to the Italian throne.*

itself, the chief of the Sûreté explained that "half" of the onlookers were actually "plainclothes police . . . explicitly ordered to knock down anyone who so much as opened his mouth."

Many, like the German Ambassador, blamed the unfortunate consequences of the Dowager Empress's visit on the inability of the French government to withstand the chauvinistic right. "There is nothing but intrigue here," Ambassador Münster wrote Chancellor Caprivi the day of Vicky's departure, "and it could not be otherwise with a Government of Parvenus, who have not been born and brought up to govern. People who mount a horse without being able to ride are a danger to themselves, the horse and others; that is the case with those at present in power." But when Münster himself came under attack for not being sufficiently sensitive to the situation—he had, in fact, accompanied Vicky on her visit to St. Cloud—he pushed the blame onto the Dowager Empress and the head of her household, Count Seckendorff.

"I still continue to be much tormented about all the reports circulated at Berlin purporsing [sic] to come from Paris . . . ," Vicky wrote Victoria several weeks later. Attacked by the conservative Berlin papers for visiting French artists in defiance of the advice of the German Ambassador, Vicky wrote Victoria that it was Ambassador Münster who had "told me to go." Accused of not wanting the Russian Ambassador invited to dinner at the German Embassy, Vicky was infuriated. "This is a direct untruth! I wished him to be asked as Münster insisted on asking the others [but he] was ill & could not come. I wanted the wife to be asked to dinner, but Münster did not . . . so I received her alone."

The conservative papers listed "other crimes" committed by the Dowager Empress. "I am supposed to have have gone to all sorts of Jewish collectors. I went to see the great Spitzer Collection. He certainly was a Jew—when he was alive! . . . at Berlin people say I had cost Herbette [French Ambassador to Germany] his place, had spoilt the Exhibition & had caused Münster the greatest trouble & inconvenience! Considering that he invited me, & was very keen about my coming, I think this most spiteful."

The Kaiser did nothing to counteract these slurs. It was more convenient to let his mother take the blame than explain that his attempt to ease relations between Germany and France had failed to take into account the power and hostility of the Boulangists. And neither the German Ambassador nor the Foreign Ministry, both of whom had clearly misjudged the climate of opinion in France, stepped forward to accept responsibility for a trip that was doomed from the start.

As of the spring of 1891, within a year of dismissing Bismarck, Wilhelm II had managed to rile both his long-term enemies, the French, and his former allies, the Russians.

IN MAY OF 1891, a year before it was due to expire, Germany renewed its Triple Alliance with Austria and Italy with diplomatic gusto. In retaliation, Alexander III of Russia invited the French fleet to call in at the Baltic port of Kronstadt, where he gave a dinner for the commander and stood with his head uncovered during the playing of the musical *bête noire* of crowned heads, the revolutionary "Marseillaise." The following month, Alexander III signed the so-called August Convention with the French. The first step toward a formal alliance, it was an agreement between Russia and France to consult each other in case either was menaced by an aggressor.

Three months later, the Dowager Empress was appalled to read that her son had delivered a speech during the September maneuvers at Erfurt, in which he referred to Napoleon I as "that Corsican parvenu."

"[H]e was a great historical personage & soldier—& a vanquished foe," Vicky wrote Victoria, who agreed that her grandson's speech was "really dreadful." "Can Caprivi or someone not prevent such things and . . . beg him not to make so many speeches?" the Queen asked. Although Wilhelm's ministers quickly had the wording changed to the "Corsican conqueror," it was the first version that the French remembered.

Relations between Germany and France did not improve over the next few years. Nor did relations between Germany and Russia, in spite of a trade treaty lowering tariffs on imported grain, for which Wilhelm II campaigned actively against the Junkers. Terribly pleased with the successful passage of the tariff treaty, the Kaiser believed that this economic rapprochement would lead to the renewal of friendship between Germany and Russia. But he was apparently unaware that the Russians and French had signed a secret military convention two months earlier, in January of 1894, which provided that if either France or Russia were attacked by Germany, the other country would come to its aid.

Under the personalized diplomacy of Wilhelm II, Germany had managed to alienate its neighbors to the east and west, joining them in the giant pincer that had haunted the darkest visions of Germany's former Chancellor, Otto von Bismarck.

CHAPTER
SIXTY-FOUR

"Wilhelm II's capacity for self-delusion was almost limitless."

ISOBEL HULL

*F*REED FROM THE RESTRAINING HAND of Bismarck, Wilhelm II's behavior grew more capricious. "Everything must be done in a hurry & be startling! & emanate or seem to emanate from one source! . . . I think a Ministry composed of Mons. Jules Verne . . . with General Boulanger . . . and certainly Richard Wagner, if he were alive, would be the sort that would best suit the taste in high quarters . . . ," Vicky wrote Victoria shortly after Bismarck's dismissal. "It seems to me that the German Emperor is to be converted into a sort of Czar, & Germany to be governed by ukases."

The Kaiser's influence on domestic policy was nearly as disastrous as it was on foreign relations; in the case of national affairs, however, Caprivi kept some control. Unlike Wilhelm II, who believed in dispensing favors to his subjects somewhat in the manner of scattering feed to chickens, Caprivi tried to fend off discontent through legislative reform. To do this, he needed to replace the conservatives, who were currently voting against the government because of the trade treaties, with the Catholic Center Party. To mollify the Center, Caprivi released church funds held by Bismarck since the days of the *Kulturkampf,* allowed the antisocialist law to lapse, and returned what remained of the Reptile Fund after twenty-four years to the Hanovers (this last accomplished with considerable prodding from the Dowager Empress).

But the Kaiser denigrated the Reichstag as a "Chatter Chamber," spoke publicly of stringing up its delegates, and still believed that he could run Germany like an old-fashioned fiefdom. Visiting Munich in the fall of 1891, he signed the city hall register "Suprema Lex, Regis Voluntas" ["The King's wish is the supreme law"]. "A Czar, an infallible Pope, the Bourbons and our poor Charles I might have written such a sentence," Vicky wrote Victoria in despair, "but a constitutional monarch in the 19th Century!!" Vicky worried that her son would finish by destroying the monarchy itself.

Wilhelm II believed that anything that was wrong with Germany could be fixed if only the working class understood how much he and the House of Hohenzollern had done for them. In his mind, reverence for God and reverence for the Kaiser should be inseparable, and he was not above using the former to achieve the latter. He had first tried this by supporting Pastor Stöcker's Christian mission. His second attempt, the international labor conference, had generated nothing more than publicity. Now he called another conference, this one on education. Wilhelm preached that by emphasizing German studies over classical history and encouraging lots of exercise, he could turn pale, nearsighted Latin scholars into healthy, hearty supporters of the monarch. His highly charged speech at his education convention created "the most painful impression" on the delegates, but since it was the Kaiser speaking, school curricula were altered.

The question of education also came up when Caprivi, trying to form a majority in parliament, promised the Center Party a school bill that would give the clergy control of religious instruction in the primary schools. The Dowager Empress said that the Chancellor and her son were "playing a most dangerous game." Others more influential agreed, and Wilhelm soon reversed course, causing his Minister of Education and Religious Affairs, who had authored the bill, to tender his resignation. Caprivi followed suit—sending the Kaiser into a nervous breakdown and total seclusion for two weeks. When he finally emerged from the palace, Wilhelm was able to convince Caprivi to resign only his portfolio as President of Prussia and retain his positions as Prussian Foreign Minister and Chancellor of the Reich. As his replacement, Caprivi recommended Count Botho zu Eulenburg, a repressive reactionary who eventually killed the school bill and lost the support of the Catholic Center Party for the government.

If Wilhelm II's government was unable to maintain a consistent policy toward Catholics, he himself was firm about Jews. "The Jews are the curse of my country," he told Lady Susan Townley, wife of the second secretary of the British Embassy. "They keep my people poor and in their clutches. In every small village in Germany sits a dirty Jew, like a spider drawing the people into the web of usury. . . . The Jews are the parasites of my Empire. The Jewish question is one of the great problems I have to deal with."

While the Jews provided an easy scapegoat for the Kaiser's frustrations, the pomp and ceremony of his office furnished an outlet for his hyperactivity. As the historian Isobel Hull said, "The Kaiser swore in recruits, dedicated regimental colors, unveiled monuments, launched ships, opened buildings, consecrated churches, reviewed troops, led parades, ate farewell dinners, inaugurated galleries, pinned medals, and performed a hundred other such activities in dizzying succession."

The Kaiser's love of conspicuous grandeur could be seen in his palace, which featured huge white salons decorated with quantities of crystal and gold. According to one visitor, Wilhelm II's throne room with its highly ornamented dais was "worthy of Solomon." The court of Wilhelm II was also the most "stiff and formal" in Europe. "Nobody spoke above a whisper"; the salons were "sibilant with hissed consonants"; only the wife of the Foreign Minister and *grandes dames* of the court were allowed to sit on the sofa.

But Wilhelm still declared himself happiest in the company of his soldiers.

He surrounded himself with adjutants, chosen largely for their great height and good looks, and military attachés, whom he referred to as his "comrades" and whom he consulted on matters of political substance in lieu of his trained advisers. Determined to control every aspect of his soldiers' lives, he drew up a code of food and drink for the officers' mess. His passion for uniforms quickly became a joke among his relatives; between 1888 and 1905, he changed dress regulations in the German army thirty-seven times. The uniform for the Garde du Corps—white breeches, shiny breastplates, and huge golden eagles atop silver helmets—looked, according to a member of the British community in Berlin in the 1890s, as if it had been "designed for the knights of Ruritania." Required to dress in uniform even during the hot summer, army officers were reduced to wearing tennis garb and carrying rackets in order to get around the Kaiser's regulations.

Not so amusing, according to Willy's mother, was her son's "fad" of giving all the members of the cavalry long lances to carry. These awkward appurtenances caused "many nasty accidents," one of which involved Moretta's husband, Adolf, whose foot was crushed in a fall from his horse.

A more devastating instance of Kaiserian jingoism occurred in the spring of 1892 when a sentry fired on three men who were making fun of him. It was bad enough that in Germany soldiers had automatic authority over civilians, but in this instance the Kaiser made a point of publicly commending the sentry. "The man no doubt acted as he was told . . . but still one person was killed & the others wounded. . . . What must people think when the sovereign praises the soldier openly for firing on another man, just as much his subject & entitled to as much protection," Vicky wrote Victoria.

Believing himself a gifted soldier, Wilhelm II adored the army maneuvers that took place in Germany each fall. This was because his general staff made sure that the Kaiser always won the war games, even if it meant fudging the critiques that followed, changing rules or even uniforms in mid-battle. It was an unwritten rule that anyone who dared to best the Kaiser would be summarily "fired." Or, as Lamar Cecil wrote in his biography of Wilhelm II, "The Army was prepared to do virtually anything to insure the continuation of the Kaiser's martial enthusiasm."

It followed that Wilhelm, the major supporter of military appropriations, was bound to run into a disagreement with Caprivi, who wanted to keep the army budget down in order to get it through the Reichstag. In the winter of 1893, after consulting "God and my ancestors," the Kaiser came up with a huge appropriation of some sixty million marks, boasting to his generals that he would "carry the Bill through at all costs," that he would "not forgo a single man or a single Mark" and would "send the whole cracked Reichstag to the devil!"

His mother was appalled by the size and manner of the demand. Funding for educational and cultural purposes was being reduced, she said, because the army "swallows up everything." Moreover, Chancellor Caprivi should have carefully prepared the electorate, instead of suddenly presenting it with "this immense demand of money at a time when all the sad consequences of the Bismarck Regime are most felt!—the depression of trade and the unsatisfactory state of agriculture, the ever increasing now almost crushing burden of taxation. . . . Wilhelm's great unpopularity & the general discontent make this bill so distasteful to the people that I fear there is not chance of its being passed!"

The bill was defeated. The Kaiser dissolved parliament and called for new elections. If the new Reichstag did not accept his military bill, he said, he would simply change the constitution. By reducing the term of army service, Wilhelm II got his way, and the bill squeaked through by a margin of sixteen votes. Wilhelm dashed off a cable to Queen Victoria about his "great victory," and within two weeks his yacht was sighted at Cowes, where he had gone for the regatta.

But in pushing the army bill through the Reichstag, Caprivi had displeased old-line Junkers, who had fought the reduction of tariffs on imported grain and now objected strongly to shortening the military tour of duty. Already anathema with the conservative courtiers who surrounded Wilhelm II, Caprivi, who did not hail from an old Junker family and who refused to kowtow to the Kaiser, was discovering that serving Wilhelm II and the Fatherland at the same time was a contradiction.

One of the Chancellor's biggest problems was the Kaiser's habit of listening to courtiers rather than political advisers. Wilhelm associated criticism with disloyalty, and those who wanted to stay close to the seat of power learned never to disagree. Waldersee discovered this when he had the temerity to criticize the Kaiser's poor performance in the maneuvers of 1890. Three months later, Wilhelm informed his Chief of Staff that he was sending him to the suburbs of Hamburg, on the coast of Germany. "I was not for a second in doubt that the end of my military career had arrived," said Waldersee. What always amazed the court was the ease with which Wilhelm could dismiss an old friend with seemingly no sense of the pain he caused. It was "as if certain feelings which we take for granted in others are suddenly simply not there," said Philipp zu Eulenburg.

Eulenburg was delighted with Waldersee's fall. An elegant flatteur, amusing raconteur, and musician, "Phili" Eulenburg had, by the time Wilhelm came to the throne, already taken Waldersee's place as the Kaiser's best friend. Eulenburg had a subtle mind and displayed artistic talent—making him the exact opposite of the stuffed uniforms with whom Wilhelm II usually surrounded himself. He was close to Holstein, who used him to get the Kaiser's ear, and also to the Kaiserin, who liked the Nordic ballads he composed and sang. "Whenever he set foot in our Potsdam home," Wilhelm II said early in their friendship, "it was like a flood of sunshine shed on the routine of life." A rigid monarchist and anti-Semite, Eulenburg had as little use as Wilhelm II for parliamentary procedures or the delegates who participated in them. He was also a strong believer in filial piety, exhibited enormous devotion to his own mother, and disapproved of the way Bismarck had gone about, in the words of Hull, "intentionally poisoning" the relationship between Wilhelm and Vicky.

Although the Dowager Empress said that Eulenburg was "not to be trusted," it was Eulenburg and his group of friends (known as the Liebenberg Circle) who managed to keep her son functioning. Within the court, it was well known that the Kaiser was unable to keep his mind on work for very long and was subject to debilitating attacks of what was known in those days as nerves. Because of his extreme highs and lows, there was considerable worry that he might one day break down permanently. Under the false veneer that Wilhelm had created for himself—warrior, autocrat, husband, father—there remained a little boy overly attached to his mother and, many believe, a repressed homosexual. When the strain got to be too much, according to Hull, the Kaiser fled on his yacht or to one of his hunting lodges with his friends, who catered to his fantasies with childish pranks and vulgar entertainments.

"I'll parade you like a clipped poodle! . . . ," one Liebenberger wrote another, planning a skit for the Kaiser's amusement. "Just think: behind shaved, in front long bangs out of black or white wool, in back under a real poodle's tail, a noticeable rectal opening, and as soon as you stand upon your hind feet, in front a big fig leaf. . . . I already see in my mind's eye H.M. laughing."

WHILE WILHELM II ESCAPED the burdens of kaiserdom, Caprivi took the criticisms leveled at the government. The most strident attacks came from Bismarck, who had retired to Friedrichsruh to nurse his grievances and write his memoirs. The former Chancellor was prone to issuing statements expressing his displeasure over the way things were being run—what Vicky called "having a hit at Caprivi"—and a number of journalists, known collectively as the "diaspora press," made names for themselves interviewing the old lion in his lair. Not too surprisingly, Bismarck attracted quite a coterie of adherents, among them industrialists who wished to bring him back to reestablish protectionism. Their biggest problem was the hostility between the ex-Chancellor and Wilhelm II. In December of 1891, Bismarck's supporters approached the Dowager Empress for help.

Their appeal provided Vicky with a moment of exquisite if brief triumph, exceeding even Bismarck's call for sympathy before his dismissal. If the Dowager Empress had been forced to admire the Iron Chancellor's intellect, she had despised the conservatives around him for their paucity of imagination, political inflexibility, and nasty intrigues. For reasons far less patriotic than those of the old Chancellor, they had separated her husband and herself from the heir to the throne.

"[T]he agitation on the part of the Conservatives & Bismarckites to bring Prince Bismarck back is very strong! . . . ," she wrote Victoria on December 12, 1891.

First they want to obtain a complete reconciliation with William. I have even been spoken to & asked whether I would not try to influence William in that direction!

You may imagine how I laughed! The very people who for years laboured & intrigued to destroy my influence & that of Fritz now would wish me to help to patch things up with Prince Bismarck!! I told them plainly that I had not the faintest influence over the son whom their wickedness has turned against his parents. . . .

I should consider it very dangerous for the country and the monarchy to let Prince Bismarck have any thing to say any more. That later on, William should be on a footing of courtesy & civility with him & that he should be received at Berlin, etc. I should consider both dignified & proper & good policy, but nothing more!

Holstein, who feared that a political reconciliation between Bismarck and the Kaiser would undermine his own policies at the Foreign Ministry, agreed. It had been announced that Herbert von Bismarck was marrying a Hungarian countess the following summer in Vienna, and diplomatic custom demanded that Bismarck Sr. request an audience with Emperor Franz Joseph when he went to Vienna for his son's wedding. Convinced by Holstein and Philipp zu Eulenburg that such an encounter would damage Austro-German relations, Wilhelm II wrote Franz Joseph a letter, asking the Austrian Emperor not to receive his "disobedient subject" until such time as the old Chancellor apologized for his transgressions. "Bismarck was always a Russian, is a Russian, and will always be Russian and in his heart a decided enemy of Austria," the Kaiser told the Emperor of Austria.

For his part, Bismarck also wanted an apology from Wilhelm II, who worried that his ex-Chancellor might publish letters Willy had written criticizing various European leaders or that the "nasty old man" would die unreconciled and martyred. In January of 1894, the Kaiser sent an emissary to Friedrichsruh with a bottle of his best wine and a letter wishing Bismarck a speedy recovery from a bout with the flu. When Bismarck expressed his regret that he could not thank the Kaiser personally, the envoy responded as expected —with an invitation to come to Berlin.

"You will be surprised [sic] to hear that Prince Bismarck is coming here to court in a few days," Vicky wrote Victoria at the end of January. "Of course it is good that the personal relations should be of a civil & pleasant nature . . . but I am also rather afraid that the fact of his appearing here will be turned into a . . . return to political power, favour & influence which I should consider disastrous."

Vicky need not have worried. When Bismarck arrived in Berlin, he was met by Prince Henry and an honor guard, who escorted him to the palace. The crowds, which Vicky had predicted would treat the occasion as "very sensational & fine fun," were estimated at 300,000 to 400,000. Arriving at the palace, he was conducted up the steps to the accompaniment of a band for his audience with the Kaiser. Although their ten-minute interview was described by the press as a "long, frank exchange of views," it was purposefully interrupted after no more than two minutes by Henry, instructed by Willy to rescue him.

During the afternoon, Wilhelm II made his own bid for popular support, riding down Unter den Linden followed by a "jubilant" crowd shouting "Long live our magnanimous Kaiser." When a Berliner questioned the enthusiasm, she was told by a member of the Foreign Ministry that "arrangements had been made for men and boys to run after the Kaiser . . . to shout this and similar stuff."

That evening, Bismarck was honored at a banquet hosted by the Kaiser. Between his initial meeting with Wilhelm II and dinner at the palace, the ex-Chancellor had paid a call on Vicky.

"I thought him unaltered!" the Dowager Empress wrote her mother. "To save him the staircase I saw him downstairs, and it happened to be the very room in which I had not seen him since the morning in May, 1887, when he came to ask me not to allow Bergmann to perform the operation on my darling Fritz's throat. . . . I reminded him of it, & he said, 'Those are past times' and added 'how lovable and noble the man was throughout his illness.' The interview only lasted about 8 minutes & then he drove off again."

For all its brevity and superficiality, Bismarck's meeting with his former enemy the Dowager Empress was apparently more friendly than his audience with his onetime admirer Wilhelm II. Theirs was a public reconciliation, not a private one. Willy's old mentor returned to Friedrichsruh unsatisfied, and the Kaiser continued to resent the old man for the rest of his life.

As Caprivi's successor, Prince Hohenlohe, noted a year or so later, "Fear of Bismarck is the reigning epidemic in Berlin."

CHAPTER
SIXTY-FIVE

> *"The Empress Friedrich is one of the most tragic figures of modern history."*
>
> PRINCESS CATHERINE RADZIWILL

*I*T CANNOT BE SAID that the Dowager Empress of Germany made a quiet or willing exit into the wings of European history. Reduced to offstage commentary on world events, she seethed her way through the early years of her widowhood in a state of perpetual frustration, barely managing to keep down the angers boiling within. Sometimes it was the thought of her beloved Friedrichskron, now the home of the unfeeling Dona, which kept her "awake at night." Or recollections of insults received: "[N]o one knows what a <u>tempest</u> of despair . . . sometimes rages within me," she wrote Victoria four years after Fritz's death. Too often, it was the state of Germany itself, careening back and forth in the hands of an erratic young despot—the son in whom she had invested so much love and effort.

One thing that stung Vicky was the difference in Wilhelm's attitude toward her mother and herself, the huge gap between his esteem for a reigning queen and his contempt for a former empress. "Calling you 'Colleague' is very <u>ridiculous</u> but also very characteristic of <u>him</u> & <u>significant</u>," she commented on a letter the Kaiser had written his grandmother. "He does <u>not</u> consider <u>me</u> his colleague, therefore I am not entitled in his eyes to the consideration . . . & respect or to the confidence & <u>deference</u> with which he now treats <u>you</u>. . . . 'She has no influence' is his opinion of my position—therefore I am neglected, forgotten, shooed aside, never consulted, <u>hardly</u> <u>ever</u> <u>written</u> to or visited!"

Victoria agreed. The Queen, who continued to be Vicky's primary source of strength, well understood the isolation of royalty and the consequent importance of family relationships. "[T]he more my sorrow & loneliness weigh upon me, the more I cling to your love & affection & sympathy which has never failed me," Vicky wrote her mother eighteen months after Fritz's death. "May God bless & protect you for many a year to come," she wrote seven years later, a few days before Victoria's seventy-eighth birthday, "& spare you to us to whom your love & kindness & sympathy are so inexpressibly precious, & to <u>none</u> <u>more</u> than to me!"

Ever the wooer, the Dowager Empress continued to seek reassurances of her mother's love. "I should indeed feel so happy if I thought you missed me a little!" she wrote in 1891. She always sympathized with Victoria's ailments—the infirmities of age, the chronic rheumatism, the recurrent headaches, the difficulties in walking—and never failed to inquire into the state of Victoria's health. Nor did she hesitate to weigh in her own aches and pains. "I am so sorry your leg is still so troublesome! My head & neck and shoulder are still very painful and give me no rest at night!" Vicky wrote when she was fifty-four and Victoria almost seventy-six.

Throughout this, as in every period of their lives, Vicky wrote her mother at least three times every week. Even a delay of twenty-four hours was followed by excessive apologies. She did not expect the Queen to reciprocate. "<u>Pray</u> do <u>not</u> trouble or worry to write to me when you have so little time. You should <u>not</u> try your dear eyes." As the years went by, she also adjusted her handwriting and ink color to make it easier for the Queen's failing sight.

Through their correspondence, mother and daughter continued to summon the spiritual presence of the sainted Albert and Fritz into their lives, buttressing and rationalizing their own joys or sadnesses with the assured approval of the dear departeds. Nearly every letter also marked the anniversary of the death day of some other relative, raised by the single act of dying into the pantheon of the noble. Even Uncle Ernest, once he was dead, exhibited "much kindness & goodnature and many a lovable quality & was so bright & attractive," according to the niece whom he had betrayed. Thirty-two years after the demise of Vicky's two-year-old son Sigismund, Queen Victoria sent her daughter a wire acknowledging the child's birthday and her loss. "It is <u>just</u> like you!" Vicky responded gratefully. "<u>No</u> one else has remembered this day."

When they were not invoking the past, the ladies occupied themselves with the future, pairing off eligible girls in the family with dynastically appropriate spouses in the hopes of furthering the family's hold on Europe. One of Queen Victoria's triumphs was the engagement of her cousin Mary's* daughter May to Bertie's eldest son, heir to the English throne.† The Tecks, ruined by debts, were unable to give May a dowry, and Victoria and Vicky had worried about finding a sensible wife for the feckless Duke of Clarence, until Victoria came up with the idea of May. "I cannot help laughing . . . when I think of . . . someone mentioning to Dona what a charming girl May was, & how nice it would be if her brother‡ thought of her!" Vicky wrote Victoria. "Dona was most offended & said to me that her brother would not dream of making such a mésalliance!!!"

"With regard to darling Bertie's sweet girls . . . ," Vicky wrote two years later, "it <u>would</u> be desirable that they should marry someone of a reigning

---

* *Princess Mary Adelaide of Cambridge, the hefty daughter of the Duke of Cambridge, married to the Duke of Teck.*

† *Albert Victor died shortly after the engagement. Bertie's second son married his brother's fiancée, and they ruled as King George V and Queen Mary from 1910 to 1936.*

‡ *Ernest Gunther of Schleswig-Holstein, deemed unmarriageable by most members of the royal families of Europe.*

family. . . . It really is not wise to leave the fate of those dear girls 'dans le vague' for years longer." When the Prince of Wales told his mother and sister that his two unmarried daughters, aged twenty-four and twenty-five, were happy at home with their mother, Vicky remained unconvinced.

Circumstances had forced the Dowager Empress of Germany into a different perspective on matrimony than her family in England. Royal mothers like Queen Victoria and the Princess of Wales (later Queen Alexandra) usually tried to keep one daughter unmarried and at home to take care of them. Victoria insisted that Beatrice continue to live with her after her marriage, and Alexandra kept her second daughter single. Vicky could not afford the same luxury. "I used always to fear that my girls would be without a home of their own if I should be suddenly taken—and after one has been through so much sorrow, one seems so much more familiar with the thought that one's life might at any moment be at an end, & so anxious to provide for the safety & comfort of one's children while one has time!"

Queen Victoria did not understand this point of view, as she showed by her reaction to the announcement of the engagement of Vicky's youngest daughter, Mossy, to Prince Friedrich Charles (Fischy) of Hesse-Kassel. "I hope & believe it is what you wish," she wrote Vicky, "but I think Mossy ought not to have left you so soon. . . . I agree with the Mohammedans that duty toward one's parents goes before every other, but that is not taught as a part of religion in Europe. As Fischy has no place of his own, could they not chiefly live with you? You ought to make conditions. . . . For you to be quite alone will never do."

But the Dowager Empress made no "conditions," and Mossy married the young Hessian Prince on the anniversary of Vicky and Fritz's wedding day, January 25, 1893. Two weeks before the wedding, Queen Victoria sent Vicky this twofold thrust: "I ought not tell you now, who have this so soon before you, what I feel about a daughter's marrying, but to me there is something so dreadful, so repulsive in that one has to give one's beloved and innocent child, whom one has watched over and guarded from the breath of anything indelicate . . . to a man, a stranger to a great extent, body & soul to do with what he likes. No experience . . . will ever help me over that, especially when the mother is a widow."

"All you say about a mother's feelings when her daughter marries are an echo of my maternal sentiments—," Vicky answered. "Still. . . . A young girl does not remain a young girl—time flies! and it would be sad to see instead of motherhood and a matronly look taking its place, a withered & perhaps discontented and disappointed old maid! I should reproach myself then, & she might reproach me & think her life & happiness has been sacrificed to me!"

It was fortunate for Vicky that the next generation kept marrying and producing children—nine within the seven years following Fritz's death—providing her with opportunities to expend the energy and experience that was not wanted elsewhere. Vicky's three younger daughters always made their mother feel needed. "I am very glad to have the opportunity of being with her [Sophie] and . . . looking after her a little . . . ," Vicky wrote Victoria from Greece six weeks before the birth of Sophie's second son. "The dear child is so pleased I have come!"

While the Dowager Empress occupied herself with the rest of the family, the Kaiserin openly admitted that her children were "purposely kept away" from her mother-in-law. At one point, when the Kaiser's three oldest sons were nine, eight, and seven, they were sent to have tea with their grandmother. "[W]e should like to come to you very often, Grandmama," they told her, "but you see they don't let us." Although Vicky wrote Victoria that she "could not help laughing," her sense of humor in this area often failed her. "[I]t makes me bitter!" she said, adding in one of her not infrequent outbursts of self-pity, "I have already been deprived of enough in this life!"

In the fall of 1892, the Kaiserin gave birth to a daughter, the couple's seventh and last child and the only girl. She was named Victoria Louise—after Queen Victoria of England and Queen Louise of Prussia.* The Dowager Empress tried to be gallant when it was made clear that the child was specifically not named for her. "I think it quite understandable that the little girl . . . should be called after you!!" she wrote Victoria.

Most of the time, however, Vicky took perverse pleasure in totting up the wrongs visited on her by Willy and Dona. In doing this, she managed to ruin even the rare occasions when they included her in their celebrations. "It is William & Dona's wedding day," she wrote Victoria at the end of February, 1892, "and I am going to the palace. I have not had a meal there since Jan 1. William has not been to see me for a month. . . ."

"William is coming here on the evening of the 8th and leaves on the morning of the 9th," she wrote from Bad Homburg in September of the same year. "I have not seen him since the beginning of April! . . . There was time to go to Norway & . . . for shooting & to England, but there was no time to see me, nor would there be now if the Manoeuvres were not in the Rhine!"

IN THE SPRING OF 1894, the Dowager Empress moved into her new home, Schloss Friedrichshof† in Kronberg. Almost overnight, her martyrdom lessened and the injured tone of her letters improved dramatically. With a home of her own, purchased with personal funds, from which no government or disgruntled child had the right to eject her, Vicky could relax for the first time since her husband's death, secure in the knowledge that even as a much-maligned Englishwoman in Germany she was comparatively safe. Now when winter came on, she no longer had to move to Berlin or travel to get out of the unheated castle at Bad Homburg.

Friedrichshof had taken four years to complete, and the Dowager Empress was very proud of it. The style was *faux* Gothic—that *altdeutsch* combination of gables, turrets, moldings, and ornamentations so dear to late-nineteenth-

---

* *The wife of Friedrich Wilhelm III, who had tried to charm Napoleon I into territorial concessions for Prussia.*

† *Now a hotel.*

century royalties. Built of stone from the surrounding Taunus Mountains, it featured two-story arched windows overlooking some 300,000 acres of park, forest, and elaborately terraced flower gardens. One small parcel of land with a small ruin on it, visible from her windows, eluded her until the Kaiser arranged to give it to her for Christmas of 1892.

Vicky hung the walls of Friedrichshof with red and yellow damask and placed her collections on display—majolica and faience, bronzes, old watches and snuff boxes. There were marble busts from the fifteenth and sixteenth centuries, as well as paintings by Rubens and Bordone.

She also collected photographs. "There is no reason why a photo should not be a good portrait and a work of art," she wrote Victoria in a day when photographers still occupied themselves almost exclusively with technique. Unlike most of her peers, Vicky recognized virtues in the nonacademic output of her time, even if she did not want to own it. When the painter and designer Edward Burne-Jones died, she wrote Victoria, "[W]hether one admires or understands his style or not & whether one cares for his works . . . I think every one must admit he was a great artist in his way!"

The Dowager Empress wanted to show her home to her mother, but she was afraid to invite the Queen before trying out her modern innovations like an electrical system with no backup oil or gas lamps. "[T]o have you under my roof is quite a different thing to having any one else! I should be miserable if anything went wrong or we had any accidents."

According to one frequent female guest, Friedrichshof was "looked upon as the most perfect and best appointed residence of its day." Men like Prince (later Chancellor) Hohenlohe found the perfection somewhat intimidating. Shown his quarters, Hohenlohe described a "large room, with a great four-post bed, and a dressing-room and bath-room leading out of it. All very handsome, tasteful, and convenient; only the bath-taps for hot and cold water are so elegant that . . . I had great difficulty in turning them on, and could scarcely turn them off again."

"As soon as I reach my room I take off my shoes and go about in my socks, for even the softest slippers might have marked the parquet, and 'She' would have discovered it . . . ," said the British Ambassador, Frank Lascelles. "Smoking in the room was, of course, out of the question, but even to smoke out of the window was risky! 'She' might have spotted it. So I used to spread *The Times* in front of the fireplace, and kneeling down on it, smoke up the chimney, though it gave me a crick in the neck."

By now, Vicky had a reputation, probably well-earned, for exaggerated housewifeliness. "Not a speck of dust was to be seen," said her librarian, who hastened to assure posterity that his employer's "charm of manner" eased the burden of her demands. As did her generosity, since she paid her servants thirty percent more than her son paid his.* "Her instincts were orderly and

---

* *Living conditions at the Kaiser's palace were no better than the wages. One unventilated toilet was provided for every twenty-six servants.*

economical," her Lord Chamberlain, Baron von Reischach said, "but the reputation she had in Germany of being parsimonious was absolutely unmerited, for she was always open-handed in the cause of charity."

Certainly the Hohenzollerns had seen to it that this Dowager Empress would never be as wealthy as her predecessors. "The demands made on her purse . . . were immeasurable," said one member of her staff. "Her Majesty had no less than forty-two charitable institutions under her protection which were regularly supported."

Vicky spent as much time as possible at Friedrichshof, arriving in April or May and remaining until late autumn. During these months, she pursued her interest in architecture and landscape gardening. She had always been an enthusiastic horsewoman, but now, surrounded by her own forests of chestnut and pine, she rode out every morning, accompanied by a gentleman-in-waiting, the master of the horse, and two grooms. She was "a fearless and sure rider," according to one member of her staff. "In her sixtieth year, she still cleared . . . the most difficult ditches and obstacles and rode by no means very gentle horses." This assessment of Vicky's horsemanship was echoed by the head of her household, a former Hussar, who said that she had "splendid hands."

For riding, Vicky wore a black habit, round black hat, and red boots. The rest of the time she dressed in a black gown with a black veil. A miniature of Fritz hung on a gold chain around her neck, along with her glasses attached to a gold chain dotted with amethysts. She usually wore two rings, one set with a sapphire and two diamonds, the other with a ruby.

After breakfast, Vicky gave the orders for the day to her chief steward and the master of the household, then retreated to work in the library, her favorite room in the castle. "There was something moving about this great storehouse of learning," said Roger Fulford, who edited the letters between the Dowager Empress and her mother, "a don's library alive with all the optimism of the Victorians, entombed in the gloom of a Berlin schloss."

Unlike many royal libraries, most of the books had been read by their owner. According to Vicky's librarian, she read with great speed and was "thoroughly versed" in everything from theology and philosophy to literature and hygiene. "Seldom has a woman possessed such comprehensive knowledge . . . even . . . economics," he commented in awe. "[A]nything she had read was always at her finger-tips, always at her command," said one frequent visitor to Friedrichshof.

Before lunch, which was served promptly at one-fifteen, Vicky drove out to oversee work on her estate or inspect neighborhood projects. She restored the castle of Kronberg and a Gothic church with fifteenth-century frescoes, paved local roads, planted shade trees, improved drainage and street cleaning in the town, and built a hospital, a school, and a library. She was, as she had always been, an enthusiastic painter, and when she was not out doing what she saw as her duty to her neighbors, she worked in a room on the second floor of her home set up as a studio.

The Dowager Empress entertained frequently, usually at luncheon. Guests were served by "noiseless footmen" in her small round dining room, with a vaulted ceiling and enormous fireplace. Coffee was passed on the terrace, after which she withdrew to her rooms, emerging around four-thirty for tea and a drive or a walk in the woods. In the evenings, as she descended the staircase for dinner, her "trailing black robes and black veil" impressed her guests.

As did her mind. She was, as one of them pointed out, a "thoroughbred, passionately championing her point of view, complaining bitterly and with tears about the injustice done her. She took as her premises fine lofty sentiments and principles and on them fashioned her own world, and everything that refused to fit in with it she discarded relentlessly. She had no conception of . . . traditional conventions, of environment, education, and the working of chance in life."

Within a short time of its completion, Friedrichshof became a stopping-off place for relatives and friends. "My house is quite full now, or rather will be in a few days when Charlotte & Bernhard & Alfred are here! Mossy, Fischy and their 2 little darlings and Henry & Irene and Vicky [Moretta] & Adolf are here. I was at the station very early this morning to see dearest Alix [Princess of Wales] on her way to Copenhagen," Vicky wrote Victoria in January of 1895. Delighted to be in the midst of life again, generous with her hospitality, the Dowager Empress was also punctilious in tracking the movement of her nieces and nephews, and never failed to comment when one or another of them did not make sufficient efforts to pay her a visit.

Political figures and other notables on their way through Frankfurt often made the detour to Kronberg, where they stayed anywhere from a few hours to a few days. "This is a very central part of the world so that many come past here," Vicky wrote Victoria the year she moved in, "& I am a sort of wayside inn!"

Guests were likely to encounter Vicky's grandchildren, who were allowed to race through the castle, according to one disgruntled member of the household, "blowing their trumpets till the walls echoed with the noise and tumult." An intellectually demanding mother and grandmother, the Dowager Empress liked to see children work hard and play hard. Although inattention to studies infuriated her, the shouting and running that disturbed other adults seemed only to make her smile. When a child was needy, she was at her best.

This was the case with Henry and Irene's hemophiliac son, Toddy, who spent weeks at a time under his grandmother's care at Friedrichshof. Another frequent long-term houseguest was Charlotte's daughter, Feo. "She is really a good little child," Vicky said after one visit, "& far easier to manage than her Mama." But Feo was no more interested in studies than Charlotte had been. "Her little head is always running on dress, and what people wear & look like," Vicky said. She blamed Feo's shallowness on a lack of parental guidance and tried to make up for it. "[T]he atmosphere of her home is not the best for a child of her age . . . .With Charlotte for an example, what else can one expect. . . ." "Her parents are rarely ever at home or together. . . . She hardly knows what home life is! She was very sorry to go away!"

Friedrichshof was also a refuge for Vicky's siblings, particularly Bertie and

Helena, whose various health problems—he was overweight, she was addicted to drugs—brought them nearly every summer to the nearby spa at Bad Homburg. Vicky never missed an opportunity to praise them to the Queen. Bertie was invariably "so kind & good," and Lenchen, whatever her problems, was always a help and a joy to have in her home.

The month after Vicky moved into Friedrichshof, Wilhelm came to see her, arriving with an entourage of twenty-three for a one-night stay. Greeted by triumphal arches and the excited citizens of Kronberg, the Kaiser was preoccupied throughout the visit by a rumor that Dona's brother, Ernest Gunther of Schleswig-Holstein, wanted to marry Princess Hélène of Orléans, the daughter of the pretender to the throne of France. The Orléans family had lived in exile in England for many years and were very close to Queen Victoria.

A Frenchwoman in the family would not do, he says, nor a Catholic in an old Protestant house. He says Dona cannot sleep & sends him letters and telegrams without end to see whether such a calamity could not be prevented. William asked me whether I knew no means of stopping such a project! I could only answer that . . . I hardly thought it probable that so charming & beautiful a Princess would accept Ernest Gunther. . . . I see no harm in the 19th Century of a German Prince marrying a Catholic. . . . I do not think it a misfortune to have a French woman in the family. . . . I think Dona's excitement and agitation & religious prejudices quite exaggerated and ridiculous! . . . William hopes you would be able to induce the parents & young lady to refuse Gunther.

Although the merest possibility of "a new & cosmopolitan element" in the Hohenzollern family pleased Vicky, who said it might lead to "less obstinacy, pigheadedness & narrow mindedness & prejudice in the future generations," Hélène did not marry Ernest Gunther, and the Kaiser's attention was soon taken by another problem closer to home. Known as the affair of the pornographic letters, it was a bizarre interlude in Wilhelm's reign in which Dona's difficult brother may have also played a part.

Starting in the fall of 1892, members of the Kaiser's court, including the moralistic Kaiserin, had begun receiving anonymous notes that threatened to expose sexual peccadilloes. These letters often included pornographic pictures in which the faces and bodies had been removed and replaced with pictures of the recipients. Over a period of two years, at least two hundred of these letters were delivered.

Acting on unproven evidence backed by intrigues within the court, Wilhelm ordered his friend Leberecht von Kotze summarily arrested. But the letters continued to arrive while Kotze was incommunicado behind bars. Wilhelm had him released, and no further efforts were made to ferret out the source of the letters. Waldersee claimed that the court had discovered that the real culprit was a close relative of Wilhelm II. At the same time, Dona's brother Ernest Gunther was prohibited from living in either Berlin or Potsdam and told that he could spend "no more than a week at a time" at court.

A few months after his first visit, Wilhelm came back to Friedrichshof. Intent on surprising his mother on her fifty-fourth birthday, he arrived unannounced, disrupting her plans. "William's sudden appearance here yesterday morning . . . upset the whole house very much!" she wrote Victoria.

> It was most kindly meant of him, but it caused great confusion and gave a great deal of trouble, as you can imagine in a small household like this with few servants—he arrived with 3 gentlemen, a party of 14 in all!
>
> Fischy was in bed, I in my bath . . . when he drew up to the door! As he spent the night here, Charlotte & Bernhard who <u>were</u> to have slept here, returned to the hotel at Frankfort! However William is in a very good humour and was <u>delighted</u> to have taken every one by surprize. The suddenness of these arrangements is anything but a pleasure or a convenience, but the intention is kind, so one must not complain. . . . Bernhard & Charlotte, Adolf & Vicky, Anna [Adolf's mother] & Illa who were all to have come to luncheon, had to be telegraphed to <u>not</u> come, as there was <u>no</u> room left with William & his suite.

Willy did the same thing the following year on his mother's fifty-fifth birthday, turning up without warning at Mossy's castle, Rumpenheim, where Vicky was visiting. Wilhelm, who expected to be praised for these attentions to his mother, complained to the British Ambassador that the English press made no mention of his kindnesses.

The Kaiser's visits did not normally include his wife, but as the years passed, the Dowager Empress was allowed to see a bit more of his children. These visits were always made "<u>with</u> their Mama, <u>never</u> . . . alone and <u>only</u> for a few <u>minutes!</u>" Vicky understood: "She <u>does</u> <u>not</u> <u>wish</u> them to be intimate with me. . . . I have <u>begged</u> <u>so</u> often & <u>so</u> much to see them that <u>now</u> I say nothing <u>any</u> more. . . . William simply forgets or does not think, but with Dona it is <u>system</u> & conviction; she thinks my influence might be <u>bad</u> for her children. Of course, I cannot quarrel with her on that account, if this is her opinion, she is only doing what seems to her her duty."

But relations had definitely improved between mother and son. He began to come to Friedrichshof more often, which she enjoyed in spite of her complaints about the "enormous" entourages he invariably brought with him. Wilhelm II also made up with his sister Sophie when she visited Germany in the summer of 1894. Eventually, there was even a thaw in the relationship between the Dowager Empress and the Kaiserin. Dona, who went to the Bad Homburg spa for her health a few years later, called on her mother-in-law and invited the Dowager Empress to attend the confirmation of one of her sons.

"MY PERSONAL RELATIONS with William are good and in no way strained," Vicky wrote Victoria in the spring of 1896; "he is quite nice to me, and I have forgiven him with all my heart the cruel wrong he did me; but of course we meet seldom and I am a complete outsider . . . unable to do <u>any</u> good, in constant anxiety about him & the course of events and the future. I even perceive that William tries to give me pleasure here and there and I am always very grateful for it."

Vicky had forgiven, but she could not forget. Everything and everyone around her, from the newspapers she opened in the morning to the guests she entertained in the evening, spoke of her son's misapprehension of the nature and uses of power. His blundering follies and ignorance of the issues of the day were destroying the country for which she had given her life. For the rest of her days, the Dowager Empress would bear a profound sadness—punctuated by outbursts of fury—and an inconsolable regret for what should have been.

Nevertheless, she always demurred when asked to intercede. As she wrote Queen Victoria in 1894, "People have implored me to use influence with William . . . but I was obliged to say I could not. . . . I fear I could do no good whatever, and would be certain to be misunderstood, and the people about him would take the opportunity of creating fresh prejudices against me."

Vicky had finally accepted the fact that there was no way to span the divide between herself and Wilhelm II—an ideological gulf that seemed to widen even as they themselves reached out toward an emotional accommodation. Although she certainly understood this, there was another element in Willy and their relationship that she did not take into account, perhaps because she did not recognize it or admit it to herself. This was her son's mental instability, which was becoming apparent to more than just his close friends.

To explain Willy's grandiosity, his mother used words like impetuous and noisy; to rationalize his recurrent rages and restlessness, she pointed to the ways in which his grandparents and others had spoiled him; to excuse his occasional breakdowns, she referred to a tendency to be easily hurt. Living in the days before distinctions were made among various kinds of mental illness, Vicky would probably not have known that her son's peculiarities were symptoms of mania, a state of mind only exaggerated by his position as Kaiser. Even Wilhelm II's personal physician, Dr. Leuthold, refused to admit that his sovereign was probably a manic-depressive.* Confronted by a "nervous breakdown" in 1897 and a "violent outbreak" three years later, the doctor admitted to Philipp zu Eulenburg that the Kaiser's "condition reflects a certain weakness of the nervous system," but he "emphatically" denied "any possibility of mental disorder."

In 1894, a satirical pamphlet entitled "Caligula, a Study of Roman Megalomania" appeared in German bookstores and sold thousands of copies. Written by Ludwig Quidde, a professor and member of the Reichstag, it compared the rampant Caesarism of Wilhelm II with that of the mad Emperor of ancient Rome. Drawing implicit parallels between Wilhelm and Caligula, both of whom had mounted the throne by skipping over a generation, Quidde also satirized other members of Wilhelm's court, including the Dowager Empress, who was compared to Caligula's mother, who hated her son.

"[N]o one can doubt that it is aimed at the Kaiser," said Waldersee, who

---

* Wilhelm himself referred to the "fits of depression" that assailed his father, and manic-depressive illness runs in families (Wilhelm II, My Early Life, p. 5).

disapproved of the pamphlet despite Wilhelm's shabby treatment of him. What upset Waldersee was the fact that Quidde dared use his own name and that the book had not been banned. Certainly everyone expected Wilhelm II to take Quidde to court—until one of the local rags speculated on the following piece of dialogue sure to take place at any future trial:

"Q: Whom had you in mind in writing this book, Professor?

"A: Caligula, of course! Whom have you in mind, Mr. Prosecutor?"

CHAPTER SIXTY-SIX

"The chief danger in the life of Kaiser Wilhelm II is that he is and remains absolutely unaware of the effect that his speeches and actions have on Princes, public men, and the masses. The life work of every Government of Wilhelm II must be to counter this danger and as far as is possible to nullify these effects. A task which soon wears one out."

FRIEDRICH VON HOLSTEIN, *1896, in a letter to Philipp von Eulenburg*

*W*ILHELM II HAD STARTED his reign convinced that the right combination of personal charm and social reform could win over labor, but after a few years on the throne, he had grown bitter and disillusioned. Neither his educational theories nor the expiration of the antisocialist bill in 1890 had seduced workers away from the Social Democratic Party, which continued to increase its representation in the Reichstag. When President Carnot of France was assassinated by an anarchist in July of 1894, the Kaiser ordered Caprivi to prepare a new, harsher antisocialist bill that would exile agitators and punish anyone who criticized the Kaiser or the House of Hohenzollern. Following Bismarck's example, Wilhelm announced that if the Reichstag did not pass this legislation, he would dissolve it; if that failed, he would ask the princes of Germany to abrogate the constitution. Caprivi said he would resign rather than become the instrument of a coup d'état. Tired of Caprivi's prickly rectitude, the Kaiser accepted his resignation in October of 1894.

Caprivi was followed into office by Prince Chlodwig zu Hohenlohe-Schillingsfürst, a Bavarian Catholic who had served as Governor of Alsace-Lorraine. A friend of the Dowager Empress and a relative of the Kaiser by marriage, Uncle Chlodwig, as he was known to the Kaiser, was already an old man of seventy-five, tired and seemingly more malleable than Caprivi. With his slightly bent frame, fringes of white hair, and thin voice, he looked more delicate than he was. "[F]or many years past he has looked worn-out and broken," Waldersee said, "but mentally he is as fresh as paint." Unlike his predecessor, Hohenlohe was on good terms with Bismarck, an advantage Wilhelm probably took into account when he chose him.

Hohenlohe visited the Dowager Empress at Friedrichshof two weeks before assuming the chancellorship. She believed that he was the "best successor" to Caprivi her son could have found, but, like everyone else, worried about the seventy-five-year-old's stamina. Two conversations with the new Chancellor changed her mind. Hohenlohe, Vicky wrote Victoria, would meet "all the great difficulties he has to fight against with the greatest calmness! Not the smallest one is William's impulsiveness. . . . I think Prince Hohenlohe's calm, conciliatory and dignified manner will by degrees have an influence! He is both wise and patient, & has great tact & experience."

There was a great deal for Hohenlohe to conciliate, according to Vicky, who said that irritation against the government had "never been louder or stronger." The Kaiserin, supported by her three closest female companions at court, known as the "Hallelujah Aunts," had recently embarked on a campaign to construct large, expensive churches—twenty-two were built by 1897—the upkeep of which fell to the citizens of Berlin. If Dona had her churches, Willy had his parades, which, his mother said, exasperated the citizenry by "upsetting . . . the thoroughfares for a couple of hours." This, added to the changeover in ministers and the "despotic & personal character of the present Government," did not increase the popularity of the now recognizedly unstable Kaiser.

Hohenlohe's slow and measured pace averted a minor crisis early in his administration. Berlin was in the middle of preparations for Bismarck's eightieth birthday (April 1, 1895), when a motion to recognize the day was defeated in the Reichstag by a collection of his old enemies—members of the liberal Catholic Center and Social Democratic parties, Poles, Danes, and Alsatians. Wilhelm ordered Hohenlohe to punish the Reichstag with dissolution, but the Chancellor managed to persuade him to wait until everyone calmed down, which they did. Meanwhile, the Kaiser traveled to Friedrichsruh with four army detachments to parade before the ex-Chancellor and present him with a golden sword "as an emblem of that great and mighty constructive period when blood and iron was the cement" of the German Empire.

The Dowager Empress criticized Wilhelm's behavior as equally excessive, particularly after the way in which he had dismissed the Chancellor. She herself wrote Bismarck a "civil note," but, as she told Victoria, "I could not heap on flattery and say what I do not think and feel! He did his country as much harm as good. . . . A certain section of the public look upon him as the 'maker' of Germany. I who know how it all came about know what his part was & was not! He is a most remarkable man—cunning and daring, astute and energetic as few people have ever been. Napoleon, Richelieu, Talleyrand . . . would recognize many of their qualities in him; but to live at Berlin under his regime . . . was misery & thraldom & more or less constant danger."

Hohenlohe's success in preventing Wilhelm from dissolving the Reichstag gave the Dowager Empress hope that he would continue to find ways to temper the words and actions of her son. The new Chancellor, who Holstein said behaved like an "under-butler," was not a confrontational man. "I was firmly determined never again to take offense at anything," Hohenlohe said early in his career as Chancellor. "If I had done otherwise I should have had to send in my resignation at least once a week." Hohenlohe's method of dealing with Wilhelm II was to listen to the Kaiser's political outbursts in silence, go home, and write out his counterarguments. Like his predecessors, he was appalled by the influence of the Kaiser's military entourage, writing his wife that this "occult government" was a "calamity" for himself and the state.

The defeat of the antisocialist bill in 1894 did not stop Wilhelm II, who demanded more draconian legislation the following year. Calling for extreme penalties for anyone convicted of making subversive comments about the Kaiser, religion, property, or the family, this bill, too, failed to pass the Reichstag. The Dowager Empress was delighted. "The government are ill advised & seem very blind as to the danger of what they are doing!" she wrote Victoria. "The most retrograde nonsense is preached & carried out; & the blind low Church, Orthodox Pietism is rampant and emanates from Court circles. It is bitter indeed to have to sit still & look on at all the blunders made!"

There were more blunders to come.

In the spring of 1895, Wilhelm's highly regarded reformist Minister of War, General Bronsart von Schellendorf, introduced a bill providing for open military trials except in cases where they might jeopardize state secrets. Supported by the Reichstag and the people, who worried about the tendency of the German army to put itself above the law, it was violently opposed by Wilhelm. When Bronsart presented the law to the Prussian ministry in the hope of gaining approval before proceeding to the Reichstag, he was supported by all of the ministers except the ultra-right-wing Minister of the Interior, Ernest von Köller, who leaked the secret proceedings of the meeting to the Kaiser and the press. Hohenlohe told Wilhelm that if Köller was not dismissed, all the other ministers would resign, himself included. Wilhelm, who could not afford to lose two chancellors within thirteen months, was forced to dismiss Köller and accept a watered-down version of the bill. For his sacrifice, he demanded and got the resignation of his progressive Minister of the Army.

After Bronsart's resignation, Wilhelm II set about ridding himself of two other members of his cabinet, who, like the former Army Minister, exhibited signs of independence. By 1897, he had managed to weed out anyone who did not believe in a Kaiser's absolute right to do as he liked, uninhibited by public opinion, parliament, or the constitution.

A CONFIRMED AUTOCRAT, Wilhelm II invariably came down on the side of entrenched power elsewhere, however ugly its manifestations. Faced with the ongoing disintegration of the Ottoman Empire and the widespread uprisings of its subjects, the Kaiser placed himself and his nation squarely behind the reactionary Sultan, Abdul Hamid II, whom he honored with state visits in 1889 and 1898.

Abdul, who was known variously as Abdul the Damned and the Red Sultan (for all the blood he shed), had come to power in 1876, just before the Russo-Turkish War. His first move had been to banish the author of a progressive constitution and to set about reestablishing absolute power for himself. This meant bloody reprisals against the various peoples of the Balkans brave or foolish enough to revolt against what Salisbury called the "feeble, corrupt & vicious" Turkish government. The Dowager Empress, who had once followed the English line in supporting the Turks, turned on the Sultan when she heard that he "allowed if not instigated" the retaliatory massacres.

Vicky found her son's attitude toward the subject peoples of the Ottoman Empire particularly repellent in the case of the inhabitants of the island of Crete, who were supported in their revolt against the Sultan by the Greeks. "William has a most unjust & blind dislike of Greece & poor King George," she wrote Victoria, "& Dona still more, which is very unfortunate; with her it is the Glucksburg relationship,* & with him prejudice & Sophie's change of religion!"

Wilhelm II could not wait to involve himself in the 1897 war between Greece and Turkey over these uprisings, exhibiting what the British Ambassador called a "wild state of excitement" as he summoned the diplomatic representatives of the other Great Powers at all hours of the day and night in an effort to organize a blockade of Greece. His hostility was so blatant that Queen Victoria made a formal protest through her embassy in Berlin. Meanwhile, his mother, who glided over the responsibility of the Greeks in fomenting the revolt, collected funds for their relief. From the time Sophie married the heir to the Greek throne, the Dowager Empress had become an impassioned and rather untrustworthy Greek apologist and supporter. "Please, darling Sophie," she wrote her daughter, "when you get the money, distribute it . . . amongst those poor refugees, but say you have collected it from and amongst your friends, as it would not do if it were officially known that I . . . sent it. I might get into trouble. And please, dear, not a word must be said that Grandmama contributed."

After a series of decisive defeats at the hands of the Turks, Greece asked the Great Powers to settle the conflict. The Kaiser took personal credit for the cessation of hostilities, which came about, he wired his grandmother, only after "the [Greek] King and the Government . . . begged for my intervention through Sophy." Vicky remarked that her son might have shared the peace laurels with the members of his Foreign Ministry, and she resented the fact that the Kaiser refused to join England, France, and Russia in guaranteeing a loan to Greece after the war.

The Dowager Empress was also deeply agitated over the plight of the Armenian victims of the Turkish massacres, which began in the mid-1890s. Declaring that "indignation ought to burn in every human bosom at such deeds," she tried to use what little influence she had to get various countries of Europe to intervene. "One wonders that the Great Powers do not interfere in a more energetic manner!" she wrote her mother during the first Armenian massacre. "The Eastern question is indeed a powder barrel, and no one likes to have anything to do with it for fear of a war which might lead to a universal conflagration, & on the strength of this reluctance on the part of the Great Powers—which in a great measure is only necessary prudence—the Turks continue their cruelties."

While other European leaders and their governments remained passive

---

* *King George I of Greece was a son of the King of Denmark. It was the Danish royal family, the Glücksburgs, who had contended for control of Schleswig-Holstein against Dona's family, the Augustenburgs.*

onlookers to the tragedy, the German Kaiser actively supported the Turks. Prodded by Vicky, Queen Victoria asked Prime Minister Salisbury about sending personal letters of appeal to the Sultan, the Kaiser, and the Czar of Russia. Salisbury was "not hopeful." Abdul Hamid, he said, was interested in only two things—"Himself" and "Islam." As to Wilhelm II: "From what I have seen of his character, I should rather dread giving him umbrage. He has not recovered from the intoxication of his accession to power; it is rather growing worse."

But Victoria appealed to Willy anyway. After a consultation with Hohenlohe, the Kaiser told his mother to tell his grandmother that "not so much as a biscuit could be sent" to the starving Armenian women and children "without the Sultan's permission," that it was "impossible to reach the poor creatures on account of the snow till spring, & by that time there would most likely be no one left to help or care for."

"If Europe does not find a means of stopping him, the Sultan will exterminate the Armenians altogether," Vicky wrote Victoria some months and many deaths later. "The German Government I think is deplorable, as the Austrian is, & as the Russian Government has been hitherto." Vicky hoped that Victoria would be able to appeal to the young Czar of Russia, Nicholas II, who was in England at the time and, according to the Queen, appeared "most anxious to act with us."

This shift in Vicky and Victoria's attitude toward Russia —a remarkable progression from distrust to hope—had come about because of a death and a marriage in the Russian royal family.

DURING THE SUMMER of 1894, Alexander III's son Nicholas had become engaged to a niece of Vicky's. Alix, or Alicky as she was known in the family, was the youngest surviving daughter of Vicky's sister Alice. Quite a handsome but strange young woman, Alicky had taken some time to overcome her religious scruples in order to convert to Orthodoxy, but shortly after the death of Alexander III in the fall of 1894, she had married the new Czar, Nicholas II.

"What a benefactor to his country, what a saviour to that poor oppressed nation, what a Godsend to Europe he might be! . . . ," Vicky had written Victoria on November 3, 1894, two days after the accession of Nicholas II. "May the truth reach his ears and wise disinterested council! . . . May the fact that you are his grandmama* be a blessing to him in many ways and dispell many a blind prejudice."

In the fall of 1896, the young Czar and Czarina visited their families in western Europe, bringing with them their first daughter. They impressed Queen Victoria as "quite unspoilt and unchanged . . . as dear & simple . . . as ever." When they came to Germany to lay the cornerstone of a Russian Orthodox church in Bad Homburg, the Dowager Empress, who brought them back to

---

* Czar Nicholas II was married to the Queen's granddaughter. He was also the Queen's grandnephew, since Bertie was his uncle (Nicholas's mother was a sister of Alexandra). Nicholas, Willy, and Bertie's son, the future George V, were all first cousins.

Friedrichschof for luncheon, was similarly pleased. "[H]is modest, simple, straightforward way is so taking & the expression of his eyes so winning . . . and the shyness he still has lends a charm to anyone in <u>that</u> <u>position</u>."

With a beloved niece sitting on the throne of Russia next to a quiet, unassuming husband, the Dowager Empress looked forward to an improvement in Germany's relationship to Russia. Not only would Nicky's German wife help undo the anti-German bias that had increased during the reign of his father, but such a well-meaning young Czar might be able to lead Russia out of the dark ages of ignorance and repression.

But in fastening her hopes on the young Romanov, the Dowager Empress of Germany did not take into account either his passivity or the personality of her son. For if the peaceful temperament of Nicholas II of Russia seemed geared to improving relations between Russia and England, the volatility of Wilhelm II almost guaranteed continued distrust. In spite of the Kaiser's conviction that he could charm the young Czar into deserting his new French allies for old German ones, Nicky was no fonder of Willy than his father, Alexander III, had been.

Meanwhile, as Bertie wrote a friend, "The character and personality of the new Tsar give assurance of the benefits which would come of an alliance between England and Russia."

CHAPTER
SIXTY-SEVEN

> *"I am the sole arbiter and master of German Foreign Policy.
> . . . May Your Government never forget this. . . ."*
>
> KAISER WILHELM II, *in a letter to* EDWARD VII, *1901*

*A*T THIS POINT in Germany's history, the Kaiser would have done well to make an accommodation with England. But his attitude toward the country of his mother's birth was as complicated and ambivalent as his feelings for his mother, and he lurched between hate and love, contempt and admiration, furious disavowal and slavish emulation. Imbued with a sense of divine right, he exploded in fury when any country or person failed to kowtow to his royalness. Nor did he understand why his hearty, often well-meaning overtures raised such antipathy in the recipients. Typical of the Kaiser's flat-footedness was his appearance at Cowes in August of 1895.

The annual English regatta was considered a purely social event, but the Kaiser had sailed in with a flotilla of warships, geared to impress Uncle Bertie. "H.M. gave the English a special treat by bringing along a fleet of four battleships and a dispatch boat," one of the member of the Kaiser's entourage noted in a report to the Wilhelmstrasse. "They block the course of the racing vessels, every few moments they get an attack of *salutirium*, the sailors are flooding Cowes, the Queen has to invite the commanders, etc!"

While at Cowes, Wilhelm II summoned Prime Minister Salisbury to his yacht, ostensibly to discuss the Armenian massacres, although the Kaiser really wanted to talk about the worrisome Franco-Russian alliance. The Kaiser and Lord Salisbury did not get along well. Wilhelm II felt correctly that the British Prime Minister did not like him. Salisbury distrusted Wilhelm's bluster and had asked the Queen to "recommend . . . calmness, both in his policy and in the speeches which he too often makes." But Victoria was worried about the Armenians, and Salisbury did as she commanded. The audience with Wilhelm II was to take place on board the *Hohenzollern*.

Due to circumstances beyond his control, the Prime Minister, who was staying with the Queen at Osborne House, was an hour late. Although he apologized, explaining that his launch had broken down and it had taken time to bring another one, the Kaiser remained angry. Preoccupied with his own hurt feelings, Wilhelm did not grasp Salisbury's veiled hints that Germany and

England might cooperate in partitioning the Ottoman Empire and allow Russia to take Constantinople. The Kaiser, who misinterpreted Salisbury's plan as an attempt to destroy Germany's efforts to regain Russia's friendship, rejected Salisbury's ideas out of hand. Wilhelm's advisers must have told him about his error, because the next day he asked to see Salisbury again, specifying that the Prime Minister should appear at 4:00 P.M.

This time Salisbury never arrived at all. He had been with the Queen when the Kaiser's message arrived, and he was not given the invitation until three-forty-five, when it was too late to get out to the Kaiser's yacht. Since the invitation had come by telephone, Salisbury, assuming it was no more than a last-minute courtesy after their unsatisfactory talks of the day before, returned to London.

The combination of two misfires, both of which Wilhelm regarded as deliberate on the part of the British Prime Minister, plus articles in the English press critical of a saber-rattling speech he had given on board one of his cruisers, convinced the Kaiser that he had been the object of an intentional snub, and he returned to Germany in high dudgeon. Two months later, he found what he thought was a third instance of British malevolence in some comments from the outgoing British Ambassador, Sir Edward Malet. Mild-mannered and concilia-tory, Malet told the German Secretary of State that he felt he was leaving Berlin with Anglo-German relations in good order, his only concern being Germany's support for the Boers in the Transvaal, which, he said, was a "possible danger to friendly relations of the two countries in the future."

When the Secretary of State repeated Malet's words, Wilhelm declared that he, the German Kaiser, had been insulted over "a few square miles of Negroes and palm trees." In spite of a flurry of diplomatic thrusts and parries—apologies forwarded by Salisbury, heels dug in by Wilhelm—nothing could convince the Kaiser that he had not been the object of purposeful mockery. He looked for a way to get back at the British—and soon found one in the highly explosive situation in the Transvaal in southern Africa.

THE BOERS (Dutch Afrikaners), who had settled the Transvaal in 1854, had signed a convention with the British in 1881 that guaranteed their autonomy in domestic affairs in exchange for submission to the British Empire in matters of foreign policy. Led by their President, the Bible-wielding Paul Kruger, the Boers resented the foreigners who came to their country to mine for gold, which was discovered in 1886. To keep them under control, Kruger passed a law which said that no one with less than five years' residency could become a citizen or vote.

Opposed to President Kruger was Cecil Rhodes, the Englishman known as "the Colossus" who controlled ninety percent of the diamond production in South Africa and held substantial investments in gold mines as well. Prime Minister of the British Cape Colony to the south, Rhodes's dream was an expansion of British rule northeastward and an eventual realization of a British railroad leading from the Cape to Cairo. To overthrow Kruger, Rhodes assembled a sizable cache of weapons and a private army, commanded by his friend Dr. Leander Starr Jameson. In October of 1895, Rhodes's army began gathering on the border of the Transvaal, waiting for a signal from the malcontents within. When the uprising failed to materialize, the army moved in anyway in what became known as the Jameson Raid. Rhodes's men were easily defeated by the Boers, who turned Jameson over to British authorities. Highly embarrassed by the incident, the British Foreign Office disavowed the renegade army.

Wilhelm II had often expressed his fondness for the "little nation" of the Transvaal, explaining that the Dutch Boers were in fact "Lower Saxon-German in origin" and hence racially related to the Germans. President Kruger appreciated the Kaiser's support. He usually portrayed his country as a helpless infant, remarking at a celebration of the Kaiser's birthday in January of 1895, "Our little republic only crawls about among the great powers, but we feel that if one of them wishes to trample on us, the other tries to prevent it." Just in case anyone missed the point, Kruger added that Germany was "a grown up power that would stop England from kicking the child republic."

This line had great appeal for the Kaiser, who pounced gleefully on the news of the failed Jameson Raid. Ignoring the German Ambassador in London, who cabled that England had condemned the raid in no uncertain terms, Wilhelm summoned his top military advisers and descended on Hohenlohe's palace. There, according to his Secretary of State, Marschall von Biberstein, he put forth "some weird and wonderful plans," including the establishment of a German protectorate over the Transvaal and mobilization of the marines.*

To counter these follies, one of his advisers suggested that His Majesty merely send Kruger a congratulatory cable. The result was the famous "Kruger telegram," written by a senior member of the Foreign Ministry after Hohenlohe threatened to resign if the Kaiser's draft was used. The watered-down version, which spoke of restoring peace and defending the Transvaal's independence, was not particularly objectionable. The fact that it was sent at all, however, was a nasty slap at the British.

"William's telegram to President Kruger I think a deplorable mistake," Vicky wrote Victoria. The Prince of Wales, who called it "a most gratuitous act of unfriendliness," agreed and asked his sister whether it was just another of Willy's impulsive acts or represented the official position of the German government. Vicky brought up the subject over lunch with Chancellor Hohenlohe.

"I asked whether a certain telegram was to be rejoiced at," she reported. "He answered that it certainly was in accordance with German public feeling at this moment, from which answer I gather that the telegram was approved."

But Queen Victoria, the Prince of Wales, and the Dowager Empress remained convinced that the wire was the work of Wilhelm II. "I feel that I cannot refrain from expressing my deep regret at the telegram you sent Presi-

---

* The most ingenious scheme actually came from one of the Kaiser's advisers, who proposed disguising the Governor of German East Africa as a lion hunter in order to get him into Pretoria to act as Chief of Staff to President Kruger.

dent Kruger," the Queen wrote her grandson. "It is considered very unfriendly towards this country, which I feel sure it is not intended to be, and has, I grieve to say, made a very painful impression here. The action of Dr. Jameson was of course very wrong and totally unwarranted; but considering the very peculiar position in which the Transvaal stands towards Great Britain, I think it would have been far better to have said nothing."

"Never was the telegram intended as a step against England or your Government . . . ," Wilhelm replied. "Rebels against the will of the most gracious Majesty the Queen are to me the most excrable [sic] beings in the world, & I was so incensed at the idea of your orders having been disobeyed . . . I thought it necessary to show that publicly . . . I was standing up for law, order & obedience to a Sovereign whom I revere & adore."

The Queen was not fooled. Her grandson's excuses, she said, were "lame and illogical." She told Vicky that "the bad feeling" over the telegram would last "some little time"—a judgment in which the Dowager Empress sadly concurred. Holstein, who had counseled against sending a telegram in the first place, claimed that the Kaiser's cable was the catalyst for the ensuing era of hostility between Germany and England. "England, that rich and placid nation, was goaded into her present defensive attitude towards Germany by continuous threats and insults on the part of the Germans. The Kruger telegram," said the *éminence grise* of the Wilhelmstrasse, "began it all."

ONE OF THE IMMEDIATE RESULTS of the Kruger telegram was that the Kaiser, who had started hinting for an invitation the previous winter, was not invited to his grandmother's diamond (sixtieth) jubilee celebrations in June of 1897, in which his mother was one of the most visible and honored participants. His exclusion disturbed him enormously. And for several years after the Kruger telegram, he was not invited to attend his favorite summer event, the Cowes regatta in England.

Two months after the jubilee, Wilhelm sailed off to pay a call on Nicholas II. The visit went well, but as soon as the Kaiser left, the Russian court began to prepare for the arrival of another head of state, President Fauré of France. It was at this meeting that the word "allied" was first used in connection with Russia and France. When Nicholas II raised his glass to the "friendly and allied" nation of France, and President Fauré of France saluted the "united and allied" nation of Russia, it was clear to the world that an alliance between an old enemy on Germany's west flank and an old friend turned cool on the east was now a reality.

One outgrowth of the Kruger telegram was the passage by the Reichstag in March of 1898 of the First Naval Law. The enlargement of the German navy was based on the premise that a stronger fleet was necessary to protect German colonies and mercantile interests abroad and give it clout in international relations, particularly vis-à-vis England. Up to this time, Wilhelm II had regarded the British navy as the protector not only of England's colonies around the world but of German interests as well. For Admiral Tirpitz, the author of the naval law, the backlash of the Kruger telegram had proved extremely "useful." As he put it many years later, "The outbreak of hatred, envy, and rage which the Kruger Telegram let loose in England against Germany contributed more than anything else to open the eyes of large sections of the German people to . . . the necessity for a fleet."

"William's one idea is to have a Navy, which shall be larger & stronger than the British Navy," Vicky had warned Victoria at the time of the Jubilee. To her daughter Sophie in Greece, she wrote about the passage of the naval bill four years later: "I am not altogether happy and enthusiastic . . . as I think other things want the money still more in Germany. . . . Of course England does not like it . . . but the abuse poured on England by the German Press day by day about everything and on every occasion is quite extraordinary. I fear it leads to a distressing conclusion in England, which is that she has no greater enemy than Germany and no more bitter foe than William."

For his part, Wilhelm II complained that he was treated by the English like "a silly boy." In March of 1898, the British Ambassador to Germany, Frank Lascelles, wrote Salisbury that the "continued hostility evinced towards him [Wilhelm] by the Prince of Wales would possibly have serious results on the relations between the two countries." To ease the situation, Wilhelm suggested that his mother mediate between his uncle and himself. The position of the Dowager Empress has "much improved of late," Lascelles wrote the Prince of Wales, adding that "the feeling which she now inspired among the people, amounted almost to veneration."

Although he must have been pleased that his sister was finally getting her due, Uncle Bertie saw no need for Vicky to intervene. "If only the son could see more of his mother and could get under her influence, how different everything would be . . . ," he said. But he denied any hostility on the part of Wilhelm's English relations. "The whole matter rests in the German Emperor's hands, and there is really no need for his mother's good offices."

The Foreign Office showed a similar lack of interest in rapprochement with the Germans, and the British Colonial Secretary, Joseph Chamberlain, found himself denounced by the Foreign Office for a speech in May of 1898 recommending an Anglo-German alliance. Vicky, who labeled Chamberlain's ideas "plain common sense," did not understand the English reaction. A few weeks later, when the Kaiser spoke to her about testing the political climate in London regarding a future alliance with Germany, she accepted the commission with alacrity.

But Wilhelm was not playing straight with his mother. While the Dowager Empress thought she was working toward an alliance between her two countries —bombarding her mother with letters about Wilhelm's sincerity, the importance of meeting him "half-way," and the danger to both England and Germany of Russian expansion in the Far East—she was being set up as a decoy by her son to distract the British while he tried to obtain colonial concessions from them.

England and Germany were currently engaged in negotiations with Portugal over a loan to be secured by Portuguese territories in Mozambique and Angola. "Germany is anxious . . . that we should settle to whom these colonies are to go, if Portugal should give them up . . . ," Salisbury wrote Queen Victoria, "but we are very anxious to make it clear that we desire to . . . protect her [Portugal] in the possession of her colonies. . . . Germany professes the same desire, but we are not quite sure of her sincerity."

Salisbury's suspicions were correct. The German Ambassador was instructed to temporize in meetings over the Portuguese territories while the Kaiser tried to bargain for other English colonies in central and South-West Africa. When his demands were rejected by Salisbury, Wilhelm claimed that his overtures of friendship had been met with "something between a joke and a snub."

It was clear that Vicky did not understand how her son had used her to camouflage his efforts to enlarge German holdings overseas. "I must write next time again about Germany and England," the Dowager Empress told Victoria in the summer of 1898, ten days before the two countries finally agreed on a hypothetical division of the Portuguese spoils. "I wonder where the hitch is, since both seem so anxious for an understanding?"

THE KAISER WAS ANXIOUS to expand Germany's colonial empire. Although his African colonies had proved more troublesome and expensive than they were worth, he was determined to add more of what Otto Pflanze called "symbols of national pride and power, proof that Germany was a world power with far-flung possessions and a rival, if not the equal, of Britain." In 1897, Wilhelm joined Russia, England, and France in a race for territory in China. Taking as a pretext the murder of two German Catholic missionaries, the Germans occupied the Chinese port of Kiaochow in 1897.

The German occupation was only one instance of the scramble for possessions that took place in China from 1897 to 1899, dividing the country into various spheres of influence. To stave off a commercial war, the American Secretary of State, John Hay, proposed the Open Door policy, which stated that the powers* should not interfere with each other's ports or levy unfair harbor or railway taxes on each other's goods. To get the Great Powers out altogether, the Boxers, a provincial Chinese militia, murdered the German Minister and laid siege to the European legations in Peking in the summer of 1900. Shocked by the Minister's death—his mother had been a childhood friend of Fritz—the Dowager Empress advanced an interesting theory about the cause of the trouble. "I fear the Germans have been much too 'go-ahead' in their doings in China which has alarmed the Chinese and made them turn against all foreigns [sic]. . . . I grieve to think that our British influence has so decreased of late years, & the Russian influence increased."

To avenge the murder of his diplomat and relieve the legations, Wilhelm II proposed sending a joint force under General Waldersee to China. Armed

---

* England, Russia, Germany, France, Italy, and Japan.

with the consent of the Russians and the acquiescence of the French, he reviewed the German forces assembled at Bremerhaven on July 27, 1900, delivering another of his now-familiar harangues, during which he announced that this was "what comes of cultures which are not founded on Christianity." All "heathen cultures," Wilhelm II declared, "collapse at the first catastrophe."

"Show yourselves Christians. . . . Give the world an example of virility and discipline! . . ." he exhorted his soldiers; "no pardon will be given and no prisoners will be made. Anyone who falls into your hands falls to your sword! Just as the Huns . . . created for themselves . . . a name which men still respect, you should give the name of German such cause to be remembered in China for a thousand years that no Chinaman, no matter whether his eyes be slit or not, will dare to look a German in the face."

But before the Kaiser's soldiers could even reach Peking, the besieged legations were rescued by an international force from other countries. When he got the news, Wilhelm II, according to his friend Philipp zu Eulenburg who was with him on a cruise, "completely lost control. . . . His violence in conversation was terrifying. . . . His Majesty cannot control himself any more when he is filled with anger."

Embarrassed by their tardy entry into Peking, the Germans undertook a series of punitive missions against the Chinese that lasted from December of 1900 to May of 1901. The Boxer Protocol, the official end to the uprising, was signed in September 1901.

Meanwhile, the relationship between Germany and England remained Vicky's most vital concern. Even after her failed attempts at mediation, she continued to hold out hope that a rapprochement might be worked out "for the good of both countries." She was pleased that Cecil Rhodes visited Berlin in the spring of 1899 and even happier when Willy wrote to tell her he was "delighted" with their meeting.

This was not surprising. Rhodes flattered the Kaiser, and in exchange for Wilhelm's permission to route his railway and telegraph lines through German East Africa, undertook to lobby for the Kaiser's reinstatement in the good graces of the English royal family. Two months before the Queen's eightieth birthday, a celebration Willy desperately wanted to attend, Rhodes wrote the Prince of Wales that Wilhelm II appeared to him to be "most anxious to work with England" and "gain your good opinion." Rhodes also hoped that the Kaiser would be invited back to Cowes. "I think . . . we ought to try and work with Germany," he said, "and the Emperor is really Germany. . . . I am sure . . . that, if you showed him good feeling when he came to England, it would immensely influence his mind."

But the Kaiser was not invited to the Queen's birthday party. He complained that he was being mistreated by his grandmother's country and wrote her about the "shame & pain I have suffered, & how my heart has bled when to my despair I had to watch how the arduous work of years was destroyed—to make the two nations understand each other." He told the British attaché in Berlin that "for years he had been the one true friend to Great Britain on the continent of Europe, and had done everything to help her policy and assist her, and that he had received nothing in return but ingratitude." Someday, he threatened, "when it was too late," the English would "regret" their actions. The attaché was not unduly alarmed: "[A] great deal of his Majesty's ill-humour is due to the fact that he was . . . bitterly disappointed at being told he was not to go to England for the birthday," he noted.

There was another reason why the Kaiser had not been invited. In March of 1899, two months before her birthday, Victoria wrote young Czar Nicholas II:

> I feel I must . . . tell you something which you <u>ought</u> to know and perhaps do not. It is, I am sorry to say, that William takes every opportunity of impressing upon Sir F. Lascelles* that Russia is doing all in her power to work against us. . . . I need not say that I do not believe a word of this. . . . But I am afraid William may go and tell things against us to you, just as he does about you to us. If so, pray tell me openly and confidentially. It is so important that we should understand each other, and that such mischievous and unstraightforward proceedings should be put a stop to.

But Wilhelm blamed his troubles with England on Prime Minister Salisbury, with whom he had once again come into conflict. This time, it was over the island of Samoa in the South Pacific, where the victor in a civil war, supported by Germany, had been attacked by English and American warships. The Kaiser had been trying to acquire the British portion of Samoa, but Salisbury was determined to keep the islands under the joint protection of England, Germany, and the United States. When, after refusing to invite him to her birthday celebration, the Queen finally decided to ask him to visit her two months later while he was attending the Cowes regatta, Willy jumped in with resentments flying:

"I think it my duty to point out that public feeling over here has been very much agitated & stirred to its depths by the most unhappy way in which Lord Salisbury has treated Germany in the Samoan business . . . ," the Kaiser wrote the Queen.

> Lord Salisbury's Government must learn to respect and treat us as equals, as long as he cannot be brought to do that, people over here will remain distrustful. . . .
> Now you will understand, dear Grandmama, why I so ardently hoped to be able to go over for your birthday. That visit would have been perfectly understood over here, as the duty of the grandson to his grandmother. . . . But a pleasure trip to Cowes,† after all that has happened, & with respect to the temperature of our public opinion here, is utterly

* *The British Ambassador in Berlin.*

† *She had not invited him to Cowes only to pay her a visit while he was there. He purposely misinterpreted her invitation in order to get his point across.*

impossible. . . . I can assure you there is no man more deeply grieved & unhappy than me! and all that on account of a stupid island which is a hairpin to England compared to the thousands of square miles she is annexing right and left unopposed every year.

"I doubt whether any Sovereign ever wrote in such terms to another Sovereign, and that Sovereign his own Grandmother, about their Prime Minister . . . ," Victoria shot back, enclosing a memorandum from Salisbury refuting Wilhelm's allegations of wrongdoing one by one. "I never personally attacked or complained of Prince Bismarck, though I knew well what a bitter enemy he was to England and all the harm he did."*

The Samoan issue was settled in early November of 1899, and three weeks later the Kaiser was invited back to England. He took Dona, two of his sons, and a large suite, including Bernhard von Bülow, the Anglophobic Foreign Minister who would succeed Hohenlohe as Chancellor within the year. "I do hope people will tell <u>Bülow</u> straight out what they think about the German press . . . ," Vicky wrote Victoria. "He has never been in England and I hope & trust it may do good."

In England, the Kaiser became more English than his relatives, abandoning his usual array of colorful uniforms in favor of suits from Savile Row, and informing his military aides, as they waited for the Queen under the round tower at Windsor, "Gentlemen, from that tower the world is ruled." When Victoria complained to Willy about the awful tone of the German press, he blamed it on the " 'poison' which Bismarck poured into the ears of the people." He explained to "dearest Grandmama" that the ex-Chancellor "hated England, and wished for an alliance with Russia," and that if he, Wilhelm II, had not forced Bismarck to resign, he did not know "what would have happened."

"The visit has been a really great success," Victoria wrote Vicky, as Willy left Windsor to visit Uncle Bertie at Sandringham. "Both William & Dona were extremely amiable & kind & I had a good deal of talk with William on all subjects & found him very sensible & <u>most</u> anxious that all should <u>go well</u> between the 2 countries & that they should be on the best of terms. . . . Dona was also very nice & kind & not stiff at all."

"I am very glad indeed to hear . . . that all has gone off so well, that they made themselves pleasant & amiable (which they can when they like). . . . All this is comforting & satisfactory," Vicky wrote back.

But as the Dowager Empress knew, her son's congeniality hardly conformed to the climate of opinion he had helped to create in Germany. In spite of Wilhelm II's assurances to his Uncle Bertie that he and Bülow had "with superhuman efforts . . . got the better of the German Press," the fires of Anglophobia were being carefully fanned by both the court and the Wilhelmstrasse over English policy in South Africa.

Six weeks before Wilhelm's visit to England, war had broken out between

---

* *This is not exactly true.*

the Boers and the English in the Transvaal, and the Germans were actively supporting their old friend, President Kruger. "The spite and rudeness of the German Press knows no bounds, and the abuse and sneers lavished on England," the Dowager Empress wrote Sophie. "Three hundred Germans in arms going to join the Boers! I want to know why the Boers, who are Dutch intermarried with the wild tribes of South Africa, are considered of closer kin to the Germans than the English, who are Anglo-Saxons."

Vicky, who had long given up on German foreign policy, ignored the general condemnation of England, following every battle with lively interest and unflagging belief in the rightness of English colonialism. She never missed an opportunity to criticize the Germans for their support of the Boers and celebrate or condole with the Queen over advances and reverses. For the first several weeks of the war, there were far more of the latter than the former. "Our forces were indeed too slender at that place to oppose such an enormous number! . . ." she wrote Victoria. "So <u>much</u> advice is given the Boers from German, French, Russian & Dutch sources that, of course, they know quite well what to do and <u>where</u> our weakest points are. . . . I am pining for more and better news."

It was not until Generals Roberts * and Kitchener arrived with reinforcements in early January of 1900 that the English began to gain the offensive. No one was more pleased than the Dowager Empress of Germany, who sent ecstatic letters to her mother in reply to victory cables from London. Forced to keep her excitement to herself, Vicky said she felt like "a perfect volcano."

By June, Johannesburg had been taken and Pretoria occupied, and in September, the Transvaal was annexed by the English. President Kruger fled to Europe, where the Kaiser, his former best friend, refused to receive him now that he was out of power and looking for help. Nevertheless, Kruger found plenty of other admirers in the Anglophobic atmosphere of Berlin.

"It is disgraceful what a fuss is being made in Germany about that nasty common old thief of a Kruger," Vicky wrote Sophie. "Luckily <u>not</u> by William or the Government. It is only because people consider him the enemy of England. That is enough to make any wretch a hero in the eyes of the Germans."

---

* *Frederick Sleigh Roberts, first Earl Roberts of Kandahar, Pretoria and Waterford, was the Supreme Commander in South Africa.*

CHAPTER
SIXTY-EIGHT

"A society that must produce a great man in each generation to maintain its domestic or international position will doom itself."

HENRY KISSINGER, *1968*

O*NE OF WILHELM'S* most vocal supporters in the belligerent nationalism that had become the hallmark of his reign was Bismarck, living out his last years at Friedrichsruh, fighting old enemies and slowly succumbing to age and the cumulative effects of many and varied illnesses. In severe pain with a gangrenous left foot, Bismarck's physical decay only heightened his irascibility.

"Did you read all the things Prince Bismarck has been publishing," Vicky asked Victoria in 1896 about a spate of articles from Friedrichsruh in which Bismarck accused England of having fomented strikes within Germany, much as he claimed she had "organized" the revolts of the Cretans and the Armenians against the Turks. "Prince Bismarck remains mischievous & dangerous to the last," she concluded, "& yet . . . still has . . . great influence."

A few weeks later, with anti-English feeling running high, the Dowager Empress herself came under attack. According to Bismarck, Vicky had told Queen Victoria—and thus the British government—about the highly secret Reinsurance Treaty, signed between Germany and Russia in 1887.*

It was indeed <u>mean</u> & <u>spiteful</u> & ungentlemanly of Prince Bismarck to try and have a fling at me <u>now</u> and take <u>advantage</u> of the feeling in Germany against England to excite public opinion & "national feeling" against me! . . . his <u>vanity</u> & <u>ambition</u> cannot let him <u>rest</u>, he must always be "poséing" [posing] before the public as the <u>defender</u> of <u>German</u> interests & the national cause <u>against</u> those who . . . are supposed to have endangered it by our so called "English tendencies" which is another word for our <u>liberal</u> <u>opinions</u> & sentiments.

While Bismarck's need to feed his popularity at the expense of others was an annoyance to Vicky, it was a severe problem for Wilhelm II. No matter what the Kaiser did to exalt his own persona or resurrect the ghost of his overeulo-

---

* *See Chapter 64. We have no way of knowing if this was true or not. Although Bismarck usually lied about Vicky, she often did discuss German policy with Victoria.*

gized grandfather, the German people looked to Friedrichsruh, not Berlin, to fill the national longing for an outsized hero. Wilhelm II scrupulously maintained all of the outward courtesies toward Bismarck—honors, holiday greetings, gifts—while trying desperately to dispel the Bismarck aura. In one speech, the Kaiser claimed that the architect of the German Empire had been nothing more than an "energetic support" for Wilhelm I. In another, he reduced Bismarck's role to one of the "handymen and pygmies" around the first German Kaiser—a distortion so ridiculous that Bismarck did not even bother to refute it.

At the end of 1897, Henry informed Willy that Bismarck looked as if he could not survive much longer. Curious as to "how long the old man will last," Wilhelm went to look for himself. "I would let myself be torn limb from limb before undertaking anything which might make difficulties or unpleasantness for you," he told his ex-Chancellor.

But Bismarck, who privately referred to Wilhelm II as that "dumb kid," trusted the Kaiser no more than Willy trusted him. Guessing that Wilhelm would try to make a circus of his funeral, Bismarck left specific instructions as to the disposal of his body.

He died on July 30, 1898. The Kaiser, who was cruising in the North Sea, set off immediately for Friedrichsruh, cabling Herbert von Bismarck that "Germany's greatest son" must be buried "by the side" of his own ancestors, the Hohenzollerns. But when he got to the Bismarck home, he was informed by Herbert that in accordance with his father's wishes, the casket had already been sealed in preparation for a brief service—so brief in fact that Wilhelm was on his way back to Berlin within half an hour of his arrival.

He returned to Friedrichsruh for Bismarck's official burial eight and a half months later. Johanna had predeceased her husband, and they were interred together in a newly constructed mausoleum on the grounds of their estate. It was noted that the Kaiser stood on one side of the proceedings with his courtiers, while the Bismarcks stood well away on the other. As a parting shaft, the old Chancellor himself had written the words engraved on his sarcophagus: "A loyal German servant of Kaiser Wilhelm I."

The death of Bismarck, according to the librarian at Friedrichshof, "greatly affected" the Dowager Empress, who immediately gave "various directions concerning the speedy completion of several pieces of work, observing 'that all may be finished when I am no longer here.'" There is a three-week hiatus in her surviving letters to Victoria, indicating that she did not want the world to share her thoughts on the demise of her old enemy.*

Wilhelm II would have done well to follow his mother's example. With Bismarck gone, the Kaiser tried to rewrite history. He told his mother that the only reason he had not joined with his father against Bismarck when they were both alive was because the other German princes would have risen in protest: "For the moment Bismarck was master of the situation and of the Em-

---

* Clearly, she asked to have them destroyed.

pire . . . ," Wilhelm said. "This man who completely stole the hearts of our people . . . seemed to be entering the lists against the House of Hohenzollern for the sake of his own family."

THREE MONTHS after Bismarck's death, Victoria congratulated Vicky on a "merciful escape" from a serious riding accident. The Dowager Empress, as she wrote her mother, was out riding with her daughter Mossy and the wife of her Lord Chamberlain when her horse shied at a steam thresher. "I tried to quiet it," she said,

> & the groom got off to lead it past the machine, but it reared in one moment & swung round, throwing me off, happily on the right side, and my habit caught in the pommel, which broke the weight of the fall, but was very dangerous as my head & shoulders were on the ground almost under the horse's hoofs. However, I got up & walked part of the way home. . . . Whether it was a kick or a tread on my right hand, I do not know, but it was extremely painful! . . . It was my favourite horse . . . a very lucky escape—nothing of any consequence happened—& I am all right today, except for a headache, and much ashamed that it should have happened.

"The Empress possessed such perfect self-control that she showed no sign whatever of the accident . . . ," her librarian reported, adding that when Vicky returned to Friedrichshof, she announced that she would "ride again the day after to-morrow. . . . To-day . . . ," she conceded, "I shall try to paint and write some letters."

A few weeks later, the Dowager Empress left for a long vacation in England. While there, she verified news she had received from the doctor who examined her after her accident—that she was suffering from breast cancer. According to the Queen's doctors, the cancer was "far too advanced" to be operable. For the moment Vicky told no one but her mother, brother Bertie, and sister Beatrice. The Queen advised her not to concentrate on it.

"I assure you my thoughts are not incessantly dwelling in a morbid way on my own health!" Vicky promised Victoria after she left Osborne for Sandringham. "It would be foolish & useless, and could only be hurtful." She repeated her determination a month later: "I will not dwell on all the conflicting thoughts, the hopes & fears etc., they shall all be hushed in the one feeling that I have a dear & kind mother, who, to the last will protect her child, even from afar! I thank God for this blessing."

But Vicky was frightened by the dizziness that overcame her while visiting friends near Edinburgh, causing her to misjudge the position of a chair and sit down, as she put it, "on the floor by the side of the chair." Nervousness had made the Dowager Empress dizzy before. It dissipated within a day or two, and she left for Italy, grateful to Bertie for lending her his private railway carriage and to the Queen for saying that she could come back to England anytime she wished.

She stayed in Bordighera, on the Italian Riviera, until May of 1899. She adored "the soft balmy creamy air" of the south and preferred the quieter, Italian part of the Riviera. Cannes and Nice, she wrote Victoria, had grown too big and too busy. Nonetheless, she paid a visit to the Queen when she arrived some weeks later for a holiday at Cimiez.

"I was at Cimiez yesterday with dear Grandmama . . . ," Vicky wrote Sophie. "Beloved Aunt Alix was there, and Uncle Bertie, his dear kind face is always sunshine to me. . . . I do not like Nice at all . . . though the hotel in which dear Grandmama is staying is splendid, with immense rooms and every comfort and luxury. But, oh, how I prefer to exist in quiet simple Bordighera, where one has the woods and mountains in immediate neighbourhood, and is so near the sea, and out of the way of smart people. Today, sweet Aunt Alix was here to see me, so dear and good of her to come over from Villafranca bay."

Outwardly, the Dowager Empress of Germany still seemed healthy; "sun-burned and robust" was how she looked to Marie Mallet, Queen Victoria's young lady-in-waiting. Her appearance even fooled her Lord Chamberlain, Baron Reischach, whom she took into her confidence on her return to Fried-richshof. She asked Reischach to take a walk with her in the castle park. "I have to disclose to you an important matter, but you must give me your word of honour beforehand that you will not mention it to any one."

"I am afraid, your Majesty, that I cannot give my word before knowing to what I am pledging myself," the stiff-minded Reischach answered.

"I am afraid I cannot help telling you, but it must not become public property," she said. He gave his word and cried when she told him about her cancer.

"There is no reason for alarm," she added. "I have trained myself the whole of my life to be able to resist illness for another ten years, for my body is as hard as steel. I should in that case attain the age of seventy, when I consider that every person has lived her life. I shall be able to enjoy my children and grandchildren for quite a long time, and can accumulate an adequate fortune for them, thanks to your skilful handling of my affairs."

Asked if her children knew of her illness, the Dowager Empress said no. Reischach replied that he could not take the responsibility on himself and that she must tell the Kaiser.

"No, not on any account" was Vicky's reaction. "I do not wish for sympathy, and I have mentioned the matter to you for practical reasons." Explaining that she could no longer lead a public life, she told the Chamberlain that she must now "live for my health entirely, and be accompanied by a medical adviser on my travels."

When Reischach asked how she knew she was suffering from cancer, Vicky said that her physician had given her the diagnosis, which had been confirmed by the doctors in England.

Reischach, who trusted neither Vicky's doctor nor English medicine, asked her to see another German doctor "of repute and standing" and inform her children if he concurred in the diagnosis. She acquiesced. Professor Renvers, who came from Berlin the next morning, confirmed the presence of cancer that had already metastasized. According to Reischach, "She might have got off with a very slight operation if she had disclosed it six months earlier." Still, the Chamberlain was impressed by the way his employer "discussed all these things, with a sangfroid and courage and fearlessness of death which many a man might have envied her. Her great qualities again appeared on this occasion; indeed, her whole personality emanated greatness."

In accordance with her promise, Vicky told the Kaiser a few weeks later when he came to see her and all her other children except Charlotte, whom she could not trust to keep quiet. To Sophie, she explained why her illness "must remain an absolute secret. . . . You know how indiscreet people at Berlin are. I am not much loved, so I should not like to have people . . . rejoicing over my misfortune and speculating on my coming decease before it is necessary."

FROM THE SPRING OF 1899 on, the Dowager Empress's health began to deteriorate. A sure sign that she was not feeling well is the fact that she did not go to England at the end of May for her mother's eightieth birthday celebrations. "It is a very great disappointment to me . . . ," she wrote Sophie. "But I am not quite well, and the fatigue . . . besides many another reason, made it impossible for me to manage."

Sophie arrived at Friedrichshof at the beginning of June with her children and stayed through the summer. She returned to Athens concerned about her mother, who had already begun to suffer discomfort. Put to bed for a week in August during Bertie's annual visit to the spa at Bad Homburg, Vicky wrote Victoria that the pain was "very wearing though not constant. It was so very annoying not to have been able to entertain dear Bertie as I should have wished."

By early October she was complaining regularly about "lumbago," which is what the doctors named as the source of her misery, rather than the metastasis of the cancer into her spine. "My lumbago is no better," she wrote Victoria in early October, "I am trying hot sand in bags. Professor Renvers has been to see me today & seemed very much satisfied, though I am feeling anything but well & suffer much pain."

Ordered by the doctors to go to a warmer climate during the German winter, she again chose Italy. "My lumbago is still very bad, and I do not look forward to the journey and the shaking of the railway," she wrote her mother. "Altogether I do not like going away and would have preferred staying at my dear Friedrichshof, but Professor Renvers wished it. . . . He wants me to be out of doors and have as much sun as possible." By the time she reached Trento, the pain was so disabling she could hardly get up and down the hotel stairs. It hurt when she lay down at night and when she tried to sit up in a chair. Walking was easier, and she managed to be outdoors a good deal. The doctor arrived at the beginning of November and ordered electrical and massage treatments.

"The constant pain is so wearing & the helplessness very trying," she wrote Victoria.

Within a few weeks, Vicky had given up carriage rides, had had a rope tied on her bed so that she could turn over, and was being treated with hot poultices and sulfur baths. "Every movement is painful," she wrote Victoria. The doctors must have grown concerned about the plausibility of the lumbago story, because in the middle of December, the Dowager Empress informed the Queen that her "condition" was not "purely lumbago," but "also neuralgia, in the region of the spine & hips."

By the beginning of 1900, she was in pain almost all day and night. "It is so trying & so wearing to suffer so much for such a long time!" she wrote Victoria. "They say it will get right & go away, etc. & only wants patience, but I own I fear sometimes I shall never be rid of it any more, as no remedy seems of any use!"

One of the physicians she had seen in England, Dr. Francis Laking, suggested morphine, which Vicky found "very useful." She was "touched & grateful" when she learned that her mother had paid Laking's bill. In early April, she went into brief remission, and Professor Renvers confirmed the improvement. Although still in pain, she wrote that she was, in fact, "beginning to look & feel more like myself again."

A few weeks later, she returned to Friedrichshof, traveling with her own bed and sofa set up in the railway carriage. Fritz and Louise of Baden met her at Karlsruhe station on her way through Baden. They both looked lined and old, but were "very kind & much disturbed that I was not well!" Mossy met the train at Heidelberg; she was joined by her husband and children at Frankfurt, along with Moretta and Adolf—all of whom traveled home with the Dowager Empress. Once at Friedrichshof, she was able to get around by means of a wheelchair and a pony carriage, both gifts of Queen Victoria.

"My dear Friedrichshof is so charming," she wrote Sophie. "It looks so tidy, clean, well-kept and in apple-pie order. It seems as if I had never been away, though it is sad indeed to be wheeled about in a chair like an old, old lady, and carried up and down stairs like a child, here, where I have always been so active."

She could not take part in the celebrations surrounding her eldest grandson's coming of age. Moreover, she scarcely knew the boy. "You can imagine the many sad & bitter & painful thoughts that filled my mind . . ." she wrote Victoria in May of 1900. "Berlin 'en fête,' our house, where I toiled for nearly 40 years, shut up, my 3 daughters in hotels for the first time!! Fate has shut me out of everything, & 2 generations pass over our heads!! It is perhaps selfish to think that, but one cannot help it sometimes!!"

That same month, the Dowager Empress celebrated the Queen's birthday by gathering her children for luncheon to toast their grandmother's health and have a group photo made to send to England. "My life is very different to what it usually is!!" Vicky wrote Victoria in early June. "But I must be very thankful considering the fearful attacks I had in winter, & that the evil has grown so much slower . . . than was expected, but of an afternoon & evening I often feel quite worn out with fighting against the discomfort & gnawing pain! . . . every one maintains I am looking <u>marvellously</u> <u>well</u>, & <u>quite</u> <u>unaltered</u>. (my looking glass often tells me another story.) Still I manage to get through what I have to do, all right."

This short respite was soon over, and the spasms of pain began to overwhelm her again. "It seems wrong to complain when one has every comfort about one," she wrote Victoria, "& so <u>many</u> have to suffer without anything to ease or soothe them!" In conversation with those around her, she compared herself to her husband, commenting that she was "not so brave" as he had been.

The death of her brother Alfred, the Duke of Coburg, at the end of July from cancer of the larynx, the same disease that had killed Fritz, was a serious blow. Like Queen Victoria, Vicky heard he was ill only a few days before his demise. She had wanted to go to Coburg to see him before he died, but was unable to travel. She was now often unable to go downstairs, even to meals.

Vicky heard that the Duke of Coburg had not been told that he was suffering from cancer. "What a mercy darling Alfred did not know the nature of his illness, and the utter hopelessness of it," she wrote Victoria. "Dear Alfred was spared mental pain and anxiety and like Fritz was convinced that he <u>would</u> improve! This is a mercy, though in my own case, I far prefer to know <u>exactly</u> how the matter stands, one can make all one's arrangement with great care & ease & thought."

At the moment she herself was bedridden. "I am suffering a deal of pain still, & the doctors keep on assuring me that it will leave off; and that I shall be able to walk better again, etc. The only position in which I am pretty comfortable is lying down, with a hot bottle on my back, & one under my arm."

Guests continued to come and go from Friedrichshof, and it was clear that Vicky's three younger daughters had decided not to leave their mother alone. Willy came to see her, as did Charlotte and Bernhard. The Dowager Empress told Charlotte the truth about herself, begging her eldest daughter to keep her secret—a promise Charlotte gave and broke within a few months.

"The house here is <u>very</u> full," Vicky wrote Victoria in the middle of August 1900, "& I sadly fear I cannot do the honours as I should like! This is not my fault as you know. They all say I look so well, but that is only the warm weather which brings a colour to one's face. One cannot look well when one is devoured with pain as I am with rarely one hour's respite."

The spasms were now occurring as often as every two hours and lasting between half and three-quarters of an hour, during which time the Dowager Empress could "only scream and groan." Her physician moved into Friedrichshof so as to be on call during the night. Although her doctors had assured her that "the pain would soon wear off," their promises had "<u>not</u> <u>come</u> <u>true</u>" and, as she now began to realize, probably never would.

CHAPTER
SIXTY-NINE

> *"I will most likely go to my grave unknown, alien, and misunder-*
> *stood, for a lonely woman is not able to achieve anything against*
> *many . . . men and their blind prejudices."*
>
> THE DOWAGER EMPRESS

F ROM MIDSUMMER OF 1900 on, the health of the Dowager Empress deteriorated rapidly. In Germany for his annual August cure at Bad Homburg,
Bertie spent even more time than usual with his sister, and Alix, the Princess
of Wales, who accompanied her husband on a visit to Friedrichshof, reported
to her son George* that "Aunt Vicky . . . is always now suffering terrible
agonies."

Shortly after her brother and sister-in-law's departure, Vicky suffered a
serious setback. Queen Victoria considered going to Germany and asked the
Kaiser's permission to send Dr. Laking, the doctor who had originally prescribed morphine for the Dowager Empress. Wilhelm refused to let the English
doctor come. "[I]t would create a most deplorable feeling here which must on
no account be roused," he wrote his grandmother.

Wilhelm also wrote Uncle Bertie that his mother must not try to go
through with a trip to England that she had been planning for some time.
"[S]he is a very bad sailor, & the slightest attack of sea sickness would probably
harm her heart & bring about another collapse, which could eventually prove
fatal," he said. The Kaiser, who seemed to rally to his mother's side primarily to
impress her English family, added, "Since today I am able to breathe more
freely, for Mama has for the first time since nearly a month left her bed, & spent
a few hours in an armchair. We have spent most anxious days here . . . & feel so
relieved to see her out of the immediate danger."

Although it was clear that Wilhelm II shared his uncle's concern over his
mother's worsening condition, her health also served as a bridge of opportunity,
carrying him safely over old animosities to topics of immediate interest. While
Uncle Bertie was in Bad Homburg, Willy had done everything he could to
corral him into political discussions. Now that the Prince of Wales was gone,
the Kaiser's report on his mother's poor health and inability to travel led quite
conveniently into one of Wilhelm's favorite topics—shipbuilding.

---

* *Later King George V.*

A few years after he was introduced to Cowes and yacht racing by the Prince of Wales, Wilhelm II had ordered the firm of G. L. Watson to construct a ship specifically to race against and beat his uncle's *Britannia*. Watson had succeeded, and Uncle Bertie, who did not relish the idea or expense of an ongoing competition with his nephew, had withdrawn from racing at Cowes. Shortly thereafter, the Prince of Wales found it necessary to order a new yacht for Queen Victoria. Willy could scarcely contain himself when he heard that the yacht, built at a British naval dockyard, was "totally unfit" for his grandmother. "I believe a private firm would have done better," he tweaked his uncle in the letter about his mother's health. "Watson for instance, who designs any number of fine steady Yachts for Amerikans & British ought I am sure be able to suggest a good one. . . ."

Whatever taunts the Kaiser had to offer, the Queen was duly grateful for the good news Bertie received about her eldest daughter. "Thank God! Vicky is going on well," she wrote her eldest son. "But it is indeed not right to let no one of her own family come to see her."

Acknowledged even by her enemies for her courage in dealing with pain, Vicky's descriptions in her letters to her mother were so graphic that Helena and Beatrice stopped reading them to the Queen. The eighty-one-year-old monarch herself had begun to fail, and the shock of her son Alfred's death in the summer of 1900 compounded her problems. Victoria had now lost three of her children —Alice, Leopold, and Alfred—and a fourth was dying a long, excruciating death.

As Vicky wrote Sophie at the end of October of 1900, "[T]he terrible nights of agony are worse than ever, no rest, no peace. The tears rush down my cheeks when I am not shouting with pain. The injections of morphia dull the pains a little for about a quarter of an hour, sometimes not at all, then they rage again with renewed intensity, and make me wish I were safe in my grave, electricity does no good, nor poultices (hot), not ice-bags, nor embrocations [rubbing with liniment], nothing! nothing! It is fearful to endure. My courage is quite exhausted."

"I am just as I was," she wrote her mother in November; "the pain is fearful when it comes on, and the night sleepless. Tomorrow I shall have been 7 weeks in bed." A week later, still bedridden, she reached her sixtieth birthday amid "a flood of letters telegrams and bouquets." Queen Victoria sent her "a splendid bath chair [wheelchair]," but she had not been able to leave her room for two months. "To think of her, who was so wonderfully active and strong, now so ill and suffering, is heartbreaking . . . ," Queen Victoria wrote in her journal that day. "We pray daily that she may suffer less."

Vicky's arms and hands had swollen, and she had to have her wedding band sawed off. "To be without my wedding ring for the 1st time since 1858, when dear Papa put it on the finger of his bride of 17 . . . ," she wrote Sophie. "It seems so dreadful to have it broken in two, and taken off by force, but it had to be." To her mother, she dictated,* "I am intensely grateful to be alive and here, & to have the hope of meeting again in some months or weeks."

But neither mother nor daughter was fit to travel. Like Vicky, who had to be carried downstairs to supervise preparations for Christmas, the Queen barely struggled through the holidays, trying to keep up appearances and rituals. It was obvious to those around her that the great old lady had very little time left. "I am miserable to think you have not been feeling well and have again been troubled with malaise!!" Vicky wrote Victoria on Christmas Day. "I wish with all my heart that all my suffering and discomfort would do for us <u>both</u> & that <u>you</u> might be spared everything that is disagreeable."

On January 1, in spite of trembling hands and failed eyesight, the Queen sent Vicky handwritten New Year's wishes. Five days later, the Queen's last letter addressed to her eldest child said that her health was bad, but she hoped for improvement. On January 16, Victoria gave her last official order, instructing the British Ambassador to Germany to decline one of the Kaiser's many proffered decorations. Three days later, the Queen's children—all but Vicky—were called home. Vicky's brother Arthur was in Berlin at the time, and the sad news, meant for him, also reached the Kaiser. Uninvited, Wilhelm II rushed to his grandmother's death watch at Osborne House.

On the morning of January 22, while the Bishop of Winchester repeated the prayers for the dying and the Queen's doctor, James Reid, plied her with oxygen, Helena, Beatrice, and Louise recited for their mother the names of her loved ones who were standing around her bed—everyone, that, is except Wilhelm II. The Kaiser was very unpopular with his aunts and uncles. When Dr. Reid asked the Prince of Wales if Wilhelm's name should not be included, the Prince said that it would "excite" his mother "too much." Later, after the others had left, the doctor ushered the Kaiser to his grandmother's bedside. When Reid returned five minutes later, she told him, "The Emperor is very kind."

She died at six-thirty that evening, supported in bed by Reid and Willy, who knelt for an hour with his right arm under his grandmother's pillow, unable to change sides with the doctor.† Overwhelmed by his Englishness, the Kaiser helped two of his uncles lift Queen Victoria's body into her coffin. Much to everyone's confusion, he bestowed on Lord Roberts, the hero of the Boer War, the German Order of the Black Eagle. Wilhelm II announced that he would remain in England until his grandmother was buried—as a member of the family, not the German Kaiser. Whether this was out of the Kaiser's desperate need to take part in every royal rite or whether, as rumor said, he stayed to

---

* *From early November of 1900 until her death, the Dowager Empress dictated many of her letters.*

† *He could not use his left arm.*

collect on loans his mother had made to his uncle Bertie, is unclear.* In any event, the Kaiser rode a showy white horse in the position of honor, directly behind the coffin and next to Bertie, now Edward VII, in the funeral procession. "William continues kindness itself and touching in his devotion, without a sign of 'brusquerie' or selfishness," Bertie wrote Vicky on the day of the funeral.

"Words cannot describe my agony of mind at this overwhelming sorrow," Vicky wrote Sophie when she heard the news. "Oh, my beloved Mama! Is she really gone? Gone from us all to whom she was such a comfort and support. To have lost her seems so impossible—and I far away could not see her dear face or kiss her dear hand once more. . . . What a Queen she was, and what a woman! What will life be to me without her. . . . In the bitterness of my grief I must admit that it was a mercy she did not suffer pain, and that she had no long illness, a peaceful end."

WILHELM II RETURNED from his grandmother's funeral to pay an overdue call on his mother—he had not seen her for three months—and wrote Uncle Bertie:

> Mama has visibly changed since I saw her in November. Her face is swollen a little, so that through its roundness & fullness the likeness to dear Grand-mama has become very marked. The progress of the malady on her left side is great. The whole of the left arm is totally paralised [*sic*] & quite useless; it is bandaged & much swollen. The right arm & hand is also swelling & causing great annoyance. The feet are very strongly swollen & the legs partly, but the pain in the back has lost its sharpness. The worst is that her digestion has become troubled & that she is frequently sick & does not care for food much. Today she even gave up some blood. Consequently she is weak & feels absolutely miserable. . . .
>
> We are all fearfully pained by what we see & hear. . . . Poor mother is simply in a horrible state of suffering & discomfort; so that one really sometimes is at loss to think whether she could not be spared the worst. This is the state of things as it is, & I felt bound to let you know the exact truth.

At the end of February 1901, Bertie came to see his sister, arriving with two attendants—Sir Francis Laking, the English doctor who had recommended morphine for her pain, and Frederick Ponsonby, one of the King's secretaries and Fritz's godson. The Dowager Empress wanted to see Laking. He was traveling as the King's physician in order not to rile her German doctors, who believed she was past help, or the Kaiser's household, who regarded his appearance as an insult to German medicine. Bertie hoped that Laking might be able

---

* *According to the French Ambassador, Paul Cambon, the Prince of Wales, who could not ask his mother for any more money to settle his debts, had borrowed between fifteen and twenty-five million French francs in a loan arranged by Baron Hirsch. The loan had been guaranteed by Vicky at the time she was Kaiserin, and Wilhelm II was determined to collect what was owed the House of Hohenzollern. (See Gordon Brook-Shepherd,* Uncle of Europe, *p. 101).*

to alleviate some of his sister's excruciating pain by giving her larger doses of painkiller than the uselessly "tiny" ones allowed by the German physicians, who refused the patient's pleas to give her more. Edward VII "took the view that it was right to risk shortening a doomed life in an effort to relieve intolerable suffering." Still, according to Ponsonby, "Laking's presence was resented not only by the German Doctors, but by the Emperor and his Suite."

It was the King's first visit abroad since he had assumed the throne, but since it was a purely personal visit to his dying sister, he had pleaded with the Kaiser not to plan any royal welcome or formalities. When he arrived at the Frankfurt station, however, Wilhelm II was waiting in the middle of a phalanx of military men, all in blazing uniforms, to greet him as he stepped off the train in modest civilian attire.

Even before his trip, Willy had tried to lure Edward VII over to the official castle at Bad Homburg by heating it and preparing rooms for him.* But as Bertie wrote his sister, "I never had the intention of going there, as my visit is only for you dearest Vicky."

Wilhelm, delighted to have another monarch to entertain, did not give up. The day of the King's arrival was bright and sunny with snow on the ground, and the Kaiser, who was exceedingly proud of a new sleigh and two gray horses, insisted on driving his uncle from Kronberg station to Friedrichshof himself. As soon as he dropped off the King, he dashed back to Bad Homburg, swearing he could make the distance in half the usual time of an hour. True to his word, he returned two hours later for lunch. In accordance with royal protocol, Edward VII then had to put on a Prussian uniform for the meal and ride back to Bad Homburg that afternoon for the requisite return call. Willy wanted to come back to Friedrichshof for dinner, but Uncle Bertie excused himself on the basis of fatigue.

Three days after their arrival, Frederick Ponsonby received a message summoning him to Vicky's rooms in the castle. It was early evening, and the Dowager Empress greeted him in her sitting room, propped up with cushions and looking, he said, "as if she had just been taken off the rack after undergoing torture." The nurse explained that the patient had been given a dose of morphine and would be able to speak in a few moments. When Vicky opened her eyes, she began immediately asking him questions. Did he like Friedrichshof? What did he think of it? Had he seen her art collection? "The impression that I was talking to a dying woman vanished," he said, "and I was suddenly conscious that I had to deal with a person who was very much alive and alert. We talked of the South African War and of the way it was being misrepresented in Europe. . . . She asked searching questions about the King's position as a constitutional monarch and expressed her admiration of our constitution."

After fifteen minutes, the "hurricane of questions" stopped, and the Dowa-

---

* Bathrooms with running water and fireplaces—refused to Vicky for the four years she lived there—had been installed in 1897 in preparation for a two-day visit by the Kaiser and his wife.

ger Empress closed her eyes again. The nurse reappeared to say that Ponsonby must go, but left them alone when Vicky asked him to stay for a few more minutes.

"There is something I want you to do for me," the Dowager Empress told Ponsonby when the nurse had left the room. "I want you to take charge of my letters and take them with you back to England. . . . I will send them to you at one o'clock to-night and I know I can rely on your discretion. I don't want a soul to know that they have been taken away and certainly Willy must not have them, nor must he ever know you have got them."

Since Vicky had never kept a diary, she had asked the Queen to return her letters, sent to England for safekeeping, so that she might tell the story of her life in Germany and contradict the accusations leveled at her and her husband by Bismarck and Willy. She had intended to take the letters back with her to England after she was finished, but had not been able to complete the task. Now she knew there would be no more trips back home. Having experienced Willy's behavior after his father's death, it was clear that the letters would not be safe once she was gone. This was her last chance to get them out of Germany.

At 1:00 A.M. that night, Ponsonby answered a knock at his door. There were four men dressed in blue serge and high riding boots, clearly not regular palace servants,* bearing two boxes "the size of portmanteaux" covered with black oilcloth. Edward VII's secretary, who thought the letters mentioned by the Dowager Empress could easily be concealed in one of his own valises, was at a loss to know how to get these huge cases out of the country. They could neither be hidden nor smuggled out of Friedrichshof, which was crawling with the Kaiser's secret police. In desperation, Ponsonby wrote CHINA WITH CARE on one packing case and BOOKS WITH CARE on the other, along with his address at home in England. When questioned by Edward's courier, he intimated that he had bought some contraband goods in Hamburg and needed help getting them past customs.

On March 1, King Edward and his party left Friedrichshof for London. Fortunately, no one dared take their eyes off the Kaiser, who was holding forth on some subject in the foyer of the castle as two strange-looking black cases, noticeably different from the luggage that had come in with the King of England, were being carried out. When he got home to England, Ponsonby took the letters to his home in Windsor and locked them up.

---

* *Ponsonby later concluded that they must have been "trustworthy servants . . . from the Stables and therefore probably quite ignorant of the contents of the boxes" (RA: Geo. V, AA 68/96, Ponsonby to the Duke of Connaught, 12/4/26).*

CHAPTER
SEVENTY

> *"Queen Victoria's eldest daughter . . . was the most remarkable*
> *English princess of modern history. . . . When we realise the gifts*
> *of her mind we sense the reality of her sorrows."*
>
> ROGER FULFORD

WHEN EDWARD VII left Vicky in March of 1901, no one could predict how much longer she had to live. The King ordered his usual suite at Bad Homburg for the middle of August to be near her, and the Kaiser made arrangement to go there or to nearby Kassel to be near the King. Meanwhile, a succession of relatives began a pilgrimage to Friedrichshof—Vicky's daughters, their husbands and children, Henry and Irene and theirs, her sisters Helena and Beatrice, her sister-in-law Alix (Queen Alexandra of England), her niece Victoria of Battenberg (later the Marchioness of Milford Haven), etc. Willy came twice to see his mother—once at the end of April and once in mid-July.

Along with these visitors and an unabated interest in world affairs, one of the things that supported the Dowager Empress during the last months of her life was her correspondence with Sophie.

"I know you have forbidden me writing and I have promised to obey," she wrote Sophie on March 7, shortly after one of Sophie's visits,

> but one little line I must send to say how my thoughts are with you on the journey. How I miss you I cannot say, nor how grateful I was for your visit, my own pet. You were so sweet to your Mama and so patient with her, sacrificed so much time to her, and read so much, and it was such a joy to have you.
>
> This is Easter Day. . . . I am spending it miserably in my bed, in great pain and torture. Irene has just arrived, Henry comes this evening. I am going to have some eggs hidden in the garden for Mossy's dear little people. . . . Have you seen all the funny and mostly very incorrect pictures in the illustrated papers about dear Uncle Bertie's visit here?

In spite of her illness, the Dowager Empress had taken on the task of improving conditions in Greece, pushing Sophie to act like a future queen by starting hospitals, soup kitchens, kindergartens, trade schools, even a branch of the S.P.C.A. She sent a German manager for one of the soup kitchens and recommended one of her own Victoria House nurses as matron of a maternity hospital. She plied Sophie and Tino with advice, good and bad, on adopting forestry conservation from the Italians and copying the English at Portsmouth in using seawater to wash down the dusty streets of Athens. "Indeed my head is always running on your railway to Salonica," she had written her daughter in early 1899. "It would make an untold difference to Greece. When one thinks how railways are being pushed into the wilds of Africa, and now in China, one wonders that yours has not been done long ago." She suggested that Sophie invite Thomas Cook of Cook's Tours to Athens to explain how to attract tourists, so that "poor little Greece would become rich at once."

The Dowager Empress even tried to learn Greek. "Every morning in bed I learn words by heart, but my memory is very bad, and when one does not <u>hear</u> a language one picks it up slowly." During these last months of her life, Vicky also tried to teach the future Queen of Greece her interpretation of the royal code:

"I feel so strongly how important it is that the Dynasty are not silent and idle spectators of what is going on, but <u>can</u> and <u>do</u> influence the affairs of the country and further the interests of the nation to its moral and material advantage by helping in every good public work, and pushing on improvement and progress in small things as in great, and thus teaching and educating people by their example, which is as important in its way as great political questions."

But as the spring of 1901 progressed, the frequency of the Dowager Empress's letters to this far-off child decreased. It had become apparent that she was failing more rapidly than the doctors had expected. Sophie was due to come home in early June.

"If the newspapers are to be trusted, this will be my last letter, as they say you leave on the 9th. . . . I have been terribly bad these last few days," Vicky wrote her Greek daughter. "The attacks of pain so violent, the struggle for breath so dreadful, when in bed or lying down, most distressing. . . . I manage to struggle through the day, I know not how, and am much out of doors, lying down, my arm hung up in a cushion, and my head too. Of an afternoon I have a drive. What joy it will be to see you and Tino and the sweet children. If you are only not bored."

The Dowager Empress survived two months more, a martyr to the doctors' refusal to give her enough morphine to ease her agony for more than a few minutes at a time. As her pain increased, the sentries outside Friedrichshof begged to be moved farther off so as not to hear her screams. Her body wasted away, and even her face, once as round as her mother's, was sunken and without color. But Willy, who visited her in the middle of July before leaving for his annual cruise, said that she still preserved her interest "in everything that is going on in the world, politics as well as litterature [*sic*] and art." From this he concluded that she was likely to survive until winter.

Before she died, the Dowager Empress dictated a will disposing of her worldly goods—her furniture, jewelry, silver, artwork, and papers. She left Friedrichshof to Mossy, her jewelry and works of art to her other children and relatives. There were gifts for every employee and "every person who in her lifetime had stood near to her," said Reischach, her Lord Chamberlain.

In spite of the fact that her three younger daughters recognized that the end was near, the official bulletins from Berlin stated that the condition of the Dowager Empress was "quite satisfactory." Not until August 4, the day before her death, was it announced that "the strength of the illustrious patient is fading fast." By then, the Kaiser, who had been cruising the North Sea in his yacht, tending to his sick friend, Philipp zu Eulenburg, was steaming back to Germany as fast as he could. Dona met him at Kiel. He berated her in front of the rest of their entourage for not remaining at Friedrichshof. (Vicky did not want her there.) Kaiser and Kaiserin arrived thirty-six hours before his mother's death.

Wilhelm II took up the vigil and scarcely left his mother's room. Up until the end, one of Vicky's three younger daughters, who had been at her bedside for several weeks, was with her. Ironically, it was Willy who was there when she died. "My sister Sophie and I had just gone into the garden to have a rest when we were called back, and we were too late to be present when she actually breathed her last," Mossy said many years later.

IMMEDIATELY AFTER his mother's death, the Kaiser's troops moved in. Cavalry had been posted around the perimeter of the property, special police patrolled the castle itself, and searchers were assigned to every room. Nothing was found.

The Dowager Empress had left precise instructions for her funeral. She had dictated them to her sister Helena during her last summer. There were to be no autopsies like that inflicted on her beloved Fritz, no embalming, no photographs or portraits, no royal lying-in-state. Her body was to be covered by the Prussian royal standard; the coffin was to be closed and placed in the town church in Kronberg before being moved for interment in the mausoleum at Potsdam. "I wish . . . the court chaplain . . . to say a short prayer, but on no account is he to make a speech," she said.

Having not been able to find and destroy his mother's letters and papers, Wilhelm II set out to undermine Vicky's last shred of credibility with the German people in case they were ever discovered. To do this, he invited his Chancellor, Bernhard von Bülow, out for a walk the day after Vicky's death and offered him some salacious tidbits:

"He told me," Bülow wrote in his memoirs, "that his mother had decided that her body should be wrapped unclothed in the English flag, the Union Jack, and be thus laid in the coffin. She had also ordered her coffin to be sent to England for she wanted to be buried there. I agreed with the Kaiser when he said that he did not think these wishes of his mother could be carried out, because they might offend the sensibilities of the German people and the dignity of our country."

A nude German Empress, clad only in the British flag, refusing to be buried in Germany—this was the sort of tale sure to be repeated all over the country:

"We hear from Berlin that the Emperor is very upset by the drama which has taken place at Cronberg, and by the griefs his mother has inflicted upon him, even after her death," Princess Marie Radziwill, one of Vicky's more ardent detractors, wrote to a correspondent in Paris.

> She left strictest orders in regard to her funeral, stressing the fact that she did not want to be buried as a German Sovereign, but as an English Princess. During her lifetime, she had ordered and sent to Cronberg a coffin from London, and an Anglican Bishop, specified by her, was to come to preside at her obsequies, which she wanted to have solemnized according to the rites of the Anglican Church.
>
> The poor Emperor found himself in a most embarassing situation, as he wanted to fulfil his mother's last wishes, but could not have a German Empress buried according to English rites. . . .
>
> You may imagine how hurt people in Berlin felt by all this. However, this Princess, who scorned in dying everything that was German, had lived in Germany the greater part of her life, and it was only up to her to make herself beloved in that country. . . . It seems to be a positive fact that the empress has herself destroyed her Memoirs, which consisted of a journal, written day by day, and all her correspondence with her mother; and these facts prove to Germans how right they were to distrust her.

THE KAISER'S EFFORTS to hide the real facts of his mother's life came out in a conversation that took place shortly after her death, when Ponsonby, who had spirited her letters out of Germany a few months earlier, returned with Edward VII for the funeral.

One evening after dinner, the King's secretary was approached by Count August zu Eulenburg, head of the Kaiser's household. Eulenburg said that no letters or papers had been found when the Dowager Empress died, although a "thorough search" had taken place. The Kaiser had instructed him to find out "whether by chance these letters were in the archives at Windsor."

Ponsonby, who had never taken the letters out of his own home, replied that he would write at once to Lord Esher, the keeper of the archives at Windsor. In due course, a note came back, saying that the letters were "certainly not in the archives."

The letters that told Vicky's story remained safely locked away in Ponsonby's house for over a quarter of a century. Not until 1928, in answer to the publication of a self-serving memoir by Wilhelm II, exiled in Holland after World War I, did Fritz's godson edit and publish these letters.

It was Vicky's one and only triumph over Bismarck and her son.

EPILOGUE

"The Kaiser is even more cowardly than vain. . . . It is not by
his will that he will start a war, but by his weakness."

EDWARD VII, 1906

"All he [Wilhelm II] wished was to feel like Napoleon, and be
like him without having to fight his battles. . . . If you are the
summit of a volcano, the least you can do is to smoke."

WINSTON CHURCHILL

*I*N LEAVING HER beloved Friedrichshof to Mossy, Vicky could not have
known that the days of great royal establishments were coming to an end. In
1925, a few years after World War I, Vicky's youngest daughter and her sons
abandoned the huge castle in favor of smaller, more practical villas they had
built on its grounds.

Twenty years later, at the end of World War II, Major Anthony Blunt,
Surveyor of the King's Pictures on assignment with British Military Intelligence,* alerted the British royal family that the contents of Friedrichshof were
"in considerable disarray" and that Vicky's papers were being "exposed to the
eyes of the inquisitive and the fingers of the acquisitive." At the time, Friedrichshof was occupied by the Americans.† Blunt and Sir Owen Morshead, the King's
Librarian, obtained General Dwight D. Eisenhower's permission to visit the
Schloss and remove archival materials. Queen Victoria's letters to Vicky and
some of Vicky's letters were sent back to England for safekeeping. In response
to Mossy's request, the Queen's letters were returned to Germany in 1951 and
have remained there ever since. In 1954, Vicky's youngest and last surviving
child died at Schönberg, near her mother's home of Friedrichshof, which has
been turned into a hotel by her descendants.

Vicky's other daughters all died before the advent of Hitler and the Second
World War. Charlotte, whose life was plagued with poor health, succumbed
first, in 1919. Historian John Röhl believes that her stomach pains, rashes, and
urinary problems were a sign of porphyria—the rare disease marked by unbearable pain and periods of insanity that had attacked her ancestors, Friedrich
Wilhelm I of Prussia and George III of England.

Vicky's second daughter, Moretta, outlived her first husband, who died in

* *Blunt was later proved to be a spy for the KGB.*

† *The Hesse family jewels were in fact stolen from under the floor of a subcellar at Friedrichshof*
and taken to the United States by two American army officers, later arrested by the military
police and sentenced to jail.

the middle of World War I, and in 1927 she married Alexander Zoubkov, thirty-four years her junior (he was twenty-seven and she was sixty-one at the time). They were married only a year before she divorced him, and one year later, in November of 1929, she herself died.

Sophie became Queen of the Hellenes in 1913, when her father-in-law was assassinated and her husband, Constantine I, ascended to the throne. Despised by the Allies during the early years of World War I for his German wife and policy of neutrality, Constantine was forced to abdicate in 1917. He was brought back to the throne by plebiscite in 1920, but was exiled again two years later. Because of the unstable situation in Greece, Sophie saw all three of her sons sit on the Greek throne at one time or another. She outlived her husband by nine years and died in Germany in 1932.

Vicky's second son, Henry, also died before World War II. An admiral in the navy, he played a minor role in the political history of Germany when he tried twice—in 1912 and after the assassination at Sarajevo but before the outbreak of hostilities in 1914—to carry messages from King George V of England to the Kaiser concerning the position England would take in the event of a general war. In both instances Henry's reports made England sound far more neutral than she was. Whether this was due to his unwillingness to upset his brother or to Wilhelm's refusal to hear bad news, the results of Henry's attempts at diplomacy only added to the confusion that preceded the outbreak of World War I.

Wilhelm's ability to disregard reality and his deep ambivalence toward England—both painfully apparent during his mother's lifetime—increased after her death. The Kaiser talked about the necessity for Germany and England to "stand together," but he permitted his ministers, who reflected the hatred of the British planted in the Germans by Bismarck, to scuttle all attempts at an Anglo-German entente. Although Willy accused his uncle Edward VII of trying to isolate Germany, it was not Uncle Bertie's ill will but Germany's huge naval buildup that caused anger and anxiety in England. When the German Ambassador to the Court of St. James's tried to explain this, the Kaiser erupted: "I do not wish for good relations with England at the price of not building the German fleet." Wilhelm apparently agreed with Tirpitz that it was possible to create and maintain a menacing array of seapower merely as a reminder to England that she could not afford to become Germany's enemy.

As relations between Germany and England deteriorated during the years before World War I, so did the Kaiser's personal reputation. Although he distanced himself from his friend Eulenburg when the latter was accused of homosexuality, the embarrassment of Eulenburg's public trial rubbed off on the crown. No sooner had the Eulenburg scandal died down than an interview with Wilhelm, published in the *Daily Telegraph* in 1908, made the German Kaiser look like a political fool. In the article, Wilhelm said that he took it as "a personal insult" when the British press distorted his "repeated offers of friendship" to England, that English suspicions of the German naval buildup were "unworthy of a great nation," and that England might one day be grateful for

German ships in the face of the growing power of the Japanese. Moreover, the Kaiser claimed that during the Boer War he had resisted Russia's and France's attempts to lure Germany into an anti-British coalition and that he had even tried to help Queen Victoria by presenting her with a battle plan similar to the one that had eventually brought victory to England.

Along with infuriating the pro-Boer Germans with his remarks, Wilhelm managed to antagonize the Japanese and further alienate the Russians and the French; in the absence of a copy of his victory plan, he became a laughingstock in England. A speech he delivered in August 1910, affirming his "divine right" and claiming that he was the "instrument of the Lord," did not improve his tarnished image.

Although the Kaiser behaved with restraint during the Balkan Wars of 1912–13, refusing to support Austria in her attempts to thwart Serbian expansion, he reversed himself in June 1914, when Archduke Franz Ferdinand was assassinated in Sarajevo by a Bosnian acting for Serbian nationalists. Franz Ferdinand was a friend as well as a member of a royal family. In a state of excitement reminiscent of previous emotional highs, Wilhelm II immediately offered Germany's full support to Austria against Russia in the event of a general war. The Kaiser's support allowed the Austrians to present the Serbs with an impossible ultimatum. Seemingly unaware of the powder keg he had helped set in place, Wilhelm declined to participate in a four power conference proposed by the English to keep the peace.

By the time the Kaiser read Serbia's capitulation to Austria and realized that the Austrians had already won their point, it was too late to stop Austria from declaring war on the Serbs. When Nicholas II of Russia tried to enlist Wilhelm's help, begging him "in the name of our old friendship to do what you can to stop your allies [Austria] from going too far," Willy told Nicky that Serbia was guilty of an "outrageous crime." He also reminded the Czar that they had "a common interest in seeing all regicides punished." From this point on, Germany's generals took matters into their own hands. Having prepared for years for a two-front offensive against Russia and France, they insisted that Austria mobilize fully and promised that Germany would do the same.

On August 1, 1914, Germany declared war on Russia. Five days later Austria followed suit. Throughout this time, the Austrians had been pursuing negotiations with the Russians, hoping to come to an agreement over Serbia. But once Germany declared war, the negotiations became superfluous. In his desire to pose before the world as the mighty leader of a unbeatable military power, Wilhelm II had helped precipitate a war that might have been avoided.

In light of this, one would have expected the Kaiser to march off to war, banners flying. But Wilhelm, now depressed by premonitions of disaster, claimed that his advisers and generals had dragged him into an unwinnable fight (partially true), that the English had always planned to destroy Germany (untrue), and that George V of England and Nicholas II of Russia had plotted "with guile and treachery in their hearts" to attack Germany when they attended the wedding of his daughter the previous year (paranoid fantasy).

Although Wilhelm did move to the front at the beginning of hostilities, he contributed little to the war effort beyond traveling back and forth in his gold-and-cream-colored train to dispense medals. Having built the navy of his dreams, he would not allow it to be jeopardized by fighting. And when Germany's defeat became inevitable, he withdrew to his castle at Wilhelmshöhe, where, according to the disgusted chief of his naval cabinet, he visited galleries with his entourage and conducted his life "as though nothing had happened." When he was finally convinced that he must abdicate to save his skin, Wilhelm fled to Holland.

From the safety of exile, the former Kaiser wrote his memoirs. "Not Germany, but the alliance of her foes, prepared the war according to a definite plan, and caused it," he claimed. The book was reviewed by Winston Churchill. "No more disarming revelation of inherent triviality, lack of understanding and sense of proportion . . . can be imagined," he said of its author. "It is shocking to reflect that upon the word or nod of a being so limited there stood attentive and obedient for thirty years the forces which, whenever released, could devastate the world."

The following year (1929), Frederick Ponsonby published a selection of the letters given him for safekeeping by the Empress Frederick. Wilhelm had tried to stop Ponsonby by claiming that he himself held the copyright; when that failed, he wrote a preface to the German edition in which he intimated that his mother had been a hysterical woman who conjured up nonexistent enemies. Vicky's English relations and her two remaining daughters, who worried about the public airing of family feuds, also disapproved of Ponsonby's book, which came out under the title, *Letters of the Empress Frederick*.

The ex-Kaiser died on June 5, 1941, the year that Russia and the United States entered World War II. Although he had contributed as much as anyone to the tragic upheavals of the twentieth century—the 10,000,000 people killed in World War I and the climate of chauvinism, scapegoating, and Jew-baiting that accompanied World War II and the Holocaust—Wilhelm II spent a comfortable and seemingly guilt-free old age, railing at the Socialists, the Jews, and the Americans, who, he said, had plotted to bring down the House of Hohenzollern and Germany.

Seven months before his death, the ex-Kaiser had written his old friend Poultney Bigelow a postcard. "Today the 100th birthday of my mother! No notice is taken of it at home! No 'Memorial Service' or . . . committee to remember her marvellous work for the . . . welfare of our German people. . . . Nobody of the new generation knows anything about her."

Notes

Abbreviations used:

ARCHIVAL SOURCES
RA: The Royal Archives, Windsor Castle
KHH: Kurhessische Hausstiftung, Schloss Fasanerie, Fulda
GStA: Geheimes Staatsarchiv Preussischer Kulturbesitz, Berlin
NYPL: New York Public Library, Poultney Bigelow Papers, Rare Books and
Manuscripts Division, Astor, Lenox and Tilden Foundations
RCP: Royal College of Physicians of London
  QVJ: Queen Victoria's Journals (Royal Archives)

NAMES
B: Bismarck
EdVII: Edward VII
F: Fritz (Friedrich III)
FWIV: Friedrich Wilhelm IV
KL: King Leopold I
PA: Prince Albert
QV: Queen Victoria
V: Vicky (Empress Frederick)
WI: Wilhelm I
WII: Wilhelm II

PUBLISHED SOURCES
Leaves: Queen Victoria. *Leaves from a Journal.*
Memoir: Anonymous. *The Empress Frederick: A Memoir.*
Letters: Frederick Ponsonby. *Letters of the Empress Frederick.*
Recollections: Anonymous. *Recollections of Three Kaisers.*

Other published sources are cited by the author's last name. Complete bibliographical information on all published works cited can be found in the Bibliography.

Note: Short forms of sources are shown in parentheses following first citation of the complete title.

CHAPTER ONE

27 "[A]n ugly . . . undressed": KHH: QV to V, 5/4/59.
27 "Just before . . . nervous": RA: QVJ, 12/1/40.
27 "the only . . . dread": RA: QVJ, 12/11/39.
28 "dark, dull . . . chimneys": KHH: QV to V, 11/21/84.
28 "Oh Madam . . . Prince": Philip Whitwell Wilson, ed. *The Greville Diary,* Vol. II, p. 214.
28 "stark naked": *Ibid.*
28 "[A]las! a . . . comfort": RA: QVJ, 12/1/40.
28 "Albert, father . . . me": Hector Bolitho, *The Prince Consort and His Brother* (Bolitho 1), p. 34.
28 "I should . . . Heaven": *Ibid.*
28 "ogre who . . . rage": Ghislain de Diesbach, *Secrets of the Gotha*, p. 196.
28 "Nothing was ready": Elizabeth Longford, *Queen Victoria*, p. 153.
29 "dear marriage day,": Arthur Christopher Benson and Viscount Esher, eds., *Letters of Queen Victoria, 1837–1861*, p. 322.
29 "seemed to . . . observing": Anonymous, *The Empress Frederick: A Memoir*, *(Memoir)*, p. 4.
29 "quite conscious . . . formed!": *Ibid.*, p. 3.
29 "no more": RA: M 11/9.
29 Princess Royal: An honorary title that may be conferred by the monarch on his or her eldest daughter. Vicky was only the fourth Princess to carry it since Charles I created it for his daughter, Princess Mary, in 1642.
29 "She is . . . out": RA: QVJ, 12/28/40.
29 "the shadow . . . marriage": KHH: QV to V, 3/24/58.
29 "froglike": Longford, p. 154.
30 "he would . . . her": Cecil Woodham-Smith, *Queen Victoria*, p. 73.
30 "I know . . . existed": *Ibid.*, p. 67.
30 "[W]e were . . . remained": Benson and Esher, Vol. 1, p. 324.
30 "the brightest . . . childhood": Woodham-Smith, p. 79.
30 "Mephistopheles": *Ibid.*, p. 80.
31 "Dear good Lehzen": *Ibid.*, p. 144.
32 "In my . . . house": Theodore Martin, *Life of the Prince Consort*, Vol. I, p. 69.
32 "He is . . . him": *Greville Diary*, Vol. II, p. 358.
32 "never forgot her": Martin, Vol. I, p. 6 note.
33 "train myself . . . man": Robert Rhodes-James, *Prince Albert*, p. 31.
33 "An irresistible . . . life": *Ibid.*, p. 32.
33 "Albert is . . . heart": Bolitho 1, p. 40.
34 "intricate turns . . . imaginary": Sarah Spencer, Lady Lyttelton, *Correspondence*, p. 326.
34 "footman-in-waiting . . . messages": RA: M 16/1.
34 *To teach . . : breast:* RA: M 12/9.
35 "The present . . . Society": RA: M 12/16.
35 "encroach . . . rights": RA: M 12/18.
35 "Her Majesty . . . vary": RA: M 12/29.
35–36 "Good Education . . . pure": RA: M 12/14, *passim.*

CHAPTER TWO

37 "*Clever children . . . others*": RA: Y 38/26, Feodora to QV, 3/23/46.
37 "We drove . . . suppose' ": Alfred E. Knight, *Victoria: Her Life and Reign*, pp. 125–26.
37 "Our fat . . . obstinate": Benson and Esher, Vol. II, p. 3, QV to KL, 1/9/44.
38 "The Princess . . . enough": Lyttelton, p. 319.
38 "Oh, dear . . . uncle": *Ibid.*, p. 332.

38 "too comical": *Ibid.,* p. 324.
38 "The evening . . . falsehoods": RA: M 13/70.
38 "the Princess . . . way": RA: M 13/68.
39 "I am . . . time": Lyttelton, p. 354–55.
39 "Good morning . . . bed": Nina Epton, *Victoria and Her Daughters,* p. 48.
39 "too severe": RA: Y 37/60 Feodora to QV, 11/23/44.
39 "We find . . . do?' ": RA: Y 91/21, QV to KL, 9/26/43.
39 "Pussette, I . . . effect": RA: Y 198/222, QV to KL, 5/28/44.
39 "I thought . . . whipping": RA: M 13/87.
39 "His Royal . . . precedent": RA: M 13/45.
40 "poisoned her . . . conscience": Woodham-Smith, p. 301.
40 "I cannot . . . alarm": RA: M 13/35.
40 "I dread . . . mind": RA: M 12/35.
40 "great pain . . . down?" Lyttelton, p. 360
40 "You must . . . again": Benson and Esher, Vol. II, p. 7.
40 "is very . . . weeks": Lyttelton, p. 338–39.
41 "I am . . . prayers": RA: M 12/39.
41 "He is . . . firmly": Roger Fulford, *The Prince Consort,* (Fulford I), p. 95.
41 "It is . . . kindness": *Ibid.*
41 "The root . . . scolding": Woodham-Smith, p. 427.
42 "the submission . . . Character": RA: M 12/55.
42 "Arithmetic, Dictation . . . Edward 6th": RA: M 12/66.
42 "Don't look . . . see it": Reginald Pound, *Albert,* p. 325.
42 "always the . . . disgraced": John C. G. Röhl, *Wilhelm II, Die Jugend des Kaisers, 1859–1888,* p. 102.
42 "the nation's child": Daphne Bennett, *King Without a Crown,* p. 130.
42 "From her . . . genius": *Memoir,* p. 33.
43 "In our . . . water": Martin, Vol. II, p. 287.
44 "only great . . . present": Epton, p. 49.
44 "dazzling . . . England!": Lyttelton, p. 394–95 *passim.*

CHAPTER THREE

45 *"The fact . . . in":* Woodham-Smith, p. 15.
46 "the Grapeshot Prince": Herbert Eulenberg, *The Hohenzollerns,* p. 236.
46 "wretched refugees": Lyttelton, p. 373.
46 "We have . . . pigeons": Dr. Kurt Jagow, *Letters of the Prince Consort,* p. 141.
47 "a loyal German": *Ibid.,* p. 119.
47 "sworn enemy . . . claims": Eulenberg, p. 243.
47 "I find . . . us": Benson and Esher, Vol. II, p. 126, QV to KL, 9/29/46.
48 "the two . . . Europe": Princess Catherine Radziwill, *The Empress Frederick (Radziwill 1),* p. 46.
49 "contamination": Longford, p. 223.
49 "I would . . . son": Jagow, p. 175, note 2, Ernest Augustus of Hanover to FWIV, 4/1/51.
49 "countless hordes . . . London": RA: F 24/89, FWIV to PA, 4/8/51.
49 "Mathematicians have . . . victims": Jagow, p. 176–77.
50 "You cannot . . . being": Radziwill 1, p. 47.
51 "With all . . . you": Hector Bolitho, ed. *Letters of Queen Victoria from the House of Brandenburg Prussia,* (Bolitho 2), pp. 23–24.
51 "Never did . . . it": RA: Y 96/25, QV to L, 5/27/51.
51 "Napoléon le Petit,": Theo Aronson, *The Fall of The Third Napoleon,* p. 17.
51 "With such . . . safe": Benson and Esher, Vol. II, p. 438.
52 "improper interference": Baron Ernest von Stockmar, ed., *Memoirs of Baron Christian Friedrich Stockmar,* p. 480.
52 "the Austrian . . . ambition": Rhodes-James, p. 222.

53 "It is impossible . . . power": Martin, Vol. III, p. 12.

53 "It is sad . . . behaviour": Egon Corti, *The English Empress* (Corti 1), p. 25.

53 "Vicky is . . . sense": Hector Bolitho, ed., *Letters from the Archives of the House of Brandenburg-Prussia,* (Bolitho 3), pp. 38–39.

53 "growing fast . . . developing": *Ibid.,* p. 49.

53 "alighting like . . . away": Woodham-Smith, p. 453.

53 Crimean War: Most of this information on the Crimean War is taken from Cecil Woodham-Smith's biography of Queen Victoria.

CHAPTER FOUR

54 *"Only four . . . dress":* S. Burchell, *Imperial Masquerade,* p. 60. Burchell attributes this statement to Edmond and Jules Goncourt.

54 "exquisitely proportioned": *Ibid.,* p. 48.

55 "All the children . . . eyes": Queen Victoria, *Leaves from a Journal" (Leaves),* pp. 27–30 *passim.*

55 "daring and lively": Allan Thomas, ed., *A New Most Excellent Dancing Master,* p. 36.

55 "Vicky behaved . . . about": *Leaves,* p. 40.

56 "ecstasies": *Ibid.,* p. 42.

56 "Make sure . . . front": Burchell, p. 69.

56 "[R]eally it . . . people": Magdalen Ponsonby, *A Lady in Waiting to Queen Victoria* (Ponsonby 1), p. 21.

56 "broiling": *Ibid.,* p. 73.

56 "[N]o description . . . enthusiastic": *Leaves,* pp. 75–76.

57 "shocking toilette . . . gold": Benita Stoney and Heinrich C. Weltzien, eds., *My Mistress the Queen,* p. 17.

57 "never-to . . . week": *Leaves,* p. 140.

57 "think and . . . else": Benson and Esher, Vol. III, pp. 176–78, QV to Stockmar, 9/1/55.

57 "looked nice . . . dresses": *Leaves,* p. 123.

57 "very communicative . . . carriage": *Ibid.,* p. 105.

58 "quite understood": *Ibid.,* p. 129.

58 "the domain . . . moustaches": Burchell, p. 100.

58 "like a . . . nymph": *Leaves,* p. 124.

58 "the like . . . seen": *Ibid.*

58 "blushing deeply": Corti 1, p. 20.

58 "very Russian . . . Junker": *Leaves,* pp. 125–26.

58 "malevolent curiosity": Otto von Bismarck, *Reflections and Reminiscences,* Vol. I, p. 190.

58 "melted in . . . Empress": *Leaves,* p. 143.

58 "get leave . . . us": Woodham-Smith, p. 466.

59 "badly dressed . . . trifles": Ponsonby 1, p. 25.

59 "nearest and . . . incredible": Benson and Esher, Vol. III, p. 176 –78.

59 "love-making was . . . virtue": *Leaves,* p. 20.

CHAPTER FIVE

60 *"Impressions one . . . soul":* Romulus Linney, prologue to *The Sorrows of Frederick and Holy Ghosts,* p. 5.

60 "present political . . . come": Corti 1, p. 18.

60 "matchmaker . . . confidential": Jagow, p. 238, PA to WI, 9/21/55.

60 "soldierly": "The Marriage of Her Royal Highness The Princess Royal," *The Morning Post,* January 26, 1858.

61 "[I]t has . . . come": Andreas Dorpalen, "Frederick III and the German Liberal Movement," *The American Historical Review*, Vol. LIV, No. 1, October 1948, p. 2.

61 "The task . . . Friedrichs-d'or": Margaretha von Poschinger, *Life of the Emperor Frederick*, p. 116.

62 "I know . . . to": *Ibid.*, p. 19.

62 "envied . . . necessity": *Ibid.*, p. 21.

63 "with every . . . views": *Ibid.*, p. 397.

63 "No one . . . out": *Ibid.*, pp. 27–30.

63 "Fritz's knowledge . . . peers": Patricia A. Kollander, *The Liberalism of Frederick III*, p. 18.

63 "manifested . . . society": Poschinger, p. 30–31.

63 "undoubtedly had . . . life": *Ibid.*, p. 37.

CHAPTER SIX

65 *"Why tinge . . . prepare"*: Mme. Lola, Montez, *The Arts of Beauty or Secrets of a Lady's Toilet*, p. 21.

65 "bewitched those . . . her": Walpurga, Lady Paget, *Scenes and Memories* p. 62. Henceforth cited as Paget 1.

65 "thin & interesting": RA: Z 25/77, V to QV, 5/18/71.

65 "almost timid": Paget 1, p. 62.

65 "That he . . . it": RA: Z 22/16, V to QV, 9/2/68.

65 "always finding . . . unjustly": *Greville Diary*, Vol. II, p. 456.

66 "Stop, gentlemen . . . handkerchief": Knight, p. 183.

66 "We looked . . . deal": Corti 1, p. 21.

66 "someone . . . hard": *Ibid.*

66 "Great rectitude . . . degree": RA: G 38/22, PA to Stockmar, 9/20–21/55.

66 "sweet, natural . . . heart": Corti 1, p. 21.

67 "something had . . . himself": Longford, p. 260.

67 "always . . . bounds": RA: Add. A 7/9.

68 "It is . . . heart": Poschinger, p. 57.

68 "like a . . . dream": Corti 1, p. 22.

68 "the love . . . day": Kollander, p. 22.

68 "in raptures . . . satisfaction": Poschinger, p. 56.

68 "The young . . . me": RA: Y 100/40 *passim*, QV to KL, 10/9/55.

68 "dear darling . . . time": Bolitho 3, pp. 57–58.

68 "paltry German . . . England": RA: Z 61/20, clipping from the London *Times*, 10/3/55.

69 "in raptures . . . mountain' ": RA: I 29/102, extract of a letter by William Cobden to a friend, 3/20/56.

69 "You ask . . . judges": Corti 1, pp. 26–27, and Richard Barkeley, *The Empress Frederick*, pp. 43–44.

70 "As for . . . stake": Martin, Vol. III, pp. 448–49.

71 "rich silk . . . lace": Barkeley, p. 47.

71 "The Princess . . . superiority": Lord Edmond Fitzmaurice, *The Life of George Leveson Gower, Second Earl Granville*, p. 172.

71 "Poor dear . . . her": RA: Add. U 171/225, QV to Feodora, 11/28/55.

71 "I resent . . . den": Longford, p. 262.

71 "I fear . . . itself": RA: S 8/29, Lady Bloomfield to QV, 9/23/56.

71 "Never were . . . itself": William S. Monypenny and George Earle Buckle, *The Life of Benjamin Disraeli*, Vol. IV, p. 46.

72 "a good-humoured . . . clever": Ponsonby I, p. 241.

72 "The Prince . . . Prince": Monypenny and Buckle, Vol. IV, p. 46.

72 "so much . . . himself": Benson and Esher, Vol. III, p. 248, QV to KL, 6/3/56.

72 "she cannot . . . feelings": Bolitho 1, p. 160.

72 "horribly shy . . . others": RA: Z 31/37, V to QV, 7/28/77.
72 "The Prince . . . rank": Benson and Esher, Vol. III, pp. 280–81.
72 "The Prince . . . yet": *Memoir*, pp. 42–43.
72 "It is . . . direction": Corti 1, p. 30.

CHAPTER SEVEN

74 *"[O]ur marriage . . . one"*: KHH: QV to V, 1/10/79.
74 "pitiable . . . beginning": RA: Z 61/40 *passim*, Stockmar to PA, 10/25/55.
74 "national union . . . herself": RA: I 31/85, PA to John Russell, 3/18/60.
74 "Vicky is . . . History": Martin, Vol. III, p. 388, and Jagow, pp. 243–44. (Note: Since translations vary, I have used Martin, with the exception of "many and . . . mind," which is quoted from Jagow.)
75 "From dear . . . else": Corti 1, p. 25.
75 "a serious . . . conscience": RA: Z 15/7 V to QV, 4/4/63.
75 This information on Vicky's trousseau comes from the Royal Archives.
75 "You have . . . country": Corti 1, p. 28.
75 "That you . . . Vicky": *Ibid.*, pp. 23–24.
76 "How the . . . accumulated!": *Memoir*, p. 51.
76 "The hours . . . day": Corti 1, p. 25.
76 "We dined . . . Albert": Longford, p. 265.
76 "suitable to . . . country": Woodham-Smith, p. 488.
76 "Her allowance . . . her": Jagow, p. 274.
76 "Whatever may . . . closed": Benson and Esher, Vol. III, p. 321.
77 "The Princess . . . them": Corti 1, p. 32.
77 "You can . . . another": *Ibid.*, p. 35.
77 "almost a . . . gentleness": Walpurga, Lady Paget, *Embassies of Other Days* (Paget 2), Vol. I, pp. 48–49.
77 "The Princess . . . make": Roger Fulford, *Dearest Child,* (Fulford 2), pp. 38–39, note 1.
77 "rather a trial": Paget 2, Vol. I, p. 90.
78 "[I]t gave . . . child": RA: QVJ, 1/18/58.
78 "That thought . . . into": KHH: QV to V, 4/15/85.
78 "radiant at . . . tones": Paget 1, p. 49 *passim.*.
78 "perfectly atrocious . . . royalties": RA: QVJ, 1/19/58.
78 "pale and agitated": *Ibid.*, 1/23/58.
78 "the happiest . . . happy": Corti 1, p. 38.
78 "Poor dear . . . display": RA: QVJ, 1/24/58.
78 This information on Vicky's jewels is from the Royal Archives.
79 "[I]t is . . . sacrificed": KHH: QV to V, 4/18/59.
79 "I felt . . . greatly": RA: QVJ, 1/25/58.
79 "Not a . . . flutter": Lyttelton, p. 418.
79 "very pretty . . . child!": RA: QVJ, 1/24/58.
79 "A procession . . . following": *Ibid.*, 1/25/58.
79 "conspicuous": RA: "The Marriage of Her Royal Highness, the Princess Royal, 1858," clipping from the *Morning Post*, 1/26/58.
80 "[T]he effect . . . manner": RA: QVJ, 1/25/58.
80 "bore himself . . . advantage": RA: "The Marriage . . ." clipping from the *Morning Post*, 1/26/58.
80 "Last came . . . plainly": RA: QVJ, 1/25/58.
81 "work in . . . Victoria": Martin, Vol. IV, p. 165.
81 "the deserving poor": RA: "The Marriage . . ." clipping from the *Morning Post*, 1/26/58.
81 "beef . . . tobacco": Barkeley, p. 59.
81 "I cannot . . . it!": RA: Z 5/1, V to QV, 1/25/58.
81 "a very . . . wife": KHH: QV to V, 1/25/58.

81   "really quite . . . now": RA: Z 5/4, V to QV, 1/26/58.

82   "Everything seems . . . Fritz": RA: QVJ, 1/27/58.

82   "I think . . . Papa!": RA: QVJ, 2/1/58.

82   "We went . . . again": RA: QVJ, 2/2/58.

83   "My heart . . . heart": Martin, Vol. IV, p. 169.

83   "My brother . . . future": Ernest II, Duke of Saxe-Coburg-Gotha, *Memoirs,* Vol. III, pp. 213–14, and *Memoir,* pp. 41–42. (Note: There are variations in translations, and I have tried to choose the clearest phrases. "My brother . . . tenderly" is from Ernest II; "to be . . . marriage" is from *Memoir;* "For many years . . . Prussia" is from Ernest II; "above all . . . future" is from *Memoir.*)

83   "Vicky is . . . Berlin": Hector Bolitho, *Albert, Prince Consort,* p. 160.

Chapter Eight

87   *"I have . . . believed":* James M. Perry, "The Royal Life," *Wall Street Journal,* 4/21/86.

87   "so unwell . . . shaky": RA: Z 5/6, V to QV, 2/3/58.

87   "to cheer . . . him": RA: Z 5/5, V to QV, 2/2/58.

87   "the dreadful . . . all": RA: Z 5/6, V to QV, 2/3/58.

87   "May God . . . ought": *Ibid* .

87   "The pain . . . advice": RA: Z 1/3, V to PA, undated, 2/3/58(?).

88   "gentle, charming . . . captivating": Paget 1, p. 51.

89   "much hurt": *Ibid.*

89   "the magnificent . . . everywhere": RA: Z 5/11, V to QV, 2/6/58.

89   "the most" . . . generals": Paget 1, p. 52.

89   "a veritable . . . flags": Corti 1, p. 42.

89   "the gilded . . . sea": *Ibid.,* p. 37.

89   "Berlin is . . . in": Rosslyn Wemyss, *Memoirs and Letters of the Right Hon. Sir Robert Morier, G.C.B.,* Vol. I, p. 166.

89   "a dreary . . . possible": *Handbook for Travelers on the Continent,* Fifth Ed., London, 1850 *(Handbook),* p. 344.

89   "sluggish, dirty . . . conferred": D. Mackenzie Wallace, *Russia,* p. 381.

90   "noxious odors . . . friends": *Handbook,* p. 344.

90   "We were . . . winds!": RA: Z 5/15, V to QV, 2/8/58.

90   "Are you . . . heart": Paget 1, p. 67.

90   "Every one . . . gold!": KHH: QV to V, 2/9/58.

90   "The whole . . . wife": Woodham-Smith, p. 504.

90   "golden opinions": *Ibid.*

90   "This kindly . . . mother": Corti 1, p. 42.

91   "history is . . . Royalties": *Ibid.,* p. 45.

Chapter Nine

92   *"I am . . . slaves":* Linney, p. 5.

93   "geographical expression": Gene Gurney, *Kingdoms of Europe,* p. 248; also G. Barraclough, ed., *The Times Atlas of World History,* p. 190.

93   "one of . . . crown": G. Barraclough, *The Origins of Modern Germany,* p. 385.

93   The stories of the Elector of Hesse and the Margrave of Ansbach-Bayreuth are taken from Robert H. Lowie, *Towards Understanding Germany,* p. 36.

93   The information on crossing borders is also from Lowie.

94   "Every nation . . . obedience": Gordon Craig, *The Germans,* p. 23.

96   Mirabeau: Quoted in E. J. Passant, *A Short History of Germany,* p. 4.

96   "a virtual foreigner": Hajo Holborn, *A History of Modern Germany, 1648–1840,* p. 238.

96   "Hats off . . . here": Nancy Mitford, *Frederick the Great,* p. 291.

96   "We went . . . Great": Holborn, p. 372.

97   "Proceed regardless . . . right!": Eulenberg, p. 192.
97   "I possess . . . washed": Radziwill 1, p. 8.
98   "If he . . . mistress": J. Christopher Herold, *The Age of Napoleon*, p. 151.
98   "The queen . . . comedy": *Ibid.*, pp. 151–52.
99   "to ensure tranquility": Golo Mann, *The History of Germany Since 1789*, p. 83.
100   "There was . . . unbearable": *Ibid.*, p. 120.
100   "German freedom . . . unity": Erich Eyck, *Bismarck and the German Empire*, p. 22.
101   "The Princess . . . knavery": Corti 1, p. 43.

CHAPTER TEN

102   *"Unmarried people . . . is"*: Corti 1, p. 55.
102   "I shall . . . talked": KHH: QV to V, 2/17/58.
102   "How do . . . melancholy!": KHH: QV to V, 2/24/58.
103   "I always . . . life!": Radziwill 1, p. 32.
103   "very firm . . . character": Eulenberg, p. 252.
103   "the Dragon . . . Rhine": Richard Hough, *Louis and Victoria* (Hough 1), p. 41.
103   "He could . . . man": Eulenberg, p. 258.
104   "Away with . . . Prussia": Anonymous, *Recollections of Three Kaisers, (Recollections),* p. 21.
104   "the very . . . horror": Eulenberg, p. 244.
104   "If we . . . ne'er-do-well": Prince von Bülow, *Memoir, 1897–1903*, p. 17.
104   "very small . . . hard": KHH: QV to V, 2/18/58.
105   "mortal enemy": Eyck, p. 22.
105   "the most . . . everybody": RA: Z 5/16, V to QV, 2/12/58.
105   "one of . . . existence": Princess Catherine Radziwill, *Secrets of Dethroned Royalty* (Radziwill 2), p. 195.
105   "so cowed . . . husband": RA: Z 5/16, V to QV, 2/12/58.
105   "is very . . . husband": RA: Z 5/69, V to QV, 5/10/58.
105   "the brave . . . make": RA: Z 5/27, V to QV, 2/26/58.
105   "No familiarity . . . in-law)": KHH: QV to V, 2/15/58.
106   "It was . . . example": RA: Z 5/19, V to QV, 2/20/58.
106   "as an asset": KHH: PA to V, 3/24/58.
106   "as my . . . Royal": KHH: QV to V, 6/6/58.
106   "[W]hen we . . . you": KHH: QV to V, 3/31/58.
106   "an affectionate . . . line": KHH: QV to V, 2/20/58.
107   "Don't tell . . . this": Paget 2, Vol. I, p. 97.
107   "If you . . . often": KHH: QV to V, 10/4/58.
107   "Letters from . . . can": RA: Z 7/20, V to QV, 10/9/58.
107   "[I]t gives . . . live!": KHH: QV to V, 2/15/58.
107   "I feel . . . happy": RA: Z 5/16, V to QV, 2/12/58.
107   "I feel . . . pardonnable": RA: Z 5/79, V to QV, 5/29/58.
108   "stared . . . way!": RA: Z 5/40, V to QV, 3/19/58.
108   "I'm sure . . . newspapers": KHH: PA to V, 3/24/58.
108   "stupid confused . . . fault": RA: Z 1/14, V to PA, 4/3/58.
108   "I quite . . . on": RA: Z 5/61, V to QV, 4/24/58.
109   "Being young . . . evening": Paget 2, Vol. I, p. 92.
109   "badly heated . . . all": Paget 1, p. 53.
109   "in constant dread": Paget 2, Vol. I, p. 94.
110   "utter discomfort . . . glass": *Ibid.*, p. 92.
110   "[W]hat a . . . here": RA: Z 5/57, V to QV, 4/14/58.
110   "The cold . . . brisk": KHH: QV to V, 2/15/58.
110   "I was . . . thermometer?": KHH: QV to V, 2/18/58.
111   "You ought . . . still": KHH: QV to V, 2/22/58.
111   "I beg . . . out": RA: Z 5/26, V to QV, 2/23/58.

Chapter Eleven

112 *"[W]e poor . . . amusement"*: KHH: QV to V, 8/10/59.

112 "the Prussian Versailles": *Handbook,* p. 360.

112 "cannot know . . . eye": RA: Z 1/22, V to PA, 5/27/58.

112 "What shall . . . self": Corti 1, p. 47.

112 "[Y]ou and . . . before": RA: Z 5/67, V to QV, 5/6/58.

113 "[T]he stairs . . . it": RA: Z 5/71, V to QV, 5/13/58.

113 "I who . . . dreadful": RA: Z 5/78, V to QV, 5/26/58.

113 "It is . . . suppressed": Corti 1, p. 46.

113 "relation between . . . good": Martin, Vol. IV, pp. 241–42.

113 "enjoyments, etc. . . . plagues": KHH: QV to V, 3/24/58.

113 "If I . . . was": KHH: QV to V, 4/14/58.

113 "I must . . . conception)": Corti 1, p. 47.

114 "That you . . . soul": RA: Z 6/4, V to QV, 6/12/58.

114 "What you . . . unecstatic": KHH: QV to V, 6/15/58.

114 "I could . . . propriety": RA: Z 6/7, V to QV, 6/19/58.

114 "I hope . . . too": RA: Z 6/12, V to QV, 6/28/58.

114 "I hope . . . endure": KHH: QV to V, 10/27/58.

114 "I know . . . child": KHH: QV to V, 11/17/58.

115 "see how . . . here": John van der Kiste, *Frederick III,* p. 35.

115 "My . . . profit": KHH: QV to V, 12/11/58.

115 "dreadfully hot . . . angel": Martin, Vol. IV, p. 287.

115 "the perpetual . . . dress": *Ibid.,* pp. 289–90, note 3.

115 "The whole . . . matters": Sir James Clark, RCP: Mss 30–31, unpublished diary, pp. 100–101.

115 "Gothic jewel": Martin, Vol. IV, p. 283.

116 "1000's of . . . reforms": Arthur Gould Lee, ed., *The Empress Frederick Writes to Sophie,* (Lee 1) p. 310.

116 "very necessary . . . introduced": KHH: QV to V, 4/2/59.

116 "[H]ow was . . . things": RA: Z 7/107, V to QV, 4/4/59.

117 "non extant . . . end!": RA: Z 36/7, V to QV, 2/11/82.

117 "Dearest Fritz . . . respect": RA: Z 6/7, V to QV, 6/19/58.

Chapter Twelve

118 *"[T]he political . . . Prussia"*: Jagow, p. 129.

118 "What a . . . unaided": Corti 1, p. 48.

119 "You may . . . done": RA: Z 1/47, V to PA, 11/6/58.

119 "The English . . . displayed": Benson & Esher, Vol. III, p. 383.

120 "ugly . . . it": Paget 2, Vol. I, p. 100.

120 "one of . . . imaginable": Radziwill 1, p. 34.

120 "Mama is . . . further": Corti, p. 36.

121 "active, restless . . . beloved": RA: Z 2/19, V to PA, 5/13/59.

121 "[I]t is . . . me": RA: Z 5/18, V to QV, 2/15/58.

121 "promise . . . clash": KHH: QV to V, 10/4/58 *passim.*

121 "I think . . . one": RA: Z 7/20 *passim,* V to QV, 10/9/58.

121 "I want . . . will": Henry Reese, *The Greville Diary,* Vol. II, pp. 387–89. (Note: This is from the three-volume edition published in 1874–78, edited by Henry Reese, but does not appear in the two-volume edition, published in 1927, edited by Wilson.)

Chapter Thirteen

123 *"It may . . . destiny"*: Longford, p. 234.

123 several versions: Up until recently, the version usually accepted was told in *Vicky,* a

biography of the Empress Frederick by Daphne Bennett, published in 1971. This account seemed plausible until one realized that the author had put Wilhelm II's birth in the wrong place (Babelsberg castle in Potsdam instead of Vicky's own palace in Berlin) and assigned the wrong nationality (Scottish) to Dr. Martin, who was German and lived and taught in Berlin. John Röhl's book, *Kaiser Wilhelm II, Die Jugend des Kaisers, 1859–1888,* not yet translated from the German, is based on the original archives and essentially confirms my account.

123 "[W]hen I . . . you?": KHH: QV to V, 11/17/58.

123 "clutching": RA: Z 63/115, Fritz's report of the birth.

124 "begged everyone . . . herself": *Ibid.*

124 "in her . . . die": *Memoir,* p. 101.

124 "long before . . . arrived": RA: Z 63/118, Sir James Clark to QV, 2/1/59.

124 "difficulty . . . child": RA: Z 63/112, Wegner to QV, 1/28/59.

124 "very painful . . . consequence": RA: ADD. U 34/2 (copy).

124 uterine stimulant: Called *secale cornutum* in Martin's report, translated by Kohut as ergotamine. Thomas Kohut, *Wilhelm II and the Germans,* p. 5.

125 "seemingly dead . . . attempts": This is taken from Martin's report, RA: ADD. U 34/2 (copy), "report about the delivery of Her Royal Highness . . . etc.," Berlin, 2/9/59: "When I found only slight and slow pulsation in the umbilical cord, I ordered a strong chloroform anaesthesia . . . in preparation for the now necessary operation . . . I lifted the upward turned legs of the Prince carefully out and, since his life was seriously endangered, guided his arm which was turned upward and back next to the head . . . Thereafter I turned . . . the rump of the child and . . . freed his right arm, which was turned upward as well, finally his head . . . carefully extracting the infant. The Prince was, as previously indicated by the weak and intermittent pulse rate in the umbilical cord . . . seemingly dead . . . but commenced breathing after the usual life saving attempts were made . . . ."

A recent article on the subject suggests that in dislodging the infant's arm and using it to rotate the body, Martin did cause the injury. The author of the article states, however, that the infant's "breech presentation complicated by nuchal arms [arms wrapped around the neck]" is the second "most difficult form of breech extraction . . . not an easy maneuver, and in less skilled hands, potentially disastrous" (William B. Ober, M.D., "Obstetrical Events That Shaped Western European History," *Yale Journal of Biology and Medicine* 65 (1992), p. 208).

125 "After careful . . . life": RA: ADD. U 34/2 (copy).

125 "so much": RA: Z 9/71, V to QV, 6/19/60.

125 "[S]ince it . . . died": RA: Z 63/116, Augusta to QV, 1/29/59.

125 "Then I . . . boy": RA: Z 63/108, Augusta, to QV, 1/27/59.

125 "Soon after . . . cheers": RA: Z 63/116, Augusta to QV, 1/29/59.

125 "rarely . . . country": RCP: Clark, pp. 195–96.

125 "God be . . . did": KHH: QV to V, 1/29/59.

126 "was observed . . . such": RA: Z 63/117, Sir James Clark to QV, 1/31/59.

126 "disastrous": RA: VIC ADD. U 34/3. Augustus Martin's answers to "malicious statements and accusations" aimed at his father, Eduard Martin.

126 "hovered for . . . death": Woodham-Smith, p. 513.

126 "You ask . . . Wegner": RA: Z 7/93, V to QV, 3/6/59.

127 "slight indications . . . birth": RA: Z 63/133, "Memorandum," by Dr. Wegner, 9/8/59.

127 "a horror . . . treated": RA: Z 29/58, V to QV, 12/11/75.

127 "We are . . . Fritzes": Corti 1, pp. 52–53.

127 "somewhat alarming": KHH: QV to V, 2/23/59.

127 "May our . . . place": RA: Z 2/10, V to PA, 3/5/59.

127 "Afterwards . . . speaking": RA: Z 7/88, V to QV, 3/3/59.

128 "flushed . . . care": RA: Z 7/91, Lady Bloomfield to QV, 3/5/59.

128 "I gather . . . through": Martin, Vol. IV, pp. 401–402.

128 "Papa . . . them": KHH: QV to V, 5/2/59.
128 "no adoration . . . child": KHH: QV to V, 3/16/59.
128 "I think . . . him": RA: Z 7/99, V to QV, 3/18/59.
129 "Your grandson . . . you": RA: Z 2/28, V to PA, 7/16/59.
129 "[H]e said . . . done": RA: Z 2/30, V to PA, 7/30/59..
129 "He does . . . sooner": RA: Z 9/4, V to QV, 12/12/59.
130 "animalic baths": RA: Z 63/133, "Memorandum," by Dr. Wegner, 9/8/59.
130 "He is . . . immensely": RA: Z 8/29, V to QV, 8/11/59.
130 "[T]he shoulders . . . child's": RA: Z 2/44, V to PA, 12/10/59.
130 "completely alone . . . self-assurance": Röhl, p. 45.
130 "I cannot . . . hereafter": RA: Z 15/15, V to QV, 4/28/63.
131 Willy's infirmity: Current authorities in child psychology would say that Willy's useless arm symbolized to his mother and female nursery attendants a lack of male sexuality (i.e., the stunted arm as a symbol of the penis). Children like Willy who are studied today usually have serious problems with gender identity. Willy's father's continual absences from the home would have pushed the child to identify even more with his mother.

Chapter Fourteen

132 *"At the . . . importance"*: Corti 1, p. 51.
132 "It is . . . then": Paget 1, p. 59.
133 "with the . . . knapsacks": Eyck, p. 43.
133 "Your anxiety . . . day": RA: Z 7/120, V to QV, 4/30/59.
133 "Wegner will . . . summer": RA: Z 7/107, V to QV, 4/4/59.
133 "Mama has . . . applauded!!!!!!!!!": Röhl, pp. 101–102.
133 "delightful intercourse . . . child": KHH: QV to V, 6/4/59.
133 "has grown . . . England": Corti 1, p. 56.
133 "I am . . . you": *Ibid.*, pp. 55–56.
134 "no longer . . . more": Röhl, p. 76.
134 "All is . . . French": RA: Z 8/6, V to QV, 6/16/59.
134 "dead silence": Paget 1, p. 59.
135 "We are . . . made": RA: Z 8/17, V to QV, 7/16/59.
135 "because they . . . possible": RA: Z 2/27, V to PA, 7/13/59.
135 "the immense . . . 'Unity' ": KHH: QV to V, 7/9/59.
135 "rather disagreeable scenes": RA: Z 2/19, V to PA, 5/3/59.
135 "too great . . . feelings": KHH: QV to V, 7/16/59.
135 "That I . . . such": RA: Z 8/19, V to QV, 7/20/59.
135 "not the . . . Europe": Corti 1, p. 58.
135 "itching to . . . French!": *Ibid.*, p. 56.
135 "I am . . . Austrians": RA: Z 8/22, V to QV, 7/29–30/59.
136 "a flood": RA: Z 8/8, V to QV, 6/21/59.
136 "waiters": RA: Z 2/24, V to PA, 6/25/59.
136 "I think . . . subject": KHH: QV to V, 7/6/59.
136 "please the family": RA: Z 8/11, V to QV, 6/30/59.
137 "I was . . . more": RA: Z 9/69, V to QV, 6/16/60.
137 "I am . . . offend": RA: Z 9/71, V to QV, 6/19/60.
137 "Yours are . . . magnificent": RA: Z 8/14, V to QV, 7/6/59.
137 "enormous suite": Paget 1, p. 59.
137 "[T]he noise . . . house": RA: Z 9/68, V to QV, 6/12/60.
138 "I think . . . presence": RA: Z 9/66, V to QV, 6/5/60.
138 "much easier": RA: Z 71/83, F to QV, 7/31/60.
138 "I do . . . Victorias": KHH: QV to V, 8/7/60.
138 "The Queen . . . me": RA: Z 9/85, V to QV, 8/10/60.
138 "ready to . . . faces": RA: Z 9/86, V to QV, 8/15/60.

CHAPTER FIFTEEN

139 *"The past . . . there"*: L. P. Hartley, prologue to *The Go-Between,* as cited in *The Oxford Book of Quotations,* pp. 242–43.

140 "notorious for . . . conduct": *Memoir,* p. 120.

140 "I only . . . progress": RA: Z 3/35, V to PA, 8/18/60.

141 "a fine . . . skin": RA: QVJ, 9/25/60.

141 "much better": RA: Z 290/46, QV to Duchess of Kent, 9/26/60.

141 "materially": Barkeley, p. 83.

141 "most important . . . delicate": Wemyss, Vol. I, p. 163.

141 "a great . . . insulting": RA: Z 3/43 *passim,* V to PA, 11/10/60.

142 "You can . . . us": RA: Z 3/46, V toPA, 11/23/60.

142 "How can . . . way!": RA: Z 5/54,V to QV, 4/13/58.

143 "I do . . . spoilt": RA: Z 10/28, V to QV, 12/21/60.

143 "her father . . . continually": RA: Z 8/54, V to QV, 9/29/59.

143 "I think . . . Alice": KHH: QV to V, 6/6/60.

143 "almost black": RA: Z 5/54, V to QV, 4/13/58.

144 "We three . . . truly": Paget 1, p. 133.

144 Princess Alexandra: Her proper title was still Princess Alexandra of Schleswig-Holstein-Sonderburg-Glücksburg, as her father was not yet King of Denmark, but Princess Alexandra of Denmark is used here for simplicity.

144 "the most . . . Princess": Paget 2, Vol. I, p. 139.

144 "I am . . . twitching": KHH: QV to V, 10/4/59.

144 "I do . . . taste": RA: Z 9/3, V to QV, 12/10/59.

144 "just the . . . admires": RA: Z 10/22, V to QV, 12/7/60.

144 "I never . . . it": RA: Z 10/25, V to QV, 12/17/60.

145 "[F]rom that . . . once": RA: Z 13/49, V to QV, 9/6/62.

145 "outrageously beautiful": Philip Magnus, *King Edward the Seventh,* p. 46.

145 "mother's . . . foolish": KHH: QV to V, 2/25/61.

145 "You know . . . safe": KHH: QV to V, 12/18/60.

145 "I am . . . person": RA: Z 10/67, V to QV, 3/11/61.

145 "I never . . . over": RA: Z 11/18, V to QV, 6/4/61.

145 "he had . . . much": RA: Z 12/16, V to QV, 9/26/61.

145 "certainly much . . . world": KHH: QV to V, 10/1/61.

145 "Bertie may . . . so": RA: Z 12/20, V to QV, 10/12/61.

CHAPTER SIXTEEN

147 *"There are . . . people"*: KHH: PA to WI, 3/12/61; also Martin, Vol. V, p. 314.

147 "We approached . . . her!": RA: Z 10/36, V to QV, 1/2/61.

148 "magnificent": Radziwill 1, p. 70.

148 "My day . . . meet": RA: Z 10/37, V to QV, 1/4/60.

148 "was an . . . positions": Philip Ziegler, *The Duchess of Dino,* p. 345.

149 "did not . . . in": RA: Z 10/37, V to QV, 1/4/61.

149 "very quick . . . early": KHH: QV to V, 1/5/61.

149 "Every day . . . pleasure": RA: Z 10/47, V to QV, 1/23/61.

150 "From his . . . affection": RA: Z 13/15, V to QV, 5/13/62.

150 "Allow me . . . day!": Corti 1, p. 70.

150 "You can . . . before": KHH: F to V, 8/25/61.

150 "If 'marriages . . . case": Corti 1, p. 71.

150 "breach of . . . respect": *Ibid.,* p. 65.

150 "Having found . . . Constitution": Wemyss, Vol. I, p. 231.

150 "bitter, aggressive . . . people": *Ibid.,* p. 66.

150 "serving . . . model": Martin, Vol. V, p. 313.

151 "The King . . . it": RA: Z 10/49, V to QV, 1/29/61.

151 "smile & . . . dreadful": RA: Z 4/3, V to PA, 1/25/61.

151 "advanced age . . . anything": Paul Wiegler, *William the First*, p. 198.

151 "[I]f there . . . line!": RA: Z 4/2, V to PA, 1/19/61.

151 "the best . . . delighted": RA: Z 4/2 *passim*, V to PA, 1/19/61.

151 "[I]f only . . . man": RA: Z 4/11, V to PA, 3/15/61.

152 "a welcome . . . sorrow": Stanley Weintraub, *Victoria*, pp. 289–90 *passim*.

152 "[I]ll natured . . . certainty": RA: Z 4/21, V to PA, 6/7/61.

152 "I cannot . . . l'infini": RA: Z 4/13, V to PA, 4/13/61.

152 "It is . . . her": Corti 1, p. 68.

153 "To our . . . Mission": RA: Z 12/20, V to QV, 10/12/61.

153 "It is . . . Berlin": RA: Z 12/22, V to QV, 10/18/61.

154 "regretted that . . . revolution!": RA: Z 4/33, V to PA, 10/26/61.

154 "I receive . . . God": Fulford 2, p. 359, n. 5.

154 "Her Royal . . . reality": Benson and Esher, Vol. III, p. 591, The Earl of Clarendon to QV, 11/5/61.

154 "exquisite grace . . . king": Martin, Vol. V, pp. 397–98.

CHAPTER SEVENTEEN

155 "[S]he not . . . father": Ernest II, Vol. III, p. 223.

155 "I ask . . . head?!": RA: Z 12/37, V to QV, 11/19/61.

155 "But how . . . disgrace": RA: Z 12/35, V to QV, 11/15/61.

156 "the poorest administrator": Gurney, p. 364.

156 "Here I . . . grey": RA: Z 12/37, V to QV, 11/19/61.

156 "It has . . . cheering": KHH: QV to V, 11/16/61.

156 "one of . . . London": Magnus, p. 51.

157 "which . . . life": Woodham-Smith, p. 536.

157 "on the . . . shudder": *Ibid.*, pp. 536–37.

157 "the greedy . . . profligacy": Woodham-Smith, p. 536.

157 "sad heart . . . more": Martin, Vol. V, p. 414.

157 "It would . . . dreadful!": Rhodes-James, p. 270.

158 "I am . . . rheumatism": Corti 1, p. 72.

158 "a cold . . . low": KHH: QV to V, 11/27/61.

158 "dear Papa . . . better!": KHH: QV to V, 11/30/61.

158 "3 days . . . night": KHH: QV to V, 12/6/61.

158 "Really the . . . news": RA: Z 12/44, V to QV, 12/8/61.

158 "I fear . . . amuse": RA: Z 12/43, V to QV, 12/7/61.

159 "almost all radicals": *Ibid.*

159 "The state . . . wrong": RA: Z 12/46, V to QV, 12/11/61.

159 "Don't be . . . days": KHH: QV to V, 12/7/61.

159 "Thank God . . . satisfactorily": KHH: QV to V, 12/10/61.

159 "The doctors . . . thin": KHH: QV to V, 12/11/61.

159 "Thank God . . . now": RA: Z 12/49, V to QV, 12/14/61.

159 "If only . . . one": Corti 1, p. 76.

159 "Why has . . . affection": RA: Z 12/50, V to QV, 12/15/61.

160 "[L]et us . . . good": RA: Z 12/51, V to QV, 12/17/61.

160 "I will . . . endeavours!": RA: Z 12/52, V to QV, 12/18/61.

160 "Yes, dearest . . . shudder!": KHH: QV to V, 1/15/62.

160 "I know . . . intentions": RA: Z 12/64, V to QV, 1/14/62.

161 "[L]ast night . . . misery!": RA: Z 12/53, V to QV, 12/21/61.

161 "alive and well": RA: Z 13/5, V to QV, 4/15/62.

161 "[H]ow admirably . . . life": KHH: QV to V, 6/11/62.

161 "dear darling . . . here!": RA: Z 12/54, V to QV, 12/23/61.

161 "Mama is . . . husband": Corti 1, p. 82.

161 "I feel . . . aspect!": RA: Z 12/56, V to QV, 12/26/61.

CHAPTER EIGHTEEN

163 *"[I]f an . . . docile"*: Fritz Stern, *The Failure of Illiberalism*, p. xvi.

163 "I have . . . all": RA: Z 13/37, V to QV, 7/19/62.

163 four political parties: This outline is taken largely from the political papers of Robert Morier, as collected by his daughter, Rosslyn Wemyss, pp. 172–77.

163 "a sort . . . provinces": *Ibid.*, pp. 175–76.

164 "entrusted with . . . Crown": *Ibid.*, p. 175.

164 "much-aligned minority": *Ibid.*, p. 173.

164 political parties: I have dropped designations like "New Prussian," "Old Prussian," and "Old Liberal" in the interests of simplification.

165 "dirty militiamen": Otto Pflanze, *Bismarck and the Development of Germany*, p. 159. (Note: This is the original paperback edition, published in 1962, which became Volume I of the subsequent three-volume hardcover edition, published in 1990.)

165 "state within . . . state": *Ibid.*, p. 164.

165 Statistics on the composition of the officer class are taken from Hajo Holborn's *A History of Modern Germany, 1840–1945*, p. 137; the figures on population and recruits are from Golo Mann's *A History of Germany Since 1789*, p. 254.

165 "intelligent conservative": John Keegan and Andrew Wheatcroft, *Who's Who in Military History*, p. 280.

165 "royal military cabinet": Holborn, p. 139. Much of this information on Roon, Manteuffel, and Prussian army reform comes from Holborn.

165 "Discipline, blind . . . familiarity": Michael Howard, *The Franco-Prussian War*, p. 20.

166 "school of . . . obedience": Pflanze, Vol. I, pp. 160–61 *passim*.

166 "spineless tactics": Holborn, p. 145.

166 "Rumour has . . . will": Corti 1, p. 83.

166 "For heaven's . . . now": KHH: V to F, 3/14/62.

167 "opposition to . . . King": KHH: F to V, 3/18/62.

167 "I hardly . . . heart": KHH: V to F, 3/20/62 *passim*.

167 "The reactionary . . . power": RA: Z 13/34, V to QV, 7/8/62.

167 "street by street": Pflanze, Vol. I, p. 165.

167 "oppositional . . . expressions": RA: Z 13/37, V to QV, 7/19/62.

167 "[Y]ou can . . . silence!": KHH: V to F, 3/20/62.

168 "a storm . . . him": RA: Z 13/48, V to QV, 9/3/62.

168 "I have . . . signature": Corti 1, pp. 92–93.

168 "constitute a . . . Crown": KHH: F to V, 9/19/62.

168 "If the . . . day": KHH: V to F, 9/20/62.

168 "poor broken . . . man": Van der Kiste, p. 71.

169 "resentful": Wiegler, p. 209.

169 "opposed to . . . man": KHH: F to V, 9/19/62.

169 "I have . . . Yes": Wiegler, pp. 209–10.

169 "not a . . . government": Bismarck, Vol. II, p. 58.

CHAPTER NINETEEN

170 *"The German . . . imagine"*: Pflanze, Vol. II, p. 32.

171 "good old . . . state": Eyck, p. 12.

171 "enormous and . . . gusto": James D. McCabe, Jr., *History of the War Between Germany and France*, p. 787.

171 "petty and tedious": Bismarck, Vol. I, p. 36.

171 "The Prussian . . . all": *Ibid.*, p. 14.

171 "wild . . . crazy": Pflanze, Vol. I, p. 53.

172 "tore the . . . reasonableness": Edward Crankshaw, *Bismarck*, p. 24.

172 "more in . . . dilemma": Henry A. Kissinger, "The White Revolutionary: Reflections on Bismarck," *Daedalus*, 97 (1968) (Kissinger 1), pp. 894–96.

172 "I think ... cleverness": A. J. P. Taylor, *Bismarck: The Man and the Statesman*, pp. 20–21.

172 "No one ... self-denial": Pflanze, Vol. II, p. 62.

172 "I believe ... King": *Ibid.*, p. 21.

173 "No one ... chance": Taylor, p. 23.

173 "not a ... capital": Pflanze, Vol. II, p. 63.

174 "If we ... anvil": *Ibid.*, p. 84. I am indebted to Pflanze for his explanation of Bismarck's actions, from which this is taken.

174 "The Prince ... Princess": Bismarck, Vol. I, p. 190.

174 "disease ... later": Eyck, p. 44.

174 "He thought ... annoyance": Crankshaw, p. 123.

175 "Take care ... says": Eyck, p. 53.

175 "My things ... highway": Pflanze, Vol. I, p. 155.

175 "a woman ... Russia": Princess Catherine Radziwill, *Germany Under Three Emperors* (Radziwill 3), p. 73.

175 "Since the ... letter": Crankshaw, pp. 123–24 *passim*.

176 "*Periculum in* ... out": Bismarck, Vol. II, p. 55.

176 "These Junkers ... eagles": Mann, p. 274.

176 "government ... affairs": Eyck, p. 58.

176 "disastrous": Corti 1, p. 96.

176 "People will ... enemy": Crankshaw, p. 132; and Alan Palmer, *Crowned Cousins* (Palmer 1), p. 140.

176 "a liar". ... ass: Eyck, p. 59.

176 "takes fright ... it": Taylor, p. 56.

176 "Germany ... blood": *Ibid* .

177 "racy excursions": Eyck, p. 59.

177 "I can ... tactics": Bismarck, Vol. II, pp. 75–77 *passim*.

Chapter Twenty

179 *"If the ... throne":* Frederick Holstein (Norman Rich and M. H. Fischer, eds.), *The Holstein Papers* (Holstein), Vol. II, p. 386.

179 "[H]e thinks ... opposition": RA: Z 13/27, V to QV, 6/17/62.

179 "You did ... ardent": KHH: QV to V, 11/28/62.

180 "like a ... thunder": Richard Hough, *Edward and Alexandra* (Hough 2), p. 80.

180 "much harm": RA: Z 12/19, V to QV, 10/7/61.

180 "he was ... Prussia": Roger Fulford, *Dearest Mama* (Fulford 3), p. 136, n. 1.

180 "The fine ... laugh": RA: Z 14/14, V to QV, 11/19/62.

180 "I am ... photographs": RA: Z 14/22, V to QV, 12/17/62.

181 "in strict incognito": RA: Z 14/20, V to QV, wire, 12/12/62.

181 "[O]h how ... miserable": RA: Z 14/19, V to QV, 12/11/62.

181 "I have ... again": KHH: QV to V, 12/17/62.

181 "of sorrow ... dreamt": RA: Z 14/23, V to QV, 12/20/62.

181 "We shall ... game": RA: Z 14/22, V to QV, 12/17/62.

182 "I tremble ... worry": KHH: QV to V, 1/6/63.

182 "since the ... still": Pflanze, Vol. I, p. 194.

182 "The King ... lead": RA: Z 14/35, V to QV, 1/31/63.

183 "As things ... cheaply": Corti 1, p. 101.

183 "chiefly ... rights": RA: Z 14/30, V to QV, 1/12?/63.

183 "Oh! if ... incomprehensible!": KHH: QV to V, 2/4/63.

183 "do all ... presence": KHH: QV to V, 2/11/63.

183 "a perfect monster": RA: Z 15/13, V to QV, 4/21/63.

183 "how exceedingly ... uninteresting": RA: Z 14/37, V to QV, 2/7/63.

183 "awfully cheered": Hough 2, p. 91.

184 "nothing else ... theirs": RA: Z 14/35, V to QV, 1/31/63.

184 "Such a ... boy!": Epton, p. 108.

184 "all kinds . . . result": Corti 1, p. 102.
184 "personal considerations . . . terrorizing": Pflanze, Vol. I, pp. 200–201. I am indebted to Otto Pflanze for this description of the measures taken by Bismarck at the time.
185 "in powder . . . difficulties!": RA: Z 15/18, V to QV, 5/11/63.

CHAPTER TWENTY-ONE

186 *"Prussia is . . . mouth"*: Karl Kraus, *"Die Fackel,"* in Peter Vinsittart, *Voices, 1870–1914,* p. 116.
186 "pitched battle": RA: Z 15/20, V to QV, 5/16/63.
186 liberal vs. conservative papers: based on figures quoted by Otto Pflanze, Vol. I, p. 202.
186 "virtual monopoly": Robert H. Keyserlingk, *Media Manipulation, the Press and Bismarck in Imperial Germany,* p. vi. I am indebted to Keyserlingk for most of this information on the Prussian press.
186 "dangerous to . . . emergency": Pflanze, Vol. I, p. 204.
187 "[F]eeling . . . disagreeable": RA: Z 15/27, V to QV, 5/30/63. Note: I have used the word "experience" to complete the Crown Princess's sentence, since she inadvertently omitted whatever word she wished to use.
187 "warning him . . . protest": RA: Z 15/28, V to QV, 6/1/63.
187 "so the . . . hope": Kollander, p. 65.
187 "must satisfy . . . king": *Ibid.,* p. 66.
187 "travelled all . . . anxiety": RA: Z 15/29, V to QV, 6/5/63.
187 "[P]eople . . . decree": Kollander, p. 68.
187 "We . . . King": RA: Z 15/29, V to QV, 6/5/63.
188 "I did . . . government": RA: Z 15/30, V to QV, 6/8/63.
188 "publicly known . . . theories": Pflanze, Vol. I, pp. 205–206, n. 41.
188 "noble and . . . sentiments": Bismarck, Vol. II, p. 112.
188 "I did . . . it": Eyck, p. 62.
188 "a sensation . . . abroad": Bismarck, Vol. II, pp. 112–13.
188 "furious letter . . . opinions": RA: Z 15/30, V to QV, 6/8/63.
188 "I realize . . . yours": Dorpalen, p. 13.
188 "impossible": RA: Z 15/30, V to QV, 6/8/63.
188 "If I . . . politics": Poschinger, p. 145.
188 "Your behaviour . . . father": KHH: WI to F, 6/10/63.
188 "the sympathy . . . latter": Bismarck, Vol. II, pp. 113–14.
189 "so much . . . other": *Ibid.,* p. 115.
189 "a regular inquisition": Palmer 1, p. 143.
189 "There is . . . clue?": Wemyss, pp. 342–43.
189 "The correspondence . . . things": KHH: QV to V, 8/5/63.
189 "graveyard stillness . . . government": Pflanze, Vol. I, p. 206.
190 "sort of . . . Eldorado": RA: Z 15/42, V to QV, 7/26/63.
190 "I have always . . . rest!": RA: Z 15/36, V to QV, 7/3/63.

CHAPTER TWENTY-TWO

192 *"A government . . . another"*: Eyck, p. 62.
192 "She is . . . well": KHH: QV to V, 6/24/63.
192 "And now . . . desolate!!": KHH: QV to V, 7/11/63.
192 "only comfort . . . pleasure": Corti 1, p. 108.
192 "[I]t does . . . Fritz": RA: Z 15/45, V to QV, 8/8/63.
192 "scenes . . . things": RA: Z 15/46, V to QV, 8/10/63.
192 "obedience . . . untenable": Pflanze, Vol. I, p. 208.
193 "Thirty reigning . . . refuse?": Taylor, p. 68.

193 "tore . . . door": Moritz Busch, *Bismarck: Some Secret Pages of History*, Vol. I, p. 131.
193 "The conflict . . . Austria": Corti 1, p. 110.
193 "horrid expression": Palmer 1, p. 144.
193 "so done . . . trembly": Fulford 2, p. 259, QV to V, 9/1/63. The original of this letter does not seem to be in the archives at Schloss Fasanerie (KHH) with the rest of Queen Victoria's letters to Vicky.
193 "made a . . . blame": Corti 1, p. 111.
194 "Repeated dissolutions . . . other": Pflanze, Vol. I, p. 208.
194 "[T]he King . . . scaffold": KHH: F to V, 9/3/63.
194 "[T]his abominable . . . England": Pflanze, Vol. I, p. 209.
194 "in order . . . destruction": The conversation is referred to in a letter from the Crown Prince to the Princess (KHH: F to V, 9/3/63). This translation is taken from three sources: the above letter, Pflanze, Vol. I, 208–209, and Corti 1, p. 112.
194 "A momentous . . . ministry": Bismarck, Vol. II, p. 118.
194 "I consider . . . spirits!": KHH: F to V, 9/16/63.
194 "My poor . . . nonsense": KHH: V to F, 9/4/63.
195 "as a . . . sacred?": Bismarck, Vol. II, pp. 121–23.
195 "I asked . . . shoulder": *Ibid.*, p. 119.
195 "When I . . . thundercloud": Pflanze, Vol. I, p. 209.
195 "I have . . . law": Corti 1, p. 113.
195 "Now begins . . . swindle": Pflanze, Vol. I, p. 209.
196 "The Prussian . . . elimination": *Ibid.*, p. 212. This information on the elections is taken from Pflanze.
196 "I am . . . anxieties": KHH: QV to V, 9/8/63.
196 "[A]s you . . . says": KHH: QV to V, 11/4/63.
196 "What am . . . passed!": RA: Z 16/3, V to QV, 12/25/63.
197 "How you . . . sad!": KHH: QV to V, 12/30/63.
197 "fully realized . . . state": Bismarck, Vol. II, p. 127.

Chapter Twenty-three

201 *"Only three . . . it"*: Eyck, pp. 77–78.
201 "a steady . . . measures": Pflanze, Vol. I, p. 213.
203 "Oh! God . . . dreadful!": George Earle Buckle, ed., *The Letters of Queen Victoria*, Second Series, Vol. I, 1862–1869, p. 117, QV to KL, 11/19/63.
203 "Schleswig is . . . heirs": Martin, Vol. II, p. 315.
203 "the Duchies . . . Papa": Giles St. Aubyn, *Edward VII*, pp. 91–92.
203 "any violent . . . contend": *Ibid.*, p. 90.
204 "Allow me . . . interests": (Bolitho 2), p. 144, QV to WI, 12/14/63.
204 "all our . . . agreeable": RA: Z 16/4, V to QV, 12/29/63.
204 "web of lies": Corti 1, p. 119.
204 "The more . . . here!": RA: Z 16/5, V to QV, 1/1/64.
205 "King Christian . . . all": RA: Z 16/6, V to QV, 1/5/64 *passim*.
205 "proudest . . . diplomatic intrigues": Busch, Vol. I, p. 130.
206 "mission were . . . nature": KHH: V to F, 1/31/64.
206 "I do not . . . him!": RA: Z 16/10, V to QV, 1/20/64.
206 "I can . . . stubbornness": Corti 1, p. 123.
207 "That you . . . preserved": *Ibid.*, pp. 126–27.
207 "What Orders . . . ashamed": *Ibid.*, p. 125.
207 "She thought . . . it": *Ibid.*, p. 127.
207 "I am . . . effect": *Ibid.*, p. 131.
207 "The sly . . . later on": *Ibid.*, pp. 128–29.
208 The first Crown Council after the accession of Christian IX: There is some question about the date. Pflanze says it did not take place until February 3, 1864, two days after the invasion of Schleswig. Bismarck says it was held "immediately after the

death" of the Danish King, which occurred on November 15, 1863; Bismarck also claims that the Crown Prince, who was in England until December 23, was present and "raised his hands to heaven as if he doubted my sanity." Since Bismarck was prone to revise history to his own benefit, the Pflanze date is probably correct. In either case, the Crown Prince could not have been present, since he left for the front on January 30, 1864 (Pflanze, Vol. I, p. 246, and Bismarck, Vol. II, p. 188).

208   "every one . . . state": Bismarck, Vol. II, p. 188.
208   "When the . . . later": KHH: V to F, 4/16/64.
208   "complete separation . . . succession": Pflanze, Vol. I, p. 248. This and other explanations of Bismarck's diplomatic machinations are taken primarily from Pflanze.

CHAPTER TWENTY-FOUR

210   *"Bismarck espouses . . . principle"*: KHH: V to F, 3/14/62.
210   "I . . . here": KHH: V to F, 3/3/64.
210   "You know . . . again": KHH: QV to V, 1/30/64.
210   "very proud . . . danger": RA: Z 16/14 *passim*, V to QV, 2/3/64.
210   "You are . . . did!": KHH: QV to V, 2/6/64.
210   "I had . . . it!": KHH: QV to V, 2/3/64.
210   "Your Mama . . . scenes": Corti 1, p. 122.
211   "grief for . . . Palmerston": *Ibid.*
211   "I think . . . again": RA: Z 16/19, V to QV, 2/22/64.
211   "I cannot . . . best!": KHH: QV to V, 2/24/64 *passim*.
211   "as he . . . name": RA: Z 16/43, V to QV, 5/4/64.
211   "[I]t makes . . . much": RA: Z 16/42, V to QV, 4/30/64.
212   "in the . . . world!": KHH: QV to V, 5/10/65.
212   "Indeed I . . . love!": RA: Z 16/45, V to QV, 5/16/64.
212   "He is . . . Carl": RA: Z 16/47, V to QV, 5/20/64.
212   "arch-spy . . . Kreuzzeitung": Corti 1, p. 133.
212   "the democrat . . . family": Elisabeth and Hélène Potocka, *Souvenirs de la Princesse Antoine Radziwill*, p. 64.
212   "Danish hobby-horse": Wemyss, Vol. I, p. 371.
212   "[A]fter all . . . Englishwoman": Corti 1, p. 132.
212   "The family . . . improved": Buckle, Second Series, Vol. I, pp. 188–89, V to QV, 5/11/64.
213   "the people's . . . right": KHH: V to F, 3/16/64.
213   "If your . . . own": Bolitho 2, p. 150, QV to WI, 5/28/64.
213   "he had . . . them": Pflanze, Vol. I, p. 251.
213   "would not . . . nerves": RA: Z 16/55, V to QV, 6/14/64.
214   "as the . . . mind": RA: Z 16/61, V to QV, 7/8/64.
214   "This summer . . . strides": KHH: V to F, 3/31/64.
215   "I am . . . approve": RA: Y 43/125, Feodora to QV, 9/26/64.
215   "My little . . . occupation": RA: Add. C 26/27, V to Caroline Barrington, 11/7/64.
215   "disliked the . . . me": RA: Add. U 143. Reel 3, QV to Alice, 12/10/64.
215   "very much . . . recover": *Memoir*, p. 199.
215   "[I]t is . . . it?": RA: Add. MSS. U 143, Reel 3, QV to Alice, 1/9/65.
216   "very self-willed . . . selfish": RA: Add. U 143, Reel 3, QV to Alice, 2/22/65.
216   "I am . . . M. de B.": RA: Z 17/4, V to QV, 11/9/64.
216   "I did . . . him": Corti 1, p. 138.

CHAPTER TWENTY-FIVE

217   *"For heaven's . . . sacrifice"*: Henry Kissinger, *Diplomacy*, (Kissinger 2), p. 129.
217   "I am . . . Duchies!": RA: Z 17/7, V to QV, 11/20/64.
218   "ungrateful & mean": RA: Z 17/88, V to QV, 9/11/65.
218   "sooner or later": Pflanze, Vol. I, p. 256.

218 "We cannot . . . war": Poschinger, pp. 221–22.
218 "German civil war": Eyck, p. 99.
219 "The German . . . power": Pflanze, Vol. I, p. 178 *passim*.
219 "an overwhelming . . . dissensions": Poschinger, pp. 225–28.
220 "Two centuries . . . initiative": Pflanze, Vol. I, p. 265.
220 "mildly critical . . . commissar": *Ibid.*, p. 277.
220 "one of . . . jurisdiction": Eyck, p. 110.
220 "For those . . . Prussia": Pflanze, Vol. I, p. 278. I am indebted to Pflanze for this information on the repression of the opposition.
220 "I have . . . them": *Ibid.*, p. 186.
220 "The middle . . . everywhere": RA: Z 17/76, V to QV, 7/4/65.
221 "hope for . . . worst": RA: Z 17/79, V to QV, 7/15/65.
221 "If you . . . least!": RA: Z 17/83, V to QV, 8/1/65.
221 "the most . . . it": Eyck, pp. 106–107. This must be a paraphrase of Clarendon's statement, as it is not in quotation marks in Eyck.
221 "Every principle . . . aside": Buckle, Second Series, Vol. I, p. 277, General Grey to Earl Russell, 9/9/65.
221 "The Gastein . . . law": Eyck, pp. 106–107.
221 "If . . . negotiation": Poschinger, pp. 229–30.
222 "stupefied . . . partition": *Ibid.*, p. 230.
222 "comes and . . . much": RA: Z 17/57, V to QV, 4/18/65.
222 "You know . . . position": KHH: QV to V, 9/11/65.
223 "poor nerves . . . merriment": KHH: QV to V, 6/21/65.
223 "Bertie and . . . hosts": RA: Z 17/96, V to QV, 11/7/65.
223 "has much . . . heart": RA: Z 18/7, V to QV, 12/19/65.
223 "Words cannot . . . you": KHH: QV to V, 12/5/65.
223 "I miss . . . it": RA: Z 18/2, V to QV, 12/7/65.

     CHAPTER TWENTY-SIX
225 *"Prussia has . . . itself"*: Quoted in Kissinger 1, p. 903.
225 "everwhere in . . . include": Poschinger, pp. 258–59.
225 "democratic, revolutionary": *Ibid.*, p. 261.
225 "either into . . . powder": Lord Augustus Loftus, *Diplomatic Reminiscences*, Second Series, Vol. I, p. 39 *passim*.
226 "natural . . . justified": Pflanze, Vol. I, p. 284.
226 "more definite guarantees": *Ibid.*, p. 292.
226 "We should . . . it": Loftus, Vol. I, p. 53.
226 "bad nights . . . it [war]": RA: Z 18/32, V to QV, 3/9/66.
226 "he may . . . generals": RA: Z 18/30, V to QV, 3/3/66.
226 "anxious to . . . war": RA: Z 18/34, V to QV, 3/16/66.
226 "vanished under . . . Bismarck": Loftus, Vol. I, p. 50.
227 "[I]t is . . . People": Buckle, Second Series, Vol. I, pp. 310–11, QV to F, 3/28/66.
227 repeating confidential conversations: The origin of Queen Victoria's mediation efforts was a conversation that took place between King Wilhelm and the English Ambassador to Berlin, Lord Augustus Loftus, at a large dinner given by Bismarck —the contents of which Bismarck conveyed to the French, thus, in Victoria's words, "abusing his master's confidence in order to defeat the pacific views of the King" (Buckle, Second Series, Vol. I, p . 311; also see Loftus, Vol. I, pp. 46–48, and Roger Fulford, *Your Dear Letter* (Fulford 4), p. 62, n. 1.
227 "Beloved Brother . . . alone": Buckle, Second Series, Vol. II, p. 317, QV to WI, 4/10/66.
227 "quite sad . . . contains": RA: Z 18/44, V to QV, 5/1/66.
227 "to the lawless . . . helplessness": Dorpalen, p. 17.
227 "Unconcerned . . . very amiable": RA: Z 18/40, V to QV, 4/6/66.
227 "The King . . . amiability": Loftus, Vol. I, p. 49.

227 "NO ONE": Buckle, Second series, Vol. I, p. 312, Alexandrine to QV, 3/28/66.
227 "by no . . . displeasing": *Ibid.*, p. 314, the Earl of Clarendon to QV, 3/31/66.
228 "destroyed the . . . Confederation": Eyck, p. 114.
228 "I have . . . proud": *Ibid.*, p. 115.
229 "I am . . . that": KHH: QV to V, 4/25/66.
229 last-minute attempts: War was nearly averted in one instance by some shrewd diplomacy on the part of Austria herself, but this was thwarted by the unstoppable race toward mobilization. In another attempt, two aristocratic brothers named Gablentz drafted a compromise giving Prussia territory and Austria financial compensation, but this was abandoned as a result of opposition from the smaller German states.
229 "last mistress . . . man": Pflanze, Vol. I, p. 301.
229 "How bad . . . are!": Eyck, p. 120.
229 "the consequences . . . all": RA: Z 18/46, V to QV, 5/9/66.
230 "I see . . . upon": RA: Z 18/54, V to QV, 6/2/66.
230 "Now it . . . King!": Eyck, p. 122.

CHAPTER TWENTY-SEVEN

231 *"Genius is . . . stop":* Taylor, p. 265.
231 "We appeal . . . narrow-mindedness": Pflanze, Vol. I, pp. 295–96.
231 "At this . . . die": Loftus, Vol. I, p. 60.
232 "Every new . . . advantage": Howard, p. 2.
232 "eminence . . . commander": Poschinger, p. 270.
232 "I like . . . him": Colonel Charles Walker, *Days of a Soldier's Life*, pp. 228–29.
232 "possessed . . . leader": Poschinger, pp. 254–55.
233 "Well, then . . . troops": *Ibid.*, p. 254.
233 "We know . . . necessary": Kollander, p. 118.
233 "You think . . . experience": Corti 1, p. 152.
234 "Your Majesty . . . comes": Walker, p. 254.
234 "[T]he honour . . . decision": *Ibid.*, pp. 233–34 *passim*.
234 "Thanks to . . . embraces": *Ibid.*, p. 231 *passim*.
234 "The future . . . straw!": Poschinger, p. 287. This anecdote, which comes third hand from the diary of Theodor von Bernhardi, does not claim to reproduce Napoleon's exact wording.
234 "War is . . . preparing": Corti 1, p. 152.
234 "Darling husband . . . won": *Ibid.*, p. 153.
235 "If we . . . neighbours": Eyck, pp. 132–33.
235 "Your Royal . . . other": Corti 1, p. 154.
235 "I must . . . them": *Ibid.*, p. 155.
235 "out of . . . consented": Bismarck, Vol. II, pp. 232–33.
235 "Inasmuch as . . . peace": *Ibid.*, p. 233. Bismarck did not say that these were the King's exact words, but rather "something to this effect."
236 "The Emperor . . . war": Eyck, p. 129.
237 "I have . . . All!": Pflanze, Vol. I, p. 310.

CHAPTER TWENTY-EIGHT

238 *"Prussia must . . . Prussia":* Pflanze, Vol. II, p. 3.
238 "the hardest trial": RA: Z 19/19, V to QV, 11/14/66.
238 "A little . . . off": RA: Z 18/63, V to QV, 6/30/66.
238 "most frightful convulsions": RA: Z 18/73, V to QV, 7/31/66.
238 "Oh to . . . day!": RA: Z 18/62, V to QV, 6/26/66.
238 "I am . . . post": Kollander, p. 117.
238 "In you . . . uppermost": *Ibid.*, p. 118.

239 "I feel . . . yet": RA: Z 18/64, V to QV, 7/2/66.
239 "wearying": RA: Z 18/68, V to QV, 7/16/66.
239 "that little . . . agony": RA: Z 18/69, V to QV, 7/20/66.
239 "house & . . . all": RA: Z 18/70, V to QV, 7/23/66.
239 "[I]t is . . . husband": KHH: QV to V, 7/28/66.
239 "lying . . . hand": Lady Anne Macdonell, *Reminiscences of Diplomatic Life*, p. 125.
240 "on every . . . countrymen": RA: Z 18/71, V to QV, 7/25/66.
240 "What do . . . them": RA: Z 18/66, V to QV, 7/9/66.
240 "not fair . . . glory": RA: Z 18/69, V to QV, 7/20/66.
240 "as fine . . . through": Poschinger, p. 275.
240 "He is . . . possible": RA: Z 18/76, V to QV, 8/10/66.
240 "my hideous self": RA: Z 18/68, V to QV, 7/16/66.
240 "as if . . . off!": RA: Z 18/77, V to QV, 8/13/66.
241 "[T]he universal . . . heart": RA: Z 19/6, V to QV, 9/22/66.
241 "I am not . . . miscalculations": RA: Z 19/6, V to QV, 9/22/66 *passim*.
241 "Only under . . . shock": Pflanze, Vol. I, p. 309.
241 "I remain . . . despotism": RA: Z 18/75, V to QV, 8/5/66.
242 "The only . . . policy": Corti 1, p. 157.
242 "is by . . . do": RA: Z 19/8, V to QV, 9/28/66.
243 "as apparently . . . sources": Keyserlingk, pp. 142–43.
244 "unspeakably miserable": Eyck, p. 135. This information about Frankfurt is taken from Eyck.
244 The Prussian . . . home": RA: Z 19/3, V to QV, 9/11/66.
245 "[Y]ou know . . . happen": RA: Z 19/17, V to QV, 11/3/66.
245 "very unpleasant . . . years": Corti 1, p. 158.
245 "A young . . . all": *Ibid.*, p. 159.
246 "Oh how . . . that": RA: Z 19/15, V to QV, 10/23/66.

CHAPTER TWENTY-NINE

247 *"The trophies . . . success"*: Pflanze, Vol. I, p. 327.
248 "delayed growth . . . power": *Ibid.*, p. 326.
248 "expansion of Prussia": Kollander, p. 124.
248 "I have . . . disappointed": RA: Z 19/74, V to QV, 3/26/67.
248 "To be . . . wait": Dorpalen, pp. 18–19.
249 "The French . . . Germany": Pflanze, p. 375.
250 "sense of honor": *Ibid.*, p. 380.
250 "People are . . . once": RA: Z 19/75, V to QV, 4/2/67.
250 "The population . . . anti-Prussian": Pflanze, Vol. I, p. 376.
250 "not to . . . France": RA: Z 20/1, V to QV, 4/27/67.
251 "I do . . . nothing": RA: Z 19/85, V to QV, 4/20/67. (Note: "Reduced" is written "not reduced" in the original, but this was clearly an error.)
251 "surprised . . . difficulty": KHH: QV to V, 4/24/67.
251 "the world . . . war": Bolitho 2, pp. 161–62, QV to WI, 4/22/67.
251 "encouraged": RA: Z 20/1, V to QV, 4/27/67.
251 "admiration for . . . likely": RA: Z 20/3 *passim*, V to QV, 4/27/67.
251 "quite delighted . . . war": KHH: QV to V, 5/15/67.
252 "half closed . . . expression": Burchell, p. 130.
252 "suffocation . . . prostitutes": Wiegler, p. 279.
252 "I cannot . . . taste": RA: Z 20/10, V to QV, 5/?/67 (sometime during the last week of May).
252 "looking so pretty": RA: Z 20/12, V to QV, 6/5/67.
253 "very hot . . . shops": RA: Z 20/11, V to QV, 6/1/67.
253 "the charming . . . knew' ": RA: Z 20/13, V to QV, 6/10/67.
253 "The King's . . . gratified him": RA: Z 20/12, V to QV, 6/5/67.

253 "like a . . . holiday": RA: Z 20/13, V to QV, 6/10/67.
253 "Dear Vicky . . . her": Alice, Grand Duchess of Hesse, *Letters to Her Majesty the Queen*, p. 167.
253 "distressed . . . loss": KHH: QV to V, 5/18/67.

CHAPTER THIRTY
255 *"I love . . . happiness"*: RA: Z 19/51, V to QV, 2/2/67.
255 "Long live . . . year": Poschinger, p. 310.
255 "surprised . . . possible": *Ibid.*, p. 308.
255 "The Prince . . . courtesy": *Ibid.*, p. 306.
256 "These Prussians . . . everything": *Ibid.*, p. 309.
256 "You know . . . power": RA: Z 21/29, V to QV, 4/10/68.
256 "conquetterie . . . Rome": KHH: QV to V, 8/14/69.
256 "gives way completely": RA: Z 23/68, V to QV, 8/17/69.
256 "has not . . . event": RA: Z 20/78, V to QV, 12/23/67.
256 "These years . . . bear": RA: Z 21/8, V to QV, 1/25/68.
256 "People are . . . 3rd": RA: Z 20/52, V to QV, 10/19/67.
256 "We should . . . us": RA: Z 20/59, V to QV, 11/6/67.
256 "get softer . . . with": RA: Z 19/5, V to QV, 9/17/66.
257 "The Queen . . . relief": RA: Z 21/38, V to QV, 5/12/68.
257 "small . . . dullness": Princess Catherine Radziwill, *Memories of Forty Years* (Radziwill 4), pp. 71–72.
257 "The plates . . . fond": *Ibid.*, p. 65.
257 "[T]here is . . . provoking": RA: S 9/44, Madeleine Blücher to QV, 12/19/67.
257 "I think . . . stay": RA: Z 22/35, V to QV, 11/2/68.
258 "As regards . . . everywhere": Bolitho 2, p. 165, QV to WI, 12/27/68.
258 "marvellously well-read . . . benevolence": Poschinger, pp. 201–12.
258 "The stories . . . discouraged": RA: Z 23/8, V to QV, 1/16/69.
258 "detested Germans . . . health": RA: Z 23/6, V to QV, 1/12/69.
259 "Dearest Bertie . . . even": RA: Z 23/9, V to QV, 1/20/69.
259 "how the . . . Rose": Walker, p . 269.
259 "I thank . . . handsome": RA: Z 23/10, V to QV, 1/23/69.
259 "very anxious": RA: Z 23/71, V to QV, 8/28/69.
260 "words of . . . friendship": Van der Kiste, p. 107.
261 "awful and disgusting": RA: Z 25/77, V to QV, 5/18/71.
261 "[I]t does . . . [cows]": RA: Add. Reel 3, U 143, QV to Alice 10/14/64.
261 "the ugly . . . myself)": RA: Z 17/18, V to QV, 12/25/64.
261 "so amiably . . . has": RA: Z 19/57, V to QV, 2/13/67.
261 "very well": RA: Z 24/24, V to QV, 1/1/70.
263 "of genius": Keegan and Wheatcroft, p. 223.
263 "We don't . . . Prussian": Pflanze, Vol. I, p. 408.
263 "very kind . . . civil": RA: Z 24/24, V to QV, 1/1/70.
263 "a military . . . world": Keegan and Wheatcroft, p. 223.

CHAPTER THIRTY-ONE
264 *"Hatred of . . . nation"*: Pflanze, Vol. I, p. 236.
264 "shocked . . . vice": RA: Z 22/24, V to QV, 10/6/68.
264 "The poor . . . incredible": KHH: QV to V, 10/10/68.
265 "utterly against . . . affair": Pflanze, Vol. I, p. 441.
265 "Germany's . . . Charles V": *Ibid.*
266 "Reliable support . . . expected!": Crankshaw, p. 260.
266 "Bismarck is . . . serious": RA: Z 24/49, V to QV, 4/26/70.
266 "most profoundly secret": RA: Z 24/38, V to QV, 3/12/70.
266 "You will . . . up": RA: Z 24/49, V to QV, 4/26/70.

266 "no doubt . . . differently": Pflanze, Vol. I, p. 442.

266 "I have . . . inclination": Crankshaw, p. 261.

266 "It is . . . attack": Howard, p. 50. The validity of the document from which this quote is taken is questioned by Otto Pflanze in *Bismarck and the Unification of Germany*, Vol. I, pp. 446–47, n. 43.

267 "I fear . . . government": RA: Z 24/68, V to QV, 7/6/70.

267 "so far . . . weakness": Howard, p. 51.

267 "The newspapers . . . possible": Pflanze, Vol. I, p. 452.

267 "I think . . . this": RA: Z 24/69, V to QV, 7/8/70.

268 "[T]hank goodness . . . circumstances": RA: Z 24/70, V to QV, 7/13/70.

268 "insufficient . . . concession": Pflanze, Vol. I, p. 455.

268 "Yes, that . . . do": *Ibid.*, p. 456. There is another, unlikely, version of the Ems dispatch story, told by Colonel (later General) Charles Walker, the British military attaché, who heard it from the Minister of the Interior, Count Botho zu Eulenburg. In this version, Bismarck, Roon, and Eulenburg dined together and Bismarck, who "appears to have had no inclination for war," was convinced to go to war by Moltke's "*urging* and assurance that there never was a better opportunity, that the army could be mobilised in thirteen days [it took sixteen], and that he had no doubts of the result." See Walker, p. 376.

268 "the most faithful": Fritz Stern, *Gold and Iron*, (Stern 2) p. 277.

268 "Down with . . . face": Pflanze, Vol. I, p. 456.

269 "our freedom . . . conquerors": *Ibid.*, p. 469–70.

269 "feverish dream . . . etiquette": RA: I 63/79, Lord Granville to QV, 7/15/70.

269 "Bismarck . . . enemy": RA: Z 33/20, V to QV, 7/5/79.

269 "violent headache . . . terribly": RA: Z 24/70, V to QV, 7/13/70.

269 "a serious turn": Friedrich III of Prussia, *The War Diary* (FIII), p. 4.

269 "are well . . . us": RA: Z 24/70, V to QV, 7/13/70.

270 "making our . . . supposed": FIII, p. 6.

270 "shoulder to . . . again": *Ibid.*, pp. 5–6.

270 "All hope . . . everywhere": RA: Z 24/71, V to QV, 7/16/70.

271 "I don't . . . ever": KHH: QV to V, 8/5/70.

271 "forbidden France . . . her": *Memoir*, p. 229..

271 "The feeling . . . disadvantages": RA: Z 24/74, V to QV, 7/25/70.

271 "frantic . . . partiality": RA: Z 25/1 *passim*, V to QV, 8/1/70.

271 "looked on . . . eyes": RA: Z 25/2, V to QV, 8/4/70.

271 "clear and . . . ill": Walker, p. 281.

271 "Words are . . . feel?": KHH: QV to V, 7/20/70.

272 "[N]o one . . . control": FIII, p. 7.

272 "In many . . . Germans": *Ibid.*, p. 10.

272 "ill disposed . . . school": Howard, p. 60.

272 "reserve force": FIII, p. 10.

272 "It is . . . Fritz!": RA: Z 24/73, V to QV, 7/22/70.

272 "hardest . . . fulfill": Walker, p. 279.

272 "He described . . . hands' ": *Ibid.*, p. 270–71.

272 "The thought . . . again!": RA: Z 24/74, V to QV, 7/25/70.

CHAPTER THIRTY-TWO

273 *"All the . . . babies"*: Vansittart, p. 39.

273 "I never . . . shoes": Walker, p. 309.

273 "still customary . . . him!": FIII, p. 13.

273 "a brilliantly . . . heights": Walker, pp. 290–91.

274 "God be . . . enhanced": FIII, pp. 22–26.

274 "almost nonchalantly . . . everywhere": Poschinger, p. 320.

274 "I detest . . . lot": Gustav Freytag, *The Crown Prince and the Imperial Crown*, p. 14.

274   "In a . . . it": Poschinger, p. 322.
274   "The Crown . . . good-fellowship": *Ibid.*, p. 326.
274   "Pray say . . . Prince": Walker, p. 297.
275   "The Battle . . . effect": RA: Z 25/4, V to QV, 8/9/70.
275   "slow understanding . . . leader": Alfred von Waldersee, *A Field-Marshal's Memoirs*, pp. 83–84.
275   "horrid blunder . . . force": Walker, p. 311.
275   "headstrong conduct": Keegan and Wheatcroft, p. 130.
275   *"Bayard sans . . . reproche"*: FIII, p. 69.
275   "Are you . . . Charles?": *Ibid.*, p. 45.
275   "I see . . . avoided": *Ibid.*, p. 118.
276   "monarchical jealousy": Poschinger, p. 397.
276   "a prominent part": *Ibid.*, p. 323.
276   "[E]verywhere . . . prisoners": *Ibid.*, p. 89.
276   "I saw . . . earth": Walker, p. 315.
276   "which alone . . . possible": Poschinger, p. 325.
276   "My dear . . . Napoleon": FIII, p. 92.
276   "threw . . . gratitude": *Ibid.*, pp. 93–94.
277   "gallant Army . . . exploits": *Ibid.*, p. 173.
277   "At last": *Ibid.*, p. 182.
277   "the Prince Field-Marshal": *Ibid.*, p. 22.
277   "the humiliation": *Ibid.*, p. 97.
277   "lacked . . . distinguished": *Ibid.*, p. 99.
277   "I cannot . . . service": *Ibid.*, p. 100.
277   "rich liveries . . . racecourse": *Ibid.*, p. 98.
277   "Poor Emperor . . . to": RA: Z 25/13, V to QV, 9/6/70.
277   "judgment from heaven": KHH: QV to V, 8/22/70.
277   "a just . . . wishes!": KHH: QV to V, 8/26/70.
278   "It is . . . thought": RA: Z 25/13, V to QV, 9/6/70.
278   "Your 2 . . . fall": KHH: QV to V, 9/17/70.
278   "so right . . . individuals": RA: Z 25/14, V to QV, 9/12/70.
278   "feel . . . down": Pflanze, Vol. I, pp. 472–73.
279   "Germany is . . . posts": R. Scott Stevenson, *Morell Mackenzie*, p. 59.
279   "Naturally our . . . them": FIII, p. 167.
279   "The Crown . . . occupation": Poschinger, p. 350.
280   "copiously . . . clarity": *Ibid.*, p. 199.
280   "until Alsace . . . ourselves": *Ibid.*, pp. 475–77.
281   "extremely averse": Walker, p. 301.
281   "annexation . . . made": FIII, p. 117.
281   "Voices are . . . hazard": RA: Z 25/13, V to QV, 9/6/70.
281   "Apparently . . . spot": FIII, pp. 202–203.
281   "In Berlin . . . openly": *Ibid.*, p. 248.
281   "The assertion . . . freemasons": Busch, Vol. I, pp. 249–51.
282   "Everything has . . . conscience": FIII, pp. 239–40.

Chapter Thirty-three

283   *"There is . . . justify"*: Anton Chekhov, *The Notebooks of Anton Chekhov,* translated by S. S. Koteliansky and Leonard Woolf (The Hogarth Press, London, 1967), p. 61.
283   "large . . . women": RA: Z 25/1, V to QV, 8/1/70.
283   "If wars . . . horrors": RA: Z 23/40, V to QV, 4/24/69.
283   "difficulty . . . anything": KHH: QV to V, 8/1/70.
283   "I know . . . enemy": RA: Z 25/2, V to QV, 8/4/70.
283   "some old . . . oilcloth": KHH: QV to V, 8/1/70.
283   "I hear . . . this": RA: Z 25/5, V to QV, 8/9/70.

284   "My wife . . . rejected!": FIII, p. 70.
284   "I am . . . description": RA: Z 25/13, V to QV, 9/6/70.
284   "I returned . . . done": RA: Z 25/18, V to QV, 9/30/70.
284   "properly appreciated . . . knowledge": FIII, p. 115.
284   "It gives . . . reply": *Ibid.*, pp. 147–48.
284   "My mother-in-law . . . children": RA: Z 25/21, V to QV, 10/9/70.
285   "very kind . . . education": RA: Z 25/22, V to QV, 10/13/70.
285   "genuine . . . affection": FIII, p . 201.
285   "I think . . . of": RA: Z 25/41, V to QV, 1/7/71.
285   "[I]t is . . . article": RA: Z 25/33, V to QV, 12/9/70.
285   "urgent and indispensable": FIII, p. 114.
286   "a self-contained . . . married": Eyck, p. 178.
286   "perhaps . . . Germany": Radziwill 3, p. 99.
286   "The Crown . . . madness": Pflanze, Vol. I, p. 491.
286   "re-establish . . . dignity": *Ibid.*, p. 492.
286   "President": *Ibid.*, p. 267.
286   "Delivering . . . longings": Ladislas Farago and Andrew Sinclair, *Royal Web*,
        p. 195.
287   "in the . . . Wilhelm": FIII, p. 272.
287   "I have . . . supplanted": Crankshaw, p. 295; "I cannot . . . supplanted!": FIII,
        p. 279, n. 3.
287   "so averse . . . done!": RA: Z 25/45, V to QV, 1/20/71.
287   "I have . . . significance": FIII, p. 273.
287   "I am . . . and I": KHH: F to V, 8/27/72.
287   "Although tomorrow . . . men": *Ibid.*
288   "Everyone is . . . large": RA: Z 25/34, V to QV, 12/6/70.
288   "invented by . . . correspondent": RA: Z 25/51, V to QV, 2/7/71.
288   "whole non-German world": FIII, p. 314.
288   "entirely destroyed . . . conditions": Pflanze, Vol. II, p. 247.
288   "two great . . . nations": Fulford 4, p. 320, n. 1.
288   "unconcealed sympathy": RA: Z 25/52, V to QV, 2/10/71.
288   "[T]he excitement . . . fury": *Ibid.*
288   "The feeling . . . people": KHH: QV to V, 3/1/71 *passim.*
289   "we Germans . . . hated": RA: Z 25/54, V to QV, 2/15/71.
289   "It was . . . poor prince": Pflanze, Vol. II, p. 33.
289   "He no . . . diplomatists": Prince Chlodwig Hohenlohe-Schillingsfürst, *Memoirs,*
        Vol. II, p. 53.
289   "The next . . . out": RA: Z 25/61, V to QV, 3/18/71.
289   "tried him . . . campaign": RA: Z 25/63, V to QV, 3/24/71.
289   "swarm of greats": RA: Z 25/85, V to QV, 6/20/71.
289   "Germania receiving . . . Broadway": Pflanze, Vol. II, p. xi.
290   "positively broiling . . . saddle": FIII, pp. 336–37.
290   "the greatest . . . seen": RA: Z 25/84, V to QV, 6/17/71.
290   "sat his . . . through": FIII, p . 337.
290   "Wilhelmkin, Wilhelmkin . . . day!": William II, *My Early Life*, (WII) p. 49.

CHAPTER THIRTY-FOUR

293   *"But for . . . widows"*: Pflanze, Vol. II, p. 45.
293   "splendid": Longford, p. 382.
293   "Beloved Mama . . . calamity": RA: Add. A 1/16, V to QV. These quotes are taken
        from what must have been the original draft of the letter, discovered after World
        War II, in 1945.
294   "congenial": RA: Y 45/82, Feodora to QV, 8/10/71.
294   "Our drive . . . children?": RA: Z 26/1, V to QV, 7/21/71.
294   "roamed with . . . voice": RA: Z 26/3, V to QV, 8/16/71.

294 "what I . . . humbug!": RA: Z 26/8, V to QV, 8/25–26/71.
295 "boiling over . . . Bismarck": Paget 2, p. 262.
295 "very healthy . . . rage": RA: Z 26/12, V to QV, 9/9/71.
295 "a short . . . angry": RA: Z 26/13, V to QV, 9/13/71.
295 "too much . . . themselves": RA: Z 26/15, V to QV, 9/19/71.
295 "the most . . . know": RA: Z 26/61, V to QV, 3/29/72.
296 "scenes at . . . Emperor's": RA: Z 26/61, V to QV, 3/29/72.
296 "dreaded . . . forwards": RA: Z 55/20, V to QV, 9/30/93.
296 "It is . . . beauty": RA: Z 26/27, V to QV, 11/13/71.
296 "neither a . . . violent": RA: Z 26/19, V to QV, 10/5/71.
296 "No member . . . them": RA: Z 26/31, V to QV, 12/4/71.
296 "Some day . . . us!": RA: Z 26/64, V to QV, 4/3/72.
297 "horribly afraid . . . event": RA: Z 26/56, V to QV, 3/2/72.
297 "I am . . . dreadful": RA: Z 26/58, V to QV, 3/8/72.
297 "immensely wretched": RA: Z 26/65, V to QV, 4/8/72.
297 "I am . . . country": KHH: QV to V, 4/10/72.
297 "May I . . . best": RA: Z 26/53, V to QV, 2/24/72.
297 "prefer . . . altogether": RA: Z 26/56, V to QV, 3/2/72.
297 "I took . . . me": RA: Z 26/67, V to QV, 4/16/72.
297 "I am . . . kind": KHH: QV to V, 10/20/72.
298 "for myself . . . remain": RA: Z 26/68, V to QV, 5/3/72.
298 "I don't . . . have?": KHH: QV to V, 5/8/72.
298 "I suppose . . . responsibility": KHH: QV to V, 5/21/72.
298 "We did . . . today": RA: Z 26/75, V to QV, 5/25/72.
298 "raptures": RA: Z 26/76, V to QV, 5/30/72.
298 "a very . . . creature": RA: Z 26/77, V to QV, 6/2/72.
298 "I wish . . . amiable": RA: Z 26/78, V to QV, 6/6/72.
299 "the prisoner . . . Vatican": William L. Langer, *The New Illustrated Encyclopedia of World History,* Vol. I, p. 674.
299 "by violence . . . coercion": Pflanze, Vol. II, p. 179.

Chapter Thirty-five

300 *"In Berlin . . . him"*: Eyck, p. 271.
300 "view of . . . France": *Ibid.,* p. 190.
301 "Never will . . . dimensions": Bismarck, Vol. III, p. 188.
301 "readily turn": Winifred Taffs, *Ambassador to Bismarck, Lord Odo Russell,* p. 54.
301 "I pity . . . hear": KHH: QV to V, 8/17/72.
301 "more like . . . else": RA: Z 27/3, V to QV, 9/12/72.
302 "It gave . . . abolished": RA: Z 27/4, V to QV, 9/20/72.
302 "It is . . . are": Pflanze, Vol. II, p. 259.
303 "The joy . . . France": Taffs, p. 14.
303 "Everybody needs . . . hate": *Ibid.,* p. 205.
303 "If we . . . return": Eyck, p. 204.
304 "abroad as . . . home": Pflanze, Vol. II, p. 195.
304 "destruction of . . . measures": Fulford, *Darling Child,* p. 114, n. 1.
304 "seriously ill . . . uncomfortable": RA: Z 27/96, V to QV, 11/11/73.
304 "Bismarck's . . . justice": Kollander, p. 165, n. 25, F to Friedberg, 8/9/74.
304 "You may . . . same!": Crankshaw, p. 309.
305 "as a . . . measures": Kollander, p. 165, n. 25.
305 "I fancy . . . enjoyed": *Ibid.,* pp. 308–309.
305 "[A]ll over . . . Priesthood": KHH: QV to V, 10/24/73.
305 "I do . . . religions": *Ibid.*
305 "I must . . . possible": KHH: QV to V, 10/11/74.
305 "I do . . . them!": RA: Z 28/66, V to QV, 10/15/74.

305 "I dare . . . know!": RA: Z 29/10, V to QV, 2/28/75.
306 "He [Bismarck]is . . . Emperor": Corti 1, p. 186.

CHAPTER THIRTY-SIX

307 *"You have . . . possible"*: Poschinger, p. 291.
307 "a ruler . . . pitiless": Crankshaw, p. 331.
307 "had to . . . manners": Eyck, p. 331.
307 "The Germans . . . dangerous": RA: Z 30/1, V to QV, 6/12/75. The word "misgoverned" has been substituted for "misgovernment" in this quote.
308 "The first . . . several litres": Pflanze, Vol. II, pp. 52–53.
308 "I can't . . . more": *Ibid.*, pp. 51–52.
309 "One of . . . such": *Ibid.*, p. 392.
309 "influence . . . appreciated": Taffs, p. 18.
309 "unscrupulous . . . Princess": Buckle, Second Series, Vol. II, pp. 247–48, Lady Emily Russell to Queen Victoria, 3/15/73.
311 "Somebody wanted . . . with": *Ibid.*, p. 217.
311 "Why should . . . it?": *Ibid.*, p. 218.
311 "the duty . . . initiative": Taffs, p. 86, Lord Russell to Lord Derby, 4/27/75.
312 "firm hope . . . Europe": Buckle, Second Series, Vol. II, p. 396, QV to Alexander II, 5/19/75.
312 "the Ultramontanes . . . circles": Bismarck, Vol. III, p. 114, B to WI, 8/13/75.
312 "inexperienced diplomatists . . . personages": Eyck, p. 221.
312 "Behind our . . . maniac": Crankshaw, p. 329.
312 war scare: On the basis of the memoirs of General Le Flô, the French Ambassador to Russia, George F. Kennan points out that the crisis was skillfully manipulated by the French partially in response to two letters allegedly from the Prince of Wales to President MacMahon of France, warning France about "the irresponsible alarmist talk . . . current in German military circles." (Bertie was in Berlin in September of 1874 for Willy's confirmation.) Kennan says that Décazes purposefully distorted Radowitz's statement in order to "extract" the warning from the Russians, thus winning the battle for public opinion "hands down" over Bismarck. He blames Bismarck's embarassment on his fear of the ultramontanes and "the jittery and belligerent German press" (although he does not say that the German press was largely controlled by Bismarck). From this, he posits "the unshakable conviction of many millions of Frenchmen, including most French statesmen, that the key . . . to France's security" lay in Russia (Kennan, *The Decline of Bismarck's European Order*, pp. 11–23).
313 "an intriguer . . . majesty": Pflanze, Vol. II, p. 360.
313 "too fond . . . up": RA: Z 31/19, V to QV, 4/7/77.
313 "He accuses . . . animal": *Ibid.*, p. 368.
313 "the traitoress": RA: Z 64/155, Lady Emily Russell to QV, 9/1/77.
313 "exalted lady . . . Rome": Busch, Vol. II, pp. 122–33.
313 "the most . . . queen": Eyck, p. 229.
313 "very nice . . . it!": RA: Z 31/28, V to QV, 5/28/77.
313 "made opposition . . . them": Busch, Vol. II, p. 134.
313 "[I]t is . . . him": RA: Z 31/24, V to QV, 4/28/77.
314 German financial and industrial growth: For a detailed examination of this subject, see Otto Pflanze, *Bismarck and the Development of Germany*, Vol. II, Chapter 1, from which this very brief summary is taken.
315 "Jews actually . . . now": Crankshaw, p. 339.
315 "I am . . . implementation": *Ibid.*, p. 341.
315 "Germany wants . . . should!": Frederick Ponsonby, *Letters of the Empress Frederick*, p. 138, V to QV, 6/5/75. Hereafter cited as *Letters*.
316 "fiasco . . . then": Eyck, p. 235.

316   "lacked . . . imagination": Pflanze, Vol. II, pp. 350–51.
316   "old feudal . . . disguise": *Ibid.*, p. 344.

CHAPTER THIRTY-SEVEN

318   *"The most . . . life"*: Crankshaw, p. 332.
318   "Even the . . . thrust": Keyserlingk, pp. 65–66.
319   "His estimate . . . truth": Poschinger, p. 378.
319   "The Prince . . . cause": Radziwill 4, pp. 90–91.
319   "I am . . . upbringing": Röhl, pp. 102–104.
320   "not the . . . wife": *Ibid.*
320   "After . . . her": Corti 1, pp. 195–96.
320   "How different . . . wife": *Recollections*, p. 68–71.
320   "love of . . . prevailed": Sir James Rennell Rodd, *Social and Diplomatic Memories, 1884–93,* (Rodd 1), p. 60.
320   "I invariably . . . battles": Hugo, Baron von Reischach, *Under Three Emperors,* p. 139.
321   "studied . . . comprehension": Poschinger, pp. 372–73.
321   "Say How . . . row": Longford, p. 386.
321   "I hope . . . unpatriotic": RA: Z 17/62, V to QV, 5/6/65.
322   "the rest . . . aparatus *[sic]*": RA: Z 21/3, V to QV, 1/8/68.
322   "I always . . . climate!": RA: Z 27/91, V to QV, 10/22/73.
322   "I had . . . night": RA: Z 23/50, V to QV, 5/26/69.
322   "comforted . . . me": RA: Z 23/59, V to QV, 6/26/69.
323   "a one-armed . . . Prussia": Thomas Kohut, *Wilhelm II and the Germans*, p. 43.
323   "My mother . . . schoolroom": *Ibid.*, p. 4.
323   "[N]o parents . . . manners": Poultney Bigelow, *Prussian Memories, 1864–1914,* p. 46.
324   "seem to . . . home": RA: Z 23/70, V to QV, 8/25/69.
324   "[I]t is . . . fair": RA: Z 25/30, V to QV, 11/26/70.
324   "The little . . . child": Alice Miller, *For Your Own Good*, p. 5.
324   "stiffly upright": Princess Victoria of Prussia, *My Memoirs*, p. 25.
325   "Come back . . . scamper": *Ibid.*, p. 3.
325   "Believe me . . . give": KHH: QV to V, 3/2/70.
325   "[W]hen one . . . anxiety": KHH: QV to V, 12/3/70.
325   "I cannot . . . head": RA: Z 18/76, V to QV, 8/10/66.
325   "[S]he had . . . longer": RA: Z 18/46, V to QV, 5/9/66.
326   "I always . . . descendants": RA: Z 24/30, V to QV, 2/5/70.
326   "I kiss . . . Mama": RA: Z 15/42, V to QV, 7/26/63.
326   "Our whole . . . first": WII, p. 61.
326   "We have . . . chooses": RA: Z 16/73, V to QV, 8/13/64.
327   "[B]ring him . . . much!": KHH: QV to V, 1/27/65.

CHAPTER THIRTY-EIGHT

328   *"[I]t is . . . pupil"*: Kohut, p. 42.
328   "make no . . . Great": RA: Z 16/74, V to QV, 8/16/64.
328   Hintzpeter: For the sake of consistency, I have adopted Vicky's spelling; according to John C. G. Röhl (*Wilhelm II, Die Jugend des Kaisers, 1859–1888*), the correct spelling is Hinzpeter.
328   "He is . . . extreme": Wemyss, Vol. II, pp. 97–98.
329   "just beginning . . . well": RA: Z 19/46, V to QV, 1/20/67.
329   "a pearl": RA: Z 22/11, V to QV, 8/19/68.
329   "a treasure": RA: Z 24/55, V to QV, 5/13/70.
329   "We feel . . . him": RA: Z 22/11, V to QV, 8/19/68.
329   "We may . . . Hintzpeter": RA: Z 25/72, V to QV, 5/3/71.

329 "Hintzpeter . . . excluded": WII, pp. 17–18.
330 "[D]espite . . . him": *Ibid.*, p. 21.
330 "Children's . . . now": RA: Z 19/30, V to QV, 12/10/66.
330 "[I]t is . . . still": KHH: V to WII, 1/16/70.
330 "It is . . . out": KHH: V to WII, 3/7/70.
330 "I cannot . . . good": RA: Z 17/54, V to QV, 4/7/65.
331 "It was . . . city": WII, p. 2.
331 "He must . . . riding": KHH: V to F, 6/29/63.
331 "When the . . . tortured": WII, p. 23. This version is disputed by Röhl in his recent book on Wilhelm II. Röhl seems to feel that Wilhelm misrepresented this part of his training in order to gain sympathy and improve his image—a ruse he often resorted to in later life.
331 "Prof. Hinzpeter . . . pupil": Princess Victoria of Prussia, p. 12.
331 "But you . . . 9": KHH: QV to V, 1/8/68.
332 "We saw . . . education": WII, p. 20.
332 "Tomorrow will . . . it": RA: Z 23/11, V to QV, 1/26/69.
332 "marched past . . . well": RA: Z 23/43, V to QV, 5/4/69.
332 "There were . . . badly": RA: Z 78/3, WII to QV, 5/20/69.
332 "constantly": KHH: V to F, 3/9/64.
332 "too engrossing . . . passion": RA: Z 16/60, V to QV, 7/6/64.
333 "Many thanks . . . heart": KHH: V to WII, 3/16/70.
333 "What impressed . . . muzzles": WII, p. 36.
333 "I am . . . education": RA: Z 25/48, V to QV, 1/28/71.
333 "I am . . . men": RA: Z 25/53, QV to V, 2/10/71.
333 "You need . . . classes": RA: Z 25/49, V to QV, 1/30/71.
334 "Once or . . . by": Wiegler, p. 423.
334 "extremely intimate": WII, p. 81.
335 "very haughty . . . himself": Röhl, pp. 186–87.
335 "When William . . . exchange": *Ibid.*, p. 99.
335 "contact with . . . too": *Ibid.*, p. 187.
335 "Thank God . . . friends": FIII, p. 285.
335 "I am . . . destroy": RA: Z 25/48, V to QV, 1/28/71.
335 "Tell Charlotte . . . girls": KHH: QV to V, 3/7/66.
335 "Stupidity is . . . task": RA: Z 19/18, V to QV, 11/5/66.
335 "more difficulties ": RA: Z 19/42, V to QV, 1/4/67.
335 "Alas, she . . . admired": RA: Z 20/25, V to QV, 7/22/67.
336 "smothered": RA: Z 17/43, V to QV, 2/28/65.
336 "You do . . . amusing": RA: Z 19/21, V to QV, 11/17/66.
336 "very backward . . . slow": RA: Z 24/53, V to QV, 5/6/70.
336 "He must . . . liberty": RA: Z 20/75, V to QV, 12/14/67.
336 "You need . . . person": RA: Z 24/55, V to QV, 5/13/70.
336 "very shy . . . Papa": RA: Z 25/63, V to QV, 3/24/71.

CHAPTER THIRTY-NINE

338 "*Ladies should . . . uselessness*": Vansittart, p. 79.
338 "Oh the . . . me!": RA: Z 17/27, V to QV, 1/18/65.
338 "I fear . . . oneself": RA: Z 28/7, V to QV, 2/2/74.
338 "a pity . . . society": RA: Z 15/36, V to QV, 7/3/63.
338 "[I]t makes . . . sleep": RA: Z 18/33, V to QV, 3/13/66.
338 "possessed a . . . mind": Reischach, pp. 111–12.
338 "hideous self": RA: Z 18/68, V to QV, 7/16/66..
338 "I fear . . . open!": RA: Z 28/7, V to QV, 2/2/74.
339 "an almost . . . shyness": Reischach, p. 91.
339 "Everybody noticed . . . her": RA: Z 64/109, Lady Emily Russell to QV, 3/17/77.
339 "I am . . . forward": KHH: QV to V, 4/12/73.

339 "[L]et me . . . Exhibition": RA: Z 27/45, V to QV, 4/22/73.
339 "quite a . . . etc.": RA: Z 27/41, V to QV, 4/9/73.
339 "It is . . . time": RA: Z 27/46, V to QV, 4/26/73.
339 "with all . . . possible": RA: Z 27/47, V to QV, 4/30/73.
340 "the most . . . way": WII, pp. 73–74.
340 "Willie is . . . him": RA: Z 27/47, V to QV, 4/30/73.
340 "The ceremony . . . it": RA: Z 27/48, V to QV, 5/2/73. The actual lapse of time between exhibitions was twenty-two, not twenty-three years.
340 "ridiculous, florid . . . corpse": Brigitte Hamann, *The Reluctant Empress*, p. 206.
340 "You can . . . good-natured": RA: Z 27/48, V to QV, 5/2/73.
341 "It gives . . . use": KHH: QV to V, 5/25/73.
341 "I hope . . . painful": KHH: QV to V, 9/14/73.
341 "literally . . . besides": The Dean of Windsor and Hector Bolitho, *Later Letters of Lady Augusta Stanley, 1864–1876*, p. 229.
342 "Anything to . . . Court": RA: Z 28/8, V to QV, 2/10/74.

Chapter Forty

343 *"To prefer . . . mistaken"*: RA: Z 34/54, V to QV, 10/13/80. (Note: Mohammedan is spelled Mahomedan in original.)
344 "territorially saturated . . . intimate": Pflanze, Vol. II, p. 419.
344 "one can . . . Bismarck": RA: QVJ, 2/7/76.
344 "of the . . . ours": Buckle, Second Series, Vol. II, p. 443, QV to the Earl of Derby, 2/9/76.
344 "national . . . alliances": Pflanze, Vol. II, p. 257.
345 "refused . . . throat": *Ibid.*, p. 420.
345 "Every wish . . . Conferences": RA: Z 29/81, V to QV, 5/29/76.
345 "Fritz had . . . done": RA: Z 29/84, V to QV, 6/13/76.
345 "I . . . fear . . . going": KHH: QV to V, 8/31/76.
345 "Alas, you . . . dress!": RA: Z 29/99, V to QV, 9/4/76.
346 "I count . . . me": Corti 2, p. 16.
346 "the finest . . . century": Longford, p. 408.
346 "Russia . . . Turks": Buckle, Second Series, Vol. II, p. 480, QV to Disraeli, 9/28/76.
346 "The Russians . . . Christians": RA: Z 29/101, V to QV, 9/16/76.
346 "You say . . . to": RA: Z 30/2, V to QV, 10/25/76.
347 "simple and honest": *Letters*, p. 144, V to QV, 10/28/76.
347 "dislikes & . . . us": RA: Z 31/20, V to QV, 4/14/77.
347 "It is . . . wrong": KHH: QV to V, 5/3/77.
348 "What . . . together": RA: Z 31/49, V to QV, 9/22/77.
348 "the re-establishment . . . Constantinople": Poschinger, p. 389.
348 "It is . . . campaigns": *Letters*, p. 154, Fritz to QV, 10/19/77.
348 "for one . . . Lion": *Ibid.*, p. 156, V to QV, 12/19/77.
348 "Except among . . . way": *Ibid.*, p. 162, V to QV, 4/5/78.
349 "golden . . . stars": Monypenny and Buckle, Vol. VI, p. 317.
349 "Bismarck . . . Kissingen": Pflanze, Vol. II, p. 438.
349 "It is . . . midnight": Monypenny and Buckle, Vol. VI, p. 327.
349 "spell": Bülow, p. 453.
349 "Der alte . . . Mann!": Monypenny and Buckle, Vol. VI, p. 311.
349 "I dined . . . smile": *Ibid.*, p. 331.
349 "very triumphant": Longford, p. 414.
350 "almost hysterical . . . Germany": George F. Kennan, *The Decline of Bismarck's European Order*, p. 40.
350 "The Congress . . . treatment": *Letters*, p. 164, V to QV, 7/13/78.
350 "It would . . . peace": Eyck, p. 251.

CHAPTER FORTY-ONE

351 *Only Prince . . . leadership*": Keyserlingk, p. 124.
351 "in floods . . . valets!": RA: Z 30/4 *passim*, V to QV, 6/4/78.
352 "be carried . . . is": Wiegler, p. 369.
352 "The Crown . . . convictions": Poschinger, p. 410.
352 "The Emperor . . . that": KHH: QV to V, 6/3/78.
352 "As I . . . attempt": Eyck, p. 239.
353 "I was . . . father": Bismarck, Vol. III, pp. 123–36.
354 "impress the . . . obstructionism": Pflanze, Vol. II, p. 402.
354 "continually told . . . habits": RA: Z 31/83, V to QV, 6/11/78.
354 "He [Marx] . . . down": Corti 1, p. 211–12.
355 "one of . . . talked": Pflanze, Vol. I, p. 228.
355 "What could . . . me?": *Ibid.*, p. 230.
356 "[Bismarck] has . . . help": Pflanze, Vol. II, p. 286.
356 "within the . . . state": *Ibid.*, p. 291.
356 Statistics: These figures as well as this abbreviated history of socialism in Germany are taken from the second volume of Otto Pflanze's three-volume work on Bismarck.
357 "incredible luck": *Ibid.*, p. 398.
357 "Here the . . . despised!": RA: Z 31/85, V to QV, 7/30/78.
357 "harmony . . . classes": Pflanze, Vol. II, p. 414.
358 "abuse . . . driving": RA: Z 31/85, V to QV, 7/30/78.
358 Railroads: The German railways had long been a problem, one that Bismarck, as a farmer and producer of timber, related to personally. Once the primary factor in joining the diverse German states, the railroads suffered from a multiplicity of rate charges—over two thousand different rates, as well as secret rebates for special customers. Although Bismarck was unable to nationalize them, he did manage to achieve state railway ownership in Prussia, which helped standardize and stabilize prices elsewhere.
358 "The work . . . gold": Pflanze, Vol. II, p. 482.
359 "[T]he great . . . move": RA: Z 33/24, V to QV, 7/16/79.

CHAPTER FORTY-TWO

360 *"To see . . . dreadful"*: KHH: QV to V, 12/3/70.
360 "The 3 . . . nature": RA: Z 60A/1, V to QV, 9/8/77.
360 "I gained . . . origin": WII, p. 76.
360 "sermonizing tone": Röhl, p. 213.
360 "Your Imperial . . . being": *Ibid.*, p. 215.
361 "[I]t is . . . possesses": *Ibid.*, p. 214.
361 "the censure . . . heretical!": RA: Z 207/47, V to QV, 1/30/77.
361 "strange boys . . . list!": WII, p. 98.
361 "violent": RA: Z 28/55, V to QV, 8/29/74.
361 "[C]eremonies of . . . schoolboy": RA: Z 29/61, V to QV, 12/29/75.
361 "We entered . . . company": WII, p. 100.
362 "ever tactful . . . familiarity": *Ibid.*, p. 101.
362 "The history . . . people": *Ibid.*, p. 108 *passim*.
362 "work very hard": RA: Z 28/70, V to QV, 10/30/74.
362 "The effect . . . brilliant": KHH: Hintzpeter to F, 10/10/74.
362 "I get . . . letters": KHH: WII to V, 11/1/74.
362 "so little . . . rage": Röhl, p. 241.
362 "I am . . . be": GStA: V to WII, 12/6/74.
363 "I get . . . do": KHH: WII to V, 12/12/74.
363 "I have . . . dream": KHH: WII to V, 2/6/75.

363 "I have . . . you": KHH: WII to V, 2/11/75.

363 "Your little . . . course!": GStA: V to WII, 3/7/75.

364 "Again have . . . yourself": KHH: WII to V, 5/13/75.

364 "You never . . . them": KHH: WII to V, 6/20/75.

364 "I did . . . laugh": GStA: V to WII, 6/22/75.

364 "About my . . . having": GStA: V to WII, 6/24/76.

364 "Willy . . . not": Letters, p. 174.

364 "silence . . . disdainful": Röhl, pp. 208–209 passim.

364 "I bore . . . happy": RA: Z 207/47, V to QV, 1/30/77.

365 "Dr. Hintzpeter . . . parents": Marie von Bunsen, Lost Courts of Europe, p. 242.

365 "must be attributed": Joachim von Kürenberg, The Kaiser, p. 14.

365 "In this . . . studies": WII, pp. 128–29.

365 "exclusively devoted . . . afterward": Lamar Cecil, "History as Family Chronicle," Kaiser Wilhelm II, New Interpretations, John J. G. Röhl and Nicholas Sombart, eds., p. 96.

365 "[H]e is . . . mischief": RA: Z 207/47, V to QV, 1/30/77.

366 "the most swagger": Michael Balfour, The Kaiser and His Times, p. 80.

366 "heavy drinking . . . left": WII, p. 133.

366 "I cannot . . . age!": KHH: F to V, 8/31/77.

366 "I never . . . can": GStA: V to WII, 12/11/77.

366 "Certainly . . . afraid": GStA: V to WII, 7/16/78.

366 "a hot-tempered . . . racket": Lady Susan Townley, Indiscretions of Lady Susan, p. 40.

366 "would want . . . Bible": Meriel Buchanan, Queen Victoria's Relations, p. 94.

366 "I could . . . been": KHH: QV to V, 4/8/80.

367 "Questioned . . . her": Buchanan, p. 95.

367 "the typical . . . officer": Recollections, p. 79.

367 "galloping squadrons": Ibid., p. 157.

367 "boisterous geniality . . . returned": Rodd 1, p. 50.

367 "had never . . . me": Röhl, p. 99.

367 "Calma is . . . smile": KHH: QV to V, 3/17/80.

368 "people . . . ill-used": KHH: QV to V, 2/18/80.

368 "very difficult . . . fact": RA: Z 34/7, V to QV, 1/29/80.

368 "[C]ould you . . . her!": KHH: papers of Friedrich III of Germany concerning the marriage of Prince Wilhelm, WII to V, 4/30/79.

368 "diplomatic talent": Ibid., WII to V, 5/6/79.

368 "Could you . . . little": RA: U 34/4, WII to V, 5/20/79.

368 "would still . . . Duchies": RA: Z 33/24, V to QV, 7/16/79.

368 "It seems . . . him": KHH: papers of Friedrich III of Germany concerning the marriage of Prince Wilhelm, Helena to V, 12/21/79.

368 "wish to . . . character": Röhl, pp. 398–99.

369 "I cannot . . . overcome": Ibid., p. 366.

369 "[A] brilliant . . . world": RA: Z 34/9, V to QV, 2/13/80.

369 "turning up . . . noses": Röhl, p. 369.

369 "Two of . . . her": Wiegler, p. 380.

369 "Willy is . . . character!": RA: Z 34/36, V to QV, 7/17/80.

369 "I am . . . it!": RA: Z 34/41, V to QV, 8/7/80.

369 "thought it . . . pheasants": RA: Z 34/42, V to QV, 8/10/80.

369 "only hope . . . disposition": Röhl, p. 377.

369 "If he . . . emotion": Ibid., p. 372.

369 "do all . . . her": KHH: papers of Friedrich III of Germany concerning the marriage of Prince Wilhelm, Helena to V, 9/16/79.

Chapter Forty-three

371 "*If I . . . maid*": Lillie de Hegermann-Lindencrone, *The Sunny Side of Diplomatic Life*, p. 303.
371 "foolish, frivolous . . . Princess": Radziwill 1, p. 144.
371 "How differently . . . like": RA: Z 31/35, V to QV, 7/21/77.
371 "I think . . . ways": KHH: QV to V, 7/25/77.
371 "great trial": KHH: QV to V, 2/6/77.
372 "How well . . . yourself": RA: Z 31/45, V to QV, 8/29/77.
372 "immense . . . trundle[d]": RA: Z 31/53, V to QV, 10/11/77.
372 "After . . . you": RA: Z 31/70, V to QV, 2/19/78.
372 "How good . . . too?": RA: Z 31/102, V to QV, 11/25/78.
372 "the kiss of death": Palmer 1, p. 170.
372 "If I . . . home!": RA: Z 32/1, V to QV, 12/15/78.
373 "forbidden": RA: Z 32/3, V to QV, 12/21/78.
373 "a cruel . . . one!": RA: Z 32/1, V to QV, 12/16/78.
373 "coldness and indifference": Röhl, p. 390.
373 "the dear . . . sympathy": RA: Z 32/1, V to QV, 12/16/78.
373 "Perhaps . . . atheist!": Radziwill 1, p. 153.
373 "He is . . . everywhere": RA: Z 32/16, V to QV, 2/10/79.
373 "I do . . . child": RA: Z 32/36, V to QV, 3/25/79.
373 "I have . . . over!": RA: Z 32/27, V to QV, 3/26/79.
374 "inspired by . . . on": Radziwill 1, p. 141.
374 "scratch out . . . violently": RA: Z 32/39, V to QV, 4/10/79.
374 "[T]he Empress . . . afraid": RA: Z 33/2, V to QV, 4/10/79.
374 "it must . . . either": RA: Z 33/4, V to QV, 5/6/79.
374 "We endeavour . . . age": Poschinger, p. 416.
375 "I hate . . . me!": RA: Z 33/45, V to QV, 11/4/79.
375 "Willy . . . slow!": RA: Z 28/30, V to QV, 5/23/74.
375 "It was . . . gone!": RA: Z 34/52, V to QV, 10/1/80.
376 "lost": RA: Z 34/53, V to QV, 10/8/80.
376 "is good . . . power!": RA: Z 34/57, V to QV, 10/29/80.
376 "your oldest . . . daughter": RA: Z 32/34, V to QV, 3/22/79.
376 "growing very . . . glass": RA: Z 34/57, V to QV, 10/29/80.
376 shared a bedroom: When Vicky's bed hangings caught fire in October of 1882, she wrote Queen Victoria, "[W]e spent the night on sofas in different rooms." RA: Z 36/53, V to QV, 10/17/82.
376 "vivid . . . smile": Rodd 1, pp. 48–49.
377 "Few women . . . looks": Rodd, *Social and Diplomatic Memories, 1894–1901*, Second Series, (Rodd 2), p. 300.
377 "give herself . . . them": RA: Z 64/109, Lady Emily Russell to QV, 3/17/77.
377 "He is . . . pretensions": Busch, Vol. II, pp. 211–12.

Chapter Forty-four

378 "*In trying . . . most*": Kissinger 1, p. 920.
378 "The old . . . earlier": Pflanze, Vol. II, p. 490.
378 "more independent . . . influenced": *Ibid.*, p. 394.
378 "When there . . . *trois*": Holborn, p. 236.
379 "nightmare of coalitions": Pflanze, Vol. II, p. 432.
379 "an autocrat . . . rule": Kennan, p. 71.
379 "Austria is . . . us": *Ibid.*, p. 72.
379 "sacred legacy": Pflanze, Vol. II, p. 502.
380 "fears . . . countries": *Ibid.*, and Eyck, p. 263.
380 "I was . . . Russia": Bismarck, Vol. III, p. 178.
380 "contrary . . . principles": Pflanze, Vol. II, p. 503.

380   "a conflict . . . dimensions": Kennan, p. 73.
380   "a strong advocate": Bismarck, p. 191.
380   "[I]f Germany . . . disappear": Kollander, p. 184.
381   "Bismarck is . . . am": Pflanze, Vol. II, p. 507.
381   "Those men . . . above": Eyck, p. 265.
381   "to see . . . emperors": Pflanze, Vol. III, p. 80.
381   "what Britain's . . . Russia": Eyck, p. 265.
381   "not a . . . gentleman": RA: Z 27/40, V to QV, 4/15/73.
381   "Bismarck proposed . . . Question?": Eyck, p. 266. There are two versions of this
        conversation—Disraeli's and Münster's. Since Münster was in the difficult position
        of reporting to Bismarck, it seems likely that Disraeli's account is more accurate.
381   "I knew . . . Austrians": Pflanze, Vol. II, p. 509.
382   "It will . . . other": *Ibid.*, p. 510.
382   "the only . . . Europe": Pflanze, Vol. III, p. 79.
382   "Prince Bismarck . . . Constantinople?": RA: Z 34/21, V to QV, 5/1/80.
383   "no . . . sleep": Pflanze, Vol. III, pp. 88–89.
383   "more concerned . . . bride": Alan Palmer, *The Kaiser* (Palmer 2), p. 20.
384   "One is . . . innocent: *Letters,* pp. 184–85, V to QV, 3/14/81.
385   "very solemn . . . accounting": Kennan, p. 78.
386   "arrange some . . . circles": Kollander, p. 190.

CHAPTER FORTY-FIVE

387   *"History as . . . history":* Arthur M. Schlesinger, Jr., *The Disuniting of America,*
        p. 37.
387   "There is . . . well": Pflanze, Vol. III, p. 21.
388   "lordly, aristocratic . . . debts": *Ibid.,* p. 11.
388   "The Bismarck . . . impotence": Pflanze, Vol. II, p. 475.
388   "Usually they . . . communism": RA: Z 35/51, V to QV, 10/27/81.
389   "Everyone . . . elements": Pflanze, Vol. III, p. 58.
389   "Have you . . . Ministers?": RA: Z 36/3, V to QV, 1/10/82.
389   "spread every . . . it": RA: Z 36/4, V to QV, 1/13/82.
389   "he first . . . horrified": RA: Z 36/3, V to QV, 1/10/82.
389   "quite satisfied . . . wife": RA: Z 36/5, V to QV, 1/18/82.
389   "full well . . . well": Poschinger, p. 400.
389   Karl von Normann: According to Patricia Kollander *(The Liberalism of Frederick
        III)*, it was the Crown Prince and Princess who wanted to send Normann away—
        Fritz so that Normann could gain diplomatic experience, and Vicky because she
        felt he was too political. In this version, Fritz himself requested Normann's new
        posting, which Holstein and Bismarck were only too happy to oblige.
389   "joint . . . position": Corti 1, p. 221.
389   "Once I . . . recall": Corti 1, p. 221.
389   "one great . . . so": Radziwill 3, p. 188.
389   "an act . . . room": Holstein, Vol. II, p. 150. The first two quotes are from Holstein;
        the last is supposedly a direct quote from Bismarck.
390   "a splendid . . . himself": *Ibid.,* p. 208.
390   "one of . . . know": RA: Z 207/18, Lord Odo Russell to Sir Henry Ponsonby,
        Christmas, 1875.
390   "a favourable . . . Victoria": Corti 1, p. 222.
390   "I don't . . . Seckendorff": *Letters,* p. 192, Lady Ponsonby to QV, undated.
390   "A great . . . Princess: Radziwill 1, pp. 159–60.
391   "No doubt . . . them": RA: Z 35/53, V to QV, 11/5/81.
392   "The border . . . unjustified": Pflanze, Vol. III, pp. 202–204.
392   "learn . . . civilization": *Ibid.,* p. 206.
393   Anti-Semitic literature: This information is taken from Holborn, p. 281.

393 "national misfortune . . . usury": Heinrich von Treitschke, *History of Germany in the Nineteenth Century,* pp. xxv–xxvi.
394 "If you . . . Germany": RA: Z 23/36, V to QV, 4/10/69.
394 "The disturbance . . . movement": RA: Z 34/62, V to QV, 12/10/80.
394 "deplorable . . . way!": RA: Z 34/68, V to QV, 12/25/80.
394 "dangerous spirit . . . presumptuousness": Pflanze, Vol. III, p. 200.
394 "not approve . . . modest": Hohenlohe-Schillingfürst, p . 281.
394 "a race": Pflanze, Vol. III, p. 201.
394 "Fritz considered . . . feelings": Corti 1, p. 293.
395 "I so . . . Jews": KHH: QV to V, 1/22/81.
395 "The Crown . . . culture": Theo Aronson, *The Kaisers,* p. 140.
395 "By the . . . me": *Recollections,* p. 69.
396 "Accident insurance . . . Reichstag": *Ibid.,* p. 156.
396 "the state . . . society": *Ibid.,* p. 159.
397 "dumb . . . louse": Pflanze, Vol. II, p. 241 *passim.*
397 "Whenever anything . . . suffer": *Ibid.,* p. 407.
397 "the eminent . . . world": *Ibid.,* p. 111.
397 "lifelong . . . statesman": Eyck, p. 274.

Chapter Forty-six

398 *"If all . . . everywhere":* RA: Z 36/35, V to QV, 7/15/82.
399 "safety valve": Pflanze, Vol. III, p. 116.
399 "I don't . . . shirts": *Ibid.,* p. 114.
399 "He will . . . them": Hohenlohe-Schillingsfürst, Vol. II, p. 267.
399 "I am . . . elections": *Letters,* p. 195, V to Lady Ponsonby, 10/17/84.
400 "During this . . . moment": Eyck, p. 275.
400 "the sole . . . England": Crankshaw, p. 396.
400 "I foresee . . . trade": *Letters,* pp. 151–52, V to QV, 7/11/77.
400 "the Queen . . . Bismarck": *Ibid.,* p. 152.
400 "England's influence . . . people": RA: Z 31/35, V to QV, 7/21/77.
401 "The German . . . then": RA: Z 36/33 *passim,* V to QV, 6/24/82.
401 "You will . . . deeply": KHH: QV to V, 7/12/82.
401 "The bombardment . . . be": RA: Z 36/34, V to QV, 7/13/82.
401 "occupy Egypt . . . East": RA: Z 36/35, V to QV, 7/15/82.
402 "a claim . . . holdings": Pflanze, Vol. III, p. 126.
402 "Here the . . . fault!": RA: Z 30/11, V to QV, 7/3/83.
402 "This German . . . direction": KHH: QV to V, 12/27/84.
402 "The acquisition . . . crosses": Pflanze, Vol. III, p. 129.
403 "I don't . . . else": *Ibid.,* p. 130.
403 "I think . . . see": RA: Z 37/54, V to QV, 12/23/83.
403 "further our . . . powers": Pflanze, Vol. III, p.130.
403 "He was . . . secret": Eyck, p. 278.
404 "to take . . . peace": *Ibid.,* p. 280.
404 "To discuss . . . it": *Ibid* .
404 "The governing . . . bureaucrat": Pflanze, Vol. III, p. 133.
405 "Can't we . . . treatment?": *Ibid.,* p. 138.
405 Statistics: See Pflanze, Vol. III, pp. 113–142, for more statistics and a comprehensive discussion of Bismarck's colonial policy, upon which this summary is based.
405 "colonial swindle": *Ibid.,* p. 140.
405 "Your map . . . Africa": *Ibid.,* p. 142.

Chapter Forty-seven

407 *"It is . . . Bulgaria":* Corti 2, p. 145.
407 "Russia has . . . later": *Ibid.,* p. 35.

408 "first time . . . rank": Palmer 1, p. 166.
409 "morganatic cousin": Corti 2, p. 20.
409 "the German": *Ibid.*, p. 37.
410 "You do . . . Bulgaria!": Buckle, Second Series, Vol. III, 1879–1885, p. 699, QV to the Marquis of Salisbury, 10/6/85. (Note: Prince Alexander saw Queen Victoria right after he saw Bismarck and gave her a detailed account of his interview with the Chancellor; hence, it seems to the author that the quote, coming from Victoria, is accurate.)
410 "at all . . . you": Corti 2, p. 41.
410 "very nice . . . vassal": RA: Z 33/10, V to QV, 5/28/79.
410 "I do . . . Russian": KHH: QV to V, 6/10/79.
410 "any help . . . give": Buckle, Second Series, Vol. III, p. 27, QV to the Marquis of Salisbury, Cypher Telegram, 6/10/79.
410 "kind and just": Corti 2, p. 42.
410 "The Russian . . . one": *Ibid.*, p. 46.
410 "It is . . . help: *Ibid.*, p. 52.
411 "Why not . . . troops?": *Ibid.*, p. 65.
411 "Good Lord . . . evening": *Ibid.*, p. 60.
411 "a hatred . . . fixation": Kennan, pp. 113–14.
412 "a kind . . . eccentricity": Epton, p. 166.
412 "All my . . . time": Corti 2, p. 101.
412 "the old . . . position!": RA: Z 30/12, V to QV, 7/28/83.
412 "to prevent . . . vassal": Buckle, Second Series, Vol. III, p. 445, QV to Earl Granville.
412 "Standing . . . Russia": *Ibid.*, p. 448, Henry Ponsonby in the name of the Queen to Earl Granville, 10/25/83. (Note: Corti, in *Alexander von Battenberg*, incorrectly dates this [p. 103] as coming from the letter of October 12, 1883, and cites Volume II instead of Volume III.)
412 "My poor . . . wait?": Corti 2, p. 96.
413 "contaminated court": Arthur Ponsonby, *Henry Ponsonby, Queen Victoria's Private Secretary* (Ponsonby 2), p. 302.
413 "club the . . . death": John C. G. Röhl, "The Emperor's New Clothes," in Röhl and Sombart, p. 32.
413 "the well-being . . . stake": WII, p. 263.
413 "Alas, we . . . worse: RA: Z 30/21, V to QV, 5/16/84.
414 "marry . . . place": Corti 2, pp. 123–24 *passim*.
414 "good reasons . . . interference": Radziwill 1, p. 168.
414 "should stand . . . good": Corti 2, pp. 128–29.
414 "I only . . . eyes": *Ibid.*, p. 130; "I assure . . . Alliance": Corti 1, pp. 222–23. These are two versions of the same quotation, cited by Corti from A. Ssawin in the Russian periodical *Krasny Archiv* in 1922. In the first instance, Corti adds the caveat, "It is assumed that these letters have not been forged by the Russians."
415 "Altogether . . . everywhere": Corti 2, pp. 130–31.
415 "Although Friedrich . . . power": Kohut, p. 87.
415 "Turkish tastes": Corti 2, p. 131.
415 "I see . . . more!": RA: Z 30/24, V to QV, 1/30/85.
415 "Private To . . . well": RA: Z 30/25, V to QV, 2/2/85.
415 "a comfort . . . me": RA: Z 30/23, Princess Victoria of Prussia to QV, 12/24/84.
416 "As a . . . rank": Corti 2, pp. 148–49.
417 "With all . . . uttermost": Radziwill 1, pp 165–66.

CHAPTER FORTY-EIGHT

418 "*None of . . . morning*": Kissinger 2, p. 140.
418 "[Y]ou who . . . relented": KHH: QV to V, 1/3/85.
418 "We were . . . much!": Corti 2, p. 150.

419 "I saw . . . Liko": KHH: QV to V, 1/3/85.
419 "There . . . this": KHH: QV to V, 3/7/85.
419 "extraordinary impertinence . . . insolence": KHH: QV to V, 1/10/85.
419 "Willie . . . him": KHH: QV to V, 2/13/85.
419 "As for . . . words": KHH: QV to V, 1/10/85.
419 "absurdly . . . Princes": Ponsonby 2, pp. 251–52.
419 "Russia . . . since!": Buckle, Second Series, Vol. III, p. 699, QV to Marquis of Salisbury, 10/6/85.
420 "only sorry . . . through": Corti 2, pp. 176–77.
421 "I think . . . moment!": RA: Z 38/9, V to QV, 4/23/86.
421 "that wonderful . . . provide": Kennan, p. 129.
421 "one of . . . arrived": Corti 2, pp. 235–36.
421 "As Russia . . . Sovereign": *Ibid.*, p. 239.
422 "golden bridge": *Ibid.*, p. 242.
422 "I am . . . first": *Ibid.*, p. 241.
422 "As Imperial . . . Reichstag": Eyck, p . 284.
422 "rather horrified": RA: Z 38/37, V to QV, 8/11/86.
422 "did not . . . subject": Radziwill 1, p. 166.
423 "It stands . . . credit": Corti 1, p. 231.
423 "*un garcon . . . foi*": Aronson 2, p. 135.
423 "If I . . . Bismarck": Corti 1, p. 233.
423 "destroyed . . . ideas": *Ibid.*
423 "The fear . . . this": RA: Z 38/31, V to QV, 7/8/86. (Note: The original is written "France & Germany"—obviously a mistake.)

CHAPTER FORTY-NINE

424 "*Treaties of . . . difficulty*": A. J. P. Taylor, *The Struggle for Mastery in Europe* (Taylor 2), p. 264.
424 "crutch": Kennan, p. 177.
424 "So called . . . service": RA: Z 38/41, V to QV, 11/8/86.
424 "For some . . . up": Kennan, p. 213.
425 "I could . . . me": *Ibid.*, p. 228.
426 "[T]he moderate . . . for": RA: Z 39/2, V to QV, 2/26/87.
426 "It is . . . party": RA: Z 39/6, V to QV, 3/9/87.
426 "There is . . . ranks": RA: Z 39/6 *passim*, 3/9/87.
427 "find itself . . . empire": Pflanze, Vol. III, pp. 250–51.
427 "We have . . . Dardanelles": *Ibid.*, pp. 243–44.
427 "can easiest . . . convenient": RA: Z 39/20, V to QV, 4/29/87.
428 "[N]ow he . . . miscalculation": RA: Z 39/19, V to QV, 4/22/87.
429 "admits . . . Sultan!": RA: Z 38/74, V to QV, 10/17/87.
430 "that animal Boulanger": Pflanze, Vol. III, p. 270.
430 "very keen . . . war": Waldersee, p. 125.
430 "We no . . . Russia": Eyck, p. 296.
430 "We Germans . . . world!": Pflanze, Vol. III, p. 272.
430 "God preserve . . . indignation!": J. Alden Nichols, *The Year of the Three Kaisers*, p. 111.
430 "I do . . . follower!": RA: Z 40/2, V to QV, 1/5/88.

CHAPTER FIFTY

432 "*[I]t is . . . men*": Corti 1, p. 256.
432 "summoned . . . politics": Bismarck, Vol. III, p. 252.
432 "as an . . . commit": Holstein, Vol. II, p. 206.
432 "[I]f the . . . government": *Ibid.*, p. 211.
432 "created a . . . true": Kollander, pp. 225–27.

433   "thrash thugs . . . position": Holstein, Vol. II, pp. 212–13.

433   "English influence . . . misfortune": *Ibid.*, p. 217.

434   "no more . . . tracheotomy": Michaela Reid, *Ask Sir James*, p. 88.

434   Survival statistics: See Pflanze, Vol. III, p. 275, n. 35, and Kollander, p. 235.

434   "to consent . . . it": RA: Z 42/37, V to QV, 8/23/88.

435   "The doctors . . . away": RA: Z 39/23 *passim*, V to QV, 5/17/87.

435   "he would . . . to": RA: Z 39/24, V to QV, 5/19/87.

435   "really very . . . advice": RA: Z 39/25, V to QV, 5/20/87.

435   "epoch-making . . . important": Stevenson, pp. 43–50.

436   "certainly . . . with": KHH: QV to V, 5/20/87.

436   "His Imperial . . . whisper": Morell Mackenzie, *The Fatal Illness of Frederick the Noble*, pp. 9–10.

436   "as a physician . . . complication": *Ibid.*, pp. 10–11.

436   "a growth . . . anatomy": *Ibid.*, pp. 12–15.

437   "annoyance and disappointment": *Ibid.*, p. 17.

437   "grieved to . . . wife": *Ibid.*, pp. 19–20.

437   "burnt . . . present": *Ibid.*, pp. 23–26 *passim*.

437   "Did any . . . pathology": *Ibid.*, pp. 24–29.

438   "Of course . . . cruel!": RA: Z 39/26, V to QV, 5/22/87.

438   "horrid preparations": RA: Z 39/25, V to QV, 5/20/87.

438   "touched to tears": RA: Z 39/29, V to QV, 5/27/87.

438   "Dear Louise . . . rude!": RA: Z 39/27, V to QV, 5/22/87.

438   "How all . . . us": RA: Z 39/31, V to QV, 5/31/87.

438   "I know . . . proper": RA: Z 39/29, V to QV, 5/27/87.

439   "grand consultation . . . disease": Mackenzie, p. 34.

439   "Virchow . . . improbable": *Ibid.*, pp. 34–35.

439   "I think . . . jubilee": RA: Z 39/38, V to QV, 6/11/87.

439   "I must . . . meet": RA: Z 39/34, V to QV, 6/3/87.

CHAPTER FIFTY-ONE

440   *"She has . . . woman"*: Radziwill 4, p. 193.

440   "It seems . . . feeble": Corti 1, p. 237.

441   "Considering the . . . affairs": Robert Massie, *Dreadnought*, p. 35.

441   "be stirred . . . England": Lamar Cecil, "History as Family Chronicle," Röhl and Sombart, pp. 100–101.

441   "William is . . . tendency!": RA: Z 39/5, V to QV, 3/7/87.

441   "had no . . . aside": Holstein, Vol. II, p. 347.

442   "Pardon me . . . excuse": Rodd 1, p. 123.

442   "rudeness . . . roots": WII, pp. 199–201 *passim*.

442   "very dangerous . . . omnipotence": RA: Z 39/19, V to QV, 4/22/87.

442   "women were . . . them": John C. G. Röhl, "The Emperor's New Clothes," Röhl and Sombart, p. 46.

442   "Clothes and . . . understands": Balfour, p. 87.

443   "one of . . . law": Radziwill 1, pp. 155–56.

443   "first because . . . think": KHH: QV to V, 3/21/87.

443   "[W]e most . . . relations": RA: Z 39/13, V to QV, 3/26/87.

443   "ordered . . . are": RA: Z 39/30, V to QV, 5/30/87.

443   "by the . . . whatever": RA: Z 39/34 *passim*, V to QV, 6/3/87.

444   "I trust . . . on!": RA: Z 39/35, V to QV, 6/5/87.

444   "sulked": RA: Z 50/48, V to QV, 6/20/91.

444   "he [Willy] only . . . them": Holstein, Vol. III, p. 219.

445   "one of . . . Wagner": The Marquis of Lorne, *V.R.I, Queen Victoria, Her Life and Empire*, p. 322.

445   "Bonnets and . . . Mantel": Longford, p. 500.

445   "natural voice again": Stevenson, p. 89.

445 "sufferings . . . relapse": Corti 1, pp. 246–47.
446 "dangerous state": RA: Z 38/96, V to QV, 11/28/87.
446 "He goes . . . master": Longford, p. 503.
446 "I flattereed . . . campaign": Holstein, Vol. II, p. 216–17, Radolinski to Holstein, 7/20/87.
446 "calm . . . Seckendorff": KHH: QV to V, 8/27/87.
446 "The Crown . . . deliverance": Holstein, Vol. II, p. 348, 9/28/87.
446 "I am . . . believes: RA: Add. A 12/1502, V to Lady Ponsonby, 9/9/87.
447 The Crown Princess's alleged affair with Seckendorff: See "The Myth About the Missed Liberal Chance: Illness and Death of Emperor Friedrich III," by Professor Dr. John C. G. Röhl, *Frankfurther Allgemeine Zeitung,* June 15, 1988.
447 "It would . . . present": RA: Z 38/57, V to QV, 8/30/87.
448 "It is . . . Italy": RA: Z 38/74, V to QV, 10/17/87.
448 "Sir M. . . . aback": RA: Z 38/83, V to QV, 11/6/87.
448 "I have . . . heroism": Mackenzie, pp. 65–66.
448 "To think . . . health": RA: Z 38/91, V to QV, 11/18/87.

CHAPTER FIFTY-TWO
449 *"I cannot . . . hope":* RA: Z 38/85, V to QV, 11/11/87.
449 "heartless . . . vain": Palmer 2, p. 29.
449 Willy's visit: There are two versions of this story. This is a composite of the Crown Princess's letter to Queen Victoria, dated November 15, 1887 (RA: Z 38/87) and Kaiser Wilhelm II's somewhat different rendering in his autobiography, *My Early Life,* p. 279.
449 "begged . . . up": WII, p. 278.
450 "many a . . . together": RA: Z 38/87, V to QV, 11/15/87.
450 "came in . . . followed": William II 2, p. 279 *passim.*
450 "with the . . . inexperienced": RA: Z 38/87, V to QV, 11/15/87.
450 "would simply . . . Fritz": RA: Z 38/87, V to QV, 11/15/87.
450 "same character . . . another" Thomas A. Kohut, "Kaiser Wilhelm II and His Parents," in Röhl and Sombart, p. 80.
451 "one of . . . Germany": Mackenzie, p. 68.
451 "They read . . . way": RA: Z 38/84, V to QV, 11/9/87.
451 "it would . . . high": WII, p. 280.
451 "put their . . . shock": RA: Z 38/85, V to QV, 11/11/87.
451 "convulsive sobbing": WII, p. 280.
451 "I have . . . end": Kollander, p. 237.
451 "And so . . . order": WII, p. 281.
452 "Christian submission": Corti 1, p. 256.
452 "[T]here is . . . Prince": Röhl, p. 690.
453 "Do not . . . Regency": RA: Z 38/88, V to QV, 11/16/87.
453 "The interference . . . think!": RA: Z 38/91, V to QV, 11/18/87.
453 "The Crown . . . monarchy": Holstein, Vol. II, pp. 357–58, 11/14/87.
454 "should not . . . government!": WII, p. 276.
454 "Now as . . . statements": Virginia Cowles, *The Kaiser,* p. 68.
454 "They have . . . me!": RA: Z 38/97, V to QV, 11/29/87.
454 "Henry . . . operation!!": *Ibid.*
454 "painfully . . . views": Corti 1, p. 255.
454 "quite a . . . pleasant": RA: Z 38/101, V to QV, 12/8/87.
455 "The conviction . . . operation": Corti 1, p. 256.

CHAPTER FIFTY-THREE
456 *"Press, Jews . . . gas?":* NYPL: Poultney Bigelow papers, Box 34A, letter Wilhelm II to Poultney Bigelow, 8/15/27.

456 "satisfactory . . . favourable": RA: Z 39/42–51, doctors' reports, 11/11/87–12/27/87.

456 "made their . . . creatures!": WII, p. 279.

456 "The less . . . it": RA: Z 38/101, V to QV, 12/8/87.

456 "Letters are . . . Germany": RA: Z 38/103, V to QV, 12/14/87.

457 "[Y]ou must . . . enough": KHH: QV to V, 12/15/87.

457 "I cannot . . . smile: Holstein, Vol. II, pp. 350–51. It is assumed by the editors of the Holstein papers that this was written by Lyncker to Radolinski, who was in Berlin at the time.

457 "did not . . . true!": Röhl, p. 700.

457 "not a . . . lonely": *Letters*, p. 268, Lady Ponsonby to QV, 12/14/87.

458 "I declare . . . pity": *Ibid.*, p. 270, Lady Ponsonby to Sir Henry Ponsonby, undated.

458 "The boy . . . it!!": RA: Z 38/97, V to QV, 11/29/87.

459 "second Luther": Lamar Cecil, *Wilhelm II,* p. 104.

459 "the most . . . Monarchy": Balfour, p. 114.

459 "Wilhelm does . . . me": Nichols, p. 40.

459 "When I . . . it": *Ibid.*

459 "For the . . . treatment": Holstein, Vol. II, p. 363.

459 "down to . . . detail": Cecil, p. 102.

459 "Thank God . . . today": RA: Z 40/14, V to QV, 2/9/87.

460 "irrevocably lost . . . past!": RA: Z 40/16, V to QV, 2/12/87.

460 "I fear . . . you": KHH: QV to V, 2/16/88.

460 "smiling as . . . hope: Holstein, Vol. III, p. 258–59 *passim,* Radolinsky to Holstein, 2/12/88.

460 "cancer was . . . possibility": *Ibid.*

460 "no longer . . . doubt": *Ibid.*, p. 109.

460 "it may be": RA: Z 40/27, V to QV, 3/6/88.

461 "Surgeons have . . . excuse": RA: Z 41/15, Morell Mackenzie to Sir James Reid, 2/23/88.

461 "sole responsible . . . Mackenzie": Stevenson, p. 109.

461 "nothing less . . . life": Rodd 1, p. 128.

461 "Would it . . . tomorrow": Wiegler, p. 442.

461 "It is . . . beginning": Nichols, pp. 167–68.

462 "His Majesty . . . Germany": Corti 1, p. 264.

462 "I thank . . . wife": *Letters*, p. 286.

CHAPTER FIFTY-FOUR

463 *"The Emperor . . . Emperor!": ("L'Empéreur est mort, vive l'Empéreur mourant!")* Corti 1, p. 266.

463 "My own . . . now": KHH: QV to V, 3/10/88.

463 "We are . . . him": Nichols, p. 173.

464 "glad to . . . fatigue": RA: Z 41/25, V to QV, 3/13/88.

464 "the people . . . windows": RA: Z 41/26, V to QV, 3/14–15/88.

464 "beautifully written": Nichols, p. 181.

465 "the faithful . . . Empire": *Letters,* pp. 289–91, F to Bismarck, 3/12/88.

465 "very good . . . well!": RA: Z 41/30, V to QV, 3/19/88.

465 "produced the . . . impression": RA: Z 41/26, V to QV, 3/14–15/88.

465 "I feel . . . more!": Pflanze, Vol. III, p. 281.

465 "not a . . . so": RA: Z 41/30, V to QV, 3/19/88.

465 "a feminine . . . months": Nichols, p. 193.

466 "The Emperor's . . . policy": Corti 1, p. 266.

466 "It is . . . months": RA: Z 41/26, V to QV, 3/14–15/88.

467 "rather over-zealous": Rodd 1, p. 131.

467 "That is . . . now": Corti 1, p. 269.

467 "On account . . . bed": RA: Z 41/27, V to QV, 3/16/88.

467 "Sure . . . listening": Nichols, pp. 255–56.

468 "Like the . . . Jews": Waldersee, p. 138.

468   "Cohn I . . . thousand": Nichols, p. 184.
468   "the national . . . graybeard": *Ibid.,* p. 193.
468   "was particularly . . . with": Corti 1, p. 288.
468   "Everything . . . question": Pflanze, Vol. III, p. 281.
469   The tension . . . throne: *Ibid.,* p. 295.
469   "I had . . . once": Corti 1, pp. 285–86.
470   "quite exhausted": RA: Z 41/30, V to QV, 3/19/88.
470   "Hohenzollern Prussia . . . woman": Nichols, p. 176.
470   "I think . . . future": RA: Z 41/27, V to QV, 3/16/88.
470   "I have . . . sea": KHH: QV to V, 3/31/88.
470   "besmirched . . . ruin": Röhl, "The Emperor's New Clothes," Röhl and Sombart, p. 33.
471   "In deep . . . way": Waldersee, p. 136.
471   "that has . . . government": Nichols, pp. 216–17.
471   "There was . . . Berlin": Rodd 1, p. 133.

CHAPTER FIFTY-FIVE

472   *"For him . . . reach":* Radziwill 3, p. 53.
472   "I can . . . Sandro: KHH: QV to V, 3/21/88.
473   "impossible": Corti 2, p. 284.
473   "What to . . . come": Nichols, p. 206.
473   "jumped up . . . clear": Corti 2, p. 285. Corti describes the scene, but gives no source; therefore, I do not consider him a primary source like the Holstein Diaries, which quote Radolinski.
473   "stamped . . . sheet": Holstein, Vol. I, p. 141.
473   "Battenberg will . . . wife": Corti 2, p. 285.
473   "The Battenberg . . . affair": Holstein, Vol. II, pp. 366–67.
474   "a crazy letter": Corti 2, p. 286.
474   "I will . . . this": *Ibid.,* p. 284.
474   "very biting": Holstein, Vol. II, p. 368.
474   "I shall . . . accordingly": Corti 2, p. 288.
474   "The worst . . . mother!": Cecil, p. 118.
475   "I count . . . wish": Corti 2, p. 293.
475   "enchanted": Nichols, p. 213.
475   "about to . . . fatherland": *Ibid.,* p. 210.
475   "I would . . . mother": Busch, Vol. II, pp. 412–19.
476   "Battenberg marriage . . . act": Nichols, p. 209.
476   "I am . . . it": *Ibid.,* p. 227.
476   "really disloyal . . . understand": *Letters,* pp. 295–96, QV to Sir Henry Ponsonby, 4/9/88.
476   "great hubbub . . . press": RA: Add. A 5/479/11.
476   "as if . . . history": *Letters,* p. 299, Colonel Leopold Swaine to the Prince of Wales, 4/13/88.
476   "So many . . . again": Ponsonby 2, p. 294.
477   "I do . . . agreeable": *Letters,* p. 301, V to QV, 4/13/88.
477   "pay no . . . silly": RA: Z 41/38, V to QV, 4/10/88.
477   Regarding the reasons for Bismarck's behavior: J. Alden Nichols *(The Year of the Three Kaisers)* posits another, more Machiavellian theory, i.e., that Bismarck was trying "to provoke the reactionaries into attacking the crown" in order to show Willy just how disloyal his friends really were (p. 213).

CHAPTER FIFTY-SIX

479   *"I must . . . do":* Corti 1, p. 279.
479   "peculiar sound": *Ibid.,* p. 275.

479 "in a . . . hands": Stevenson, pp. 121–22.
479 "as soon as possible": *Ibid.*, pp. 117–18 *passim.*
479 "in a . . . again": Mackenzie, pp. 145–49.
480 "ill treated me": Stevenson, p. 123.
480 "Bergmann for . . . afternoon": Corti 1, p. 275.
480 "knew not . . . deftly": Stevenson, p. 118 *passim.*
480 "The battle . . . people": Rodd 1, p. 137.
480 "There was . . . cannula": Stevenson, p. 123.
481 "attributable . . . stabbing": Mackenzie, pp. 154–55.
481 "very serious . . . pus": RA: Z 41/39, Morell Mackenzie to Sir James Reid 4/18/88, 4/20/88.
481 "Everywhere . . . come": Nichols, p. 241.
481 "hopeless . . . day": Waldersee, p. 141.
481 "In the . . . exception": Holstein, Vol. II, pp. 270–71.
481 "Her Majesty . . . concern": Nichols, pp. 247–48.
482 "It appears . . . weighed": *Ibid.*
482 "He was . . . Bismarck": Buckle, Third Series, Vol. I, 1886–1890, p. 402, QVJ, 4/24/88.
482 "I was . . . both": KHH: QV to V, 5/21/88.
482 "almost nervous": Ponsonby 2, p. 297.
482 "agreeably surprised . . . gentle": Buckle, Third Series, Vol. I, 1886–1890, p. 404, (QVJ, 4/25/88).
482 "He spoke . . . clever' ": Corti 1, p. 276, and Nichols, p. 249.
483 "What a woman!": Crankshaw, p. 408.
483 "Grandmama behaved . . . Charlottenburg": Busch, Vol. II, p. 423.
483 "Prince Bismarck . . . minimised": *Letters,* p. 303, Sir Edward Malet to the Marquis of Salisbury, 4/28/88.
483 "unbuttoned his . . . heart": *Ibid.*, p. 304.
483 "Vicky took . . . three!": RA: QVJ, 4/25/88.
483 "[I]t was . . . lot": Buckle, Vol. I, 1886–1890, pp. 407–408 (extract from QVJ, 4/26/88, "In the Train").
483 "high time the old lady died": Röhl, "The Emperor's New Clothes," Röhl and Sombart, p. 32. This remark is not in quotation marks in Röhl.
484 "in full . . . Emperor!": Corti 1, p. 278.
484 "I have . . . to-day!": Radziwill 1, pp. 216–18.
484 "If I . . . out": Corti 1, p. 278.
484 "had control . . . patriotism!": *Ibid.*, pp. 294–95.
484 "I dare . . . Germany?": *Ibid.*, p. 278.
484 "William fancies . . . one!": RA: Z 41/47, V to QV, 5/12/88.
484 "as demonstratively . . . well": RA: Z 41/50 *passim,*V to QV, 5/18/88.
484 "He is . . . this!": RA: Z 41/49, V to QV, 5/19/88.
484 "I am . . . it": KHH: QV to V, 5/21/88.
484 "I am . . . sport": Holstein, Vol. II, p. 376.
485 "droll": Nichols, p. 265.
485 "been waiting . . . people": *Ibid.*, p. 305 *passim.*
485 "ungracious": *Ibid.*, p. 322.
486 "that the . . . coup": *Ibid.*, p. 306.
486 "Mama and . . . too": *Ibid.*, p. 328.
486 "very careful . . . sensible": *Ibid.*, p. 331.
486 "Fritz has . . . sure": RA: Z 41/59, V to QV, 6/8/88.
486 "Do you . . . understanding": Nichols, p. 334. For a detailed and cogent analysis of this affair, see J. Alden Nichols, *The Year of Three Kaisers,* from which this summary is taken.

CHAPTER FIFTY-SEVEN

487 *"No one . . . day"*: Eyck, pp. 298–99.
487 "God damn . . . affairs": Nichols, p. 318.
488 "imperial dignity . . . silence": Poschinger, pp. 452–53.
488 "I have . . . this": Corti 1, p. 279.
488 "What will . . . improve?": *Ibid.*
488 "not going . . . long!": RA: Z 41/61, V to QV, 6/12/88.
488 "sealed their . . . scenes": RA: Z 68/126, Radolinski to QV, 6/22/88.
488 "[H]is face . . . go": Corti 1, pp. 297–98.
489 "Our day . . . again": Cecil, p . 123.
489 "I hardly . . . terrace!": RA: Z 41/62, V to QV, 6/13/88.
489 "I am . . . now": GStA: F's diary, 6/14/88.
489 "a special . . . keeping": Corti 1, p. 300.
489 "What is . . . me?": *Ibid.*, p. 301.
489 "Are the . . . me?": GStA, F's diary, 6/14/88.
489 "left and . . . palace": Corti 1, p. 301, *passim.*
490 "Oh, very, very!": *Ibid.*
490 "Victoria . . . children": Kollander, p. 259.
490 "Gradually . . . quiet!": Corti 1, p. 302.
490 "appeared unmounted . . . found!": *Ibid.*, pp. 302–303.
490 "The measures . . . me": Kürenberg, p. 81.
491 "shrubbery": Nichols, p. 339.
491 "In spite . . . with": Waldersee, p. 146.
491 "German medicine . . . skullduggeries": Kollander, p. 261.
491 "I was . . . remains": Corti 1, p. 304.
491 "The dead . . . chattering": Kürenberg, pp. 81–82.
492 "Try, my . . . world": RA: GV AA 17/24, the Prince of Wales to the Duke of York, 6/16/88.
492 "Instead of . . . infamous": Cowles, p. 74.
492 "immature bad boy": Cecil, p. 268.
492 "Prince Bismarck . . . happens": St. Aubyn, p. 280.
492 "the saddest . . . Liberalism": Nichols, p. 338 *passim.*
493 "[H]aving . . . iron": Wemyss, Vol. I, p. 164.

CHAPTER FIFTY-EIGHT

497 *"It is . . . wicked"*: RA: Add. U 172/143, QV to Victoria of Hesse, 7/4/88.
497 "William II . . . also": Corti 1, p. 308.
497 "follow . . . path": *Letters,* p. 322.
497 "I became . . . generation": WII, p. 3.
497 "I close . . . stuffed!!": RA: Z 42/5, V to QV, 6/29/88.
497 "recovered from . . . sickness": Waldersee, p.146.
497 "Prince Bismarck . . . condole!": Corti 1, p. 308.
497 "cold reception": *Letters,* p. 324, Colonel Swain to Sir Henry Ponsonby, 7/4/88.
497 "The Queen . . . accession": Buckle, Third Series, Vol. I, pp. 421–22, QV to Sir Henry Ponsonby, 6/28/88.
498 "as if . . . position": Corti 1, p. 310.
498 "I think . . . you!!": RA: Z 42/9, V to QV, 7/8/88.
498 "sickening": Buckle, Third Series, Vol. I, p. 433, QV to the Prince of Wales, 7/24/88.
498 "the peace . . . world": RA: I 56/84, WII to QV, 7/6/88.
498 "Trust that . . . government": Buckle, Third Series, Vol. I, p. 429, cable QV to the Marquis of Salisbury, 7/7/88.
498 "All one . . . happy": RA: Z 44/4, V to QV, 2/27/89.
498 "William is . . . too": RA: Z 42/33, V to QV, 7/27/88.

498 "The last . . . you": RA: Z 42/31, V to QV, 8/16/88.
499 "some mistake . . . visitors": RA: Z 42/42, V to QV, 9/1/88.
499 "Since our . . . entertaining": RA: Z 43/10, V to QV, 9/28/88.
499 *Der greise . . . Kaiser]*": *Letters*, p. 347.
499 "I am . . . support": Corti 1, p. 309.
499 "terrible intrigues": Buckle, Third Series, Vol. I, p. 420, QVJ, 6/25/88.
499 "I am . . . you": RA: I 56/82, QV to WII, 7/3/88.
500 "enormous amount . . . year": RA: I 56/84, WII to QV, 7/6/88.
500 "Capital . . . course": RA: Z 60A/4, V to QV, 7/13/88.
500 "it's the . . . penny": Kohut, p. 76.
501 "I do . . . munificence": Reischach, p. 118.
501 the Duchess de Galliera: The Dowager Empress was not the only royal beneficiary
    of the Galliera largesse: the Duchess bequeathed her palace in Paris to Franz Joseph
    of Austria. At the time of the Duke's death, which preceded that of the Duchess,
    the Galliera estate was worth approximately 200 million French francs, of which
    Vicky received five million.
501 "William . . . it": RA: Z 43/7, V to QV, 9/24/88.
501 "I never . . . Berlin!": RA: Z 44/39, V to QV, 5/7/89.
502 Regarding the increase in Wilhelm II's income: See Michael Balfour, *The Kaiser
    and His Times*, p. 125.
502 "bear . . . creators": RA: Z 45/30, V to QV, 7/23/89.
502 "[It] is . . . me!": RA: Z 45/24, V to QV, 7/6/89.
502 "When . . . misgivings": Corti 1, p. 309.
502 "It pains . . . Friedrich' ": RA: Z 42/24, V to QV, 7/30/88.
502 "purloined . . . there": RA: Z 60A/3, V to QV, 7/12/88.
502 "State papers . . . year": RA: Z 41/66, V to QV, 6/20/88.
503 "[A]s Friedberg . . . all": RA: Z 60A/3, V to QV, 7/12/88.
503 "[I]n case . . . England": RA: Z 42/19, V to QV, 7/21/88.
503 "only documents . . . no!": RA: Z 43/2, V to QV, undated (possibly 9/13/88).
503 "Scarcely . . . work": Corti 1, p. 307.
503 "was no . . . tube": Stevenson, p. 143.
503 "Gentlemen . . . dead": Corti 1, pp. 307–308.
504 "The operation . . . relief": Lee 1, p. 218.
504 "*he would* . . . Nation": Rodd 1, pp. 146–47.
504 "[I]t was . . . right": *Ibid.*, p. 152.
504 "They have . . . so!": RA: Z 43/24, V to QV, 10/16/88.
504 "It is . . . St. Petersburg!": RA: Z 43/25, V to QV, 10/17/88.

CHAPTER FIFTY-NINE

506 "*Nothing was . . . matters*": Anne Topham, *Memories of the Fatherland*, p. 33.
506 "His dear . . . Sedan": RA: Z 42/27, V to QV, 8/6/88.
506 "The Marmor . . . me": RA: Z 43/7, V to QV, 9/24/88.
507 "not allowed . . . sympathisers": Eyck, p. 305.
507 "genuine . . . Emperor": Busch, p. 435.
507 "The Diary . . . apocryphal' ": RA: Z 43/9, V to QV, 9/27/88.
507 "I have . . . Arnim' ": RA: Z 43/11, V to QV, 11/29/88.
507 "high treason": *Letters*, p. 348.
507 "There is . . . have!": RA: Z 43/20, V to QV, 10/11/88.
508 "manner . . . them": Rodd 1, pp. 158–59. Rodd says that he does "not pretend to
    quote precisely the words used, but the substance . . . is correct."
508 "poor old Geffcken": RA: Z 43/13, V to QV, 10/2/88.
508 "clumsy invention . . . honor": Pflanze, Vol. III, p. 305.
509 "I must . . . off": Reischach, p. 110.
509 "completely . . . invented": Bülow, Vol. II, p. 530.
509 "so many . . . now": Bunsen, p. 218.

509 "resolutely . . . notice": RA: Z 44/37, Lady Ponsonby to QV, 5/4/89.
509 "Gustav . . . others!": RA: Z 43/31, V to QV, 10/30/88.
510 "a very . . . Europe": RA: Z 44/37, Lady Ponsonby to QV, 5/4/89.
510 "that fat . . . influence": Holstein, Vol. II, p. 382.
510 "great surprise . . . admiration": RA: Z 45/36, V to QV, 8/5/89.
510 " 'an English . . . believes": RA: Z 44/33, V to QV, 4/27/89.
510 "nothing . . . perchance": RA: Z 43/6, V to QV, 9/22/88.
510 "suffering . . . selfish": RA: Z 43/1, V to QV, 9/13/88.
510 "How I . . . myself!": RA: Z 43/11, V to QV, 9/29/88.
510 "Some of . . . this!": RA: Z 43/25, V to QV, 10/17/88.
511 "completely . . . so": RA: Z 43/20, V to QV, 10/11/88.
511 "says William . . . grandfather": RA: Z 43/27, V to QV, 10/20/88.
511 "The result . . . libel": RA: Z 47/9, V to QV, 12/24/89.
512 "a brave . . . woman": Freytag, p. 41.
512 "subordination . . . absolute": *Ibid.,* p. 49.
512 "quite incomprehensible . . . careful": GStA: Louis of Hesse to V, 10/13/88.
512 "only Louis . . . fears": RA: Z 52/43, V to QV, 4/17/92.
512 "thereby showing . . . house": *Letters,* Colonel Leopold Swaine to Sir Henry Ponsonby, November 1888.
513 "interfered": RA: Z 57/13, V to QV, 11/30/94.
513 "duty . . . habits": RA: Z 43/34, Augusta to V, 11/7/88.
513 "continual intercourse . . . sometimes": RA: Z 42/36, V to QV, 8/22/88.
513 "really like . . . one": RA: Z 42/37, V to QV, 8/23/88.
513 "fawns on William": RA: Z 43/20, V to QV, 10/11/88.
513 "William & . . . year": RA: Z 43/32, V to QV, 11/2/88.
513 "to hide . . . events' ": RA: Z 44/5, V to QV, 2/28/89.
103 "As to . . . strangers": RA: Z 44/8, V to QV, 3/4/89.
513 "in Russia": RA: Z 44/10, V to QV, 3/8/89.
513 "I am . . . suffocating": RA: Z 44/21, V to QV, 4/1/89.
514 "more prudent": Buckle, Third Series, Vol. I, p. 443, the Marquis of Salisbury to the Prince of Wales, 10/24/88.
514 "Letter received . . . again": *Ibid.,* p. 443, QV to the Marquis of Salisbury, 10/24/88.
514 "Bernhard . . . Government": RA: Z 43/32, V to QV, 11/2/88.
514 "The Empress . . . elements": Corti 1, p. 313.
514 "The Clique . . . country": RA: Z 43/32, V to QV, 11/2/88.
514 "[I]t would . . . years": RA: Z 49/10, V to QV, 8/27/90.

CHAPTER SIXTY

515 "*[I]t is . . . even!*": RA: Z 42/6, V to QV, 7/2/88.
515 "affairs of state": Cowles, p. 89.
515 "a scandal": Buckle, Third Series, Vol. I, p. 489, the Prince of Wales to Prince Christian of Schleswig-Holstein, 4/3/89.
515 "uncle's rooms . . . company": Cowles, p. 89.
515 "gross insult . . . this": RA: Add. A 5 479/34 *passim,* the Prince of Wales to V, 10/31/88.
515 "I am . . . that": RA: Z 43/32, V to QV, 11/2/88.
516 "[I]t is . . . impossible": Buckle, Third Series, Vol. I, p. 441, QV to the Marquis of Salisbury, 10/15/88.
516 "Here Bertie . . . him!": RA: Z 43/32, V to QV, 11/2/88.
516 "I believe . . . manners": RA: Z 60A/9, V to QV, 1/19/89.
517 "less satisfactory . . . possible": Buckle, Third Series, Vol. I, p. 477 *passim,* the Marquis of Salisbury to V, 3/9/89.
517 "William must . . . apology": Corti 1, p. 321.
517 "William yesterday . . . me": RA: Z 44/9, V to QV, 3/7/89.
517 "I quite . . . passed": RA: Z 44/13, V to QV, 3/15/89.

517 "invention": Buckle, Third Series, Vol. I, p. 491, Prince Christian of Schleswig-Holstein to the Prince of Wales, 4/8/89 (secret telegram).
517 "a few . . . Vienna": *Ibid.,* p. 492, the Prince of Wales to Prince Christian, 4/10/89.
517 "if he . . . occurred": *Ibid.,* p. 500, Sir Henry Ponsonby to Prince Christian, 5/25/89.
517 "matters worse . . . story": *Ibid.,* p. 501, Sir Henry Ponsonby to Prince Christian (?), 6/1/89.
518 "show his . . . right": Corti 1, p. 323.
518 "sacrificed . . . expediency": Buckle, Third Series, Vol. I, p. 501, Sir Francis Knollys to Prince Christian, 6/8/89.
518 "I hope . . . me!": RA: Z 45/26, V to QV, 7/13/89.
518 "Wronged . . . offence!": RA: Z 46/13, V to QV, 9/27/89.
518 "I can . . . wish": RA: Z 45/10, V to QV, 6/3/89.
518 "very amiable . . . legs": Buckle, Third Series, Vol. I, pp. 521–22, QVJ, 8/2–8, 1889
519 "the admirable . . . him": *Ibid.,* p. 523, the Marquis of Salisbury to QV, 8/8/89.
519 "the triumphant . . . fêted": *Letters,* pp. 389–90, V to QV, 9/27/89.
519 "All these . . . situation": RA: Z 45/38, V to QV, 8/9/89.
519 "a good . . . cleverness": KHH: QV to V, 9/4/88.
520 "On arriving . . . either": RA: Z 46/26, V to QV, 10/20/89.
520 "considerably relieved": RA: Z 46/32, V to QV, 11/4/89.
520 "the humble . . . Fleet": RA: I 58/21, WII to QV, 2/24/90.
521 "I certainly . . . war": Cecil, p. 132.
521 "quite disdainfully . . . Great": WII, p. 27.
521 "The Kaiser . . . genius": Balfour, p. 126.

CHAPTER SIXTY-ONE

522 *"How one . . . despot":* RA: Z 48/2, V to QV, 3/15/90.
522 "I never . . . nothing": RA: Z 46/13, V to QV, 9/27/89.
523 "necessary . . . zeal": Pflanze, Vol. III, p. 331.
523 "I will . . . unbecoming": RA: Z 45/2, V to QV, 5/18/89.
523 "The efforts . . . limits": Pflanze, Vol. III, p. 348.
523 "Not all . . . owned": *Ibid.,* pp. 348–49.
523 "a mine . . . himself": RA: Z 47/34, V to QV, 2/19–21/90.
523 "he had . . . confidence ": RA: Z 44/31, V to QV, 4/20/89.
523 "If I . . . military": Pflanze, Vol. III, p. 303.
524 "my ideas . . . Beggars": *Ibid.,* pp. 356–57.
524 "his distinguished . . . duty": *Ibid.,* pp. 320–21.
524 "If his . . . position": *Ibid.,* pp. 356–58.
525 "That puts . . . opinion": Cowles, pp. 91–92.
525 "boiling": Pflanze, Vol. III, p. 358.
525 "They are . . . Bismarck's": Eyck, p. 315.
525 "gone too . . . chancellor": Pflanze, Vol. III, pp. 358–59 *passim.*
525 "My beloved . . . genius!": RA: Z 47/32, V to QV, 2/15/90.
525 "There is . . . not?": RA: Z 47/34, V to QV, 2/19–21/90.
525 "a move . . . sense?": KHH: QV to V, 2/19/90.
526 "never mentioned . . . expect": RA: Z 47/34, V to QV, 2/19–21/90.
526 "Prince Bismarck . . . you": Princess Marie Louise, *My Memories of Six Reigns,* p. 94.
526 "I want . . . sympathy": Pflanze, Vol. III, p. 365.
527 "So far . . . to": RA: Z 47/34, V to QV, 2/19–21/90.
527 "the socialist menace": Pflanze, Vol. III, p. 364.
527 "No surrender! . . . side": *Ibid.*
527 "like a . . . way": *Ibid.,* p. 365.
528 "[T]he breach . . . Chancellor": Holstein, Vol. III, p. 328, Prince Reuss to Holstein.

528 "I have . . . man": Pflanze, Vol. III, p. 370.
528 "in Friedrichsruh . . . time": *Ibid* .
529 "I am . . . write": *Ibid.*, p. 96.
529 "deepest . . . heart": *Ibid.*, p. 373.
529 "that false face": Cowles, p. 97.
529 "tried to . . . same": *Ibid.*, p. 98 *passim* Note: Cowles has translated the second person singular familiar form to "thee," for which I have substituted the more common "you."
530 "train . . . schoolboy": Buckle, Third Series, Vol. I, pp. 584–87, Memorandum, Sir Edward Malet, 3/22/90.
530 "I cannot . . . peace": RA: Z 48/5, V to QV, 3/22/90.
530 "the manner . . . press": Bigelow, p. 47.
530 "Prince . . . not": RA: Z 48/6, V to QV, 3/25/90.
530 "Like a . . . added": Pflanze, Vol. III, p. 377.
531 "The Emperor . . . again": Radziwill 3, p. 349.
531 "a state . . . honours": Cowles, p. 97.
531 "Yesterday Prince . . . done:" RA: I 58/32, WII to QV, 3/27/90.

CHAPTER SIXTY-TWO

532 *"I always . . . either!"*: RA: Add. A 4/28, the Prince of Wales to V, 5/9/91.
532 "Louise . . . yesterday!": RA: Z 47/14, V to QV, 1/6/90.
532 "She was . . . friends!": RA: Z 47/15, V to QV, 1/3/90.
532 "You would . . . remembered": RA: Z 47/16, V to QV, 1/11/90.
533 "I have . . . me": Lee 1, p. 56.
533 "knows nothing . . . wounded": *Ibid.*, p. 57.
533 "ready now . . . me!": RA: Z 47/17 *passim*, V to QV, 1/13/90.
534 "could only . . . pocket": RA: Z 47/19, V to QV, 1/17/90.
534 "prevent my . . . influence!": RA: Z 47/17, V to QV, 1/13/90.
534 "I am . . . hard": RA: Z 47/19, V to QV, 1/17/90.
534 "I think . . . order": RA: Z 47/22, V to QV, 1/23/90.
534 "great ceremony . . . foolish": RA: Z 47/40, V to QV, 3/10/90.
534 "a most . . . row": RA: Z 47/32, V to QV, 2/15/90.
534 "little present . . . belong": RA: Z 54/5, V to QV, 11/22/92.
535 "a perfect . . . yet!": RA: Z 54/76, V to QV, 6/26/93.
535 "[I]t is . . . spoilt!": RA: Z 48/26, V to QV, 6/3/90.
536 "[I]t again . . . Diary": RA: Z 48/31, V to QV, 6/13/90.
536 "Dona seemed . . . is!": RA: Z 48/5, V to QV, 3/22/90.
536 "means to . . . way": RA: Z 49/44, V to QV, 12/16/90.
536 "Dona keeps . . . reason": RA: Z 50/13, V to QV, 2/6/91.
537 "as the . . . godmother": RA: Z 50/8, V to QV, 1/25/91.
537 "Wherever William . . . on": RA: Z 50/18, V to QV, 2/14/91.
537 "cut out . . . maid": RA: Z 49/40, V to QV, 12/5/90.
537 "in dread . . . marriage": RA: Z 45/10 *passim*, V to QV, 6/3/89.
537 "I shall . . . reason!": RA: Z 45/17, V to QV, 6/19/89.
537 "I think . . . painful": KHH: QV to V, 6/18/89.
538 "I should . . . me": RA: Z 45/18, V to QV, 6/21/89.
538 "In her . . . die": RA: Z 48/30, V to QV, 6/12/90.
538 "frantic telegram . . . hours": RA: Z 50/23, V to QV, 2/22/91.
538 "I feel . . . provided!": RA: Z 48/21, V to QV, 5/17/90.
539 "took off . . . from her": RA: Z 69/153, William Haggard to Sir Henry Ponsonby, 7/21/90.
539 "a skilled doctor": RA: Z 69/182, William Haggard to Sir Henry Ponsonby, 7/29/90.
539 "William is . . . account!": RA: Z 49/5, V to QV, 8/13/90.
539 "I hear . . . country": Corti 1, pp. 337–38.

540 "The version . . . soon": RA: Z 50/6, V to QV, 1/20/91.
540 "I trust . . . home": RA: Z 50/29, V to QV, 3/29/91.
540 "one has . . . it": Corti 1, pp. 338–39.
540 "RECEIVED . . . SOPHIE": Lee 1, pp. 85–86.

CHAPTER SIXTY-THREE

541 *"What . . . successor?"*: Massie, p. 111.
541 "How much . . . life!": RA: Z 49/37, V to QV, 11/22/90.
541 "It does . . . world": RA: Z 49/43, V to QV, 12/13/90.
541 "I thought . . . office": RA: Z 48/6, V to QV, 3/25/90.
542 "rarely sober": RA: Z 48/11, V to QV, 4/8/90.
542 "I . . . policy": Corti 1, p. 334.
542 "A man . . . balls": Cecil, p. 189.
542 "If Bismarck . . . policy": Massie, p. 114.
543 "I am . . . Alliance": RA: I 58/45, WII to QV, 5/22/90.
543 "intriguing with . . . back": Buckle, Series Three, Vol. I, pp. 598–99, QVJ, 4/25–26, 1890.
544 "fishing for uniforms": Aronson 2, p. 227.
544 "bound to . . . exceptions": RA: I 58/21, WII to QV, 2/24/90.
544 "I am . . . me": RA: Z 50/12, V to QV, 2/3/91.
545 "very blond . . . charming": Gaston Routier, *Un Point d'Histoire Contemporaine: Le Voyage de l'Impératrice Frédéric à Paris*, p. 4.
545 "good . . . pictures": RA: Z 50/22, V to QV, 2/20/91.
545 "Vive Russia . . . Germans": Routier, p. 57.
545 "Without the . . . public": *Ibid.*, p. 29.
546 "half . . . mouth": Holstein, Vol. III, p. 370.
546 "There is . . . power": Corti 1, pp. 340–41.
546 "I still . . . spiteful": RA: Z 50/29, V to QV, 3/29/91.
547 "[H]e was . . . foe": RA: Z 50/29, V to QV, 9/26/91.
547 "really dreadful . . . speeches?": KHH: QV to V, 9/22/91.

CHAPTER SIXTY-FOUR

548 *"Wilhelm II's . . . limitless"*: Isobel Hull, *The Entourage of Kaiser Wilhelm II*, p. 64. The wording has been changed slightly here; the original reads "Wilhelm's capacity".
548 "Everything must . . . ukases": RA: Z 48/11, V to QV, 4/8/90.
548 "Chatter Chamber": Cecil, p. 195.
548 "A Czar . . . Century!!": RA: Z 51/46, V to QV, 11/16/91.
549 "the most . . . impression": Cecil, p. 197.
549 "playing a . . . game": RA: Z 52/20, V to QV, 2/16/92.
549 "The Jews . . . with": Townley, p. 45.
549 "The Kaiser . . . succession": Hull, p. 41.
549 "worthy of . . . consonants": Townley, pp. 54–61.
550 "comrades": Cecil, p. 127.
550 "designed for . . . Ruritania": Townley, p. 54.
550 "fad . . . accidents": RA: Z 51/16, V to QV, 8/29/91.
550 "The man . . . protection": RA: Z 52/48, V to QV, 5/14/92.
550 "fired": Bunsen, p. 232.
550 "The Army . . . enthusiasm": Cecil, p. 129.
550 "God . . . ancestors": *Ibid.*, p. 202.
550 "carry the . . . devil!": Waldersee, p. 192.
550 "swallows up everything": RA: Z 54/10, V to QV, 12/7/92.
550 "this immense . . . passed!": RA: Z 54/26, V to QV, 1/7/93.
551 "great victory": RA: I 59/101, telegram, WII to QV, 7/14/93.

551 "I was . . . arrived": Waldersee, p. 179.
551 "as if . . . there": John Röhl, "The Emperor's New Clothes," Röhl and Sombart, p. 33.
551 "Whenever he . . . life": WII, p. 187.
551 "intentionally poisoning": Hull, p. 80.
552 "not to . . . trusted": RA: Z 48/27, V to QV, 6/4/90.
552 "I'll parade . . . laughing": Hull, p. 69.
552 "having . . . Caprivi": RA: Z 53/48, V to QV, 11/9/92.
552 "diaspora press": Pflanze, Vol. III, p. 387.
552 "[T]he agitation . . . more!": RA: Z 52/5 *passim*, V to QV, 12/12/91.
553 "disobedient subject . . . Austria": Pflanze, Vol. III, p. 396.
553 "nasty old man": *Ibid.*, p. 402.
553 "You will . . . disastrous": RA: Z 55/53, V to QV, 1/25/94.
553 "very sensational . . . fun": RA: Z 55/54, V to QV, 1/25/94 .
553 "long, frank . . . views": Bunsen, p. 175.
554 "jubilant . . . stuff": *Ibid.*, p. 176.
554 "I thought . . . again": RA: Z 55/56, V to QV, 1/27/94.
554 "Fear of . . . Berlin": Cecil, p. 220.

CHAPTER SIXTY-FIVE

555 *"The Empress . . . history"*: Radziwill 1, p. 244.
555 "awake at . . . me": RA: Z 53/46, V to QV, 10/28/92.
555 "Calling you . . . visited": RA: Z 54/68, V to QV, 6/2/93.
555 "[T]he more . . . me": RA: Z 47/18, V to QV, 1/14/90.
555 "May God . . . me!": RA: Z 59/1, V to QV, 5/21/97.
556 "I should . . . little!": RA: Z 50/25, V to QV, 3/25/91.
556 "I am . . . night!": RA: Z 56/35, V to QV, 8/1/94.
556 "Pray do . . . eyes": RA: Z 55/14, V to QV, 9/6/93.
556 "much kindness . . . attractive": *Ibid.*
556 "It is . . . day": KHH: V to QV, 9/15/96.
556 "I cannot . . . mésalliance!!!": RA: Z 51/49, V to QV, 11/26/91.
556 "With regard . . . longer": RA: Z 55/73, V to QV, 4/26/94.
557 "I used . . . time!": RA: Z 56/16, V to QV, 6/8/94.
557 "I hope . . . do": KHH: QV to V, 6/22/92.
557 "I ought . . . widow": KHH: QV to V, 1/11/93.
557 "All you . . . me!": RA: Z 54/28, V to QV, 1/13/93.
557 "I am . . . come!": RA: Z 54/70, V to QV, 6/11–13/93.
558 "purposely kept away": RA: Z 53/47, V to QV, 11/4/92.
558 "[W]e should . . . laughing": RA: Z 52/21, V to QV, 2/20/92.
558 "[I]t makes . . . life!": RA: Z 53/28, V to QV, 8/27/92.
558 "I think . . . you!!": RA: Z 53/36, V to QV, 9/23/92.
558 "It is . . . month": RA: Z 52/25, V to QV, 2/27/92.
558 "William is . . . Rhine!": RA: Z 53/29, V to QV, 9/3/92.
559 "There is . . . art": KHH: V to QV, 8/29/96.
559 "Whether one . . . way!": RA: Z 59/35, V to QV, 6/22/98.
559 "[T]o have . . . accidents": RA: Z 55/29, V to QV, 11/3/93.
559 "looked upon . . . day": Bunsen, p. 190.
559 "large room . . . again": Hohenlohe-Schillingfürst, Vol. II, p. 469.
559 "As soon . . . neck": Bunsen, pp. 194–95 *passim*.
559 "Not a . . . seen": G. A. Leinhaas, *Reminiscences of Victoria, Empress Frederick,* p. 16.
559 "charm of manner": *Ibid.*, pp. 41–42.
559 "Her instincts . . . charity": Reischach, p. 92.
560 "The demands . . . supported": Leinhaas, p. 45.
560 "a fearless . . . horses": *Ibid.*, p. 17.

560 "splendid hands": Reischach, p. 92.
560 "There was . . . schloss": Fulford 1, p. 12.
560 "thoroughly . . . economics": Leinhaas, pp. 21–22.
560 "anything she . . . command": Bunsen, p. 204.
561 "noiseless footmen": *Ibid.*, p. 190.
561 "trailing black . . . veil": *Ibid.*, p. 192.
561 "thoroughbred . . . life": Bunsen, p. 191.
561 "My house . . . Copenhagen": RA: Z 57/27, V to QV, 1/18/95.
561 "This is . . . inn!": RA: Z 56/29, V to QV, 7/13/94.
561 "blowing their . . . tumult": Leinhaas, p. 41.
561 "She is . . . Mama": RA: Z 52/53, V to QV, 5/24/92.
561 "Her little . . . expect": RA: Z 55/20, V to QV, 9/30/93.
561 "Her parents . . . away!": RA: Z 56/52, V to QV, 10/5/94.
562 "so kind & good": RA: Z 56/45, V to QV, 9/13/94.
562 "A Frenchwoman . . . Gunther": RA: Z 56/1, V to QV, 5/2/94.
562 "a new . . . generations": RA: Z 56/6, V to QV, 5/11/94.
562 "no more . . . time": Henry W. Fischer, *Private Lives of Kaiser William II and His Consort*, Vol. II, p. 406.
563 "William's . . . suite": RA: Z 57/8, V to QV, 11/22/94.
563 "with their . . . minutes!": RA: Z 57/32, V to QV, 2/5/95.
563 "She does . . . duty": KHH: V to QV, 7/17/96.
563 "enormous": KHH: V to QV, 10/22/96.
563 "My personal . . . it": KHH: V to QV, 4/12/96.
564 "People have . . . me": RA: Z 56/14, V to QV, 6/5/94.
564 manic depressive illness: The psychiatrist who first wrote about manic depression was Emil Kraepelin (1856–1926), a German who published *Manic Depressive Insanity* in 1921. (See *Manic Depressive Illness*, by S. K. Goodwin and K. R. Jamison [New York: Oxford University Press, 1990], p. 844.) According to Wilhelm II's most psychiatrically oriented biographer, Thomas Kohut, psychiatrists from the United States and five other European countries diagnosed Wilhelm II as a manic-depressive at about the same time (after world War I)—a diagnosis with which Kohut disagrees on the grounds that they never examined Wilhelm and based their conclusions at least as much on history as on medicine. Kohut refers back to the Kaiser's great-great-grandfather, Czar Paul I of Russia, who was mentally ill, but does not, like this author, believe Wilhelm II was a manic-depressive. (See Kohut, *Wilhelm II and the Germans*, (p. 6 and 252, n. 11 and 12.)
564 "nervous breakdown": Bülow, p. 48.
564 "violent outbreak . . . disorder": *Ibid.*, pp. 452–53.
564 "[N]o one . . . Kaiser": Waldersee, p. 192.
565 "Q: Whom had . . . Prosecutor?": Balfour, p. 180.

CHAPTER SIXTY-SIX

566 *"The chief . . . out"*: Holstein, Vol. III, pp. 612–13.
566 "[F]or many . . . paint": Waldersee, p. 194.
566 "best successor": RA: Z 57/1, V to QV, 10/31/94.
566 "all the . . . experience": RA: Z 57/23, V to QV, 1/4/95.
567 "never been . . . stronger": RA: Z 57/6, V to QV, 11/15/94.
567 "Hallelujah Aunts": Hull, p. 26.
567 "upsetting . . . Government": RA: Z 57/6, V to QV, 11/15/94.
567 "as an . . . cement": Corti 1, p. 349.
567 "civil note . . . danger": RA: Z 57/41 *passim*, V to QV, 4/6/95.
567 "under-butler": Balfour, p. 192.
567 "I was . . . week": Küremberg, p. 118.
567 "occult government . . . calamity": Cecil, p. 215.
568 "The government . . . doing!": RA: Z 58/56, V to QV, 12/5/95.

568 "The most . . . made!": RA: Z 58/61, V to QV, 12/21/95.

568 "feeble . . . vicious": RA: Z 51/32, the Marquis of Salisbury to QV, 9/17/91.

568 "allowed if . . . instigated": RA: Z 58/59, V to QV, 12/14/95.

569 "William has . . . religion!": RA: Z 51/20, V to QV, 9/5/91.

569 "wild . . . excitement": Cecil, p. 322.

569 "Please, darling . . . contributed": Lee 1, p. 246.

569 "the [Greek] . . . Sophy": RA: H 40/56, WII to QV, 5/13/97.

569 "indignation ought . . . deeds": KHH: V to QV, 2/26/96.

569 "One wonders . . . cruelties": RA: Z 58/49, V to QV, 11/12/95.

570 "not hopeful . . . worse": Buckle, Third Series, Vol. II, p. 586, the Marquis of Salisbury to Sir Arthur Bigge, 12/29/95.

570 "not so . . . for": KHH: V to QV, 1/4/96.

570 "If Europe . . . hitherto": KHH: V to QV, 9/29/96.

570 "most anxious . . . us": Corti 1, p. 353.

570 "What a . . . prejudice": RA: Z 57/2, V to QV, 11/3/94.

570 "quite unspoilt . . . ever": KHH: QV to V, 9/26/96.

571 "[H]is modest . . . position": KHH: V to QV, 10/17/96.

571 "The character . . . Russia": Sir Sidney Lee, *Edward VII* (Lee 2), Vol. I, p. 692.

Chapter Sixty-seven

572 "I am . . . this": RA: X 37/51, WII to EdVII, 12/30/01.

572 "H.M. . . . commanders, etc!": Jonathan Steinberg, *Yesterday's Deterrent: Tirpitz and the Birth of the German Battle Fleet*, p. 76.

572 "recommend . . . makes": Massie, p. 211.

573 "possible danger . . . trees": Cecil, pp. 284–85.

574 "little nation . . . republic": Massie, p. 221.

574 "some weird . . . plans": *Ibid.*, p. 223.

574 "William's telegram . . . mistake": KHH: V to QV, 1/4/96.

574 "a most . . . unfriendliness": Buckle, Third Series, Vol. III, p. 7, Sir Francis Knollys to Sir Arthur Bigge, 1/4/96.

574 "I asked . . . approved": Lee 2, Vol. I, p. 727.

574 "I feel . . . nothing": Corti 1, p. 352.

575 "Never was . . . adore": RA: O 45/140a, WII to QV, 1/8/96.

575 "lame and . . . time": Cecil, p. 288–89.

575 "England, that . . . all": Holstein, Vol. I, p. 160.

575 "friendly . . . allied": Corti 1, p. 354.

576 "useful . . . fleet": Massie, p. 231.

576 "William's . . . Navy": RA: Z 56/20, V to QV, 6/21/94.

576 "I am . . . William": Lee 1, p. 277.

576 "a silly . . . countries": Corti 1, p. 354.

576 "much improved . . . veneration": RA: I 61/39, Sir Frank Lascelles to the Prince of Wales, 3/25/98.

576 "If only . . . offices": Lee 2, Vol. I, p. 736.

576 "plain common sense": RA: Z 59/28, V to QV, 5/18/98.

576 "half-way": Buckle, Third Series, Vol. III, p. 258, V to QV, 7/15/98.

577 "Germany is . . . sincerity": *Ibid.*, pp. 263–64, the Marquis of Salisbury to QV, 8/10/98.

577 "something between . . . snub": *Ibid.*, p. 262, the Marquis of Salisbury to QV, 8/4/98.

577 "I must . . . understanding?": RA: Z 59/38, V to QV, 7/20/98.

577 "symbols of . . . Britain": Pflanze, Vol. III, p. 141.

577 Open Door: All the countries accepted the Open Door except Russia, which held out certain reservations, and Germany. Wilhelm II said that he and the Czar wanted "China to remain whole & undivided, not split up in spheres of interest, & open door!" (RA: T 10/126, WII to the Prince of Wales, 7/31/00).

577 "I fear . . . increased": RA: Z 60/85, V to QV, 7/4/00.
578 "what comes . . . face": Balfour, pp. 226–27.
578 "completely lost . . . anger": Bülow, pp. 452–53.
578 "for the . . . countries": RA: Z 59/41, V to QV, 8/26/98.
578 "delighted": Lee 1, p. 300.
578 "most anxious . . . mind": Buckle, Third Series, Vol. III, p. 350, Cecil Rhodes to the Prince of Wales, March 1899 (undated).
578 "shame & . . . other": RA: I 62/14, WII to QV, 5/27/99.
578 "for years . . . birthday": Buckle, Vol. III, pp. 358–59, and n. 1, p. 359, Colonel Grierson to Sir Frank Lascelles, 5/3/99.
579 "I feel . . . to": *Ibid.*, pp. 343–44, QV to Nicholas II, 3/1/99.
579 "I think . . . year": RA: I 62/14, WII to QV, 5/27/99.
580 "I doubt . . . did": Buckle, Vol. III, pp. 381–82, QV to WII, 6/12/99.
580 "I do . . . good": RA: Z 60/33, V to QV, 11/3/99.
580 "Gentlemen . . . ruled": Palmer 1, p. 192.
580 " 'poison . . . happened": Buckle, p. 421, QVJ, 11/21/99.
580 "The visit . . . all": KHH: QV to V, 11/25/99.
580 "I am . . . satisfactory": RA: Z 60/40, V to QV, 11/27/99.
580 "with superhuman . . . Press": RA: W 60/89, WII to the Prince of Wales, 2/23/00.
581 "The spite . . . Anglo-Saxons": Lee 1, p. 312.
581 "Our forces . . . news": RA: Z 60/31, V to QV, 11/2/99.
581 "a perfect volcano": RA: Z 60/67, V to QV, 4/28/00.
581 "It is . . . Germans": Lee 1, p. 340.

CHAPTER SIXTY-EIGHT

582 *"A society . . . itself"*: Kissinger 1, p. 889.
582 "Did you . . . influence": KHH: V to QV, 10/29/96.
582 "It was . . . sentiments": KHH: V to QV, 11/20/96.
583 "energetic support . . . pygmies": Pflanze, Vol. III, p. 425.
583 "how long . . . last": Taylor 1, p. 264.
583 "I would . . . you": Corti 1, p. 356.
583 "dumb kid": Pflanze, Vol. III, p. 426.
583 "Germany's greatest . . . side": *Ibid.*, p. 428.
583 "A loyal . . . Wilhelm I": *Ibid* .
583 "greatly affected . . . here": Leinhaas, p. 40.
583 "For the . . . family": Corti 1, p. 356.
584 "merciful escape": KHH: QV to V, 9/11/98.
584 "I tried . . . happened": RA: Z 59/43, V to QV, 9/6/98.
584 "The Empress . . . letters": Leinhaas, pp. 50–51 *passim.*
584 "far too advanced": Reid, p. 107.
584 "I assure . . . hurtful": RA: Z 59/53, V to QV, 12/8/98.
584 "I will . . . blessing": RA: Z 59/55, V to QV, 1/11/99.
584 "on the . . . chair": RA: Z 59/48, V to QV, 10/31/98.
585 "the soft . . . air": RA: Z 59/69, V to QV, 3/13/99.
585 "I was . . . bay": Lee 1, pp. 299–300.
585 "sunburned and robust": Marie Mallet, *Life with Queen Victoria*, p. 156.
585 "I have . . . greatness": Reischach, pp. 185–87.
586 "must remain . . . necessary": Lee 1, p. 322.
586 "It is . . . manage": *Ibid.*, p. 302.
586 "very wearing . . . wished": RA: Z 60/21, V to QV, 9/8/99.
586 "My lumbago . . . pain": RA: Z 60/25, V to QV, 10/10/99.
586 "My lumbago . . . possible": RA: Z 60/28, V to QV, 10/24/99.
587 "The constant . . . trying": RA: Z 60/31, V to QV, 11/2/99.
587 "Every . . . painful": RA: Z 60/41, V to QV, 12/14/99.
587 "condition . . . hips": RA: Z 60/42, V to QV, 12/15/99.

587 "It is . . . use!": RA: Z 60/52, V to QV, 1/30/00.
587 "very useful ": RA: Z 60/62, V to QV, 3/14/00.
587 "touched & grateful": RA: Z 60/60, V to QV, 3/9/00.
587 "beginning to . . . again": RA: Z 60/65, V to QV, 4/7–8/00.
587 "very kind . . . well!": RA: Z 60/66, V to QV, 4/21/00.
587 "My dear . . . active": Lee 1, p. 331.
587 "You can . . . sometimes!!": RA: Z 60/70, V to QV, 5/10/00.
587 "My life . . . right": RA: Z 60/78, V to QV, 6/7/00.
588 "It seems . . . them!": RA: Z 60/83, V to QV, 6/29/00.
588 "not so brave": Radziwill 4, p. 216.
588 "What a . . . it": RA: Z 60/89, V to QV, 8/15/00.
588 "Dear Alfred . . . thought": RA: Z 60a/61, V to QV, 8/6/00.
588 "I am . . . arm": RA: Z 60/89, V to QV, 8/15/00.
588 "The house . . . respite": RA: Z 60a/63, V to QV, 8/18/00.
588 "only scream . . . true": Lee 1, p. 336.

CHAPTER SIXTY-NINE

589 "I will . . . prejudices": Reischach, p. 142.
589 "Aunt Vicky . . . agonies": RA: G.V.AA 32/22, the Princess of Wales to the Duke of York, 8/30/00.
589 "[I]t would . . . roused": RA: I 62/111b, WII to QV (cable), 10/12/00.
589 "[S]he is . . . fatal": RA: I 62/111c, WII to the Prince of Wales, 10/21/00.
589 "Since today . . . one": Ibid.
590 "Thank God . . . her": RA: T 10/131, QV to Prince of Wales, 10/22/00.
590 "[T]he terrible . . . exhausted": Lee 1, p. 337.
590 "I am . . . bed": RA: Z 60a/65, V to QV, 11/10/00.
590 "a flood . . . [wheelchair]": RA: Z 60a/67, V to QV, 11/21/00.
590 "To think . . . less": Corti 1, p. 363.
590 "To be . . . be": Lee 1, pp. 340–41.
591 "I am . . . weeks": RA: Z 60a/67, V to QV, 11/21/00.
591 "I am . . . disagreeable": RA: Z 60a/74, V to QV, 12/25/00.
591 "excite . . . kind": Reid, pp. 210–11.
592 "William . . . selfishness": RA: Add. A4/198, EdVII to V, 2/1/01.
592 "Words cannot . . . end": Lee 1, p. 343.
592 "Mama has . . . truth": RA: L 4/82, WII to EdVII, 2/9/01.
593 "tiny": RA: Z 60A/70, V to QV, 12/8/00.
593 "took the . . . suffering": St. Aubyn, p. 315.
593 "Laking's . . . Suite": RA: Geo. V, AA 68/96, Sir Henry Ponsonby to the Duke of Connaught, 12/4/26.
593 "I never . . . Vicky": RA: Add. A 4/202, EdVII to V, 2/21/01.
593 "as if . . . CARE": Letters, pp. ix–xii.

CHAPTER SEVENTY

595 "Queen Victoria's . . . sorrows": Fulford 1, pp. 11–12.
595 "I know . . . here?": Lee 1, pp. 343–44.
596 "Indeed my . . . ago": Ibid., p. 293.
596 "poor little . . . once": Edmund Swinglehurst, The Romantic Journey: The Story of Thomas Cook and Victorian Travel, p. 74.
596 "Every morning . . . slowly": Lee 1, p. 329.
596 "I feel . . . questions": Ibid., p. 286.
596 "If the . . . bored": Ibid., p. 347.
596 "in everything . . . art": RA: X 37/44, WII to EdVII, 7/24/01.
597 "every person . . . her": Reischach, p. 192.
597 "quite satisfactory . . . fast": Gordon Brook-Shepherd, Uncle of Europe, p. 106.

597 "My sister . . . last": Lee 1, p. 348.
597 "I wish . . . speech": Reischach, p. 189.
597 "He told . . . country": Bülow, pp. 528–29.
597 "We hear . . . her": Marie Radziwill, *Lettres de la Princesse Radziwill au Général de Robilant, 1889–1914,* Vol. II, pp. 117–20.
598 "thorough search . . . archives": *Letters,* p. xv. In a letter to the Duke of Connaught dated December 4, 1926, Ponsonby said that it was "about a year later" when Eulenburg approached him about the letters, but in the book containing the letters, he said it was during the time of the funeral. (Considering the Kaiser's eagerness to get hold of them, Eulenburg may well have spoken to him twice. RA: George V, AA 68/96, 12/4/26).
598 Vicky's letters: Subsequent and more extensively edited versions of both sides of the correspondence appeared in five volumes, compiled by Roger Fulford, from 1964 to 1981; a final volume, edited by Agatha Ramm, came out in 1990. The unedited letters have never been published.

EPILOGUE

599 *"The Kaiser . . . weakness":* Gordon Brook-Shepherd, *Royal Sunset,* p. 116
599 *"All he . . . smoke":* Winston Churchill, *Great Contemporaries,* p. 37.
599 "in considerable . . . acquisitive": RA: Add. A 1/1, Memorandum of Sir Owen Morshead to Sir Alan Lascelles, 7/22/45.
600 "stand together": Cowles, p. 191.
600 "I do . . . fleet": *Ibid.,* p. 250.
600 "a personal insult . . . nation": Massie, p. 685.
601 "divine right . . . Lord": Cowles, p. 283.
601 "in the name . . . punished": Massie, pp. 869–70.
601 "with guile . . . hearts": Cowles p. 353.
602 "as though . . . happened": *Ibid.,* p. 393.
602 "Not Germany . . . world": *Ibid.,* p. 419.
602 "Today the . . . about her": NYPL: Poultney Bigelow Papers, Box 34A.

Selected Bibliography

In addition to books and periodicals, the following archival sources were used:

The Royal Archives, Windsor Castle; The Hesse Family Archive (Kurhessische Hausstiftung), Schloss Fasanerie, Fulda, Germany; The Secret German State Archive, Prussian Section (Geheimes Staatsarchiv Preussischer Kulturbesitz), Berlin; The New York Public Library, Poultney Bigelow Papers, Rare Books and Manuscripts Division, Astor, Lenox and Tilden Foundations; The Royal College of Physicians of London.

Of the authors and books listed below, several were particularly important in the preparation of this book. Of these, the one I consulted most often was Otto Pflanze's remarkable three-volume work, *Bismarck and the Development of Germany*. Others are John Röhl's *Wilhelm II, Die Jugend des Kaisers, 1859–1888;* Erich Eyck's *Bismarck and the German Empire;* Lamar Cecil's *Wilhelm II;* and J. Alden Nichol's *The Year of Three Kaisers.* I must also mention two pioneer works: Sir Frederick Ponsonby's *Letters of the Empress Frederick,* published in 1929, and Egon Corti's *The English Empress,* translated from the German in 1957. Without these, today's biographer would be missing great chunks of the story.

Albert, Harold A. *Queen Victoria's Sister: the Life and Letters of Princess Feodora.* London: Robert Hale, 1967.

Albisetti, James C. *Schooling German Girls and Women.* Princeton: Princeton University Press, 1988.

Allinson, A. R., ed. and trans. *The War Diary of Emperor Frederick II 1870–1871.* London: Stanley, Paul and Company, Ltd., 1927.

Alice, H. R. H., Countess of Athlone. *For My Grandchildren.* Cleveland: World Publishing Co., 1966.

Alice, Grand Duchess of Hesse: Letters to Her Majesty the Queen. London: John Murray, 1884.

Anderson, Pauline. *The Background of Anti-English Feeling in Germany 1840–1902.* New York: Octagon Books, 1969.

Anonymous. *The Empress Frederick, A Memoir.* New York: Dodd, Mead, 1914.

Anonymous. *The Private Life of the Queen by a Member of the Household.* New York: D. Appleton & Co., 1897.

Anonymous. *Recollections of Three Kaisers.* London: Herbert Jenkins Ltd., 1929.

Anonymous. *Things I Shouldn't Tell.* Philadelphia: J. B. Lippincott Company, 1925.

Aronson, Theo. *The Fall of the Third Napoleon.* Indianapolis: Bobbs-Merrill Co., 1970.

———. *The Kaisers.* Indianapolis: Bobbs-Merrill Co., 1971.

———. *A Family of Kings.* London: Cassel & Co., 1976.

Asprey, Robert. *Frederick the Great: The Magnificent Enigma.* New York: Ticknor and Fields, 1986.

Auchincloss, Louis. *Persons of Consequence: Queen Victoria and Her Circle.* New York: Random House, 1979.

Balfour, Michael. *The Kaiser and His Times.* London: The Cresset Press, 1964.

Barkeley, Richard. *The Empress Frederick.* London: Macmillan/New York: St. Martin's Press, 1956.

Barraclough, G. *The Origins of Modern Germany.* Oxford: Basil Blackwell Publishing, 1952.

Beal, Erica. *Royal Cavalcade.* London: St. Paul and Co., 1939.

Benson, Arthur Christopher, and Reginald Baliol, Viscount Esher. *Letters of Queen Victoria 1837–1861.* London: John Murray, 1907.

Benson, E. F. *The Kaiser and English Relations.* London: Longmans, Green and Company, 1890.

———. *Queen Victoria.* London: Longmans, Green and Company, 1935.

———. *Queen Victoria's Daughters.* New York: Century Company, 1939.

Bennett, Daphne. *King Without a Crown: Albert, Prince Consort of England.* Philadelphia: J. B. Lippincott, 1977.

———. *Vicky: Princess Royal of England and German Empress.* New York: St. Martin's Press, 1971.

Bernardy, Françoise de. *Albert and Victoria.* New York: Harcourt, Brace and Company, 1953.

Bigelow, Poultney. *Prussian Memories 1864–1914.* G. P. Putnam's Sons, 1915.

Bismarck, Otto von. *Reflections and Reminiscences.* Tauchnitz Edition, 1898.

Bloomfield, Georgiana, Baroness. *Reminiscences of Court and Diplomatic Life.* Two volumes. London: Kegan, Paul, Trench and Co., 1883.

Blowitz, Henri de. *Memoirs.* New York: Doubleday Page and Co., 1903.

Blücher, Evelyn, Princess. *An English Wife in Berlin.* London: Constable and Co., Inc., 1920.

Bolitho, Hector. *Albert the Good.* New York: D. Appleton & Co., 1982.

———. *Albert, Prince Consort.* New York: Bobbs-Merrill Co., Inc., 1964.

———, ed. *The Prince Consort and His Brother: 200 New Letters.* New York: D. Appleton-Century Co. Ltd., 1934.

———, ed. *Letters of Queen Victoria from the Archives of the House of Brandenburg-Prussia.* Translated by Mrs. J. Pudney and Lord Sudley. New Haven: Yale University Press, 1938.

Boykin, Edward, ed. *Victoria, Albert and Mrs. Stevenson.* New York: Rinehart and Company, 1957.

Briggs, Åsa, ed. *The Nineteenth Century.* New York: Bonanza Books, 1985.

Brook-Shepherd, Gordon. *Royal Sunset.* Garden City, N.Y.: Doubleday and Co., Inc., 1987.

———. *Uncle of Europe.* New York: Harcourt Brace, 1975.

Buchanan, Meriel. *Queen Victoria's Relations.* London: Cassel & Co., 1954.

Buckle, G. E. *Letters of Queen Victoria* (2nd and 3rd series). London: John Murray, 1926–1931.

Bülow, Bernhard, Prince von. *Memoirs, Volume II: 1897–1903.* New York: Putnam, 1930–32.

———. *Imperial Germany.* New York: Dodd, Mead and Company, 1914.

Bunsen, Mme. Charles de. *In Three Legations.* London: T. Fisher Unwin, 1909.

Bunsen, Marie von. *Lost Courts of Europe.* New York: Harper and Bros., 1930.

Burchell, S. C. *Imperial Masquerade.* New York: Atheneum, 1971.

Burghclere, Lady. *A Great Lady's Friendships: Letters to Mary, Marchioness of Salisbury, Countess of Derby (1862–1890).* London: Macmillan, 1933.

Busch, Moritz. *Bismarck, Some Secret Pages of History*. Two volumes. New York: Macmillan, 1898.

Carr, William. *A History of Germany 1815–1945*. 2nd edition. New York: St. Martin's Press, 1979.

Cecil, Lamar. *Wilhelm II*. Chapel Hill: University of North Carolina Press, 1989.

Chamier, J. Daniel. *Fabulous Monster*. New York: Longmans, Green and Co., 1934.

Chekhov, Anton. *The Notebooks of Anton Chekhov*. Translated by S. S. Koteliansky and Leonard Woolf. London: The Hogarth Press, 1967.

Churchill, Winston. *Great Contemporaries*. Chicago: The University of Chicago Press, 1937 (reprint 1973).

Clark, Ronald W. *Balmoral: Queen Victoria's Highland Home*. New York: Thames and Hudson, Inc., 1981.

Connell, Brian. *Regina vs. Palmerston: The Correspondence Between Queen Victoria and Her Foreign and Prime Minister, 1837–1865*. Garden City, N.Y.: Doubleday & Company, Inc., 1961.

Corti, Egon Caesar Conte. *Alexander von Battenberg*. London: Cassel and Co., Ltd., 1954.

———. *The English Empress*. London: Cassel and Co., Ltd., 1957.

Cowles, Virginia. *The Kaiser*. New York: Harper and Row, 1963.

———. *The Romanovs*. New York: Harper and Row, 1971.

Craig, Gordon. *The Germans*. New York: G. P. Putnam's Sons, 1982.

———. *Germany 1866–1945*. New York: Oxford University Press, 1978.

———. "Portrait of a Political General: Edwin von Manteuffel and the Constitutional Conflict in Prussia." *Political Science Quarterly*, Vol. LXVI, no. 1, March 1951.

Crankshaw, Edward. *Bismarck*. New York: The Viking Press, 1981.

Cunliffe, Marcus. *The Age of Expansion 1848–1917*. Springfield, Mass.: G. & C. Merriam Company, 1974.

Curzon, Mary, Lady. *Lady Curzon's India*. John Bradley, ed. New York: Beaufort Books, 1985.

Daisy, Princess of Pless. *Better Left Unsaid*. New York: E. P. Dutton & Co., Inc., 1931.

———. *What I Left Unsaid*. New York: E. P. Dutton & Co., Inc., 1936.

Deutsch, André. *Queen Victoria: Leaves from a Journal*. London: André Deutsch, Ltd., 1961.

Diesbach, Ghislain de. *Secrets of the Gotha*. New York: Meredith Press, 1968.

Demeter, Karl. *The German Officer Corps*. London: Weidenfeld and Nicholson, 1965.

Dewhurst, Jack. *Royal Confinements*. New York: St. Martin's Press, 1980.

Dickens, A. G., ed. *The Courts of Europe*. New York: McGraw-Hill Book Co., 1977.

Dorpalen, Andreas. "Frederick III and the German Liberal Movement." *The American Historial Review*, Vol. 54, no. 1, October 1948.

———. "Empress Augusta and the Fall of the German Monarchy." *The American Historical Review*, Vol. 58, 1952.

Dulcken, H. W. *The Life of William the First*. London: Ward, Lock & Co., 1888.

Duff, David. *Hessian Tapestry*. London: Frederick Miller, 1967.

———. ed. *Queen Victoria's Highland Journal*. Exeter: Webb & Bower, 1980.

Eilers, Marlene. *Queen Victoria's Descendants*. New York: Atlantic International Publications, 1987.

Emden, Paul H. *Behind the Throne*. London: Hodder and Stoughton, 1934.

Epton, Nina. *Victoria and Her Daughters*. New York: Norton, 1971.

Ernest II, Duke of Saxe-Coburg-Gotha. *Memoirs*. Translated by Percy Andrae. London: Remington & Co., 1890.

Eulalia of Spain, H. R. H. *The Thread of Life*. London: Cassell and Company, Ltd., 1912.

Eulenberg, Herbert. *The Hohenzollerns*. Translated by M. M. Bozman. New York: The Century Co., 1929.

Eyck, Erich. *Bismarck and the German Empire*. New York: The Norton Library, 1964.

———. "The Empress Frederick." *The Quarterly Review*, Vol. 289, 1951.

Eyck, Frank. *The Prince Consort*. Boston: Houghton Mifflin Co., 1959.

Farago and Sinclair. *Royal Web.* New York: McGraw-Hill Book Co., 1982.

Finestone, Jeffrey. *The Lost Courts of Europe.* New York: The Vendome Press, 1981.

Fischer, Henry W. *Private Lives of Kaiser William II and His Consort, from the papers and diaries of Ursula, Countess von Eppinghoven.* Three volumes. New York: Fred de Fau & Company, 1909.

Fisher, John, Lord. *Memories.* London: Hodder and Stoughton, 1919.

Fitzmaurice, Lord Edmond. *The Life of George Leveson Gower, the Second Earl Granville.* Two volumes. New York: Longmans, Green & Co., 1905.

Ford, J. A., trans. & ed. *The Correspondence of William I & Bismarck, with Other Letters from and to Prince Bismarck.* Two volumes. New York: Frederick A. Stokes Co., 1901.

Friedrich III. *A Diary.* London: Sampson Low, Marston, Searle & Rivington, 1888.

———. *The Emperor's Diary of the Austro-German War, 1866, and the Franco-German War, 1870–1871 to which is added Prince Bismarck's Rejoinder.* Henry W. Lucy, ed. London: George Routledge & Sons, 1888.

———. *War Diary.* London: Stanley Paul, 1927.

Friedrich Leopold of Prussia, H. R. H. Princess. *Behind the Scenes at the Prussian Court.* Major Desmond Chapman-Huston, ed. London: John Murray, 1939.

Friendly, Alfred. *Beaufort of The Admiralty.* New York: Random House, 1977.

Freytag, Gustav. *The Crown Prince and the Imperial Crown.* London: George Bell and Sons, 1890.

———. *Reminiscences of My Life.* Translated by Katerine Chetwynd. Two volumes. London: F. V. White and Co., 1890.

Fulford, Roger. *Hanover to Windsor.* New York: Fontana-Collins, 1960.

———. *The Prince Consort.* London: Macmillan, 1949.

———. *Darling Child.* New York: Evans Brothers Ltd., 1976.

———. *Dearest Child.* New York: Holt Rinehart and Winston, 1964.

———. *Dearest Mama.* New York: Holt, Rinehart & Winston, 1969.

———. *Your Dear Letter.* New York: Charles Scribner's Sons, 1971.

———, ed. *Beloved Mama.* New York: Evans Brothers Ltd., 1981.

Gay, Ruth. *The Jews of Germany.* New Haven: Yale University Press, 1992.

Gerard, James W. *My Four Years in Germany.* New York: George H. Duran Company, 1917.

Gerard, Noel, *Princess Alice.* London: Constable, 1974.

Goff, Margaret, Lady. "Life Like a Dome." Unpublished manuscript.

Goodwin, S. K., and K. R. Jamison. *Manic Depressive Illness.* New York: Oxford University Press, 1990.

Gower, Lord Ronald. *My Reminiscences.* Two volumes. London: Kegan, Paul, Trench, & Co., 1883.

Grey, The Hon. C. *The Early Years of His Royal Highness the Prince Consort.* London: Smith, Elder & Co., 1867.

Guedalla, Philip. *The Hundred Years.* London: Hodder and Stoughton Limited, 1936.

Gurney, Gene. *Kingdoms of Europe.* New York: Crown Publishers Inc., 1982.

Hamann, Brigitte, *The Reluctant Empress.* Translated by Ruth Hein. New York: Knopf, 1986.

Handbook for Travellers on the Continent. 5th ed. London: John Murray, 1850.

Hare, Augustus C. *The Life and Letters of Frances, Baroness Bunsen.* New York: George Routledge & Sons, 1879.

Hegermann-Lindencrone, Lillie de. *The Sunny Side of Diplomatic Life.* New York: Harper & Brothers, 1914.

Herold, J. Christopher. *The Age of Napoleon.* New York: Crown Publishers Inc., 1983.

Hibbert, Christopher. *Queen Victoria in Her Letters and Journals.* London: John Murray, 1983.

———. *The Royal Victorians: King Edward VII, His Family and Friends.* Philadelphia: J. B. Lippincott, 1978.

Hobhouse, Hermione. *Prince Albert, His Life and Work.* London: Hamish Hamilton Ltd., 1983.

Hohenlohe-Schillingfürst, Prince Chlodwig. *Memoirs.* Two volumes. New York: Macmillan, 1906.

Holborn, Hajo. *A History of Modern Germany 1648–1840 and 1840–1945.* Two volumes. Princeton University Press, 1969.

Holmes, Sir Richard, ed. *Edward VII, His Life and Times.* Vol. I. London: The Amalgamated Press, Ltd., 1910.

Holstein, Frederick. *The Holstein Papers.* Norman Rich and M. H. Fischer, eds. Cambridge: Cambridge University Press, 1955–1963.

Hough, Richard, ed. *Advice to a Grand-daughter.* London: Heinemann, 1975.

———. *Edward and Alexandra.* New York: St. Martin's Press, 1993.

———. *Louis and Victoria: The First Mountbattens.* London: Hutchinson & Co., Ltd., 1974.

Howard, Michael. *The Franco-Prussian War.* London: Rupert Hart-Davis, 1961.

Hull, Isobel. *The Entourage of Kaiser Wilhelm II.* Cambridge: Cambridge University Press, 1982.

Hunter-Steibel, Penelope. *Of Knights and Spires: Gothic Revival in France and Germany.* New York: Rosenberg and Steibel, Inc., 1989.

Jagow, Dr. Kurt, ed. *Letters of the Prince Consort.* New York: E. P. Dutton & Company, Inc., 1938.

James, Robert Rhodes. *Prince Albert.* New York: Alfred A. Knopf, 1984.

Judd, Denis. *Eclipse of Kings: European Monarchies of the Twentieth Century.* London: MacDonald and Jane's, 1976.

———. *The Royal Victorians.* New York: St. Martin's Press, 1975.

Keegan, John, and Andrew Wheatcroft. *Who's Who in Military History.* New York: William Morrow and Co., Inc., 1976.

Kennan, George. *The Fateful Alliance.* New York: Pantheon Books, 1984.

———. *The Decline of Bismarck's European Order.* Princeton: Princeton University Press, 1979.

Kennedy, Paul. *The Rise of Anglo-German Antagonism.* London: The Ashfield Press, 1980.

Kerr, John. *Queen Victoria's Scottish Diaries.* Moffat, Scotland: Lochar Publishing, 1992.

Keyserlink, Robert H. *Media Manipulation, the Press and Bismarck in Imperial Germany.* Montreal: Renouf Publishing Co., 1977.

Kirsch, Richard. *Bismarck.* Sussex, England: Wayland Publishers, 1976.

Kissinger, Henry. *Diplomacy.* New York: Simon & Schuster, 1994.

———. "The White Revolutionary: Reflections on Bismarck." *Daedelus,* no. 97, 1968.

Knight, Alfred E. *Victoria: Her Life and Reign.* London: S. W. Partridge & Co., 1896.

Koch, H. W. *A History of Prussia.* New York: Dorset Press, 1978.

Kohut, Thomas. *Wilhelm II and the Germans.* New York: Oxford University Press, 1991.

Kollander, Patricia A. *The Liberalism of Frederick III.* Thesis submitted to Brown University, 1992.

Kuřenberg, Joachim von. *The Kaiser.* New York: Simon & Schuster, 1955.

Langer, William L. *The New Illustrated Encyclopedia of European History.* Two volumes. New York: Harry N. Abrams, Inc., 1975.

Lee, Arthur Gould. *The Empress Frederick Writes to Sophie.* London: Faber & Faber, 1955.

Lee, Sir Sidney. *King Edward VII.* Two volumes. New York: The Macmillan Co., 1925.

Leinhaas, G. A. *Reminiscences of Victoria, Empress Frederick.* Mainz: 1902.

Lincoln, W. Bruce. *The Romanovs.* New York: The Dial Press, 1981.

Linney, Romulus. *The Sorrows of Frederick and Holy Ghosts.* New York: Harcourt, Brace, Jovanovitch, 1977.

Loftus, Augustus, Lord. *The Diplomatic Reminiscences of Lord Augustus Loftus.* Two volumes. London: Cassel and Co., Ltd., 1894.

Longford, Elizabeth. *Darling Loosy: Letters to Princess Louise 1856–1935.* London: Weidenfeld & Nicholson, 1991.

————. *Queen Victoria*. New York: Harper and Row, 1964.

————, ed. *Louisa, Lady in Waiting*. London: Jonathan Cape, 1979.

Lorne, The Marquis of. *V.R.I. Queen Victoria Her Life and Empire*. New York: Harper & Bros., 1901.

Lowie, Robert H. *Towards Understanding Germany*. Chicago: University of Chicago Press, 1954.

Ludwig, Emil. *Bismarck: The Story of a Fighter*. New York: Blue Ribbon Books, 1930.

————. *Wilhelm Hohenzollern: The Last of the Kaisers*. New York: G. P. Putnam's Sons, 1922.

Lyttelton, Sarah Spencer, Lady. *Correspondence*. The Hon. Mrs. Hugh Wyndham, ed.. London: John Murray, 1912.

Macdonell, Anne, Lady. *Reminiscences of Diplomatic Life*. London: Adam & Charles Black, 1913.

Mackenzie, Morell. *The Fatal Illness of Frederick the Noble*. London: Sampson, Low, Marston, Searle, & Rivington, 1888.

Maehl, William H. *Germany in Western Civilization*. Tuscaloosa: University of Alabama Press, 1981.

Magnus, Philip. *King Edward the Seventh*. London: John Murray, 1964.

Mallet, Marie. *Life with Queen Victoria*. London: John Murray, 1968.

Mann, Golo. *The History of Germany Since 1789*. New York: Penguin Books Ltd., 1974.

Marie Louise, H. H. Princess. *My Memories of Six Reigns*. London: Evans Brothers Limited, 1956.

Marie, Princess of Battenberg. *Reminiscences*. London: George Allen and Unwin Ltd., 1925.

The Marriage of the Princess Royal, on Jan. 25, 1858, To His Royal Highness Prince Frederick William of Prussia. London: R. MacDonald, 1858.

Martin, Theodore. *Life of the Prince Consort*. Six volumes. London: Smith, Elder & Co., 1867-1880.

Massie, Robert. *Dreadnought*. New York: Random House, 1991.

Masur, Gerhard. *Imperial Berlin*. New York: Basic Books Inc., 1970.

Maurois, André. *Disraeli*. New York: D. Appleton and Co., 1928.

Maxwell, Sir Herbert E. *The Life and Letters of George William Frederick, the 4th Earl of Clarendon*. London: Edward Arnold, 1913.

McCabe, John D., Jr. *History of the War Between Germany and France*. Philadelphia: National Publishing Company and Jones Brothers & Co., 1871.

Meineke, Friedrich. *The Age of German Liberation*. Berkeley: University of California Press, 1977.

Miller, Alice. *For Your Own Good*. Translated by Hildegard and Hunter Hannum. New York: Farrar, Straus & Giroux, 1983.

Mitford, Nancy. *Frederick the Great*. New York: E. P. Dutton, Inc., 1970.

Moltke, Count Helmuth von. *The Franco-German War*. New York: Harper & Brothers, 1892.

Mommsen, Wolfgang J. "Kaiser Wilhelm II and German Politics." *Journal of Contemporary History*, Vol. 25, 1990.

Monypenny, William S., and George Earl Buckle. *Life of Disraeli*. Six volumes. New York: Macmillan, 1929.

Montez, Lola. *The Arts of Beauty*. Reprint. New York: The Ecco Press, 1978.

Morrow, Ian F. D. *Bismarck*. New York: Collier Books, 1970.

Mosse, W. E. *The European Powers and the German Question 1848–1871*. New York: Octagon Books, 1981.

Nevill, Barry St.-John. *Life at the Court of Queen Victoria*. Salem: Salem House, 1984.

Nichols, J. Alden. *The Year of Three Kaisers*. Chicago: University of Illinois Press, 1987.

Nowack, Karl Friedrich. *Kaiser and Chancellor*. New York: Macmillan Co., 1930.

Nowakowski, Tadeusz. *The Radziwills: The Social History of a Great European Family*. New York: Delacorte Press, 1966.

Paget, Walpurga. *Embassies of Other Days*. New York: Hutchinson & Co., 1923.

———. *Scenes and Memories*. New York: Charles Scribner's Sons, 1912.

Palmer, Alan. *Crowned Cousins*. London: Weidenfeld & Nicolson, 1985.

———. *The Kaiser*. New York: Charles Scribner's Sons, 1978.

Parker, Geoffrey. *The Thirty Years' War*. New York: Military Heritage Press, 1984.

Passant, E. J. *A Short History of Germany 1815–1945*. Cambridge: Cambridge University Press, 1966.

Peacocke, Marguerite D. *The Story of Buckingham Palace*. London: Odhams Press Limited, 1952.

"Le Petit Homme Rouge." *The Court of the Tuileries, 1852–1870*. London: Chatto & Windus, 1912.

Pflanze, Otto. *Bismarck and the Development of Germany*. Three volumes. Princeton: Princeton University Press, 1963–1990.

Politikos. *The Sovereigns of Europe*. New York: D. Appleton & Co., 1897.

Ponsonby, Arthur. *Henry Ponsonby, Queen Victoria's Private Secretary*. London: Macmillan, 1942.

Ponsonby, Sir Frederick. *Letters of the Empress Frederick*. London: Macmillan, 1929.

———. *Recollections of Three Reigns*. New York: E. P. Dutton and Co., Inc., 1952.

Ponsonby, Mary. *A Lady-in-Waiting to Queen Victoria*. Magdalen Posonby, ed. New York: J. H. Sears & Co., Inc. 1927.

Pope-Hennessey, James. *Queen Victoria at Windsor and Balmoral. Letters from her Granddaughter, Princess Victoria of Prussia*. New York: George Allen and Unwin, Ltd., 1959.

Poschinger, Margarethe von. *Life of the Emperor Frederick*. London: Chapman & Hall, 1902.

———, ed. *Diaries of the Emperor Frederick*. Translated by Frances A. Welby. London: Chapman & Hall Ltd., 1902.

Potocka, Elisabeth and Hélène. *Souvenirs de la Princess Antoine Radziwill*. Paris: Librairie Plon, 1931.

Potocki, Mary Margarete Radziwill, Princess. "From the Distant Past." Unpublished manuscript.

Pound, Reginald. *Albert*. New York: Simon and Schuster, 1973.

Prince, Morton. *The Psychology of the Kaiser*. Boston: Richard G. Badger, 1915.

Procession from the Palace to the Chapel Royal of the Wedding of the Princess Royal to Prince Frederick of Prussia (woodcut).

Radziwill, Princess Catherine. *The Empress Frederick*. London: Cassel and Company, Ltd., 1934.

———. *Germany Under Three Emperors*. New York: Funk & Wagnalls, 1917.

———. *Memories of Forty Years*. New York: Funk & Wagnalls, 1915.

———. *My Recollections*. London: Isbister & Company, 1904.

———. *Secrets of Dethroned Royalty*. New York: John Lane Co., 1920.

———. *Those I Remember*. London: Cassel and Company, Ltd., 1924.

Radziwill, Marie. *Lettres de la Princesse Radziwill au General de Robilant, 1889–1914*. Two volumes. Bologna: Nicola Zarichelli, 1933.

Ramm, Agatha. *Sir Robert Morier*. Oxford: Oxford University Press, 1973.

———, ed. *Beloved and Darling Child*. London: Alan Sutton, 1990.

Reese, Henry, ed. *The Greville Diary*. Three volumes. London: Henry Reese, Ltd., 1874–1878.

Reid, Michaela. *Ask Sir James*. London: Hodder & Stoughton, 1987.

Reischach, Hugo, Baron von. *Under Three Emperors*. Translated by Prince Blücher. London: Constable and Company, Ltd., 1927.

Remak, Joachim, ed. *The First World War: Causes, Conduct, Consequences*. New York: John Wiley & Sons, Inc., 1971.

Rhodes-James, Robert. *Prince Albert*. New York: Alfred A. Knopf, 1984.

Richardson, Joanna. *Victoria and Albert*. New York: Quadrangle/The New York Times Book Co., 1977.

Roberts, Dorothea. *Two Royal Lives*. New York: Scribner and Welford, 1889.

Rodd, Sir James Rennell. *Social and Diplomatic Memories 1884–93*. London: Edwin Arnold & Co., 1922.

———. *Social and Diplomatic Memories 1894–1901*. Second Series. London: Edwin Arnold & Co., 1923.

———. *Frederick: Crown Prince and Emperor*. London: David Stott, 1888.

Roberts, Jane. *Royal Artists*. London: Grafton Books, 1987.

Röhl, John C. G. "Der Mythos der verpassten liberalen Chance. Krankheit und Tod Kaiser Friedrichs III." *Frankfurter Allgemeine Zeitung*, June 15, 1988.

———. *Germany Without Bismarck*. Berkeley: University of California Press, 1967.

———. *Wilhelm II, Die Jugend des Kaisers, 1859–1888*. Munich: C. H. Beck, 1993.

Röhl, John, and Nicolaus Sombart, eds. *Kaiser Wilhelm II, New Interpretations*. Cambridge: Cambridge University Press, 1982.

Routier, Gaston. *Un Point d'Histoire Contemporaine: Le Voyage de l'Impératrice Frédéric à Paris en 1891*. Paris: Henri Daragon, 1901.

Schwartz, Helen and Marvin, eds. *Disraeli's Reminiscences*. New York: Stein and Day, 1975.

Schwering, Count Axel von. *The Berlin Court Under William II*. London: Cassel & Co., 1915.

Sewell, Lieutenant Colonel J. P. C., ed. *Personal Letters of King Edward VII*. London: Hutchinson & Co., Ltd., 1931.

Sheehan, James J. *The Career of Lujo Brentano; A Study of Liberalism and Social Reform in Imperial Germany*. Chicago: University of Chicago Press, 1966.

———. *German Liberalism in the Nineteenth Century*. Chicago: University of Chicago Press, 1978.

———. *Imperial Germany*. New York. Franklin Watts, 1976.

Semon, Henry C., and Thomas A. McIntyre, eds. *The Autobiography of Sir Felix Simon*. London: Jarrolds Publishers, 1926.

St. Aubyn, Giles. *Edward VII, Prince and King*. New York: Atheneum, 1979.

Sinclair, Andrew. *The Other Victoria*. London: Weidenfeld and Nicholson, 1981.

Snyder, Louis. *Diplomacy in Iron: The Life of Herbert von Bismarck*. Malabar, Florida: Robert E. Kreiger Publishing Co., 1985.

Squire, J. C., ed. *If It Had Happened Otherwise*. New York: St. Martin's Press, 1972.

Steinberg, Jonathan. *Yesterday's Deterrent: Tirpitz and the Birth of the German Battle Fleet*. New York: The Macmillan Company, 1965.

Stern, Fritz. *The Failure of Illiberalism*. New York: Alfred A. Knopf, 1972.

———. *Gold and Iron*. New York: Vintage books, 1977.

Stevenson, R. Scott. *Morell Mackenzie*. London: William Heinemann Medical Books, Ltd., 1946.

Stockmar, Baron Ernest von. *Memoirs of Baron Christian Friedrich Stockmar*. Friedrich Max Mudler, ed. Boston: Lee and Shepherd, 1873.

Stone, Norman. *Europe Transformed 1879–1919*. Glasgow: Fontana Paperbacks, 1983.

Stoney, Benita, and Heinrich C. Weltzien, eds. *My Mistress the Queen*. London: Weidenfeld and Nicholson, 1994.

Stuart, Dorothy Margaret. *The Mother of Victoria*. London: Macmillan & Co., Ltd., 1941.

Swinglehurst, Edmund. *The Romantic Journey: The Story of Thomas Cook & Victorian Travel*. New York: Harper & Row, 1974.

Taffs, Winifred. *Ambassador to Bismarck, Lord Odo Russell*. London: Frederick Muller, 1937.

Taylor, A. J. P. *Bismarck: The Man and the Statesman*. New York: Vintage Books, 1967.

———. *The Last of Old Europe*. New York: The New York Times Book Co., 1976.

———. *The Struggle for Mastery in Europe*. London: Oxford University Press, 1974.

Taylor, Edmond. *The Fall of the Dynasties*. Garden City, N.Y.: Doubleday and Company, Inc., 1963.

Taylor, Lucy. *"Fritz" of Prussia*. London: T. Nelson & Sons, 1891.

Thomas, Allan, ed. *A New Most Excellent Dancing Master*. Stuyvesant: Pendragon Press, 1992.

Topham, Anne. *Memories of the Fatherland*. London: Methuen & Co., Ltd., 1916.

———. *Memories of the Kaiser's Court*. New York: Dodd, Mead and Company, 1914.

Townley, Lady Susan. *Indiscretions of Lady Susan*. London: Thorton Butterworth Ltd., 1922.

Treitschke, Heinrich von. *History of Germany in the Nineteenth Century*. Chicago: University of Chicago Press, 1975.

Tschudi, Clara. *Augusta, Empress of Germany*. New York: E. P. Dutton & Co., 1900.

Tuchman, Barbara W. *The Proud Tower*. New York: The Macmillan Company, 1966.

van der Kiste, John. *Frederick III*. Gloucester, England: Alan Sutton, 1981.

———. *Queen Victoria's Children*. Gloucester, England: Alan Sutton, 1986.

Vansittart, Peter. *Voices, 1870–1914*. New York: Franklin Watts, 1985.

Vasilli, Count Paul (pseudonym of Catherine Radziwill?). *Behind the Veil at the Russian Court*. New York: John Lane Co., 1932.

———. *Berlin Society*. New York: S. W. Green's Sons, 1884.

Victoria, Queen. *Leaves from a Journal*. London: André Deutsch Ltd., 1961.

Victoria, H. R. H. Princess of Prussia. *My Memoirs*. London: Eveleigh, Nash and Grayson, 1929.

Viktoria Luise, H. R. H. Princess of Prussia. *The Kaiser's Daughter*. Englewood Cliffs: Prentice-Hall, Inc., 1965.

Viereck, George Sylvester. *The Kaiser on Trial*. Richmond, Va.: The William Byrd Press, Inc., 1937.

Wake, Joanne. *Princess Louise, Queen Victoria's Unconventional Daughter*. London: Collins, 1985.

Waldersee, Alfred von. *A Field Marshall's Memoirs*. London: Hutchinson & Co., 1924.

Walker, General Sir C. P. Beauchamp. *Days of a Soldier's Life*. London: Chapman & Hall, Ltd. 1894.

Wallace, D. Mackenzie. *Russia*. New York: Henry Holt & Co., 1881.

Warner, Marina. *Queen Victoria's Sketchbook*. New York: Crown Publishers Inc., 1979.

Weintraub, Stanley. *Victoria*. New York: E. P. Dutton, 1987.

Wemyss, Mrs. Rosslyn. *Memoirs and Letters of the Right Hon. Sir Robert Morier, G. C. B., from 1826–1876*. London: Edward Arnold, 1911.

Whitfield,. *Beloved Sir James; The Life of Sir James Clarke*. Privately printed, 1982.

Whittle, Tyler. *The Last Kaiser*. New York: New York Times Books, 1977.

Wiegler, Paul. *William the First*. Boston: Houghton Mifflin, 1929.

William II. *My Early Life*. London: Methuen & Co., 1926.

———. *My Memoirs, 1878–1918*. London: Cassell and Company, Ltd., 1922.

Williamson, David. *Debrett's Kings and Queen of Europe*. Topsfield, Mass.: Salem House Publishers, 1988.

Wilson, Lawrence. *The Incredible Kaiser*. New York: A. S. Barnes and Co., Inc., 1963.

Wilson, Philip Whitwell, ed. *The Greville Diary*. Two volumes. New York: Doubleday, LePage & Co., 1927.

Windsor, the Dean of, and Hector Bolitho. *Letters of Lady Augusta Stanley (1849–1863)*. London: Gerald Howe Ltd., 1927.

———. *Later Letters of Lady Augusta Stanley (1864–1876)*. New York: Jonathan Cape & Harrison Smith, 1929.

Wistrich, Robert S. *Anti-Semitism*. New York: Pantheon Books, 1991.

Woodham-Smith, Cecil. *Queen Victoria*. New York: Dell, 1972.

York, H. R. H. the Duchess of, with Benita Stoney. *Victoria & Albert: Life at Osborne House*. London: Weidenfeld and Nicholson, 1991.

Ziegler, Philip. *The Duchess of Dino*. London: Collins, 1988.

Acknowledgments

WRITING A BOOK based largely on private letters and journals is not possible without the generosity and cooperation of family and archivists. I wish to acknowledge the gracious permission of Her Majesty Queen Elizabeth II to research in and publish extracts from the Royal Archives at Windsor Castle. I thank Landgraf Moritz von Hessen, who gave me similar permission for the Hesse Family Archive in the Schloss Fasanerie in Fulda, Germany. Without these two halves of the mother-daughter correspondence, there would have been no book.

Success or failure of archival research depends greatly on the help of the archivists themselves. In that regard, I am most grateful to Sheila de Bellaigue, Registraar of the Royal Archives at Windsor, and her kind and competent staff: Pam Clark, Allison Derrett, and Pat West. Lady de Bellaigue is a trustworthy historian, a gifted translator, and a patient friend. I should like also to mention Lady de Bellaigue's predecessor, Elizabeth Cuthbert, who was at Windsor when I began my research. I am grateful to Frau Nicolette Luthmer in the Hessische Hausstiftung; in the Geheimes Staatsarchiv Preussischer Kulturbesitz in Berlin, Dr. Isselin Guntermann and Dr. Letkemann; at the Royal College of Physicians in London, librarian Jeff Davenport; and at the New York Society Library, Mark Piel.

I should like to thank Jon Vanden Heuvel, who vetted the manuscript for me and researched questions about German history. Thanks are also due to my translators: Patricia Kollander, who was also my initial guide through the Fulda archive; Elisabeth Hevner; and Robert Torrey. For advice on medical matters, I am indebted to Dr. Eleanor Galenson, Dr. Martin Post, Dr. Desider Rothe and Senta Driver. I thank Thomas Bachman, who assisted me on my first trip to Germany. Friends who helped include Frances Brody, who provided information on her great-uncle, Eduard Lasker; Schuyler Chapin, who offered books, information, and a lifelong interest in the subject matter; Annabel Davis-Goff, who lent me her grandmother's memoirs; Isobel d'Ornano, who provided those of her great aunt; Barbara Goldsmith, who found a cache of the Kaiser's letters in the New York Public Library; Louise and Henry Grunwald, with whom I explored Berlin and Potsdam; and Robert Fizdale, Grace Hechinger, Selma Hirsh, Dr. Kay Jamison, Deborah Jowitt, David Kahn, Carter Omens, Nick Pileggi, Lee Radziwill, Timothy Ryback, and Jude Scott-Fox, all of whom provided help and information in different and substantive ways.

To my editor, Alice Mayhew, I owe an enormous debt of gratitude. Beyond her well-known gift for editing, she offered support, enthusiasm, and a staggering knowledge of modern European history. I also want to thank her assistant, Roger Labrie, for his patience in answering daily queries and fielding daily concerns. I am indebted to Eve and Frank Metz, whose interest in the project helped me enormously; to Edith Fowler, who designed the interior of the book and the photo sections with great skill and understanding; to Natalie Goldstein, who had the unenviable task of researching the obscure pictures; and to Leslie Ellen, whose thoughtful help with the copy was invaluable. I want to thank Frances Dimond, Curator of the Photograph Collection at the Royal Archives, for finding most of the photos. This is our second project together, and there is no one I know with a better eye for the informing image. My English editor, Ion Trewin, gave me excellent advice, as did George Weidenfeld, who encouraged me to write the book. I also want to thank my agents and friends, Lynn Nesbit and Amanda Urban, for concern that went beyond the project at hand.

There are two people without whom I could not have muddled through the past eight years: my old pal and fellow writer Barbara Thompson Davis, who gave of her time and profound intelligence to read endless versions of the manuscript, discuss minute problems, and offer imaginative solutions. I will never be able to thank her enough for her friendship and generosity. And my beloved husband, Alan Pakula, whose enthusiasm for the project sustained me when I might have given up. A loving source of creative ideas, editing skills, and forbearance, he never fails to amaze me with his own talent, while at the same time he makes my work possible.

Index

(continued from page 6)

PHOTO CREDITS